PEDIATRIC
NEUROPSYCHOLOGY

Related Titles of Interest

Handbook of Behavior Therapy with Children and Adults: A Developmental and Longitudinal Perspective
Robert T. Ammerman and Michel Hersen (Editors)
ISBN: 0-205-14583-3

Handbook of Prescriptive Treatments for Children and Adolescents
Robert T. Ammerman, Cynthia G. Last, and Michel Hersen (Editors)
ISBN: 0-205-14825-5

Handbook of Child and Adolescent Assessment
Thomas H. Ollendick and Michel Hersen (Editors)
ISBN: 0-205-14592-2

The Sourcebook of Pediatric Psychology
Roberta A. Olson, Larry L. Mullins, Jeffrey B. Gillman, and John M. Chaney
ISBN: 0-205-15182-5

Pediatric Psychology: Psychological Interventions and Strategies for Pediatric Problems
Michael C. Roberts
ISBN: 0-205-14465-9

Behavioral Medicine: Concepts and Procedures
Eldon Tunks and Anthony Bellissimo
ISBN: 0-205-14484-5

PEDIATRIC NEUROPSYCHOLOGY

Interfacing Assessment and Treatment for Rehabilitation

Ervin S. Batchelor, Jr.

Carolina Center for Development and Rehabilitation
Charlotte, NC

Raymond S. Dean

Ball State University

Editors

Allyn and Bacon

Boston • London • Toronto • Sydney • Tokyo • Singapore

Copyright © 1996 by Allyn & Bacon
A Simon & Schuster Company
Needham Heights, Massachusetts 02194

Library of Congress Cataloging-in-Publication Data

Pediatric neuropsychology : interfacing assessment and treatment for
  rehabilitation / Ervin S. Batchelor, Jr. and Raymond S. Dean, editors.
     p. cm.
  Includes bibliographical references and index.
  ISBN 0-205-16486-2 (paper). -- ISBN 0-205-16091-3 (cloth)
  1. Pediatric neuropsychology.   2. Pediatric neurology.
I. Batchelor, Ervin S.   II. Dean, Raymond S.
  [DNLM: 1. Nervous System Diseases--in infancy & childhood.
2. Neuropsychology--in infancy & childhood.   3. Child Development
Disorders--rehabilitation.   WS 340 P37135 1995]
RJ486.5.P43   1995
618.9´28--dc20
DNLM/DLC
for Library of Congress   94-35616
                                                   CIP

Printed in the United States of America

10 9 8 7 6 5 4 3 2 1   99 98 97 96 95

This book is dedicated to two very special boys:
Master Evan and Master Jake

CONTENTS

PREFACE

Researchers in pediatric neuropsychology have made tremendous strides toward understanding the relationship between the developing brain and the evolution of complex aspects of human behavior. *Pediatric Neuropsychology* is an integrated discussion of the most common neurological conditions impacting on normal neuropsychological development. Strategies for assessing and treating a variety of disorders affecting brain function in children are given. This book is rather timely, given the shift of neuropsychological evaluation from an emphasis on diagnosis to utilizing interpretation of test results to formulate treatment approaches. In fact, neuropsychologists are becoming more and more responsible for program development and direction, cognitive rehabilitation, and psychotherapy for patients with central nervous system dysfunction and their families. These chapters offer the scientist/practitioner's perspective on examining and treating neuropsychological deficits associated with specific diagnostic categories of neurologically impaired children. The individuals contributing to this book have demonstrated research and clinical expertise in each of the respective areas on which they comment.

Pediatric Neuropsychology is written for an audience of professionals possessing some basic knowledge of neurology and neuropsychology. It is an excellent reference for those interested in understanding the nature of neurological disorders in children and the neuropsychological deficits that accompany each. Further, the book offers fundamental principles for treating children, and their families, who are coping with specific neurological disorders.

Chapter 1 sets the tone for the book, offering an overview of contemporary issues complicating researchers' attempts to establish diagnostic and treatment paradigms accommodating various factors, including recovery from illness or injury, and the developing brain.

In Chapter 2, the author provides a compelling argument to combine qualitative and quantitative strategies of neuropsychological assessment in order to obtain adequate information for establishing diagnoses and formulating appropriate treatment strategies unique to each diagnostic category. Issues of sensitivity and specificity are discussed for the pediatric population, with due consideration given to limitations of the tests and strategies used for testing that may influence test results. Specific suggestions are offered to facilitate the development of treatment strategies based on referral questions and diagnoses.

The author of Chapter 3 provides a brief historical perspective on behavioral neurology and its interface with psychology. Emphasis is placed on providing validity to neuropsychological assessment based on neuroradiologic studies. In addition, various neuro-imaging techniques are overviewed. Fundamental treatment approaches are also considered, including behavioral and psychopharmacological interventions.

Chapter 4 offers a review of various structural, metabolic, chromosomal, teratogenic, and systemic conditions arising in the perinatal-neonatal period that may result in profound central nervous system defects.

Neurodegenerative diseases appearing in childhood are thoroughly characterized in Chapter 5. Cognitive and behavioral dysfunctions associated with many are discussed. Instead of habilitation and rehabilitation for problems of this sort, the course of illness characterizing decline in functioning is described. Suggestions are noted for managing the physiological and psychological needs of both the patients and their families.

In Chapter 6, evaluation and treatment of pediatric head trauma are reviewed. The most common neuropsychological deficits are identified for this population. Complications in rehabilitation and community reentry are also discussed.

The author of Chapter 7 provides a review of neuropsychological and neurobehavioral deficits associated with brain tumors. Variations in the types of tumors, onset of symptoms, diagnoses, and treatment are offered. Physiological, cognitive, and emotional treatment approaches are discussed, as well as community reintegration adjustment.

Chapter 8 provides an extensive discussion of cerebrovascular disorders in the pediatric population. Neuropsychological findings associated with these cerebrovascular disorders are reviewed. Medical and neuropsychological strategies for treatment are integrated with an emphasis on cognitive rehabilitation.

The authors of Chapter 9 provide a comprehensive review of the neuropsychological foundations for learning disabilities. Strategies for assessing learning disabilities are reviewed in detail. Also, a variety of treatment strategies that have been researched are discussed.

In Chapter 10, the authors delineate four primary medical disorders that affect central nervous system dysfunction: asthma, human immunodeficiency virus (HIV), diabetes mellitus, and end-stage renal disease. Neuropsychological deficits associated with each of these disorders are mentioned. Emotional consequences of medical disorders are also reviewed, and approaches to treatment are discussed.

Disorders of attention are the focus of Chapter 11. Neuropsychological constructs presumed to underpin attentional functioning are presented. Psychopharmacological intervention, behavioral modification, cognitive-behavioral strategies, and educational approaches are discussed and integrated as approaches to managing attentional deficits in children.

Seizure disorders are characterized in Chapter 12. Neuropsychological deficits associated with various types of seizure disorders are identified. Specific strategies for managing children with seizures in the school setting are also summarized.

Chapter 13 offers a comprehensive discussion of the classification and etiology of mental retardation. Two specific habilitation strategies are proposed favoring that of a more individualized treatment approach, combining strategies of accentuation of strengths through task analysis and cognitive habilitation.

Chapter 14 gives due consideration to current treatment paradigms being developed to measure outcome. Treatment effectiveness is shown to be measured in a variety of ways, depending on the nature and purpose of treatment as well as outcome desired. Some attention is allocated to placement outcomes and improvements measured by neuropsychological testing. This chapter provides an opportunity for those interested in understanding more about the implications of the treatment process on recovery and an opportunity to explore the pitfalls and rewards of this type of research.

This book should be enjoyed equally by rehabilitation professionals, physicians, and allied health professionals. However, we specifically designed the book to be utilized in an advanced training setting, such as an internship, residency, or postdoctoral fellowship program study for pediatric neurologists, neuropsychologists, and neuropsychiatrists. We intend that the children with neurological impairment who are served by the audience of this collaborative project will ultimately benefit.

ACKNOWLEDGMENTS

We would like to thank the following individuals who were kind enough to review this book and offer their suggestions: Patricia Bennett (Manhasset Public Schools, Manhasset, NY); Kevin R. Krull (Health Sciences Center, University of Oklahoma); and Monica Smith (Northern Indiana Associates in Psychology, Mishawaka, IN). Also, we would like to thank Randall Evans (Learning Services Corporation) for his resources supporting conceptualization of the final chapter.

ABOUT THE EDITORS

Ervin S. Batchelor, Jr., obtained his Ph.D. in school psychology with specialization in clinical neuropsychology at Ball State University. He was the first postdoctoral fellow in neuropsychology for the Behavioral Neurology Unit at Beth Israel Hospital, Harvard Medical School. He is presently serving as Executive Director at Carolina Center for Development and Rehabilitation. Dr. Batchelor has authored and coauthored over 20 journal articles and book chapters in the area of pediatric neuropsychology. This is his first edited text in the area.

Raymond S. Dean obtained his Ph.D. in child clinical/school psychology from Arizona State University, and trained with Ralph Reitain in an internship setting. He currently holds a Distinguished Professorship at Ball State University. Dr. Dean is past president of APA, Division 40 and the National Academy of Neuropsychology. He is current editor of *Journal of School Psychology* and past editor of *Archives of Clinical Neuropsychology*. He has authored and coauthored numerous papers in the field. Further, he has edited and coedited several texts on neuropsychology.

CONTRIBUTING AUTHORS

Janet M. Arceneaux
Ball State University
Muncie, IN

Robert F. Asarnow
University of California
Los Angeles, CA

Jeffrey T. Barth
University of Virginia Health Sciences Center
Charlottesville, VA

Erin D. Bigler
Brigham Young University
Provo, UT

Thomas J. Boll
University of Alabama
Birmingham, AL

Virginia Bonnefil
Baylor College of Medicine
Houston, TX

Carl B. Dodrill
Harborview Medical Center
Seattle, WA

David W. Dunn
Indiana University Medical Center
Indianapolis, IN

Judith A. Harding
Boston Children's Hospital
Boston, MA

Stephen R. Hooper
University of North Carolina
Chapel Hill, NC

Michele D. Kleiman
University of Connecticut Medical School
Farmington, CT

Judith A. LaMarche
University of Alabama
Birmingham, AL

Richard Lewis
Pomona College
Claremont, CA

Roger Light
Daniel Freeman Memorial Medical Center
Inglewood, CA

Kenneth D. McCoy
Ball State University
Muncie, IN

Raymond K. Mulhern
St. Jude Children's Research Hospital
Memphis, TN

Elizabeth Neumann
Clinical Psychologist—Private Practice
Big Bear Lake, CA

Francis J. Pirozzolo
Baylor College of Medicine
Houston, TX

Allan Ribbler
Montanari Residential Treatment Center
Hialeah, FL

Thomas V. Ryan
University of Virginia Health Sciences Center
Charlottesville, VA

Paul Satz
University of California
Los Angeles, CA

Brenda H. Stone
University of Rhode Island
Kingston, RI

Molly H. Warner
Swedish Medical Center
Seattle, WA

J. Michael Williams
Hahnemann University
Philadelphia, PA

Kelli S. Williams
Magee Rehabilitation Hospital
Philadelphia, PA

W. Grant Willis
University of Rhode Island
Kingston, RI

PEDIATRIC
NEUROPSYCHOLOGY

1

INTRODUCTION

ERVIN S. BATCHELOR, JR.

Pediatric neuropsychology has evolved from studies in behavioral neurology, pediatric medicine, and experimental neurobiology integrated with child clinical psychology, school psychology, adult clinical neuropsychology, special education, and other advances in objective measurement of human behavior. This is evident in neuropsychological test batteries, procedures, and measures developed for children, which are downward extensions of adult neuropsychological batteries, or previously established neurological assessment strategies. Other child neuropsychological test batteries are based on theories of neurological development in concert with neurologically based procedures. Treatment approaches in pediatric neuropsychology have been expanded to include models of cognitive development, along with special education techniques to facilitate recovery and habilitation of sensory-motor functions, language and visual-spatial abilities, information processing, and complex executive functioning. Systems work, crisis intervention, short-term grief, and adjustment therapies have been necessarily integrated to meet the emotional needs of patients and their families.

Recently, much progress has been made toward understanding neuropsychological development in humans (see Dean [1985] and Gaddas [1985] for a review). We are just now on the verge of understanding neuropsychological development in children. Luria (1973) has outlined a relatively comprehensive course of corroborative relationships between structural and functional development of the human brain. It appears that the organization and relegation of brain functions to specific hemispheric regions have genetic propensities that evolve over the first 14 to 15 years of life (Levy & Reid, 1976; MacLean, 1970). Over some 40 weeks of gestation, the fetal brain grows to an average weight of 350 grams, approximately 10% of the neonate's birth weight. The majority of cell generation and migration rapidly takes place during the gestational period but continues slowly after birth throughout infancy and childhood. The majority of myelinization in the cerebrum occurs after birth, during the first 2 years of life but extends well into puberty. At age 1 year, the infant's brain weight will grow to 1,500 grams, or 70% of the adult size brain (2,200 grams) (Himwich, 1970).

In theory, the present neuroanatomical organization of brain structure and function has evolved by the addition of increasingly complex structures that have enhanced the organism's potential for successfully interacting with its environment. Each structural addition has facilitated the organism in more complex integration of sensory experience and motoric options for efficient survival responses (Dean, 1985).

MacLean (1970) described the upper spinal cord, brain stem, basal ganglia, and midbrain diencephalon as the protoreptilian brain and the primary evolutionary stage of development. The paleomammilian brain marks the second evolutionary stage, which includes the protoreptilian structures plus the limbic system (cingulate, insula, and portions of cerebral cortex). This life form had no language and was primarily driven by fear, hunger, thirst, and need to procreate. The paleomammilian organism was probably a very kinesthetic animal, depending primarily on senses of taste, smell, and touch for survival. The neomammilian brain gave rise to more refined cortical structures that facilitated development of auditory and visual processing, language, visual-spatial constructions, and analytical thought.

The course of functional development, from conception to adulthood, appears to approximate its evolutional phylogeny (Goldman, 1972). Somatosensory experience is present in the 4-week-old-embryo. The fetus can be tested for deafness at 6 months of age. A newborn can distinguish the smell and taste of its mother at birth. However, it is not until two weeks after birth that the infant can differentiate between visual patterns. It is clear that the new born is heavily dependent on its sense of touch, smell, and taste to negotiate its environment. Indeed, it is primarily through the kinesthetic modalities that the infant first gains some control over its environment. Indeed, it is primarily through the kinesthetic modalities that the infant first gains some control over its environment. By comparison, auditory and visual skill development takes much longer to mature. The kinesthetic sensory modalities support early auditory and visual development. For example, vibrations through the skin facilitate auditory experience; the baby's hand and body movements stimulate visual development and sensory integration for vestibular functioning.

This process very likely involves critical early periods of somatosensory/motor experience, which facilitate further development of central nervous system structure and function. All infants are primary kinesthetic learners. However, 60% of all children grow to be primary visual learners, and about 30% of all children develop a primary auditory learning style. Only 10% of those reaching maturity will remain primary kinesthetics. Without mastering visual-written and/or auditory-verbal means of learning and communicating, children in most cultures are effectively identified as being either disabled or impaired.

Ordinary individual differences and aberrations in neurological development related to brain dysfunction may well change the course of what otherwise might have been considered "normal" ontogeny. Children who are deprived of sensory input during critical periods of development often suffer delays in skill acquisition. This is obvious for those children who, because of chronic ear infections between the ages of birth and 48 months, suffer speech and language problems; or children with congenital visual impairments who have significant difficulty developing visually guided motor skills. One may hypothesize that lack of appropriate sensory input, or sensory feedback from motoric behavior during critical periods, may result in aberrations in development of neural pathways required to facilitate acquisition of more complex neuropsychological functions. Many researchers have argued that diffuse lateralization of cortical functions may account for children who have normal brain structure presenting with subtle information-processing deficits, classic attention deficits, dyslexia, dyscalculia, or dysgraphia (Dean, 1985; Geschwind, 1974; Levy & Reid, 1976; Satz, Bakker, Tenuissen, Goebel, & Van der Vlugt, 1975).

Researchers have just begun to investigate the implications of incurred brain injury, congenital and developmental anomalies of brain structure and function for subsequent neuropsychological development in children. There seems to be a number of interacting factors that may impact this issue. The endogenous factors include genetics (Levy & Reid, 1976), preferred learning strategies, premorbid developmental status, and nature, type, location, extent, and severity of the lesion(s) (Geschwind, 1974) (see Chapter 2 for further discussion). The chronological factors consist of gestational age at birth (Dean, 1985), the age of onset, and duration of illness. The important exogenous factors are sociocultural and psychological status of the family, and the child's psychological reaction to the illness (Dean, 1986).

When considering these variables, attempts to formulate models of brain development and behavioral functioning for children with various neurologic disorders becomes increasingly complex. Each model must automatically assume a chronology by interaction of endogenous premorbid conditions. Any assumptions made about normal development of the organism must consider the child's age at the time of onset. Where prematurity is involved in an infant or young child with neurological impairment, developmental age of the child may be most accurately calculated by subtracting the number of weeks of prematurity from the child's chronological age since birth (Dean, 1985). Following neurological insult, those children having preexisting neuropsychological deficits will probably be compromised more than children having normal cognitive and emotional functioning.

The etiology of the illness will largely determine the course and potential outcomes for the individual patients. Thus, a multitude of models for abnormal neurological development may be entertained. Yet, there does appear to be some predictability of recovery, assuming the illness is not progressive and terminal. Certain types of injuries—such as mild cerebral edema, tissue strain, or mild contusions—may cause temporary damage and transient loss of function. However, permanent tissue damage due to more extensive injury may well disrupt the normal course of neurological development of a particular structure (depending on age) and/or function.

Interestingly, the developing brain does have the capacity for plasticity (one hemisphere assumes responsibility for mediating functions normally relegated to the damaged contralateral hemisphere). While the debate continues over the exact mechanisms of this process, it appears that there are critical periods for plasticity that coincide with critical periods for neuropsychological skill acquisition. Relegation and lateralization of cognitive function follow a relatively well-defined course that approximates the development and maturation of the secondary and tertiary areas of the cerebral cortex (Bryden & Allard, 1978; Dean, 1985; Peiper, 1963; Satz et al., 1975). Between the ages of 5 and 7, the secondary association areas of the cerebral cortex become fully myelinated (Luria, 1973). Damage to either hemisphere prior to this period seems to have less effect on the subsequent skill acquisition than would normally be subsumed by the lesioned foci (Dikman, Matthews, & Harley, 1975; Pirozollo, Campanella, Christensen, & Lawson-Kerr, 1981). Conversely, damage to either hemisphere after this period usually results in more devastating effects on development of cognitive functioning.

The degree of plasticity is also affected by the severity of damage to a given hemisphere. Those patients receiving complete hemispherectomies fare better than those with only partial removal of a hemisphere (Pirozollo et al., 1981).

Tertiary association areas fully mature between the ages of 10 and 12 years. Few studies have reported plasticity effects in humans beyond the age of 10 years. From this viewpoint, damage to neural pathways in the cerebrum after 10 years of age will likely result in some permanent loss of specific function.

The brain fully matures between the ages of 14 and 15 years of age. Yet, normal cognitive development will typically continue through the second decade of life. However, it is clear that, for children with static encephalopathy, some cognitive skills will peak well before this time, and in cases of the progressive intrinsic brain disease of metabolic disorders, cognitive functions may never emerge or prematurely degenerate. In the normal brain, dendritic growth and arborization may continue well through the fourth or fifth decade, at which time cerebrovascular and neurodegenerative changes emerge. Cognitive function then gradually declines.

Children with compromised central nervous systems are more likely to suffer emotional and behavioral problems than those without brain injury (Shaffer, 1974). In many cases of incurred brain injury or disease process that begin childhood, it is extremely difficult to dissociate endogenous from exogenous variables affecting emotional reactivity and behavioral control. In cases of certain congenital neurologic disorders that are static or progressive in nature, certain emotional and behavioral correlates are fairly predictable. For example, autistic children are characteristically socially inept, display self-stimulatory behaviors, establish ritualistic play and activity habits, remain primarily kinesthetic learners through adulthood, have impaired attention and complex language deficits, and frequently display aggression when frustrated. However, the emotional and behavioral components of other congenital conditions, such as attention deficit disorders, vary significantly with age, subtype, severity of condition, and environmental factors. Some of these children will develop irritable moods, oppositional behavior, and antisocial tendencies. Others will manifest a depressed mood, withdrawing from peers and family. Still others may display cyclical mood swings. There is another subgroup of these children who experience cognitive deficits but no behavioral problems.

It appears that the ability to select appropriate responses, control impulses, modulate affect, and allocate emotional balance develops between 12 and 50 postnatal months of life. It is during this time that the more primitive reflexes (e.g., Moro reflex, tonic neck) are suppressed, indicating development of higher cortical and cerebellar control (Dean, 1985; Van dur Vlugt, 1979; Yakovlev & Lecours, 1967). If damage occurs to the cerebrum during this developmental phase, these primitive reflexes may not disappear or may return if already suppressed, suggesting decreased inhibition of lower regions of the neuroaxis, which include the diencephalon and limbic areas (see Dean [1985] for complete discussion). Intense emotional reactivity originates from deep limbic structures, the diencephalon and hypothalamus (see Ross [1985] for further discussion). Thus, damage to the cerebrum between birth and 50 months may well produce conditions ripe for disinhibition of emotions and behavioral dyscontrol. Damage to the frontal and/or temporal lobes, limbic and diencephalic structures, at any time during development, may also result in changes in personality, affective instability, mood liability, or behavioral disturbance.

The child's psychological reaction to a central nervous system injury or illness often contributes to the diagnostic puzzle—the formulation and implementation of treatment. Many issues must be considered. The expected outcome should be the first concern. Children with poor prognosis or terminal illness will respond to their illness much differently than those whose outcome is more optimistic. For children with cancer, the psychological picture is often confusing because of inconsistency in the validation of prognosis by various doctors. Thus, it is difficult to accurately assess mood and adjustment.

The nature, course, and severity of illness will also affect the child's perception of the infirmity. Many children often move into denial, or assume an aggressive posture regarding mild to moderate disabilities, as they attempt to reject or defend against stigmatization by peers. Others may migrate into a learned helplessness state and subsequently react with depression. Still others may confront mild disabilities head-on and make appropriate adjustments with minimal psychological support. Their sociocultural background and familial status clearly add to the complexity and resolution of their recovery.

Families often appropriately rescue and protect children with neurologic conditions. However, far too frequently, family members learn to build or change their lives around this individual, neglecting themselves or the needs of the patient's siblings;. In some cases of mild disability (e.g., learning disability or attention deficit disorder), families will develop similar symptoms as a means of normalizing the child's condition or seeking equal attention. And, in some extreme and rare situations, the parents will create circumstances under which serious, even life-threatening, conditions may develop (e.g., Munchausen's Disease by Proxy). In any of these cases, the child is poorly served by the parents. Parents should be involved in the care of the child where possible and assume as much responsiblity for treating the child without overprotecting, keeping the child in the role of the pateint. Often, along with children, parents must grieve losses and may be the initial target for psychological and educational interventions.

It is common knowledge that sociocultural factors are related to psychiatric disorders and learning problems in children and adults. It should come as no surprize that children born in low socioeconomic status (SES) families are at greater risk for developing perinatal complications (Batchelor, Gray, Dean, & Lowery, 1988). Thus, it becomes essential to carefully examine medical records of such children in order to assess the neuropsychological status and make proper diagnoses. Children with disadvantaged sociocultural backgrounds will have fewer opportunities to develop a strong knowledge base required for development of higher cortical functions such as organization, analytical reasoning, and problem solving. From this view, certain aspects of the culturally disadvantaged individual's cognitive development may plateau at an early age.

Further, such individuals' performances may well be skewed on culturally influenced standardized tests. Treating the socioculturally deprived child who has a neurologic disorder is difficult, often because the family is limited in their ability to benefit from psychological and education interventions. These families tend to accept the child's disability and expect little in the way of improvement or recovery. This situation may be relieved where institutionalization is an available option. However, financial limitations often accompanying these families typically prohibit appropriate courses of treatment.

Beyond this text, little has been written about the impact that treatment may have on long-term recovery of neuropsychological functioning and future neuropsychological development. Presently, neuropsychologists are examining the relationship between assessment and treatment for purposes of rehabilitation. Presumably, such an established link will create an opportunity for both researchers and clinicians to attain a better understanding of the parameters of utilizing pediatric neuropsychological test results to formulate treatment plans that can offer empirical outcome data.

To date, there is little in the way of established paradigms for researching treatment strategies formulated from neuropsychological assessment. According to Bigler (see Chapter 3), the first problem stems from lack of agreement among researchers on appropriate strategies or test protocols used for assessment. This issue is clearly pivotal, but difficult to manage in the laboratory, given variations in the natures and courses of illnesses and potential outcome for the child. In cases of progressive decline in functioning (e.g., Sturge-Weber Syndrome or Batton's Disease), rehabilitation is not an appropriate consideration. Here, the neuropsychologist's role may be minimal, establishing a baseline and documenting the deterioration in functioning, and preparing the family for necessary perceived changes in lifestyle, education, and case management. In cases of minor head injury, the neuropsychologist may direct comprehensive outpatient rehabilitation services for the child and family, seeing that appropriate transition back to the home and school is successful. Thus, the choice of test batteries will depend on the type of information to be derived from assessment. And outcome measures will clearly vary, depending on expected prognosis, diagnosis, test protocols, therapeutic modalities, and treatment goals.

Along these same lines, variations in test batteries may differ, based on availability of funding. Indigent patients seen by private practitioners in acute community-based hospital settings are less likely to receive comprehensive testing than affluent individuals who might be seen in postacute, freestanding rehabilitation units served by faculty and postdoctoral students.

A second concern extends from the first and involves differences in strategies used for interpreting test results (see Batchelor, Chapter 2). It is not uncommon to find two competent neuropsychologists trained in separate programs, who derive slightly dissimilar interpretations of underlying functional deficits based on the same test results. There may be no fault with the examiners here, but rather with the tests that too frequently measure simultaneous aspects of brain function. This type of error can be critical in an attempt to accurately conceptualize strategies for treatment, should habilitation/rehabilitation be appropriate. Such differences in interpretation may be due to variations in training models and theoretical biases of trainers, which are often represented in the types of tests administered, interpretive strategies applied, and types of information used for corroboration, if any.

The third issue has to do with the degree of clinical experience and the clinicians' fundamental knowledge of the functional and structural development of the brain—that is, their understanding of neuropsychological phenomena associated with abberations in development for specific neuropsychological conditions. This portion of the puzzle is currently emerging as a primary feature in the literature, particularly for some disorders (e.g., attention-deficit disorder, traumatic brain injury, autism, cerebrovascular accidents); while others (e.g., central nervous system metabolic disorders, agenesis of the corpus callosum, neurofibromatosis, and Arnold Chairi malformations) remain obscured. It is from this view that the following chapters offer some insights regarding the existing literature describing significant neurological conditions in children, what contributions have been made by neuropsychology, and how treatment strategies may be conceptualized, given the complications of conditions created by circumstances surrounding these disorders.

This text represents a practical yet empirically conservative view of esteemed scientist-practitioners who have expertise in assessing specific pediatric neurologic populations, and knowledge of how this information may be utilized to formulate reasonable treatment strategies. These chapters have been organized in such a way as to consider specific neurologic conditions and related endogenous, exogenous, and chronological variables. Contributing authors have attended to the cognitive, emotional, and behavioral correlates invoked in rehabilitation to varying degrees, depending on available research. This text does not include a chapter covering some of the important neuropsychiatric disorders (e.g., childhood schizophrenia and Tourette's Syndrome) and pervasive developmental disorders (e.g., autism and Asperger's Syndrome). However, significant attention has been given to these topics elsewhere.

REFERENCES

Batchelor, E. S., Gray, J. W., Dean, R. S., & Lowery, R. (1988). Interactive effects of socioeconomic factors & perinatal complications. *NASA Program Abstracts, F-169*, 115–116.

Bryden, M. P., & Allard, F. (1978). Dichotic listening and the development of linguistic processes. In M. Dinsbourne (Ed.), *The asymmetrical function of the brain*. New York: Cambridge University Press.

Chelune, G. J., & Edwards, P. (1981). Early brain lesions: Ontogenetic-environmental considerations. *Journal of Consulting and Clinical Psychology, 49*.

Dean, R. S. (1985). Foundation and rationale for neuropsychological bases of individual differences. In L. Hartledge & C. Telzrons (Eds.), *Neuropsychology of individual differences: A developmental perspective* (pp. 7–39). New York: Plum Press.

Dean, R. S. (1986). Neuropsychological aspects of psychiatric disorders. In J. E. Obrzut & G. W. Hynd (Eds.), *Child neuropsychology: Clinical practice (Vol. 2)* (pp. 83–112). London: Academic Press.

Dikman, S., Matthews, C. G., & Harley, J. P. (1975). The effect of early versus late onset of major motor epilepsy upon cognitive intellectual performance. *Epilepsy, 16*.

Gaddas, W. H. (1985). *Learning disabilities and brain function* (2nd ed.). New York: Springer-Verlag.

Geschwind, N. (1974). The anatomical basis of hemispheric differentiation. In S. J. Dimond & J. G. Beaumont (Eds.), *Hemispheric function in the human brain*. New York: Halstead Press.

Geschwind, N., & Levitsky, W. (1968). Human brain: Left-right asymmetries in temporal speech region. *Science, 161*.

Goldman, P. S. (1972). Development determinants of cortical plasticity. *Acta Neurobiologiae Experimentalis, 32*.

Himwich, W. A. (1970). *Developmental neurobiology*. Springfield, IL: Charles C. Thomas.

Levy, J., & Reid, M. (1976). Variations in writing posture and cerebral organization. *Science, 194*, 337–339.

Luria, A. R. (1973). *The working brain: An introduction to neuropsychology*. London: Penguin Press.

MacLean, P. D. (1970). The triune brain, emotional and scientific bias. In F. O. Schmitt (Ed.), *The neurosciences: Second study program*. New York: Rockefeller University Press.

Peiper, A. (1963). *Cerebral function in infancy and childhood*. (Translation by B. & M. Nagler from the German 3rd rev. ed.) New York: Consultants Bureau.

Pirozzolo, F. J., Campanella, D. J., Christensen, K., & Lawson-Kerr, K. (1981). Effects of cerebral dysfunction on neurolinguistic performance in children. *Journal of Consulting and Clinical Psychology, 49*.

Ross, E. D. (1985). The modulation of affect and non-verbal communication by the right hemisphere. In M. M. Mesulam (Ed.), *Principles of behavioral neurology* (pp. 239–258). Philadelphia: F. A. Davis.

Satz, P., Bakker, D. J., Tenuissen, J., Goebel, R., & Van der Vlugt, H. (1975). Developmental parameters of the ear asymmetry. A multivariate approach. *Brain and Language, 2*.

Shaffer, D. (1974). Psychiatric aspects of brain injury in childhood: A review. In S. Chess & A. Thomas (Eds.), *Annual progress in child psychiatry and child development*. New York: Brunner/Mazel.

Van der Vlugt, H. (1979). Aspects of normal and abnormal neuropsychological development. In M. S. Gazzaniga (Ed.), *Handbook of behavioral neurobiology: Vol. 2. Neuropsychology*. New York: Plenum Press.

Yakovlev, P. I., & Lecours, A. R. (1967). The myuelogenetic cycles of regional maturation of the brain. In A. Minkowski (Ed.), *Regional development of the brain in early life*. Oxford: Blackwell.

Yakovlev, P. I., & Rakie, P. (1966). Patterns of decussation of bulbar pyramids and distribution of pyramidal tracts on two sides of the spinal cord. *Transactions of the American Neurology Associations, 91*.

2

NEUROPSYCHOLOGICAL ASSESSMENT OF CHILDREN

ERVIN S. BATCHELOR, JR.

INTRODUCTION

In recent years, many have discussed assessment of children with neurologic disorders (e.g., Dean, 1985a; Dunn & Epstein, 1987; Hynd & Obrzut, 1981; Hynd & Willis, 1988; Languis & Wittrock, 1986). Several disciplines are involved in assessment, including neurosurgeons, neurologists, neuropsychologists, psychologists, neurophysiologists, physiatrists, psychiatrists, physical therapists, speech and language therapists, occupational therapists, and special educators, just to name a few. Members of each discipline have presented overlapping concerns, but may well approach the assessment process with different agenda. For example, the neurosurgeon is typically concerned with acute care of emergent symptoms, whereas the physiatrist is more likely to be consulted if the patient has mobility problems associated with injury long after the neurosurgeon has evaluated and treated the patient. Through careful review of medical records, psychiatrists are finding that many of their adolescent inpatients have a history of early insults to the brain and are assessing neurobehavioral problems (Dean, 1986). The nature of evaluations will change little for professionals such as the physical therapist, special educator and the like, given their place on the continuum of service provided to children with neurologic disorders. However, the role of neurologists and neuropsychologists are likely to change.

Neurologists and neuropsychologists have found niches along the continuum of care, ranging from the emergency room to outpatient long-term follow-up. The purpose and nature of their assessments change according to the setting, referral question, and circumstances under which examinations are conducted. The quality of assessment is restricted to the expertise and biases of

9

the examiners' availability of neurodiagnostic tools, interaction between the two disciplines, and patient funding.

As state-of-the-art neuropsychological, neurophysiological, and neuroimaging techniques evolve, neurologists are recognizing the value of the neuropsychologist's role in assessment and treatment (e.g., Weintraub & Mesulam, 1985). Likewise, trained neuropsychologists find kinship with neurologists, as both often service the patient in similar ways with respect to assessment in various settings (see Chapter 3).

The purpose of this chapter is to introduce a contemporary perspective on assessment that frequently requires a team effort of the neurologist and neuropsychologist. Herein, the author will argue for a comprehensive and integrative assessment process that utilizes the tools relied on by both disciplines. This complementary approach is designed to more clearly facilitate understanding of the patient's deficits and needs for treatment. With due respect, such an undertaking is not meant to exclude other specialists' contributions (e.g., neurosurgeons, physiatrists, psychiatrists, and psychologists) in the process of interfacing diagnosis and treatment in the rehabilitation of children with neurologic disorders. Rather, this approach will hopefully elucidate the value of more cooperative efforts among all professionals involved in habilitation and rehabilitation.

ASSESSMENT CONCERNS IN PEDIATRICS

Prior to discussing approaches to neuropsychological assessment in children, several caveats and considerations should be discussed. Because a child's development is a dynamic, continuous and relatively rapid process, there may be little consistency in premorbid history from which to establish a baseline of performance. Premorbid history of prenatal and perinatal events, and developmental milestones may be poorly documented, making it difficult to formulate a baseline for comparison, particularly in preschool children (Gray, Dean, & Rattan, 1987). From an environmental viewpoint, children reared in low socioeconomic settings often have remarkable perinatal and psychiatric histories (Batchelor, Gray, Dean, & Lowery, 1988; Dean, 1986). In the cases where parents are substance abusers or are cognitively impaired, information about the patient's developmental history is often inaccurate and incomplete (Gray et al., 1987). Under these conditions, attempts to sort out the familial, cultural, and physiological influences in performance outcome are often complicated (Dean, 1985a, 1986). As one can imagine, the interaction of these factors may also limit the clinician's ability to make accurate prognostic statements (Dean, 1985a, 1986). Thus, the need for corroboration of information about the child's presenting condition emerges.

The pediatric neuropsychologist requires extensive knowledge of the relationship between central nervous system development (including cerebral organization, laterality, and plasticity) and the emergence of cognitive functions from birth through early adulthood. A basic understanding of these relationships is prerequisite for appropriate selection, administration, and accurate interpretation of neuropsychological instruments used in making inferences regarding brain function. By comparison, neuropsychological assessment of children is far more complicated than that of adults (e.g., Dean, 1986; Reed, Reitan, & Klove, 1965). Several factors have been reported. Analysis of anatomical differences in children with abnormal brains have revealed anomalies in structure (e.g., Galaburda, Signoret, & Ronthal, 1985; Wada, Clarke, & Hamm, 1975). Because the brain goes through some rather dramatic changes over the first 14 years of life (Boll, 1974), aberrations in central nervous system functioning at various stages of development may result in dynamic variations on test profiles and expectations for recovery of functioning (Dean, 1986; Hartledge & Reynolds, 1981; Reed et al., 1965). Thus, organization of brain function in children is poorly understood (Hynd & Willis, 1988).

Individual differences in hemispheric development give rise to the hypothesis that rates of consolidation may vary as the brain organizes functions. Sex differences in organization of function may contribute to variations in neuropsychological test performance in both normal (McGlone & Davidson, 1973) and clinical populations (e.g., Batchelor and Dean, 1990). Premorbid history (Benton, 1974), age of onset (Boll, 1974), acuteness of illness (Hartledge & Hartledge, 1977), severity, and extent of lesion (Dean, 1986) interact to produce variations in assessment and treatment outcome (Dean, 1986). The brain appears to have the amazing capacity to reorganize cognitive functions during critical periods of development, 2 to 7 years of age (see Chelune & Edwards, 1981; Dean, 1985b; Dikeman, Matthews, & Harley, 1975; Pirozzolo, Campanella, Christensen, & Lawson-Kerr, 1981), which further complicates this state of affairs. Where evidence supports the hypothesis of brain damage, it becomes is an arduous task to disassociate physiological changes from cognitive and emotional reactions to these changes (Dean, 1985a, 1986). From this view, inferences regarding localization of brain dysfunction may be of limited value for children with developmental central nervous system disorders, brain injury, or intrinsic brain disease (Dean, 1986; Hartledge & Reynolds, 1981; Reed et al. 1965). Together, these factors tend to complicate interpretive, diagnostic, and prognostic processes. So being, neuropsychological assessment should be approached in such a way that test results can also be corroborated from multiple sources to maximize potential for making accurate diagnostic and prognostic statements.

Qualitative and Quantitative Aspects of Data

Quantitative data implies that information is arrived at via objective means. By definition, quantitative data must be reliable and valid. Reliability and validity directly depend on the psychometric properties of the tests; competency in administration and consistency of examiners' reporting observations; patients' consistency in performance; families' ability to supply accurate information to the examiner through surveys and/or direct questioning; and accuracy of prior medical records. In contrast, qualitative data are obtained with less objectivity. Qualitative data may be described as information obtained by means that have not yet been established as reliable, but may well meet the requirements for face or content validity. Table 2.1 offers a continuum of information typically utilized by the neuropsychologist and/or neurologist that may help to eliminate an illusive dicotomy that has historically evolved between advocates of quantitative and qualitative approaches to neuropsychological assessment.

To illustrate this point, the reliability of norms for neuropsychological tests ranges from knowledge derived from extensive personal experience to regionally standardized scores controlling for age, sex, IQ, education, and socioeconomic status. Validity of tests will depend on reliability, the extent to which the test results accurately represent constructs describing the behavior measured, interpretive strategy, and source of norms for comparison. The same holds true for usage

TABLE 2.1   Continuum of Qualitative and Quantitative Data

Qualitative Data		Quantitative Data	
Patient history from interviews with parents and patient, surveys, and questionnaires	Patient history from medical, day-care, psychological, and school records		
Parents' observations of behavior, mood, affect, and comportment	Clinician observations of behavior, mood, affect, and comportment		Standardized behavior rating scales, personality inventories, mood-specific indices, behavioral programming designed to operationalize and monitor specific behavior
Internal norm-referenced neuropsychological test scores; process analysis of test performance	Standardized norm-referenced scores (small sample)	Standardized norm-referenced test scores (national sample)	Standardized regionally norm-referenced test scores controlling for age, sex, IQ, and SES
	Neurologic Soft Signs		Neurologic Hard Signs
		Visual inspection of neurodiagnostic studies (e.g., PET, CT, MRI, EEG, BEAM, EP, SPECT, posturography)	Computer-based statistical interpretation of neurodiagnostic procedures using machine-specific norms
			Biologic specific markers (e.g., liver function tests, thyroid function tests, lumbar puncture studies, electrolyte studies, biopsies, drug screens)

of neuroradiological procedures. Unless quantitative approaches are consistently applied in neuroimaging techniques, interpretation of the data ultimately depends on the clinician's expertise (Turkheimer, 1989).

In the clinical setting, it is rare that stringent quantitative guidelines are applied to interpretation of all data sources. Thus, there is almost always some subjectivity and qualitativeness in the interpretation of neurological, neuropsychological, neurophysiological, or neuroradiological test results. It is virtually meaningless to interpret results without due consideration given to the child's presenting symptoms, behavioral observations, and background information (Dunn & Epstein, 1987). These latter sources typically yield more qualitative or subjective information. Thus, overall interpretative strategies for neuropsychological assessment may be most accurately viewed on a continuum of qualitative and quantitative information.

It was mentioned earlier that parents' reports of patient history may well be unreliable and subjective. Lezak (1995) has aptly stated that data derived from test administration clearly differs from that information obtained through clinical interviews, questionnaires, medical records, and behavioral observations. A similar notion has been implied by Bigler (1991) for other neurodiagnostic techniques. Neuropsychological (Lezak, 1995), neuroradiological, neurological, and neurophysiological measures are merely sets of exposures and observations of a more fluid set of circumstances. Extrapolations and generalizations based on interpretations and inferences from isolated measures of the child's behavior are necessarily limited with respect to reliability and validity (Lezak, 1995). From this viewpoint, most of these types of data will also be subject to varying degrees of objectivity and dependent on the nature and environment of the stimulus, the administration of the stimulus, the patient, other informative sources, and the techniques applied to data collection and interpretation. Because of the need to integrate existing data from a continuum of qualitative and quantitative sources, it becomes essential for clinicians to understand the limitations and strengths of each data source and corroborate where necessary.

Information Derived from Neuropsychological Tests

Parallel to the issue of objectivity in assessment are concerns about the sensitivity, specificity, and appropriateness of tests being administered to children. Sensitivity refers to the extent to which a test can accurately predict brain impairment. Thus, sensitivity is often gauged on the statistical power (see Pedhazur, 1973) of a test, and depends heavily on standardized administration, reliability, and all aspects of validity. By design, measures of sensitivity exclude the qualitative aspects of task performance. And as will be discussed, measures of sensitivity in pediatrics are relatively nonspecific.

The primary objective of sensitive measures have been to separate normal children from those with brain damage (Selz & Reitan, 1979). We know that injury to the developing brain is more likely to result in a more generalized, rather than specific, pattern of deficits (e.g., Boll, 1974; Boll & Reitan, 1972a, 1972b,

1972c). Perhaps this finding accounts for why combined scores rendered from a standardized childrens' test battery (see Selz & Reitan, 1979) have been more successful in predicting brain damage. However, no single neuropsychological test has demonstrated validity in this clinical application (Boll, 1978).

In lieu of rules for predicting brain impairment utilizing standardized test procedures discussed by Selz and Reitan (1979), the Full Scale IQ Score obtained via the Wechsler Scales seems to be the best indicator of generalized cerebral dysfunction (Boll & Reitan, 1972a, 1972b, 1972c; Hynd & Willis, 1988). Black (1976) has offered evidence indicating that a 20-plus-point discrepancy is statistically significant in populations of children with brain damage. However, relative to Black's (1976) report, variations exist between verbal intelligence quotient (VIQ) and performance intelligence quotient (PIQ) scores within the normal population (Kaufman, 1979). Thus, the implications for lateralization and localization of impairment based on VIQ-PIQ discrepancies must be very carefully considered (see Hynd & Willis, 1988; Teeter, 1986).

Sensitivity of neuropsychological tests may vary due to test design for age appropriateness and individual differences in critical periods for emerging cognitive functions (see Dean, 1985a). This assertion may, in part, account for the limited utility of single measures for predicting brain damage. Individual differences in brain development may also explain the low reliability and validity of neuropsychological tests reported at early ages, limiting predictive and inferential value of standardized scores for very young children (e.g., Bayley, 1949; McCall, Hogarty, & Hurlburt, 1972; Rattan & Rattan, 1987).

Specificity refers to the nature of the behavioral, cognitive, and emotional functions underlying a given task, to the extent that the process in which errors result in scores and the scores, themselves, can be inferred to localize brain dysfunction. The specificity of pediatric neuropsychological tests may be influenced by sex, premorbid status, age, the nature of the task, neuropsychological functions underpinning the task, potential for variations in cognitive strategies for accurate task completion, administrative procedures, and the test environment. When examining pediatrics, both the sensitivity and specificity of tests may also be affected by the interaction between the age of onset and recovery curve, location and extent of lesion, premorbid integrity of the central nervous system, sociocultural background, and emotional status (Dean, 1986).

Confounding the issue of specificity are the multitude of studies where children with brain damage yield a diffuse pattern of deficits on neuropsychological testing (e.g., Boll & Reitan, 1972a, 1972b, 1972c). With the advent of positron emission tomography (PET) (see Gur [1985] and Pawlik & Heiss [1989] for review) and brain electrical activity mapping (BEAM) (e.g., Duffy, Denkla, Bartels, Sandini, & Kiessling, 1979), evidence suggests that even simple information processing may simultaneously involve multiple levels and regions of the neuroaxis. Factor-analytic studies (e.g., Batchelor, Sowles, Dean, & Fischer, 1991) have provided data to support the notion that the same tests measure separate neuropsychological constructs at different age levels. More specifically, it appears that the complexity of neuropsychological functioning increases with age (Batchelor et al., 1991; Crockett, Klonoff, & Bejerring, 1969). Thus, as one would suspect, individual differences in brain development for both normal and clinical populations complicate the interpretation of neuropsychological test results for purposes of establishing specificity (Dean, 1985b; Hynd & Willis, 1988).

From this viewpoint, the pediatric neuropsychologist should be skeptical of making inferences regarding localization of brain dysfunction in children based solely on neuropsychological test data. Indeed, neuropsychological test results used to infer localized brain dysfunction in children clearly requires corroboration with other sources such as electroencephalography (EEG), magnetic resonance imaging (MRI), computed axial tomography (CAT), evolked potentials (EP), and PET. Indeed, specificity in pediatric neuropsychological assessment may best be utilized as a term to describe and qualify specific cognitive and emotional deficits, excluding the notion of inference for localization of brain dysfunction.

Some would argue that standardized neuropsychological batteries may show generalized performance deficits because the tests are designed to measure multiple, salient, and/or overlapping constructs, obfuscating subtle specific patterns of performance indicative of brain dysfunction (Kaplan, 1990; Weintraub, 1990).

Unfortunately, this plausable contention awaits empirical evaluation. There are a multitude of neuropsychological instruments available for children with and without norms that have been designed by advocates of the "process" approach to assess specific aspects of cognitive functioning (Kaplan, 1988; Lezak, 1983; Spreen & Strauss, 1991; Weintraub & Mesulam, 1985). Task analysis of these tests are necessary for accurate interpretation of results (Kaplan, 1988), within theoretical neurobehavioral and neurocognitive models that parallel functional and structural development (see Dean, 1985b). However, inferences regarding localization of brain dysfunction in children remain hypothetical until further researched. (See Chapter 3 for further discussion of this issue.)

As expected, there seems to be a trade-off between specificity and sensitivity for neuropsychological instruments used to assess children. Although the full-scale intellectual quotient (FSIQ) is the single-most sensitive measure of cerebral integrity, this measure offers little information regarding the specific aspects of cognitive processing. On the other hand, measures such as Continuous Performance Tests offer specific information about sustained attention, but poor results on such tests would not be used alone to infer brain damage. Proper selection, administration, and interpretation of neuropsychological instruments may approximate a balance between sensitivity and specificity when considered in light of data obtained through other relevant sources.

In isolation, neuropsychological tests have limited potential to consistently measure the full scope of developing neuropsychological functions utilizing a set of standardized test items that meet researchers' requirements set for reliability and validity, while simultaneously capturing sensitivity of the brain's integrity and specificity of cognitive functions as they are relegated to specific brain regions over the developmental course. Thus, any approach to pediatric neuropsychological assessment will require utilization of several tests that accurately diagnose brain impairment and characterize the nature of neuropsychological deficits within and between domains of brain function.

APPROACHES TO NEUROPSYCHOLOGICAL ASSESSMENT

Historically, there have been two major venues in clinical neuropsychology: The battery and the process approaches. The "battery" approach (e.g., Golden, Hammeke, & Purisch, 1978; Halstead, 1947, 1951; Reitan, 1969; Reed et al., 1965; Selz & Reitan, 1979) relies heavily on the examiner's ability to predict neuropsychological dysfunction based on an interpretation of combined standardized test scores. Currently, there are three fundamental neuropsychological test batteries designed for children: the Reitan-Indiana Neuropsychological Test Battery for Children, 5–8 years (Reitan, 1969); the Halstead-Reitan Neuropsychological Test Battery for Children, 9–14 years (Reitan, 1969); and the Luria-Nebraska Neuropsychological Battery for Children (Golden, Hammeke, & Purisch, 1978). These test batteries have been extensively studied and critiqued (see Hynd & Willis, 1988). Cutoff scores are used to differentiate those with and without brain damage.

Pathognomonic neurological signs are considered along with patterns of performance on neuropsychological tests to compare functioning on either side of the body. Based on these comparisons within a theoretical model of developmental neurology, lateralization and/or localization of dysfunction may be sometimes inferred. To date, there are no comprehensive standardized neuropsychological test batteries marketed for infants, toddlers, or preschoolers. However, there are a number of psychometric instruments used to make inferences about normal brain development for young children (see Bayley, 1949; Davison, 1974; Lezak, 1995; Spreen & Strauss, 1991; Tupper, 1986). The "battery" approaches have been conceptualized as primarily a quantitative strategy of neuropsychological assessment (e.g, Lezak, 1995; Reitan & Wolfson, 1985).

Based in behavioral neurology, advocates of the "process" approach (e.g., Kaplan, 1988; Weintraub & Mesulam, 1985) regard less concern for standardized test performance, and focus more on patient history, presentation of symptoms, strategy for task completion, and analysis of errors observed and documented. Information is synthesized from these sources and used to formulate hypotheses about specific domains of neuropsychological impairment (e.g., attention, language, memory, visual-spatial skills, higher-order functions, sensation, perception, motor abilities, executive functions, emotions, and motivation).

Hypotheses based on test data are generated from instruments designed with low levels of specificity. Generally, these are standardized tests measuring multiple constructs. These hypotheses are then systematically evaluated by selecting and administering neuropsychological tests with higher levels of specificity. These latter tasks are designed to measure as few constructs as possible and are selected to double disassociate within and between domains of function thought to underpin tests from which the original hypotheses were formulated. From this view, no set of standardized tests is prescribed. Instead, the examiner chooses and/or develops appropriate tests to administer based on the hypotheses conceptualized regarding each patient's unique set of deficits. Hypotheses are either confirmed or nullified by comparing all aspects of task performance on each of the measures selected. In this way, specific deficits in task performance are accurately identified and described. Inferences are then made regarding brain function underlying performance deficits. From this viewpoint, the "process" approach is more qualitative in nature (Kaplan, 1988; Lezak, 1995).

The most salient consideration for selecting an approach to neuropsychological assessment should be to determine how the information will be utilized in outcome. For purposes of this chapter, the value of neuropsychological data is realized in one's ability to use the information to determine need for further diagnostic procedures; provide results that can be corroborated with other neurodiagnostic measures in order to confirm diagnoses; formulate appropriate treatment strategies and establish realistic goals for each patient; and establish a baseline for future retesting. In order to obtain this scope of information, both quantitative and qualitative neuropsychological data must be obtained (Lezak, 1995).

SYSTEMATIC COLLECTION OF QUALITATIVE AND QUANTITATIVE DATA

Data collection is perhaps the most laborious aspect of neuropsychological assessment. However, the process by which data are obtained yields the fruits of labor for harvesting interpretation. It is important to understand the nature of each data source and where it falls on the continuum of qualitative/quantitative information. Most neuropsychologists would agree: It is better to have too much rather than too little information. As data become more qualitative, they should be corroborated in order to be considered reliable and limit the number of false positives. Thus, multiple sources of data are necessary for diagnosis and treatment.

Patient and family history should be obtained by the patient's parents, grandparents, and other involved caregivers if possible. History inventories can be used to cross-reference information obtained in interviews as well as medical, psychological, and school records. Teachers and physicians may also be asked to complete questionnaires to obtain specifics. Any discrepancies revealed should be addressed with the sources. If questionnaires are used, then multiple-choice formats have been shown to be the most reliable (Gray et al., 1987).

Symptoms may be identified from clinical interviews, symptom inventories, medical and school records, behavioral rating scales, systematic behavioral observation, and contact with professionals involved in the care of the child. Symptoms should be clarified with the patient and parents, and may be organized under the following headings: behavioral, somatic, cognitive, and emotional. The clarification process needs careful attention, because children presenting with perceptual symptoms, as well as their parents, may be unable to accurately describe the clinical condition.

Obtaining developmental, social, and educational histories are often the best methods of reconstructing the child's behavioral background. It is essential to note the gestational period; any exposure to teratogens, the mother's medical history during pregnancy, and complications experienced each trimester (see Gray et al., 1987). Specific details regarding labor and delivery may be telling for many neurological conditions. The perinatal period should carefully reviewed as apnea episodes, bradicardia, seizures, chemistry imbalances, infectious diseases, allergies, remote organ failure, neurologic cardiovasular, or neuroendocrine problems may develop during this time. Developmental milestones for sensory-motor and language functions should be carefully assessed. Changes in sleep, appetite, thirst, and energy level need to be documented as part of the developmental history. Any medical problems and associated changes in behavior during infancy and childhood must be considered. Of particular concern are chronic inner-ear infections, previously ignored head injuries, chemical exposures, and prolonged surgical procedures, particularly of the heart, lungs, or brain.

Family history offers information regarding the child's genetic predisposition to central nervous system disorder, neuropsychiatric disturbances, or remote organ disease affecting central nervous system dysfunction. Questionnaires are sometimes effective, but directed questioning is usually required as extended family members are not often considered when parents are completing surveys.

The child's social and educational background are often closely related. There is also a relationship between quality of prenatal and postnatal care and socioeconomic status (see Batchelor et al., 1988). Thus, parents' educational level, occupation, and work history are important. How and where the child spent, or is spending, the early childhood years should be considered. The frequency with which the child attends to and moves between schools may also be a factor. Repeated grades and special services provided should be noted. An exploration on interpersonal skills and style with peers, younger and older children, and adults playing different roles (i.e., parents and teachers) should be made. A history of potential abuse or neglect must not be overlooked, as head injury and hypoxic episodes (Munchausen's Syndrome by Proxy) are not uncommon under these circumstances.

The clinical interview offers the neuropsychologist a chance to obtain information about symptoms that help clarify the nature of the child's problem(s). Some would argue that an accurate history of the presenting symptoms are essential for formulating hypotheses about test selection (Kaplan, 1988) and diagnosis (Dunn & Epstein, 1987). The style of interview is directed by the age of the child, the presenting complaints, and the integration of developmental, medical, family, social, and educational histories. However, it is often helpful to ask some routine questions (in the form of questionnaires and in person) to ensure nothing has been missed. These routine questions may be looked at as a review of neuropsychological systems, much as physicians consider a review of physical systems. Specific sensory-motor, emotion, and cognitive changes—recent or remote— may provide insight into premorbid status and/or long-standing cyclical patterns of behavior(s). Finally, onset of symptoms and course of illness must be clearly understood. Table 2.2 offers a guideline to obtain qualitative information during the clinical interview that cannot always be accurately characterized through other means.

A synthesis of information may be derived from the clinical interview and medical, developmental, social, educational, and family history. These data will enable the neuropsychologist to formulate hypotheses regarding premorbid status and neuropsychological strengths and weaknesses. Although the types of problems are often clear by this point in the assessment process, the sources may not be. Herein lies the purpose of neuropsychological testing, neurological examination, and other neurodiagnostic procedures. Hypotheses for assessment must be based in a model of brain development that makes allowances for aberrations

TABLE 2.2 Review of Neuropsychological Systems

1. Arousability: Sleep/Wake Patterns
2. Excitability: Activity Level Throughout the 24 Cycle: Subjective Report of Energy by the Patient
3. Distractibility by Stimuli in Various Modalities: Speed of Processing Verbal/Visual/ Motor
4. Comportment: Impulse Control/Frustration Tolerance/Ability to Self-Monitor
5. Mood and Modulation of Affect: Stability vs. Liability
6. Motivation: Interests vs. Noninterests (level of energy put forth; strengths vs. weaknesses)
7. Motor Skills (Gross and Fine)
8. Vestibular Functioning: Balance and Stability
9. Sensorium: Elementary/Complex (changes across modalities including hallucinations/illusions; ability to tolerate intensity stimuli in various modalities)
10. Ability to Tolerate Change in Activities
11. Language: Comprehension, Repetition, Word Finding, Discourse, Speed, Pressure, Articulation, Fluency
12. Thought Processes: Intrusions, Ruminations, Cosmological, Illogical, Confusion, Disjointed, or Disorganized Thoughts; Cognitive Slippage; Concrete vs. Abstract Content
13. Visual-Spatial Skills: Choice of Play Activities, Work Activities, Style of Play and Work, Dysmetria
14. Orientation: Time, Person, Place, Space
15. Memory: Retrograde-Antograde; Episodic, Auditory/Verbal, Visual-Spatial-Motor
16. Organization: Self in Context of Activity, House, School, Play
17. Compulsions/Phobias
18. Unusual Experiences (e.g. deja vu, jamais vu, clairvoyance, fainting, black-out spells, depersonalization, dizziness, vertigo, hypersensitivity, hyperreligiousity, sweats, periods of confusion, stereotypes, tics, copralalia
20. Ability to Modulate between Intra-Personal and Extra-Personal Space
21. Lateral Preference for Peripheral Sensory and Motor Tasks

in organization of cognitive functioning, unique learning styles, and wide variations in performance expectations for various clinical populations (see Dean,
1985a).

Most neuropsychologists would agree that if neuropsychological testing is
warranted, then some measure of general functioning is indicated. The Wechsler
Series offers information that is relevant to both issues of sensitivity and specificity. As previously mentioned, the general summary scores (FSIQ, VIQ-PIQ discrepancy) are sensitive indicators (Black, 1976; Boll & Reitan, 1972a, 1972b, 1972c;
Hynd & Willis, 1988). However, each of the subtests of the Wechsler Intelligence
Scale for Children-Revised (WISC-R) have been correlated with neuropsychological measures (see Batchelor et al., 1991; Fischer, 1987) and have been used to formulate hypotheses regarding deficits within and between domains of cognitive
functioning (Kaplan, 1988). Based on hypotheses formulated from background
information, behavioral observations, and performance on subtest measures of
general ability (Fischer 1987; Lezak, 1995), other tests designed to assess specific
domains of functioning are often selected. Neuropsychological testing should be
comprehensive, encompassing measures of sensation and motor functions, attention, perception, language, visual-spatial skills, organization, memory and
new learning, motivation, emotions, and personality. Abstract reasoning and
problem solving, as well as executive abilities, should also be included, where developmentally appropriate.

The neuropsychologist should be equipped with the ability to utilize a number of tests that are developmentally appropriate. Some should measure as few
constructs as possible. Others should measure overlapping constructs, in order to
double disassociate neuropsychological deficits and corroborate findings. Tests
yielding scores with strong predictive validity may provide answers to questions
regarding generalized brain dysfunction and may offer hypotheses about specific
cognitive strengths and weaknesses. Qualitative aspects of neuropsychological
tests may be utilized to compensate for information lost in standardized testing
designed to obtain higher degrees of sensitivity. Moreover, by administering
both qualitative and quantitative measures, neuropsychologists will increase the
likelihood of producing data that are sensitive to generalized brain damage. This
approach can also be interpreted to more accurately identify a constellation of
cognitive deficits that may lead to hypotheses about more specific aspects of
brain dysfunction. These inferential formulations may then be considered in concert with other existing data for diagnostic purposes and treatment planning.

INTEGRATION AND INTERPRETATION OF QUALITATIVE AND QUANTITATIVE DATA

Once data are obtained from neuropsychological assessment, the neuropsychologist in the rehabilitation setting must determine if and what further diagnostic
procedures are indicated; document different aspects of the patient's history, the
clinical interview, and the results and interpretation of the neuropsychological

tests; and determine what treatment strategies will be useful based on the analysis and interpretation of the test results. There have been several different interpretive strategies postulated for making inferences regarding brain functioning (see Kaplan, 1988; Lezak, 1995; Reitan, 1967).

Reitan (e.g., 1967) has discussed three related but independent interpretive methods. The levels of performance approach compares the patient's test scores to standardized norms. This inter-individual method may be misleading as there are some brain-injured individuals who score high on standardized tests, and some without brain damage who score low on these same measures (Jarvis & Barth, 1984; Reitan & Wolfson, 1985).

Performance patterns have also been recognized as potential indicators of brain damage (Babcock, 1930; Matarazzo, 1972; Reitan, 1967; Wechsler, 1955). This intra-individual approach may also lead to false conclusions about the presence or absence of brain damage (Jarvis & Barth, 1984) given that a number of other variables such as socioeconomic status, educational opportunities, and parental influences may account for discrepant performance patterns.

More neurologically based, a third method involves the comparison of sensory, motor, and reflex functioning on either side of midline. While nonspecific, a higher incidence of neuropsychological soft signs (e.g, essentially measures of coordinated gross and fine musculature) have been found in clinical pediatric populations (see Tupper [1986] for review). Peripheral lesions notwithstanding, replicable asymmetries in reflexes and functions governed by the cranial nerves are almost always pathognomonic signs of central nervous system damage. However, the examiner must keep in mind that complex sensory-perceptual or motor abilities cannot be reliably tested until the child fully comprehends the task requirements.

Further, complex sensory-motor abilities and reflexes develop at variable rates, giving rise to considerations for individual differences (Dean, 1985b). Certain primitive reflexes (e.g., the Moro) emerge and disappear over the course of normal central nervous system development. However, brain damage is suspicious should reflexes be unexpectedly absent or return after they have disappeared. This method of inference is limited for reasons similar to the first. Discrete lesions in the teriary zones of the cerebral cortex, as well as some subcortical and midbrain structures, may easily be missed.

A fourth method of inferring brain damage comes from qualitative analysis of errors made in the process of completing the task (Kaplan, 1988; Lezak, 1995). "Organic signs" have been defined as aberrant responses or response sets (Lezak, 1995). A number of authors have described specific test results that are postulated signs of organicity in adults (e.g., Fuller & Laird, 1963; Satz, 1966; Wechsler, 1958). Kaplan (1988) has eloquently characterized a variety of errors and response modalities that have been linked to brain damage in adults. However, the efficacy of this approach has not been clearly demonstrated with children.

Because assessment of the developing brain presents with unique challenges, and no single interpretive method is fool-proof, interpretation of neuropsychological data warrants consideration and corroboration of all available sources.

Conclusion of brain dysfunction founded on significant neuropsychological findings alone should be made based on compelling evidence. Test results must be interpreted with consideration of background information, neurological findings, and other available neurodiagnostic information.

Further procedures are often indicated and will vary with the information obtained in the neuropsychological evaluation. Referrals are made based on need for corroborative evidence and/or symptoms that may be identified by the neuropsychologist, but not adequately assessed with neuropsychological tests (e.g., visual distortion, vestibular dysfunction, seizure disorder, etc.). The recommendation for specific procedures should be based on clarification of the presenting symptoms, hypotheses formulated from interpretation of test results, knowledge of neuroanatomy, and relationships between structure and function.

For example, vestibular dysfunction may result from damage to all aspects of the visual system; the vestibulospinal tracts; the eighth cranial nerve and its afferent tracts; the four brain stem vestibular nuclei; the second, third, fourth, and fifth cranial nerves and respective nuclei; the inferior or superior colliculei; and the tectum, medial, or lateral geniculate bodies of the thalamus. Based on the patient's presenting symptoms and neuropsychological test results, the neuropsychologist may hypothesize damage to the propreoceptive, auditory, and/or visual systems. Recommendations would be made accordingly for comprehensive neurological assessment, posturography, as well as visual evoked and/or auditory evoked potentials. In follow-up, corroborative evidence would be supplied and the source(s) of the problem identified. Where possible, treatment would be provided.

Neuropsychologists' assessment may stand alone for purposes of diagnosing higher cortical dysfunction and forming a baseline for reevaluation. Interpretation of valid test results must be made within the context of symptom presentation, background information, and knowledge gained in the clinical interview. The value of any interpretive statement indicating neuropsychological deficits depends on the clinician's understanding of the specificity and sensitivity of the test result(s) used to make inference. It is useful to know that the patient's brain is damaged. For this purpose, quantitative interpretive approaches (e.g., Selz & Reitan, 1979) and assessment of pathognomonic signs corroborated by other neurodiagnostic test results are recommended. However, in order to develop appropriate strategies for treatment, information regarding specific processing deficits within the affected cognitive domains is required. Such information may be derived, in part, from patterns of performance. However, task analysis provides the opportunity for the clinician to examine specific aberrations in cognitive functioning underlying performance deficits. Qualitative analysis informs us of how the patient fails to succeed at the task. Once deficits are clearly characterized, specific treatment interventions can be developed and implemented for remediation or compensation. Adjustment issues resulting from neuropsychiatric and psychiatric complications must also be conceptualized and integrated to formulate an adequate perspective on the scope of treatment necessary to serve the child's motivational and emotional needs.

Evaluation of the emotional/motivational/behavioral aspects of the child's functioning is essential to all comprehensive neuropsychological assessments and should be at least screened, regardless of the presenting complaints.

The debate continues regarding the etiology of emotional/motivational/behavioral sequelae associated with children who are brain damaged. There is evidence to support changes in the child's personality consistent with what would be expected from the location of injury after the brain has incurred insult (Levin & Eisenberg, 1979). However, Klonoff and Parris (1974) have noted behavioral responses (e.g., denial and low self-concept) to brain injury that are common in the normal population. In either case, children with neurological impairment are six times more likely than normals to experience emotional/motivational/behavioral sequelae as a direct result or secondary to brain damage (Dean, 1986).

Theorectically, injury to the brain could result in both direct neurobehavioral sequelae and emotional reactivity. While researchers view this area as fertile ground for future investigation, clinicians continue to struggle with decision making in assessment of emotional dysfunction as a primary presenting symptom. A relatively recent and comprehensive discussion of this topic can be found in Dean's (1986) review of the literature. For purposes of neuropsychological assessment, objective measures are perhaps the safest means of obtaining reliable data in neurologically impaired populations. Children with impaired sensory, perceptual, motor, visual-spatial, language, and/or executive plan functions may perform poorly on projective measures for reasons other than emotional/motivational/behavioral disturbance.

Other significant factors worthy of consideraton to be integrated for interpretation include onset and course of the emotional/motivational/behavioral symptom; the extent to which organic impairment can be linked to the primary symptom based on knowledge of previous research and neuroanatomy of the lesion; treatment effectiveness of previous somatic regimens (medication, surgery, and the like); length of hospitalization and response to treatment; and varying severity of individual symptoms (Dean, 1986). Causative statements linking brain damage to emotional/motivational/behavioral sypmtoms should be rendered with caution. However, to the extent to which these sequelae complicate the developmental habilation or rehabilitation process, due consideration must be given in treatment plans utilizing whatever appropriate strategies are indicated (e.g., crisis intervention, behavioral management, medication, surgery in epilepsy, rehabiliation psychotherapy, family therapy).

Once all information is appropriately integrated, interpreted, and reported, the neuropsychological test results can then be used to establish a baseline for reevaluation. In this way, effectiveness of treatment can be quantified as outcome. Alone, neuropsychological test results may not encompass all aspects of the patient's rehabilitation needs. Modified outcome studies designed to demonstrate effectiveness of treatment based on neuropsychological test results and other aspects of rehabilitation programming can be extrapolated from Evans and Ruff's (1992) work with adults. Combining strategies to assess treatment outcome involving both medical and neuropsychological approaches may further explicate the value and role of neuropsychological assessment in treating children with neurologic disorders.

REFERENCES

Babcock, H. (1930). An experiment in the measurement of mental deterioration. *Archives of Psychology, 117,* 105.

Batchelor, E. S., & Dean, R. S. (1990). Sex differences in neuropsychological performance of children with reading disorders. *International Journal of Neurosciences, 50,* 95–102.

Batchelor, E. S. Gray, R. S., Dean, R. S. & Lowery, R. (1988). Interactive effects of socioeconomic factors and perinatal complications. *NASP Program Abstracts, F,-169,* 115–116.

Batchelor, E. S., Sowles, G., Dean, R. S., & Fischer, W., (1991). Construct validity of the Halstead-Reitan Neuropsychological Battery for children with learning disorders. *Journal of Psychoeducational Assessment, 9,* 16–31.

Bayley, N. (1949). Consistency and variability in the growth of intelligence from birth to eighteen years. *Journal of Genetic Psychology, 75,* 165–196.

Benton, A. L. (1974). Clinical neuropsychology in childhood: An overview. In R. M. Reitan & L. A. Davison (Eds.), *Clinical neuropsychology: Current status and applications.* Washington, DC: V. H. Winston & Sons.

Bigler, E. D. (1991). Neuropsychological assessment, neuroimagining and clinical neuropsychology: A synthesis. *Archives of Clinical Neuropsychology, 6,* 113–132.

Black, F. W. (1976). WISC Verbal-Performance discrepancies as indicators of neurologic dysfunction in pediatric patients. *Journal of Clinical Psychology, 30,* 165–167.

Boll, T. J. (1974). Behavioral correlates of cerebral damage in children aged 9 through 14. In R. M. Reitan & L. A. Davison (Eds.), *Clinical neuropsychology: Current status and applications.* Washington, DC: V. H. Winston & Sons.

Boll, T. J. (1978). Diagnosing brain impairment. In B. B. Wolman (Ed.), *Clinical diagnosis of mental disorders.* New York: Plenum Press.

Boll, T. J., & Reitan, R. M. (1972a). Comparative ability interrelationships in normal and brain damaged children. *Journal of Clinical Psychology, 28,* 152–156.

Boll, T. J., & Reitan, R. M. (1972b). Motor and tactual perceptual deficits in brain damaged children. *Perceptual and Motor Skills, 34,* 343–350.

Boll, T. J., & Reitan, R. M. (1972c). The comparative intercorrelations of brain-damaged and normal children on the trail making test and the Wechsler-Bellevue Scale. *Journal of Clinical Psychology, 28,* 491–493.

Chelune, G. J., & Edwards, P. (1981). Early brain lesions: Ontogenic-environmental considerations. *Journal of Consulting and Clinical Psychology, 49,* 777–790.

Crockett, D., Klonoff, H., & Bejerring, J. (1969). Factor analysis of neuropsychological tests. *Perceptual and Motor Skills, 29,* 259–262.

Davison, L. A., (1974). Current status in clinical neuropsychology. In R. M. Reitan & L. A. Davison (Eds.), *Clinical neuropsychology: Current status and applications.* Washington, DC: V. H. Winston & Sons.

Dean, R. S. (1985a). Neuropsychological assessment. In J. D. Cavenar, R. Michels, H. K. H. Brodie, A. M. Cooper, S. B. Guz, L. L. Judd, G. L. Klerman, & A. J. Solnit (Eds.), *Psychiatry.* Philadelphia: Lippincott.

Dean, R. S. (1985b). Foundation and rationale for neuropsychological bases of individual differences. In L. Hartledge & K. Telzrow (Eds.), *Neuropsychology of individual differences* (pp. 7–39). New York: Plenum Press.

Dean, R. S. (1986). Neuropsychological aspects of psychiatric disorders. In J. E. Obrzut & G. W. Hynd (Eds.), *Child neuropsychology: clinical practice* (vol. 2, pp. 83–112). London: Academic Press.

Dikeman, S., Matthews, C. G., & Harley, J. P. (1975). The effect of early versus late onset of major motor epilepsy upon cognitive intellectual performance. *Epilepsia, 2,* 472–482.

Duffy, F. H., Denkla, M. B., Bartels, P. H., Sandini, G., & Kiessling, L. S. (1979). Dyslexia: Automated diagnosis by computerized classification of brain electrical activity. *Annals of Neurology, 7,* 421–428.

Dunn, D. W., & Epstein, L. G. (1987). *Decision making in child neurology.* Toronto, Canada: B. C. Decker, Inc.

Evans, W. R., & Ruff, R. M. (1992). Outcome value: A perspective on rehabilitation outcomes achieved in acquired brain injury. *Journal of Head Trauma, 7,* 24–38.

Fischer, W. (1987). Neuropsychological interpretation of intelligence tests. In R. S. Dean (Ed.), *Introduction to assessing human intelligence.* Springfield, IL: Charles Thomas.

Fuller, G. B., & Laird, J. T. (1963). The Minnesota Perceptodiagnostic Test. *Journal of Clinical Psychology, Monograph Supplement, 16.*

Galaburda, A. M., Signoret, J. C., & Ronthal, M. (1985). Left posterior angiomatous anomaly and developmental dyslexia: Report of five cases. *Neurology (Cleveland) 35 (Suppl.),* 198.

Golden, C. J., Hammeke, T. A., & Purisch, A. D. (1978). Diagnostic validity of a standardized neuropsychological battery derived from Luria's neuropsychological tests. *Journal of Clinical and Consulting Psychology, 46,* 1258–1265.

Gray, J. W., Dean, R. S., & Rattan, G. (1987). Assessment of perinatal risk factors. *Psychology in the Schools, 24,* 15–21.

Gur, R. C. (1985). Imaging regional brain physiology in behavioral neurology. In M. M. Mesulam (Ed.), *Principles of behavioral neurology* (pp. 139–186). Philadelphia: F. A. Davis Press.

Halstead, W. C. (1947). *Brain and intelligence: A quantitative study of the frontal lobes.* Chicago: The University of Chicago Press.

Halstead, W. C. (1951). Biological intelligence. *Journal of Personality, 20,* 118–130.

Hartledge, C. C., & Hartledge, P. L. (1977). Psychological testing in neurological diagnosis. In J. Youman (Ed.), *Neurological surgery.* Philadelphia: Saunders.

Hartledge, L. C., & Reynolds, C. R. (1981). Neuropsychological assessment and individualization of instruction. In G. W. Hynd & J. E. Obrzut (Eds.), *Neuropsychological assessment and the school-age child: Issues and perspectives.* Orlando, FL: Grune & Stratton.

Hynd, G. W., & Obrzut, J. E. (Eds.). (1981). *Neuropsychological assessment and the school-age child: Issues and perspectives.* Orlando, FL: Grune & Stratton.

Hynd, G. W., & Snow, J. H. (1986). Assessment of neurological and neuropsychological factors associated with severe learning disabilities. In D. J. Lazarus & S. S. Strichart (Eds.), *Psychoeducational evaluation of children with low intellectual handicaps.* Orlando, FL: Grune & Stratton.

Hynd, G. W., & Willis, W. G. (1988). *Pediatric neuropsychology.* Orlando, FL: Grune & Stratton.

Jarvis, P. E., & Barth, J. T. (1984). *Halstead-Reitan Test Battery: An interpretive guide.* Odessa, FL: PAR.

Kaplan, E. (1988). A process approach to neuropsychological assessment. In T. J. Boll & B. K. Bryant (Eds.), *Clinical neuropsychology and brain function: Research measurement and practice* (pp. 129–167). Washington, DC: APA.

Kaplan, E. (1990). Lectures in neuropsychology. Boston V.A. Hospital, Boston.

Kaufman, A. S. (1979). *Intelligent testing with the WISC-R.* New York: Wiley Interscience.

Klonoff, H., & Parris, R. (1974). Immediate, short term and residual effects of acute head injuries in children: Neuropsychological and neurological correlates. In R. M. Reitan & L. A. Davison (Eds.), *Clinical neuropsychology: Current status and applications.* Washington, DC: V. H. Winston & Sons.

Languis, M., & Wittrock, M. C. (1986). Integrating neuropsychological and cognitive research: A perspective for bridging brain-behavior relationships. In J. E. Obrzut & G. W. Hynd (Eds.), *Child neuropsychology: clinical practice* (vol. 2, pp. 209–239). London: Academic Press.

Levin, H. S., & Eisenberg, H. M. (1979). Neuropsychological impairment after closed head injury in children and adolescents. *Journal of Pediatric Psychology, 4,* 389–402.

Lezak, M. D. (1995). *Neuropsychological assessment.* New York: Oxford University Press.

Matarazzo, J. D. (1972). *Wechsler's measurement and appraisal of adult intelligence* (5th ed.). New York: Oxford University Press.

McCall, R. B., Hogarty, P. S., & Hurlburt, N. (1972). Transitions in infant sensory-motor development and the prediction of childhood IQ. *American Psychologist, 27,* 728–748.

McGlone, J., & Davidson, W. (1973). The relation between spatial ability with special reference to sex and hand preference. *Neuropsychologia, 11,* 105–113.

Pawlik, G., & Heiss, W.-D. (1989). Positron emission tomography and neuropsychological function. In E. D. Bigler, R. A Yeo, & E. Turkheimer (Eds.), *Neuropsychological function and brain imagining.* New York: Plenum Press.

Pedhazur, E. J. (1973). *Multiple regression in behavioral research: Explanation and prediction.* New York: CBS College Publishing

Pirozzolo, F. J., Campanella, D. J., Christensen, K., & Lawson-Kerr, K. (1981). Effects of cerebral dysfunction of neurolinguistic performance in children. *Journal of Consulting and Clinical Psychology, 49,* 791–806.

Rattan, A. I., & Rattan, G., (1987). A historical perspective on the nature of intelligence. In R. S. Dean (Ed.), *Introduction to assessing human intelligence.* Springfield, IL: Charles Thomas.

Reed, H. B. C., Reitan, R. M., & Klove, H. (1965). The influence of cerebral lesions on psychological test performance in children. *Journal of Consulting Psychology, 29,* 247–251.

Reitan, R. M. 1967). Psychological assessment of deficits associated with brain lesions in subjects with normal and subnormal intelligence. In J. L. Khanna (Eds.), *Brain damage and mental retardation: A psychological evaluation.* Springfield, IL: Charles Thomas.

Reitan, R. M. (1969). *Manual for administration of neuropsychological test batteries for adults and children.* Indianapolis, IN: Author.

Reitan, R. M., & Wolfson, D. (1985). *The Halstead-Reitan Neuropsychological Test Battery: Theory and clinical interpretation.* Tucson, AZ: Neuropsychology Press.

Satz, P. (1966). Specific and nonspecific effects of brain lesions in man. *Journal of Abnormal Psychology, 71,* 65–70.

Selz, M., & Reitan, R. M. 1979. Rules for neuropsychological diagnosis: Classification of brain function in older children. *Journal of Consulting and Clinical Psychology, 47,* 258–264.

Spreen, O., & Strauss, E. (1991). *A compendium of neuropsychological tests.* New York: Oxford Press.

Teeter, P. A. (1986). Neuropsychological batteries for children. In J. E. Obrzut & G. W. Hynd (Eds.), *Child neuropsychology: Clinical practice* (vol. 2, pp. 187–227). London: Academic Press.

Tupper, D. E. (1986). Neuropsychological screening and soft signs. In J. E. Obrzut & G. W. Hynd (Eds.), *Child neuropsychology: Clinical Practice* (vol. 2, pp. 139–186). London: Academic Press.

Turkheimer, E. (1989). Techniques of quantitative measurement of morphological structures of the central nervous system. In E. D. Bigler, R. A Yeo, & E. Turkheimer (Eds.), *Neuropsychological function and brain imaging.* New Hork: Plenum Press.

Wada, J. A., Clarke, R., & Hamm, A. (1975). Cerebral hemisphere asymmetry in humans. *Archives of Neurology, 32,* 239–246.

Wechsler, D. (1955). *Wechsler adult intelligence scale manual.* New York: Psychological Services Corp.

Wechsler, D. (1958). *The measurement and appraisal of adult intelligence* (4th ed.). Baltimore: Williams & Wilkins.

Weintraub, S. (1990). Personal supervision. Dept. of Behavioral Neurology, Beth Israel Hospital, Boston.

Weintraub, S., & Mesulam, M.-M. (1985). Mental states assessment of young and elderly adults in behavioral neurology. In M.-M. Mesulam (Ed.), *Principles of behavioral neurology* (pp. 71–123). Philadelphia: F. A. Davis Press.

3

BRIDGING THE GAP BETWEEN PSYCHOLOGY AND NEUROLOGY
Future Trends in Pediatric Neuropsychology

ERIN D. BIGLER

Traditionally, medicine has focused on relevant clinical history, physical exams, and diagnostic laboratory tests that lead to a diagnosis. Once a diagnostic conclusion has been reached, that diagnosis typically guides effective treatment, usually in the form of pharmacotherapy, surgical intervention, or some other type of physical intervention (e.g., casting for bone fracture). Clinical psychology also has followed a tradition of diagnostic assessment but often diagnostic conclusions are not complete without lengthy behavioral observations and monitoring. Whereas the physician may have precise diagnostic tools (e.g., cell blood count [CBC]) that are *definitive* for the presence or absence of a particular disorder, traditionally, psychology has not enjoyed such diagnostic precision.

In medicine and psychology these different orientations of viewing a particular problem have often dictated quite different methodologies for examining a patient complaint. For example, in the child who presents with symptoms of "inattention," the physician first may approach the evaluation problem in terms of various metabolic studies that examine thyroid and blood sugar levels and a physical exam to rule out any systemic disease. Other laboratory studies may be requested (e.g., EEG to rule out seizure disorder).

In contrast, from a psychological perspective, the clinician may focus more on family dynamics, current school and behavior problems, stress issues, personality and temperament factors, family background (in particular any family history for depression, hyperactivity, or related disorders), and a host of additional behavioral variables. Actual behavioral testing would attempt to elucidate deficits in attention, concentration, or impulse control. For example, if this were determined to be a case of Attention-Deficit Hyperactivity Disorder (ADHD) (see Nussbaum & Bigler, 1990), for the nonpsychiatric physician, the treatment most likely would be in the form of some stimulant medication alone. From the psychologic-psychiatric perspective, however, the clinician would be just as interested in how the child is doing in his or her family, school, and social environment, and may set up some type of behavioral management program or engage the child in some form of individual or family therapy.

There was a time when these two orientations were somewhat at odds with one another, with each ideologic "camp" (i.e., medicine vs. behavioral intervention) claiming better success rates and more effective treatment. Fortunately, for the bonafide ADHD child it is now well documented that the disorder should not be treated in isolation but rather through a merging of both the medical and behavioral treatment aspects (Nussbaum & Bigler, 1990; Whalen & Henker, 1991). In part, this is because medicine has recognized further the important role that behavior plays in biologic function, and psychology has recognized the expanding role that biology plays in psychological function. Thus, even though there has been a convergence of late, it is to be expected that a natural gap remains between neurology and pediatric neuropsychology because of their historical origins and orientations in medicine and psychology.

This "gap" between psychology and neurology is rapidly closing, however, as the two disciplines recognize the essential interdependence that they have upon one another and that the future progress of the child is dependent upon a mutual understanding of both the biologic and psychologic. In this chapter, the historical perspective of the "gap" will be discussed, followed by current areas where the gap still exists, and concluded with a discussion on how the gap may be closed.

PSYCHOLOGY AND NEUROLOGY: HISTORICAL PERSPECTIVE

Neurology has a rich and meritorious history of assessing basic nervous system function by a physical exam, reflex testing, and laboratory studies. Such procedures provided "objective" or "hard" findings as to the existence of brain dysfunction. For more than three-quarters of this century, the sentiment in neurology was that these objective findings *had* to be present before the neurologist would unequivocally state the presence or absence of brain damage. On the other end of the spectrum, clinicians who studied behavior of children with verified brain damage observed that some of the symptoms displayed by brain-damaged children (i.e., poor motor coordination, impaired visual-spatial functioning, poor attention span, impulsivity, hyperactivity, etc.) were identical to those in children who had no history of "brain damage" nor had any "physical" findings of neurologic impairment. Such findings become synonymous with "soft" neurologic signs, and the great debate was on whether these children truly had neurologic deficits or simply a pseudo-neurologic condition wherein the behavior merely mimicked "brain damage" (Rutter, 1983).

During the 1950s through the 1980s, there were great debates as to which side was correct (see Rie & Rie, 1980; Rutter, 1983). Mesulam (1985) aptly states that during this period of time, the objective "organic" approach was considered as the "insensitive sledgehammer" and behavior "as the soft underbelly of neurology" (p. viii).

In 1966, Luria's tome entitled *Higher Cortical Functions in Man* was translated into English. Concerning this seminal contribution to learning and its impact on bridging the gap between neurology and psychology, Hans-Lukas Teuber made the following statement in the book's preface: "Professor Luria's book thus marks a further and decisive step toward the eventual coalescence of neurology and psychology, a goal to which only a few laboratories in the East and West have been devoted over the last decades." Influenced by Luria's work, along with the standardization of a number of clinical neuropsychological tests from the 1950s through early 1970s (e.g., Benton Visual Retention Test, Boston Diagnostic Aphasia Exam, Halstead-Reitan Neuropsychological Test Battery), neuropsychology's position by the late 1970s and early 1980s had become solidified and neurology was expanding its role in understanding "behavior." As led by Norman Geschwind, this merging of behavior and neurology was signaled by M-Marsel Mesulam's text *Principles of Behavioral Neurology* in 1985. Mesulam, a physician, recognized the critical interdependence of neurology and neuropsychology in the development of behavioral neurology by this statement: "Since the single most fundamental aspect of behavioral neurology is the systematic assessment of mental state, the neuropsychologist has played one of the most important roles in the development of the entire field" (p. viii).

Neurology as a subspecialty of medicine is in its second century (Gowers, 1888). In contrast, neuropsychology has emerged as a clinical discipline only in the last half of this century. From the 1950s to the 1980s, neuropsychology went from single paper-pencil tests (e.g., the Bender Visual-Motor Gestalt Test) to elaborate tests that assess neurocognitive functioning (see Bigler, 1988; Lezak, 1983).

Prior to the advent of neuroimaging studies, neuropsychology was particularly dependent on the neurologic exam, laboratory procedures (e.g., EEG), and neurosurgical confirmation or autopsy to verify structural anatomic areas of damage (Bigler, 1991). Although great strides were made during this era, several restrictions were imposed on the generalization of neuropsychological data and clinical application of neuropsychological findings because of the imprecise methods for lesion quantification. However, with the introduction of various neuroimaging methods wherein in-vivo studies could be done concomitant with neuropsychological tests, greater precision in brain-behavioral relationships has resulted (Bigler, Yeo, & Turkheimer, 1989; Damasio & Damasio, 1989).

This cross-fertilization or bridging between neurology and psychology first emerged with adults and then extended to children. Part of the delay in extending to children has been the problem with developmental issues both in neurologic development as well as cognitive skill, motor, sensory-perceptual, and language acquisition. Additionally, there are no comprehensive standardized neuropsychological test batteries for children.

An example of the change that has occurred in pediatric neurology can be gained from examining past textbooks. In 1969, Patrick Bray, a pediatric neurologist, published his classic text in pediatric neurology entitled *Neurology in*

Pediatrics. The cover of the text had a reflex hammer and an EEG tracing, again underscoring the reliance on objective test findings. This text had 514 pages yet only 19 dealt with "mental, behavior, and learning disorders." In contrast, Herskowitz and Rosman, also pediatric neurologists, published in 1982 the pediatric neurology text entitled *Pediatrics, Neurology and Psychiatry—Common Ground.* The entire text is devoted to an integration of understanding underlying neurologic function, psychologic/psychiatric, and developmental issues in behavior. Thus, Herskowitz and Rosman focused on the necessity to integrate clinical information at the physical, neurological, and psychological (or behavioral) levels in the treatment of the whole child.

Based on this brief historical review, it is apparent that the gap between neurology and psychology has, in part, been bridged. What is needed now is an increased span of the bridge, its moorings and footings, and to develop more bridges. This will be the focus of the subsequent topic headings.

NEUROIMAGING

Various neuroimaging methods have emerged rapidly as the premier in-vivo methods to study structural integrity of the brain (Bigler et al., 1989). Foremost, current neuroimaging techniques utilizing magnetic resonance imaging (MRI) provide exquisite anatomic detail for both the normal as well as pathological brain (see Figure 3.1). Other neuroimaging methods (see review by Pawlik &

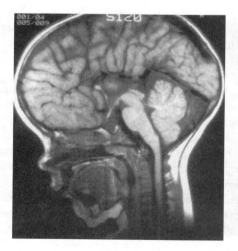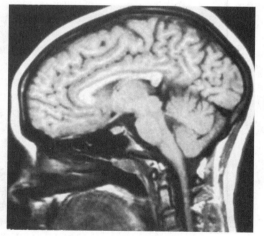

FIGURE 3.1 Mid-sagittal MRI views from a normal child (left) and one with congenital agenesis of the corpus callosum (right). Note the exquisite anatomic detail that the MRI provides. See Bigler, Rosenstein, Roman, and Nussbaum (1988).

Heiss, 1989)—such as single photon emission computed tomography (SPECT), positron emission tomography (PET), or regional cerebral blood flow (CBF)—provide metabolic information in addition to anatomic data that can be provided by MRI methods or computerized tomography (CT) (see Figures 3.1 and 3.2). Also there are a variety of ways of undertaking regional cerebral blood flow studies (Abou-Khalil, Siegel, Sackellares, Gilman, Hichwa, & Marshall, 1987; Chugni, Phelps, & Mazziotta, 1987) and some other metabolic methods for brain imaging, but the ones just mentioned are those most commonly in use at this time.

FIGURE 3.2 (Far left) Computed tomographic scan of patient with Broca's aphasia showed moderately large lesion that spared Broca's area. (Second from left) Positron emission tomographic scan obtained from same level as computed tomographic scan. PET scan demonstrates left-to-right metabolic asymmetry throughout left hemisphere. The Gray scale displays quantitative metabolic rates expressed in milligrams per 100g per minute. (Middle left) Computed tomographic scan of patient with Wernicke's aphasia. Computed tomographic scan demonstrates large lesion in posterior cerebral cortex of the dominant hemisphere. (Center right) Positron emission tomographic scan shows prominent metabolic asymmetry in posterior regions, with mild-to-moderate frontal lobe asymmetry. The Gray scale displays quantitative metabolic rates expressed in milligrams per 100g per minute. (Second from right) Computed tomographic scan of patient with conduction aphasia. Computed tomographic scan demonstrates moderate-sized lesion in posterior cerebral cortex of the dominant hemisphere. (Far right) Positron emission tomographic scan shows typical pattern observed in 8 of 10 patients with asymmetry in posterior left hemisphere, while prefrontal regions were symmetric. The Gray scale displays quantitative metabolic rates expressed in milligrams per 100g per minute. From "Cerebral Glucose Metabolism in Wernicke's, Broca's and Conduction Aphasia" by E. J. Metter, D. Kempler, C. Jackson, W. R. Hanson, J. C. Mazziota, & M. E. Phelps, 1989, *Archives of Neurology, 46*. Copyright 1989, American Medical Association. Reprinted by permission. These images demonstrate the use of anatomic and metabolic imaging to depict lesion boundaries.

The rapid growth of these technologies has far outstripped the ability to keep up with behavioral studies to further elicit brain (anatomic)-behavior relationships. For example, in Figure 3.3, the MRI depicts marked dilation of the ventricular system in a young male child who has obvious hydrocephalus. The anatomic detail is exquisite in its demonstration of the pathologic state of hydrocephalus. However, just viewing the brain's pathologic state does not necessarily tell much about what behavioral or cognitive deficits might be expected. In fact, looking at the extent of the ventricular dilation in this case, one might suspect a rather severe degree of mental retardation. That, however, is not the case. Neuropsychological data on this child (see Figure 3.3 caption) demonstrated relatively spared language abilities with normal verbal intelligence but significant visual-spatial deficits. Thus, some aspects of cognitive/mental functioning are quite intact in this child, which may not have been predicted if one just restricted interpretation to the amount and degree of structural damage.

Accordingly, a major area that has had to be "bridged" between neurology and psychology is the utilization of this anatomic information in terms of better understanding brain-behavior relationships. There have been several recent texts

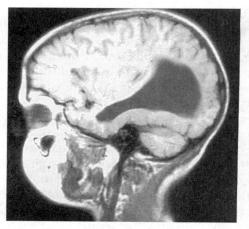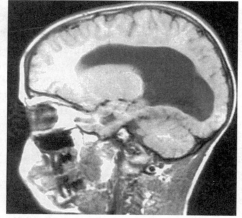

FIGURE 3.3   The two saggital MRI views depict marked ventricular dilation in this 9-year-old child with congenital hydrocephalus. Despite the prominent hydrocephalus and obvious structural changes in the brain, this child had some remarkable intact functions. For example, at age 9, his verbal IQ score on the Wechsler Intelligence Scale for Children (WISC-R) was 95, along with a sequential processing score of 85 on the Kaufman Assessment Battery for Children (KABC). The child did have significant perceptual-motor deficits (PIQ $\leq$ 45; KABC simultaneous processing score = 57). These results demonstrate the problem with attempting to directly relate major structural defects with behavioral outcome. See Bigler, 1988.

(Bigler et al., 1989; Damasio & Damasio, 1989) that have dealt with this subject, but it is anticipated that this will become an even more prevalent area of investigative research. The MRI and other neuroimaging methods lend themselves readily to digital input of the data, which allows a more precise quantification for determining lesion location, abnormal tissue densities, structural volumetric values, and the like (Bigler, 1991). For example, there has been some very exciting research that has utilized MRI techniques to image the brain of learning-impaired individuals (Duara et al., 1991; Jernigan, Hesselink, Sowell & Tallal, 1991; Larsen, Holen, Lundberg, & Odegaard, 1990). Each of these studies demonstrated neuroanatomic differences between language and learning-impaired children, in contrast to nonaffected children. No diagnostic markers were identified as yet, but this research orientation has tremendous potential.

NEUROIMAGING-NEUROPSYCHOLOGICAL ASSESSMENT INTERFACE

As alluded to earlier, neuroimaging and neuropsychological assessment have typically been considered two distinct separate methods for examining the central nervous system—one focuses on structure and anatomy, the other on function and behavior. However, with the detailed refinement in imaging capability provided by MRI, it is apparent that this information could be utilized in a way in which greater precision in brain-behavior relationships could be accomplished.

For example, one could take a sample of patients with focal, lateralized lesions and develop a method using CT or MRI technology to localize the central point of the lesion and the volume of the lesion (Figure 3.4(1)). Also, one would want to pay attention to other structural changes that may occur in the brain (atrophy, ventricular dilation, homologous areas of the brain that may change in size or form, etc.). Next, that data could be utilized to determine the various regions that are "important" in controlling a particular neuropsychological function. Last, the final step would require an integration of this anatomic information with the behavioral—not in gross fashion (i.e., left hemisphere) but rather an image that demonstrates the overlapping "importance" of a particular behavior with a particular brain region.

We have essentially accomplished this, in part with the method of establishing "importance" functions that relate lesion locality and behavioral results for any given brain lesion or neuropsychological function (Turkheimer, Yeo, Jones, & Bigler, 1990; Turkheimer, Yeo, & Bigler, 1990; Yeo, Turkheimer, & Bigler, 1990). Figure 3.4 demonstrates the importance function of errors on the Reitan-Indiana Aphasia Screening Test, tactile sensory-perceptual exam of the Reitan-Klove sensory perceptual examination, and double simultaneous visual stimulation (Reitan & Wolfson, 1985). Note the areas of maximal involvement where the correspondence between localized areas of damage and their greatest effect on a behavioral measure approaches unity and how the importance function dissipates as it moves away from the "most" important region. Utilizing such importance functions based on group data, it can be applied to the individual patient

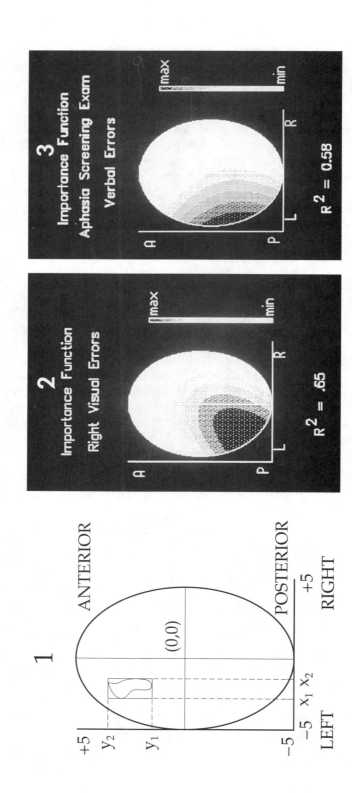

34

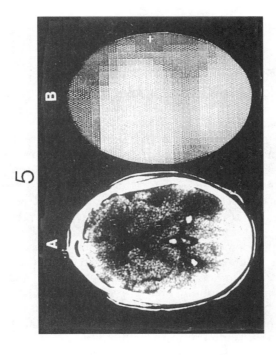

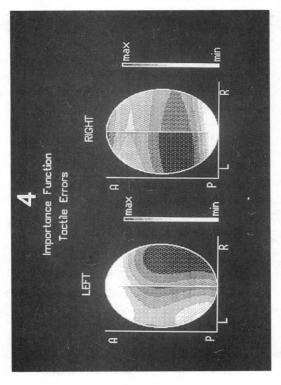

FIGURE 3.4 (1) Demonstration of estimation of lesion location as a rectangle extending from x_1 to x_2 and y_1 and y_2. (2) Right visual extinction and (3) verbal errors on the Reitan-Indiana Aphasia Screen Test. (4) Importance functions for tactile errors. (5) Importance function based on neuropsychological data from a patient (B) with right cerebral damage secondary to a cerebrovascular accident. The actual CT image is A. See Yeo, Turkheimer, and Bigler, 1990.

as well. In Figure 3.4, the importance function generated by neuropsychological data is given along with the actual CT findings. To date, no such methods have been applied to childhood disorders, but we anticipate to do so and likewise anticipate this information and line of research will be extremely useful in both applied and basic research areas.

In addition to the preceding methodology, it is apparent also that the research of others is suggesting a variety of unique ways to examine the brain. For example, Jernigan and Tallal (1990) have examined white and grey matter factors in the developing brain and see a reduction in white/grey matters ratios with aging. Piven, Berthier, Starkstein, Nehme, Pearlson, and Folstein (1990) have utilized MRI methods to identify developmental cerebrocortical malformations in autistic children. Harbord, Finn, Hall-Craggs, Robb, Kendall, and Boyd (1990) have also demonstrated developmental stages of myelination with MRI methods. Since myelination and white/grey matter ratios appear to be very critical in terms of developmental staging, a better and more precise understanding of white/grey morphometries in relationship to behavior and development appears to be a critical area of future research. This could lead to a better understanding of the anatomic basis of "developmental delay" syndromes and may provide key insights concerning the neuroanatomic factors in certain learning disorders. This line of research will undoubtedly provide for a further bridging of pediatric neuropsychology and neurology. With current quantitative neuroimaging methods, all major brain structures can now be distinguished and volumes calculated (Blatter et al., 1994). Future research will apply these methods, which are depicted in Figure 3.5, to address all of these neurodevelopmental issues.

There is another method—behavioral imaging (see Gur, Trivedi, Saykin, & Gur, 1988)—that provides a graphic display of neuropsychological performance superimposed on a pictorial image of the brain (see Figure 3.6). This method provides a way of imaging neuropsychological deficit performance based on expert ratings as to the importance of that area. While this procedure provides graphic display of potential areas of neuropsychological impairment, the method is not based on an empirical derivation of that deficit, only the impression of a panel of experts as to what that region of the brain actually controls or is involved in. Thus, there are limitations to this methodology (see Yeo et al., 1990). To date, there have been no neuropsychological studies using this method with children.

Another imaging quantification method holds promise for pediatric neuropsychology as well. This method deals with computer-generated planimetric two-dimensional maps of the cerebral cortex using MRI data (Jouandet, Tramo, Herron, Hermann, Loftus, Bazell, & Gazzaniga, 1989). This procedure allows the determination of surface area, which in turn is utilized to generate a cortical "landscape" (see Figure 3.7). The clinical significance of this information is not known at this time but it appears to be another excellent morphometric tool that may aid in examining the relationship between the developing brain and behavior.

In summary, the interface of brain imaging methodology with neuropsychological testing should strengthen the bridge between neurology and psychology.

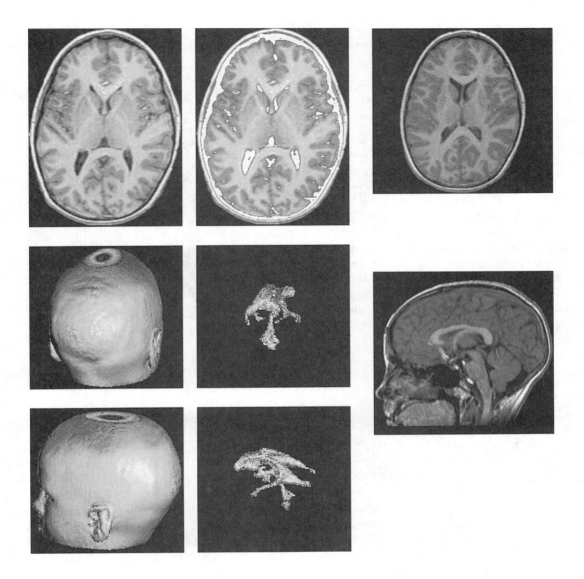

FIGURE 3.5 Standard axial (top) and saggital (left) magnetic resonance images. (Left) The upper-left image depicts the standard axial image enhanced to separate white and gray matter, along with cerebral spinal fluid (CSF) and then subjected to a threshold technique to isolate the ventricle (upper right). For each MRI slice, the ventricle is similarly identified and isolated, such that a 3-D image of the ventricle can be extracted. The 3-D ventricle in various positions is depicted in the figures in the lower left. Details for doing this type of three-dimensional image presentation have been outlined by Bigler (1992). For these illustrations, 3-D image reconstruction of the skull has been achieved and displayed to the left of the isolated ventricle, so that orientation of the ventricle can be easily distinguished. The study of the ventricular system is an indirect index as to the integrity of many brain structures (Anderson & Bigler, 1995; Gale, Johnson, Bigler, & Blatter, 1995). These type of quantitative magnetic resonance imaging methods will provide a means by which structural brain changes associated with development and/or disease can be studied.

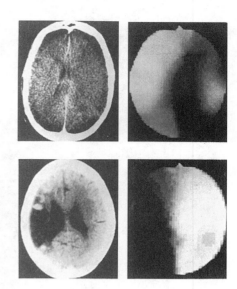

FIGURE 3.6   Behavioral imaging. (Left) CT scans depicting cerebral infarcts in the right (A) and left (C) hemisphere. (Right) Behavioral imaging results depicting (in various shades of gray with the darker image suggesting greater behavioral deficit) corresponding to the CT. From "Behavior Imaging" by R. C. Gur, S. S. Trivedi, A. J. Saykin, & R. E. Gur, 1988, *Neuropsychiatry, Neuropsychology, and Behavioral Neurology, 1.* Reprinted by permission of Raven Press.

This appears to be a most fruitful area of research in the future and one that will have tremendous clinical application, particularly in child neuropsychology.

NEUROLOGICAL, NEUROPSYCHOLOGICAL, AND DEVELOPMENTAL TESTING: PREDICTION OF FUTURE LEVEL OF FUNCTION

Predicting the outcome of function, particularly in cases where some form of early brain insult occurs or when significant developmental delays are present, has been a major diagnostic/prognostic problem in the field of pediatrics and neurology. Since the 1970s, this has become even more of a concern because of advances in medical technologies that permit the survival of very low birth weight infants and infants who are the product of life-threatening neonatal complications.

The prediction of outcome is extremely critical, because of what we know of the immature nervous system and its interaction with environmental stimulation and neuroplasticity. Huttenlocher (1990) and others in the area of developmental neurobiology have demonstrated critical periods of neuronal growth. It may be that if appropriate stimulation does not occur during these critical periods, there may be a diminution in neuroplasticity and recovery of function. Accordingly, at-risk infants or infants clearly identified as neurologic syndromes are in need of interactive therapies as early as possible. A study (Palmer et al., 1988) demonstrated that in 12- to 19-month-old spastic diplegic infants, a general stimulation treatment program that included "learning games" in addition to physical therapy was more effective than physical therapy alone in terms of general motor development. This would be fitting with the neurodevelopmental model that suggests all

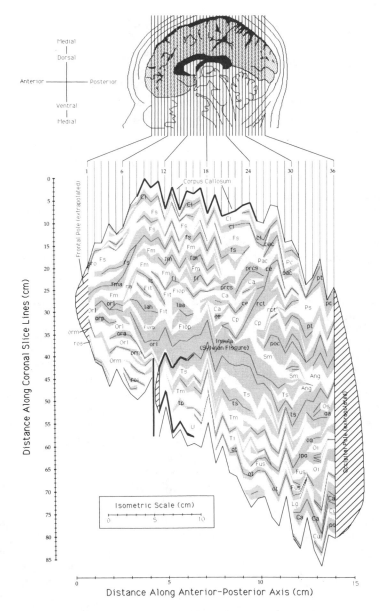

FIGURE 3.7 "Cortical landscapes" derived from MRI, left hemisphere. Gyrus names are capitalized; sulcus names are lowercase. Shaded regions represent intra-sulcal cortex; unshaded regions represent superficial cortex. Cross-hatched areas designate the extrapolated portions of the frontal and occipital poles that extended beyond the anterior and posterior limits of the scan sections. At the top is an orientation compass and a mid-sagittal representation of the hemisphere (not to scale) showing the approximate levels of coronal sections. The vertical and horizontal scales indicate MR distances; the isometric scale is used for area measurements. From Jouandet, Tramo, Herron, Hermann, Loftus, Bazzell, and Gazzanga (1989) with permission.

systems are integrated and that general stimulation per se results in improvement in specific systems. Also, this would suggest that a treatment program that has general stimulation (i.e., activities that are not designed to be specific rehabilitative aids) in addition to specific stimulation (physical therapy) may be superior to a program where specific stimulation is provided solely.

One of the problems with predicting outcome is the multitude of behavioral variables that need to be taken into consideration. Most of the outcome studies have looked at various physical findings or laboratory findings and then followed up with developmental testing. There have been few studies that have looked at neuropsychological variables and those studies have typically done only longitudinal early lifespan neuropsychological evaluation and have not yet reported findings in terms of late childhood, adolescent, or adult outcome. Thus, it appears that the most important problem facing the child neuropsychologist working in this area is a way to determine at the earliest possible date when a function deviates from normal.

Unfortunately, comprehensive developmental neuropsychological batteries essentially do not exist as of this writing (see Stoddart & Knights, 1986), and currently one has to rely on standardized developmental tests, pediatric neurologic exams, or laboratory studies (EEG, evoked response studies, ultra sound, etc.). The majority of prediction studies fall into the category of either infants with neonatal complications and/or low birth rate and prematurity (Drillien, Pickering, & Drummond, 1988; Gillberg & Gillberg, 1989; Gillberg, Gillberg, & Groth, 1989; Huttenlocher, Levine, Huttenlocher, & Gates, 1990; Iloeje, 1988; Largo, 1990; Shafer, Stokman, Shaffer, Ng, O'Connor, & Schonfeld, 1986; Taylor, Powell, Cherland, & Vaughan, 1988; Singer, Kercsmar, Lagris, Orlowski, Hill, & Doerschuk, 1989; Vohr, Garcia-Coll & Oh, 1989) or children that display developmental lag (Amiel-Tison & Ellison, 1986; Hadders-Algra, Touwen, & Huisjes, 1986; Kitchen, Rickards, Ryan, Ford, Lissenden, & Boyle, 1986; Lindahl, Michelsson, & Donner, 1988; Lindahl, Michelsson, Helenius, & Parre, 1988; Parkinson, Scrivener, Graves, Bunton, & Harvey, 1986; Portnoy, Callias, Wolke, & Gamsu, 1988; Stewart, Costello, Hamilton, Baudin, Townsend, Bradford, & Reynolds, 1989; Vohr, Coll & Oh, 1988). Essentially, all of these studies demonstrate that abnormal neurologic or developmental signs are, at least, partially predictive of subsequent deficit. This is not surprising, but what is surprising is that many of the predictive tests are what have been referred to as "soft" neurologic signs, which have generally been thought to have an imprecise relationship to cognition and behavior.

Huttenlocher, Levine, Huttenlocher, and Gates (1990) have extended these results and the importance of "soft" neurologic or developmental signs and their relationship to predicting outcome. To accomplish this, they studied children who were the product of normal pregnancy, birth, and delivery at 3 and 5 years of age on a series of standardized screening neurologic procedures (Touwen & Prechtl, 1970). Twelve neurologic tests were determined to differentiate normal from at-risk children for learning disabilities at one or at both ages. These neurologic tests are presented in Table 3.1. Follow-up of the 5-year-old group at age 7 demonstrated on linear relationship between performance on these neurologic tests and the Weschler Intelligence Scale for Children-Revised (see Figure 3.8).

TABLE 3.1 Final Set of Neurological Tasks with Scoring Criteria

Task	Description	Passing Performance
Walk on toes	Walk across room on toes after task is demonstrated by tester.	Walks on toes with feet
Walk on heels	Walk across room on heels after task is demonstrated by tester.	Walks on heels with both feet
Tandem gait forward	Walk heel to toe on a line marked by tape after demonstration by tester.	Walks with sufficient balance to avoid stepping off line
Tandem gait backward	Walk heel to toe on tape line after demonstration by tester.	Walks with sufficient balance to avoid stepping off line
Touch localization	Child is asked to close eyes and to point or to report where he is touched. The examiner touches, in turn, the dorsum of one hand, the other hand, and both hands.	Reports all stimuli correctly
Restless movements	Child sits on a chair with feet off the floor; hands in lap; he or she is asked to sit completely still for 1 minute (timed).	Child remains seated throughout the 1-minute test and is motionless for at least half the test period
Downward drift	Stand with outstretched pronated hands for 20 seconds, eyes closed.	No downward drift of either arm
Hand coordination	Child is asked to initiate rapid alternating supination and pronation of one hand at a time.	Smooth supination-pronation for at least 3 cycles with each hand
Hopping	Child is asked (or shown) to hop on one foot.	Able to hop on each foot
Alternate tapping	Child is asked to imitate 3 tapping tasks: (1) tap 5 times with right index finger (at a rate of about 2 taps/sec); (2) tap 5 times with left index finger; (3) tap alternately with left and right index finger for 4 cycles.	Performs all 3 tasks
Complex tapping	Child is asked to imitate 2 tapping tasks: (1) tap twice with left index finger and then twice with right finger, repeating the pattern 5 times at a rate of about 2 taps/sec; (2) tap once with left index finger and twice with right index finger, repeating the pattern 5 times.	Either task performed correctly

Source: Data from Huttenlocher et al., 1990.

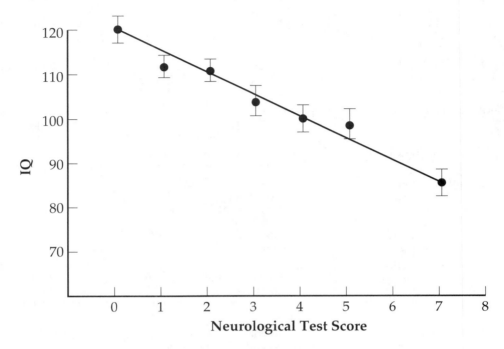

FIGURE 3.8   Regression line correlating neurologic findings with outcome. This regression line demonstrates the relationship between neurological test score (see Table 3.1) at age 5 years and full scale IQ on the Wechsler Intelligence Scale for Children at age 7. The error bars represent one SEM. See Huttenlocher, Levine, Huttenlocher, and Gates, 1990.

These results are quite impressive and indicate early stability and persistence of deficits. The more important implication of this line of research, however, is underscoring the need to identify these children as early as possible to attempt to correct the deficit via integrative and interactive therapies. The children in Huttenlocher and colleagues study were not at risk at birth, as mental retardation, cerebral palsy, and other factors were controlled for. Thus, this excellent study demonstrated that children, for whatever reason, who show some "soft" neurologic signs early on are at much higher risk for developmental and cognitive problems later in life.

To date, there has been no detailed longitudinal study of such children. This research (i.e., neonatal predictive factors and *long-term* neuropsychological outcome) is very much in need of being done. Likewise, such research would have to look back in time to attempt to determine other relationships, particularly antecedent factors during prenatal and neonatal periods that may have had subtle neurodevelopmental effects. For example, the study by Smith and Knight-Jones

(1990) in a group of 43 children who were the product of very low birth weight (<1501g) who at age 5 "were apparently normal, with no observable handicap or need for special education provision" (p. 600), there was only 1 child with a full-scale IQ score greater than 110. On the McCarthy Scales, this group of children had a general cognitive index of 88.56, in contrast to normal control children who had a score of 101.00. The implication here is that even in children that outwardly appear "normal," significant neurodevelopment effects may be related to low birth weight, which in turn may have a deleterious effect on brain and cognitive development. This type of research will aid significantly in further bridging the gap between neurology and psychology.

Along these lines, the work by Jernigan and Tallal (1990) holds considerable promise. As reviewed earlier in this chapter, their work has looked at a quantification procedure for determining white/grey matter development (Holland, Haas, Norman, Brant-Zawadzki, & Newton, 1986). It may be that children with neurodevelopmental delay have subtle morphologic abnormalities that can be detected by MRI. For example, Willerman, Schultz, Rutledge, and Bigler (1991) demonstrated a relationship between MRI findings and IQ between two groups controlled for age and education, but results were disparate in measured IQ levels (mean IQ of 89 vs. 137). These results were particularly impressive in that the findings indicated a significant difference in various volumetric measures of the brain in critical association areas (see Figure 3.9). Such findings have implications for the relationship between potential neuropsychological deficits and cognitive impairment that is based on a morphologic difference in the brain.

The combination of neurologic and neuropsychological screening methods with magnetic resonance imaging, ultra sound, evoked potential, and quantitative EEG measures (to be discussed below) should provide a way to determine which are the most sensitive early predictors. Then the task at hand would be to determine what modifies behavior and the extent of neuroplasticity that could be expected via such techniques.

ELECTROPHYSIOLOGY STUDIES

The routine EEG has not been of particular utility in evaluation of children with developmental delays. However, we have entered an era of computer-assisted EEG data analysis, in particular quantitative EEG topography mapping and more sophisticated and elaborate methods for averaging evoked responses. Duffy's original work (see Duffy, Denckla, Bartels, & Sandini, 1980) in this area demonstrated electrophysiologic irregularities in dyslexic boys that to a degree differentiated reading disorder subtypes. More recent work by Duffy and McAnulty (1990) has corroborated their earlier findings (see Figure 3.10) and extended them to demonstrate that quantitative electrophysiologic changes can be recorded that appear to demonstrate neurophysiologic correlates in response to environmental effects of a reading therapy program. Duffy interprets this work as suggesting that dyslexia may be a more dynamic or plastic process than

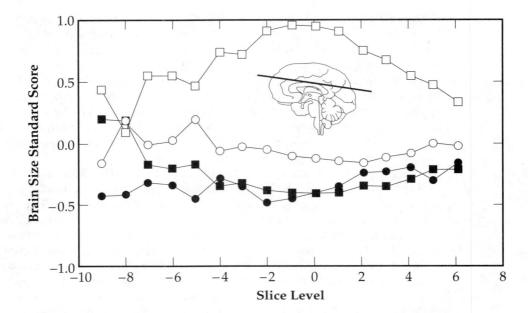

FIGURE 3.9 IQ-brain size correlations. Brain area in standard scores (mean
= ± SD = 1) by high versus average IQ and sex, adjusted for
height and weight. Squares refer to men and circles to women;
empty symbols refer to high IQ, filled symbols to average IQ.
Slice "0" is at the midventricle level as shown in the insert; 5
mm thick MRI images are separated by 2.5 mm. Large brain
area-IQ differences in men near ventricles (calices -3 to +1
above 0) include neural substrates of language and association.
A repeated measures analysis of variance on ventricle size
across slices -3 to +1 reveals no effect of sex, IQ, or their
interaction (all ps > .20) so ventricles are included in area
measurements. Tissue above or below graphed levels are
excluded because all subjects could not be represented.

previously appreciated. Others (Flynn & Deering, 1989; Pinkerton, Watson, &
McClelland, 1989) also have demonstrated differentiation by EEG quantitative
methods of reading disabilities subtypes. Since these studies rely on neuropsychological differentiation of the children prior to EEG identification, it is anticipated that this line of research will provide a better understanding of EEG parameters and learning disability along with other developmental disorders and
their relationship to neuropsychological test performance and outcome.

Also, there may be electrophysiologic indices in infancy that may be predictive of outcome. To date, this research has focused primarily on motor outcome
using various types of sensory evoked potentials (Gorke, 1986; Willis, Duncan,

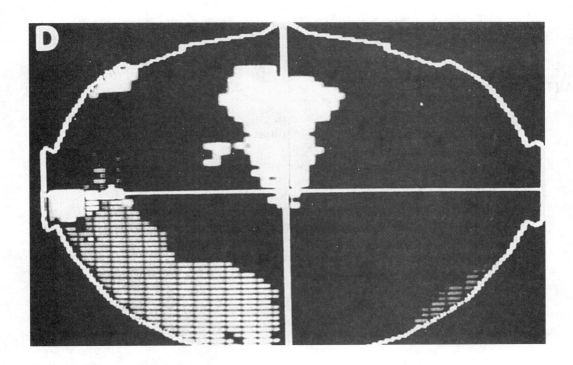

FIGURE 3.10 Brain electrical activity mapping (BEAM) composite depicting EEG abnormalities in dyslexia boys. This image shows a schematic outline of the head, nose above, left ear to the left, right ear to the right, vertex in the center, and occiput below. It represents a summary t-statistic SPM displaying all regions of between-group differences that differentiated boys with dyslexia-pure from normal readers. Regions shown reach or exceed the P < 0.02 two-tailed probability level across all EEG and/or EP states. Note that regions delineated include the classic left mid-temporal and left anterior temporal regions typically associated with language function. Note, also, the prominent bilateral media frontal involvement. The very same regions were delineated elsewhere by blood flow studies during language function in normal subjects. Thus dyslexia-pure appears to be associated with electrophysiological "difference" in all regions normally involved in language function, including the medial frontal region. Reprinted with permission from *Neuropsychologia, 28,* F. H. Duffy & G. McAnulty, "Neurophysiological Heterogeneity and the Definition of Dyslexia: Preliminary Evidence for Plasticity," copyright 1990, Pergamon Press Ltd.

Bell, Pappas, & Moniz, 1989). EEG topography mapping studies are now being done with infants wherein quantitative EEG information will be utilized to predict or follow outcome. Since these studies are currently in progress, it will be some time before more definitive statements can be made, but, as this research progresses, further bridges will be established between pediatric neurology and neuropsychology.

ULTRASOUND

Ultrasound has become the method of choice for imaging the developing fetal brain because of its noninvasive qualities (Lui, Boag, Daneman, Costello, Kirpalani, & Whyte, 1990). Although the resolution of ultrasound is markedly less than that achieved by CT or MRI, certain brain structures and landmarks (ventricle, skull) can typically be readily identified (see Figure 3.11).

Numerous studies (Beverly, Smith, Beesley, Jones, & Rhodes, 1990; Bozynski, Nelson, Ganaze, Rosati-Skertich, Matalon, Vasan, & Naughton, 1988; Costello, Hamilton, Baudin, Townsend, Bradford, Stewart, & Reynolds, 1988; Iivanainen, Launes, Pihko, Nikkinen, & Lindroth, 1990; Rodriguez, Clause, Berellen, & Lyon, 1990; Trounce, Fagan, Young, & Levene, 1986) have demonstrated the negative

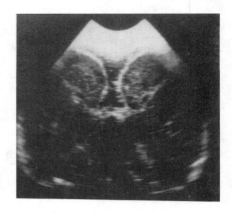

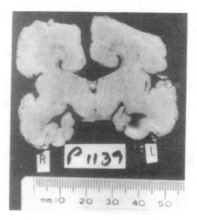

FIGURE 3.11 Comparison of ultrasound (top) to post mortem section (bottom). Note that ultrasound does provide for gross brain structure (i.e., ventricles, interhemispheric fissure and Sylvian fissure) determination. Reprinted with permission from *Developmental Medicine and Child Neurology*, 28, J. Q. Trounce, D. G. Fagan, I. D. Young & M. I. Levene, "Disorders of Neuronal Migration: Sonographic Features," copyright 1986, MacKeith Press.

relationship between gross abnormalities on an ultrasound and outcome. There have been no detailed behavioral or psychological studies following these children during their later childhood or adolescent development, and such studies are needed. Most of these studies have followed the children only up to about age 7. This appears to be a very fruitful area for potential research that could have widespread clinical significance and likewise provide a further bridging between neurology and psychology.

PREVENTIVE MEASURES

It is obvious that the best outcome occurs in children who have no neurologic risk factors and therefore preventive methods will continue to be the most important way of reducing the consequences of either a developmental disorder or the effects of brain injury. A host of prenatal factors are now recognized that can affect the developing fetus (Zuckerman & Hingson, 1986). Specifically, neonates exposed to teratogens in utero are at the highest risk for sustaining brain injury (Goldstein & Levin, 1990; Naugle, 1990). (See Chapter 4 for further review.)

For example the Zuckerman and Hingson (1986) study demonstrated that women who smoke marijuana, drink two or more drinks per day and smoked at least one pack of cigarettes per day deliver babies who are 1.1 pounds smaller, one week short of gestation, and seven times more likely to have compatible features with fetal alcohol syndrome. Long-term, longitudinal neuropsychological studies have not been done in a prospective way with such children, but it is anticipated that such environmental damaging effects will have a mark negative impact on outcome. Other studies have demonstrated a wide-range of central nervous system effects secondary to maternal substance use/abuse (Laegreid, Olegard, Conradi, Hagberg, Wahlstrom, & Abrahamsson, 1990).

Thus, any preventive measures that reduce neurodevelopmental risk factors will likely result in more positive outcomes. To date, neuropsychology typically has been in a position to impact the child only *after* the damage or deficit has occurred. It appears that in the future, neuropsychology and pediatric neurology should place an even greater focus on preventive and antecedent factors.

TREATMENT ISSUES OF NEUROBEHAVIORAL DISORDERS IN CHILDREN

The core behavioral symptoms typically associated with childhood neurologic disorders involve deficits in attention/concentration, poor impulse control, and emotional lability (Nussbaum & Bigler, 1990). Obviously, such symptoms commonly occur in nonneurologic disorders with purely "psychogenic" origins. Nonetheless, in the child with neurologic disorder when these symptoms are present, they typically are addressed through behavioral and pharmacological treatment strategies. Both approaches will be discussed here with a focus on future trends.

Behavioral Strategies

The rationale behind most behavioral strategies in treating children with neurologically related behavior problems is that through environmental structuring, there will be a reduction in the potential number of extraneous stimuli impacting the child (Deaton, 1990). By reducing the number of extraneous and inappropriate stimuli, this, in turn, maximizes the child's chance of responding to appropriate, meaningful, and significant stimuli. In other words, this is an attempt to externally control the options to which a child may respond to impulsively. Once the environment is properly controlled, then more traditional behavior therapy strategies can be implemented (Horton & Sautter, 1986; McGuire & Rothenberg, 1986).

The problem with behavioral treatment strategies with neurologically impaired children is that they often are very time intensive and may require constant monitoring and artificial manipulation of the environment. All of these factors are problematic for generalization of the treatment effect to the more naturalistic setting. As such, behavioral treatment of the neurologically impaired child often falls short of the intended goals.

Pharmacological Strategies

Depending on the nature of the symptoms and the neurological diagnosis, children with neurobehavioral disorders may benefit from a wide spectrum of psychoactive agents (McGuire & Sylvester, 1990). These medications include anticonvulsants, neuroleptics, benzodiazepines, antidepressants, antihistamines, hypnotics, lithium, stimulants, and Beta-adrenergic agents. In terms of contemporary as well as past treatment for neurobehavioral disorders, pharmacological treatment has been the treatment of choice and is often implemented in isolation without concomitant behavioral intervention. For such treatment, the indisputable medication of choice has been stimulant medication. In such a scenario, the child presents with symptoms of hyperactivity and poor attention span and often without any formal testing is placed on a stimulant medication regimen. If the targeted behaviors seem to "improve," then nothing else is done. Such an approach obviously misses many of the complex interactions between brain and behavior and behavior and environment. A strict medication approach implies a unitary treatment for this multimodality problem (Rappoport, 1983).

In bridging the treatment gap in terms of future trends in pediatric neuropsychology, the behavioral intervention strategies clearly fall into the purview of the neuropsychologist, whereas the medication approach falls to the physician. What should be the focus is the child, so that these two approaches meet with the child in the center of the treatment, not being pulled in one direction or the other. There is ample clinical and empirical evidence to support the integration of the two approaches, which typically results in greater positive outcome than either approach individually (see Whalen & Henker, 1991).

All of this should not be taken as an indication that further research into the separate influence of medication or behavioral intervention strategies should not be done—far from it. Neither of these methods or their combination is as effective as needed. There is considerable work to be done in this area. Similarly, the behavioral strategy approaches (Deaton, 1990) have just begun to cross-fertilize with cognitive rehabilitation strategies (Prigatano, 1990), and this constitutes another important future development in the treatment of childhood neurobehavioral disorders. Last, there is a tremendous need for innovative therapies in this area. A significant number of children with neurobehavioral disorders simply do not benefit from the current treatment armamentarium. Possibly determining effective treatment methods for such incalcitrant treatment cases will open the door to the more routine. Let us hope.

One other point of "bridging" in this area of treatment needs to be discussed. Pharmacological treatment of neurobehavioral disorders in children may be effective in reducing some target abnormal behaviors, but the long-term sequelae of pharmocologic treatment on the developing brain are not well understood. This represents a critical area where the medical and clinical neuropsychological need to mesh, to avoid untoward iatrogenic effects of pharmacological treatment for a childhood neurobehavioral disorder (see related work by Dikmen, Temkin, Miller, Machamer, & Winn, 1991).

THE NEED FOR A COMMON LANGUAGE

One major factor that has hindered bridging the gap between neuropsychology and pediatric neurology is the lack of a common language. Much of the responsibility for this lies with neuropsychology because there is not a uniform consensus about what constitutes a standardized battery for assessing neuropsychological impairment in children. As of this writing, a comprehensive child neuropsychological battery does not exist that has been fully standardized with age, education, and developmental issues controlled for.

Contemporary child neuropsychological batteries essentially have been "pieced" together by utilizing various tests that have some age standardization (e.g., Benton Visual Retention Test, Beery Visual-Motor Integration Test) with those that do not (see Bigler & Nussbaum, 1989). For example, the Halstead-Reitan Neuropsychological Test Battery for older children is basically a downward extension of the adult battery and is not stratified by age, education, or IQ, even though all those factors may significantly influence neuropsychological performance. Until neuropsychology has a test battery that controls for age, education, IQ, and potentially other important developmental issues, it will be difficult to make universally accepted statements about neuropsychological impairment in children. Without universal acceptance of what constitutes a true neuropsychological impairment, dialogue between neuropsychologists and pediatric neurologists will continue to be less than complete. This issue may be the most important one for neuropsychology to address in this decade.

However, as pointed out in Chapter 2 of this text, while attempts to extensively quantify neuropsychological test performance may capture sensitivity to brain damage, subtleties associated with specific deficits and aberrations in performance style may be missed. Such information may be crucial in understanding unique aspects of processing deficits in treating children with higher cortical dysfunction. From this viewpoint, it would seem essential for both physicians and psychologists to first work toward some common understanding of normal and abnormal behavioral manifestations of brain functioning, particularly aspects of complex attention and integration of sensory experiences, memory, motivation, organization of verbal and nonverbal cognition, abstract thinking, problem solving, insight, foresight, executive functions, and self-monitoring of behavior. Without agreement on a detailed and relatively comprehensive model of neurobehavioral development, psychologists will be limited in their ability to develop appropriate assessment strategies. Further, results of their tests will continue to be misinterpreted and miscommunicated. Thus, any treatment strategies formulated from test results will be of limited research value when comparing across laboratories, clinics, and medical centers.

CONCLUSIONS

The natural division between neurology and psychology has evolved from neurology's focus on objective physiological and anatomical tests and psychology's reliance on behavioral observation and testing to infer underlying neurologic deficits. The bridge between neurology and neuropsychology comes from neurology's greater interest in "behavior" and psychology's expanding view of neurobiologic factors underlying behavior. In the past, the separation was largely one of orientation in the absence of common tools that could be used to assess neurological and psychological function. With the technological advances of the last two decades, the two disciplines can share common methodologies and must strive for a common "language" between neurology and neuropsychology. What this means for the child with a neurological disorder is that there will be a better and more complete understanding and treatment of the problem. The so-called winner in this bridging between neurology and psychology will be the child.

REFERENCES

Abou-Khalil, B. W., Siegel, G. J., Sackellares, J. C., Gilman, S., Hichwa, R., & Marshall, R., (1987). Positron emission tomography studies of cerebral glucose metabolism in chronic partial epilepsy. *Ann Neurol 22*, 480–486.

Amiel-Tison, C. and Ellison, P. (1986). Birth asphyxia in the fullterm newborn: Early assessment and outcome. *Developmental Medicine & Child Neurology 27*, 671–682.

Anderson, C. and Bigler, E. D. (1995). Ventricular dilation, cortical atrophy and neuropsychological outcome following traumatic brain injury. *Journal of Neuropsychiatry, 7.* 42–48.

Beverly, D. W., Smith, I. S., Beesley, P., Jones, J. and Rhodes, N. (1990). Relationship of cranial ultrasonography, visual and auditory evoked responses with neurodevelopmental outcome. *Developmental Medicine & Child Neurology, 32*, 210–219.

Bigler, E. D. (1988). The neuropsychology of hydrocephalus. *Archives of Clinical Neuropsychology, 3*, 81–100.

Bigler, E. D. (1991). Neuropsychological assessment, neuroimaging and clinical neuropsychology: A synthesis. *Archives of Clinical Neuropsychology, 6*, 113–132.

Bigler, E. D. (1992). Three-dimensional image analysis of trauma-induced degenerative changes: An aid to neuropsychological assessment. *Archives of Clinical Neuropsychology, 7*, 449–456.

Bigler, E. D. & Nussbaum, N. L. (1989). Child neuropsychology in the private medical practice. In C. R. Reynolds & E. Fletcher-Janzen (Eds.), *Handbook of clinical child neuropsychology*. New York: Plenum Press, pp. 557–572.

Bigler, E. D., Rosenstein, L. D., Roman, M. and Nussbaum, N. L. (1988). The clinical significance of congenital agenesis of the corpus collosum. *Archives of Clinical Neuropsychology, 3*, 189–200.

Bigler, E. D., Yeo, R. A., & Turkheimer, E. (1989). *Neuropsychological function and brain imaging*. New York: Plenum Press.

Blatter, D. D., Bigler, E. D., Gale, S. D., Johnson, S., Anderson, C., Burnett, Parker, Kurth, S. and Horn. (1994). Quantitative volumetric analysis of brain MRI: Normative database spanning five decades (16–65). *American Journal of Neuroradiology, 16*, 241–251.

Bozynski, M. E. A, Nelson, M. N., Ganaze, D., Rosati-Skertich, C., Matalon, T. A. S., Vasan, V. and Naughton, P. M. (1988). Cranial ultrasonography and the prediction of cerebral palsy in infants weighing ****£1200 grams at birth. *Developmental Medicine & Child Neurology, 30*, 342–348.

Bray, P. F. (1969). *Neurology in pediatrics*. Chicago: Year Book Medical Publishers.

Chugani, H. T., Phelps, M. E., and Mazziotta, J. C. (1987). Positron emission tomography study of human brain functional development. *Ann Neurol 22*, 487–497.

Costello, A. M. de L., Hamilton, P. A., Baudin, J., Townsend, J., Bradford, B. C., Stewart, A. L. and Reynolds, E. O. R. (1988). Prediction of

neurodevelopmental impairement at four year from brain ultrasound appearance of very preterm infants. *Developmental Medicine and Child Neurology, 30*, 711–722.

Damasio, H. and Damasio, A. R. (1989). *Lesion analysis in neuropsychology*. New York: Oxford University Press.

Deaton, A. (1990). Behavioral change strategies for children and adolescents with traumatic brain injury. In E. D. Bigler (Ed.), *Traumatic brain injury*. Austin, TX: Pro-Ed, pp. 231–249.

Dikmen, S. S., Temkin, N. R., Miller, B., Machamer, J. & Winn, H. R. (1991). Neurobehavioral effects of phenytoin prophylasix of posttraumatic seizures. *Journal of the American Medical Association, 265*, 1271–1277.

Drillien, C. M., Pickering, R. M. and Drummond, M. B. (1988). Predictive value of screening for different areas of development. *Developmental Medicine and Child Neurology, 30*, 294–305.

Duara, R., Kushch, A., Gross-Glenn, K., Barker, W., Jallad, B., Pascal, S., Loewenstein, D. A., Sheldon, J., Rabin, M., Levin, B. & Lubs, H. (1991). Neuroanatomic differences between dyslexic and normal readers on magnetic resonance imaging scans. *Archives of Neurology, 48*, 410–416.

Duffy, F. H. and McAnulty, G. (1990). Neurophysiological heterogeneity and the definition of dyslexia: Preliminary evidence for plasticity. *Neuropsychologia, 28*, 555–571.

Duffy, F. H., Denckla, M. B., Bartels, P. and Sandini, G. (1980). Dyslexia: regional differences in brain electrical activity by topographic mapping. *Annals of Neurology, 7*, 412–420.

Flynn, J. M. and Deering, W. M. (1989). Subtypes of dyslexia: Investigation of Boder's System using quantitative neurophysiology. *Developmental Medicine & Child Neurology, 31*, 215–223.

Gale, S. D., Johnson, S., Bigler, E. D. and Blatter, D. D. (1995). Nonspecific white matter degeneration following traumatic brain injury. *Journal of the International Neuropsychological Society, 1*, 17–28.

Gillberg, I. C. and Gillberg, I. C. (1989). Children with preschool minor neurodevelopmental disorders. IV: Behavior and school achievement at age 13. *Developmental Medicine and Child Neurology, 31*, 3–13.

Gillberg, I. C., Gillberg, C. and Groth, J. (1989). Children with preschool neurodevelopmental disorders. V: Neurodevelopmental Profiles at age 13. *Developmental Medicine and Child Neurology, 31,* 14–24.

Goldstein, F. C. and Levin, H. S. (1990). Epidemiology of traumatic brain injury: Incidence, clinical characteristics, and risk factors. In E. D. Bigler (Ed.), *Traumatic brain injury.* Austin, TX: Pro-Ed, pp. 51–67.

Gorke, W. (1986). Somatosensory evoked cortical potentials indicating impaired motor development in infancy. *Developmental Medicine & Child Neurology, 28,* 633–641.

Gowers, W. R. (1888). *A manual of diseases of the nervous system.* Philadelphia: P. Blakiston, Son & Co.

Gur, R. C., Trivedi, S. S., Saykin, A. J. and Gur, R. E. (1988). Behavioral imaging. *Neuropsychiatry, Neuropsychology, and Behavioral Neurology, 1,* 53–60.

Hadders-Algra, M., Touwen, B. C. L. and Huisjes, J. J. (1986). Neurologically deviant newborns: Neurological and behavior developmental at the age of six years. *Developmental Medicine and Child Neurology, 28,* 569–578.

Harbord, M. G., Finn, J. P., Hall-Craggs, M. A., Robb, S. A., Kendall, B. E. and Boyd, S. G. (1990). Myelination patterns on magnetic resonance of children with developmental delay. *Developmental Medicine and Child Neurology, 32,*.

Holland, B. A., Haas, D. K., Norman, D., Brant-Zawadzki, M., and Newton, T. H. (1986). MRI of normal brain maturation. *American Journal of Neuroradiology, 7,* 201–208.

Horton, A. M. & Sautter, S. W. (1986). Behavioral neuropsychology: Behavioral treatment for the brain injured. In D. Wedding, A. M. Horton & J. Webster (Eds.), *The neuropsychology handbook.* New York: Springer, pp. 259–277.

Huttenlocher, P. R. (1990). Morphometric study of human cerebral cortex development. *Neuropsychologia, 28,* 517–527.

Huttenlocher, P. R., Levine, S. C., Huttenlocher, J. and Gates, J. (1990). Discrimination of normal and at-risk preschool children on the basis of neurological tests. *Developmental Medicine and Child Neurology, 32,* 394–402.

Iivanainen, M., Launes, J., Pihko, H., Nikkinen, P. and Lindroth, L. (1990). Single-photon emission computed tomography of brain perfusion: Analysis of 60 pediatric cases. *Developmental Medicine and Child Neurology, 32,* 63–68.

Iloeje, S. O. (1988). Trophic limb changes among children with developmental apraxia. *Developmental Medicine and Child Neurology, 30,* 791–796.

Jernigan, T. L., Hesselink, J. R., Sowell, E. & Tallal, P. A. (1991). Cerebral structure on magnetic resonance imaging in language- and learning-impaired children. *Archives of Neurology, 48,* 539–545.

Jernigan, T. L. and Tallal, P. (1990). Late childhood changes in brain morphology observable with MRI. *Developmental Medicine and Child Neurology, 32,* 379–385.

Jouandet, M. L., Tramo, M. J., Herron, D. M., Hermann, A., Loftus, W. C., Bazell, J. and Gazzaniga, M. S. (1989). Brainprints: Computer-generated two-dimensional maps of the human cerebral cortex in-vivo. *Journal of Cognitive Neuroscience, 1,* 88–117.

Kitchen, W. H., Rickards, A. L., Ryan, M. M., Ford, G. W., Lissenden, J. V. and Boyle, L. W. (1986). Improved outcome to two years of very low-birth weight infants: Fact or artifact. *Developmental Medicine and Child Neurology, 28,* 579–588.

Laegreid, L., Olegard, R., Conradi, N., Hagberg, G., Wahlstrom, J. and Abrahamsson, L. (1990). Congenital malformations and maternal consumption of benzodiazepines: A case control study. *Developmental Medicine and Child Neurology, 32,* 432–441.

Larsen, J. P., Holen, T., Lundberg, I. & Odegaard, H. (1990). MRI evaluation of the size and symmetry of the Planum temporale in adolescents with developmental dyslexia. *Brain & Language, 39,* 289–301.

Largo, R. H. (1990). Predicting developmental outcome at school age from infant tests of normal, at-risk and retarded infants. *Developmental Medicine and Child Neurology, 32,* 30–45.

Lezak, M. G. (1983). *Neuropsychological assessment.* New York: Oxford University Press.

Lindahl, E., Michelsson, K. and Donner, M.

(1988). Prediction of early school-age problems by a preschool neurodevelopmental examination of children at risk neonatally. *Developmental Medicine and Child Neurology, 30,* 723–734.

Lindahl, E., Michelsson, K., Helenius, M. and Parre, M. (1988). Neonatal risk factors and later neurodevelopmental disturbances. *Developmental Medicine & Child Neurology, 30,* 571–589.

Lui, K., Boag, G., Daneman, A., Costello, S., Kirpalani, H. and Whyte, H. (1990). Widened subarchnoid space in pre-discharge cranial ultrasound: Evidence of cerebral atrophy in immature infants. *Developmental Medicine and Child Neurology, 10,* 882–887.

Luria, A. R. (1966). *Higher cortical functions in man* (2nd ed.). New York: Basic Books.

McGuire, T. L. & Rothenberg, M. B. (1986). Behavioral and psychosocial sequelae of pediatric head injury. *Journal of Head Trauma Rehabilitation, 1,* 1–6.

McGuire, T. L. & Sylvester, C. E. (1990). Neuropsychiatric evaluation and treatment of traumatic brain injury. In E. D. Bigler (Ed.), *Traumatic brain injury.* Austin, TX: Pro-Ed, pp. 209–229.

Mesulam, M. M. (1985). *Principles of behavioral neurology.* Philadelphia: F. A. Davis.

Metter, E. J., Kempler, D., Jackson, C., Hanson, W. R., Mazziotta, J. C., and Phelps, M. E. (1989). Cerebral glucose metabolism in Wernicke's, Broca's and conduction aphasia, *46,* 27–34.

Naugle, R. I. (1990). Epidemiology of traumatic brain injury in adults. In E. D. Bigler (Ed.), *Traumatic brain injury.* Austin, TX: Pro-Ed, pp. 69–103.

Nassbaum, N. L. & Bigler, E. D. (1990). *Identification and treatment of attention deficit disorder.* Austin, TX: Pro-Ed.

Ohr, B. R., Garcia-Coll, C., and Oh, W. (1988). Language and neurodevelopmental outcome of low-birthweight infants at three years. *Developmental Medicine and Child Neurology, 31,* 582–590.

Palmer, F. B., Shaprio, B. K., Wachtel, R. C., Allen, M. C., Hiller, J. E., Harryman, S. E., Mosher, B. S., Meinert, C. L. and Capute, A. J. (1988). The effects of physical therapy on cerebral palsy: A controlled trial in infants with spastic diplegia. *New England Journal of Medicine, 318,* 803–808.

Parkinson, C. E., Scrivener, R., Graves, L., Bunton, J. and Harvey, D. (1986). Behavioral differences of school-age children who were small-for-dates babies. *Developmental Medicine and Child Neurology, 28,* 498–505.

Pawlik, G. & Heiss, W. D. (1989). Poitron emission tomography (PET) and neuropsychological function. In E. D. Bigler, R. Yeo & E. Turkheimer (Eds.), *Neuropsychological function and brain imaging.* New York: Plenum Press, pp. 137–198.

Pinkerton, F., Watson, D. R. and McClelland, R. J. (1989). A neurophysiological study of children with reading, writing and spelling difficulties. *Developmental Medicine & Child Neurology, 31,* 569–581.

Piven, J., Berthier, M. L., Starkstein, S. E., Nehme, E., Pearlson, G. and Folstein, M. D. (1990). Magnetic resonance imaging evidence for a defect of cerebral cortical development in Autism. *American Journal of Psychiatry, 147,* 734–739.

Portnoy, S., Callias, M., Wolke, D. and Gamsu, H. (1988). Five-year follow-up study of extremely low-birthweight infants. *Developmental Medicine and Child Neurology, 30,* 590–598.

Prigatano, G. P. (1990). Recovery and cognitive retraining after brain injury. In E. D. Bigler (Ed.), *Traumatic brain injury.* Austin, TX: Pro-Ed, pp. 273–295.

Rappoport, J. L. (1983). The use of drugs: Trends in research. In M. Rutter (Ed.), *Developmental neuropsychiatry.* New York: Guilford Press, pp. 385–403.

Reitan, R. M. & Walfson, D. (1985). *The Halstead-Reitan Neuropsychological Test Battery: Theory and Clinical Interpretation.* Tucson, AZ: Neuropsychology Press.

Rie, H. E. & Rie, E. D. (1980). *Handbook of minimal brain dysfunctions.* New York: Wiley.

Rodriguez, J., Claus, D., Berellen, G. and Lyon, G. (1990). Periventricular leukomalacia: Ultrasonic and neuropathological correlations. *Developmental Medicine and Child Neurology, 32,* 347–355.

Rutter, M. (1983). *Developmental neuropsychiatry.* New York: Guilford Press.

Shafer, S. Q., Stokman, C. J., Shaffer, D., Ng, S. K. C., O'Connor, P. A. and Schonfeld, I. S. (1986). Ten-year consistency in neurological test performance of children without focal neurological deficit. *Developmental Medicine and Child Neurology, 28,* 417–427.

Singer, L. T., Kercsmar, C., Lagris, G., Orlowski, J. P., Hill, B. P. and Doerschuk, C. (1989). Developmental sequelae of long-term infant tracheostomy. *Developmental Medicine and Child Neurology, 31,* 224–230.

Smith, A. E. A. and Knight-Jones, E. B. (1990). The abilities of very low-birthweight children and their classroom controls. *Developmental Medicine and Child Neurology, 32,* 590–601.

Stewart, A. L., Costello, A. M. de L., Hamilton, P. A., Baudin, J., Townsend, J., Bradford, B. C. and Reynolds, E. O. R. (1988). Relationship between neurodevelopmental status of *very preterm* infants at one and four years. *Developmental Medicine and Child Neurology, 31,* 756–765.

Stoddart, C. and Knights, R. M. (1986). Neuropsychological assessment of children: Alternative approaches. In J. E. Obrzut and G. W. Hynd (Eds.), *Child neuropsychology (Volume 2: Clinical practice).* Orlando, FL: Academic Press, pp. 229–243.

Taylor, D. C., Powell, R. P., Cherland, E. E. and Vaughan, C. M. (1988). Overflow movements and cognitive, motor and behavioral disturbance: A normative study of girls. *Developmental Medicine and Child Neurology, 30,* 759–768.

Touwen, B. C. L. and Prechtl, H. F. R. (1970). The neurological examination of the child with minor nervous dysfunction. *Clinics in Developmental Medicine,* No. 38. London: S.I.M.P./Heinemann Medical.

Trounce, J. Q., Fagan, D. G., Young, I. D. and Levene, M. I. (1986). Disorders of neuronal migration: Sonographic features. *Developmental Medicine and Child Neurology, 28,* 467–471.

Turkheimer, E., Yeo, R. A. & Bigler, E. D. (1990). Basic relations among lesion location, lesion volume and neuropsychological performance. *Neuropsychologia, 28,* 1011–1019.

Turkheimer, E., Yeo, R. A., Jones, C. & Bigler, E. D. (1990). Quantitative assessment of covariation between neuropsychological function and location of naturally occurring lesions in humans. *Journal of Clinical and Experimental Neuropsychology, 12,* 549–565.

Vohr, B. R., Coll, C. G. and Oh, W. (1988). Language development of low-brithweight infants at two years. *Developmental Medicine and Child Neurology, 30,* 608–615.

Vohr, B. R., Garcia-Coll, C., and Oh, W. (1989). Language and neurodevelopmental outcome of low-birthweight infants at three years. *Developmental Medicine and Child Neurology, 31,* 582–590.

Whalen, C. K. & Henker, B. (1991). Therapies for hyperactive children: Comparisons, combinations and compromises. *Journal of Consulting and Clinical Psychology, 59,* 126–137.

Willerman, L., Schultz, R., Rutledge, J. N. & Bigler, E. D. (1991). In-vivo brain size and intelligence. *Intelligence, 15,* 223–228.

Willis, J., Duncan, M. C., Bell, R., Pappas, F. and Moniz, M. (1989). Somatosensory evoked potentials predict neuromotor outcome after periventricular hemorrhage. *Developmental Medicine and Child Neurology, 31,* 435–439.

Yeo, R. A., Turkheimer, E. and Bigler, E. D. (1990). Neuropsychological methods of localizing brain dysfunction: Clinical versus empirical approaches. *Neuropsychiatry, Neuropsychology and Behavioral Neurology, 3,* 290–303.

Zuckerman, B. S. and Hingson, R. (1986). Alcohol consumption during pregnancy: A critical review. *Developmental Medicine and Child Neurology, 28,* 649–654.

4

DISORDERS APPEARING IN THE PERINATAL AND NEONATAL PERIOD

FRANCIS J. PIROZZOLO   VIRGINIA BONNEFIL

The publication of this book is timely, as it comes at a period of rapidly expanding knowledge about the human nervous system. Scientific progress in the neurosciences, in genetics, and in the clinical disciplines that bear on the issues addressed in this book is advancing at an astounding pace. In order to appreciate the complexity of clinical issues confronted in pediatric neuropsychology, it is ever more apparent that developmental neurobiology is the cornerstone or basic science of this clinical discipline.

Disturbances in the development of the nervous system—at the molecular, cellular, or systems levels—underlie many of the abnormal behaviors clinicians see in childhood. The recent literature appearing in neuropsychology (e.g., Gray & Dean, 1991; Eslinger, 1991; Molfese, 1989; Livingstone, Rosen, & Drislane, 1991) provides some preliminary glimpses of the future of pediatric neuropsychology. It is plausible that, for many of the most common neuropsychological and neuropsychiatric disorders, researchers may soon find biological etiologies.

The purpose of this chapter is to briefly review the disorders that appear in perinatal and neonatal life. Because of space limitations, the chapter will necessarily represent only a cursory look at some of the more important disorders that disturb behavioral development. In addition, certain disorders, such as epilepsy, have an extensive literature in the neurosciences, but because they have both perinatal and later-life onsets they will not be treated, in spite of rapid and exciting advances in the understanding of the amino acid neurotransmitters or neuromodulators that may contribute to their etiology. Similarly, space does not permit the review of intriguing recent data (e.g., Livingstone et al. 1991) on the possibility that developmental dyslexia may result from a disorganized magnocellular system in the lateral geniculate nucleus of poor readers. Future research will provide conclusive evidence of the replicability of these early findings, their role in producing the pathognomonic reading defects, and whether antibodies that destroy proteins found only in the magnocellular system are the cause of these hypoplasias.

DEVELOPMENTAL NEUROBIOLOGY AND DISORDERS OF CNS MATURATION

Tremendous advances being made at the molecular, cellular, and systems levels in our understanding of central nervous system (CNS) development offer great promise for unraveling some of the mysteries of developmental disorders. Realization by clinician investigators that disturbances in brain development are likely to be important in the pathogenesis of psychiatric illness. Indeed, this view has gained favor not only among child psychiatrists, for whom firsthand experience with infantile autism and childhood schizophrenia make it an obvious conclusion, but also among researchers in adult psychopathology, who are increasingly adopting a developmental perspective in their studies on schizophrenia as well as on bipolar disorder and major depressive illness.

Brain development proceeds by the temporal unfolding of events that are regulated by processes both intrinsic and extrinsic to the brain. Intrinsic processes are largely genetically cued and produce an immature brain that has the capability to assimilate, process, integrate, and react to information from the environment. Extrinsic processes begin *in utero* and continue throughout life; they use environmental stimuli to modulate brain development. The differentiation between intrinsic and extrinsic processes has heuristic appeal, but it should be understood that even those "hard-wired" developmental processes that may seem to take place independently of environmental modification are, in fact, highly susceptible to shaping by external stimuli. Indeed, it is probably the fact that the development of their genetically programmed brains can be modified by environmental stimulation and experience that distinguishes higher-order organisms.

The stages of brain development include formation of the neural tube, neurogenesis, neuronal migration, and neuritic differentiation. Disturbances in the early stages of development usually produce more severe consequences than those in the later stages. For example, failure of neural tube closure is associated with severe defects, many of which are incompatible with life. Disruptions in neurogenesis lead to focal agenesis or hypoplasias of discrete brain areas, whereas disturbances in neuronal migration cause agyrias, microgyrias, or dysplasias.

All of the preceding deficits are detectable grossly or microscopically. In contrast, disruptions in the elaboration of synaptic connections are detectable when dramatic, but may go unnoticed if cellular morphology is not grossly affected. However, it may be precisely in this end-stage area of neuronal differentiation that the pathology underlying developmental disorders creates two areas of investigation receiving attention currently: the regulation of synapse formation and the control of neuronal pruning.

Normal synapse formation is critical for the establishment of proper connection between neurons, neuronal tracts, and areas of the brain. What we do not understand are the consequences of disruptions in synaptogenesis that are too subtle to be detected in the microscope, but which nonetheless may lead to clinical dysfunctions—whether severe, as in autism, or milder, as in dyslexias. In the same vein, there is great interest in clarifying the processes of hyperinnervation and pruning back of cerebral neurons.

What is emerging is the notion that subtle disruptions in normal brain development may underlie neuropsychiatric disorders, creating an interesting and somewhat frustrating problem for researchers: Because no obvious structural abnormalities have been described for neuropsychiatric disorders, we must search for subtle, perhaps evanescent, structural defects, the consequences of which are, nonetheless, clinically far reaching. This poses a formidable challenge and demands the development of new, more sensitive and sophisticated methodologies to tackle the problem. Two important new areas of research are the characterization of developmentally regulated genes—which may encode structural proteins, transcription factors, or growth factors or their receptors—and the development of innovative imaging procedures that permit noninvasive access to the brain during discrete developmental periods.

DISORDERS OF EMBRYONIC INDUCTION, CELL MIGRATION, AND PROLIFERATION: MORPHOGENETIC ANOMALIES

There are numerous disorders that are associated with disturbances in neuropsychological function that are a result of dysraphic states (Table 4.1). These developmental disorders are malformation syndromes that involve failures of the brain or other cranial features to form as a result of failures in the induction of mesoderm and neuroectoderm. The most frequently occurring induction disorder is that in which the neural folds fail to fuse dorsally to form the neural tube. This class of dysraphic disorder includes anencephaly, the most frequently occurring major CNS malformation (MacMahon & Naggan, 1967). Females predominate in this form of rachischisis in the range from 3:1 to 7:1. The incidence is believed to be around 0.7 per thousand.

Spina bifida occulta, cranium bifidum, myelomeningocele, and menigocele are inductive disorders that result from fusion failures of the vertebral column, posterior midline of the skull, and herniations of the cord and meninges and cord, respectively. Reviews by Benda (1952), Laurence and Tew (1967), and Hunt and Holmes (1976) detail the causes and consequences of such dysraphic states. Although many patients with these disorders are profoundly mentally retarded, some are only mildly impaired. Attempts have been made to find criteria, including intelligence test results, that predict the survival rate, surgical, and other treatment outcomes. It has been shown, for example, that IQ can be predicted by the thickness of the cortical mantle at birth (Hunt & Holmes, 1976) and

TABLE 4.1   Perinatal Malformations and Complications

I. Posterior midline CNS axial skeletal defects; dysraphisms
    A. Anencephaly
    B. Spina bifida and cranium bifida
    C. Arnold Chiari malformations
    D. Diplomyelia
    E. Diastematomyelia
    F. Syringomyelia
    G. Hydromyelia
    H. Myelomeningocele
    I. Meningocele
II. Developmental anomalies of the base of the skull and upper cervical vertebrae
    A. Platybasia
    B. Klippel-Feil syndrome
    C. Cleidocranial dysotosis
III. Anterior midline defects
    A. Holoprosencephaly
IV. Disorders of cellular migration and proliferation
    A. Schizencephaly
    B. Lissencephaly (Agyria)
    C. Macrogyria (Pachygyria)
    D. Micropolygyria
    E. Agenesis of the corpus callosum
    F. Microcephaly
    G. Macrocephaly
    H. Craniostenosis
    I. Hydrocephalus
    J. Hydranencephaly
    K. Achondroplasia
    L. Osteopetrosis
V. Prenatal Infections
    A. Syphilis
    B. Toxoplasma gondii
    C. Rubella
    D. Cytomegalovirus
    E. Herpes simplex
VI. Chromosomal defects
    A. Down syndrome
    B. Cri du chat
    C. Turners syndrome
    D. Russel-Silver syndrome

TABLE 4.1 *Continued*

VII. Other
  A. Hypoxia
  B. Hypoglycemia
  C. Hypercarbia
  D. Acidosis
  E. Physical trauma
  F. Intoxications
  G. Arterial or venous insufficiencies
  H. Endema

by the presence of radiolucent skull defects known as lacunar skull (Fishman, et al., 1977).

Another series of dysraphic states arising out of the early inductive period is the Arnold-Chiari malformation firs described by Cleland a century ago (Cleland, 1883) and further characterized by Chiari several years later (Chiari, 1891). These malformations may be asymptomatic or they may have profound effects on the behavior of the patient. Cognitive disorders may be a consequence of the resulting hydrocephalus, displacement of posterior brain structures, meningitis, or heterotopias of cerebral cortex, including polygyria or microgyria.

SYNDROMES ASSOCIATED WITH ENLARGED HEAD

The syndrome of enlarged head, macrocrania, megaloencephaly, macrencephaly, megacephaly, macrocephaly, and hydrocephalus are syndromes of diverse causes (Table 4.2). Examples of normal neuropsychological development come from each diagnostic class, yet mental retardation is a common feature of these malformation syndromes.

The diagnosis of megaloencephaly refers to enlarged brain, whereas the terms *megacephaly* and *macrocephaly* refer to enlarged head. Megacephaly can be established by measurement of head circumference of more than two standard deviations above the mean for age, sex, race, and gestational age. Since many factors influence the size of the head, such as the size and thickness of the cranium, these factors may not be associated with cognitive deficit. The differential diagnosis of megaloencephaly and hydrocephalus is the most important consideration, as opposed to large head size alone.

Megaloencephaly implies an increase in neural elements (and therefore increased brain size and/or weight). True megaloencephaly is a proliferation disorder that may affect the cerebrum, cerebellum, and brain stem equally. Dekaban and Sakuragawa (1977) examined clinical data and neuropathological specimens of 31 patients with megaloencephaly. Some 25 cases presented with mental retardation, with 18 cases presenting other major neurologic handicaps. Eight

TABLE 4.2   Differential Diagnosis of Megalocephaly

Early infantile
  Normal variant
  Hydrocephalus
    Induction disorders: spina bifida cystica, cranium bifidum, Arnold-Chiari malformations, aqueductal stenosis
    Mass lesions: neoplasms, AVMs, cyst formations
    Infections: pre-, peri- and postnatal
    Hemorrhage: peri- and postnatal hemorrhage
  Subdural effusion
Late infantile
  Normal variant
  Hydrocephalus
    Space-occupying lesions
    Post-bacterial or granulomatous meningitis
    Dysraphism
    Posthemorrhagic
  Subdural effusion
  Increased intracranial pressure
    Pseudotumor cerebri
  Primary skeletal cranial dysplasias
  Megaloencephaly
    Metabolic CNS disorders
    Proliferation syndromes (neurocutaneous)
    Cerebral gigantism
    Achondroplasia
    Primary megaloencephaly
Early and late childhood
  Normal variant
  Hydrocephalus
    Space-occupying lesions
    Induction disorder
    Postinfectious
    Hemorrhagic
  Megaloencephaly
    Proliferation syndromes
    Familial
    Pseudotumor cerebri

brains were normal in gross appearance and cytoarchitecture, whereas 10 brains had severe gross malformations and 11 had architectonic abnormalities such as heterotopias and cortical laminar disorganization.

Hydrocephalus is an example of a complicated clinical phenomenon that has diverse etiologies and multiple consequences. There is a sex-linked trait that is due to atresia of the aqueduct. Other forms of hydrocephalus that follow viral, bacterial, or aseptic meningitis are associated with obstructing fibrosis of the arachnoid tissue. Congenital malformations, such as in the Arnold-Chiari malformation and the Dandy-Walker syndrome, also account for a high percentage of infantile hydrocephalus. Hydrocephalus caused by tumors or arachnoid cysts, trauma or infection, and occult (or normal pressure) and arrested hydrocephalus are still other examples of the numerous pathological entities that are known to affect young children. Neurosurgical treatment—including removal of tumors or cysts in the foramina of Magendie or Luschka, ventricular bypass, ventriculoperitoneal shunting, ventriculovascular shunting, and choroid plexus extirpation—reduces mortality and improves cognitive function in a majority of patients (Milhorat, 1972).

OTHER MORPHOGENETIC ANOMALIES

Schizencephaly is a "true agenesis" syndrome (Yakovlev & Wadsworth, 1946), characterized by symmetric clefts in the cerebral hemispheres. These clefts are thought to be a consequence of the arrest in the development of the ventricle wall. Other cell migration anomalies are seen in conjunction with schizencephaly, including lissencephaly, heterotopias, and disorganized white matter.

Porencephaly is a term used to describe a variety of morphogenetic defects that communicate with the ventricular system and are characterized by intracerebral and extracerebral cavities and cysts. Unlike schizencephalies, which arise exclusively from early prenatal migration and diverticulation errors, porencephalies are of the prenatal, perinatal, or postnatal origin. The incidence of these disorders is unknown.

The syndrome of hydranencephaly is characterized by absence of the cerebral hemispheres despite normal meninges and skull. Two forms of hydranencephaly have been differentiated: one with complete absence of supratentorial neural structures and one with remnants, including basal ganglia, mesencephalon, and cerebellum. The latter group may appear normal at birth, but very few cases will survive the first year.

Lissencephaly is the syndrome of failed sulcation. The appearance of the surface of the cerebral cortex is smooth, resembling that of a normal 12-week-old fetus. Complete lissencephaly is very rare (Norman, 1963), and partial lissencephaly—which is the syndrome of decreased sulcation, agyria, and pachygyria—is also very uncommon (Dignan & Warkany, 1978).

The tremendous interest in lissencephaly, agyria, pachygyria, and polymicrogyria is related to the dramatic findings on autopsy and to findings that show correlation between cognitive defects (e.g., childhood dyslexia) and pachygyria, polymicrogyria, and microgyria (Drake, 1968; Galaburda & Kemper, 1979; Pirozzolo, 1979).

METABOLIC DISEASES

Inborn metabolic errors have a relatively low incidence in the population. Nevertheless, metabolic conditions that give rise to perinatal problems are the subject of intense research interest, and this is due, first, to the theoretical consideration that these disorders provide insight into the role of certain biochemical substances in normal brain function. Second, certain metabolic disorders are reversible (e.g., phenylketonuria and galactosemia), and the treatment for these conditions has been successful. Third, it is significant that developmental problems are seen in each of the nine classes of metabolic disorders, although it has not been observed in all examples of each class of disorders. Menkes (1980) has classified metabolic disorders into the following classes: (1) disorders of amino acid metabolism and associated with neurologic symptoms; (2) disorders of the amino acid transport; (3) disorders of carbohydrate metabolism; (4) mucopolysaccharidoses; (5) mucolipidoses and disorders of glycoprotein metabolism; (6) disorders manifested by intermittent metabolic acidosis; (7) disorders of lipid metabolism; (8) disorders of metal metabolism; and (9) disorders of purine metabolism.

Phenylketonuira (PKU) serves as a clear example of a metabolic defect. As with other metabolic conditions, PKU cannot be understood as a condition in which there is a simple omission or reduction of an important enzyme. Folling (1934) first recognized the PKU syndrome in 10 mentally retarded patients who excreted large amounts of phenylpyuric acid. Jervis (1947) later showed that the metabolic defect responsible for PKU is an inability to convert phenylalanine into paratyrosine because of the absence of phenylalanine hydroxylase activity, which catalyzes the conversion. In addition to elevated phenylalanine levels, tryptophan and tyrosine metabolism are disrupted, which causes decreased levels of serum 5-hydroxytryptamine and urine 5-hydroxyindoleacetic acid (Pare et al., 1958). Deficiencies in the enzyme dihydropteridine reductase and the cofactor biopterin have also been shown to be associated with disrupted phenylalanine metabolism.

The defect is transmitted as a simple recessive autosomal trait and has an incidence of about 1 in 14,000 (Berman et al., 1969). PKU children have traditionally been considered to have high incidence of seizures, EEG abnormalities, hyperactivity, and psychopathological behavior. Data suggest that male PKU patients with and without mental retardation have the most significant evidence of psychopathology (Fisch et al., 1981).

Dietary treatment, especially when it has been implemented before the age of 6 months, has been successful in bringing PKU children up to normal intellectual levels and in reducing other behavioral disorders as well. When PKU children are identified early in life and treatment is initiated near birth, normal cognitive function can be expected. In a large-scale study, Williamson and colleagues (1981) followed 132 PKU children who were treated at an early age and found that IQs at age 6 can be predicted by (1) mother's IQ; (2) age of treatment initiated; and (3) treatment compliance. These data strongly suggest that early treatment results in "recovery" to an expected level of intelligence.

Dietary treatment is, of course, not without problems since phenylalanine is an essential amino acid and its reduction can cause severe metabolic consequences. In addition, phenylalanine toxicity does extend beyond early childhood even though it is partially reversible. Recent data suggest that older treated PKU children experience declines in verbal IQ and that this may be independent of phenylalanine blood level (Knoll et al., 1980).

NUTRITIONAL DEFICIENCIES

It is not surprising that maternal physiology affects fetal development in a significant way. Two characteristics of the relationship between fetus and mother are, however, a bit surprising. First, it is abundantly clear that maternal suboptimal nutrition is not shared equally by the fetus—that is, the fetus appears to have some protection from maternal malnutrition. Second, the CNS also has been assumed to have some special protection since it is said to suffer less than other organs do from undernutrition.

Recent research would challenge the latter assumption. One major research model of intrauterine growth retardation (the Wigglesworth procedure) involves ligation of the uterine artery. Animals generally have little or no behavioral abnormalities (although they are vulnerable to metabolic disorders such as hypoglycemia).

A second research model produces a drastically different neuropathological and neurobehavioral picture. The protein restriction model of natural malnutrition has consistently shown that the brain is not spared and is, in fact, symmetrically affected with other organs. Both neuropathological (e.g., reduced neuronal population, myelination, and neurotransmitter deficiencies) and neurobehavioral effects are seen.

The conversion of nutrients from the diet into an active form depends on an interaction between the nutrients and protein molecules in several steps, including (1) enzymatic hydrolysis; (2) binding with specific proteins for absorption; (3) enzymatic conversion into a storage form (when supply exceeds demand and storage into enzyme (when demand exceeds supply); (4) binding with plasma proteins for transport to various organs; (5) binding with proteins on the cell surface, in cytoplasm, and/or in the nucleus; (6) enzymatic conversion into an active form (or coenzyme for vitamins); and (7) binding of an active form with apoenzyme to form the holoenzyme.

The entry of substances from the blood into the brain occurs as a result of lipid solubility or through carrier-mediated transport systems (Pardridge & Oldendorf, 1977). Brain metabolism may be controlled by the availability of the substrate, which is, in turn, under the influence of dietary nutrients. Thus, catecholamine and serotonin pathways, for example, are under the influence of tyrosine and tryptophan concentrations in the blood, which are modulated by dietary protein. It would not be surprising then to see mental defects in the face of disturbances of dietary intake and neurotransmitter metabolism, especially since the two neurotransmitter systems are known to be involved in the regulation of certain behavioral functions. Indeed, there are clinical data to show that nutritional deficiencies can lead to conditions of intellectual impairment.

Chronic niacin and thiamine deficiencies are dramatic examples of how nutritional deficiencies affect mental function. Kety (1975) estimated that 10% of all institutionalized mental patients at the turn of the centry suffered from pellagra. Cretinism (and subsequent mental retardation) resulting from iodine deficiency is another example of such a relationship. There is also no doubt that severe states of malnutrition (in neonates and in pregnant mothers) cause or contribute to mortality. The correlation is not so clear, however, in less severe states of malnutrition, although intuition tells us that such deficiencies must adversely affect mental development. Some authors (e.g., Pollitt, 1969; Frisch, 1971; Kinsborne, 1980) have queried whether the far more common occurrence of mild malnutrition has permanent effects on cognitive function, with research data not supporting lasting intellectual deficits.

Marasmus results from severe restriction of both calories and proteins. Marasmic infants have organ and muscle atrophy but are alert and have good appetites. Unfortunately, these children have very poor living conditions, malnourished parents, low motivation and energy levels, and inadequate learning opportunities, rendering conclusions about the cause of their intellectual deficit very difficult to make. Similarly, children with kwashiorkor, resulting from diets low in protein (relative to calories), have abundant evidence of mental retardation (Chase & Martin, 1970), but these children are extremely apathetic, deprived, and listless. The directions of cause and effect among these variables are not clear. Kinsbourne (1980) has suggested that severe malnutrition affects the developing brain and that even minor malnutrition affects the child's learning strategies even when learning capacity is normal.

HEPATOLENTICULAR DEGENERATION

Brain disorders that accompany liver disease are numerous, but the most clearly understood are Wilson's disease (hereditary hepatolenticular degeneration) and acquired hepatocerebral degeneration. Wilson's disease is a familial, progressive neurodegenerative disorder that is linked to disturbances in copper metabolism. Onset is usually in the first three decades, affected patients suffering from cirrhosis of the liver, extrapyramidal motor signs, Kayer-Fleischer corneal rings, and intellectual impairment. Neuropathologically, cavitation, and atrophy predominate in the putamen with lesions also involving the globus pallidus, caudate, thalamus, and other areas of brainstem and cerebellum.

The mechanism responsible for this metabolic defect is still not completely understood. Patients with Wilson's disease absorb excessive amounts of copper and have decreased plasma copper-binding gamma-globulin. It may be that the cerebral degeneration is secondary to cirrhosis of the liver and not a direct effect of copper on brain function (Adams & Sidman, 1968).

In the acquired form of hepatocerebral degeneration, there can be equally significant mental retardation. Chronic liver disease is not associated with Kayser-Fleischer corneal rings or copper metabolic disturbances, but with neuropathologic changes resembling those seen in Wilson's disease, although these changes are usually not as prominent. Clinical symptomatology is similar to that observed in Wilson's disease with tremor, rigidity, choreoathetosis, ataxia, dysarthria, and altered mental status as the hallmark features. Hyperammonemia may also be present.

Other major metabolic disorders associated with mental retardation are galactosemia, glycogen storage disease, familial hypoglycemia, fructose intolerance, hypoparathyroidism, lipidoses, and mucopolysaccharidoses.

PRENATAL INFECTIONS

Although human immunodeficiency virus (HIV) has received the most research attention in recent years, other prenatal and postnatal infections can play a role in disturbed neuropsychological development. Rubella is one of the more common prenatal infections that can produce mental retardation, congenital disfigurement, blindness, deafness, and language disorders. Driefuss (1975) has found that rubella can produce cellular necrosis, gliosis, and retardation or inhibition of cell growth. In addition, perivascular inflammatory cell changes and low-grade leptomeningitis can result from this infection. Other infections that can produce various degrees of mental retardation include cytomegalic inclusion disease and granulomatous meningoencephalitis (toxoplasmosis). All of these prenatal infections may lead to occlusion of the aqueduct producing hydrocephalus. Abscesses may increase intracranial pressure by producing a mass effect, or they may be the source of infection, with resulting sequelae.

CHROMOSOMAL DEFECTS

As discussed previously, genetics is one of the fastest growing sciences, providing startling new discoveries on an almost daily basis. The scientific world awaits completion of the massive Human Genome Project, which will provide even further knowledge about genetic disease. The incidence of chromosomal defects has been difficult to establish. Some authorities (e.g., Valentine, 1975, p. 86) contend that "chromosome disorders are among the commonest to afflict mankind." Evidence for this position comes from a study by Carr (cited by Valentine), which showed that 22% of spontaneous abortions under 154 days' gestation have chromosomal aberrations, whereas 40% of fetuses aborted between 26 and 60 days have chromosomal aberrations. Studies of the causes of mental retardation (e.g., Gustavson, 1977) suggest that chromosomal disorders account for only a small minority of cases of mental retardation, whereas polygenic inheritance of unfavorable combinations of genes account for as many as 80% of the cases of mental deficiency (Kinsbourne, 1980). However, the Fragile X syndrome and Down syndrome are among common chromosomal causes of mental retardation.

FRAGILE X SYNDROME

Recent research has established that the Fragile X [fra(X)] syndrome is second only to trisomy 21 as a genetic cause of mental retardation. It has a prevalence of about 1 in 1,350 males and 1 in 2,033 females (Webb et al., 1986). Despite its relative high frequency, the disorder has been recognized for less than 20 years, and this is probably due to the fact that unlike other genetic and chromosomal causes of dementia retardation, individuals affected with the fra(X) have relatively few physical anomalies. Fra(X) males may have minor craniofacial abnormalities such as large head circumference, facial asymmetry, and prominent ears and foreheads. Mitral valve prolapse, scoliosis, and hyperextensible joints are common findings. A pathonomic feature of adult fra(X) males is macroorchidism.

Fra(X) expression is seen in only one-half of female carriers, with only one-third of these carriers being mentally impaired. Whereas males generally have more significant mental retardation, speech disturbance, and hyperactivity, and approximately one-fourth of fra(X) males have seizures, fra(X) females are less severely affected. A neuropsychological pattern observed by Kemper and colleagues (1986) and Miezejeski and colleagues (1984) found that man fra(X) carriers have high verbal IQs and low performance IQs, with impairments in arithmetic, digit span, block design, and object assembly.

The Fragile X syndrome is caused by the inheritance of a marker on the X chromosome at position q27. The exact nature of the biochemical defect underlying the fragile site on the X chromosome is not known, although it is believed to involve the availability of thymidine. Excess availability of thymidine will induce fra(X) sites (Sutherland et al., 1985). Thymidine synthesis can be blocked by inhibiting thymidylate synthetase using 5-fluorodeoxyuridine, methotrexate, trimethoprim, flurodeoxycytidine, and trifluorothymidine, and this has been shown in numerous studies (e.g., Sutherland, 1977).

An hypothesis on the molecular basis of the fra(X) mutation suggests that a recombination or amplification of a DNA sequence occurs at a site rich in pyrimidines (such as trymidine) and that unequal crossing over during meiosis occurs, which could cause a rearrangement and amplification or deletion of sequences that affect nearby genes.

DOWN SYNDROME

John Langdon Down, medical superintendent of the Earlswood Asylum for Idiots in Surrey, England, was the first to describe the clinical symptomatology associated with the chromosomal defect of mongolism, or Down syndrome. He had attempted to devise a classification scheme of the diagnosis of congenital forms of mental retardation. He was frustrated by the many different causes of mental retardation and could only contribute the observation that one family of mental defect was consistently associated with certain physiognomic characteristics. He described the typical "mongolian" faces of broad, flat face, obliquely placed eyes, and heavy epicanthic folds.

Down correctly assumed that this mental retardation syndrome was not the result of an "accident after uterine life" and that these patients were congenitally mentally defective. He speculated that the cause of this syndrome was tuberculosis in the parents. Interestingly, Down observed that mongolism accounted for 10% of mental retardates that came to his attention, an incidence surprisingly close to current estimates.

Down syndrome is the best known cause of mental retardation. In the United States, the current incidence of Down syndrome is believed to be approximately 1 in 1,000 live births (Adams et al., 1981), which is in contrast to the higher incidence of 1.33 per 1,000 live births as recently as 1960.

LeJuene (1959) was the first to associate Down syndrome with an extra chromosome in the G group. Ninety-five percent of all cases result from nondisjunction, with only a small percentage of cases being associated with translocation.

Clinically, Down syndrome is characterized by mental retardation, growth retardation, epicanthal folds, simian palmar crease, and hypotonia. Patients with Down syndrome are also known to have increased incidence of abnormalities associated with premature aging, such as increased susceptibility to diabetes mellitus, neoplasms, cataracts, and a dementia that pathologically resembles Alzheimer's disease (Martin, 1978). In addition, the incidence of disorders such as leukemia, endocrine dysfunction, and neurotransmitter abnormalities and deficiencies are known to be greatly decreased.

PERINATAL TRAUMA

Neurobehavioral impairments are frequently associated with trauma to the brain at or near the time of delivery. This nonprogressive brain syndrome, which is also known as cerebral palsy, affects more than 2 out of every 1,000 live births (Hansen, 1960), and there is reason to believe that a very high percentage of these survivors have degrees of mental retardation (Menkes, 1980). Despite the fact that birth injuries have been known to cause neurologic handicaps since Little's classic description of spastic diplegia in an infant who was a product of a difficult labor (Little, 1862), the exact pathogenesis is still unknown. Among the possible agents that could produce these encephalopathic events are hypoxia, hypoglycemia, hypercarbia, acidosis, physical trauma, arterial or venous insufficiency, and edema.

It should be added, however, that even in normal delivery there is considerable compression of the head and, infrequently, minimal intracranial damage as indicated by the presence of red blood cells in the cerebrospinal fluid (Walton, 1977). An early study (Roberts, 1925) showed that 14% of neonates have significant evidence of blood in the cerebrospinal fluid, although very few of these children manifested neurologic abnormalities. Given that normal births produce such a picture, it is not surprising that breech deliveries, difficult forceps deliveries, and other abnormal conditions producing excessive compression on the fetal head or traction on the brain stem and spinal cord might be associated with severe traumatic lesions.

Holland (1922) was the first to study the etiology of these traumatic birth injuries. He suggested that tears of the tentorium, resulting from longitudinal stress on the falx, were associated with large basal hemorrhages that could be attributed to a ruptured internal cerebral vein. In his series, the tentorium was torn in 48% of the cases and the falx torn in 3%. Difficult forceps delivery—accompanied by flexion, hyperextension, and torsion of the brain stem and spinal cord—produce lacerations, especially of the cerebral peduncles. Overriding the parietal bones is also commonly associated with lacerations of the superficial cerebral veins and, less commonly, with laceration of the superior sagittal sinus.

While these direct traumatic effects give rise to obvious neurologic sequelae, they probably do not account for the majority of birth injuries (Courville, 1971). It is assumed that hypoxia causes a great majority of the pathological changes in perinatal injury. It is also assumed that hypoxia may work independently to produce these changes or that it may work with a secondary phenomenon (e.g., edema, secondary circulatory disturbance).

Many classification schemes have been suggested for this class of disorders, but there is no univeral agreement about these important acquired anomalies. Ingram (1964) has described the following categories of cerebral palsy: (1) quadriplegia or tetraplegia, (2) diplegia, (3) hemiplegia; (4) bilateral hemiplegia, (5) ataxia, and (6) dyskinesia (dystonic, choreoid, and athetoid forms).

The relationship between the cognitive and motor defects in cerebral palsy is not well understood. Indeed, many children may present without motor signs and have profound disturbances of cognitive function. It is thought that disturbances of motility such as diplegia, which impair progression through the stages of psychomotor development, may serve to retard the child's cognitive development. Evidence of the role of motor dysfunction in retarding cognitive develoepmnt comes from the observations that many children with impaired motor function early in life seem to have accelerated cognitive development (despite low measured IQ) in later childhood and reach normal to supranormal intellectual levels.

The effects of asphyxia have been well described in laboratory animals, in human neonates, and in adult humans. The differential effects between adults and children are important, and theoretical considerations must be given to the difference between metabolic insults that occur in the second and third trimester. In adults, hypoxia is most commonly associated with events such as cardiac arrest, carbon monoxide poisoning, and anoxia secondary to respiratory and circulatory failure. Neurons, the neural elements most sensitive to anoxia, suffer the most damage in the CNS. The structures selectively damaged by hypoxia in the adult are thought to be the pyramidal cells of the hippocampus, Purkinje cells of the cerebellum, basal ganglia, and the deeper layers of the cerebral cortex. The entire cortex can be altered after only a few minutes by hypoxia. While the deeper layers of cortex are usually differentially affected (especially those lying deep in cortical sulci), it is not uncommon to find adjacent white matter changes as well. Damage to the vascular endothelium can contribute to the picture of disruption, although direct neuronal involvement is most likely to account for the preponderance of anoxic effects. Other alterations include microglial activation and astrocytic proliferation, with the outcome closely associated with the extent of necrosis. In severe anoxic conditions, macrophages and capillary proliferation appear.

Ulegyria is a common consequence of vascular lesions in the perinatal period. It is characterized by mantle sclerosis, the localized destruction of the inferior parts of the convolution with relative sparing of the crown. This gives rise to the "mushroom cap" appearance of gyri. In more severe forms of ulegyria, ventricular dilatation often occurs.

Perinatal trauma causes lesions in the basal ganglia in up to 35% of the cases. The most distinctive lesion in the basal ganglia after perinatal trauma is *status marmoratus,* or the marbled state. Symmetric demyelination and hypermyelination give the appearance of marbling in this region.

Passive Exposure to Toxic Substances: Licit and Illicit
Drug Abuse

In the last decade, there has been an alarming incidence of damage to fetuses due to passive, *in utero* exposure to psychoactive substances used by mothers. Many case reports are appearing in the scientific literature pointing to associations between maternal drug use and infant mortality and morbidity. This section will briefly review this issue (for a more extensive discussion, see Bonnefil & Pirozzolo, 1992).

It is now widely accepted that alcohol use during pregnancy can have significant damaging effects on neonates (Burd & Martsolf, 1989; O'Connor et al., 1986; Schandler et al., 1988; Streissguth & LaDue, 1987). The number of infants born to cocaine-abusing mothers has dramatically increased in the last decade (Chasnoff et al., 1989b; Frank et al., 1988). An equally alarming trend is the concomitant increase in the number of infants born seropositive for HIV (Nicholas et al., 1989; Pizzo et al., 1988). Pediatric HIV seropositivity is most often the result of maternal or paternal substance abuse (Nicholas et al., 1989).

Neuropsychological Effects of Passive Exposure to
Psychoactive Substances

CNS Depressants—Alcohol.   Alcohol is a well-established teratogen, and prenatal exposure can cause a number of adverse perinatal outcomes, depending on the dose, duration of exposure, and other conditions (Streissguth & LaDue, 1987). The early stage of pregnancy appear to be the most critical period for adverse fetal effects, particularly the first several weeks after conception (McKay, 1983) (see Table 4.3).

TABLE 4.3   Neuropsychological Sequelae in Infants Passively Exposed to Psychoactive Substances *In Utero*

Substance	Neuropsychological Sequelae
CNS Depressants	
Alcohol	Tremors, hyperactivity, mild to severe deficits ranging from FAE (including deficits in attention, learning, memory, organization, and problem solving) to FAS (characterized by dysmorphogenesis, growth retardation, mental retardation, fine and gross motor impairments, and disturbances in social inhibition)
Barbiturates	*
Benzodiazepines	*
CNS Stimulants	
Caffeine	*
Cocaine	Tremulousness, irritability, hypertonia, sleep and feeding disturbances, abnormal reflexes, decreased motor function, poor orientation and state regulation behavior, abnormal EEGs
Amphetamines	*
Tobacco	Lowered IQ scores, learning difficulties, deficits in verbal, reading, and mathematical skills, hyperactivity/impulsivity, neurological soft signs
Hallucinogens	
Marijuana	Impaired fetal growth, acute tremors, exaggerated startle reflex, irritability, impaired habituation to visual stimuli
LSD	*
PCP	Acute tremulousness, irritability, hypertonicity, hyperreactivity to stimuli with intermittent lethargy; poorly organized state behavior
Ecstasy	*
Opioids	Acute neonatal abstinence syndrome with subsequent motor incoordination, impaired visual-motor-perceptual functioning; mild mental retardation/developmental delays at preschool age
Inhalants	*

*While there have been reports of relationships between these substances and teratogenic or neuropsychological effects in animals or humans, at present there is no scientific consensus on the nature and magnitude of neuropsychological sequelae in humans.

Excessive maternal use of alcohol in pregnancy is known to cause the fetal alcohol syndrome (FAS), first described in 1973 by Jones and colleagues (Streissguth & LaDue, 1989). FAS is characterized by a cluster of symptoms, including physical growth retardation; dysmorphogenesis, including craniofacial anomalies; and CNS manifestations, including mental retardation (Ernhart et al., 1989; Pirozzolo, Bonnefil, & Brawler, 1991). FAS is the third most common cause of mental retardation in Western countries, following trisomy 21 (Down syndrome) and Fragile X syndrome, which are more prevalent genetic causes; FAS is the most frequent known teratogenic cause of mental retardation (Pirozzolo, 1985; Streissguth & LaDue, 1987; Yu et al., 1991). Estimates of the prevalence of FAS among women who drink heavily during the period shortly after conception range from 2.5 to 3.5% (Burd & Martsolf, 1989; Ernhart et al., 1989). This is greater than 20 times the prevalence in the normal population (Ernhart et al., 1989). It has also been estimated that 8% of cases of mild mental retardation may be due to prenatal exposure to alcohol. The recurrence risk for FAS among siblings is as high as 25% (Ernhart et al., 1989; Streissguth & LaDue, 1989).

Dose-response relationships have been established in laboratory animals (and suggested in humans) for adverse behavioral and teratogenic outcomes. It is clear that neuropsychological deficits can be seen at lower doses than those necessary to produce malformations. It has been suggested that there may be an analogous dose-response continuum of neurobehavioral, developmental, and dysmorphic consequences if in utero exposure to excessive alcohol consumption that overlaps with the full-blown syndrome of FASA (Burd & Martsolf, 1989). This pattern would include less-severe clinical manifestations of fetal alcohol effects (FAE) (Streissguth & LaDue, 1987).

The mechanism of action of alcohol on the embryo and fetus is thought to be via the placental and blood-brain barriers. Fetal blood alcohol level reaches approximately the same concentration as that of the mother; however, the fetus clears the alcohol from its system more slowly than does the mother, presumably because of hepatic immaturity.

Quite apart from the global mental retardation evident in FAS, neuropsychological deficits associated with prenatal alcohol exposure can include varying intellectual decrements, learning deficits, attentional and memory deficits, fine and gross motor impairments, deficits in organization and problem solving, tremor, and hyperactivity (Streissguth et al., 1989). FAS patients, in addition to having intellectual and dysmorphic characteristics, display psychosocial problems such as lack of inhibition, poor social judgment, over-friendliness, over-inquisitiveness, and excessive demands for physical contact and affection (Streissguth & LaDue, 1987).

Cocaine.   Although cocaine use during pregnancy is a less common than alcohol, research reports of the consequences of cocaine use continue to be presented. Cocaine is the illicit drug of choice among the poor and the affluent alike and its use has been increasing to the point that it currently competes with marijuana as the primary illicit drug used by women of childbearing age in the United States (Anday et al., 1989; Chasnoff et al., 1989b; Hume et al., 1989; Oro & Dixon, 1987). This has led to a recent dramatic increase in the number of infants born to cocaine-abusing mothers (Chasnoff et al., 1989b). Estimates of the incidence of urban infants exposed to cocaine in utero range from 10 to over 17% of those seeking routine prenatal care (Bauchner et al., 1988; Frank et al., 1988; MacGregor et al., 1989). It has been suggested that the majority of infants with prenatal exposure to illicit drugs are born to mothers who are cocaine abusers (Fulroth, Phillips, & Durand, 1989).

As is true for any other individual substance of abuse, analysis of neurobehavioral correlates of *in utero* exposure to cocaine as well as epidemiologic patterns are difficult because of such confounding variables as socioeconomic status, prenatal care, nutritional status, and concomitant use of other drugs, such as alcohol, heroin, tobacco, and marijuana. Some investigators advocate urine screening along with questionnaires or interviews to ascertain the prevalence of drug use among pregnant women. In studies where urine assays have been employed in order to verify cocaine use during pregnancy, approximately one-fourth of those testing positive for cocaine metabolites had denied in interviews that they had used cocaine (Bauchner et al., 1988; Frank et al., 1988).

In addition to passive exposure to the fetus to cocaine via transplacental transmission (Cherukuri et al., 1988) or via breast milk (Chasnoff, Douglas, & Squires, 1987), cases have been reported of infants and young children who experienced severe acute effects of cocaine toxicity via passive inhalation of the smoke of freebase crack cocaine (Bateman & Heagarty, 1989).

Several consistent findings have emerged from research on neurological and neurobehavioral consequences of prenatal cocaine exposure. One is that neonates exposed to cocaine *in utero* exhibit a characteristic pattern of neurobehavioral effects. Using a combination of neurobehavioral and psychophysical assessment measures including the Brazelton Neonatal Behavior Assessment Scale; Brazelton, Als, & Tronick, 1979), researchers have shown that cocaine-exposed neonates display signs of drug withdrawal, including hypertonia, tremulousness, tachypnea, decreased sleep time, and feeding disturbances, as well as abnormal reflexes and decreased motor function, orientation, and state-regulation behavior (Chasnoff et al., 1989a; Chasnoff et al., 1989b; Fulroth et al., 1989). These infants demonstrate disrupted patterns of glabellar and auditory startle reflexes (Anday et al., 1989) and display abnormal EEGs, suggestive of CNS irritability (Doberczak et al., 1988). Although upon retesting, many of the abnormal neurobehavioral symptoms in cocaine-exposed infants decrease, abnormalities of orientation and state regulation persist for at least one month (Chasnoff et al., 1989b), abnormal EEGs have returned to normal in many cases by 3 to 12 months of age (Doberczak et al., 1988).

A dose-response relationship between extent of abuse and neuropsychological outcome has not been demonstrated in the research literature. However, it does appear that exposure to cocaine in the first trimester of pregnancy places the infant at risk for neurobehavioral deficits, although the risk may be diminished somewhat if the mother does not use cocaine throughout the pregnancy (Chasnoff et al., 1989a). Because the blood-brain barrier is not well established in the first trimester, the presumed mechanism of action of cocaine on neurotransmitters may result in interference with neuronal development (Grimm, 1987).

One potential sequelae of prenatal cocaine exposure is impairment in infant-caregiver interactions. It is possible that the characteristic irritability and tremulousness of the cocaine-exposed infant will interfere with these interactions and, especially if combined with environmental deprivation, result in an exacerbation of long-range adverse outcomes (Chasnoff et al., 1987; Cohen, 1991; Rodning, Beckwith, & Howard, 1989; Sameroff & Chandler, 1975).

Amphetamines.   Recent evidence suggests that amphetamine abuse has declined somewhat in the past two decades (Middaugh, 1989; O'Malley et al., 1988). Thus, research studies of prenatal amphetamine exposure are relatively few. Amphetamines are pharmacologically similar to cocaine, and it is reasonable to assume that findings regarding perinatal consequences of amphetamine exposure might be similar to those seen with cocaine. It is believed that amphetamines and corticosterone (released by amphetamines), when taken during pregnancy, exert their effects in a transplacental manner, and thus will have an influence on the developing neural and endocrine systems (Middaugh, 1989).

The literature (both animal and human) on detrimental neurobehavioral effects of prenatal amphetamine exposure suggests that prenatal amphetamine exposure results in adverse perinatal outcomes, such as reduction in length at birth, low birth weight, small head circumference, and shorter gestation (Middaugh, 1989). In addition, some evidence also suggests that amphetamine-exposed infants exhibit poor feeding behavior and excessive drowsiness throughout the first year of life (Oro & Dixon, 1987).

Long-term neuropsychological consequences of prenatal amphetamine exposure have not been documented in humans (Middaugh, 1989). The presence of long-term neurobehavioral deficits in laboratory animals (including impaired learning, slower habituation, and increased motor activity), together with amphetamines' known influence on monoaminergic and pituitary-adrenal systems, strongly suggests the neurotoxicity of amphetamine abuse during human pregnancy (Middaugh, 1989).

Tobacco.   The incidence of maternal cigarette smoking during pregnancy has not been well documented. In Western countries, there has been a 25% per capita decrease in cigarette smoking since the mid-1960s. This 25% reduction is due, however, to a decrease from 52 to 33% among adult male smokers. In contrast, the rate among women has decreased from 34 to 28%. For both males and females who use tobacco, the percentage of heavy smokers (25 or more cigarettes per day) has increased over the same period. Surprisingly, the greatest prevalence rates of smoking among females are among those of childbearing age (over 30% of women between 20 and 34 years of age smoke) (Mactutus, 1989), which makes tobacco use a significant risk to fetal humans.

In a meta-analysis of studies of the developmental consequences of passive exposure to cigarette smoking, Rush and Callahan (1989) noted inconsistent and, in some cases, contradictory findings. For example, many studies found no significant relationships between perinatal maternal smoking and measures of mental or psychomotor development in offspring. One study found a highly significant relationship between amount of cigarette smoking prior to pregnancy and an index of psychomotor development. Similar inconsistent results were found for such neonatal neurobehavioral measures as state regulation, irritability, and habituation (Rush & Callahan, 1989).

In contrast, consistent patterns of impaired academic functioning were associated with prenatal exposure to tobacco. The patterns include lower IQ scores as well as poorer verbal, reading, and mathematical skills among children prenatally exposed to smoking. Other neuropsychological deficits, such as learning disabilities, hyperactivity, and so on, were reported among prenatally exposed children.

Hallucinogens—Marijuana. Marijuana use has apparently begun to decline among adolescents (Murray, 1986; O'Malley et al., 1988). It is nevertheless a widely abused drug which now competes with cocaine as the most widely used illicit drug among young adults in Western countries (Hutchings, Brake, & Morgan, 1989; O'Malley et al., 1988). In 1985, approximately 31% of American women in their late teens to early 20s admitted to having used marijuana within the past year (Zuckerman et al., 1989).

Marijuana use during pregnancy has been estimated at approximately 12% among women in nonghetto urban areas (Fried & Watkinson, 1988). It is plausible that the true prevalence is higher (Zuckerman et al., 1989), due to under-reporting.

The dosage of delta-9-hydrocannabinol (Δ-9-THC, marijuana's major psychoactive component) is variable in different samples of marijuana. It is difficult therefore to establish dose-response relationships for marijuana use, especially in humans. In rats, quantifiable amounts of Δ-9-THC have been administered, and clear dose-response relationships are known (Hutchings et al., 1989).

It has been suggested that the concentration of Δ-9-THC in street-grade marijuana has increased 250% since it psychopharmacological effects were first systematically investigated (Schwartz et al., 1989). This marked increase in potency, combined with a relatively high (despite its illicit status) prevalence of use by pregnant women and women of childbearing age, suggests the importance of understanding potential short- and long-term consequences of its use during pregnancy.

Controversy persists over whether prenatal exposure to marijuana smoking has teratogenic or adverse neuropsychological effects in infants and children. Impaired fetal growth has been associated with maternal marijuana smoking (Zuckerman et al., 1989). Tremors, exaggerated startle reflex, and a tendency toward increased irritability have also been shown. Prenatal exposure to marijuana has also been associated in the neonate with impaired habituation to visual (but not auditory) stimuli, habituation being considered indicative of CNS integrity (Fried, 1989). At 9 and 30 days of age, signs of generalized irritability, such as increased startle response, persist in marijuana-exposed infants, whereas specific visual system reflexes, such as pupil dilation, nystagmus, doll's eye reflex, and acoustic blink, are not associated with maternal marijuana smoking (Fried, 1989). At 1 and 2 years of age, no relationship between prenatal exposure to marijuana and adverse motor, cognitive, or language neuropsychological outcome has been found

(Fried, 1989; Fried & Watkinson, 1988), suggesting that the reflex irritability seen in neonates parentally exposed to marijuana may be a mild abstinence syndrome similar to that seen in opioid-exposed neonates. It is possible that the adverse effects of prenatal marijuana exposure may resole by 12 to 24 months, leaving no measurable neuropsychological sequelae (Fried, 1989).

PCP. A recent rise in the use of PCP is especially disturbing when seen among women of reproductive age (Fico & Vanderwende, 1989). Increased prevalence of PCP use has led to clinical reports of adverse effects of prenatal PCP exposure. Placental transfer of PCP is thought to take place in humans because it has been shown to occur in rats (Fico & Vanderwende, 1989). Neonates born to PCP-abusing women have been reported to be tremulous, hyperreactive to stimuli, irritable, hypertonic, and intermittently lethargic (Fico & Vanderwende, 1989; Golden et al., 1987). Despite frequent reports of neurobehavioral abnormalities in PCP-exposed neonates, adverse mental or psychomotor developmental sequelae are not in evidence by age 2, in comparison with controls. Poor neurobehavioral outcome may be attributable to environmental variables rather than to prenatal drug exposure (Chasnoff et al., 1986).

Opioids. Although the majority of infants born with prenatal exposure to illicit drugs are born to cocaine abusers, one-fourth of those are born to mothers who abuse both cocaine and opiates (Fulroth et al., 1989). Statistics are not available on the number of infants born to opioid-using mothers, although estimates are as high as 10,000 per year in the United States alone (Hans, 1989). An increasing proportion of patients entering drug-treatment programs are women of childbearing age; in the early 1980s, the number of women in such programs reached 30%.

The neonatal abstinence (drug withdrawal) syndrome has been a well-known acute effect of opiate addiction in pregnant women for almost a century (Wilson, 1989). This syndrome is characterized by signs of CNS arousal such as hyperactivity, hyperexcitability, hyperacusis, sleeplessness, tremulousness, and prolonged high-pitched crying. It usually subsides in three to six weeks, followed by a subacute withdrawal phase, with restlessness, agitation, tremors, and sleep disturbance lasting from four to six months (Hutchings, 1985). It has recently been observed that, when heroin was used in combination with cocaine by pregnant women, neonatal abstinence symptoms were more severe than in neonates exposed to either heroin alone or cocaine alone.

Heroin and methadone are not teratogens and do not include dysmorphogenesis (Hutchings, 1985). Studies that have investigated at long-term neuropsychological effects of prenatal heroin or methadone exposure have yielded contradictory findings. There are reports of increased incidence of low-average IQ, mild mental retardation, and mild developmental delays at preschool age (Lifschitz et al., 1985). Other reports of no consistent differences in cognitive performance at ages 2 and 4 (Hans, 1989; Hutchings, 1985) also exist. Reports of impaired motor coordination, some of the characteristic symptomatology associated with attention deficit disorder (Hutchings, 1985; Marcus, Hans, & Jeremy, 1984;

Wilson, 1989), and impairments of visual-motor-perceptual function (Wilson, 1989) are fairly consistent across studies.

Pediatric AIDS and Substance Abuse

The epidemiology of HIV infection in neonates is a particularly complex issue. The National Centers for Disease Control (CDC) data probably underestimate the incidence of maternal and pediatric-acquired immune deficiency syndrome (AIDS), because most data have come only from patients with severe clinical manifestations of AIDS, and do not include the 80 to 90% who are HIV seropositive but asymptomatic or less severely afflicted (Nicholas et al., 1989). As of June, 1994, 5,734 children under age 13 had been diagnosed with AIDS in the United States. By June, 1994, there were 51,235 cases of women diagnosed with AIDS. Drug abuse was an associated factor in approximately one-half of these cases.

The proportion of children with AIDS who were vertically infected is estimated at 80%. The likelihood of a seropositive mother infecting her infant is estimated at 40% (Nicholas et al., 1989).

The mechanism of transmission of the HIV virus from mother to infant is currently under investigation. It is presumed that intrauterine transmission is the most likely route. HIV infection has been documented in fetuses as young as 12 weeks' gestational age (Nicholas et al., 1989). It has also been suggested that HIV transmission might occur during childbirth, since HIV is blood- and body fluid-borne, but no such cases have been documented. It has also been suggested that HIV might be transmitted through breast milk. Although the U.S. Public Health Service recommends against breast-feeding by HIV-infected women, this route of transmission has not been documented (Nicholas et al., 1989).

Several confounding variables make HIV transmission statistics difficult to interpret. For example, high rates of IV drug use are correlated with large numbers of sexual encounters. In addition, pediatric and adult AIDS is most prevalent in urban areas where it is more likely that even adolescents who are not using drugs themselves will have sexual liaisons with IV drug users (Nicholas et al., 1989; Olson et al., 1989; Pizzo et al., 1988). The situation is also complicated by the increasing prevalence of youthful cocaine users, many of whom inject cocaine intravenously, thereby increasing their risk of exposure to HIV.

NEUROPSYCHOLOGICAL DEFICITS
AND PEDIATRIC AIDS INFECTIONS

Neuropsychological effects of pediatric infection with HIV have been well documented over the last five years. Estimates of neurological complications in children with AIDS range from 50 to 90% (as compared with 30 to 50% in HIV positive but undiagnosed children and as compared with 30 to 60% in adults) (Belman et al., 1988; Epstein, Sharer, & Goudsmit, 1988; Janssen et al., 1989; Ultmann et al., 1987). Severe developmental delays have been found in over 95% of pediatric patients seropositive for HIV antibody (Price et al., 1989). In children with AIDS, cortical atrophy appears more severe than in adults (Olson, et al., 1989; Petito, 1988). Calcifications of the basal ganglia are more likely to be seen in children with HIV infection (Belman et al., 1986; Belman et al., 1988; Olson et al., 1989).

The major adverse neuropsychological effect of pediatric HIV infection is progressive encephalopathy, the pediatric counterpart of the AIDS dementia complex (ADC) in adults. It was formerly believed that opportunistic infections with such disease agents as cytomegalovirus (CMV) might produce the progressive encephalopathy seen in children with AIDS (Epstein et al., 1985), but it now appears that the progressive encephalopathy and resulting dementia are caused by direct infection of the brain with HIV (Belman et al., 1988; Epstein et al., 1988; Petito, 1988; Price et al., 1988). Opportunistic infection (such as with CMV) or reactivation of latent infection (such as with toxoplasmosis) are rare in children (Belman et al., 1988; Epstein & Sharer, 1988).

Different neurologic manifestations occur during different stages of pediatric HIV infection (Janssen et al., 1989). The onset of progressive encephalopathy in HIV-infected children may range from 2 months to 5 years after the initial exposure to the virus, with an average of 18 months (Epstein & Sharer, 1988). However, a small but growing number of children who were vertically infected are clinically well at between 6 and 10 years of age, although they show evidence of immune dysfunction. This suggests an extremely long incubation period for the development of immune deficiency in some children (Nicholas et al., 1989), which would parallel the development of progressive encephalopathy. Some children have presented with evidence of cognitive dysfunction prior to immunologic abnormalities (Epstein et al., 1988).

Symptoms of pediatric HIV encephalopathy include loss of developmental milestones, cognitive deterioration, and progressive motor deficits. Delays or abnormalities in the acquisition of gross and fine motor skills as well as language skills have been noted to be more pronounced than deficits in socially adaptive behaviors (Belman et al., 1988; Ultmann et al., 1987). Neuropsychological assessment has revealed that the overwhelming majority of children with symptomatic AIDS fall within the range of borderline IQ to profoundly mentally retarded (Belman et al., 1988).

STATE OF AFFAIRS IN REHABILITATION OF CHILDREN WITH EARLY INSULT TO CENTRAL NERVOUS SYSTEM

Because of the wide variability in neurobehavioral sequelae characteristic of disorders resulting during the perinatal period, space does not permit complete discussion of habilitation and/or rehabilitation efforts for children with early neurologic disorders. (See Chapter 5 for further discussion.) Suffice it to say that, in many cases, comprehensive medical management strategies are typically indicated for those children with neurological disorders that typically result in short life expectancies (e.g., children born HIV positive, agenesis of the brain, anencephalus). However, for many other children surviving early neurologic injury, the neuropsychological sequelae dictate the nature of treatment that should follow. The primary objective in all cases is to initially facilitate and maintain medical stability. Where seizures are involved, containment may well prevent further decline in cognitive, emotional, and behavioral function. Neurosurgical procedures indicated in treatment of some disorders (e.g., retractible seizures, hydrocephalus, spina bifida, myelomeningocele) may also serve to minimize neurobehavioral consequences.

Environmental conditions such as socioeconomic status likely play a significant role in the long-range outcome of survivors of early neurological insults. Families who can afford allied health-care professionals to provide early intervention may optimize the chances of the child's functional adaptation to his or her environment. The nature of services range from restructuring the child's environment to optimize quality of life to teaching remedial and compensatory strategies for managing activities of daily living and learning.

Medical ethics place great limitations on researchers' and neuropsychological assessments in formulating and evaluating treatment plans for children with early neurologic injuries. One difficulty in researching this issue is the tendency for children with early brain damage to demonstrate little cognitive development or show generalized decline in cognitive dysfunction (see Chapter 2), which may be less amenable to cognitive habilitation efforts, as compared to other disorders (e.g., attention deficit, specific learning disorders) that may respond to such treatment approaches. Another confounding factor in research paradigms using neuropsychological data to develop and monitor treatment approaches are poorly understood aberrations in central nervous system development and correlations to neurobehavioral development. Consequently, longitudinal studies designed to characterize patterns of neurobehavioral changes associated with each disorder may be necessary prior to researching assessment-treatment paradigms. From this view, many clinicians must continue to use management strategies emphasizing quality of life issues and expectations for functional outcomes in guiding treatment.

REFERENCES

Adams MM, Erickson JD, Layde PM, Oakley GP: Down's syndrome: Recent trends in the United States. *Journal of the American Medical Association:* 246: 758–760, 1981.

Adams RD, Sidman RL: *Introduction to neuropathology.* New York: McGraw-Hill, 1968.

Anday ED, Cohen ME, Kelley NE, Leitner DS: Effect of in utero cocaine exposure on startle and its modification. *Developmental and Pharmacological Therapeutics:* 12: 137–145, 1989.

Bateman DA, Heagarty MC: Passive freebase cocaine ("crack") inhalation by infants and toddlers. *American Journal of Diseases of Children:* 143: 25–27, 1989.

Bauchner H, Zuckerman B, McClain M, Frank D, Fried LE, Kayne H: Risk of sudden infant death syndrome among infants with in utero exposure to cocaine. *Journal of Pediatrics:* 113: 831–834, 1988.

Belman AL, Diamond G, Dickson, D, Horoupian D, Llena J, Lantos G, Rubinstein A: Pediatric acquired immunodeficiency syndrome: Neurologic syndromes. *American Journal of Diseases of Children:* 142: 29–35, 1988.

Belman AL, Lantos G, Horoupian D, Novick BE, Ultmann MH, Dickson DW, Rubinstein A: AIDS: calcification of the basal ganglia in infants and children. *Neurology:* 36: 1192–1199, 1986.

Benda CE: *Developmental disorders of mentation and cerebral palsies.* New York: Grune & Stratton, 1952.

Berman JL, et al,: Causes for high phenylalanine with normal tyrosine. *American Journal of Diseases of Children:* 117: 54, 1969.

Bonnefil G, Pirozzolo FJ: Neuropsychological consequences of substance abuse. In F Bolier & J Grafman (Eds.), *Handbook of neuropsychology, Vol. VII* (S. Segalowitz, Volume editor). Amsterdam: Elsevier, 1992.

Brazelton TB, Als H, Tronick E, Lester BM: Specific neonatal measures: The Brazelton Neonatal Assessment Scale. In JP Osofsky (Ed.), *Handbook of infant development.* New York: John Wiley and Sons, pp. 116–135, 1979.

Burd L, Martsolf JT: Fetal alcohol syndrome: diagnosis and syndromal variability. *Psychology and Behavior:* 46: 39–43, 1989.

Chase HP, Martin HP: Undernutrition and child development. *New England Journal of Medicine:* 282: 579, 1970.

Chasnoff IJ: Drug use and women: Establishing a standard of care. *Annals of the New York Academy of Sciences:* 562: 208–210, 1989.

Chasnoff IJ, Burns KA, Burns WJ: Cocaine use in pregnancy: Perinatal morbidity and mortality. *Neurotoxicity and Teratology:* 9: 291–293, 1987.

Chasnoff IJ, Burns KA, Burns WJ, Schnoll SH: Prenatal drug exposure: Effects on neonatal and infant growth and development. *Neurobehavioral Toxicology and Teratology:* 8: 357–362, 1987.

Chasnoff IJ, Douglas EL, Squires L: Cocaine intoxication in a breast-fed infant. *Pediatrics:* 80: 836–838, 1987.

Chasnoff IJ, Griffith DR: Cocaine: Clinical studies of pregnancy and the newborn. *Annals of the New York Academy of Sciences:* 562: 260–266, 1989.

Chasnoff IJ, Griffith DR, MacGregor S, Dirkes K, Burns KA: Temporal patterns of cocaine use in pregnancy. Perinatal outcome. *Journal of the American Medical Association:* 261: 1741–1744, 1989a.

Chasnoff IJ, Landress HJ, Barrett ME: The prevalence of illicit-drug or alcohol use during pregnancy and discrepancies in mandatory reporting in Pinellas County, Florida. *New England Journal of Medicine:* 322: 1202–1206, 1990.

Chasnoff IJ, Lewis DE, Griffith DR, Willey S: Cocaine and pregnancy: Clinical and toxicological implications for the neonate. *Clinical Chemistry:* 35: 1276–1278, 1989b.

Cherukuri R, Minkoff H, Feldman J, Parekh A, Glass L: A cohort study of alkaloidal cocaine ("crack") in pregnancy. *Obstetrics and Gynecology:* 72: 147–151, 1988.

Chiari H: Ueber veranderungen des kleinhirns infolge von hydrocephaie des grosshirns. *Deutsche Medizinische Wechenschrift:* 42: 1172, 1891.

Christensen E, Melchior J: Cerebral palsy—A clinical and neuropathological study. *Clinical and Developmental Medicine:* 25: 1, 1891.

Cleland J: Contribution to the study of spina bifida, encephalocele and anencephaus. *Journal of Anatomic Physiology:* 17: 257, 1883.

Cohen SE: Early intervention with the at-risk infant. In JW Gray & RS Dean (Eds.), *Neuropsychology of perinatal complications.* New York: Springer, pp. 204–224, 1991.

Courville CV: *Birth and brain damage.* Pasadena: MF Courville, 1971.

Dekaban HS, Sakuragawa N: Megalencephaly. In PJ Vinken & GW Bruyn (Eds.), *Handbook of clinical neurology* (Vol. 30) (pp. 131–152). Amsterdam: North-Holland Publishing Company, 1977.

Dignan P, Warkany J: Congenital malformations: Lissencephaly agyria and pachygyria. In J Wortis (Ed.), *Mental retardation and developmental disabilities* (Vol. 10) (pp. 77–91). New York: Brunner/Mazel, 1978.

Doberczak TM, Shanzer S, Senie RT, Kandall SR: Neonatal neurologic and electroencephalographic effects of intrauterine cocaine exposure. *Journal of Pediatrics:* 113: 354–358, 1988.

Drake W: Clinical and pathological findings in a child with a developmental learning disability. *Journal of Learning Disabilities:* 1: 468–475, 1968.

Dreifuss FE: The pathology of central communicative disorder in children. In EL Eagles (Ed.), *Human communication and its disorders* (Vol. 3) (pp. 383–392). New York: Raven Press, 1975.

Drillien CM, Drummond MB: *Neurodevelopmental problems in early childhood: Assessment and management.* London: Blackwell Scientific Publications, 1977.

Eimas P: Speech perception in early infancy. In LB Cohen and P Salapatek (Eds.), *Infant perception* (pp. 108–121). New York: Academic Press, 1975.

Epstein LG, Sharer LR: Neurology of human immunodeficiency virus infection in children. In ML Rosenblum (Ed.), *AIDS and the nervous system.* New York: Raven Press, pp. 79–101, 1988.

Epstein LG, Sharer LR, Goudsmit J: Neurological and neuropathological features of human immunodeficiency virus infection in children. *Annals of Neurology:* 23 (supplement): S19–S23, 1988.

Epstein LG, Sharer LR, Joshi VV, Fojas MM, Koenigsberger MR, Oleske JM: Progressive encephalopathy in children with acquired immunodeficiency syndrome. *Annals of Neurology:* 17: 488–496, 1985.

Ernhart CB, Sokol RJ, Ager JW, Morrow-Tlucak M, Martier S: Alcohol-related birth defects: Assessing the risk. *Annals of the New York Academy of Sciences:* 562: 159–172, 1989.

Eslinger P (Ed.): *Special issue of developmental neuropsychology: The frontal lobes.* Hillsdate, NJ: Lawrence Erlbaum, 1991.

Estroff TW, Schwartz RH, Hoffmann NG: Adolescent cocaine abuse. *Clinical Pediatrics:* 28: 550–555, 1989.

Fantz RL: Pattern vision in newborn infants. *Science:* 140: 296–297, 1963.

Fico TA, Vanderwende C: Phencyclidine during pregnancy: Behavioral and neurochemical

effects in the offspring. *Annals of the New York Academy of Sciences:* 562: 319–326, 1989.

Fisch RO, Sines JK, Chang P: Personality characteristics of nonretarded phenylketonurics and their family members. *Journal of Clinical Psychiatry:* 42: 106–113, 1981.

Fishman MA, et al.: Lacunar skull deformity and intelligence. *Pediatrics:* 59: 296, 1977.

Folling A: Uber ausscheidung von phenylbrenztraubensaure in den harn als stoffwechselanomalie n verbindung mit imbezillitat. *Z. Physiology and Chemistry:* 227: 169, 1934.

Frank DA, Zuckerman BS, Amaro H, Aboagye K, Bauchner H, Cabral H, Fried L, Hingson R, Kayne H, Levenson SM, Parker S, Reece H, Vinci R: Cocaine use during pregnancy: Prevalence and correlates. *Pediatrics:* 82: 888–895, 1988.

Fried PA: Postnatal consequences of maternal marijuana use in humans. *Annals of the New York Academy of Sciences:* 562: 123–132, 1989.

Fried PA, Watkinson B: 12- and 24-month neurobehavioral follow-up of children prenatally exposed to marijuana, cigarettes and alcohol. *Neurotoxicology and Teratology:* 10: 305–313, 1988.

Frisch RE: Does malnutrition cause permanent mental retardation in human beings? *Psychiatr. Neurol. Neurochir.:* 74: 463–479, 1971.

Fulroth R, Phillips B, Durand DJ: Perinatal outcome of infants exposed to cocaine and/or heroin in utero. *American Journal of Diseases of Children:* 143: 905–910, 1989.

Galaburda AM, Kemper TL: Cytoarchitectonic abnormalities in developmental dyslexia: A case study. *Annals of Neurology:* 6: 94–100, 1979.

Gallagher JJ: Knowledge to practice: A researchable issue. In HM Wisniewski & DA Snider (Eds.), *Mental retardation: Research, education and technology transfer.* New York: New York Academy of Sciences, pp. 106–130.

Golden NL, Kuhnert BR, Sokol RJ, Martier S, Williams T: Neonatal manifestations of maternalphencyclidine exposure. *Journal of Perinatal Medicine:* 15: 185–191, 1987.

Goldings AS, Steward RM: Organic lead encephalopathy: Behavioral change and movement disorder following gasoline inhalation. *Journal of Clinical Psychiatry:* 43: 70–72, 1982.

Gray JW, Dean RS (Eds.): *Neuropsychology of perinatal complications.* New York: Springer 1991.

Grimm VE: Effect of teratogenic exposure on the developing brain: Research strategies and possible mechanisms. *Developmental and Pharmacological Therapeutics:* 10: 328–345, 1987.

Guinan ME, Hardy A: Epidemiology of AIDS in women in the United States 1981–1986. *Journal of the American Medical Association:* 257: 2039–2042, 1987.

Gustavson KH: Severe mental retardation in a Swedish county. I. Epidemiology, gestational age, birthweight and associated CNS handicaps in children born 1959–1970. *Acta Pediatrica Scandinavica:* 66: 874, 1977.

Haith MM: The response of the human newborn to visual movement. *Journal of Experimental Child Psychology:* 3: 112–117, 1966.

Hans SL: Developmental consequences of prenatal exposure to methadone. *Annals of the New York Academy of Sciences:* 562: 195–207, 1989.

Hansen E: Cerebral palsy in Denmark. *Acta Psychiatrica Scandinavica:* 35: 136, 1960.

Holland E: *The causation of faetal death.* London: Ministry of Health Reports, 1922.

Hume RF Jr, O'Donnell KJ, Stanger CL, Killam AP, Gingras JL: In utero cocaine exposure: Observations of fetal behavioral state may predict neonatal outcome. *American Journal of Obstetrics and Gynecology:* 161: 684–690, 1989.

Hunt GM, Holmes AE: Factors relating to intelligence in treated cases of spina bifida cystica. *American Journal of Diseases of Children:* 130: 823, 1976.

Hutchings DE: Issues of methodology and interpretation in clinical and animal behavioral teratology studies. *Neurobehavioral Toxicology and Teratology:* 7: 639–642, 1985.

Hutchings DE, Brake SC, Morgan B: Animal studies of prenatal delta-9-tetrahydrocannabinol: Female embryolethality and effects on somatic and brain growth. *Annals of the New York Academy of Sciences:* 562: 133–144, 1989.

Ingram TTS: *Paediatric aspects of cerebral palsy.* Edinburgh: Churchill Livingstone, 1964.

James W: *The principles of psychology* (Vol. 1). New York: Holt, 1980.

Janssen RS, Cornblath DR, Epstein LG, McArthur J, Price RW: Human immunodeficiency virus (HIV) infection and the nervous system. *Neurology:* 39: 119–122, 1989.

Jervis GA: Studies on phenylpyruvic oligophrenia: Position of metabolic error. *Journal of Biological Chemistry:* 169: 651, 1947.

Jervis GA: The mental deficiencies. In S Avieti (Ed.), *American handbook of psychiatry.* New York: Basic Books, 1959.

Kemper MB, Hagerman RJ, Ahmad RS, Mariner R: Cognitive profiles and the spectrum of clinical manifestations in heterozygous fra(X) females. *American Journal of Medical Genetics:* 23: 139–156, 1986.

Kety SS: Nutrition and psychiatric illness. In G Serban (Ed.), *Advances in behavioral biology, Vol. 14: Nutrition and mental functions* (pp. 321–340). New York: Plenum Press, 1975.

Kinsbourne M: Disorders of mental development. In J Menkes (Ed.), *A textbook of child neurology* (pp. 41–62). Philadelphia: Lea & Febiger, 1980.

Knoll E, Wehle F, Thalhammer O: Psychometry and psychological observations in early treated children with phenylketonuria during 12 years. *Klinische Paediatrie:* 192: 599–607, 1980.

Laurence KM, Tew BJ: Follow-up of 65 survivors from the 425 cases of spina bifida born in South Wales between 1956 and 1962. *Developmental Medicine and Child Neurology Supplement:* 13: 280–227, 1967.

LeJeune J: Le monogolisme: Premier exemple d'aberration autosomique humaine. *Annales de Genetique:* 41: 1, 1959.

Lifschitz MH, Wilson GS, Smith EO, Desmond MM: Factors affecting head growth and intellectual function in children of drug addicts. *Pediatrics:* 75: 269–274, 1985.

Little WJ: On the influence of abnormal parturition, difficult labor, premature birth, and asphyxia neonatorum on the mental and physical conditions of the child, especially in relation to deformities. *Trans. Abstet. Soc. London:* 3: 293, 1862.

Livingstone M, Rosen G, Drislane F: Developmental dyslexia. *Proceedings of National Academy of Sciences:* 256: 1157–1160, 1991.

MacGregor SN, Ketih LG, Bachicha JA, Chasnoff IJ: Cocaine abuse during pregnancy: Correlation between prenatal care and perinatal outcome. *Obstetrics and Gynecology:* 74: 882–885, 1989.

MacMahon B, Naggan L: Ethnic differences in the prevalence of anencephaly and spina bifida in Boston, Massachusetts. *New England Journal of Medicine:* 227: 1119, 1967.

Mactutus CF: Developmental neurotoxicity of nicotine, carbon monoxide, and other tobacco smoke constituents. *Annals of the New York Academy of Sciences:* 562: 105–122, 1989.

Marcus J, Hans SL, Jeremy RJ: A longitudinal study of offspring born to methadone-maintained women. III. Effects of multiple risk factors on development at 4, 8, and 12 months. *American Journal of Drug and Alcohol Abuse:* 10: 195–207, 1984.

Martin GM: Genetic syndromes in man with potential relevance to the pathology of aging. *Birth Defects Original Article Series:* 14: 5–39, 1978.

Mckay SR: Substance abuse during the childbearing year. In G Bennett, C Vourakis, & DS Woolf (Eds.), *Substance abuse: Pharmacologic, developmental, and clinical perspectives.* New York: John Wiley and Sons, pp. 135–155, 1983.

Menkes JH (Ed.): *A textbook of child neurology.* Philadelphia: Lea & Febiger, 1980.

Middaugh LD: Prenatal amphetamine effects on behavior: Possible mediation by brain monoamines. *Annals of the New York Academy of Sciences:* 562: 308–318, 1989.

Miezejeski CM, Jenkins EC, Hill AL, Wisniewski K, Brown WT: Verbal versus nonverbal ability, fragile X syndrome, and heterozygous carriers. *American Journal of Human Genetics:* 36: 227–229, 1984.

Milhorat TH: *Hydrocephalus and the cerebrospinal fluid.* Baltimore: Williams and Wilkins, 1972.

Molfese V: *Perinatal risk and infant development.* New York: Guilford, 1989.

Murray JB: Marijuana's effects on human cognitive functions, psychomotor functions, and personality. *Journal of General Psychology:* 113: 23–55, 1986.

Nakano KK: Anencephaly: A review. *Developmental Medicine and Child Neurology:* 15: 383, 1973.

Nicholas SW, Sondheimer DL, Willoughby AD, Yaffe SL, Katz SL: Human immunodeficiency virus infection in childhood, adolescence, and pregnancy: A status report and national research agenda. *Pediatrics:* 83: 293–308, 1989.

Norman RM: Malformation of the nervous system, birth injury and diseases of early life. In W Blackwood (Ed.), *Greenfield's neuropathology* (2nd ed.) (pp. 112–131). London: Arnold, 1963.

O'Connor MJ, Brill NH, Sigman M: Alcohol use in primiparous women older than 30 years of age: Relation to infant development. *Pediatrics:* 78: 444–450, 1986.

Olson RA, Huszti HC, Mason PJ, Seibert JM: Pediatric AIDS/HIV infection: An emerging challenge to pediatric psychology. *Journal of Pediatric Psychology:* 14: 1–21, 1989.

O'Malley PM, Bachman JG, Johnston LD: Period, age and cohort effects on substance use among young Americans: A decade of change, 1976–1986. *American Journal of Public Health:* 78: 1315–1321, 1988.

Oro AS, Dixon SD: Perinatal cocaine and methamphetamine exposure: Maternal and neonatal correlates. *Journal of Pediatrics:* 111: 571–578, 1987.

Pardridge WM, Oldendorf W: Transport of metabolic substrates through the blood brain barrier. *Journal of Neurochemistry:* 28: 5–12, 1977.

Pare CMB, Sandler M, Stacey RS: Decreased 5-hydroxytryptophan decarboxylase activity in phenylketonuria. *Lancet:* 2: 1099, 1958.

Petito CK: Review of central nervous system pathology in human immunodeficiency virus infection. *Annals of Neurology:* 23 (supplement): S54–S57, 1988.

Pirozzolo FJ: *The neuropsychology of developmental reading disorders.* New York: Praeger Publishers, 1979.

Pirozzolo FJ: Mental retardation: An introduction In PJ Vinken, GW Bruyn, & H Klawans (Eds.), *Handbook of clinical neurology* (Vol. 46). Amsterdam: Elsevier, pp. 1–39, 1985.

Pirozzolo FJ, Bonnefil V, Brawley, T: Development of the embryonic, fetal, and neonatal nervous system. In JW Gray & RS Dean (Eds.), *Neuropsychology of perinatal complications.* New York: Springer, pp. 22–58, 1991.

Pizzo PA, Eddy J, Falloon J, Balis FM, Murphy RF, Moss H, Wolters P, Brouwers P, Jarosinski P, Rubin M, Broder S, Yarchoan R, Brunetti A, Maha M, Nusinoff-Lehrman S, Poplack DG: Effect of continuous intravenous infusion of Zidovudine (AZT) in children with symptomatic HIV infection. *New England Journal of Medicine:* 319: 889–896, 1988.

Pollitt E: Ecology, malnutrition and mental development. *Psychosomatic Medicine:* 31: 193, 1969.

Price DB, Inglese CM, Jacobs J, Haller JO, Kramer J, Hotson GC, Loh JP, Schlusselberg D, Menez-Bautista R, Rose AL, Fikrig S: Pediatric AIDS: Neuroradiologic and neurodevelopmental findings. *Pediatric Radiology:* 18: 445–448, 1988.

Roberts MH: Spinal fluid in newborn with special reference to intracranial hemorrhage. *Journal of American Medical Association:* 85: 500, 1925.

Rodning C, Beckwith L, Howard J: Prenatal exposure to drugs and its influence on attachment. *Annals of the New York Academy of Sciences:* 562: 352–354, 1989.

Roffwarg HP, Muzio JN, Dement WC: Ontogenetic development of the human sleep-dream cycle. *Science:* 152: 604–619, 1966.

Rush D, Callahan KR: Exposure to passive cigarette smoking and child development: A critical review. *Annals of the New York Academy of Sciences:* 562: 74–100, 1989.

Sameroff AJ, Chandler MJ: Reproductive risk and the continuum of caretaking casualty. In FD Horowitz (Ed.), *Review of child development research* (Vol. 4). Chicago: University of Chicago Press, pp. 187–244, 1975.

Schandler SL, Brannock JC, Cohen MJ, Antick J, Caine K: Visuospatial learning in elementary school children with and without a family history of alcoholism. *Journal of Studies on Alcohol:* 49: 538–545, 1988.

Schwartz RH, Gruenewald PJ, Klitzner M, Fedio P: Short-term memory impairment in cannabis-dependent adolescents. *American Journal of Diseases of Children:* 143: 1214–1219, 1989.

Streissguth AP, LaDue RA: Fetal alcohol. Teratogenic causes of developmental disabilities. In SR Schoroeder (Ed.), *Toxic substances and mental retardation: Neurobehavioral toxicology and teratology.* Washington, DC: American Association on Mental Deficiency, pp. 1–32, 1989.

Streissguth AP, Sampson PD, Barr HM: Neurobehavioral dose-response effects of prenatal alcohol exposure in humans from infancy to adulthood. *Annals of the New York Academy of Sciences:* 562: 145–158, 1989.

Sutherland GR: Marker X chromosomes and mental retardation. *New England Journal of Medicine:* 296: 1415, 1977.

Sutherland GR, Banker E, Fratini A: Excess thymidine induces folate-sensitive fragile sites. *American Journal of Medical Genetics:* 22: 433–443, 1985.

Ultmann MH, Diamond GW, Ruff HA, Belman AL, Novick BE, Rubinstein A, Cohen HF: Developmental abnormalities in children with acquired immunodeficiency syndrome (AIDS): A follow-up study. *International Journal of Neuroscience:* 32: 661–667, 1987.

Valentine GH: *The chromosome disorders* (3rd ed.). Philadelphia: Lippincott, 1975.

Walton J: *Brain's diseases of the nervous system.* Oxford: Oxford University Press, 1977.

Warkany J: Malformation syndromes associated with mental retardation. In PJ Viaken, GW Bruyn, H Klawans (Eds.), *Handbook of clinical neurology* (pp. 350–366). Amsterdam: Elsevier, 1985.

Webb TP, Bundey SE, Thake AI, Todd J: Population incidence and segregation ratios in the Martin Bell syndrome. *American Journal of Medical Genetics:* 23: 573–580, 1986.

White BL: *Human infants: Experience and psychological development.* Englewood Cliffs, NJ: Prentice-Hall, 1971.

Williamson ML, Koch R, Azen C, Chang C: Correlates of intelligence test results in treated phenylketonuric children. *Pediatrics:* 68: 161–167, 1981.

Wilson GS: Clinical studies of infants and children exposed prenatally to heroin. *Annals of the New York Academy of Sciences:* 562: 183–194, 1989.

Yakovlev P, Wadsworth RC: Schizencephalies: A study of congenital clefts in the cerebral mantel. *Journal of Neuropathology and Experimental Neurology:* 5: 116–139, 1946.

Yu S, Pritchard M, Kremer E, Lynch M, Nancarrow J, Baker E, Holman K, Mulley JC, Warren ST, Schlessinger D, Sutherland GR, Richards RI: Fragile X genotype characterized by an unstable region of DNA. *Science:* 252: 1179–1181, 1991.

Zuckerman B, Frank DS, Hingson R, Amaro H, Levenson SM, Kayne H, Parker S, Vinci R, Aboagye K, Fried LE, Cabral H, Timperi R, Bauchner H: Effects of maternal marijuana and cocaine use on fetal growth, *New England Journal of Medicine:* 320: 762–768, 1989.

5

COGNITIVE AND BEHAVIORAL MANIFESTATIONS OF NEURODEGENERATIVE DISEASES

DAVID W. DUNN

Neurodegenerative disorders are characterized by progressive deterioration of the central nervous system, peripheral nervous system, or muscle, and are caused by a known or presumed genetic metabolic abnormality. The number of disorders classified as neurodegenerative diseases is large and continuously expanding. Dyken and Krawiecki list over 600 neurodegenerative disorders involving the central nervous system (Dyken & Krawiecki, 1983). Though many of these disorders are rare and poorly defined, taken as a whole, they are a common problem from both a medical and neuropsychological perspective.

There are numerous ways of classifying these disorders. Since most are hereditary, an optimal classification would include the chromosomal locus and the subsequent metabolic derangement responsible for the disorder. The number of disorders that can be so classified is increasing rapidly. As a recent example, the gene responsible for Duchenne's muscular dystrophy has been located at Xp21, and dystrophin, the normal protein produced by this gene, has been characterized. With continuing progress it is likely that most of the neurodegenerative disorders can be described in a similar fashion. For the present time, many of the disorders will need to be listed by the predominant area of anatomic change, an approach used in the review by Dyken and Krawiecki, as well as in this chapter (Dyken & Krawiecki, 1983).

Categories to be considered are diffuse encephalopathies, disorders with widespread changes in the central nervous system, polioencephalopathies, with predominant damage to the cerebral cortex and neurons, leukoencephalopathies, disorders of white matter, basal ganglia disorders, the spinocerebellar degenerations, disorders of the peripheral nervous system including anterior horn cell diseases, and the muscular dystrophies.

EVALUATION AND DIFFERENTIAL DIAGNOSIS OF NEURODEGENERATIVE DISORDERS

The first step in establishing a diagnosis of a neurodegenerative disease is separating progressive from static disorders. It requires documenting either a plateau in development or a loss of previously acquired milestones. There are several instances in which this may be difficult. First, certain of the progressive disorders may mimic a static encephalopathy. This may occur when the onset of the neurodegenerative disease is so early and so severe that no development is seen. As an example, some of the urea cycle abnormalities present with an overwhelming metabolic disturbance in the neonatal period after which there is no further development.

Differentiating static from progressive disorders may be a problem when a progressive disease has either a very late onset or a very slow course. This may be seen with the very gradual onset of clumsiness and incoordination in Friedreich ataxia or in the very late onset of behavioral problems and chorea in Huntington disease. At times, static encephalopathies may mimic a progressive degenerative disease. The first symptoms of a static encephalopathy may not become apparent until the child has reached a certain age or level of maturation. For example, the child with hemiplegic cerebral palsy may not show significant signs before 12 to 18 months of age when the parents first notice the child's problems in walking. In addition, complications of static encephalopathies may suggest a progressive course. The child with seizures may have a progressive loss of cognitive function because of frequent intractable seizures or side effects from medication. Improved seizure control and changes in medication may reverse the regression.

The second step in the evaluation of the child with an apparent neurodegenerative disorder is to separate hereditary degenerative disorders from other, often treatable, disorders. Children with chronic diseases may have delayed development from the fatigue associated with chronic physical illness and apparent loss of milestones from the psychological stress of repeated hospitalization. Anemia and thyroid dysfunction may result as a failure to gain milestones. Psychiatric disturbances such as autism or childhood depression may mimic certain of the neurodegenerative diseases, and child abuse or neglect may result in developmental delay or regression. An occasional child has progressive loss of milestones due to either drug or toxin exposure. Both phenytoin and sodium valproate have led to a progressive organic brain syndrome, which is reversible with discontinuing medication. Structural lesions should be ruled out with appropriate neuroimaging utilizing either computed tomography or magnetic resonance imaging. Hydrocephalus or tumors involving the central nervous system can lead to progressive loss of function and personality changes. Finally, certain infectious diseases may result in progressive loss of abilities. Subacute sclerosing panencephalitis, a chronic measles infection that was much more common prior to widespread immunization, causes an early change in behavior and school performance, followed by seizures, myoclonic jerks and eventually dementia. Neonatally acquired acquired immune deficiency syndrome (AIDS) may cause a progressive deterioration of cognitive abilities and motor function.

The third step in differential diagnosis of the neurodegenerative disorders is to establish a definitive diagnosis. This is most important for those treatable metabolic neurodegenerative diseases. Many of the aminoacidurias such as phenylketonuria or galactosemia can be treated with diet. Chelation therapy can be used for the child with Wilson disease. Vitamin therapy may be effective in a number of metabolic disorders. Examples include replacement of biotin in multiple carboxylase deficiency and Vitamin E for one of the progressive ataxias. Up-to-date listings of the treatable disorders can be found in textbooks on child neurology and inherited disease (Adams and Lyon 1982; Menkes 1990).

Neuropsychological testing is an important part of the evaluation of the child with a potential neurodegenerative disease. With the initial testing, the child's functioning is compared to that of healthy children of his or her own age. Since this gives a picture of the child's ability at only one moment in time, the testing should be repeated in approximately 6 months to determine if the disorder is progressive or static in nature. Neuropsychological testing can also help reveal selective versus diffuse neurologic dysfunction. The batteries selected will depend on the age and functional ability of the child. Hynd and Willis (1988) recommend a dynamic approach to choice of test measures. They note that the Luria Nebraska Neuropsychological Battery for Children is deficient in its assessment of gross motor and visual spatial abilities, and the Halstead-Reitan Batteries for Children is weak in the assessment of academic and semantic-linguistic abilities. When these areas are of concern, standard tests will need to be supplemented with tests that assess specific areas of cognitive function no adequately addressed by the specific test battery (Hynd & Wills, 1988).

Where specific test batteries are not appropriate, developmentally appropriate measures that systematically assess the patient's current level of functioning are indicated (see Chapter 2 for further details). Neuropsychological testing may be utilized, in conjunction with other medical data, for differential diagnosis of progressive versus static neurologic disorder.

An example of modifications required in test selection made for changing abilities in children with neurodegenerative disease is given by Swift, Dyken and DuRant. In their studies of children with subacute sclerosing panencephalitis, they assessed all children with the AADM Adaptive Behavior Scale Part I and then selected a test of cognitive ability based on each child's level of functioning. Normal to mildly impaired children were tested using either the Wechsler Intelligence Scale for Children, Revised, or the Wechsler Adult Intelligence Scale. In children with moderate to severe involvement, they used the Stanford Binet Intelligence Scale using the low mental ages. The even more severely affected children were assessed using the Cattell Infant Intelligence Scale. From these measures plus interviewing or observation, they then constructed a neuropsychological disability scale including scores for gross motor, self-care, social skills, language and verbal intelligence, visual motor skills, performance IQ, and academic skills. They found that this was effective in following the longitudinal course of these children. Their approach can be used as an excellent model for future neuropsychological studies involving follow-up of children with progressive degenerative diseases.

COGNITIVE AND BEHAVIORAL DYSFUNCTION IN NEURODEGENERATIVE DISORDERS

Much of the literature discussing the neuropsychological functioning of children with neurodegenerative diseases has concentrated on studying the child with a single disorder and evaluating the implications of that disease for functioning of the child (Nolan & Pless, 1986). The effects of specific disorders on the child's intellectual, behavioral, and emotional life will be discussed later in this chapter. However, many of the children with neurodegenerative diseases and their families share common sets of problems. Recent studies of the effects of chronic illnesses on children and families has stressed the use of a noncategorical approach in which the specific illness is less important than the constellation of responses to the general problems experienced (Stein & Jessop, 1984; Stein 1990). Both a developmental and a systems theory perspective can be utilized to understand the individual child's problem (Whelan & Walker, 1989). The effects of any degenerative disease depend, in part, on the age at which development plateaus and when regression first begins, and on the developmental stage to which the child has regressed by the time of evaluation.

An additional problem is imposed by the variable rates of regression; thus, a child may be at one stage in cognitive development and an entirely different stage in motor development (Dosen 1989). The child's problems depend on both the effects of the illness on the child and the effect the disorder has on the interaction of the child with family members and society. Both factors should be considered in ongoing evaluation. Optimal therapy for the child with a neurodegenerative disease involves confining dysfunction to the effects of the illness and preventing secondary handicapping cognitive and behavioral conditions (Yando and Zigler, 1984). There must be a continuing effort to encourage development in unaffected areas and to assist the child in maximizing his or her potential in all areas.

While rehabilitation may be a misnomer in treating neurodegenerative diseases, multidisciplinary treatment is often required to address the diverse and ever-changing needs of the patient and family. Typically, a team approach is necessary, involving the skills of many different people: parents; physicians; specialists; neuropsychologists; speech and language, respiratory, occupational, and physical therapists; special educators; and nurses. Treatment plans must incorporate goals to maintain medical stability and minimize complications. Because of health-care costs and the fact that parents frequently desire some control over their child's declining health, parents usually need support and psychotherapy to make initial adjustment of a diagnosis. Their responses vary with premorbid status. Later, parents typically request and receive training in the care of the patient. Children must also be supported in order to respond to treatments.

The child with a neurodegenerative disease faces many problems. Most of these children will develop dementia—a chronic, persistent, irreversible loss of mental function—as a feature of their disorder (Dyken & McCleary, 1986). In adults, there is often a distinction made between cortical dementia, affecting memory and skilled activities, and subcortical dementia, affecting mood, attention, and the ability to manipulate and process knowledge. In childhood, this distinction is usually difficult to make. The degree of cognitive dysfunction seems to correlate with the severity of the illness, and is most pronounced in the polioencephalopathies, leukodystrophies, and diffuse encephalopathies.

The child with a chronic neurodegenerative disease is at increased risk for behavioral problems, with most studies suggesting a 1.5 to 3 times normal risk for emotional problems (e.g., Whelan & Walker, 1989). Certain factors may be important in increased vulnerability for behavioral difficulties. Age of onset seems to show little relationship to the frequency of emotional problems; however, the developmental stage at which a degenerative disease emerges may determine the types of problems experienced. Onset during infancy leads to problems in establishing attachment with the primary caretakers, whereas onset in early adolescence may result in difficulty with issues of autonomy (Stein & Jessop, 1984). Disease severity may be a factor, with children becoming more socially withdrawn as the severity of disease increases. However, in contrast to cognitive dysfunction, other behavioral problems do not appear to be linked with disease severity (Harper, 1983). Both Rutter and Blacher noted that cognitive abilities, and the effect of the illness on temperament and personality were major factors in determining risk of emotional problems (Rutter, 1981; Blacher, 1984). In addition, Rutter found that seizures increased the risk of difficulties (Rutter, 1977). Blacher suggested that the child's personal appearance, visual and hearing competence, affective responsiveness, communication skills, mobility, and social skills were all important factors in determining the emotional well-being of the child with brain impairment (Blacher, 1984).

The presence of a child with a neurodegenerative disease imposes considerable stress on a family. Though the effects of these illnesses on families has received little specific attention, studies of stress and coping in families with children who have mental retardation or chronic disabilities should reveal similar problems. Miller described stages in parental reaction to the diagnosis of a handicap in a child (Miller, 1968). Shock and disintegration occur first, followed during the second stage by denial, blame, guilt, sorrow, and early attempts at coping. The final stage is reintegration as the family proceeds with the task of living with the child. Eiser (1985) lists three major challenges for the families. First is the cognitive effort of learning about the disorder and the potential problems that will develop. The second is the emotional challenge of dealing with anger, guilt, and sorrow, and accepting the child. Finally, there is the behavioral challenge of incorporating the many new demands imposed by a disabled child on the routines of the family. The additional stresses of the neurode generative disorders are the progressive and ultimately fatal course of the disease, and the genetic etiology with the attendant issues of risk for other family members and guilt about genetic causation of the disorder.

The parents of a child with a neurodegenerative disease assume new and unfamiliar roles, seeing themselves as teacher, therapist, and parent (Wright, Granger, & Sameroff, 1984). They perform daily range of motion exercises, assist with transfers as the child becomes less mobile, deal with incontinence, and, when there are problems eating, learn either new feeding techniques or how to handle gastrostomy tube feedings. The mother, who usually bears the brunt of new demands for care, does have an increased risk of psychiatric morbidity—a risk, at least in one study, not shared by the father (Romans-Clarkson et al., 1986).

Siblings are also affected by the presence of a child with a neurodegenerative disease. In addition to the gradual loss of a playmate, they often suffer from the decreased time that parents have available due to the demands of the child with the disability. Siblings may have to help care for their disabled sibling and assume new tasks as the parents begin to devote more time to care-giving demands. Most studies have shown that siblings of children with neurologic disabilities are at increased risk for behavioral and emotional problems, although the factors important in vulnerability are not well understood (Eiser, 1985). Breslau found that siblings had an increase in aggressiveness in comparison to controls, and, over time, an increase in depressive symptoms and social isolation. This was particularly pronounced when there was maternal depression and in families from lower socioeconomic classes (Breslau & Prabucki, 1987).

The societal responses to children with neurodegenerative disease and to the needs of the family are also important in understanding the effects of illness on the child and family. The mother's level of stress has been found to relate more to the availability of social supports and less to the severity of the child's illness (Wright et al., 1984). The availability of respite care and the accessibility and adaptability of both school and placement facilities are important in helping families.

The response of the medical community is important in determining the functioning of the family, but this often presents a problem. Many pediatricians are oriented toward acute illnesses and deal poorly with the child with a chronic intractable problem (Stein, 1990). Families have complained of the physician's failure to accept the family's assessment of their own needs, and of the medical community's failure to help families obtain resources available in the community (Halpern & Parker-Crawford, 1982). Each family must negotiate the care to be given their child, and must integrate the multiple ongoing therapies into family activities often with little help or understanding of the overall problems of the child and family.

Support groups can often be of help in decreasing the family's sense of isolation, educating the family about available resources, and serving as advocates for the family in the community. The one concern occasionally expressed about support groups is the presence of individuals with varying degrees of severity of illness. The family with a minimally affected child may find their level of stress considerably increased after attending support meetings at which they see severely involved individuals. Family members with severely involved children may also react negatively to those support groups that try to emphasize only the mildly affected and behaviorally normal child.

DIFFUSE ENCEPHALOPATHIES

In their discussion of neurodegenerative diseases of children, Dyken and Krawiecki (1983) define the diffuse encephalopathies as disorders with widespread anatomic changes or diseases with poorly localized but apparently diffuse changes. They list 130 diffuse encephalopathies, including many of the neurocutaneous syndromes, metabolic disorders such as amino acidurias and organic acidurias, and a number of poorly understood and probably heterogeneous disorders such as infantile spasms. Most of these disorders are quite rare. In their personal series from two university-based pediatric neurology programs, Dyken and Krawiecki (1983) had seen 18 of the 130 diffuse encephalopathies during a 10-year period. Of the 341 patients with neurodegenerative diseases admitted to their service, 78 were children with diffuse encephalopathies. In this section, we will concentrate on neurofibromatosis and tuberous sclerosis, both neurocutaneous syndromes, and Rett syndrome.

Neurofibromatosis type 1 (NF 1) is an autosomal dominant disorder affecting 1 in 3,000 to 5,000 individuals. NF 1 was defined at a recent NIH Consensus Conference as being present when an individual has two of the following seven criteria: (1) six or more cafe-au-lait spots; (2) two dermal neurofibromas or one plexiform neurofibroma; (3) axillary freckling; (4) optic nerve glioma; (5) two or more iris nodules; (6) characteristic abnormality of bone including sphenoid wing dysplasia or thinning of long bone cortex, and (7) a definite history of NF 1 in a first-degree relative (NIH, 1987). More recent studies have determined a gene locus at 17q11.2 (Collins et al., 1989).

Neurofibromatosis is listed as a neurodegenerative disease because of the potential for progressive addition of deficits as the individual ages. Four severity grades for neurofibromatosis have been listed. Grade 1 consists of only minimal features of NF and no adverse effect on well-being; grade 4, the most severe form, defined NF with severe compromise of health or complications that were either very difficult to treat or intractable (Riccardi & Eichner, 1986). These researchers found that only 6% of this patient population were classified as severity grade 4 at 5 years of age; but by 60 years of age, 49% were listed as severity grade 4. Some individuals with NF have no features of degenerative disease and remain in good health with only minimal symptoms.

The natural history of this disease is characterized by complications that may occur at typical ages. Cafe-au-lait spots, most of the bone dysplasias, and the most troublesome plexiform neurofibromas usually appear by 4 years of age. If mental retardation is to be a feature of this disorder, it is usually evident as developmental delay within the first years of life. Optic gliomas may occur as early as birth or as late as the teenage years but seldom begin after this period. During the school-age years, concerns are possible learning disabilities and poor coordination. Iris nodules and axillary freckling usually appear between 6 and 12 years of age. Scoliosis may occur during the elementary school years or the teenage years. With the exception of the plexiform neurofibromas, neurofibromas first appear in the teenage years, increasing in number and size during young adulthood. During the adult years, the risk of malignancy begins to increase (Huson, Compston, & Harper, 1989).

Cognitive disturbances are common in neurofibromatosis but past studies have been of variable quality. Many of the older studies did not separate NF 1 from other possible variants of neurofibromatosis, and many suffer from small numbers and ascer tainment bias. Two epidemiological studies have shown an increase risk of cognitive disturbance in individuals with neurofibromatosis. Borberg (1951) noted an average full-scale IQ of 85–90 in his patient population with neurofibromatosis. More recently, Huson and colleagues (1989) found that 9 of 34 children with NF 1 were involved either in special schools or remedial classes and 25 of 90 adults with NF 1 had previously been in either special schools or remedial classes. Eldridge and associates (1989) compared cognitive function in children with NF 1 versus siblings with no evidence of neurofibromatosis. For the NF subjects, they eliminated all children with known or suspected learning disabilities and individuals with known central nervous system tumors or seizures. They found that the children with NF 1 had an average full-scale IQ score of 93 ± 11.7, whereas sibling controls had an average score of 105 ± 13.8.

Mental retardation may be a complication of either central nervous system tumors or intractable seizures in the individual with neurofibromatosis. As an isolated finding, mental retardation has been reported in 5 to 10% of NF patients. Huson and colleagues (1989) noted moderate to severe mental retardation in 3.2% of their sample. Samuelsson and Axelsson (1981) reported that 5% of their population had a full-scale IQ of <70. Riccardi and Eichner (1986) found that 8.4% of their clinic population were mentally handicaped, which was not thought to be coincidental. In their total NF population, 5.9% had an IQ score in the 60–90 range, and 3.9% had an IQ of <60.

General estimates for learning disability as a complication of NF 1 range from 25 to 50%, which is clearly higher than that of the population at large. Riccardi and Eichner (1986) found developmental delay in 21% of their population below 18 months of age, and learning disabilities in 30% of their group. Huson and associates (1989) found that 29.8% of her population-based NF group were enrolled in either remedial classes or had specific learning difficulties. Samuelsson and Riccardi (1989), reviewing data from a study in Sweden, noted that 30 of 71 patients required remedial classes. In our series of studies, 41% of the children have required some special class placement, and in a questionnaire study, others found that between 41 and 43% of children had some degree of learning difficulty (Dunn, 1987; Stine & Adams, 1989).

In the majority of studies, the major difference between NF patients and controls has been in visual-perceptual function. Stine and Adams (1989) found significant delay in visual-perceptual motor skills. Eliason (1988) found that the best predictor for NF patients versus learning-disabled non-NF patients was the poor performance of NF patients on the judgment of line orientation or the Benton multiple-choice test. Varnhagen and colleagues (1988) found significant differences on the spatial memory subtest of the Kaufman Assessment Battery for Children, further supporting the suggestion of increased problems with visual-spatial integration in NF 1 children. Finally, Eldridge and associates (1989) noted that 8 of the 9 affected children in their study had a significant visual-spatial orientation deficit as assessed by the Iowa Judgment of Line Orientation Test. In addition to problems with visual perceptual skills, NF children show problems with spelling and arithmetic (Stine & Adams, 1989). Further, NF children have more frequent WISC-R verbal performance discrepancies than children without NF diagnosed with learning disability (Eliason, 1988). In contrast, Chapman, Korf, and Urion (1989) in a comparison of children with NF 1 and age- and sex-matched controls found similar neuropsychological profiles with the exception of problems in memory. The NF 1 group scored significantly worse on the Rey Osterrieth complex figure (delayed recall condition) and the Spencer test of memory for sentences than controls, suggesting possible damage in the hippocampi.

The reasons for the cognitive defects in individuals with neurofibromatosis have not been well defined. In the majority of studies there has been no correlation between disease severity and cognitive function. Rosman and Pearce (1976), in an autopsy study of brains from individuals with neurofibromatosis, found gross malformations in deep cerebral structures and heterotopias in those individuals with NF and retardation. The brains from individuals with neurofibromatosis with an apparently normal IQ showed only microscopic changes. Dunn and Roos (1989) reviewed magnetic resonance imaging (MRI) in children with neurofibromatosis and attempted to correlate the presence of areas of abnormal signal with learning disability. They found a similar incidence of abnormal MRI in children with and without learning disability. Thus, at the present time, although the speculation continues that the cognitive defects are in some way related to cerebral malformations, this has yet to be proven conclusively.

Although most would agree that there is an increased risk of cognitive disturbance in individuals with NF 1, the risk of behavioral problems is poorly defined. Some of the children with NF and learning disability may also have attention deficit disorder (ADD) (Aron, 1984). Samuelsson and Axelsson (1981) noted that 18% of the children in their study had behavioral difficulties, but the type of behavior disorders was not clarified. In their series of adults with, NF they noted that 33% had psychiatric disorders, mostly depression, and/or organic mood disorders. In a follow-up on this group, Samuelsson and Riccardi (1989) studied the NF patients in her original series using a comprehensive psychopathological rating scale and found that 22% of the group had moderate to severe mental illness. There was no typical syndrome and the most common diagnoses were depression, anxiety with vegetative dysfunction, and organic brain syndrome.

Gillberg and Forsell (1984) reported 3 children with childhood psychosis and neurofibromatosis. In our series, 1 of 55 children with neurofibromatosis was autistic, 1 depressed, and 9 had probable attention deficit disorder (Dunn, 1987). In other studies, there has not been an excess of emotional problems. Varnhagen found no differences between NF and control groups on the Eysenck personality questionnaire, and only minimal differences with slight increase in aggressiveness in the NF children as compared to controls on the profile of mood states and preadolescent mood scale (Varnhagen et al., 1988). Riccardi and Eichner (1986) did not find an excess number of individuals with emotional problems in their patient population with neurofibromatosis.

It is surprising that psychological difficulties are not more common in neurofibromatosis. During the early school years, the combination of learning disability and poor coordination may adversely effect the child's self-esteem. During the teenage years, the stress of a chronically disabling and disfiguring condition may become an increasing burden. These problems may lead to isolation and withdrawal and thus an inability to learn and practice social skills. It is perhaps notable that in the series of Samuelsson and Riccardi (1989) 41% of their adult patients were unmarried. Particularly in a time when good health and physical appearance are important qualities to the general public, having obvious stigmata of neurofibromatosis can be difficult. One individual with neurofibromatosis reported being asked "Are you retarded or do you just look that way?" The infrequent occurrence of major psychiatric problems is thus a truly positive statement about the resilience and strength of many individuals with neurofibromatosis.

For families, many of the problems of neurofibromatosis are the same as experienced by any family with a child who is impaired. They must deal with the grief of not having a so-called perfect child and must cope with the ongoing stress of a potentially debilitating illness. Families must adapt to the unpredictability of the disorder. This may be a special problem when both parent and child are affected. Will the parent develop a neurofibrosarcoma or other malignancy that renders him or her unable to care for the child or will the child develop a significant disability that may or may not be curable?

Tuberous sclerosis is less common than neurofibromatosis but defining the true incidence has been quite difficult. Estimates have ranged from 1 in 10,000 to 1 in 170,000 (Gomez, 1988). Tuberous sclerosis is an autosomal dominant disorder, although between 67 and 86% of cases occur sporadically. A definitive diagnosis of tuberous sclerosis is based on finding two of the following lesions: (1) cortical tubers; (2) subependymal nodules; (3) retinal hamartoma; (4) facial angiofibromas; (5) ungual fibroma; (6) fibrous plaque on the forehead or scalp; or (7) multiple renal angiomyolipomas. Other frequent symptoms or signs of tuberous sclerosis include seizures, retardation, hypopigmented macules, cardiac rabdomyoma, and polycystic kidneys. In the series from Mayo, 96% of patients with tuberous sclerosis had skin lesions, 90% subependymal nodules, 84% seizures, and 47% retinal hamartomas (Gomez, 1988).

Defining the incidence of cognitive difficulties in tuberous sclerosis is complicated by the problem of ascertainment bias. The incidence of retardation is particularly high in neurologic series in which initial work-up was done for seizures or delay. For example, in one series from an EEG laboratory, 88 of 100 patients were described as mentally retarded (Pampiglione & Moynahan, 1976). In approximately 70%, the retardation was noted by 1 year of age; and in 80%, by 2 years of age. In comparison, in a series of 300 individuals with tuberous sclerosis in which both patients and asymptomatic but affected relatives were studied, 44% had normal intelligence and 47% were listed as mentally subnormal (Gomez, 1988).

In tuberous sclerosis, the developmental delay seems to follow the onset of seizures. Hunt and Dennis (1987) found that 73 to 94% of the children with tuberous sclerosis had normal development prior to their first seizure. Gomez (1988) also noted that with very few exceptions the children in his series with developmental delay had progressed normally until seizures began. He also found that there was occasional reestablishment of development once seizures were controlled. Gomez (1988) has found a significant correlation between age of onset of seizures and retardation. In his series, almost all of the children with tuberous sclerosis whose seizures began prior to 2 years were retarded; 41% of the children with seizure onset between the second and fifth birthday were retarded; and when seizure onset was after 5 years of age, only 1/3 were retarded. In his series, there was no child with tuberous sclerosis and retardation without seizures. He additionally reported two sets of male homozygous twins with tuberous sclerosis (Gomez et al., 1982). In each set, one twin had frequent seizures and the other had either no seizures or only infrequent episodes. The twin with frequent seizures was mentally subnormal and the twin with infrequent or no seizures was mentally normal, again suggesting that the presence of seizures is important in the occurrence of retardation in these children.

The reason for the association of seizures and cognitive dysfunction has not been established. Gomez (1988) suggested two possibilities. The first is that areas of cortical and subcortical hamartomas, if appropriately located, cause both seizures and retardation. CT studies have not supported this contention. Kingsley, Kendall, and Fritz (1986) found no association between the nodular calcifications in the subependymal zones or the cortical and white matter lesions and cognitive function. Magnetic resonance imaging has been more suggestive. Roach, Williams, and Laster (1987) found that individuals with significant neurologic impairment had more areas of high-signal MRI lesions involving the cerebral cortex. They suggested that MRI might help predict eventual severity of the disorder for the newly diagnosed child. Gomez, Rafecas, and Hauser (1987) also found that the presence of low attenuation cortical lesions on MRI was an adverse prognostic factor for intelligence and seizure control in those children with tuberous sclerosis who developed seizures prior to 1 year of age.

The second hypothesis for the association of seizures and cognitive dysfunction in tuberous sclerosis is that the seizures are a major factor adversely affecting cognitive development. With this hypothesis, the presence or absence of hamartomatous lesions is not as important as is the occurrence and persistence of seizures during the first years of life. Some support for this contention comes from Snyder's series on infantile spasms (Snyder, 1967). He found that individuals with tuberous sclerosis who were treated with prednisone and who had a prompt reduction in seizure number had a better cognitive outcome. Others have been less optimistic. Riikonen and Simell (1990) studied 24 patients with infantile spasms and tuberous sclerosis. They found that 16 had an initial good response to ACTH therapy, although 10 later relapsed. The long-term outcome was bleak, with only 1 of the 24 children having an IQ of >85 and only one being seizure free. At the present time, seizures should be treated aggressively though this may not have any long-term beneficial effect on cognitive development.

Behavior problems are associated with tuberous sclerosis, particularly when tuberous sclerosis is combined with seizures. In Riikonen and Simell's series, 4 of the 24 patients with tuberous sclerosis and infantile spasm developed infantile autism, 5 hyperkinetic behavior, and 1 other significant behavior problems (Riikonen & Simell, 1990). In Hunt and Dennis's (1987) series, 58% developed autistic behavior by 5 years of age, and 53% had hyperkinetic behavior. All the children with behavioral problems had both tuberous sclerosis and seizures. Curatolo and Cusmai (1987) supported this contention that there was a high incidence of autism in children with tuberous sclerosis and infantile spasms. They felt that the occurrence of behavior problems and learning disabilities might be related to the location of CNS hamartomas, noting the association of left temporal hamartomas with severe language impairment and of right parietotemporal lesions with autism.

Rett syndrome is a recently defined neurodegenerative disease, occurring predominately or exclusively in girls, in which there is a progressive loss of cognitive and motor function, and stereotypic hand movements. Though these girls are always normal initially, they stop developing between 6 and 18 months of age. Play become less active, speech is reduced, and there is mild hypotonia. This is followed by a rapidly destructive stage beginning between 1 and 4 years of age and lasting for a period of weeks to months. During this period, the child loses hand function and begins the characteristic hand wringing and other abnormal stereotypic hand movements. There is loss of language, and the child may develop seizures and periods of hyperventilation. A third plateau stage occurs during school age and may last for years. Major features are prominent ataxia and apraxia. Finally, there is a period of deterioration with progressive spasticity, minimal movements, growth retardation, and scoliosis (Rett's group, 1988).

Cognitive development is severely impaired. Most of these children seem to have a failure of intellectual progression and not a true dementing illness. Fontanesi and Haas (1988) studied 18 girls with Rett syndrome using the Vinelend Adaptive Behavior Scale, standard medical and developmental histories, and tests of basic sensory-perceptual function. They found that the age of onset of symptoms was the best predictor for adaptive functions with the exception of fine motor and language skills, which were markedly impaired. Studying object permanency in Rett syndrome, Olsson and Rett (1987) found that 18 of their 26 girls older than 2 years of age showed no object permanency, a stage seen normally at a developmental age of 4 to 6 months; at best, several had skills equivalent to a developmental age of 7 to 10 months. Fontanesi and Haas found that their children with Rett syndrome did somewhat better, and suggested that these children may have more capacity to learn than expected from their very poor language and hand function. They may respond best to the same techniques used for the motor handicapped nonverbal cerebral palsy child (Fontanesi & Haas, 1988).

To a certain extent, the behavior of these children is similar to that of autistic children. They differ in that the children with Rett syndrome do have a repertoire of social behavior, including approaching, smiling, laughing, and establishing prolonged eye contact. Children with Rett syndrome have stereotypic hand movements, hyperventilation, and a general paucity of movements during the third and fourth stages of their illness, findings consistently absent in autism. In contrast, the autistic children show much more social rejection, hyperactivity, stereotypic play, and attachment to objects (Olsson & Rett, 1987).

POLIOENCEPHALOPATHIES

In the polioencephalopathies, the brunt of the disorder is borne by the neurons in the cerebral cortex. These disorders present with seizures, cognitive regression, and often visual loss. Dyken and Krawiecki (1983) list 36 different polioencephalopathies, a number of which have several subtypes. In their clinics, the neuronal ceroid lipofuscinoses accounted for 24 of the 54 patients in this category.

The neuronal ceroid lipofuscinoses (NCL) are the most common form of the poliodystrophies. In most series, approximately one-third of the cases are late infantile onset and another one- to two-thirds juvenile onset. Infantile and adult forms are much less common. The diagnosis is usually confirmed by demonstrating granular, curvilinear, or fingerprint inclusion bodies in either the skin or white blood cells. In the infantile form, seizures, visual loss, and regression begin between 3 and 18 months of age. Motor and cognitive regression proceeds rapidly, with most of the children in a vegetative state within 2 years. Death occurs in the first decade. In the late infantile form, seizures start by 2 or 3 years of age. There is usually rapid loss of cognitive function, followed by visual loss and motor regression. These children may survive in a vegetative state, with death usually occurring during the latter half of the first decade of life.

The juvenile form of NCL has a more protracted course. Visual loss is noted by 5 to 8 years of age. Seizures and motor regression occur later. In Wisniewski and colleagues' (1988) series, the children with juvenile onset NCL developed visual loss at a mean of 6.2 years, with seizures and motor regression beginning at 9.4 years. A vegetative state was reached by 18.4 years. Cognitive dysfunction began at a mean of 7.4 years. In one of the few studies to follow cognitive function, Santavuori and associates (1985) did WISC, WAIS, or WPPSI at one- and two-year intervals. They reported that the group of juvenile NCL patients not receiving antioxidant therapy had a mean full-scale IQ of 62 at 10 to 12 years of age, falling to below 52 by 16 to 19 years of age. The group of juvenile NCL patients receiving antioxidant therapy went from a mean full-scale IQ of 79.3 at 10 to 12 years of age to a mean of 77.3 at 16 to 19 years of age, and 52.7 by 20 years of age. These children usually develop mild to moderate speech loss by approximately

18 years of age and severe dysarthria by 16 to 17 years of age. This speech has been described as accelerated and monotonous, with both stuttering and echolalia. Perseveration and word-finding difficulties have also been noted (Santavuori et al., 1985).

Behavior is often disturbed. Many researchers have noted problems with restlessness, irritability, labile emotions, and erratic behavior in children with juvenile NCL (Sorensen & Parnas, 1979; Elze, et al., 1978; Hofman, 1990). Elze and colleagues (1978) commented on the low frustration tolerance, and Hofman (1990) found problems with sleep and episodic delirium. Hallucinations were a problem in 3 of 18 children with NCL reported by Elze (1978). Sorensen and Parnas (1979) stated that 34 of 44 children with juvenile NCL had psychotic features, with visual hallucinations being the most common disturbance. Although I was unable to identify studies that specifically addressed the effect of juvenile NCL on family members, in our experience the combination of severe neurologic deficit plus agitated, delirious behavior has often been particularly trying for families; many of these children are eventually institutionalized.

The adult form of NCL is the least common. Boustany, Alroy, and Kolodny (1988) found 6 cases in a series of 65 patients. It starts at an average of 25 years of age, with a combination of behavior disturbance, dementia, extrapyramidal signs, and seizures. Lipofuscin is found in fibroblasts and white cells and cortical atrophy is prominent on CT scan.

Of the several forms of GM_2 gangliosidosis, the classic infantile Tay-Sachs form is the most common. Frequency of carriers in the Jewish population of New York City was 1 in 30 versus 1 in 300 in the non-Jewish population (Baraitser, 1985). The frequency of this disorder has been reduced significantly by screening for carrier states. The children with Tay-Sachs disease present first with listlessness and irritability, usually between 1 and 3 months of age. Myoclonus and tremor begin by 2 to 4 months of age and a progressive loss of abilities is noted by 4 to 8 months of age. Most of the children are blind by 10 to 12 months, seizures begin within the latter half of the first year or the beginning of the second year of life, and death occurs between the second or third year of life (Schulte, 1984).

The juvenile form is less common. These children begin to show deterioration of gait and a tremor by 1 to 2 years of age. Speech regression and a loss of cognitive function occur by 3 to 4 years of age. The children then develop seizures, spasticity, and ataxia, and eventually a decerebrate state usually between 5 and 14 years of age. Death occurs during the second decade.

Though the neuronal ceroid lipofuscinoses and GM2 gangliosidoses are most common, there are a number of other polioencephalopathies. GM1 gangliosidosis or generalized gangliosidosis is an autosomal recessive disorder with at least 4 different subtypes. An infantile form leads to death by 2 years of age and is characterized by coarse facial features, hepatomegaly, and motor and cognitive regression. The juvenile and adult forms are associated with prolonged survival, mild dementia, and ataxia. Dystonia may be a feature of the adult form. The sialidoses consist of an infantile form, which begins with myoclonic seizures and results in growth delay, coarse facial features, hepatosplenomegaly, and cherry red maculas, with death occurring by age 5. Two juvenile forms manifest by myoclonic seizures, cherry red maculas, loss of visual acuity, and variable psychomotor retardation, with potentially a prolonged survival.

Of the four types of Niemann-Pick disease, the most common is Type 1, an autosomal recessive disorder beginning in infancy, with death by 3 to 5 years of age. It is characterized by failure to thrive, hepatosplenomegaly, and loss of cognitive and motor milestones. In both the mucopolysaccharidoses and the mucolipidoses, there is usually variable combinations of coarsening of facial features, organomegaly, and bony abnormalities. Severe cognitive loss is associated with MPS type 1 (Hurler) and MPS 3 (San Filippo) and moderate dementia with MPS type 2 (Hunter). Severe dementia is part of mucolipidoses type 2 and 4, mannosidosis, and fucosidosis.

Menkes disease, an x-linked recessive disorder with a frequency estimated at 1 in 35,000, is a disorder of copper metabolism that results in early onset of seizures and failure of cognitive development with progressive loss of cortical function from recurrent cerebrovascular infarctions (Baraitser, 1985). Alpers seems to be a heterogeneous group of diseases in which there is onset in infancy of seizures and failure of cognitive development. Death occurs as early as 3 months of age or as late as 8 years of age.

LEUKODYSTROPHIES

The leukodystrophies consist of six main disorders: Alexander disease, Canavan sclerosis (spongy degeneration of the cerebral white matter), globoid-cell leukodystrophy, Pelizaeus-Merzbacher disease, metachromatic leukodystrophy, and the adrenal leukodys trophies. Canavan, Alexander, and globoid-cell leukodystrophies all present during the first year of life, with rapidly progressive motor and cognitive regression, often associated with seizures. Globoid-cell leukodystrophy is confirmed by finding a deficiency of galactosylceramide beta galactosidase, and Canavan by documenting aspartoacylase deficiency or N-acetylaspartic aciduria. No biochemical marker for Alexander disease is available. Pelizaeus-Merzbacher disease also starts within the first six months of life. It is a sex-linked recessive disorder characterized by abnormal eye movements, cerebellar dysfunction, and progressive spasticity. No biochemical markers are available.

Metachromatic leukodystrophy (MLD) is an autosomal recessive disorder characterized by low or absent arylsulphatase A levels. The approximate incidence is 1 in 40,000 (Menkes, 1990). The infantile form starts with motor regression, apparent by 6 months to 2 years of age. These children develop both hypertonia and areflexia, often with cerebellar dysfunction. Death usually occurs within the first decade. MacFaul and colleagues (1982) note that speech disturbances begin several months after onset of gait problems, and mental deterioration occurs within 1 to 2 years of the onset of the disorder (MacFaul et al., 1982). Apathy and irritability are frequent behavioral changes seen in these children. Juvenile MLD begins in the early school years, with learning difficulties plus clumsiness or behavior problems. These children develop inexorably progressive loss of motor function (extrapyramidal, cerebellar, and pyramidal). Death occurs in the second or third decade. The adult form is relatively uncommon, presenting with a combination of organic brain syndrome and progressive motor dysfunction.

Adrenoleukodystrophy (ALD) consists of several disorders, the two most common being the childhood form of ALD and the adult onset adreno-myeloneuropathy (AMN). Both are sex-linked recessive disorders. Childhood ALD starts between 4 and 8 years of age and AMN between 20 and 30 years of age. The diagnosis is confirmed by demonstrating an increase in very long chain fatty acids. In childhood ALD, the most common presenting problems are changes in behavior or school performance, noted in 10 of 17 patients reported by Schaumberg and associates (1975). Progressive memory loss and poor school performance were accompanied by either withdrawn behavior or bizarre aggressive outbursts. Definite evidence of Addison's disease is present in the majority of cases at the beginning of the disorder. Gait disturbances and visual loss were other common early signs. Prior to the onset of gait or visual disturbances, the diagnosis may be difficult. Of Schaumburg's 17 patients, 3 were initially thought to have schizophrenia, 1 psychopathic behavior, and 1 post-traumatic syndrome versus schizophrenia.

The progression of this disorder is rapid. Moser (1987) found a mean interval of only 1.9 years between onset of neurologic symptoms and decline into a vegetative state. Adult AMN differs from the childhood form in that the presentation is usually a combination of ataxia and paraparesis. Cognitive and behavioral disturbances do not seem to be major problems. Moser noted cerebral involvement in only 20% of his patients with AMN.

NEURODEGENERATIVE DISEASES OF THE BASAL GANGLIA

Neurodegenerative diseases involving basal ganglia, called corencephalopathies by Dyken and Krawiecki, are primarily disorders of the extrapyramidal system and are usually associated with movement disorders, including rigidity, dystonia, chorea, athetosis, ballismus, or tremor (Dyken & Krawiecki, 1983).

One of the most common disorders involving this region is dystonia musculorum deformans, or torsion dystonia. This may be a heterogenous group of disorders. Genetically, it may be autosomal dominant, autosomal recessive, or sex linked. A number of cases are sporadic. Dystonia may start in childhood or adult years, often with only a single extremity affected initially. However Marsden, Harrison, and Bundey (1976) found that 85% of those with an onset before age 10, and 60% with an onset between ages 10 and 20, eventually developed generalized dystonia. In comparison, only 4% of those with an onset after age 20 developed a generalized illness. More than half of the children with generalized dystonia become severely disabled.

Torsion dystonia is remarkable for its lack of intellectual impairment. In fact, Eldridge and colleagues (1970) found that when compared to age, sex, religion, and socioeconomically matched controls, dystonic children had a significantly higher mean IQ. Similarly, evaluating 68 individuals with dystonia using the WISC or WAIS, Riklan, Cullinan, and Cooper (1976) found an average verbal IQ of 108.3 (range 73–143), an average performance IQ of 99.1 (range 57–154), and an average full-scale IQ score of 105.2 (range 62–154). They also found that there were differences based on age of onset. Patients whose age of onset was 8 years of age or less had an average verbal IQ score of 104, performance IQ 95.2, and full-scale IQ 100.3, versus those with age of onset of 9 to 13 years who had an average verbal IQ of 114, performance IQ of 103.1, and full-scale IQ of 110.5.

The individuals with torsion dystonia do not appear to have a higher incidence of behavioral or emotional difficulties than expected in anyone with a chronic debilitating neurologic condition. Fahn and Marsden (1987) noted that these individuals may have problems in establishing interpersonal relationships, and pointed out the adverse effect of dystonia on sexual attractiveness. They have found that their patients often benefit from involvement in support groups offering the opportunity to meet with other similarly affected individuals.

One frequent problem with dystonia has been the incorrect diagnosis of hysteria or conversion reactions. Lesser and Fahn (1978) found that 37 of 84 patients with dystonia had previously received a diagnosis of emotional disorder, and many had received ongoing psychotherapy with no improvement.

When dystonia is accompanied by cognitive impairment or significant behavior disturbances, one should consider the symptomatic dystonias—that is, dystonia that follows perinatal asphyxia or other central nervous system injuries, Hallervorden-Spatz syndrome, Niemann-Pick type C disease, Wilson disease, or Huntington disease. Children with dystonia following perinatal asphyxia or CNS injury have a nonprogressive encephalopathy. Hallervorden-Spatz syndrome, a rare autosomal recessive disorder, presents around 10 years of age with dystonia, often in the lower extremities, progressing eventually to generalized rigidity. In Dooling, Schoene, and Richardson's (1974) review, 49 of 58 cases had dementia or retardation. In addition, 4 of the patients had psychiatric impairment, including 2 with psychotic symptoms, 1 with frequent rage reactions, and 1 with intermittent confusional states. Niemann-Pick disease type C, also known as juvenile dystonic lipodosis, is characterized by dystonia, dementia, impairment of upward gaze, and splenomegaly.

For anyone interested in neuropsychology, the most important basal ganglia disorders are Wilson disease and Huntington chorea. Wilson disease is an autosomal recessive disorder caused by a defect in copper transport with resultant copper deposition, particularly prominent in the liver and brain. Hepatic involvement is more common in the younger age group. In Walshe's (1976 series, patients with predominantly hepatic involvement developed symptoms and signs at a mean age of 12 years with a range of 3 to 32 years, compared to individuals with predominately neurologic presentation who developed initial signs at an average of 19 years of age with a range of 9 to 39 years. The most common early neurologic complaints are tremor, dysarthria, and drooling. Ataxia and dystonic postures occur later.

Intellectual decline may be one of the presenting symptoms of Wilson disease. Deteriorating school performance occurs early in affected children. Walshe (1976) notes that these children not only have declining cognitive function but also problems writing and speaking, a short attention span, and mood swings. The cognitive dysfunction is preventable and treatable, and even when initial psychometric testing shows no deficit in comparison to age norms, there may be continuing improvement with restriction of copper intake and therapy with D-penicillamine. Testing 9 adults before starting therapy and retesting 8 at 16 to 30 months and 4 at 63 to 73 months after treatment showed continuing improvement in the Wechsler Verbal Scale, the Shipley-Hartford tests, the Wechsler Memory Scale Quotient, and the recall portion of the Bender Gestalt test (Goldstein et al., 1968).

Behavioral problems may be a presenting complaint in 10 to 25% of individuals with Wilson disease. Scheinberg, Sternlieb, and Richman (1968) found behavioral problems in 30 of 49 patients and noted that in 13 of these 30 patients, behavioral problems were the initial symptoms of Wilson disease. They classified 9 patients as psychotic and 6 as neurotic. In the remainder, the emotional problems were considered a reaction to physical disabilities. Although adolescents had frequent behavioral problems, none of Scheinberg's 6 patients less than 12 years of age had significant emotional disturbance. Although there does not appear to be any one behavioral disorder charac teristic of Wilson disease, the frequent occurrence of emotional lability suggests that the frontal lobes may be particularly susceptible to the toxic effects of increased levels of copper (Scheinberg et al., 1984). Just as cognitive decline reverses, there does seem to be improvement in behavioral disturbance with D-penicillamine therapy and restriction of dietary copper.

Huntington disease is an autosomal dominant disorder with a frequency of approximately 4 to 7 per 100,000 (Baraitser, 1985). This disorder starts with chorea, dementia, or psychosis, usually between the ages of 35 and 45. The progression of the disorder is slow, with death occurring between 51 and 55 years of age. Less than 5% of patients may present prior to 15 years of age. These children more often have the rigid or akinetic form of Huntington disease. Jervis (1963) noted rigidity in 14 of 21 cases of juvenile onset Huntington disease, with only 8 of 21 developing chorea. Seizures were also common, occurring in 11 of the 21 cases. The dementia so characteristic of the adult form of Huntington disease is even more pronounced in the childhood form. In 4 cases, the IQs ranged from 38 to 70 at the time of initial diagnosis (Jervis, 1963).

Hansotia, Cleeland, and Chun (1968) documented the progressive nature of the cognitive impairment in childhood Huntington disease. In their first patient, initial school testing using Otis Form A showed an IQ of 84, followed 2 years later by an IQ of 66 on Otis Beta Form. After one year, more thorough neuropsychological testing showed a WISC full-scale score of 62 with a performance of 69 and a verbal of 62, falling the following year to a full-scale score of 47 with a performance score of less than 46 and a verbal of 48. The patient's older brother had minimal symptoms of juvenile Huntington chorea. His initial WAIS scores were within an average range, with a full-scale score of 93, verbal of 100, and performance of 86. However, in comparison to their siblings, the two children with Huntington chorea showed significant abnormalities in the Halstad Category Test and the Tactual Performance Test. In addition, there were difficulties in simple motor-sensory tests. These changes in cognitive function are often the presenting complaint in children with Huntington. In Hansotia and associates' (1968) review, 9 of 20 children presented with declining school performance, 10 of 20 started with abnormal movements and clumsiness, and 1 child first developed seizures.

Behavioral disturbances are also a common part of the presentation in the adult form of Huntington disease. Dewhurst, Oliver, and McKnight (1970) noted anxiety, personality disorders, depression, and paranoia in approximately half of their patients prior to initial clinical manifestations of Huntington disease. Although behavioral disturbances were not mentioned in the children described by Hansotia and colleagues or by Jervis, aggressive outbursts were noted in 3 of the 5 children described by Oliver and Dewhurst (Hansotia et al., 1968; Jervis, 1963; Oliver & Dewhurst, 1969). This may be due to the more rapid progression of the disorder, with death occurring, on the average, 8 years after the first onset of symptoms in children suffering from Huntington chorea.

With the localization of the gene for Huntington disease on chromosome 4, it is now possible to identify individuals who will later develop Huntington disease. Jason and colleagues (1988) found neuropsychologic impairment in presymptomatic individuals carrying the gene for Huntington disease. However, Strauss and Brandt (1990) have not been able to confirm this finding. They studied 12 individuals carrying the Huntington gene, 15 family members without the gene, and 15 normal controls. In a series of neuropsychological tests—including WAIS, Wisconsin Card Sort, Stroop Word Color Test, The Money Road Map, a test of verbal memory, Symbol Digit Modalities, visual vigilance, and choice reaction time—they found no difference between presymptomatic individuals and controls. At most, they found only nonstatistically significant greater interference on the Stroop Word Color Test in individuals with the Huntington gene, suggesting that prior to the onset of clinical signs of Huntington disease there is no impairment in neuropsychological function.

SPINOCEREBELLAR DEGENERATIONS

Spinocerebellar degenerations, progressive cerebellar ataxias, or inherited ataxias are terms that imply deterioration of the cerebellum, pons, medulla, and the spinal cord. Though there are several different classifications for these disorders, one useful approach outlined by Stumpf (1985) is initially to divide the spinocerebellar degenerative disorders into categories based on pattern of inheritance. Stumpf found that dominant, recessive and sporadic ataxias each accounted for approximately one-third of the patients.

The autosomal dominant ataxias have in common a usual presentation in the adult years, with only 5 to 10% of the individuals developing symptoms during childhood. Included in this group of diseases are several of the olivopontocerebellar atrophies, the Holmes-type of spinocerebellar degeneration and some forms of familial spastic paraplegia. These individuals frequently have additional signs of brain stem dysfunction and occasionally develop variable degrees of dementia late in the course of these disorder. The autosomal recessive spinocerebellar degenerations start at a younger age. Gilman and colleagues (1981) discuss 20 recessive ataxias; of this group, 18 begin during the childhood years. Only 1 (Roussy-Levy syndrome) presents during the teenage or young adult years and 1 (OPCA type 2) during the adult years. Approximately one-third of the recessive ataxias presently defy classification.

The first step in evaluation of the spinocerebellar degenerative diseases is to distinguish those disorders for which specific therapy is available. These disorders are discussed by Stumpf (1985) and are listed in Table 5.1.

It is difficult to define the true incidence of cognitive and behavioral disorders in the spinocerebellar degenerations. A major problem in reviewing the literature is the lack of agreement on diagnostic criteria for the many disorders in this category. In addition, it is often difficult to distinguish primary effects of the degenerative disease from secondary effects. Gilman and colleagues (1981) noted frequent alterations of mentation but stated that most were due to secondary effects such as brain stem compression or hydrocephalus. Occasionally, there is

TABLE 5.1   Treatable Inherited Ataxias

Disorder	Metabolic defect or sign	Treatment
Urea cycle defects	Hyperammonemia	Protein restriction Benzoate
Multiple carboxylase deficiency	Biotinidase Deficiency	Biotin
Vitamin E deficiency	Low serum Vitamin E	Vitamin E
Abetalipoproteinemia	Low cholesterol Low triglycerides Low Vitamin A & E Absent β lipoproteins	Vitamin E
Refsum disease	Elevated serum Phytanic acid	Restrict dietary Phytanic acid
Hartnup disease	Renal aminoaciduria Tryptophan malabsorption	Niacin Acetazolamide
Familial periodic paralysis	Unknown defect	Acetazolamide

Source: Based on Stumpf, 1985.

more diffuse involvement of the central nervous system, which better explains the association between the ataxia and cognitive or behavioral deficits. Table 5.2 lists those disorders that seem to be characterized both by cognitive deficit and ataxia.

A possible association between cerebellar dysfunction and psychiatric disorders has been discussed by a number of investigators (Hamilton et al., 1983). Weinberger and associates (1980) have noted cerebellar atrophy in individuals with schizophrenia. Courchesne and colleagues (1988) reported hypoplasia of vermal lobules VI and VII in individuals with autism. In contrast to the studies that looked for cerebellar dysfunction in individuals with psychiatric disturbance, studies of individuals with progressive degenerative diseases affecting the cerebellum have found an inconsistent association between initial cerebellar dysfunction and subsequent psychiatric impairment.

Keddie (1969) reported paranoid psychosis in three members of a family with an autosomal dominant psychosis, but found no additional descriptions of psychosis in individuals with hereditary ataxias. In their series of patients with a variety of different cerebellar disorders, Gilman and colleagues (1981) found that approximately 10% suffered from hallucinations, paranoid ideas, depression, or mania. Berent and associates (1990), using the Symptom Checklist 90 (revised) to

TABLE 5.2   Ataxia Associated with Mental Retardation

Recessive Disorders

Ataxia telangiectasia

Behr syndrome

Cockayne syndrome

Congenital ataxia with aniridia

Hartnup disease

Joubert syndrome

Marinesco-Sjogren syndrome

Spongy degeneration with pontocerebellar atrophy

Troyer syndrome

Dominant Disorders

Olivopontocerebellar atrophy III

Olivopontocerebellar atrophy V

Aminoacidurias and Organic Acidurias

Arginase deficiency

Arginiosuccinase deficiency

Arginiosuccinate synthetase deficiency

Intermittant branched chain ketoaciduria

Isovaleric acidemia

Ornithine transcarbamylase deficiency

study individuals with olivopontocerebellar atrophy, reported an increased incidence of depression, anxiety, and subjective emotional discomfort.

The best delineated autosomal recessive cerebellar ataxia is Friedreich ataxia. This disorder begins before puberty, 10 years being the mean age of onset. The earliest signs are clumsiness and orthopedic problems. Scoliosis and pes cavus (high arched feet with hammer toes) are seen in three-fourths of the patients. The incoordination seen in all patients is a combination of cerebellar and posterior column ataxia. The speech is dysarthric in at least 80% of the individuals, reflexes are absent, nystagmus occurs in three-fourths of the patients, and muscle atrophy in two-thirds. Approximately 20% of the individuals have diabetes mellitus. Eventually, a cardiomyopathy develops in almost all patients. The cardiomyopathy is usually the cause of death.

There is a surprising lack of consensus on the occurrence of cognitive dysfunction in Friedreich ataxia. Neither Harding (1981) nor Stumpf (1985) consider cognitive dysfunction as part of the disorder. Barbeau (1976) listed progressive intellectual impairment as an accessory sign in Friedreich ataxia, and found it particularly common in individuals with both ataxia and diabetes mellitus. In his review of spinocerebellar degenerations, Greenfield (1954) commented that it is "well known that many cases of Friedreich ataxia tend to regress mentally during the course of the disease." He stated that approximately 15% of individuals will show some degree of cognitive regression. Davies studied 20 patients using the Mill-Hill Vocabulary Test, Raven Progressive Matrices, and the Wechsler-Bellevue Verbal Scale, comparing the Friedreich patients to a control group of 15 individuals with chronic debilitating conditions (Davies, 1949). On the Mill-Hill test, the Friedreich's ataxia group was no different from the general population, and on the Wechsler test there were no ataxia patients with an IQ below 75. He did find that in 3 or 4 of the 20 patients there was impairment of recent memory and problems with attention and concentration, suggesting a mild and nonprogressive cognitive impairment. Overall, the data seem to suggest that cognitive impairment is not a major part of Friedreich ataxia.

Just as there is a problem in determining the frequency of cognitive impairment in Friedreich ataxia, the frequency of behavioral disturbance is poorly defined. In Davies's series of 20 patients, he found 2 with psychotic features, 1 with significant depression, and 2 with episodic clouding of consciousness (Davies, 1949). In his review of the literature, Greenfield (1954) noted previous descriptions of emotional lability, vagueness and lack of precision in responding to questions, and occasional hallucinations and paranoid ideas. He acknowledged the problem with separating the effect of social isolation due to the disorder from behavioral symptoms caused by the cerebellar degeneration, but stated that most authorities feel that the behavioral dysfunction is due to a mild degree of dementia. Stumpf (1985) emphasized the need for psychological support. He has found that patients with Friedreich ataxia always consider and occasionally do commit suicide.

The other relatively common spinocerebellar degeneration is hereditary spastic paraplegia. In Dyken and Krawiecki's (1983) series, hereditary spastic paraplegia was the most commonly seen spinocerebellar degeneration. In contrast to the rather homogeneous picture seen with Friedreich ataxia, hereditary spastic paraparesis encompasses a number of different disorders. There are definitely both autosomal dominant and recessive forms. Spastic paraparesis has been divided into pure and complex forms. In her discussion of pure hereditary spastic paraplegia, Harding (1981) excluded cases if there was any evidence of dementia, though other authors have allowed the inclusion of cases with retinal changes or retardation. Most authorities use the presence of ataxia, dysarthria, or ocular cerebellar signs as a reason for exclusion from the pure hereditary spastic paraparesis group.

In the pure forms of spastic paraplegia, the average age of onset for the autosomal dominant cases is approximately 20 years, with one-third of the patients developing symptoms prior to 5 years of age. The autosomal recessive cases seem to begin earlier, although with a considerable range. The first symptom is almost invariably trouble walking; there is increased muscle tone, hyperreflexia, and extensor plantar responses. The disease progression is quite slow. In Harding's (1981) series, only one patient lost the ability to walk prior to 50 years of age. Neither cognitive impairment nor behavior problems seemed to be major problems. Harding does not mention either cognitive impairment or behavior disturbances in any of the 52 cases of autosomal dominant pure hereditary spastic paresis she studied. She found only one mildly mentally retarded boy among the 5 cases of autosomal recessive pure spastic paraplegia.

In the complicated forms of hereditary spastic paraparesis, cognitive regression is more common. However, this is a heterogeneous group of diseases and many affect only a single pedigree. Dyken and Krawiecki (1983) note a frequent occurrence of mental deficiency and seizures in unaffected family members, thus suggesting that this is a polygenetic disorder.

LOWER MOTOR UNIT DISORDERS

A number of progressive degenerative diseases may involve the lower motor unit. In the spinal muscular atrophies, there is progressive degeneration of anterior horn cells. The peripheral nerves are damaged in metabolic and the hereditary motor and/or sensory neuropathies. Congenital myasthenic syndromes are due to abnormalities in the neuromuscular junction. The muscular dystrophies involve deterioration of muscle fibers.

With the spinal muscular atrophies (SMA), there is progressive loss of anterior horn cells and, in more severe cases, loss of brain stem motor nuclei (Gamstorp & Sarnat, 1984). The majority of cases of spinal muscular atrophy are autosomal recessive with a gene locus on chromosome 5q (Brzustowicz et al., 1990). There are three main types. Type I, Werdnig-Hoffmann disease, is the most severe form. Disease frequency has been estimated as between 1 in 5,000 and 1 in 50,000 (Baraitser, 1985). The onset is prenatal in 30% of the cases and within the first 3 months of life in almost all affected infants. These children never learn to sit. Death occurs by 7 months in 50% of the patients and by 18 months in 95% (Pearn & Wilson, 1973).

Both chronic infantile and juvenile (Kugelberg-Welander) SMA progress at a variable slow rate. The combined frequency for these two disorders is approximately 1 in 24,000 live births (Baraitser, 1985). The chronic infantile or intermediate type usually begins within the first year of life with a median age of onset of 6 months. These infants may develop symptoms as early as 2 months of age. Most learn to sit, although only a few are able to walk without support. Most children with chronic infantile SMA remain wheelchair-bound. The majority develop some degree of scoliosis by 3 years of age. There is usually no bulbar involvement and the children may survive into adulthood. Pearn and Wilson (1973) found an average life expectancy of 8 to 15 years of age, though survival to a much older age is possible.

In almost all studies, these children have at least average intelligence. Reviewing school records for 27 children with types 2 and 3 spinal muscular atrophy, Benady (1978) noted that 4 of the children had superior IQs, 4 were low average, and 19 average. In her testing of 15 children with the Goodenough-Harris Draw-a-Person Test, the average score was 95 (range 81–115). These children are at risk for cognitive delay because their recurring hospitalizations and their lack of mobility may cause them to miss educational, cultural, and social activities.

Behavioral problems have surprisingly not been a major concern, though one would expect that the isolation from peers, the multiple hospitalizations, and the marked dependency would put these children at significant risk for social problems. Nevertheless, Pearn and Wilson (1973) described them as well adjusted. Not all authorities have been as impressed with their emotional health. Castroviejo (1984) suggests that these children's total dependency on parents and family members leads to a sense of frustration and repressed aggression, which became manifest as tyrannical behavior. The type 2 and 3 spinal muscular atrophy children spend so much time around adults that they develop language more rapidly than the usual child of their age. Castroviejo describes these children as being articulate but demanding and willing to use their illness to manipulate adults, though out of the home, he found them shy with little confidence.

The demands on the family are significant. These children need frequent chest physiotherapy to prevent respiratory problems, help from occupational or physical therapists for positioning and wheelchair needs, and repeated visits to clinics. For optimal mobility and stimulation, electric-powered wheelchairs, electric typewriters, and other computer-assisted learning devices are essential for these children.

The families also must deal with significant emotional stress. The spinal muscular atrophies are autosomal recessive disorders; thus, both parents must deal with the guilt of genetic disease. All three of the main disorders are progressive with no current therapy to prevent deterioration. For the families of children with type 1 SMA, a constant worry is the possibility that these children will die suddenly of respiratory problems, a potential occurrence during any upper-respiratory tract infection. Families of both type 1 and type 2 SMA children will need to make an early decision about the use of long-term ventilatory support. If intubated, the children with Werdnig-Hoffmann syndrome will probably remain constantly on a respirator. Some of the children with type 2 SMA may require only night-time ventilatory support. Since it may not be possible to distinguish type 1 from type 2 SMA, some families may have been given an incorrect prognosis, expecting death of the child within the first 18 months of life. If the child has type 2 SMA and lives well into his or her elementary school years, the parents will have to readjust psychologically and begin to make more pragmatic plans for the constant ongoing care the child will require. Having already dealt with the expectations of death, parents may be better able to cope with many of the other stressors involved in taking care of a chronically ill child.

Beset by constant demands for care and time, and hampered by lack of previously learned norms for parenting such children, parents can often derive significant benefit from parent support groups. These support groups will not only provide ongoing practical suggestions for parents but will also lessen the isolation felt by many families (Yates, 1984).

MUSCULAR DYSTROPHIES

Duchenne muscular dystrophy is the most common inherited myopathy, with an incidence of 1 in 3,000 to 3,500 boys (Baraitser, 1985). During the first year, motor development may appear normal. Subsequently, the gait becomes impaired and there are problems running and climbing stairs. These boys usually develop weakness of the arms by 6 to 9 years of age, lose the ability to walk by 12 years of age, and die of respiratory or cardiac failure late in the teenage years.

Duchenne muscular dystrophy is an X-linked disorder, with a gene locus at Xp21. Dystrophin, the protein product of the gene, is absent in boys with Duchenne muscular dystrophy. This discovery has led to hopes that the missing protein could be replaced or that technical advances in the future might allow gene therapy to replace the defective gene (Dubowitz, 1989).

Boys with Duchenne muscular dystrophy often have developmental delay in both motor and language function, allowing a reasonably early diagnosis. Smith, Sibert, Wallace, and Harper (1989) studied 33 boys with a mean age of 3.5 years and a definite diagnosis of Duchenne muscular dystrophy and compared them to an age-matched group of controls on the Griffith mental development scale and the Raynell language scale. The boys with Duchenne muscular dystrophy had significantly lower scores on the Griffith subscales of locomotor and speech and hearing skills. On the Raynell language scales the boys with Duchenne muscular dystrophy were significantly lower in both comprehension and expression.

Although there has been a considerable range in IQ scores, most studies have found the mean IQ of groups of boys with Duchenne muscular dystrophy shifted one standard deviation below controls. Emery (1988) found that 20% of the boys tested had a full-scale IQ of <70 and 3% a full-scale IQ of <50. In most studies, these boys score lower on verbal than performance scores. Karagan and associates (1980) found the maximum deficit was in memory for verbal labels, pattern, and number test. Repeated assessments have shown that this is a non-progressive loss of cognitive function. The female carriers of the Duchenne gene have normal distribution of IQ scores.

There is comparatively less information on behavior problems with Duchenne muscular dystrophy. Leibowitz and Dubowitz (1981) used the Rutter behavior questionnaires for 55 sets of parents of children with Duchenne muscular dystrophy and 52 teachers of children with muscular dystrophy. On the parent questionnaire, 18 out of 55 children scored in a range indicating potential emotional disturbance; 7 were listed as primarily antisocial and 11 as neurotic. On the teacher questionnaire, 19 of the 52 children scored above the cutoff point, indicating some degree of emotional disturbance; 10 were listed as antisocial, 6 as neurotic, and 3 as mixed type behavior disorder.

The boys with Duchenne muscular dystrophy had more impairment than both normal and physically disabled children without central nervous system damage. Their degree of impairment was similar to that seen in children with central nervous system damage. Other authors have also noted behavior problems. Buchanan and colleagues (1979) commented on behavioral difficulties that they felt were often a response to frustration. Emotional problems were found particularly in those children who had not been informed of the diagnosis and in those children who had been led to believe that there might be future improvement.

The families of these children experience a considerable number of problems. Both parents experience the grief of having to deal with a chronic, progressive, and ultimately fatal disease. The child's mother may experience more guilt, as this is an X-linked genetic disorder. In one study of 25 families of children with Duchenne muscular dystrophy, 76% identified a psychological problem as their major difficulty (Buchanan et al., 1979). In this set of 25 families, there had already been 6 divorces, and 6 additional families were experiencing considerable strain. In 13 of the 25 families, there was a tendency to overprotect the child, manifest by social isolation and lack of discipline. Between 60 to 70% of these families had noted emotional distress on the part of siblings. Commonly seen was jealousy because of the extra attention given the affected child, and on the part of the girls, both a protective attitude toward their affected sibling and an anxiety about being potential carriers of the gene.

Families of children with Duchenne muscular dystrophy often undergo a cycle of loss, adaption, and then loss again. Particular problems seemed to be the beginning of the school years and the time when the child becomes wheelchair-bound. Now these families may begin to experience additional stress because of hope engendered by the rapid developments in molecular genetics. The families can begin to see the tantalizing developments and the chance for a cure just over the horizon, and yet they are faced with their child's disease relentlessly progressing. Loss and death may occur before a cure is available.

Myotonic muscular dystrophy is an autosomal dominant disorder with a prevalence of 5 per 100,000 (Baraitser, 1985). In the typical form, it begins in late adolescence with slowly progressive stiffness and hand weakness. There is also an infantile or congenital form of myotonic muscular dystrophy seen in infants carrying the gene for myotonic muscular dystrophy whose mothers also have myotonic muscular dystrophy. These children are severely hypotonic. Half of these infants have respiratory difficulty at birth and half have deformity of the feet. They slowly improve, although there is always delay in achieving motor milestones. Most learn to walk. By the end of the first decade, they begin to show typical signs of the adult form of myotonic muscular dystrophy.

The infants with congenital myotonic muscular dystrophy and the adults with myotonic muscular dystrophy differ significantly in cognitive development. Dyken and Harper (1973) found that infants with congenital myotonic muscular dystrophy who had experienced respiratory distress in the newborn period had a mean full-scale IQ of 57 ± 14 versus a mean full-scale IQ of 91 ± 7 in infants with congenital myotonic muscular dystrophy who had experienced no distress. In a subsequent study, Harper (1975) found that 48 of 70 infants with congenital myotonic muscular dystrophy had definite evidence of mental retardation and only 9 had no evidence of retardation. When test results were available, he found a mean full-scale IQ of 66 ± 16. There was no association between the presence or absence of neonatal respiratory distress and cognitive development in this latter study.

In contrast, the adult with myotonic MD shows less prominent cognitive impairment. Bird and associates (1983) found a mean Wechsler full-scale score of 90.3, mean verbal score of 91.7, and mean performance score of 90.3 in 29 adults with myotonic MD. Of the 29 adults, 6 had a Wechsler full-scale score of less than 70 and 2 had a full-scale score of greater than 120. Censori and colleagues (1990) noted that 10 of 20 adults with myotonic MD had Raven's Colored Progressive Matrices scores, which were two standard deviations below the mean for controls. Both of these research teams found selective impairment of spatial manipulation and orientation.

Behavioral disturbance is common in both adult and infantile myotonic MD. Using interview and MMPI scores, Bird and colleagues (1983) reported prominent personality abnormalities without a typical pattern in 32% of their patients. Brumback and Wilson (1984) noted elevation of the MMPI depression scale in 50% of their myotonic MD patients.

There are a number of other less common muscular dystrophies. The congenital muscular dystrophies begin at birth with weakness, hypotonia, and joint contractures. In one form, there is a myopathy and hypodensity of cerebral white matter on neuroimaging. These children have a normal or only mildly impaired intellectual ability. In the two other forms, Fukuyama CMD and cerebro-ocular dysplasia-muscular dystrophy, there is muscle involvement and atrophy or malformation of the cerebrum. The affected children all have significant retardation (Echenne et al., 1986). Fascioscapulohumeral dystrophy, an autosomal dominant disorder with a frequency of 3 to 10 cases per million, starts as facial weakness first noticed at the end of the first decade, followed by weakness of the shoulder and arm muscles and slow progressive involvement of other muscle groups. Most patients have normal intellectual development. In Karagan and Sorensen's

5)

(1981) study, the patients with FSH muscular dystrophy had a mean full-scale IQ of 107 with a verbal IQ of 102 and a performance IQ of 111. Limb girdle muscular dystrophy is a heterogeneous group of disorders that are most commonly autosomal recessive and begin during the second or third decade. As in FSH muscular dystrophy, the individuals usually do not have cognitive impairment. In Karagan and Sorensen's study of seven individuals with limb girdle dystrophy, the mean full-scale IQ was 102 ± 14.

FUTURE RESEARCH

Most of the present research into the neurodegenerative diseases has concentrated on understanding the genetic and biochemical pathogenesis of these disorders. The long-term goal is both the prevention of neurodegenerative disease and the establishment of specific therapies for the disorders. Unfortunately, for many of the disorders, cure and prevention are still years in the future. Since improvements in medical care have resulted in longer survival for many of these children, we still need to be aware of the many day-to-day problems faced both by children with neurodegenerative diseases and their families. The cognitive and behavioral problems associated with neurodegenerative disease have received too little attention. Many of the studies of cognitive and behavioral effects of neurodegenerative disorders are plagued by small numbers, vague definitions, and single measurements at only one moment in the course of the disorder. Better longitudinal studies of the behavioral and cognitive problems associated with neurodegenerative disease are essential for giving us the means to maximize the potential of these children and to prevent the secondarily disabling complications of these chronic disorders.

REFERENCES

Adams RD, Lyon G (1982). *Neurology of Hereditary Metabolic Diseases of Children*. Washington, Hemisphere Publishing Corp.

Aron AM (1984). Learning disabilities in children with NF. *Newsletter of the National Neurofibromatosis Foundation*, Winter/Spring, 4–5.

Baraitser M (1985). *The Genetics of Neurological Disorders* (revised edition). New York, Oxford University Press.

Barbeau A (1976). Friedreich's ataxia 1976—an overview. *Can J Neurol Sc, 3*, 389–396.

Benady SG (1978). Spinal muscular atrophy in childhood: Review of 50 cases. *Develop Med Child Neurol, 20*, 746–757.

Berent S, Giordani B, Gilman S, et al. (1990). Neuropsychological changes in olivopontocerebellar atrophy. *Arch Neurol, 47*, 997–1001.

Bird TD, Follett C, Griep E (1983). Cognitive and personality function in myotonic muscular dystrophy. *J Neurol Neurosurg Psychiatry, 46*, 971–980.

Blacher J (1984). A dynamic perspective on the impact of a severely handicapped child on the family. In Blacher J, (Ed). *Severely Handicapped Young Children and Their Families*. Orlando, Academic Press, pp. 3–49.

Borberg A (1951). Clinical and genetic investigations into tuberous sclerosis and

Recklinghausen neurofibromatosis. *Acta Psychiatr Neurol Suppl 71*, 1–239.

Boustany RN, Alroy J, Kolodny EH (1988). Clinical classification of neuronal ceroid-lipofuscinosis subtypes. *Am J Med Genetics Suppl 5*, 47–58.

Breslau N, Prabucki K (1987). Siblings of disabled children. *Arch Gen Psychiatry, 44*, 1040–1046.

Brumback RA, Wilson H (1984). Cognitive and personality function in myotonic muscular dystrophy. *J Neurol Neurosurg Psychiatry, 47*, 888–890.

Brzustowicz LM, Lehner T, Castilla LH et al. (1990). Genetic mapping of chronic childhood-onset spinal muscular atrophy to chromosome 5q11.2–13.3. *Nature, 344*, 540–541.

Buchanan DC, LaBarbera CJ, Roelofs R, Olson W (1979). Reaction of families to children with Duchenne muscular dystrophy. *Gen Hosp Psychiat, 1*, 262–269.

Castroviejo IP (1984). Commentary: Clinical aspects of spinal muscular atrophy. In: Gamstorp I, Sarnat HB. (Eds). *Progressive Spinal Muscular Atrophies*, New York, Raven Press, pp. 43–54.

Censori B, Danni M, Del Pesce M, Provinciale L (1990). Neuropsychological profile in myotonic dystrophy. *J Neurol, 237*, 251–256.

Chapman CA, Korf BR, Urion DK (1989). A specific memory deficit in a group of children with neurofibromatosis and learning disability. *Ann Neurol, 26*, 483.

Collins FS, Ponder BAJ, Seizinger BR, Epstein CJ (1989). Editorial: The vonRecklinghausen neurofibromatosis region on chromosome 17-genetic and physical maps come into focus. *Am J Hum Genet, 44*, 1–5.

Courchesne E, Yeung-Courchesne R, Press GA, Hesselink JR, Jernigan TL (1988). Hypoplasia of cerebellar vermal lobules VI and VII in autism. *N Engl J Med, 318*, 1349–1354.

Curatolo P, Cusmai R (1987). Autism and infantile spasm in children with tuberous sclerosis. *Develop Med Child Neurol, 29*, 551.

Davies DL (1949). The intelligence of patients with Friedreich's ataxia. *J Neurol Neurosurg Psychiat, 12*, 34–38.

Davies DL (1949). Psychiatric changes associated with Friedreich's ataxia. *J Neurol Neurosurg Psychiat, 12*, 246–250.

Dewhurst K, Oliver JE, McKnight AL (1970). Socio-psychiatric consequences of Huntington's disease. *Br J Psychiat, 116*, 255–258.

Dooling EC, Schoene WC, Richardson EP (1974). Hallervorden Spatz syndrome. *Arch Neurol, 30*, 70–83.

Dosen A (1989). Diagnosis and treatment of mental illness in mentally retarded children: A developmental model. *Child Psychiatr Hum Develop, 20*, 73–84.

Dubowitz V (1989). The Duchenne dystrophy story: From phenotype to gene and potential treatment. *J Child Neurol, 4*, 240–250.

Dunn DW (1987). Neurofibromatosis in childhood. *Curr Prob Pediatr, 17*, 445–497.

Dunn DW, Roos KL (1989). Magnetic resonance imaging evaluation of learning difficulties and incoordination in neurofibromatosis. *Neurofibromatosis, 2*, 1–5.

Dyken PR, Harper PS (1973). Congenital dystrophic myotonia. *Neurology, 23*, 465–473.

Dyken P, Krawiecki N (1983). Neurodegenerative diseases of infancy and childhood. *Ann Neurol, 13*, 351–364.

Dyken PR, McCleary GE (1986). Dementia in infantile and childhood neurological disease. In: Obrzut JE, Hynd GW (Eds.). *Child Neuropsychology* (Vol. 1). Orlando, Academic Press, pp. 175–189.

Echenne B, Arthuis M, Billard C et al. (1986). Congenital muscular dystrophy and cerebral CT scan anomalies. *J Neurol Sciences, 75*, 7–22.

Eiser C (1985). *The Psychology of Childhood Illness*. New York, Springer-Verlag.

Eldridge R, Denckla MB, Bien E, et al. (1989). Neurofibromatosis type 1 (Recklinghausen's disease) neurologic and cognitive assessment with sibling controls. *AJDC, 43*, 833–837.

Eldridge R, Harlan A, Cooper IS, Riklan M (1970). Superior intelligence in recessively inherited torsion dystonia. *Lancet, 1*, 65–67.

Eliason MJ (1988). Neuropsychological patterns: Neurofibromatosis compared to developmental learning disorders. *Neurofibromatosis, 1*, 17–25.

Elze KL, Koepp P, Lagenstein I, et al. (1978).

Juvenile type of generalized ceroid-lipofuscinosis (Spielmeyer-Sjogren syndrome). *Neuropaedriatrie, 9,* 3–27.

Emery AEH (1988). *Duchenne Muscular Dystrophy,* (revised edition). New York, Oxford University Press.

Fahn S, Marsden CD (1987). The treatment of dystonia. In: Marsden CD, Fahn S (Eds). *Movement Disorders 2.* Boston, Butterworths, pp. 359–382.

Fontanesi J, Haas RH. (1988). Cognitive profile of Rett's syndrome. *J Child Neurol, 3,* S20-S24.

Gamstorp I, Sarnat HB (1984). *Progressive Spinal Muscular Atrophies.* New York, Raven Press.

Gillberg C, Forsell C (1984). Childhood psychosis and neurofibromatosis—More than a coincidence? *J Autism Develop Disorders, 14,* 1–8.

Gilman S, Bloedel JR, Lechtenberg R (1981). *Disorders of the Cerebellum.* Philadelphia, FA Davis Company.

Goldstein NP, Ewert JC, Randall RV, Gross JB (1968). Psychiatric aspects of Wilson's disease: Results of psychometric tests during long-term therapy. *Birth Defects Original Article Series, 4,* 77–84.

Gomez MR (Ed) (1988). *Tuberous Sclerosis.* New York, Raven Press.

Gomez MR, Kuntz NL, Westmoreland BF (1982). Tuberous sclerosis, early onset of seizures, and mental subnormality: Study of discordant homozygous twins. *Neurology, 32,* 604–611.

Gomez MR, Rafecas JC, Houser OW (1987). The diagnostic and prognostic significance of low-attenuation lesions in the head computed tomography scan of patients with tuberous sclerosis. *Ann Neurol, 22,* 419–420.

Greenfield JG (1954). *The Spinocerebellar Degenerations.* Oxford, Blackwell Press.

Halpern R, Parker-Crawford F (1982). Young handicapped children and their families: Patterns of interaction with human service institutions. *Infant Mental Heal J, 3,* 51–63.

Hamilton NG, Frick RB, Takahashi T, Hopping MW (1983). Psychiatric symptoms and cerebellar pathology. *Am J Psychiat, 140,* 1322–1326.

Hansotia P, Cleeland CS, Chun RWM (1968). Juvenile Huntington's chorea. *Neurology, 18,* 217–224.

Harding AE (1981). Friedreich's ataxia: A clinical and genetic study of 90 families with an analysis of early diagnostic criteria and intrafamilial clustering of clinical features. *Brain, 104,* 589–620.

Harding AE (1981). Hereditary "pure" spastic paraplegia: A clinical and genetic study of 22 families. *J Neurol Neurosurg Psychiat, 44,* 871–883.

Harper DC (1983). Personality correlates and degree of impairment in male adolescents with progressive and non-progressive disorders. *J Clin Psychol, 39,* 859–867.

Harper PS (1975). Congenital myotonic dystrophy in Britain I. Clinical aspects. *Arch Dis Child, 50,* 505–513.

Hofman IL (1990). *The Batten-Spielmeyer-Vogt Disease.* Doorn, Bartimeus Foundaton.

Hunt A, Dennis J (1987). Psychiatric disorder among children with tuberous sclerosis. *Develop Med Child Neurol, 29,* 190–198.

Huson SM, Compston DAS, Harper PS (1989). A genetic study of von Recklinghausen neurofibromatosis in south east Wales. Guidelines for genetic counselling. *J Med Genet, 26,* 712–721.

Hynd GW, Willis WG (1988). *Pediatric Neuropsychology.* Orlando, Grune and Stratton, Inc.

Jason GW, Parjurkova EM, Suchowersky O, et al. (1988). Presymptomatic neuropsychological impairment in Huntington's disease. *Arch Neurol, 45,* 769–773.

Jervis GA (1963). Huntington's chorea in childhood. *Arch Neurol, 9,* 50–63.

Karagan NJ, Richman LC, Sorensen JP (1980). Analysis of verbal disability in Duchenne muscular dystrophy. *J Nerv Ment Dis, 168,* 419–423.

Karagan NJ, Sorensen JP (1981). Intellectual functioning in non-Duchenne muscular dystrophy. *Neurology, 31,* 448–452.

Keddie KMG (1969). Hereditary ataxia, presumed to be of the Menzel type, complicated by paranoid psychosis, in a mother and two sons. *J Neurol Neurosurg Psychiat, 32,* 82–87.

Kingsley DPE, Kendall BE, Fritz CR (1986). Tuberous sclerosis: A clinicoradiological evaluation of 110 cases with particular reference to atypical presentation. *Neuroradiology, 28,* 38–46.

Leibowitz D, Dubowitz V (1981). Intellect and behavior in Duchenne muscular dystrophy. *Develop Med Child Neurol, 23,* 577–590.

Lesser RP, Fahn S (1978). Dystonia: A disorder often misdiagnosed as a conversion reaction. *Am J Psychiatry, 135,* 349–352.

MacFaul R, Cavanagh N, Lake BD, Stephens R, Whitfield AE (1982). Metachromatic leucodystrophy: Review of 38 cases. *Arch Dis Child, 57,* 168–175.

Marsden CD, Harrison MJG, Bundey S (1976). Natural history of idiopathic torsion dystonia. In: Eldridge R, Fahn S (Eds). *Advances in Neurology* (Vol. 14). New York, Raven Press, pp. 177–186.

Menkes JH (1990). *Textbook of Child Neurology.* Philadelphia, Lea and Febiger.

Miller LG (1968). Toward a greater understanding of the parents of the mentally retarded child. *J Pediatr, 73,* 699–705.

Moser HW (1987). Adrenoleukodystrophy: From bedside to molecular biology. *J Child Neurol, 2,* 140–150.

National Institutes of Health (1987). Neurofibromatosis Concensus Development Conference Statement. Washington, DC.

Nolan T, Pless IB (1986). Emotional correlates and conse-quences of birth defects. *J Pediatr, 109,* 201–216.

Oliver J, Dewhurst K (1969). Childhood and adolescent form of Huntington's disease. *J Neurol Neurosurg Psychiat, 32,* 455–459.

Olsson B, Rett A (1987). Autism and Rett's syndrome: Behavioral investigations and differential diagnosis. *Develop Med and Child Neurol, 29,* 429–441.

Pampiglione G, Moynahan EJ (1976). The tuberous sclerosis syndrome: Clinical and EEG studies on 100 children. *J Neurol Neurosurg Psychiat, 39,* 666–673.

Pearn JH, Wilson J (1973). Acute Werdnig-Hoffmann disease. Acute infantile spinal muscular atrophy. *Arch Dis Child, 48,* 425–430.

Pearn JH, Wilson J (1973). Chronic generalized spinal muscular atrophy of infancy and childhood. Arrested Werdnig-Hoffmann disease. *Arch Dis Child, 48,* 768–774.

Rett's Syndrome Criteria Workshop Group (1988). Diagnostic criteria for Rett's syndrome. *Ann Neurol, 23,* 425–428.

Riccardi VM, Eichner JE (1986). *Neurofibromatosis: Phenotype, Natural History, and Pathogenesis.* Baltimore, Johns Hopkins University Press.

Riikonen R, Simell O (1990). Tuberous sclerosis and infantile spasms. *Develop Med Child Neurol, 32,* 203–209.

Riklan M, Cullinan T, Cooper IS (1976). Psychological studies in dystonia musculorum deformans. In: Eldridge R, Fahn S (Eds). *Advances in Neurology* (Vol. 14). New York, Raven Press, pp. 189–200.

Roach ES, Williams DP, Laster DW (1987). Magnetic resonance imaging in tuberous sclerosis. *Arch Neurol, 44,* 301–303.

Romans-Clarkson SE, Clarkson JE, Dittmer ID, et al (1986). Impact of a handicapped child on mental health of parents. *Br Med J, 293,* 1395–1397.

Rosman PN, Pearce J (1976). The brain in multiple neurofibromatosis (von Recklinghausen disease): A suggested neuropathological basis for the associated mental defect. *Brain, 90,* 829–837.

Rutter M (1977). Brain damage syndromes in childhood: Concepts and findings. *J Child Psychol Psychiatr, 18,* 1–21.

Rutter M (1981). Psychological sequelae of brain damage in children. *Am J Psychiatry, 138,* 1533–1544.

Samuelsson B, Axelsson R (1981). Neurofibromatosis. *Acta Derm Venereol, 95,* 67–71.

Samuelsson B, Riccardi VM (1989). Neurofibromatosis in Gothenburg, Sweden II. Intellectual compromise. *Neurofibromatosis, 2,* 78–83.

Samuelsson B, Riccardi VM (1989). Neurofibromatosis in Gothenburg Sweden III. Psychiatric and social aspects. *Neurofibromatosis, 2,* 84–106.

Santavuori P, Westermarck T, Rapola J, et al (1985). Antioxidant treatment in Spielmeyer-Sjogren's disease. *Acta Neurol Scand, 71,* 136–145.

Schaumberg HH, Powers JM, Raine CS, Suzuki K, Richardson EP (1975). Adrenoleukodystrophy. A clinical and pathological study of 17 cases. *Arch Neurol, 32,* 577–591.

Scheinberg IH, Sternlieb I (1984). *Wilson's Disease.* Philadelphia, WB Sanders Company.

Scheinberg IH, Sternlieb I, Richman J (1968). Psychiatric manifestations in patients with Wilson's disease. *Birth Defects Original Article Series, 4,* 85–87.

Schulte FJ (1984). Clinical course of GM2 gangliosidoses. *Neuropediatrics, 15,* 66–70.

Smith RA, Sibert JR, Wallace SJ, Harper PS (1989). Early diagnosis and secondary prevention of Duchenne muscular dystrophy. *Arch Dis Child, 64,* 787–790.

Snyder CH (1967). Infantile spasms: Favorable response to steroid therapy. *JAMA, 201,* 198–200.

Sorensen JB, Parnas J (1979). A clinical study of 44 patients with juvenile amaurotic family idiocy. *Acta Psychiat Scand, 59,* 449–461.

Stein REK (1990). Adaption of Children with Chronic Physical Disorders. In: Green M, Haggerty RS (Eds). *Ambulatory Pediatrics IV,* Philadelphia, WB Saunders, pp. 293–298.

Stein REK, Jessop DJ (1984). General issues in the care of children with chronic physical conditions. *Pediatr Cl N Am, 31,* 189–198.

Stine SB, Adams WV (1989). Learning problems in neurofibromatosis patients. *Clin Orthop, 245,* 43–48.

Strauss ME, Brandt J (1990). Are there neuropsychological manifestations of the gene for Huntington's disease in asymptomatic, at-risk individuals? *Arch Neurol, 47,* 905–908.

Stumpf DA (1985). The inherited ataxias. *Pediatr Neurol, 1,* 129–133.

Stumpf DA (1985). The inherited ataxias. *Neurol Cl, 3,* 47–57.

Swift AV, Dyken PR, DuRant RH (1984). Psychological follow-up in childhood dementia: A longitudinal study of subacute sclerosing panencephalitis. *J Pediatr Psychology, 9,* 469–483.

Varnhagen CK, Lewin S, Das JP, et al. (1988). Neurofibromatosis and psychological processes. *Develop Behavioral Pediatr, 9,* 257–265.

Walshe JM (1976). Wilson's Disease. In: Vinken PJ, Bruyn GW, Klawans HL (Eds). *Handbook of Clinical Neurology* (Vol. 27). New York, American Elsevier Publishing Co. Inc., pp. 379–414.

Weinberger DR, Kleinman JE, Luchins DJ, et al. (1980). Cerebellar pathology in schizophrenia: A controlled postmortem study. *Am J Psychiat, 137,* 359–361.

Whelan TB, Walker ML (1989). Coping and adjustment of children with neurological disorders. In: Reynolds CR, Fletcher-Janzen E. (Eds). *Handbook of Clinical Child Neuropsychology.* New York: Plenum Press.

Wisniewski KE, Rapin I, Heaney-Kieras J (1988). Clinocopathological variability in the childhood neuronal ceroidlipofuscinoses and new observations on glycoprotein abnormalities. *Am J Med Genetics, Suppl 5,* 27–46.

Wright JS, Granger RD, Sameroff AJ (1984). Parental acceptance and developmental handicap. In: Blacher J (Ed). *Severely Handicapped Young Children and Their Families.* Orlando, Academic Press, pp. 51–90.

Yando R, Zigler E (1984). Severely handicapped children and their families: A synthesis. In: Blacher J (Ed). *Severely Handicapped Young Children and Their Families.* Orlando, Academic Press, pp. 401–416.

Yates TT (1984). Commentary: Adaptation to progressive neuromuscular disease: Role of Parent Groups. In: Gamstorp I, Sarnat HB (Eds). *Progressive Spinal Muscular Atrophies.* New York, Raven Press, pp. 201–207.

6

NEUROPSYCHOLOGICAL CONSEQUENCES AND TREATMENT OF PEDIATRIC HEAD TRAUMA

THOMAS V. RYAN

JUDITH A. LAMARCHE

JEFFREY T. BARTH

THOMAS J. BOLL

INTRODUCTION

The cognitive and behavioral sequelae following severe traumatic brain injury devastate both the patient and the family (Levin, Benton, & Grossman, 1982). The nature and extent of such injuries frequently preclude a return to premorbid educational, occupational, social, and recreational functioning. These sequela in children are even more complex than in adults.

Acquired craniocerebral trauma typically occurs in young males who may be subsequently removed from the work force with the majority of their lives ahead of them (Kalsbeek, McLaurin, Harris, & Miller, 1980). Subtle post-traumatic deficits may produce substantial economic and adaptive losses over a lifetime (Boll, 1988; Lees-Haley, 1986). Heightened awareness of this problem has resulted in legislative initiatives calling for increased rehabilitation funding. Neuropsychologists have also been exploring the amelioration of functional deficits via a variety of cognitive remediation techniques (Diller, 1987). The purpose of these combined efforts has been to reintegrate potentially productive individuals into the community and to reduce the possibility of their long-term economic dependence on society's support system.

The premorbid personality, behavior, and neurocognitive characteristics of the traumatic brain-injured population are predisposing factors for both children and adults. As with adults, children who sustain this type of injury "are far from a random sample of the general population" (Rutter, Chadwick, & Shaffer, 1983, p. 84). Pediatric head trauma is even more complex due to its age-dependent developmental variability. The pediatric practitioner must consider the developmental phase and the time when the injury occurred. The adverse affect of injury is extended by disruption of subsequent cognitive, physical, and psychological development. Therefore, consideration of specific factors such as severity, location, chronicity, psychosocial environment, and family impact is always confounded by the maturational level of the individual. Overall, evaluation of head trauma must be multidimensional, and this seems to be particularly true when that individual is a child.

The following review examines the current state and future direction of assessment, treatment, and research issues involved in the neuropsychological study of pediatric head trauma.

EPIDEMIOLOGICAL FACTORS

Traumatic brain injury is now the most common neurological disability (Kurtze, 1982). Although precise statistics regarding the incidence and prevalence of pediatric head trauma are not readily available due to the absence of a centralized information network, it is estimated that more than one million children sustain traumatic brain injuries annually, representing one-sixth of all pediatric hospital admissions (Levin, Benton, & Grossman, 1982).

Rivara and Mueller (1986) described a number of recent epidemiological studies that have attempted to utilize "standard and uniformly applied criteria for brain injury within specified populations" (p. 8). Fatal and nonfatal head injuries were examined, with head trauma being defined as evidence of brain dysfunction (i.e., neurologic signs, unconsciousness, etc.). There appeared to be a steady increase in accidents across age, peaking between 15 to 19 years, with boys' rates generally higher and more serious than that of girls. Accidents occurred for boys at a rate of 150 to 200 per 100,000 prior to age 5 increasing to more than 400 per 100,000 at age 15, compared to 100 to 170 per 100,000 for girls less than age 5 and over 300 per 100,000 at age 15 (Klauber et al., 1981). Two other studies, however, suggested that these rates declined somewhat for girls ages 5 to 15 (Annegers et al., 1980; Kraus et al., 1984).

Compared to adults, children have a lower mortality rate following severe closed head trauma (Bruce, Schut, Bruno, Woods, & Sutton, 1978). This statistic may be largely due to a difference in the type of accident most commonly incurred in each population. Motor vehicle accidents account for approximately 50% of nonpenetrating adult head injuries. In children, however, motor vehicle accidents account for only 33%, with falls comprising 50% (Levin, Eisenberg, Wiig, & Kobayashi, 1982). Childhood head injuries are more likely to be closed than penetrating (Boll & Barth, 1981; Spreen, Tupper, Risser, Tuokko, & Edgell, 1984). Children's head injuries are also less likely than those of adults to be evaluated by a neuropsychologist. Consequently, their actual consequences are underappreciated (Boll, 1983). Absence of neuroradiologic evidence of structural tissue damage may be misinterpreted as absence of damage. In cases of acceleration/deceleration, rotation, or other mild closed head trauma, the associated shearing, tension, and compression commonly produce neurocognitive deficits and associated psychological and behavioral disruption that are not apparent on computerized tomography (CT) or magnetic resonance imaging (MRI). Lesions involving the white matter of the brain secondary to shear-strain mechanical forces of closed head injury have been well documented (Levin, Benton, & Grossman, 1982).

The immediate primary damage may produce permanent residual deficit. Acute medical treatment is essential to minimize the effects of secondary damage (Pang, 1989). Effective prevention, from primary to tertiary, and treatment require educational and financial commitment to other than medical-surgical systems if long-term sequelae are to be reduced.

Rutter (1981), in his review of the pediatric psychological difficulties following severe head trauma, indicated that there was a definite correlation between premorbid and post-injury problems. He stated that his own findings were "striking in showing a strong relationship between children's pre-injury behavior and their psychiatric state at the 1-year follow-up," and that "pre-injury behavior was a strong predictor of children's psychiatric problems after severe head injury" (pp. 1539–1540). Significant disruption and compromise of central neuronal structure apparently resulted in exacerbation of preexisting psychological/psychiatric difficulties. A loss of cognitive function subsequent to head trauma only worsened the child's capacity to compensate for and effectively cope with the trauma (Begali, 1987). In addition, Rutter indicated that adverse psychosocial factors also influence eventual psychiatric outcome. The rate of psychiatric/behavioral disorders for head-injured children from psychosocially disadvantaged backgrounds was from 20 to 25%. Individuals from socioeconomic and family backgrounds that were not considered adverse, however, evidenced rates of less than 7%. Family support and cohesion, in conjunction with adequate social and economic resources, positively influenced eventual neurobehavioral outcome as well as psychological adjustment. Families frequently reacted negatively to the behavioral difficulties of a young head-injured member and/or oftentimes used denial in the form of unrealistic expectations for recovery (McGuire & Rothenberg, 1986). Although the dynamics of an individual family were unclear, the need for social support and professional intervention was evident.

Klonoff (1971) examined predisposing socioeconomic factors for head-injured children. Injuries were categorized as "slight" (i.e., those children who only visited an emergency room) or severe" (i.e., those subsequently admitted to the hospital). These two clinical groups were then compared with control subjects matched on the variables of age, sex, school grades, IQ (or school readiness scores), race, and geographical location. The control group was comprised of children who were obtained from educational settings within the Vancouver, Canada, school district. For both slight and severe head injuries, boys outnumbered girls by a ratio of 12:7. Most injuries occurred between the ages of 1 and 4.

Environmental factors—such as congested residency, lower-income housing, marital dysfunction of parents, and lower occupational functioning for fathers—were characteristic of the clinical groups. Falls were found to be the most frequent cause of trauma. Klonoff pointed out the need for a follow-up evaluation and further explanation of the variable of severity.

In summary, it appears as though psychosocial adversity negatively influences neurobehavioral outcome. Children who develop significant behavioral difficulties following severe brain injury may not receive the same quality of medical, academic, or vocational interventions as would a physically disabled individual without psychological sequelae. Staff and family members may naturally respond negatively to the inappropriate, disruptive child. Although therapeutic interventions can address these emotional and behavioral aspects of head trauma, broader treatment efforts should be targeted toward prevention in the psychosocially adverse climate from which the child initially emerged. Epidemiological data suggest that head-injured children coming from psychosocially disadvantaged backgrounds tend to develop more behavioral and psychiatric difficulties.

Identification of the sequelae of severe closed head injury sustained during childhood is an initial step toward efficacious treatment. Further research is needed to better understand premorbid risk factors and to develop more effective prevention as well as intervention strategies.

FACTORS INFLUENCING OUTCOME

Age

Although type, location, and severity of the head trauma are directly related to eventual neurobehavioral recovery, none of these variables has generated as much attention among neuropsychologists as the factor of age at injury. Childhood injuries create two sets of problems, both of which require responses from the medical, educational, and family systems: (1) the cognitive, physical, and psychosocial effects of the head trauma per se and (2) and dysfunctions related to developmental delays, arrests, and/or loss of previously achieved skills.

The developmental patterns of particular abilities must be considered when interpreting research findings and individual test results. If language has not been exhibited prior to injury, it is difficult to ascertain the extent of language disruption. The cerebral substrate for visual recognition memory occurs later than for verbal memory (Levin et al., 1988). Thus, the ontology of the cognitive ability must be considered. Deficits in the higher cognitive functions of reasoning, problem solving, abstraction, and symbol manipulation may not be apparent until adolescence.

Recovery from pediatric traumatic brain injury has been associated with the "plasticity" of the developing central nervous system (i.e., the capacity of the immature brain to recover, and possibly compensate for, trauma-related structural deficits). As early as Broca's investigation of speech centers in 1861, scientists noted preservation of speech in early childhood. The ability of the young brain to recover neurobehavioral functioning led to the development of *Kennard's Principle*. The brain appeared to place a premium on language functions, even at the expense of other competing abilities.

Harris (1957) attempted to examine age-related factors in an early report on childhood head injuries. He compared data from 150 children to that of 450 adults who were seen at the Royal Infirmary in Edinburgh, Scotland, from 1950 to 1954. The so-called postconcussional syndrome was relatively rare in the children (6%) compared to the adults (25%). Harris stated that "greater reorganization of the nervous functions appears to be possible in the child" (p. 488) and "recovery from brain injury is probably more rapid and complete the younger the individual." He continued: "It is interesting that if the brain injury occurred at an early age (before 2 years) and involved the left cerebral hemisphere, several of these patients became left-handed and developed speech normally" (p. 490). Thus, he suggested the theory of pediatric neural plasticity by noting what appeared to be children's capacity to recover cognitively better than adults.

Satz and Fletcher (1981) reviewed a number of issues relating to neurodevelopmental recovery of function, and aptly pointed out the pitfalls involved with this type of research. They criticized other authors (Chelune & Edwards, 1981; Pirozzolo, Campanella, Christensen, & Lawson-Kerr, 1981) for failing to account for interactive environmental factors in the recovery process. Satz and Fletcher also emphasized the different types of recovery possible following early brain trauma in their statement "theories of recovery must separate restoration of function (e.g., diaschisis) from reorganization of function (e.g., functional substitution)" (p. 856). They concluded that the term *plasticity* is much too generalized and nonspecifically applied. Unfortunately, neurocognitive sequelae are not as spontaneously remitting as such a simplistic interpretation might imply.

Brink, Garrett, Hale, Woo-Sam, and Nickel (1970) found that although some degree of plasticity was demonstrated in focal lesions, plasticity was unlikely to be demonstrated in diffuse closed head injuries. Age was also noted to affect the type of recovery pattern. The older, more neurodevelopmentally mature, child at the time of closed head injury, the better the functional prognosis.

Lyons and Matheny (1984) utilized the co-twin control method to examine the effects of age on neurobehavioral functioning following skull fracture. Monozygotic twins were administered the Wechsler Preschool and Primary Scales of Intelligence (WPPSI) at age 6 years. Parents rated their children on Personality/Temperament factors. One twin from each pair had suffered low-velocity skull fractures with brief periods of unconsciousness. Five patients were injured between 12 and 36 months old; the remaining eight were injured between 36 and 48 months of age. Results showed no significant differences for the group whose fracture occurred between 12 and 36 months old. Those sustaining injuries after 36 months of age performed significantly worse than their twin counterparts on four performance subtests. Results were interpreted as confirming "the notion of greater plasticity of cognitive functions in younger children" (p. 492).

The result of research on age-related recuperative processes following cerebral trauma is complicated by methodological difficulties and contradictory results. Neuropsychological treatment may have lagged far behind pediatric assessment because of the belief that the developing brain is plastic and that it can and will incorporate compensatory strategies independent of clinical intervention.

Severity

As early as 1932, Russell suggested that coma duration and post-traumatic amnesia were reliable indicators of severity. Richardson (1963) provided a relatively early account of the difficulty in determining the length of post-traumatic amnesia with children. Estimates of amnesia, and subsequent return of full consciousness, are often dependent on untrained observers, particularly emotionally biased family members.

Facco and associates (1986) explained the differential prognostic value of clinical data obtained shortly following severe head trauma in 49 children and 56 adults. Clinical outcome was assessed six months following severe injury (i.e., coma greater than six hours in the absence of intracranial hematomas). Subsequent mild disability was rated as a "good" outcome, and severe disability, vegetative state, or death was considered "poor" outcome. Outcome predictors included the Glasgow Coma Scale (GCS), posturing, oculocephalic and light reflexes, the presence of associated injuries, and the need for ventilator support. For adults, however, only posturing and oculocephalic and light reflexes were significantly related to outcome. Coma duration was evidently a good prognosticator for children, but not for adults. Ventilator support was found to be correlated with poor outcomes in children, but not for adults. Results indicated that "all clinical data recorded on admission proved to be significantly related to the outcome in children, excluding the presence of associated injuries" (p. 68). These authors concluded that different prognostic clinical data should be used for generating predictions for children than for adults.

Heiskanen and Kaste (1974) studied 36 children aged 16 and under in order to determine neurological and psychoeducational sequelae following severe head trauma (4- to 10-year follow-up). These authors reported that "after a coma lasting two weeks, a child is rarely able to succeed even moderately well at school, and more than half of the patients in this present study whose periods of unconsciousness exceeded two weeks were not able to continue in normal schools" (p. 13). They relied solely on clinical interviews with patients and their families to document coma duration. Stover and Zeigler (1976) examined the relationship between length of coma and functional recovery (e.g., return to preinjury levels with regard to ambulation, activities of daily living, in 36 boys and 12 girls aged 2 to 19). Those remaining in coma for seven days or longer had not returned to full preinjury status at a 2-year follow-up. However, some individuals remaining in coma for as long as three months reached a functionally independent status. In general, brain damage was positively correlated with impairments such that the more severely injured also seemed to require longer hospitalizations, more intensive therapeutic interventions, and longer rehabilitation. The full degree of impairment and eventual outcome in children is difficult to predict. Individual variability is compounded by the developmental level at the time of injury and the premorbid mastery of knowledge and skills. The level of previously acquired, residual abilities often influences the subsequent learning ability. Psychosocial adjustment is obviously age dependent as well, and may be similarly influenced by neurocognitive impairment.

More recently, Fletcher, Ewing-Cobbs, Miner, Levin, and Eisenberg (1990) examined the potential behavioral changes following closed head injury in children at 6 and 12 months post-injury. They incorporated objective, standardized measures of behavioral adjustment in a group of 45 children (ages 3 to 15 at the time of trauma) who were screened for premorbid psychiatric disturbances. Level of severity was strongly related to outcome. Compared to the mild and moderately injured subjects, those individuals with severe trauma experienced more social withdrawal as well as school-related difficulties when rated by their parents. The severely injured group also obtained more deficient adaptive behavior scores than did their mild or moderately injured cohorts. These results confirmed earlier studies that suggested that the more extensive the severity of initial brain damage, the more guarded the eventual outcome.

Location

A. R. Luria (1973) has described the importance of the prefrontal regions of the cortex as an area "in intimate communication with nearly every other principal zone of the cortex;" and that "portions of the frontal lobes are in fact a super-structure above all other parts of the cerebral cortex, so that they perform a far more universal function of general regulation of behavior" than other association areas (p. 89). Complex neurocognitive behaviors subserved by the frontal lobes include reasoning, problem solving, planning, and execution of goal-directed behaviors. Developmentally, these areas are thought not to reach full maturity until adolescence or early adulthood. Damage to these areas in early childhood may have far-reaching implications for eventual recovery and functional adaptation that may not be manifested for years. This interaction between early frontal lobe damage and arrested or retarded development of higher cognitive functions could be termed "the sleeper effect" (Rourke, 1983; Rourke, Fisk, & Strang, 1986).

The location of the damage also appears to be crucial in the determination of which particular aspects of language are transferred to contralateral right hemisphere zones. Rasmussen and Milner (cited in Kolb & Wishaw, 1985) utilized carotid sodium amytal interviews (WADA) and dichotic-listening tasks to study patients who sustained left hemisphere lesions early in life. They found the following: (1) extreme left anterior and posterior lesions did not result in a contralateral shift in language, (2) lesions that invaded both Broca's and Wernicke's areas resulted in the development of complete right hemisphere speech, and (3) large anterior left frontal and posterior left lesions were associated with deficits in language production. This study suggested the feasibility of associating function with structure by neuroradiologic scans.

Comparison of localized versus generalized head injuries with children of various ages revealed that scholastic achievement and cognitive measures were more impaired when the child sustained localized (i.e., involvement of only one hemisphere) head trauma prior to age 5. Subjects were studied immediately following recovery from post-traumatic amnesia, at 4 months, 1 year, and finally at 2¼ years post-injury. Apparently, potential for recovery depends not only on the stage of language development but also on the potential for interhemispheric transfer of information (Rutter, 1982; Chadwick, Rutter, Thompson, & Shaffer, 1981). As Fletcher, Miner, and Ewing-Cobbs (1987) indicated, "In children, recovery of function is an issue involving not only sparing and restoration of various behaviors, but also the complex issue of how growth and development proceed in an abnormal brain" (p. 289). Critical periods of vulnerability are factors to consider in pediatric traumatic brain injury.

Due to the time delay between early childhood injury and the realization of frontal lobe damage, difficulties often occur in adolescence when the planning, organization, direction, and initiation or inhibition of complex behaviors become critical to implementing the natural changes of adolescent development. This age/location interaction is particularly significant with the relatively late maturation of frontal demand. Failure to achieve subsequent neurocognitive stages may result in frustration and low self-esteem for the child. Formal psychometric assessment may reveal a downward pattern for the brain-injured individual relative to the expected progression of cognitive mastery levels of their noninjured peers. In other words, a child injured at age 5 or 6 may appear neurologically normal but fall behind classmates as they progress through the elementary grades. Furthermore, neurobehavioral deficits may be evidenced quite differently six months, one year, or five years post-injury. Psychological and cognitive interventions may therefore need to vary according to the time that has elapsed since the acute trauma.

Rourke (1988) has developed a model of dysfunction that suggests that interruption of fiber pathways may create a specific syndrome of nonverbal learning disabilities. The subtlety of this type of disability may not be detected by neuroradiologic studies or by traditional psychoeducational assessments. According to Rourke, deficits may be confined to the nondominant hemisphere due to that hemisphere's "greater dependence upon white matter functioning, especially with regard to its apparent specialization for the intermodal integration of novel stimuli" (p. 313). The amount of white matter destroyed, as well as the developmental stage at the time of injury, would appear to be crucial factors involved in determining the extent of impact on cognition and behavior. Individuals demonstrating this type of disability may be more vulnerable to depression and even suicide at a later age (Rourke, Young, & Leenaars, 1989). The socioemotional difficulties arising from right cerebral hemisphere dysfunction may be associated with increased risk for affective disorder. For example, the nonverbal learning disabled (NLD) child may not be capable of accurately assessing prosody. Due to visuospatial difficulty, this individual may not engage in appropriate exploration of the immediate physical and social environment. These authors suggested that such avoidance resulted in social isolation and emotional withdrawal. Neuropsychologists and other professionals working with the head-injured child need to recognize the possibility that this type of disturbance may manifest itself at a later time.

Chronicity

Chronicity of residual impairments implies that spontaneous recovery, the expected performance enhancement from rehearsal/practice effect, or learning of test-taking strategies with multiple sequential neuropsychological evaluations has not occurred.

Flach and Malmros (1972) examined 125 patients in a follow-up study that occurred 10 years after children sustained head injuries. Evaluations consisted of administration of the following measures: The Wechsler Adult Intelligence Scale (WAIS) or (Wechsler Intelligence Scale for Children (WISC), the Weigl-Goldstein-Sheerer Color Form Test, the Bender Gestalt Visual Motor Test, Fog and Hermann's Test of Aphasia, and a Digit Span test. In 57 patients (46%) these authors found disturbance of varying intensity, with the most frequent being "mental deterioration reflected by a reduced Performance IQ in Wechsler's intelligence tests and by a wide dispersion of the results of the subtests" (p. 15).

Klonoff, Low, and Clark (1977) conducted a five-year follow-up assessment of 231 pediatric head trauma cases (131 were below the age of 9 years old; 100 were above the age of 9 at the time of injury). This study has provided the most accurate information to date regarding long-term sequelae. Evaluation procedures included the Reitan-Indiana Neuropsychological Test Battery for children, intellectual measures, other neurocognitive procedures, a neurological examination, and EEG recordings. EEG recordings showed the most rapid recovery, whereas neuropsychological data suggested a much slower rate of improvement. Results indicated that by the fifth year, the majority (76.3%) of head-injured subjects evidenced significant neurobehavioral recovery, whereas the remaining 23.7% continued to demonstrate impaired neurocognitive performances. Presumably, then, the neuropsychological tests were more sensitive to subtle deficits. Neurological deficits that emerged during clinical examinations were least likely to evidence change over time. This study strongly suggested the importance of the assessment instrument as well as the time since injury in both treatment planning and in prognostic statements.

Cognitive Sequelae

McFie (1961) examined the relationship between localized lesions and intellectual impairment in children. His subjects ($n = 40$) ranged in age from 5 to 15 years. Localization information was obtained via pneumoencephalography, surgery or necropsy, and repeat EEGs. The etiologies and/or neuropathologies for these lesions were not reported. Tests administered included the Wechsler-Bellevue scales, WISC, Terman-Merrill Memory for Designs Test, and clinical interviews. He found that right hemisphere lesions, particularly right parietal lesions, were associated with impaired scores on the Memory for Designs Test. This author suggests that "more widespread cerebral regions are concerned in the development of this function in the child than in its later use by the adult" (p. 364). Cognitive sequelae following pediatric head trauma have included impaired memory and learning, visuoanalytic problem solving, and a slowed rate of information processing.

Brink, Garrett, Hale, Woo-Sam, and Nickel (1970) described a sample of 46 children who sustained head injuries leading to a coma duration of one week or more, examined approximately one to seven years post-injury. Subjects were between the ages of 2 and 18 years at the time of injury, although there tended to be a bimodal distribution of younger (ages 2 to 6) and older (14 to 18 years) children in their sample. Severity was assessed according to length of coma, with this sample evidencing an average of seven weeks and a median of four weeks. Psychological assessment consisted of administering and interpreting the Wechsler and Stanford Binet scales. In this study, coma duration was directly correlated with measured post-injury intellectual abilities. More specifically, the longer a child remained in coma, the lower their post-injury IQ scores.

These authors also pointed out that the "older patients (those over 10 years of age) achieved significantly higher scores than those in the younger group, most of whom were less than 6 years old at the time of injury" (Brink et al., 1970, pp. 567–568). This differentiation was apparently unrelated to the factor of severity, as the average coma duration was lower for patients in the younger group. It may well be that the adaptive abilities necessary for successful performance on typical intellectual measures were more ingrained over time and less resistent to disruption. Individuals who sustained head injuries later in life have also likely spent more quality time in appropriate academic environments. Many of the functions purportedly assessed by standard intellectual instruments (particularly verbal abilities) have been shown to correlate with number of years of formal education.

Levin and Eisenberg (1979) examined a series of 42 children and adolescents who sustained closed head injuries. Two age groups (6 to 12 years and 13 to 18 years) were evaluated on neurocognitive measures assessing language functions, learning and memory, somatosensory and motor capacities, as well as visuospatial abilities. These authors found support for the hypothesis that severity of injury (i.e., coma duration) was directly related to the extent of neurocognitive deficits observed. In general, acquired aphasia is followed by a more complete and rapid recovery in children than in adults. The typical adolescent neuropsychological deficit profile "indicated that impairment of storage and retrieval processes in learning and memory were the most common sequelae" (p. 290). Residual deficits in language, memory, visuospatial ability, and motor proficiency persisted in the more seriously injured patients.

In a prospective study of children who sustained head injuries, Chadwick, Rutter, Brown, Shaffer, and Traub (1981) evaluated 31 subjects with severe craniocerebral trauma and 29 with mild head injuries on a number of cognitive and intellectual measures. Severely impaired subjects were those whose injuries resulted in a post-traumatic amnesia (PTA) of at least seven days; mild head injuries were defined as those which resulted in a post-traumatic amnesia of between one hour and less than one week. These subjects were then matched to an orthopedic control group of 28 children. Evaluations were conducted at the 4-month, 1-year, and 2¼-year follow-up periods. Results from clinical groups indicated that timed measures of visuomotor and visuospatial functioning (e.g., WISC Performance subtests) evidenced greater impairment than did tasks of verbal functioning. These authors concluded that "severity of injury was found to exert a powerful influence not just on the degree and persistence of intellectual impairment but also on the speed and extent of recovery." They added that "the rate of recovery was most rapid in the few months immediately after the injury, but the recovery phase generally continued throughout the first year after the accident" (p. 60). With regard to performance, Chadwick and associates suggested that scholastic difficulties (e.g., reading accuracy), were persistently impaired following very severe head trauma.

Although children with mild and moderate traumatic brain injury may return to adequate levels of measured academic achievement more quickly, this does not mean that there are no long-term problems. Does this measured competence always translate into classroom competence? Impairments in learning ability may preclude use of stored academic skill and result in poor current learning even with adequate background skills. Furthermore, fatigue and irritability may well result in academic difficulty, feelings of discouragement, and general loss of self-esteem, which may become as large a burden as the effects of the injury.

Levin, Eisenberg, Wiig, and Kobayashi (1982) compared visual and verbal memory in a group of 15 children who sustained severe head trauma (less than 8 on the Glasgow Coma Scale) to a group of 15 adolescents matched for trauma severity. Subjects also were matched by gender, lesion, and lateralization. Instruments used to examine cognitive functions included the Selective Reminding Test, as well as a visual recognition memory test. Levin and colleagues found that children in the severely impaired range continued to evidence relative deficits in visual recognition memory. They suggested that adolescents may have used verbal mediation to recognize the recurring pictures. They noted, however, that the deficit of visual memory relative to verbal memory may be influenced by the nature of the instruments used rather than a pattern of particular deficits.

The Selective Reminding Test required recall over discrete trials, whereas the visual recognition memory test required sustained attention and comparison throughout the presentation of all stimuli. Long-term verbal memory deficits, however, appeared to be rather persistent in those children and adolescents who sustained severe head trauma initially, when compared with their age-matched mild or moderately compromised counterparts. Leven and colleagues (1982) concluded that "the severity of diffuse brain injury, rather than the presence or lateralization of a focal lesion, is the primary determinant of cognitive recovery in both children and adolescents," and that "the duration of impaired consciousness, rather than the initial Glasgow Coma Scale score, had the strongest relationship to cognitive outcome" (p. 672).

How do these results mesh with theories of plasticity? Levin and associates (1982) suggested that perhaps this apparent paradox could be explained by the child's brain being more holistic, less differentiated, and less specified, making it appear more resistant/resilient to focal damage but also more susceptible to diffuse, secondary damage. This theoretical stance supported the conclusion by Brink and colleagues (1970) that some degree of plasticity may be apparent in focal lesions, but the opposite relationship was found in diffuse closed head injuries.

Mahoney and associates (1983) also documented continued neurobehavioral improvement in a group of 34 children who sustained severe head injury (i.e., coma duration greater than 24 hours). Follow-up periods for 32 of the 34 subjects ranged from as soon as nine months after discharge from the hospital to as long as four years (mean of 21 months). Although group statistics regarding cognitive and intellectual data were not presented, these authors suggested that "in contrast to adults with severe trauma and prolonged coma, significant and even spectacular recovery is common, and vigorous management coupled with cautious optimism is indicated both during the acute phase and for many months thereafter" (p. 761). Most (31) of the subjects' full-scale intelligence quotient (FSIQ) were greater than 80 at follow-up, although 21 children displayed "some cognitive or behavioral difficulty" (p. 759). These IQ scores are certainly below average, and may well have represented a significant decline from a previously higher level of functioning.

Kaufman and colleagues (1985) assessed neuropsychological outcome from gunshot wounds to the head in four adults and two children approximately one year following injury. They found no differences in terms of recovery for adults versus children, and characterized the subjects as experiencing "moderate disability in which cognitive impairment and motor deficits were the major contributing factors" (p. 756). Further study with a sample size greater than six and a matched control group is warranted.

Bawden, Knights, and Winogron (1985) compared timed versus untimed performance on a group of 51 children who were subdivided according to level of severity (i.e. mild, moderate, and severe). Level of impairment was determined through the use of a "global index," including length of unconsciousness, presence or absence of neurological signs (including the use of CT and EEG data), and Glasgow Coma Scale scores. Subjects were matched on such variables as age, sex, and injury-to-testing interval. The neuropsychological measures utilized included portions of the Halstead-Reitan Test Battery for children, the Reitan Indiana Test Battery for young children, and the WISC-R. Tests were classified according to rate of speed required (low, moderate, and highly speeded measures). These authors found that severely head injured children demonstrated impairment on the performance portions of the WISC-R, but not on the verbal subtests. They concluded that "severely head-injured children performed significantly slower than mildly or moderately head-injured children on several tests of motor speed and on a test requiring motor speed as well as visual-spatial skills," and that they "exhibited a significantly lower score on the summary measure for the highly speeded tests than on the summary measure for the low speeded tests" (p. 50).

Filley, Cranberg, Alexander, and Hart (1987) reported on an archival study of 53 children and adolescents (18 years old or less) who sustained closed head injuries. Data for assessing long-term recovery was obtained by record review. They found duration of coma to be the most significant index of severity. The Glasgow Outcome Scale, school performance, and social and vocational functioning were utilized to determine recovery. These authors found that children who sustained diffuse injuries attained a more positive outcome than those children who sustained both diffuse and focal damage. Although follow-up evaluations demonstrated cognitive improvements, particularly with regard to Performance IQ, these authors indicated that their "findings are in accord with those of others showing lasting cognitive deficits" (p. 198).

It has been hypothesized that childhood deficits may not become apparent until a later developmental time. Clinical versus control longitudinal studies could compare subjects who were head injured during childhood to peers who were not, on measures that assess complex reasoning and abstract concept formation at childhood injury, adolescence, and adulthood.

IMPLICATIONS FOR ACADEMIC FUNCTIONING

If one measure of a successful adult rehabilitation program is vocational reintegration, then the parallel measure for a child is academic reintegration. The relative success of such an endeavor depends not only on previously discussed factors such as premorbid functioning, age at injury, severity and location of the injury, and so on but rehabilitation also depends on environmental resources. The school system may seek professional consultation with regard to assessment, recommendations for cognitive remediation, and assistance with behavioral management. Educators, parents, and rehabilitation specialists need to coordinate expectations and programs for the child or adolescent who returns to the classroom following significant craniocerebral injury.

Researchers interested in the sequelae of pediatric head trauma have recognized the importance of individualized treatment planning in the classroom for quite some time. Shaffer, Bijur, Chadwick, and Rutter (1980) examined the issue of reading disability following head trauma. They studied 98 British children who sustained unilateral compound depressed skull fractures with associated dural tear and neuronal damage. Subjects were interviewed and examined at least two years post-injury utilizing the Wechsler Intelligence Scale for Children as well as an analysis of reading ability. One-third of the clinical sample evidenced a reading level approximately two years below their chronological age at the time of the assessment. This considerable lag in reading ability was also related to post-traumatic seizures in boys. The authors concluded that children who have had a severe or complicated head injury are in need of careful monitoring, particularly for later reading difficulties. The schools must be staffed and funded to provide individualized treatment (Ewing-Cobbs, Fletcher, & Levin, 1986; Begali, 1987). Flexible placement in the local school is important in the traumatic brain-injured population because of the characteristically more dramatic intraindividual differences in deficits and skill levels and the varying rates of recovery.

Haas, Cope, and Hall (1987) studied 80 patients sequentially admitted to a California Medical Center for inpatient rehabilitation following severe, blunt head trauma. Patients had been in a coma for at least six hours. Previous records were then examined for evidence of "poor scholastic achievement," which was defined as two or more failed subjects in one semester, school dropout, or a premorbid diagnosis of learning disability. Results indicated that poor scholastic achievement was associated with severity of head trauma. The authors hypothesized that children with poor academic achievement may have engaged in more risk-taking behaviors, and thereby increased their chances of sustaining head trauma. Furthermore, "both the rate and the degree of the recovery process may be affected by premorbid limitations in academic performance" (p. 55). Haas and colleagues suggested that preventive measures for children identified as at risk may be more important than treatment programs after the fact.

FAMILY IMPACT

Clinical observation made in the rehabilitation setting confirms the importance of the family as support system in the long-term neurobehavioral recovery and adjustment following traumatic head injury. Relatively little is known from an empirical standpoint regarding family adjustment to stages of recuperation in the young head-injured patient. Added to a decrease in frustration tolerance and social judgment, the changes in the victim from premorbid attitudes and behavior may produce considerable stress for the entire family. The increase in irritability, impulsivity, forgetfulness, distractibility, fatigue, apathy, is a strain on all interpersonal relationships (Boll, 1983; Martin, 1988). This stress may manifest itself in a family's unwillingness to make arrangements for discharge or in later caregiver stress. There are many points on a continuum of minimal to maximal family support and involvement. The rehabilitation team must be sensitive to and supportive of the functioning of the family constellation as a critical factor in the success of the long-term recovery process (McGuire & Rothenberg, 1986).

The initial reaction of parents following the traumatic head injury of a child is typically denial, panic, fear, and anxiety. Casey, Ludwig, and McCormick (1987) found that "parents did not feel competent enough to judge the severity of the child's injury," although "parental anxiety was correlated with perceived severity, and those parents who could not rate the injury's severity were most likely to be anxious" (p. 162). These authors concluded that parental concerns often remained unrecognized by the attending medical professionals. The medical stabilization of the child is necessarily the focus of intervention immediately following an injury. Support for the family is a secondary consideration in the acute phase. Professional guidance in the form of family psychotherapy and counseling may be recommended. In the rehabilitation and chronic adjustment phases, family support and education regarding the cognitive and behavioral sequelae are often available through organizations such as a local chapter of the National Head Injury Foundation.

Families move through various psychological stages of recovery much like the individual grief process. These stages consist of initial reactions of shock, denial, and anger, and gradually over time move from bargaining and depression to acceptance and adjustment (Kubler-Ross, 1969). Not all families will move through all stages, and it would seem as though eventual psychological acceptance of the child's limitations and adjustment of the family system would depend on the overall emotional health and stability of the family prior to the crisis. Blazyk (1983) states that "for the family, the crisis associated with head injury begins almost immediately" and that "reactions occur within the family which may have long-term effects on their eventual adjustment to this event" (p. 58). In order to promote healthy, optimal adjustment within the family, early intervention in the form of emotional support and education regarding pediatric head injury may be an important piece of the total treatment picture. However, the reality of family responsibility for a severely compromised child may be perceived as overwhelming. Management of behavioral problems may tax or exceed current special education and vocational rehabilitation facilities.

The psychological dynamics of a family's experience do not occur in isolation. McGuire and Rothenberg (1986) reported that the staff may experience discrepancies between realistic expectations and the parents' hopes. Denial and/or anger are common grief reactions associated with traumatic brain injury. By achieving a greater understanding of the nature and typical recovery factors involved with pediatric head trauma, educators and clinicians may facilitate family adjustment to support the recovery and rehabilitation process.

Rosenthal (1984) has outlined a number of family intervention methods that are most appropriately utilized in the rehabilitation setting. He described four major components: (1) education to promote improved family understanding of the patient's limitations; (2) counseling to help the family cope with the physical, cognitive, and behavioral losses, to express uncomfortable feelings, and to encourage acceptance; (3) psychotherapy, which is particularly indicated in premorbidly dysfunctional families; and (4) family support groups. Rosenthal also suggested training family members as therapists, although great care must be taken to ensure that family patience, love, and affection are not diminished.

Waaland and Kreutzer (1988) recently reviewed the literature on family reactions to pediatric head trauma. They indicated that there was little published on either the family system sequelae or on appropriate family treatment effectiveness. Based on their clinical experience, these authors suggested a treatment plan for the relatives, friends, and significant others involved in the acute as well as the chronic care. The ideal plan would incorporate the following aspects: (1) increasing the coping skills and adaptive abilities of parents through clinical intervention; (2) providing substantial education to parents and families regarding the typical cognitive, behavioral, and academic sequelae following pediatric head trauma; (3) increasing the availability of social support networks; (4) addressing the informational and emotional needs of siblings; (5) becoming an advocate for both the parents and child in the educational system; and (6) allowing for the opportunity of extended care, particularly as the impaired child reaches new developmental demands requiring additional individual and family adjustment. This appears to be a comprehensive, practical approach to the complex and multidimensional problems of traumatic brain injury in childhood.

Finally, it is clear that the family is an extremely important factor involved with the eventual neurobehavioral recovery. Further research is necessary to evaluate the following factors: rate of recovery in relation to emotional adjustment of the family; premorbid family functioning versus outcome; assessment of differential response rates to various family based interventions; pre- and post-injury role changes within the families; and a more detailed delineation of "typical" stages of family recovery. By treating the families of the head-injured victims, we will be effectively treating the young patients themselves.

REMEDIATION OF DEFICITS

Prior to the institution of any therapeutic program that intends to address cognitive and intellectual deficits with children, it is essential that the process begin with a careful neuropsychological examination. The therapist must first delineate individual neurocognitive strengths and weaknesses in order to design appropriate treatment strategies.

Relatively little is known regarding cognitively based intervention techniques for children following head trauma. Outcome studies assessing similar treatment with adult populations have met with limited success, particularly with more severely impaired individuals (Prigatano et al., 1984; Ryan & Ruff, 1988). Developmental and maturational issues make evaluation of pediatric treatment even more complex than evaluation of adult treatment. For example, the remediation of adult deficits consists of retraining lost functions and teaching adaptive coping mechanisms. Children may not have acquired a particular skill or functional ability by the time of injury. Treating information processing deficits in the school-aged child, for instance, may be more aptly termed *cognitive training* rather than *retraining*. Lost functions cannot be identified until the child has achieved the age at which it is reasonable to expect performance of developmentally appropriate tasks. Thus, such training/retraining actually needs to continue throughout maturation.

Rourke and colleagues (1986) described "three outstanding tasks that should be addressed before an efficacious program of academic remediation is implemented for the brain-impaired child" (p. 159). The initial step consists of a thorough and reliable neuropsychological (versus purely psychoeducational) evaluation. Then, these test results should be translated into an individualized academic treatment program. The third task consists of clear, concise communication of the test results and the academic remediation program of the child's parents, teachers, and others involved with the immediate care. In the absence of empirically proven cognitive training techniques with children, this approach would seem to be the most practical and effective strategy currently available to professionals.

All too often, children who sustain head injuries are classified as learning disabled (Ewing-Cobbs et al., 1986). Although it is obvious that cognitive deficits secondary to the head trauma negatively affect learning, the label of learning disability does not accurately describe the etiology or sequelae of craniocerebral damage. A separate category may be needed that is conceptually different from LD, MR, and ED special education diagnoses. This may also emphasize to teachers that a special and individualized approach needs to be taken with youngsters who have sustained head injuries, which may be different from the curriculum for children with learning disabilities.

Finally, it may be important to draw the distinction between cognitively based treatment provided in the hospital setting versus the longer-term interventions in the academic setting. Acute care cognitive training, particularly during the first six months post-injury, should probably follow the model of restitution of function (Rothi & Horner, 1983). That is, during the initial natural recovery phase, "lost" or impaired information processing abilities should be stimulated while cerebral edema decreases and vascularization of damaged areas improves. During the later phases of recovery, treatment typically centers on academic reintegration and compensation from a functional perspective for impaired and developmentally retarded abilities.

SUMMARY

Overall, it appears as though the psychological and neuropsychological dynamics of pediatric head trauma are imperfectly understood. Our knowledge of the mechanism and sequelae of childhood craniocerebral trauma increases as research continues. Epidemiological statistics indicate that psychosocial adversity is a significant risk factor for injury and a complication for recovery. Other factors that seem to be crucial in determining the child's eventual neurobehavioral outcome include the family integrity, socioeconomic environment, age at which the trauma occurs, type and location of trauma, and, most importantly, the severity of the injury. These variables are not discrete, but rather interact in a complex fashion.

Some researchers suggested that the immature brain exhibits some degree of functional flexibility, or "plasticity." Research has shown that some degree of plasticity may be associated with focal lesions, the opposite finding occurred in relation to more diffuse closed head injuries: The older the child at the time of the injury, the better the prognosis.

Typically, neurocognitive deficits found following significant head trauma in childhood include impairments in the areas of memory, new learning, spatial problem solving, reading, and a slowed rate of information processing. These deficits have far-reaching implications for social, academic, and, eventually, vocational integration. Unique and specialized intervention programs need to be developed for both the child and the family during the acute crisis, the rehabilitation process, and the chronic/adjustment phase. Monitoring and supervision may be necessary throughout the developmental changes of the maturational process.

Pediatric head trauma has reached a level of serious concern. This may be true for several reasons. First, although recovery of cognitive and intellectual functions may proceed well into the fifth year post-injury, deficits may remain in comparison to their premorbid expectations and to their noninjured peers. Children with head injuries may, with varying degrees, lose the potential to learn. As their peers continue to develop and advance normally, the head-injured child may remain intellectually static, thereby experiencing a relative decline. In addition, pediatric head trauma is a significant future concern because the deficits children may exhibit later may be "hidden" on first inspection. In fact, impairments in frontal lobe functioning may not be detected until the developmental demands for independence and self-initiated academic, social, and vocational performance challenge the child. A confounding problem is the increased risk of further injury due to behavioral and psychological difficulties such as impulsivity, disinhibition, decreased concentration, and poor judgment. The possibility of subsequent head injuries tends to increase.

Finally, although our understanding of pediatric head trauma has expanded over the past 15 years, we have a responsibility to the children, their families, and society to increase our understanding and research database. This point takes on a special significance when one considers the hidden deficits and maturational challenges of these impaired children. This should be accomplished on both individual and programmatic levels. Clinicians and educators are now left with the burgeoning problems of social, academic, and vocational integration. As professionals, they must assume the responsibility for the development, implementation, and comparative efficacy of appropriate intervention and treatment strategies. Clinical research efforts must now be directed to these areas at the same time preventive measures are undertaken on a large-scale basis through widespread education.

REFERENCES

Annegers, J.F., Grabow, J.D., Kurland, L.T., & Laws, E.R. (1980). The incidence, causes and secular trends in head trauma in Olmstead County, Minnesota, 1935–1974. *Neurology, 30*, 912–919.

Bawden, H.N., Knights, R.M., & Winogron, H.W. (1985). Speeded performance following head injury in children. *Journal of Clinical and Experimental Neuropsychology, 7* (1), 39–54.

Begali, V. (1987). *Head injuries in children and*

adolescents: *A resource and review for school and allied professionals.* Brandon, VT: Clinical Psychology Publishing.

Bigler, E.D. (1988). The neuropsychology of hydrocephalus. *Archives of Clinical Neuropsychology, 3,* 81–100.

Blazyk, S. (1983). Developmental crisis in adolescence following severe head injury. *Social Work in Health Care, 8,* (4), 55–67.

Boll, T.J. (1988). Minor head trauma in children: Out of sight but not of mind. *Journal of Clinical Child Psychology, 12,* 74–80.

Boll, T.J. (1983). Neuropsychological assessment of children. In Karoly, P. (Ed.), *Handbook of child health assessment: Biopsychosocial perspectives.* New York: Wiley.

Boll, T.J., & Barth, J.T. (1981). Neuropsychology of brain damage in children. In Filskov, S. & Boll, T.J. (Eds.), *Handbook of clinical neuropsychology.* New York: Wiley.

Brink, J.D., Garrett, A.L., Hale, W.R., Woo-Sam, J., & Nickel, V.L. (1970). Recovery of motor and intellectual function in children sustaining severe head injuries. *Developmental Medicine and Child Neurology, 12,* 565–571.

Bruce, P., Schut, L., Bruno, L.A., Woods, J.H., & Sutton, L.N. (1978). Outcome following severe head injury in children. *Journal of Neurosurgery, 48,* 679–688.

Casey, R., Ludwig, S., & McCormick, M. (1987). Minor head trauma in children: An intervention to decrease functional morbidity. *Pediatrics, 80,* (2) 159–164.

Chadwick, O., Rutter, M., Brown, G., Shaffer, D., & Traub, M. (1981). A prospective study if children with head injuries: II. Cognitive Sequelae. *Psychological Medicine, II,* 49–61.

Chadwick, O., Rutter, M., Thompson, J., & Shaffer, D. (1981). Intellectual performance and reading skills after localized head injury in childhood. *Journal of Child Psychology and Psychiatry, 22,* 117–139.

Chelune, G.J., & Edwards, P. (1981). Early brain lesions: Ontogenetic-environmental considerations. *Journal of Consulting and Clinical Psychology, 49,* (6), 777–790.

Diller, L. (1987). Neuropsychological rehabilitation. In Meier, M., Benton, A., Diller, L.

(Eds.), *Neuropsychological rehabilitation.* New York: Guilford Press.

Ewing-Cobbs, L., Fletcher, J.M., Levin, H.S. (1986). Neurobehavioral sequelae following head injury in children: Educational implications. *Journal of Head Trauma Rehabilitation, 1,* (4), 57–65.

Facco, E., Zuccarello, M., Pittonia, G., Zanardi, L., Chiaranda, M., Davia, G. & Giron, G.P. (1986). Early outcome predictions in severe head injury: Comparison between children and adults. *Child's Nervous System, 2,* 67–71.

Filley, C.M., Cranberg, L.D., Alexander, M.P. & Hart, E.J. (1987). Childhood and adolescence. *Archives of Neurology, 44,* 194–198.

Flach, J., & Malmros, R. (1972). A long-term follow-up study of children with severe head injury. *Scandinavian Journal of Rehabilitative Medicine, 4,* 9–15.

Fletcher, J.M., Miner, M.E., & Ewing-Cobbs, L. (1987). Age and recovery from head injury in children: Developmental issues. In Levin, H.S., Grafman, J., & Eisenberg, H.M. (Eds.), *Neurobehavioral Recovery from Head Injury.* New York, NY: Oxford University Press.

Fletcher, J.M., Ewing-Cobbs, L., Miner, M.E., Levin, H.S., Eisenberg, H.M. (1990). Behavioral changes after closed head injury in children. *Journal of Consulting and Clinical Psychology, 58* (1), 93–98.

Haas, J.F., Cope, D.N., & Hall, K. (1987). Premorbid prevalence of poor academic performance in severe head injury. *Journal of Neurology, Neurosurgery, and Psychiatry, 50,* 52–56.

Harris, P. (1957). Head injuries in childhood. *Archives of Disease in Childhood,* 488–491.

Heiskanen, O., & Kaste, M. (1974). Late prognosis of severe brain injury in children. *Developmental Medicine and Child Neurology, 16,* 11-14.

Jennett, B., & Teasdale, G. (1977). Aspects of coma after severe head injury. *Lancet, 1,* 878–881.

Kalsbeek, W.D., McLaurin, R.L., Harris, B.S., & Miller, J.D. (1980). The National Head and Spinal Cord Injury Survey: Major findings. In Anderson, D.W. and McLaurin, R.L. (Eds.), *Report on the National Head and Spinal*

Cord Injury Survey. Bethesda, MD: National Institutes of Health.

Kaufman, H.H., Levin, H.S., High, W.M., Childs, T.L., Wagner, K.A., & Gildenbery, P.L. (1985). Neurobehavioral outcome after gunshot wounds to the head in adult citizens and children. *Neurosurgery, 16* (6), 754–758.

Klauber, M.R., Marshall, L.F., and Barett-Connor, E. (1981). Prospective study of patient hospitalizations with head injury in San Diego County, 1978. *Neurosurgery, 9,* 236–241.

Klonoff, H. (1971). Head injuries in children: Predisposing factors, accident conditions, accident proneness and sequelae. *American Journal of Public Health, 61,* 2405–2417.

Klonoff, H., Low, M.D., & Clark, C. (1977). Head injuries in children: A prospective five year follow-up. *Journal of Neurology, Neurosurgery, and Psychiatry, 40,* 1211–1219.

Kolb, B., & Whishaw, I.Q. (1985). *Fundamentals of human neuropsychology* (2nd ed.). New York: W.H. Freeman.

Kraus, J.R., Black, M.A., and Hessol, N. (1984). The incidence of brain injury and serious impairment in a defined population. *American Journal of Epidemiology, 119,* 186–201.

Kubler-Ross, E. (1969). *On death and dying.* New York: Macmillan.

Kurtze, J.F. (1982). The current neurologic burden of illness and injury in the United States. *Neurology, 32,* 1207–1214.

Lees-Haley, P. (1986). Earnings regression analysis: Proving a child's lost earnings. *Trial,* 37–38.

Levin, H.S., Benton, A.L., & Grossman, R.G. (1982). *Neurobehavioral consequences of closed head injury.* New York: Oxford University Press.

Levin, H.S., & Eisenberg, H.M. (1979). Neuropsychological outcome of closed head injury in children and adolescents. *Child's Brain, 5,* 281–292.

Levin, H.S., Eisenberg, H.M., Wigg, E.R. & Kobayashi, K. (1982). Memory and intellectual abilities after head injury in children and adolescents. *Neurosurgery, 11* (5), 668–672.

Levin, H.S., High, W.M., Swing-Cobbs, L., Fletcher, J.M., Eisenberg, H.M., Minor, M.E.,
and Goldstein, F.C. (1988). Memory functioning during the first year after closed head injury in children and adolescents. *Neurosurgery, 22,* 1043–1052.

Luria, A.R. (1973). *The working brain: An introduction to neuropsychology.* New York: Basic Books.

Lyons, M.J. & Matheny, A.P. (1984). Cognitive and personality differences between identical twins following skull fractures. *Journal of Pediatric Psychology, 9* (4), 485–494.

Mahoney, W.J., D'Souza, B.J., Haller, J.A., Rogers, M.C., Epstein, M.H. & Freeman, J.M. (1983). Long-term outcome of children with severe head trauma and prolonged coma. *Pediatrics, 71* (5), 756–762.

Martin, D.A. (1988). Children and adolescents with traumatic brain injury: Impact on the family. *Journal of Learning Disabilities, 21,* 464–470.

McFie, J. (1961). Intellectual impairment in children with localized post-infarctile cerebral lesions. *Journal of Neurology, Neurosurgery, and Psychiatry, 24,* 361–365.

McGuire, T.L., & Rothenberg, M.B. (1986). Behavioral and psychosocial sequelae of pediatric head injury. *Journal of Head Trauma Rehabilitation, 1* (4), 1–6.

Pang, D. (1989). Physics and pathophysiology of closed head injury. In Lezak, M.D. (Ed.), *Assessment of the behavioral consequences of head trauma* (pp. 1–17). New York: Alan R. Liss, Inc.

Pirozzolo, F.J., Campanella, D.J., Christensen, K., & Lawson-Kerr, K. (1981). Effects of cerebral dysfunction on neurolinguistic performances in children. *Journal of Consulting and Clinical Psychology, 49* (6), 791–806.

Prigatano, G.P., Fordyce, D.J., Zeiner, H.K., Roueche, J.R., Pepping, M., & Wood, B.C. (1984). Neuropsychological rehabilitation after closed head injury in young adults. *Journal of Neurology, Neurosurgery, and Psychiatry, 47,* 505–513.

Richardson, F. (1963). Some effects of severe head injury: A follow-up study of children and adolescents after protracted coma. *Developments in Medicine and Child Neurology, 5,* 471–482.

Rivara, F.P., & Mueller, B.A. (1986). The epidemiology and prevention of pediatric head injury. *Journal of Head Trauma Rehabilitation, 1* (4), 7–15.

Rosenthal, M. (1984). Strategies for intervention with families of brain- injured. In Edelstein, B.A. & Coutoure, E.T. (Eds.), *Behavioral assessment and rehabilitation of the traumatically brain damaged*. New York: Plenum Press.

Rothi, L.J., & Horner, J. (1983). Restitution and Substitution: Two Theories of Recovery With Application to Neurobehavioral Treatment. *Journal of Clinical Neuropsychology, 5* (1), 73–81.

Rourke, B.P. (1983). Reading and spelling disabilities: A developmental neuropsychological perspectaive. In U. Kirk (Ed.), *Neuropsychology of language, reading and spelling*. New York: Academic Press.

Rourke, B.P. (1988). The syndrome of nonverbal learning disabilities: Developmental manifestation in neurological disease, disorder, and dsyfunction. *the Clinical Neuropsychologist, 2* (4), 293–330.

Rourke, B.P., Fisk, J.L., & Strang, J.D. (1986). *Neuropsychological assessment of children: A treatment-orientated approach*. New York: Guilford Press.

Rourke, B.P., Young, G.C., & Leenaars, A.A. (1989). A childhood learning disability that predisposes those afflicted to adolescent and adult depression and suicide risks. *Journal of Learning Disabilities, 22* (3), 169–175.

Russell, W.R. (1932). Cerebral involvement in head injury. *Brain, 55,* 549.

Rutter, M. (1981) Psychological sequelae of brain damage in children. *The American Journal of Psychiatry, 138* (12), 1533–1544.

Rutter, M. (1982). Developmental neuropsychiatry: Concepts, issues, and prospects. *Journal of Clinical Neuropsychology, 4* (2), 91–115.

Rutter, M., Chadwick, O., & Shaffer, D. (1983). Head injury. In Ruter, M. (Ed.), *Developmental Neuropsychiatry* (pp. 83–111). New York: Guilford Press.

Ryan, T.V., & Ruff, R.M. (1988). The efficacy of structured memory retraining in a group comparison of head trauma patients. *Archives of Clinical Neuropsychology, 3* (2), 165–179.

Satz, P., & Fletcher, J.M. (1981). Emergent trends in neuropsychology: An overview. *Journal of Consulting and Clinical Psychology, 49* (6), 851–865.

Shaffer, D., Bijur, P., Chadwick, O.F.D., & Rutter, M.L. (1980). Head injury and later reading disability. *Journal of the American Academy of Child Psychiatry, 19,* 592–610.

Spreen, O., Tupper, D., Risser, A., Tuokko, H., & Edgell, P. (1984). *Human developmental neuropsychology*. New York: Oxford University Press.

Stover, S.L., & Zeiger, H.E. (1976). Head injury in children and teenagers: Functional recovery correlated with the duration of a coma. *Archives of Diseases in Childhood*.

Waaland, P.K., & Kreutzer, J.S. (1988). Family response to childhood traumatic brain injury. *Journal of Head Trauma Rehabilitation, 3* (4), 51–63.

Woods, B.T., & Teuber, H.L. (1973). Early onset of complimentary specialization of cerebral hemispheres in man. *Transactions of the American Neurological Association, 98,* 113–117.

7

INTRACRANIAL TUMORS

RAYMOND K. MULHERN

The routine availability of neuropsychologists to children with brain tumors has only recently been accomplished. Traditional patterns of referral prior to the 1970s centered on the neurosurgeon/radiation oncologist relationship. With the development of comprehensive pediatric cancer clinics at major university medical centers, and the increasing role of chemotherapy given at these centers in the treatment of malignant brain tumors, it is now more commonplace for these children to be exposed to an interdisciplinary team approach, which includes neuropsychologists. As a consultant to the child's treating physician, the psychologist will commonly address questions relating to the patient's current functional status, the relationship of neuropsychological deficits to tumor location and associated factors such as hydrocephalus, the potential for recovery of function and rehabilitative recommendations following treatment, as well as the patient's and family's acceptance of the child's diagnosis and their adjustment to the child's treatment.

Because the number of children with brain tumors is relatively small and only 50% are treated at comprehensive centers (Duffner, Cohen, & Freeman, 1985), even large centers may take several years to accumulate enough patients to complete a clinical trial comparing different treatment approaches. Similar difficulties in patient accrual limit our neuropsychological knowledge of these patients. Generally speaking, published studies have followed the sequence illustrated in Figure 7.1, in which global descriptions of patients have been gradually replaced by more disease-and treatment-specific findings. Within this process, changes in the

This work was supported in part by the American Lebanese Syrian Associated Charities (ALSAC). Correspondence concerning this article should be addressed to Raymond K. Mulhern, Division of Behavioral Medicine, St. Jude Children's Research Hospital, Memphis, Tennessee 38101.

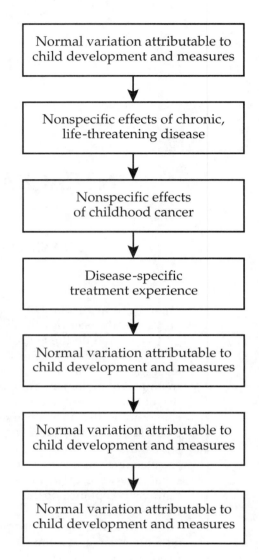

FIGURE 7.1 Conceptual progression of neuropsychological research with pediatric patients treated for brain tumors.

child's neuropsychological status that could be attributed to factors other than central nervous system (CNS) abnormalities, such as the effects of chronic disease in general, must be ruled out. This chapter will review the current neuropsychological literature on pediatric patients with brain tumors, including relevant epidemiology and medical therapies. Since the ability to identify particular chronic disabilities and specific groups at high risk for impairment is recent, there is a serious deficiency of empirical papers that have examined rehabilitative methods. A major conclusion of this review is that accelerated efforts are needed to define effective neuropsychological interventions with these children.

MEDICAL BACKGROUND

Brain tumors in children account for approximately 20% of all childhood malignancies, second only to the leukemias in terms of incidence. Annually, between 1,200 and 1,500 children below the age of 16 will be newly diagnosed. The approximate incidence is 2.4 per 100,000 in the general population of similarly aged children (Duffner et al., 1985; Leviton, 1984). The diagnosis of brain tumors peaks between the ages of 3 and 9 years, with a slightly greater risk in males than females (1.2:1). Brain tumors are quite heterogeneous in terms of site and histology; pediatric patterns do not reflect those found in adult patients.

For the sake of convenience, tumors are globally described as occurring above (supratentorial) or below (infratentorial) the tentorium, a membrane separating the cerebral hemispheres from the cerebellum. In the first six months of life and in the second decade of life, supratentorial tumors are more common than infratentorial tumors. Overall, only 15 to 25% of all pediatric brain tumors originate in the cerebral hemispheres. Common histological subtypes associated with various tumor locations are shown in Table 7.1.

Although the infratentorial volume accounts for only 10% of the total intracranial volume, 50 to 55% of childhood brain tumors originate in this area. Over 70% of all cerebellar tumors are diagnosed in the childhood years. Brain stem tumors account for an additional 10 to 15% of childhood tumors; approximately 75% of all brain stem tumors are diagnosed in childhood.

The etiology of primary pediatric brain tumors is unknown. However, *secondary* tumors of the central nervous system are noted 10 to 15 years following treatment for other pediatric malignancies such as leukemia. Greatest risk for these tumors is associated with previous cranial radiation therapy.

Presenting Signs and Symptoms

There are no pathognomonic signs for brain tumors. The presenting signs and symptoms depend on tumor location but are also found in other neurologic and

TABLE 7.1 Common Pediatric Brain Tumor Locations and Histologies

Domain	Region	Common Tumor Histologies
Supratentorial	Cerebral hemispheres	Astrocytoma
	Lateral ventricles	Carcinoma
	Hypothalamus	Astrocytoma
	Optic chiasm	Glioma
	Suprasellar	Craniopharyngioma
	Pineal	Pinealoma
Infratentorial	Cerebellum	Medulloblastoma
	Brain stem	Glioma
	4th ventricle	Ependymoma

nonneurologic diseases. Cohen and Duffner (1984) have summarized neurologic symptoms of brain tumors, dividing symptoms into those that are nonspecific and those that are localizing.

Among the most common nonspecific signs are those secondary to increased intracranial pressure (hydrocephalus), most often because of tumor obstruction of the flow of cerebral spinal fluid within the ventricles of the brain. Irritability, lethargy, diplopia, vomiting, headache, and unexplained changes in behavior and personality may occur. Longstanding hydrocephalus may result in optic atrophy with permanent visual loss and mental retardation. The syndrome of obstructive hydrocephalus is most often observed in children with midline tumors of the cerebellum that occlude the fourth ventricle. Vomiting may also occur through direct stimulation of the floor of the fourth ventricle by tumor invasion. Projectile vomiting is rare. Because of the frequent presenting features of headache and vomiting, many children with brain tumors are initially treated as if they have a flu-like illness. Headache location is not necessarily helpful in terms of differential diagnosis, although headache and vomiting shortly after awakening is often associated with intracranial tumor. Behavioral changes—including lethargy, declining school performance, and social withdrawal—may also be noted.

Localizing Signs and Symptoms

Common localizing signs and symptoms, adapted from the discussion by Duffner and associates (1985), are presented in Table 7.2. As neurologists, these authors have focused on overt manifestations of tumor invasion of normal brain structures as evidenced by clinical neurologic exam or by results of laboratory studies. Neuropsychological findings are discussed separately later in this chapter.

Among the most frequently observed signs associated with brain stem tumors are cranial nerve abnormalities (e.g., facial paresis), including ocular motor signs such as esotropia. For cerebellar tumors, ataxia (the classic staggering and wide-based gait) is the most commonly observed sign. Tumors of the third ventricle region may be manifested by growth abnormalities such as precocious puberty secondary to disruption of the hypothalamic-pituitary axis. Visual loss because of invasion of the optic chiasm may also be noted in tumors of this region. Tumors of the cerebral hemispheres are accompanied by seizures in approximately 30% of cases. Sensory and motor signs contralateral to the tumor location may be observed. Declines in school performance are common.

Neuro-Imaging

From the point of view of medical management, computerized tomography (CT) has had a revolutionary effect on the treatment of patients with brain tumors, allowing for the identification of tumors in the absence of localizing signs and without dangerous and invasive procedures such as angiography and pneumoencephalography (Packer, Zimmerman, & Bilaniuk, 1986). Increased precision in imaging can suggest specific tumor types as well as the source of increased

TABLE 7.2 **Neurologic Signs and Symptoms of Localizing Value in Pediatric Brain Tumors**

Tumor Region	Signs and Symptoms
Brain Stem	Cranial neuropathies Long tract signs Ataxia Ocularmotor dysfunction
Cerebellum	Truncal ataxia Appendicular ataxia Scanning speech Hypotonia Nystagmus toward involved hemisphere
3rd Ventricle Region	Visual acuity loss Endocrinopathies Personality changes
Cerebral Hemispheres	Hemiparesis Hemisensory loss Cognitive changes Seizures Visual field abnormalities

intracranial pressure, if present (Finlay & Goins, 1987). Magnetic resonance imaging (MRI) is increasingly available to patients suspected of brain tumors with the advantages of even greater sensitivity than CT without requiring the patient to receive the ionizing irradiation that accompanies CT studies. Intravenous contrast solutions will occasionally be used with CT and MRI to further enhance the images. An illustration of concurrent CT and MRI preoperative findings for the same child are shown in Figure 7.2.

Electroencephalography (EEG), brain stem auditory evoked potentials (BAEP), visual evoked potentials (VEP), and somatosensory evoked potentials (SEP) are also used to help localize the extent of tumor invasion on the basis of neurologic function of the patient. All neuro-imaging and EEG-based assessments are usually conducted prospectively to monitor patient status and tumor progression or regression in response to treatment.

PRINCIPLES OF MEDICAL MANAGEMENT

Surgery

Primary medical treatment of pediatric brain tumors involves surgery, radiation therapy, and, more recently, chemotherapy. Although some low-grade tumors may be successfully cured with surgery alone, most tumors will require a multimodality approach to therapy. In addition to the insult to the CNS caused by the

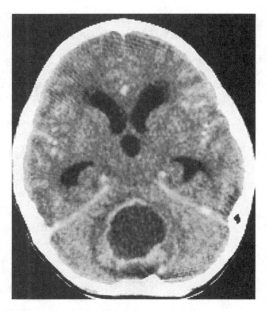

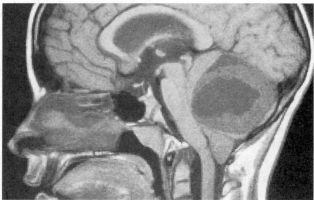

FIGURE 7.2   Transverse computed tomography
(CT) scan (left panel) and sagittal magnetic
resonance imaging (MRI; right panel) of a 10-year-
old boy with a midline cerebellar tumor.
Following surgery, the tumor was staged as a
medulloblastoma, the common malignant tumor
of childhood.

tumor and associated pathology such as hydrocephalus, each therapeutic modality is associated with recognized risks of sensory, motor, and cognitive deficits.

Until the 1970s, the operative morbidity and mortality for pediatric brain
tumors was extremely high, at least partially because of aggressive attempts to

obtain maximal tumor resection in the absence of any other potentially curative therapy. The more recent use of stereoscopic microsurgery, bipolar coagulation forceps, and especially lasers (CO_2, Nd:YAG) have allowed for decreased patient morbidity and greater precision of resections. The ultrasonic surgical aspirator emulsifies tumor at the tip, allowing selective tissue removal depending on water content. CT-directed stereotactic biopsy enables tissue sampling from exquisitely sensitive structures, such as the brain stem, that would not otherwise be approachable without considerable mortality. Despite these technical advances, the neurosurgeon provides curative therapy for the minority of patients with brain tumors.

Radiation Therapy

Ionizing irradiation will be necessary, in some form, for most children with malignant brain tumors. Delivered in one or more fractions per day, fields may encompass the tumor region only, a wide local field may be used, or, for highly malignant tumors, irradiation is given to the entire neuraxis with a "boost" to the tumor location (Kun, 1984). In cases of cranial irradiation, total doses may reach 55 Gy, a level two to three times higher than that given to children with leukemia who require CNS irradiation. As with neurosurgery, radiation therapy has experienced significant recent improvements in technology. Most recently, the linear accelerator has enabled greater accuracy in delivering irradiation to the desired field with less absorption by surrounding bone. Hyperfractionated irradiation, used to maximize tumor kill and reduce trauma to surrounding normal brain, is now under investigation. The implantation of radioactive pellets to the tumor, known as brachytherapy, remains experimental. Because of the late cognitive sequelae noted with high-dose cranial irradiation to be discussed latter, recent efforts have been made to reduce the dose in patients who are at lower risk for occurrence and to use chemotherapy as an adjunctive treatment to delay, minimize, or avoid the use of radiation therapy.

Chemotherapy

Chemotherapy is the most recent addition to the armamentarium of those treating pediatric brain tumors. As with other pediatric malignancies, multiple agents are usually used in combination or sequentially to maximize tumor kill. Short-term complications (e.g., nausea and vomiting) are common. Some active agents, such as cisplatin, also have significant long-term toxicities in interaction with radiation therapy such as progressive hearing loss and diffuse encephalopathy (Duffner et al., 1985).

With contemporary treatment approaches that combine the therapeutic modalities of chemotherapy, radiation therapy, and surgery, survival remains quite variable and depends largely on tumor histology and, secondarily, tumor location. For less aggressive tumors—such as low grade astrocytomas, craniopharyngiomas, and optic and hypothalamic gliomas—the five-year survival rates generally exceed 70%. On the other hand, cerebellar medulloblastoma, the single most common tumor of childhood, can be cured in only 30 to 60% of the cases, depending on presenting features such as metastasis at diagnosis. At the most discouraging end of the survival spectrum are high-grade gliomas, such as glioblastoma multiforme, and infiltrating tumors of the brain stem, which are rarely cured (Kun, 1984).

Late Physiologic Toxicities

The normal elements of the CNS of the child with a brain tumor are at risk for damage secondary to medical treatment of the tumor. Surveys have found that 25 to 30% of surviving patients have clinically significant visual (optic atrophy, hemianopsia), auditory, and motor disabilities (hemiparesis, ataxia) or seizures that grossly affect their performance of age-appropriate activities of daily living (Mulhern, Crisco, & Kun, 1983). Short stature, due to irradiation of the spine, or growth hormone deficiency, due to irradiation of the hypothalamic-pituitary axis, is not an uncommon problem in long-term survivors. Perhaps more than most other clinical populations, close attention should be focused on these somatic toxicities in the interpretation of neuropsychological testing performance, especially with older children who have learned to mask sensory and motor deficiencies through behavioral compensation. Unexpected changes in intracranial pressure, toxic reactions to multiple seizure medications, and the acute but reversible effects of chemotherapy and irradiation make otherwise reliable assessments more difficult.

NEUROPSYCHOLOGICAL PERSPECTIVES

Unlike some other neurologically based childhood disorders, formal neuropsychological testing has played only a minor role in the primary identification of patients with brain tumors. Most psychologists will first encounter these patients postsurgically, although aggressive recruitment may permit assessment of children who are in no acute distress prior to surgical intervention. Nevertheless, major treatment centers will have almost invariably determined that the child has a brain neoplasm, will have a fairly precise notion of tumor location and extent based upon CT and MRI, and may even know the tumor histology based on tissue obtained from biopsy or surgical resection *before* neuropsychological consultation is requested. How, then, is the role of neuropsychology defined in such a setting?

At our center, all patients are referred within one to two weeks of their surgery, often conducted elsewhere, and children are prospectively followed until they are 5 years or more from the completion of therapy. The overinvoked medical phrase "This kid looks great" is no longer a rationale for not referring patients for routine neuropsychological evaluation. By seeing virtually all patients treated at our center, we avoid the selection biases of referring physicians that might occur if we did not see consecutively diagnosed children. Over this prolonged period of contact, we are perceived as the experts in assessing the cognitive-behavioral status of the patient, in associating neuropsychological changes with the patient's tumor status and its treatment, and in making remedial and rehabilitative recommendations to the patient's treating physician and family.

RISK OF INTELLECTUAL IMPAIRMENT

We have recently completed an extensive review of the literature that summarizes 21 empirical studies of the neuropsychological status of children treated for brain neoplasms (Mulhern, Hancock, Fairclough, & Kun, 1992). An analysis of these studies by disease and treatment factors that place children at risk for neuropsychological impairments follows. Refer to Tables 7.3 and 7.4 for assistance during the discussion.

The vast majority of neuropsychological studies of children with brain tumors have used IQ as the primary outcome measure. At least in part, this seems to be a result of initial intentions to describe the global cognitive status of the child without attempts to assess discrete relationships between neuroanatomic location and neuropsychologic function. More recently, studies of children with temporal lobe and cerebellar tumors have begun to focus on more site-specific effects (Carpentieri & Mulhern, 1993; Cavazzuti, Winston, Baker, & Welch, 1980; Mulhern, Williams, LeSure, & Kun, 1986), and these will be discussed separately.

Radiation Therapy

The goal of radiation therapy is the selective destruction of malignant cells. Irradiation produces intracellular ionization that causes DNA damage and cell death within the first or second attempt at division. Cells of more rapidly growing normal organ systems are therefore most vulnerable to the adverse side effects of radiation therapy (Kun, 1984). Radiation therapy is given usually in daily fractions to maximize the ratio of tumor to normal cell kill.

In the content of pediatric brain tumors, irradiation-induced encephalopathies are a major interest area for neuropsychologists. Although acute and subacute irradiation side effects such as anorexia, confusion, and somnolence are reversible within weeks of stopping treatment, late CNS effects may be irreversible if not progressive. Radiation damage to the normal tissues of the central nervous system may manifest as cortical atrophy, vascular damage (mineralizing microangiopathy), or white matter destruction (leukoencephalopathy). Areas of involvement are invariably associated with the field and dose of irradiation delivered. However, correlation of neuro-imaging abnormalities and neuropsychological abnormalities are not consistently high, except in extremely debilitated patients. This enhances the value of neuropsychological testing in clinical settings.

Of the 21 studies in Table 7.3, 17 have examined the effects of radiation therapy on the intellect of long-term survivors of pediatric brain tumors. Of these 17

TABLE 7.3 Summary of Presenting Features and Results of Studies of Intellect in Long-Term Survivors of Pediatric Brain Tumors

Study	Sample Size*	Patient Age at Treatment (yr)	Tumor Location+			Radiation Therapy Effect	Age at Treatment Effect	Time Since Treatment Effect
			CH	3V	PF			
Bordeaux et al. (1988)	14	5–16	5	2	7	No	NR‡	NR
Cavazzuti et al. (1983)	35	2–NR	0	35	0	No	NR	NR
Cavazzuti et al. (1980)	20	6–33	20	0	0	NR	NR	Yes
Clopper et al. (1977)	20	2–16	0	20	0	NR	NR	NR
Danoff et al. (1982)	38	1–16	3	23	12	Yes	Yes	NR
Duffner et al. (1988)	16	2–16	4	6	6	Yes	Yes	NR
Duffner et al. (1983)	10	1–16	0	0	10	Yes	NR	Yes
Ellenberg et al. (1987)	43	1–15	5	16	22	Yes	Yes	NR
Hirsch et al. (1979)	59	0–2	0	0	59	Yes	NR	Yes
Hirsch et al. (1989)	42	1–15	42	0	0	NR	NR	NR
Kun et al. (1983)	30	2–16	7	8	15	Yes	No	Yes
Kun & Mulhern (1983)	18	2–15	6	1	11	No	No	Yes
LeBaron et al. (1988)	15	1–15	0	0	15	No	NR	Yes
Mulhern et al. (1989)	14	1–3	3	3	8	Yes	NR	NR
Mulhern et al. (1988)	7	5–15	7	0	0	NR	Yes	Yes
Mulhern & Kun (1985)	26	2–15	8	7	11	Yes	Yes	NR
Mulhern et al. (1986)	6	3–8	0	0	6	No	NR	Yes
Packer et al. (1989)	32	2–18	0	3	29	Yes	Yes	Yes
Riva et al. (1989)	15	3–15	0	0	15	Yes	NR	NR
Silverman et al. (1984)	9	3–25	0	0	9	Yes	Yes	NR
Spunberg et al. (1981)	13	0–2	2	3	8	No	NR	NR

*Includes only those patients with psychological testing.
+CH = cerebral hemisphere, 3V = third ventricle, PF = posterior fossa.
‡NR = Not reported.

investigations, 11 concluded that cranial irradiation had an adverse effect and 6 failed to find negative effects of radiation therapy on IQ. Among the 11 studies finding adverse effects, 6 used formal statistical procedures, whereas 4 concluded adverse effects based on clinical judgment and descriptive data only. Statistical procedures were utilized in 4 of the 6 studies that failed to find that radiation therapy placed the patient at risk for IQ changes.

The deleterious effects of radiation therapy have been demonstrated using a variety of designs, primarily comparing the presence versus absence of brain irradiation or comparing brain fields/volumes irradiated; no studies relating irradiation dose to IQ toxicity were noted. Serial studies of irradiated patients, as well as comparisons between irradiated and nonirradiated patients and between irradiated patients and normal controls have all concluded that radiation therapy has adverse effects on intellectual development. Two studies have also demonstrated greater decrements among children receiving whole brain (cranial) irradiation compared to those receiving only a localized field of treatment (Ellenberg et al., 1987; Kun et al., 1983).

Age at Treatment

Seven of the nine investigations that have examined the relationship between age at diagnosis and IQ found that a younger age at diagnosis was related to lower level of intellectual function. This is presumably because of the increased vulnerability of the rapidly developing structures of the CNS of young children. The association is difficult to specify because of variation in the definition of "younger." Some investigators were defined young children as those below 3, 6, 7, 7.5, and 8 years. Statistically significant age effects were reported in three of these seven studies (Ellenberg et al., 1987; Mulhern & Kun, 1985; Packer et al., 1989). The relationship between age at diagnosis and IQ level reported in the other investigations was purely descriptive. Of the two studies that did *not* find age at diagnosis to be related to intellectual functioning, one found a significant relationship between age at diagnosis and selective attention, with younger children performing more poorly than older children (Kun & Mulhern, 1983).

Time Since Treatment

The relationship between time since treatment and intellectual level was evaluated longitudinally by eight studies. Serial follow-up permits examination of time-lagged treatment effects as well as patient recovery of function (Mulhern et al., 1983). Three investigations found a statistically significant decline in intellectual functioning over time from preirradiation to over 4 years post-treatment. However, in one investigation this was only true for those patients receiving cranial (whole brain) irradiation and those irradiated at a younger age (Packer et al., 1989). Kun and Mulhern (1983) reported that at 3 to 70 months postirradiation, subnormal intellectual functioning was evident in 9 of 18 patients. Some 10 to 23 months later, full-scale intelligence quotients (FSIQs) were stable in 12 patients, improved in 3, and deteriorated in 3. Some 6 to 23 months later, FSIQ was stable in 8 and improved in 1 patient. No tests of significance were performed to analyze this trend. Similarly, Kun and colleagues (1983) evaluated patients following surgery before irradiation and again 10 to 26 months later, following irradiation. At the second evaluation, 2 patients were improved, 5 stable, and 3 deteriorated with regard to intellectual status.

Mixed results were found within three investigations. Cavazzuti and associates (1980) found improvements in verbal memory functioning over time for patients with right temporal tumor evaluated postoperatively and declines in verbal memory functions for patients with left temporal tumors evaluated postoperatively. Ellenberg and colleagues (1987) reported a significant rise in IQ from 1 to 4 months postdiagnosis, which declined thereafter. This relationship appeared to be mediated by tumor location. Finally, Mulhern and Kun (1985) evaluated patients post surgery but preirradiation and again 6 months after irradiation. The relationship between time since treatment and intellectual ability varied for older versus younger children: Younger children evidenced a greater decline over time in memory functioning than older children. Furthermore, among the older children, females showed more improvement than males over time on Full-Scale, Verbal, and Performance IQ.

Tumor Location

Ellenberg and associates (1987) examined the IQ scores of the third ventricular region, posterior fossa region, and cerebral hemisphere region brain tumor patients at four time intervals. Although the IQ scores of patients with hemispheric tumors were lower than those with third ventricular and posterior fossa tumors over all time intervals, this difference was only significant at the 4-month postdiagnosis evaluation, perhaps due to small sample sizes at the other intervals. Mulhern and associates (1985) found a greater *increase* in IQ scores over time for patients with posterior fossa tumors than for those with third ventricle region or hemispheric region tumors but this relationship held for only for younger children. Kun and colleagues (1983) found that a greater proportion of children with hemispheric than posterior fossa tumors showed clinical deterioration of IQ following irradiation.

Hydrocephalus

The association between chronic hydrocephalus and mental retardation is well documented. However, the effects of episodic and temporary increases in intracranial pressure are not well understood. Of the four studies that examined the relationship between hydrocephalus and intellectual deficit, three found nonsignificant results (Danoff et al., 1982; Kun et al., 1983; Mulhern et al., 1985). In contrast, Ellenberg and colleagues (1987) reported that patients with a history of hydrocephalus scored significantly lower than those without, both initially and at 4 months. However, an improvement in IQ over the 3-month interval was noted both for patients with and without a history of hydrocephalus. This investigation also compared patients with hydrocephalus who had normalization of intracranial pressure without ventriculoperitoneal shunts to those who required shunting. No significant IQ differences existed between these groups initially. At the 4-month interval, a significant IQ increase was noted for those patients with shunts but not for those patients without shunts.

Surgical Resection

In recognition of the potential damage to normal brain structures that may accompany surgical exploration and tumor resection, several investigators have analyzed the effects of surgery on IQ. Of the nine studies that examined the relationship between surgical resection and level of intellectual functioning, only two compared the differential effects of various levels of aggressiveness of surgery on IQ. Ellenberg and colleagues (1987) found no significant differences in mean IQ for groups of patients who received gross total resection and those who received partial surgical resection or biopsy only. Similarly, Cavazzuti and associates (1983) found no differences between IQ or memory quotients in patients undergoing radical tumor resection versus those undergoing biopsy, cyst aspiration, or shunting. However, it was reported that memory quotient *improved* after shunting or evacuation of cyst and radiotherapy. Although IQ was within normal limits for both groups, scores on sorting tasks were lower among radically resected patients.

Of the seven studies that evaluated overall surgical effects, two found no ill effects on IQ (Cavazzuti et al., 1983; Hirsch et al., 1989) and one noted improvements in the test scores of some patients following surgery (Cavazzuti et al., 1983). The results of the other investigations were mixed because the postoperative declines in intellectual functioning were not discussed separately from irradiation effects, chemotherapy effects, and/or tumor location.

Sensory and Motor Impairments

The impact of visual, auditory, and motor impairments secondary to the brain tumor and its treatment has seldom seen analyzed with reference to IQ performance. Cavazzuti and colleagues (1983) assessed 35 long-term survivors of craniopharyngioma: 18 had received conservative surgical procedures followed by local field radiation therapy and 17 had received aggressive attempts at gross total resections. Among the 17 patients with aggressive surgery were two subgroups, those whose tumors that never recurred and those whose tumor recurred, requiring second surgery and irradiation. Although no permanent visual impairments were noted among irradiated and nonirradiated patients without recurrence, one-third of the patients requiring repeat resection had clinically relevant visual impairments. No statistically significant differences between the IQ values of the three groups were noted with all group mean scores falling in the normal range for age.

Mulhern and associates (1985) reported on the sensory and motor status of 26 children with a variety of malignant tumors. Some 25% of the patients had one or more significant visual, auditory, or motor deficits. Although no statistically reliable correlation between these deficits and IQ was found, 5 of the 6 patients with IQ <80 were visually impaired.

Multivariate Analyses of Intellect

The discussion of patient- and treatment-related risk factors for IQ deficits has thus far assumed that these factors operate independently; however, such factors as dose and field of cranial irradiation are highly dependent on tumor location and histology. Only one investigation has attempted to analyze risk factors in combination, primarily because of the large sample size needed for such an analysis. Ellenberg and colleagues (1987) serially evaluated 43 consecutively diagnosed children with brain tumors at the Children's Hospital of Los Angeles. Multiple regression analyses used IQs at 1 to 4 years of follow-up as the criterion variables. The following factors, listed in descending order of importance, were significant univariate predictors of lower IQ: (1) lower IQ at 1 month postdiagnosis, (2) younger age at diagnosis, (3) cranial (whole brain) radiation therapy field, and (4) cerebral hemisphere tumor site. The authors also found a statistically significant interaction between age at diagnosis and radiation therapy field: Younger children receiving local or no cranial irradiation had higher IQs than comparably treated older children, whereas younger children receiving whole brain irradiation had lower IQs than comparably treated older children.

NEUROPSYCHOLOGICAL IMPAIRMENTS

Several studies have utilized formal measures of neuropsychological functioning in addition to IQ testing. Broadly speaking, the measures can be categorized into those measuring higher conceptual abilities, those assessing specific memory functions, and those assessing visual-motor, visuo-graphic, or fine motor functions (Table 7.4).

Problems with cognitive flexibility and problem-solving skills, as measured by the Category Test and Trails Test, have been noted by LeBaron and associates (1988) among 15 children treated for posterior fossa tumors. These deficits were presumably secondary to irradiation of their cerebral hemispheres as opposed to dysfunction related to the tumor itself. Riva and associates (1989) also evaluated 8 children previously treated for posterior fossa medulloblastoma with surgery and radiation therapy, as well as 7 children treated for posterior fossa astro cytoma with surgery alone. The Trail-Making Test (Forms A and B) and a computer-administered Continuous Performance Test of vigilance were given to all patients. Both groups of patients performed significantly worse than sibling controls on Trails but not the Continuous Performance Test. The authors propose that tumor or surgically related disturbance of the ascending reticular activating system was the common mechanism for observed deficits in attentional abilities because of the close neuroanatomic proximity of these structures to the posterior fossa.

Cavazzuti and colleagues (1980, 1983) have extensively evaluated long-term survivors of temporal lobe tumors as well as patients with craniopharyngioma. In the first study (Cavazzuti et al., 1980), 20 children with temporal lobe tumors (left hemisphere = 10, right hemisphere = 10), were evaluated with the Weschler Memory Scale and Wisconsin Card Sorting Test. Of the 20 patients, 19 displayed cognitive disturbances commonly associated with both dominant and nondominant cerebral hemisphere insults. Pre- to postoperative improvements in verbal memory were noted in most patients with right temporal lobe tumors; however, all these patients performed worse after surgery on measures of nonverbal memory. Two patients demonstrated preoperative impairment of frontal lobe function as measured by the Wisconsin Card Sorting Test, which persisted postsurgery. Among those patients with left temporal lobe tumors, verbal memory problems following surgery seemed inversely proportional to the severity of these deficits seen prior to surgery but most showed some deterioration. Most patients with left temporal lobe tumors had improvement in nonverbal memory function following surgery.

More recently, Carpentieri and Mulhern (1993) found auditory-verbal memory dysfunction among children irradiated for dominant and nondominant temporal lobe tumors. The investigators suggest that radiation therapy scatter to the temporal lobe contralateral to the tumor may explain such memory impairments. Dennis and colleagues (1991) extensively studied performance on recognition, content, and sequence memory tasks among 43 children surviving brain tumors in various regions. Although a high proportion had memory scores in the clinically deficient range, no predictor variables except verbal IQ were identified.

Using the same tests as in their earlier study, Cavazzuti and colleagues (1983) examined patients who had been treated for craniopharyngioma, a common tumor of the suprasellar region, with radical surgical resection using a subfrontal approach or with conservative surgery and local irradiation. Memory function and IQ were equivalent in both groups but patients who received radical surgical resection showed significantly more preservative responses on the Wisconsin Card Sorting Test.

Three independent investigations using either the Halstead-Reitan Neuropsychological Battery (Duffner et al., 1983; LeBaron et al., 1988) or the Luria-Nebraska Neuropsychological Battery (Mulhern et al., 1988) with survivors of posterior fossa tumors have found common problems associated with cerebellar insults. A high frequency of visual-motor and visuo-spatial deficits as well as problems with fine and gross motor steadiness, speed, and coordination were noted. These deficits are probably associated with cerebellar dysfunction secondary to tumor and/or surgical resection. Specific tests of visual-motor functions have also been given independently of these batteries (e.g., Developmental

TABLE 7.4 Summary of Common Methods of Assessment of Pediatric Patients with Brain Tumors

Study	Sample Size	Time Since Treatment (yr)	Psychological Tests Administered		
			Intellect	Emotional Adjustment	Neuropsychological
Bordeaux et al. (1988)	14	1–2	McC, W		
Cavazzuti et al. (1983)	35	1–19	B, W		WCS
Cavazzuti et al. (1980)	20	0–1	W		WMS, WCS
Clopper et al. (1977)	20	2–20	W		
Danoff et al. (1982)	38	1–21	W		
Duffner et al. (1988)	16	0–3	SB, McC, W		
Duffner et al. (1983)	10	1–6	SB, W		HRNB
Ellenberg et al. (1987)	43	1–4	B, McC, W		
Hirsch et al. (1979)	59	2–11	NEMI, W		
Hirsch et al. (1989)	42	1–17	NR		
Kun et al. (1983)	30	0–5	McC, W		

154

Study	N	Age range	Intelligence	Personality/Behavior	Neuropsychological
Kun & Mulhern (1983)	18	0–10	McC, W	PIC	
LeBaron et al. (1988)	15	4–9	W	PIC	
Mulhern et al. (1988)	14	0–5	B, McC	CBCL	WMSS, HRNB
Mulhern & Kun (1985)	7	2–7	W		
Mulhern et al. (1986)	26	0–1	McC, W	PIC	
Packer et al. (1989)	6	1–7	KABC	PIC	
Riva et al. (1989)	32	0–2	B, SB, W		LNNB
Silverman et al. (1984)	15	0–9	W		VMI
Spunberg et al. (1981)	9	3–8	W		CPT, TMT
	13	5–20	McC, W	PHSCS, CAT, TAT	BVMGT

B—Bayley Scales of Infant Development
BRVAT—Benton Revised Visual Retention Test
BVMGT—Bender Visual-Motor Gestalt Test
CAT—Children's Apperception Test
CBCL—Child Behavior Checklist
CPT—Continous Performance Test
HRNB—Halstead-Reitan Neuropsychological Battery
KABC—Kaufman Assessment Battery for Children
LNNB—Luria-Nebraska Neuropsychological Battery
McC—McCarthy Scales of Children's Abilities

NEMI—Nouvelle Echelle Metrique de l'Intelligence
PHSCS—Piers-Harris Self-Concept Scale
SB—Stanford-Binet Intelligence Test
TAT—Thematic Apperception Test
TMT—Trials Making Test
W—Wechsler Intelligence Scale
WCS—Wisconsin Card Sort
WMS—Wechsler Memory Scale
WMSB—Wisconsin Motor Steadiness Battery

Test of Visual-Motor Integration, Wisconsin Motor Steadiness Battery, Bender Visual Motor Gestalt Test) with similar findings. Packer and associates (1989) reported poor performance on these tasks among irradiated children with malignant posterior fossa tumors as well as nonirradiated children with benign posterior fossa tumors. Spunberg and colleagues (1981) reported that 12 of 13 children with posterior fossa tumors had deficient visual-motor skills.

At least one report has been made of the role of neuropsychological testing in the process of diagnosis of a brain tumor (Mulhern et al., 1986). In this case report, a 10-year-old boy had successfully completed his treatment for leukemia 5 years previously. He had been followed with annual neuropsychological evaluations as part of an institutional study of the late cognitive effects of treatment for leukemia. On the basis of an abnormal sensory-perceptual exam, the patient was referred for neuro-imaging. Specifically, the child had exhibited normal tactile perception of his right digits with marked imperception on the left, implicating the right parietal lobe posterior to the precentral gyrus. A subsequent CT scan revealed a right posterior parietal brain tumor as a second malignancy.

EMOTIONAL ADJUSTMENT

Seven studies have examined the emotional adjustment of pediatric brain tumor patients. Maladjustment was not statistically evaluated in any of the early studies, but the results generally indicated at least some increase in social-emotional problems in this patient population. Mulhern and Kun (1985) found that at an initial evaluation, 50% of patients showed behavioral disturbances not representative of their premorbid functioning; 42% were still identified as disturbed at a second evaluation several months later. Kun and colleagues (1983) have reported a significant trend toward psychotic symptomatology among pediatric patients with brain tumors. The authors also observed that even patients evaluated prior to irradiation had a high incidence of adjustment problems. After subtotal supratentorial or cranial irradiation, 9 of 12 patients continued to evidence abnormal social-emotional functioning, and 1 of the patients manifested new behavioral problems after local irradiation to the posterior fossa. Similarly, 56% of patients evidenced clinically significant disturbances in another investigation in which psychotic symptomatology was noted in 4 of 15 patients (LeBaron et, al., 1988). LeBaron and associates (1988) found that the behavior problems reported most frequently included somatic complaints, social withdrawal, and depression. One-third of his patient sample received scores deviant enough to warrant clinical intervention. Another investigation using projective measures of emotional functioning found that although these patients had no severe emotional disturbances, they evidenced poor planning and organizational skills as well as a passive-dependent and immature personality styles (Spunberg et al., 1981).

Mulhern and associates (1988) found evidence of organic personality syndrome in two of seven patients treated for temporal lobe tumors. These patients were characterized as having significant problems with seizure control and learning problems in school. Relatively few studies have examined the potential impact of poorly controlled seizures or the toxicity of multiple anticonvulsant therapy on emotional adjustment in these patients. However, similar concerns for children with seizures in the absence of a brain tumor have frequently been expressed (Bourgeouis et al., 1983; Ellenberg, Hertz, & Nelson, 1986).

More recent and better controlled studies have given a more favorable picture of the emotional adjustment of children after treatment. Mulhern and colleagues (1993) compared the acute emotional adjustment of children recently diagnosed with brain tumor to that of children with other cancers and found no difference in the incidence of behavior problems, although both groups exceeded normative expectations. Carpentieri and colleagues (1993), in a follow-up study, again found no difference in behavior problems between children with brain tumors and other cancers at two years postdiagnosis. However, the children with brain tumors had more difficulties in school-related activities and overall social competence. Regression analyses for behavior problems revealed that sociodemographic factors, tumor location, and tumor volume were predictive of more difficulties.

SCHOOL PERFORMANCE

Not surprisingly, many children treated for brain tumors will have school-related problems. Among children treated for posterior fossa tumors, academic achievement problems may relate to slow psychomotor speed or from the effects of radiation therapy on other structures remote to the tumor (LeBaron et al., 1988). Silverman and associates (1984) and Mulhern and Kun (1985) report an obvious decline in mathematical skills among children receiving whole brain irradiation in the absence of reading or spelling disabilities. The latter study suggested that this may have been secondary to the diminished attentional and concentration abilities also observed in these patients.

Spunberg's (1981) long-term follow-up of infants who had been treated for brain tumors revealed that 6 of 13 eventually required self-contained special educational classes. This is a higher incidence than that noted by Kun and colleagues (1983) in a review of 30 children treated for tumors at various ages. In the Kun and colleagues (1983) series, 10 children were in special education, most commonly self-contained classrooms for the learning disabled.

In at least one of the preceding investigations, declining IQ in parallel with declining academic achievement over time prompted the learning disability placements (Mulhern & Kun, 1985). This is most often observed as a slowing in the rate of acquisition of new knowledge relative to age-appropriate expectations rather than because of a loss of previously acquired knowledge or skills. Duffner and associates (1983) reported that virtually all of their 10 children treated for malignant posterior fossa tumors with cranial irradiation had significant school problems. Of the 10, 4 maintained normal IQ levels for age but had not been able to achieve commensurate with their normal age peers.

SUMMARY

Neuropsychological testing for children with brain tumors has become routine at most major cancer centers. However, because of low incidence and significant heterogeneity among patients in terms of tumor location, age at onset, and therapeutic interventions, it has been difficult to develop individual series with sufficient numbers of patients to result in definitive statements. Our present review of intellectual, emotional, neuropsychological, and school functioning of pediatric patients treated for brain tumors does, however, suggest that children with malignant tumors are at substantial risk for dysfunction in each of these psychological domains.

Gross sensory and motor deficits secondary to the tumor or surgical approaches to tumor resection may result in functional impairment with or without concurrent cognitive deficiencies. Changes in psychometric intelligence may be observed acutely following surgery but are more frequently noted several months to years following the completion of radiation therapy. With respect to intellect, emotional adjustment, and school functioning, a consistent pattern of risk factors has emerged surrounding the use of irradiation: Children who are preschool age or younger, those with supratentorial tumors, and those who receive supratentorial and/or whole brain radiation therapy are at greatest risk for dysfunction.

Formal neuropsychological studies of these patients are few but suggest that for children with cerebellar tumors, chronic problems with motor steadiness and visual-motor coordination are common. Deficiencies in higher cognitive abilities, including those commonly associated with frontal lobe functions, have also been observed in children with cerebellar tumors, presumably because the fields of radiation therapy encompassed substantial portions of their cerebral hemispheres. Since 30% or fewer children diagnosed with brain tumors will have tumors located in the cerebral hemispheres, knowledge about their neuropsychological status as long-term survivors has been severely limited. Children with dominant and nondominant temporal lobe tumors exhibit similar deficits in verbal and nonverbal memory function that one would expect in generalizing from the adult literature.

The studies reviewed here give some insight into the quality of life of children surviving brain tumors. Recently, Mostow and associates (1991) compared long-term survivors of pediatric brain tumors to their siblings in terms of their activities of daily living. Compared to siblings, former patients had a significantly higher incidence of unemployment, chronic health condition, and inability to drive an automobile. Former patients with a history of tumors of the cerebral hemispheres and radiation therapy were at greatest risk for problems with the demands of everyday living.

CONCLUSIONS AND RECOMMENDATIONS

Patient Care

For pediatric neuropsychologists as well as the oncologists, radiation therapists, neurosurgeons, and other medical staff involved in the treatment of children with cancer, brain tumors represent one of the most complex, labor-intensive, and frustrating groups of neoplasms. Malignant tumors are invariably fatal if left untreated but the consequences of a cavalier approach to aggressive therapy are disasterous in terms of the patient's subsequent quality of life. It is strongly recommended that discussions of patient status and major decisions relating to changes in patient treatment be presented in the context of an interdisciplinary team in which the pediatric psychologist or pediatric neuropsychologist plays an integral role. At our institution, weekly staffings are held for new patients presenting to the Brain Tumor Clinic as well as established patients with recurrent problems. In addition to the psychologist, child neurology, pediatric neurosurgery, physical/occupational therapy, radiation therapy, medical oncology, social work, and nursing representatives attend. Neuro-opthalmology, neuro-endocrinology, and other subspecialty consultants are requested for selected patients.

Common clinical issues in the team meeting address the anticipated efficacy: toxicity ratio of alternative medical therapies, the patient's neurologic and neuropsychologic function, especially as it relates to discharge planning and school re-entry, and patient/family adjustment to the child's diagnosis, treatment, and residual deficits. Clearly, the psychologist should have a major impact on the assessment and disposition of the patient in all of these areas. From our experience, multiple routine contacts with the patient and family beginning soon after diagnosis are more beneficial than a single extended consultation. In part, this advantage results from oftentimes unexpected changes in patient status, both positive and negative, which can occur within a few weeks. Once the child's primary attending physician makes the initial referral, which is routine for all newly diagnosed patients with brain tumors, we assume the responsibility for scheduling followup as is clinically indicated.

Although the child's primary physician may be from one of several disciplines (e.g., neurology, neurosurgery, radiation therapy, medical oncology), one can assume that they have had significant exposure to the importance of neuropsychological issues in the care of their patients with brain tumors through national conferences and journals sponsored by their professional associations. In fact, inspection of the papers published by psychologists in this area reveals that the vast majority have appeared in neurosurgical and oncology journals. Hopefully, this trend has modified traditional referral patterns to include neuropsychology without obscuring the existence of these empirical studies from psychologists.

In general, we advocate a comprehensive patient assessment within two to four weeks following surgery if the patient is neurologically stable and yearly thereafter for five years, even if the patient's progress is unremarkable. Traditional psychometric measures of intellect, academic achievement, and emotional adjustment are combined with a thorough screening of sensory, perceptual, motor, and language functions that may be expected to have a significant impact on the child's performance of age-appropriate activities of daily living in the natural environment. Our emphasis on generating recommendations for interventions of practial importance is reflected by the use of the Vineland Adaptive Behavior Scales (Sparrow, Balla, & Cicchetti, 1984) as a routine segment of the assessment battery.

The results of these evaluations are particularly useful in consulting with the child's school for needed services. These most commonly include physical therapy, occupational therapy, speech therapy, and liaison between the regular classroom teacher and an iterant teacher for the visually impaired. In some cases, the child's educational needs cannot be met in a regular classroom environment and special educational placement is necessary. An intimate understanding of the patient's capabilities and limitations by the neuropsychologist enables an advocacy role to develop, which is generally well-received by the schools since they have had little, if any, prior experience with children treated for brain tumors.

Future Research

Increasing involvement of neuropsychologists in the clinical care of patients with brain tumors will also enhance the availability of patients as participants in various clinical studies. If patients are routinely referred, standardized batteries may be developed for particular patient groups receiving identical therapy and the results combined across institutions to facilitate more timely accrual of data. Such an approach has been implemented by institutions participating in several Pediatric Oncology Group (POG) and Childhood Cancer Group (CCG) protocols. Although the primary purpose of neuropsychological testing in these protocols is to assess the late toxicities of tumor and its treatment, other questions of more parochial interest to neuropsychologists have been successfully incorporated into the design of the protocols. The use of neuropsychological testing to assess the differential toxicities of medical therapies has already influenced the contemporary medical treatment of children with brain tumors (e.g., Mulhern et al., 1989).

Few institutions currently have the capacity to perform elegant neuropsychological investigations and the large patient populations to conduct multivariate analyses that are probably more easily accomplished by a consortium of institutions. Nevertheless, relatively small series and case studies have been successfully used to identify unique characteristics of homogenous subsamples of patients with brain tumors. As the field of neuropsychology continues to progress toward a balance between assessment and intervention, patients with brain tumors may provide an intriguing population to test rehabilitative and habilitative programs. No publications are known to this author that test the usefulness of cognitive or behavioral rehabilitation methods with children treated for brain tumors. The application of neuropsychological interventions to particular focal problems, such as verbal memory deficits secondary to dominant temporal lobe tumor, may be relatively straightforward. A more complex problem will be how to minimize or prevent the progressive loss of general learning capacity observed among young children receiving cranial radiation therapy.

REFERENCES

Bordeaux, J. D., Dowell, R. E., Copeland, D. R., Fletcher, J. M., Francis, D. J., & Van Eys, J. (1988). A prospective study of neuropsychological sequelae in children with brain tumors. *Journal of Child Neurology, 3,* 63–8.

Bourgeouis, B. F. D., Prensky, A. L., Palkes, H. S., Talent, B. K., & Busch, S. G. (1983). Intelligence in epilepsy: A prospective study in children. *Annals of Neurology, 14,* 438–444.

Carpentieri, S., & Mulhern, R. K. (1993). Patterns of memory dysfunction among children surviving temporal lobe tumors. *Archives of Clinical Neuropsychology, 8,* 345–357.

Carpentieri, S., Mulhern, R. K., Douglas S., Hanna, S., & Fairclough, D. (1993). Behavioral resiliency among children surviving brain tumors: A longitudinal study. *Journal of Clinical Child Psychology, 22,* 336–346.

Cavazzuti, V., Fischer, E. G., Welch, K., Belli, J. A., & Winston, K. R. (1983). Neurological and psychophysiological sequelae following different treatments of craniopharyngioma in children. *Journal of Neurosurgery, 59,* 409–417.

Cavazzuti, V., Winston, K., Baker, R., & Welch, K. (1980). Psychological changes following surgery for tumors in the temporal lobe. *Journal of Neurosurgery, 53,* 618–626.

Clopper, R. R., Meyer, W. J., Udverhelyi, G. B., Money, J., Aarabi, B., Mulvihill, J. J., & Piasio, M. (1977). Postsurgical IQ and behavioral data on 20 patients with a history of childhood craniopharyngioma. *Psychoneuroendocrinology, 2,* 365–372.

Cohen, M. E., & Duffner, P. K. (1984). Principles of diagnosis. In M. E. Cohen & P. K. Duffner (Eds.), *Brain tumors in children: Principles of diagnosis and treatment* (pp. 9–21). New York: Raven Press.

Danoff, B. F., Cowchock, S., Marquette, C., Mulgrew, L., & Kramer, S. (1982). Assessment of the long-term effects of primary radiation therapy for brain tumors in children. *Cancer, 49,* 1582–1586.

Dennis, M., Spiegler, B. J., Hoffman, H. J., Hendrick, E. B., Humphreys, R. P., & Becker, L. E. (1991). Brain tumors in children and adolescents-I. Effects on working, associative and serial-order memory of IQ, age at tumor onset and age of tumor. *Neuropsychologia, 29,* 813–827.

Duffner, P. K., Cohen, M. E., & Freeman, A. I. (1985). Pediatric brain tumors: An overview. *Ca—A Cancer Journal for Clinicians, 35,* 33–47.

Duffner, P. K., Cohen, M. E., & Parker, M. S. (1988). Prospective intellectual testing in children with brain tumors. *Annals of Neurology, 23,* 575–579.

Duffner, P. K., Cohen, M. E., & Thomas, P. (1983). Late effects of treatment on the intelligence of children with posterior fossa tumors. *Cancer, 51,* 233–237.

Ellenberg, J. H., Hertz, D. G., & Nelson, K. B. (1986). Do seizures in children cause intellectual deterioration? *New England Journal of Medicine, 314,* 1085–1088.

Ellenberg, L., McComb, J. G., Siegel, S. E., & Stowe, S. (1987). Factors affecting intellectual outcome in pediatric brain tumor patients. *Neurosurgery, 21,* 638–644.

Finlay, J., & Goins, S. C. (1987). Brain tumors in children: I. Advances in diagnosis. *American Journal of Pediatric Hematology/Oncology, 9,* 246–255.

Hirsch, J. F., Renier, D., Czernichow, P., Benveniste, L., & Pierre-Kahn, A. (1979). Medulloblastoma in childhood: Survival and functional results. *Acta Neurochirurgia, 48,* 1–15.

Hirsch, J. F., Rose, C. S., Pierre-Kahn, A., Pfister, A., & Hoppe-Hirsch, E. (1989). Benign astrocytic and oligodendritic tumors of the cerebral hemispheres in children. *Journal of Neurosurgery, 70,* 568–572.

Kun, L. E. (1984). Principles of radiation therapy. In M. E. Cohen & P. K. Duffner (Eds.), *Brain tumors in children: Principles of diagnosis and treatment* (pp. 47–70). New York: Raven Press.

Kun, L. E., & Mulhern, R. K. (1983). Neuropsychologic function in children with brain tumors: II. Serial studies of intellect and time after treatment. *American Journal of Clinical Oncology, 6,* 651–665.

Kun, L. E., Mulhern, R. K., & Crisco, J. J. (1983). Quality of life in children treated for brain tumors: Intellectual, emotional and academic function. *Journal of Neurosurgery, 58,* 1–6.

LeBaron, S., Zeltzer, P. M., Zeltzer, L. K., Scott, S., & Marlin, A. E. (1988). Assessment of quality of survival in children with medulloblastoma and cerebellar astrocytoma. *Cancer, 62,* 1215–1222.

Leviton, A. (1984). Principles of epidemiology. In M. E. Cohen & P. K. Duffner (Eds.), *Brain tumors in children: Principles of diagnosis and treatment* (pp. 22–46). New York: Raven Press.

Mostow, E. N., Byrne, J., Connelly, R. R., & Mulvihill, J. J. (1991). Quality of life in long-term survivors of CNS tumors of childhood and adolescence. *Journal of Clinical Oncology, 9,* 592–599.

Mulhern, R. K., Carpentieri, S., Shema, S., Stone, P., & Fairclough, D. (1993). Factors associated with social and behavioral problems among children recently diagnosed with brain tumor. *Journal of Pediatric Psychology, 18,* 339–350.

Mulhern, R. K., Crisco, J. J., & Kun, L. E. (1983). Neuropsychological sequelae of childhood brain tumors: A review. *Journal of Clinical Child Psychology, 12,* 66–73.

Mulhern, R. K., Hancock, J. R., Fairclough, D., & Kun, L. E. (1992). Neuropsychological status of children treated for brain tumors: A critical review and integrative analysis. *Medical and Pediatric Oncology, 20,* 181–191.

Mulhern, R. K., Horowitz, M. E., Kovnar, E. H., Langston, J., Sanford, R. A., & Kun, L. E. (1989). Neurodevelopmental status of infants and young children treated for brain tumors with pre-irradiation chemotherapy. *Journal of Clinical Oncology, 7,* 1660–1666.

Mulhern, R. K., Kovnar, E. H., Kun, L. E., Crisco, J. J., & Williams, J. M. (1988). Psychologic and neurologic function following treatment for childhood temporal lobe astrocytoma. *Journal of Child Neurology, 3,* 47–52.

Mulhern, R. K., & Kun, L. E. (1985). Neuropsychologic function in children with brain tumors: III. Interval changes in the six months following treatment. *Medical and Pediatric Oncology, 13,* 318–324.

Mulhern, R. K., Wasserman, A. L., Kovnar, E. H., Williams, J. M., & Ochs, J. (1986). Serial neuropsychological studies of a child with acute lymphoblastic leukemia and subsequent glioblastoma multiforme. *Neurology, 36,* 1534–1538.

Mulhern, R. K., Williams, J. M., LeSure, S. S., & Kun, L. E. (1986). Neuropsychological performance of children surviving cerebellar tumors: Six case studies. *International Journal of Clinical Neuropsychology, 8,* 72–76.

Packer, R. J., Sutton, L. N., Atkins, T. E., Radcliffe, J., Bunnin, G. R., D'Angio, G., Siegel, K. R., & Schut, L. (1989). A prospective study of cognitive function in children receiving whole brain radiotherapy and chemotherapy: Two year results. *Journal of Neurosurgery, 70,* 707–713.

Packer, R. J., Zimmerman, R. A., & Bilaniuk, L. T. (1986). Magnetic resonance imaging in the evaluation of treatment-related central nervous system damage. *Cancer, 58,* 635–640.

Riva, D., Pantaleoni, C., Milani, N., & Belani, F. F. (1989). Impairment of neuropsychological functions in children with medulloblastomas and astrocytomas in the posterior fossa. *Child's Nervous System, 5,* 107–110.

Silverman, C. L., Palkes, H., Talent, B., Kovnar, E., Klouse, J. W., & Thomas, P. R. M. (1984). Late effects of radiotherapy on patients with cerebellar medulloblastoma. *Cancer, 54,* 825–829.

Sparrow, S. S., Balla, D. A., & Cicchetti, D. V. (1984) *Vineland Adaptive Behavior Scales.* Circle Press, MN: American Guidance Service.

Spunberg, J. J., Chang, C. H., Goldman, M., Auricchio, E., & Bell, J. J. (1981). Quality of long-term survival following irradiation for intracranial tumors in children under the age of two. *International Journal of Radiation Oncology and Biological Physics, 7,* 727–736.

8

CEREBROVASCULAR DISORDERS

JUDITH A. HARDING   MICHELE D. KLEIMAN

Cerebrovascular disorders (CVD) are among the most common etiologies of chronic disability and death in the United States and other Western countries. Brust (1981) estimated that at least 2 million people are affected by vascular disorder in the United States, most of whom are adults.

CVD is now being recognized in larger numbers in the pediatric population, despite recent trends suggesting a decline in adults. Although dietary improvement, increased exercise, and hypertension control appear to reduce the incidence of CVD among adults, increased numbers of affected children are appearing, at least in part, as the result of improved medical care, less invasive and more precise tests for diagnosis, and increased risk factors such as oral contraceptive use by adolescent girls and improved therapies for heart disease, prematurity, and malignancies (Roach & Riela, 1988).

An epidemiological study of children in Rochester, Minnesota, from 1965 to 1974 found an overall average annual incidence rate of CVD in children through 14 years of age of 2.52/100,000/year, with 1.89/100,000/year for hemorrhagic strokes and 0.63/100,000/year for ischemic strokes. This study excluded strokes related to intracranial infection, trauma, or birth. Other authors have quoted an average annual incidence of hemorrhagic and ischemic strokes in childhood at 2.1/100,000/year (Schoenberg, Mellinger, & Schoenberg, 1978).

Cerebrovascular disease in children is relatively uncommon when compared with adults. It is rarely secondary to atherosclerosis, hypertension, or diabetes mellitus, but it may occur with a large number of other systemic and neurologic diseases. Neurologic deficits may arise through (1) disruption of blood flow to the brain parenchyma, usually secondary to cerebral vascular thrombosis or embolism, leading to cerebral infarction; (2) intracranial hemorrhage or

Authors are listed alphabetically. Both authors contributed equally to this chapter.

subarachnoid hemorrhage—bleeding into or around the brain; or (3) transient cerebral ischemia or irritation due to the preceding mechanisms or from the presence of cerebrovascular malformations. Many disorders produce symptoms through more than one of the these mechanisms.

In this chapter, the presentation and neuropsychological evaluation of children with cerebrovascular diseases will be addressed. Many of these conditions present with similar symptoms, based on the location of the affected vessel(s). First, we will discuss a review of common clinical presentations due to involvement of the major intracerebral vessels. Next, we will provide a brief description of the more common vascular diseases that affect the central nervous system in children. This will be followed by a discussion of the neuropsychological findings in children with cerebrovascular disorders. Rehabilitation approaches will then be briefly reviewed.

COMMON CLINICAL PRESENTATIONS

Clinical presentation of children with cerebrovascular disease is extremely variable and depends on the patient's age, the location of the involved vessels, the severity of vascular involvement, collateral circulation, and the presence of other systemic medical problems. Whereas older children and adolescents with cerebral infarction or hemorrhage typically present with a recognizable constellation of symptoms similar to those found in adults, infants and young children often have less specific symptoms that may not readily be identified as secondary to cerebrovascular disease. Recent advances in neuro-imaging techniques, as well as screening for metabolic and coagulation abnormalities, have greatly improved the ability to diagnose and treat these diseases at an early stage, with consequent improvement in survival and decreased long-term morbidity in affected children.

Cerebral infarction may be defined as a focal area of necrosis of brain parenchyma that occurs secondary to insufficiency of arterial blood supply or stasis of the cerebral venous drainage. Impaired arterial cerebral blood flow may be due to vascular thrombosis or embolism and results in a diminished supply of oxygen and glucose to the brain. If very brief, there is temporary impairment of neuronal function, producing a transient neurologic deficit (i.e., transient ischemic attacks [TIA]). If longer, cerebral infarction occurs, with death of neurons. Within several hours, localized metabolic acidosis, dilatation of the surrounding blood vessels, and break down of the blood-brain barrier occur, leading to cerebral edema, which causes worsening of the neurologic deficit. Cerebral infarction secondary to venous stasis is often hemorrhagic, as increased venous pressure may result in rupture of cortical veins.

Arterial Occlusion

Blood is supplied to the brain by the two internal carotid and the two vertebral arteries, with one of each on either side of the body. The two internal carotid arteries enter at the base of the brain and each divides into two major arteries: the anterior cerebral artery and the middle cerebral artery. The anterior cerebral arteries supply the anterior and medial aspects of the cortex, whereas the middle cerebral arteries supply the lateral cerebral hemispheres. The two vertebral arteries enter at the base of the brain and combine to form the basilar artery, which divides into several smaller arteries that irrigate the cerebellum. The basilar artery then separates into the posterior cerebral arteries, which supply the medial temporal lobes and posterior occipital lobes.

The major cerebral arteries are joined at the Circle of Willis, an arterial wreath surrounding the optic chiasm at the base of the brain. The two anterior cerebral arteries are joined by the anterior communicating artery, and the posterior communicating artery connects the proximal posterior cerebral arteries to the internal carotid arteries (see Figure 8.1). This anatomical pattern serves to equalize blood flow throughout the brain and provides alternative perfusion pathways when localized vascular occlusions occur. As there are individual variations within the Circle of Willis, at times these anastomotic channels are inadequate to

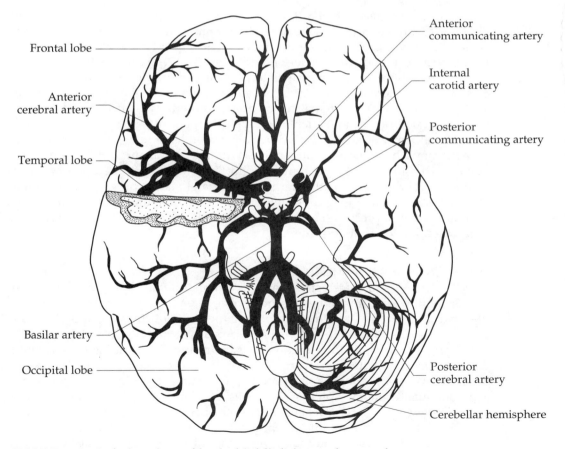

FIGURE 8.1 **Inferior view of brain highlighting major arteries.**

compensate for vascular occlusion, and cerebral ischemia results. This is especially true in elderly individuals who may have widespread atherosclerotic cerebrovascular disease.

Internal Carotid Artery (ICA)

Occlusion of the internal carotid artery is usually thrombotic or secondary to trauma with vascular dissection. Some 20 cases of childhood stroke following intraoral trauma have been reported, most commonly after a fall onto an object (or with an object in the mouth), damaging the tonsillar region adjacent to the internal carotid artery (Woodhurst, Robertson, & Thompson, 1980). A period of 2 to 24 hours may elapse between the injury and neurologic symptoms. Stroke may occur due to occlusion of the internal carotid artery or to formation of a thrombus with subsequent embolization (usually to the middle cerebral artery) (Woodhurst et al., 1980; Pearl, 1987). Prognosis following this type of injury is guarded, with a 30% mortality, 60% incidence of permanent paresis, and, in 10% of patients, resolution of a transient deficit (Pearl, 1987).

With ICA occlusion, blood flow is disrupted to all or most of the territory of the middle cerebral artery. If the anterior communicating artery is small, the ipsilateral anterior cerebral artery territory will also be affected. In some patients, the posterior cerebral artery is derived from the carotid circulation (instead of the basilar circulation), in which case its territory is compromised as well. Thus, occlusion of the internal carotid artery may cause infarction of nearly the entire ipsilateral hemisphere, with sparing of deeper structures such as basal ganglia, thalamus, and brain stem. Patients will typically present with symptoms of middle cerebral artery occlusion, including contralateral hemiplegia, hemianesthesia, homonymous hemianopsia, and aphasia (if the dominant hemisphere is involved). Due to the large amount of brain tissue damaged, there is frequently massive cerebral edema with alteration of mental status, progressing to coma. Uncontrolled swelling may cause herniation of the temporal lobe uncus leading to brain stem compression and death, at times despite aggressive management, as in cases due to intraoral trauma.

Middle Cerebral Artery (MCA)

Middle cerebral artery occlusion produces a similar initial clinical picture to ICA occlusion, however, it is more commonly due to embolic phenomena. The middle cerebral artery has two main divisions: the superior division, supplying the rolandic area, and the inferior division, supplying the temporoparietal area. Emboli more often occlude the superior division, resulting in a dense sensorimotor deficit of the contralateral face, arm, and leg. If the dominant (usually left) hemisphere is involved, a global aphasia occurs. Over time, this typically evolves into a predominantly motor aphasia—with hesitant, simplified, dysmelodic speech and relatively spared comprehension of both speech and written language. The inferior division of the middle cerebral artery is less often occluded by emboli than the superior division, although embolic involvement remains more common than occlusion by thrombus. A homonymous hemianopsia occurs, with Wernicke aphasia also present if the dominant hemisphere is affected. Speech is fluently articulated but paraphasic, and comprehension of both spoken and written language is severely impaired. This reflects involvement of the auditory association areas, or their disconnection from the primary auditory cortex in the superior part of the temporal lobe (Adams & Victor, 1985, p. 37).

Anterior Cerebral Artery (ACA)

Isolated occlusion of the anterior cerebral arteries is rare, and clinical syndromes vary related to an individual's arterial pattern within the Circle of Willis. Unilateral occlusion usually results in sensorimotor deficit of the contralateral foot and leg, with a lesser degree of upper extremity paresis, and sparing of the face. If the left anterior cerebral artery is involved, a sympathetic apraxia of the left arm and leg can result. Behavioral disturbances may include abulia with slowness and lack of spontaneity in all activities, and distractibility. If both anterior cerebral arteries arise from a single stem, occlusion leads to infarction of the medial portions of both cerebral hemispheres—resulting in paraplegia, incontinence, abulia, and aphasia.

Basilar Artery

A picture of basilar artery occlusion can arise by occlusion of the basilar artery itself, of both vertebral arteries, or of a single dominant vertebral artery. Posterior circulation strokes are not common in children and usually are associated with underlying conditions such as homocystinuria, Moya-Moya disease, or Down syndrome. The complete basilar syndrome consists of bilateral sensory and motor deficits, with cerebellar, cranial nerve, and other brainstem findings. Patients are frequently comatose due to ischemia of the high midbrain reticular activating system. Occlusion of branches of the basilar artery produces syndromes that have been well characterized in adults but rarely affect children. The reader can refer to a neurology textbook for further information on this subject.

Posterior Cerebral Artery

Both posterior cerebral arteries arise from the basilar artery in about 70% of individuals, whereas in approximately 20% of individuals, one arises from the basilar and the other from the internal carotid. In the remaining population, both posterior cerebral arteries arise from the anterior circulation. Small branches supply the thalamus, basal ganglia, inferomedial temporal lobe, and medial occipital lobe. Occlusion of the small branches supplying the basal ganglia may lead to an extrapyramidal movement disorder. Occlusion of the cortical branches to temporal and occipital lobes affects the primary visual receptive area and causes a homonymous hemianopsia, often with sparing of central vision. Visual hallucinations may occur in blind portions of the visual field. If the dominant hemisphere is affected, other associated difficulties can include alexia (with or without agraphia) anomia, visual agnosias, and memory impairment. If there are bilateral lesions of the occipital lobes due to either basilar artery occlusion or bilateral successive vascular insults, total cortical blindness may result.

Venous Occlusion

Sinovenous occlusion has been documented in association with numerous systemic disturbances, mostly those causing altered cerebral hemodynamics. Disorders most often related to sinovenous thrombosis in children include (1) dehydration, congestive heart failure, shock (Imai, Everhart, & Sanders, 1982); (2) hematologic disorders such as sickle cell anemia, polycythemia, thrombocytosis, and leukemia (Imai et al., 1982; Roach, 1989); and (3) localized inflammatory conditions, including mastoiditis, meningitis, sinusitis, and otitis media (although less prominent now, with effective early treatment due to improved antibiotic coverage) (Roach, 1989). A hypercoagulable state may also result from coagulation abnormalities (due to deficiency of antithrombin III, protein S or protein C, malignancy, chemotherapy, inflammatory bowel disease, oral contraceptives, pregnancy, and the puerperium) (Imai et al., 1982). Superior sagittal sinus thrombosis has been reported rarely following closed head injury, possibly due to release of thromboplastin following cerebral contusion (Hesselbrock, Sawaya, Tomsick, & Wadhwa, 1985).

Clinical presentation depends on the site of the sinovenous occlusion, the nature of the underlying disease, and, most importantly, whether or not cortical vein thrombosis with venous infarction has occurred (see Figure 8.2). Early symptoms that occur with occlusion of the large superior sagittal sinus (or of a dominant transverse sinus) are increased intracranial pressure with severe headache and vomiting. Frequently, there is associated impairment in the level of consciousness, with confusion and lethargy.

Thrombosis of the anterior portion of the superior sagittal sinus may not be associated with severe symptoms, as many of the superficial cortical veins are able to drain posteriorly. If the middle or posterior superior sagittal sinus is occluded, intracranial pressure is elevated due to poor venous drainage. With cortical vein occlusion, epileptic seizures and hemorrhagic venous infarctions in both hemispheres often occur with motor and sensory deficits, aphasia, and blindness. Prognosis for patients with major sinus thrombosis and bilateral large hemorrhagic infarctions is poor, with high morbidity and mortality. In a study of 38 adult patients, neurologic sequelae and death were more common in patients presenting with focal signs. However, in those with only intracranial hypertension, and no evidence of venous infarction, the only serious sequelae was optic atrophy (Bousser, Chiras, Bories, & Gastaigne, 1985). In these survivors, prognosis for recovery of function is far better than in arterial thrombosis. Patients with isolated cortical vein thrombosis often have complete recovery, although a chronic seizure disorder may persist (Roach, 1989).

Thrombosis of the cavernous sinus may follow a facial cellulitis or infection of a paranasal sinus. Fever, headache, and alteration of consciousness may progress to include visual loss and proptosis (due to ophthalmic venous obstruction) with

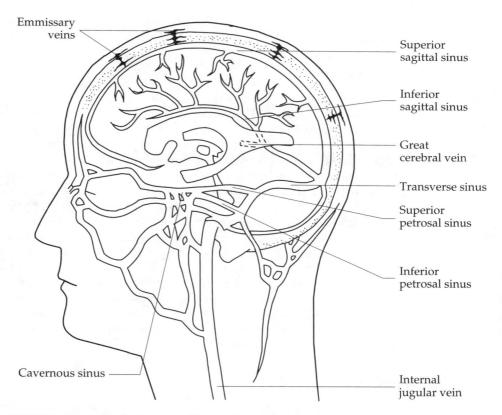

Emmissary veins

Superior sagittal sinus

Inferior sagittal sinus

Great cerebral vein

Transverse sinus

Superior petrosal sinus

Inferior petrosal sinus

Cavernous sinus

Internal jugular vein

FIGURE 8.2   Medial view of brain illustrating venous system.

limited extraocular movements (due to compression of cranial nerves within the cavernous sinus). Thrombosis frequently spreads to the opposite cavernous sinus with a high mortality in the acute stage (Roach, 1989).

Diagnosis can often be made by cranial cerebral tomography scan (CCT) or magnetic resonance imaging (MRI). Cerebral edema with multiple parasagittal hemorrhagic infarctions can be seen in sagittal sinus thrombosis. If there is thrombosis of the posterior portion of this sinus, an empty delta sign is often seen on contrast CT. However, in 5 of 25 patients in one study, CCT was normal, even in cases with focal neurologic signs (Bousser et al., 1985). Cavernous sinus thrombosis, although difficult to visualize with CCT, may be better evaluated by MRI. Demonstration of a venous intraluminal filling defect by cerebral angiography is confirmatory. Treatment includes antibiotics, if an infectious etiology is apparent, anticonvulsants for seizures, and treatment of intracranial hypertension. The use of anticoagulants remains controversial, due to the risk of hemorrhagic infarction (Imai et al., 1982). However, some authors advocate therapy with heparin if there is a deteriorating clinical course, despite aggressive symptomatic treatment.

Bousser and colleagues (1985) reported no deaths in 23 heparin-treated patients and a complete recovery in 19 of these.

Thrombotic Stroke

Thrombotic stroke occurs when large or small arteries, venous sinuses, or cortical veins are slowly occluded due to a variety of mechanisms. The deficit tends to evolve over several minutes to hours, and, especially in young children, it is often impossible to ascertain the precise time of onset. The conditions that may lead to arterial thrombotic vascular occlusions in children are multiple and include (1) primary vasculopathies (e.g., Moya-Moya disease, fibromuscular dysplasia); (2) systemic diseases with prominent vascular involvement (e.g., homocystinuria, sickle cell anemia); and (3) diseases causing vascular inflammation (vasculitides). Atherosclerosis, hypertension, and diabetes, frequent systemic conditions predisposing adults to cerebral thrombosis, are rare in children. Following a thrombotic vascular occlusion, improvement in neurologic function is often slow, occurring over weeks to months. A fairly uniform clinical picture has been identified for occlusion of each large cerebral artery in adults. A similar deficit occurs whether the mechanism is via vascular thrombosis or embolism. Venous infarctions and intracerebral hemorrhages may approximate an established "arterial" syndrome if in a similar location, although damage may extend into more than one arterial territory.

Embolic Stroke

Another important mechanism for childhood stroke is cerebral embolism. Typically, there is sudden onset of the deficit, often followed by a more rapid recovery than seen in thrombotic stroke. Partial neurologic improvement may occur minutes to hours following the onset of symptoms, due to fragmentation of the embolus with migration of portions into smaller, more distal arterial branches. Renewed blood flow to the ischemic areas can then occur, accounting for the increased incidence of hemorrhagic infarction following embolic phenomena. Embolism most often affects the carotid circulation (especially the middle cerebral artery) due to the larger volume of blood carried there and its relatively direct communication with the aorta (Roach, 1989). Symptoms depend on the size of the embolus, site of arterial obstruction, and age of the patient.

The history of initial development of symptoms is an important factor in clinically distinguishing thrombotic from embolic stroke. In young children, however, it is often difficult to differentiate the two by history. As the onset of symptoms is usually not reported, the duration of the child's deficit may not be known. A past history of transient neurologic deficits in a similar arterial distribution points to a thrombotic mechanism, while a history of multifocal deficits is more consistent with recurrent emboli. Focal seizures are more common with embolic than thrombotic infarction, yet less frequent than seen with cortical vein or dural sinus thrombosis (Roach, 1989).

Embolic stroke in children, as in adults, occur frequently due to cardiac disease. Congenital heart disease with right-to-left shunt permits embolic fragments to bypass the lungs and lodge in cerebral arteries. Valvular heart disease, due to bacterial endocarditis, rheumatic heart disease or implanted prosthetic valves, allows formation of vegetations that may then emoblize. Portions of intracardiac tumors (i.e., atrial myxoma) may also embolize. An increase in corrective surgical procedures for congenital heart defects has led to a parallel rise in the number of post-open-heart-surgery embolic strokes.

Cardiac arrhythmias, particularly atrial fibrillation, are commonly associated with embolic stroke in adults. Although relatively uncommon in children, arrhythmias may be associated with certain congenital heart defects, congestive heart failure, cardiomyopathy, or myocardial infarction.

Paradoxical emboli occur when there is a direct passage of blood from the venous to the arterial circulation, usually due to congenital heart disease or large AV (arteriovenous) pulmonary fistulae. In hereditary hemorrhagic telangiectasia, bleeding occurs from telangiectasias of skin, mucosa, and many internal organs. In approximately 15% of these patients, pulmonary fistulae (which constitute extra-cardiac right to left shunts) are present and gradually increase in size, becoming hemodynamically significant in young adulthood (Adams, Subbiah, Bosch, 1977), with symptoms of chronic hypoxemia and polycythemia such as cyanosis, digital clubbing, exertional dyspnea, and extra-cardiac murmur. Transient nonfocal neurologic symptoms such as headaches, dizziness, and distal extremity numbness occur in 30 to 67% of patients, due to hypoxemia and polycythemia. Septic and nonseptic cerebral emboli passing through the pulmonary shunt may cause focal neurological symptoms due to abscess formation.

Arterial-arterial emboli are frequently seen in adults with atherosclerotic vascular disease but may occur rarely in children, often in association with premature atherosclerosis due to familial hyperlipidoses (Daniels, Bates, Luken, Benton, Third, & Glueck, 1982). A 1% incidence of embolism during cerebral angiography is similar to that seen in adults, (Roach, 1989).

Air embolism is an iatrogenic phenomenon, occurring when air enters the arterial (or venous) circulation during medical procedures (cardiopulmonary bypass, venous and arterial catheterization, cerebral angiography, mechanical verticalition, or thoracentesis) (Menkin & Schwartzman, 1977). Fat embolism most commonly follows long-bone fractures or is associated with cardiothoracic surgery. Systemic fat embolism causes a combination of severe respiratory distress and neurologic dysfunction due to small multifocal white-matter infarctions. The prognosis is usually poor. Cerebral embolization of shotgun pellets has been reported in children (Vasick & Tew, 1982). Foreign bodies may not embolize immediately, and neurological symptoms can be delayed for hours to days (Roach, 1989) following the initial trauma. Surgical removal of intravascular foreign bodies is recommended to restore blood flow and prevent infection and erosion of the endothelial wall (Vasick & Tew, 1982).

Prognosis depends on the size and location of the embolic stroke. Younger children tend to have a better recovery, although many children have residual neurologic deficits (Roach, 1989). The use of anticoagulation in children with embolic stroke remains controversial, as microscopic foci of hemorrhage are often present, even if not apparent on neuroimaging studies. If a large infarction or evidence of hemorrhage is not present, some authors recommend initial use of heparin in the acute phase for children at risk for recurrent nonseptic emboli (Roach, 1989). Most important, in the long term, is the prevention of recurrent emboli by identifying and treating any underlying predisposing conditions.

Vascular Malformations

Intracranial hemorrhage in children, similar to thrombotic or embolic stroke, is far less common than in adults. Vascular malformations and trauma account for the vast majority of cases.

Arteriovenous Malformations

Arteriovenous malformations are congenital lesions due to failure of involution of a primitive arteriovenous network (Kelly, Mellinger, & Sundt, 1978). They are characterized by a direct between connection between intracerebral arteries and veins, without an interposed capillary bed. Involvement of the surrounding brain with areas of gliosis, fibrosis, and inflammation may account for subtle neurologic deficits that are found at times in the absence of hemorrhage. Although some authors have reported that seizures (usually of focal motor or complex partial type) are the most frequent presenting symptom (Swaiman, 1989), others have found that more children present with hemorrhage (Kelly et al., 1978; Roach, 1989).

The majority of arteriovenous malformations (AVMs) in children are supratentorial and lateralized to one hemisphere (80 to 85%), with lesions in the posterior fossa (5 to 10%) and deep midline malformations (5 to 10%) occurring much less frequently (Kelly et al., 1978). An increased incidence in males has been reported, with a ratio approaching 2:1. Symptoms depend most on the location and size of the lesion, as well as the patient's age. Older children and adolescents may present with catastrophic hemorrhage that is subarachnoid and/or intraparenchymal. Headache, nausea, vomiting, and alteration of consciousness often evolve rapidly, with neck rigidity and autonomic disturbance. Focal neurologic signs vary depending on the region of brain involved.

Small AVMs that are located deep in the cerebral hemisphere are often silent prior to rupture, with subsequent massive bleeding (Kelly et al., 1978). Alternatively, large hemispheric lesions may come to medical attention following the onset of focal seizures, episodic migraine-like headaches, or a slowly progressive motor deficit. In these cases, when hemorrhage occurs, it is less likely to be massive but will often recur. Others (Fults & Kelly, 1984) have reported no difference in the frequency of rupture of small and large arteriovenous malformations. Some children may exhibit "saltatory deterioration" or progressive symptoms due to repeated small hemorrhages or intermittent thrombosis of portions of the malformation with consequent infarctions of the surrounding brain (Roach, 1989).

Diversion of blood flow from the surrounding brain parenchyma into the vascular lesion may produce intermittent focal signs due to cerebral ischemia.

The presentation of AVMs in neonates and infants is dramatically different from that in older children. Most notable is the Vein of Galen malformation. An aneurysmal dilatation of the vein, due to high pressure, occurs with an adjacent tangled network of vessels, that connects to the carotid or vertebral circulation. In neonates, severe high-output congestive heart failure and cranial bruit result from this hemodynamically significant arteriovenous shunt (Kelly et al., 1978; Knudson & Alden, 1979; Roach, 1989; Swaiman, 1989). A large or enlarging head circumference is often present. Associated findings include a systolic heart murmur, cardiomegaly, hepatomegaly, respiratory distress, and pulmonary edema. These neonates usually die of cardiac failure. Some infants may present later in the first year with hydrocephalus, dilated scalp veins, and convulsions (if subarachnoid bleeding has occurred), but without evidence of cardiac failure (Swaiman, 1989). Increased intracranial pressure and noncommunicating hydrocephalus may occur due to compression of the adjacent cerebral aqueduct. Less frequently, older children may present with headache, intracranial hemorrhage, convulsions, and/or focal neurologic signs, due to a Vein of Galen malformation.

A similar difference in presentation occurs between infants and older children with large supratentorial AVMs. As with the Vein of Galen malformation, children less than 1 year of age commonly present with congestive heart failure, cranial bruits, and obstructive hydrocephalus, if the lesion extends deeply or has bled (Kelly et al., 1978).

Diagnosis is made definitively by four-vessel cerebral angiography, although most lesions can be visualized with contrast-enhanced CT. Following medical stabilization, the definitive treatment of AVMs is surgical. Since the risk of intracranial hemorrhage is approximately 3% each year (Roach, 1989), and somewhat higher during the first five years after an initial hemorrhage, surgical resection of accessible lesions is advisable in children, who have a high cumulative risk of rebleeding during their lifetime. For large or surgically inoperable lesions, arterial embolization by selective catheterization is a further option. Prophylactic anticonvulsants are frequently used in patients with hemispheric AVMs, as well as in those who have had a recent hemorrhage.

Other types of cerebral vascular malformations, such as capillary telangiectasias and cavernous and venous angiomas, are frequently asymptomatic and discovered incidentally but occasionally may present with hemorrhage or seizures. Of particular note is the leptomeningeal angioma found in patients with Sturge-Weber syndrome. Associated findings include a facial "port-wine nevus" cutaneous angioma (usually ipsilaterally), mental retardation, seizures, and contralateral hemiparesis, hemiatrophy, and homonymous hemianopia. Despite normal neurological development early in life, progressive deterioration often occurs, with recurrent episodes of seizures and hemiparesis, caused by repeated thrombosis of abnormal venous structures beneath the leptomeningeal malformation (Roach, 1989). Although nearly all patients develop seizures, only half are retarded. Intracranial hemorrhage has been reported in only one case.

Infrequently, the neurologic and radiographic features of Sturge-Weber may occur without an associated cutaneous port-wine nevus. Alternatively, less than half of children with port-wine nevi have leptomeningeal angiomas and should not be classified as having Sturge-Weber syndrome.

The radiographic "trolley-track" appearance of parallel convoluted lines in the parieto-occipital region, seen on x-ray or CT, is characteristic. Management includes seizure control and monitoring of intraocular pressure. Daily low-dose aspirin to prevent recurrent venous thrombosis may prevent progressive neurologic decline (Roach, 1989).

Aneurysms

Intracranial aneurysms are the most common cause of subarachnoid hemorrhage in teenagers, although AVMs are found more frequently in children with subarachnoid bleeding (Roach, 1989). Saccular ("Berry") aneurysms are the type most commonly seen in children. They usually occur at a bifurcation of the internal carotid artery and one of its main branches, due to a localized congenital defect in the vessel wall. Approximately 5% of children will have more than one aneurysm (Shucart & Wolpert, 1974). Several other congenital lesions have been found in association with intracranial aneurysms, most notably coarctation of the aorta and polycystic renal disease. There have been several reports of familial intracranial aneurysm, as well as aneurysms occurring infrequently in association with Ehler-Danlos syndrome and Marfan's syndrome.

Different arteries are more commonly involved in aneurysm formation in adults than in children. A proportionately higher percentage of internal carotid artery aneurysms and posterior fossa aneurysms occur in children (Roach, 1989). Although most aneurysms occur within the subarachnoid space, they may extend into brain parenchyma as they enlarge. This explains the component of intraparenchymal hemorrhage that accompanies subarachnoid hemorrhage in about 50% of patients with aneurysmal rupture. Unlike arteriovenous malformations, patients with aneurysms rarely have premonitory symptoms prior to the hemorrhage. Presentation is sudden, with severe headache and stiff neck, followed by a decreased level of consciousness. Unless intraparenchymal hemorrhage has occurred, there may be no focal neurologic findings. Seizures, although a common presenting feature of AVMs, are not seen with aneurysms unless subarachnoid hemorrhage has already occurred.

Mycotic aneurysms occur when septic emboli from a bacterial or fungal source damage the walls of an intracranial artery. They are often multiple and occur within brain parenchyma at distal arterial branches, most commonly along the middle cerebral artery. Hemorrhage into the brain parenchyma thus occurs more commonly than with saccular aneurysms.

Evaluation of subarachnoid hemorrhage is made by initial noncontrast CT and lumbar puncture. Four-vessel angiography is necessary to ensure that multiple aneurysms are not present. Initial medical stabilization with prophylactic anticonvulsants, pain medication, minimal stimulation, and control of intracranial pressure and systemic blood pressure is imperative. Surgical clipping of the aneurysm is necessary to prevent rebleeding.

COMMON VASCULAR DISEASES

Vasculopathies

Moya Moya Disease

Moya Moya syndrome, a rare vaso-occlusive disease of the intracranial circulation, is characterized by progressive occlusion of the internal carotid arteries and the proximal portions of the vessels of the Circle of Willis. Multiple small collateral channels develop ("rete mirable") in the basal ganglia and around the base of the brain causing the "puff-of-smoke" appearance that is pathognomonic by cerebral angiogram. Most cases occur sporadically, with symptoms beginning in childhood and with a slightly higher incidence in females. Although initially recognized in the Japanese, the Moya-Moya syndrome has since been identified in multiple ethnic groups. This angiographic pattern has been described in children with multiple disorders, including sickle cell anemia, Down syndrome, and neurofibromatosis, as well as children with renovascular hypertension and idiopathic pulmonary hypertension, suggesting the presence of systemic structural vascular abnormalities.

There are three common clinical presentations: (1) recurrent transient ischemic attacks in different vascular distributions, with permanent residua following some, and a slowly progressive deterioration of cognitive and neurologic function; (2) the pattern of alternating hemiplegia; and (3) a sudden, single, "stroke-like" episode with residual deficit. Transient ischemic attacks (TIAs) occur with highest frequency during the four years following diagnosis. The long-term prognosis is less favorable in those children with an early age of onset of symptoms, associated hypertension, or telangiectasias accompanying the cerebrovascular occlusive disease (Roach, 1989).

Fibromuscular Dysplasia

Fibromuscular dysplasia (FMD), a disease of small- to medium-sized arteries, is characterized by multiple small, saccular dilatations alternating with rings of hypertrophied muscle along the arterial wall ("string-of-beads" appearance). The cervical internal carotid arteries are most commonly affected, although in children the intracranial carotid artery and its branches may also be involved. Intracranial aneurysms have been reported in association with FMD in adults. It is most often a disease of young women, rarely affecting children, and is symptomatic in approximately half of the patients affected. Patients typically present with TIAs or multifocal cerebral infarcts. In one study, only 7 of 41 patients had symptoms of focal neurologic dysfunction referable to the distribution of an affected vessel (Sandok, Houser, Baker, & Holley, 1971). Diagnosis is made by cerebral angiography.

Homocystinuria

Homocystinuria is an inborn error of methionine metabolism, with frequent vascular complications. Deficiency of one of three enzymes responsible for methionine breakdown is inherited in an autosomal recessive manner. Thromboembolism affects vessels of all sizes in the brain, lung, kidney, and eye, and is thought to be secondary to homocystine-induced damage to the vascular endothelium, with secondary platelet activation. Associated neurologic problems include mild to severe mental retardation, delayed motor development, a high incidence of psychiatric difficulties (in up to 50%), and seizures (in 10 to 15%) (Roach, 1989). Some patients with deficiency of the enzyme cystathionine beta synthase are improved with Pyridoxine supplementation. These patients have less severe mental retardation, delayed appearance of systemic dysfunction, and a diminished number of thromboembolic episodes. Methionine restriction in the neontal period may lead to normal development, although it is uncertain if this reduces the incidence of thromboembolic complications.

There are several other multisystem diseases with a prominent associated vasculopathy in which cerebrovascular symptoms are rare before early adulthood. These include pseudoxanthoma elasticum, Fabry's disease, and Dego's disease.

Migraine

Migraine headaches are frequent in children, with a 4% incidence between the ages of 7 and 15 years. Migraine begins prior to 10 years of age in 20% and prior to 20 years of age in 50% of affected adults (Prensky & Sommer, 1979). Boys are affected more frequently in early childhood, whereas, following puberty, girls are more often affected. Inheritance is autosomal-dominant with a greater penetration in females. From 70 to 90% of patients have a positive family history. Symptoms associated with headache include nausea, vomiting, abdominal pain, and relief after sleep in 70 to 90%, positive throbbing quality in 58%, unilateral headache in 36%, and aura in 17 to 30% (Prensky & Sommer, 1979).

Common migraine is the most frequent variant in children and adolescents (70%) (Swaiman, 1989). There is no visual aura; instead, there is an "autonomic" aura consisting of irritability, lethargy, and pallor. Generalized frontal headache, nausea and vomiting, abdominal pain, and improvement with rest are characteristic.

Classic migraine occurs in approximately 15% of children (Swaiman, 1989). It is characterized by a preceding visual or somatosensory aura, usually lasting less than 20 minutes, followed by throbbing headache, nausea and vomiting, abdominal pain, and improvement following sleep. Neurologic abnormalities are usually insignificant and evanescent.

In *complicated migraine*, focal neurologic disturbances occur in association with typical migraine symptomatology. These are thought to be due to intracranial vasoconstriction with cerebral ischemia and edema following typical migraine symptomatology. The clinical presentation is defined by the vascular territory that is affected. Although most patients recover completely, some are left with neurologic sequelae. Focal neurologic symptoms may precede, accompany, or follow the headache, and usually outlast the discomfort.

In *ophthalmoplegic migraine*, orbital pain is associated with a limitation of eye movements due to a third-nerve palsy. This is thought to be caused by edema of the internal carotid artery within the cavernous sinus or edema of the distal basilar artery.

In *hemiplegic migraine*, hemiparesis is associated with contralateral headache, probably secondary to vasoconstriction and ischemia in the middle cerebral artery distribution.

In *basilar artery migraine*, occipital headache is accompanied by varied symptoms referable to the brain stem. These may include unilateral or bilateral sensory or motor abnormalities, dizziness, vertigo, ataxia, dysarthria, nausea, and vomiting, often with occipital headache.

Acute confusional migraine is most common in adolescents and consists of headache, associated with confusion and agitation, which typically resolves in four to six hours.

Precipitants to migraine headache in predisposed individuals include anxiety, fatigue, mild head trauma, stress, exercise, travel, diet, menses, illness, medications (i.e., birth control pills) and foods such as chocolate, MSG, aged cheese, and red wine.

Mild closed head injury has been associated with complicated migraine-like attacks involving varied vascular distributions. In one study, three-fifths of affected children had a positive family history for migraine headaches, although only one-fifth had a history of migraine unassociated with trauma (Haas, Pineda, & Lourie, 1975). Rarely, migraine has been associated with ischemic brain infarction (20 of 4,874 patients at the Mayo Clinic) (Broderick & Swanson, 1987)

Treatment of children with common migraine is initially attempted with analgesic medications. If headaches are persistent, or focal neurologic symptoms associated, prophylactic treatment may be initiated most frequently with propranolol, amitriptyline, or calcium channel blockers. In children with focal neurologic symptoms, additional evaluation should include a neuro-imaging study. Use of EEG is controversial, as 9% of patients with migraine may have epileptiform abnormalities, and many more have nonspecific EEG changes (Swaiman, 1989).

In young children, several phenomena of episodic, transient dysfunction are thought to represent "migraine equivalents," although headache may or may not be related. These include paroxysmal vertigo, paroxysmal torticollis, and cyclic vomiting.

Alternating hemiplegia of infancy is a rare disorder thought to be a form of complicated migraine that occurs in infants and young children (usually between the ages 2 and 3 years). Episodes of hemiparesis may alternate between right and left sides of the body and last for up to three weeks, although most resolve within 24 hours. At times, focal seizures are associated. Headaches occur in half of the patients studied (Verret & Steele, 1971). Many of these children have a strong family history of migraine and at times for alternating hemiplegia. Unlike adult migraine patients, progressive intellectual deterioration, persistent neurologic deficits (especially dyskensesis), and seizure disorders often occur. Some children develop typical migraine attacks as they get older, while fewer become entirely asymptomatic.

Blood Pressure

High Blood Pressure
Hemorrhages resulting from hypertension are rare in children and produce variable effects. Typically, they result in focal deficits that can be single or multiple. Cognitive functional systems can be mildly to severely disrupted, depending on the site of the lesion (Walton, 1977). Acute hypertensive encephalopathy may lead to extensive edema, resulting in severe diffuse deficits, with convulsions, decerebrate rigidity, coma, or death from cerebral hemorrhage (Berg & Linton, 1989).

Low Blood Pressure
Low blood pressure, or hypotension, usually has only mild effects on brain functioning (Ariel & Strider, 1983); however, at times, it can lead to moderate or severe diffuse cognitive impairment. Symptoms in children include excessive fatigue, convulsions, amnesia, or loss of specific cognitive abilities, all of which suggest ischemia of brain tissue (Gold, 1984). Sequelae are variable and often fluctuating such that diagnosis of brain dysfunction or permanent impairment is difficult.

Inflammatory Vascular Disorders

Vasculitides are a group of disorders characterized by blood-vessel inflammation and necrosis, with marked variability in the size, type, and distribution of the vessels affected. Frequently, multiple organ systems are involved. In the central nervous system, difficulties may arise secondary to arterial thrombosis or embolism, intraparenchymal or subarachnoid hemorrhage, or sinovenous occlusion (Roach, 1989). Fortunately, the majority of these disorders do not usually affect children.

Takayasu's Arteritis
Takayasu's arteritis is an inflammatory process of possible autoimmune etiology, causing inflammation that leads to occlusion of large arteries (e.g., the aorta and its main branches). Symptoms are predominantly cardiovascular and neurologic, with renal involvement also occurring. Young women are most often affected, with a female-to-male ratio of 8.5:1. Age at onset is between 10 and 20 years in 77% of patients but has been reported as early as 4 years of age (Roach, 1989). The disease typically begins with symptoms of nonspecific systemic inflammation, joint pain, and increased blood pressure. Acute cardiac or neurologic symptoms may occur, but usually a prolonged chronic phase with intermittent exacerba-

tions of cardiovascular and neurologic symptoms follows the initial phase, with a progressive and gradual deterioration of function due to vascular occlusion.

In addition to intracranial venous and arterial occlusions, myocardial infarction, pulmonary emobolism, and renovascular hypertension are serious complications. Young patients often present acutely with heart failure (67% of patients less than 15 years of age) (Lupi-Herrera et al., 1977; Sanchez-Torres, Marcushamer, Mispireta, Horwitz, & Vela, 1977). Alternatively, patients may present with recurring TIAs or a single, massive stroke-like event. Nonspecific neurologic symptoms—such as headache, vertigo, dizziness, and syncope—occur in 80 to 90% of patients, likely secondary to arterial hypertension. Focal neurologic abnormalities occur in 7 to 36% of patients, including paresis, sensory changes, aphasia, bulbar signs, and visual disturbance (Moore & Cupps, 1983). Neurologic symptoms are usually secondary to carotid occlusion and referable to anterior and middle cerebral artery distributions. Arteriography demonstrates symmetrical narrowing or occlusion of large arteries with variable collateral circulation and occasional aneurysm formation. The use of high-dose corticosteroids may suppress the early inflammatory component but has questionable efficacy once the occlusive phase of the disease has been reached. Cytotoxic therapy with cyclophosphamide appears to slow disease progression in some patients not responsive to steroids alone. Surgical bypass procedures (on aorta, renal, or carotid arteries) may improve arterial insufficiency. The five-year survival rate in a study of 32 patients was 94% (Roach, 1989).

Systemic Lupus Erythematosus

In systemic lupus erythematosus, approximately 3% of children develop focal neurologic deficits due to cerebrovascular occlusions, usually late in the course of the disease, although there is a 13 to 30% incidence of central nervous system involvement (with 75% due to metabolic, hematologic, or infectious factors) (Swaiman, 1989). A small-vessel vasculitis leads to thrombosis of small arteries in the brain, kidney, and other organs. Psychiatric disturbance—consisting of mood swings, anxiety, depression, personality change, or psychosis—occurs in 25% of patients. Other less common neurologic symptoms include visual disturbance in 6% of patients and peripheral nervous system involvement in 5%. Treatment with corticosteroids and immunosuppressive agents has improved a 10-year survival rate to 75 to 85% (Swaiman, 1989).

Many systemic vasculitic disorders—such as juvenile rheumatoid arthritis, acute rheumatic fever, and mixed connective tissue disease—begin in childhood. However, associated neurologic symptoms in most of these have been attributed to systemic factors such as metabolic encephalopathy, steroid effects, and renovascular hypertension.

Polyarteritis Nodosa

Polyarteritis nodosa, another systemic vasculitic disease, is more common in adults but may affect older children and adolescents. Prior to the use of corticosteroid therapy, there was an 80% mortality rate from neurologic, renal, and cardiovascular involvement. Diffuse involvement of small- and medium-sized arteries has been shown by postmortem study and supported by evidence of segmental narrowing on cerebral angiography. Nonfocal neurologic symptoms may occur soon after diagnosis and include seizures, headaches, disturbance of higher cortical function, and affective disorders. Focal neurologic deficits, visual dysfunction, or increased intracranial pressure may occur later in the disease course, which is chronic with intermittent exacerbations. Peripheral neuropathy or myalgias can be associated. With the use of corticosteroids and immunsuppressive agents, mortality has been decreased to 5%.

Kawasaki's Disease

Kawasaki's disease, also known as infantile polyarteritis nodosa, is an acute systemic vasculitis, usually occurring in children between 6 weeks and 18 months of age, with a male-to-female ratio of 3:1 (Nelson, Behrman, & Vaughn, 1987). The typical presentation includes high fever, cervical lymphadenopathy, conjunctival injection, and skin and mucosal lesions. More serious complications include coronary artery aneurysms, hypertension, and renal failure. Although lethargy, irritability, and aseptic meningitis are common, stroke is rare. Cerebrovascular occlusion of medium-sized arteries has been documented angiographically in six patients with polyarteritis nodosum and acute hemiplegia, and thought to be secondary to thrombosis of inflamed vessels. Intravenous gamma globulin therapy markedly reduces the incidence of coronary artery aneurysms, although the effect on cerebrovascular disease remains unclear. Neurologic prognosis is excellent, in the absence of cerebral infarction.

Schoenlein-Henoch Purpura

Schoenlein-Henoch purpura (HSP), a generalized small-vessel hypersensitivity vasculitis, is most common in childhood, with a median age of onset of 6 years (Belman, Leicher, Moshe, & Mezey, 1985). Inflammation of the small arterioles of the brain, kidney, skin, and gastrointestinal tract appears to be initiated by deposition of IgA immune complexes. Typical features of HSP include a rash on the buttocks and legs, arthritis, fever, crampy abdominal pain, nausea and vomiting. Renal failure and hypertension are common. Seizures may occur in up to 53% of these patients, and headache is seen in 25 to 43%. Mental status changes range from irritability, apathy, or hyperactivity to stupor and coma. Treatment is symptomatic. Patients with focal neurologic involvement due to ischemia or hemorrhage may have residual impairment, whereas children without focal findings have a complete neurologic recovery.

Infection

The most common cause of cerebral vasculitis in children is intracranial infection. Bacterial meningitis is most frequently the culprit, as the cerebral vessels are located in close proximity to the inflamed meninges and traverse the infected subarachnoid space. Rarely, vasculitis may be associated with viral infection. The incidence of stroke in children with bacterial meningitis may be as high as 30%, with children below 1 year of age at increased risk (Roach, 1989). Focal neurologic signs are reflective of the vessels involved. Cerebral vasoconstriction has been demonstrated angiographically in children with tuberculous, fungal, and syphilitic meningitis as well as bacterial infections. Following treatment of the infection, repeat arteriography may show complete resolution of the vasculitic changes. Other infections that have been associated with stroke in children include Mycoplasma pneumoniae (Lerer & Kalavsky, 1973), Rocky Mountain spotted fever (Gorman, Saxon, & Snead, 1981), and cat scratch disease (Lewis & Tucker, 1986).

Blood Dyscrasias (Disturbances)

Stroke can occur secondary to abnormalities of red blood cells, white blood cells, platelets, or coagulation factors. Thrombosis of cortical veins (and occasionally arteries) or venous sinuses may be precipitated by vascular stasis from abnormally large numbers of circulating red blood cells (polycythemia), white blood cells (leukocytosis), or platelets (thrombocytosis), as well as certain coagulation factor abnormalities (particularly protein C, protein S, or antithrombin 3 deficiencies). Abnormalities of red blood cell morphology, particularly sickle cell anemia, are a frequent cause of stroke in children.

Hemoglobinopathies

Sickle Cell Anemia

Sickle cell anemia is the hemoglobinopathy most often associated with stroke in children. A point mutation occurs in the globin beta chain, with a substitution of valine for glutamic acid at position G (Grotta, Manner, Pettigrew, & Yatsu, 1986; Nelson et al., 1987). This causes distortion of the red blood cell shape under conditions of lowered oxygen concentration, present normally in the venous circulation. The resulting increased blood viscosity and reduced flow lead to further tissue hypoxia and acidosis, which, in a cyclic manner, causes increased sickling of red blood cells. The sickle cell gene is inherited in an autosomal recessive manner, with 8.5% of the U.S. African-American population heterozygous for the gene (Hgb SA). These individuals have 35 to 45% Hgb S and, although sickling does not occur under physiologic conditions, it may with extreme stress (such as shock, acidosis, flying in an unpressurized aircraft, or with use of oral contraceptives). Between 0.03 and 0.16% of the U.S. African-American population is homozygous for the sickle cell gene and has sickle cell anemia (HgbSS). In these individuals, 80 to 98% of the hemoglobin contains abnormal beta chains, with the remainder being fetal hemoglobin (Hgb F) (Nelson et al., 1989).

Cerebrovascular complications occur in 8 to 17% of patients with sickle cell anemia (Portnoy & Herion, 1972), usually in those with the most severe systemic disease, manifested by more frequent vaso-occlusive crises, cardiomegaly, lower Hgb values, abnormal liver profiles, and higher reticulocyte counts and frequent infection. Clinical studies have found that 80% of stroke patients with sickle cell anemia are 15 years of age or younger, with a mean age of 6 (Wood, 1978) to 7.7 years (Grotta et al., 1986). Cerebrovascular symptoms infrequently are the first manifestation of the disease (Portnoy & Herion, 1972). Also, 75% of strokes are infarcts (Grotta et al., 1986), 20% are intracerebral hemorrhages (Swaiman, 1989), and 1 to 2% are subarachnoid hemorrhages. Occasionally, sinovenous occlusion or fat emboli (secondary to bone infarction) occur. Patients with hemoglobin SC have an intermediate course, often remaining asymptomatic until adolescence or adulthood, at which time vaso-occlusive phenomena and stroke may occur.

Stroke most often occurs in relation to infection, vaso-occlusive crisis, or both, frequently with accompanying dehydration (Swaiman, 1989). Most commonly, hemispheric "watershed infarcts" occur in the boundary zones between cerebral arteries, due to inadequate cerebral perfusion. Alternatively, either large or small arteries or veins may become occluded in the cerebral hemispheres, brain stem, or spinal cord, with variable symptoms that depend on the location and extent of the infarct. Recurrent strokes lead to progressive neurologic dysfunction. The co-existence of both old and recent strokes in many patients often leads to a clinical picture consisting of multifocal deficits. A pseudobulbar palsy may be seen, with speaking and swallowing difficulty, emotional lability, and poor ambulation. Diagnosis is made by cerebral tomography scan or magnetic resonance imaging.

Angiography should be performed only after reducing the percentage of sickle cell Hgb to less than 20% by exchange transfusion (Wood, 1978). A Moya-Moya angiographic pattern with complete or partial occlusion of the ICA and the presence of prominent collateral circulation has been seen occasionally (Stockman, Nigro, Mishkin, & Oski, 1972). The use of supplemental oxygen and intravenous fluids during vaso-occlusive crises or infections may aid in preventing stroke. However, if neurological symptoms are evolving, transfusion therapy to decrease the percentage of sickled red blood cells must be attempted.

Prior to exchange transfusion programs, 60% of children younger than 15 years of age suffered recurrent strokes (Roach, 1989; Wood, 1978); 80% of these occurred within three years (Roach, 1989) of the initial stroke. Chronic exchange transfusion therapy has been remarkably successful in decreasing the incidence of stroke recurrence to 10% (Sarnaik, Soorya, Kim, Ravindranath, & Lusher, 1979). In some patients, regression of arteriographnic abnormalities and increased cerebral blood flow have been documented (Huttenlocher, Moohr, Johns, & Brown, 1984; Sarnaik et al., 1989). Unfortunately, transfusion therapy must be continued over a prolonged time period, as patients may suffer recurrent strokes within one year following discontinuation of transfusion therapy after a one- to two-year course (Sarnaik et al., 1979). Research in gene manipulation techniques as well as medical treatments to diminish red blood cell sickling are ongoing.

Like cerebral infarction, intracranial hemorrhage in sickle cell patients most often occurs associated with vaso-occlusive crisis. Patients with hemorrhage tend to be older (73% older than 14 years of age), in contrast to patients with first infarcts (66% younger than 15 years of age). Adolescents and adults often have an underlying aneurysm or AVM (7/9 patients older than 14 years) (Van Hoff, Ritchey, & Shaywitz, 1985), whereas in children the cause is often unclear and may be due to increased vascular fragility secondary to chronic arterial changes (Roach, 1989).

Prognosis for children with sickle cell disease and cerebrovascular lesions is variable. Those with cerebral infarction tend to have a low mortality (4 to 13%) but a higher neurologic morbidity (50 to 70%), with persistent motor and/or intellectual problems. On the other hand, patients with intracranial hemorrhage have a higher mortality (60%) but a lower incidence of neurologic sequalae if they survive the acute phase (Van Hoff et al., 1985). The incidence of progressive neurologic impairment due to recurrent stroke has markedly decreased with the institution of exchange transfusion protocols.

Polycythemia

Polycythemia in children, unlike adults, is usually secondary to chronic hypoxia caused by cyanotic congenital heart disease or severe pulmonary disorders. Other illnesses that less often lead to polycythemia include renal disease, hereditary hemorrhagic telangiectasia, and cerebellar hemangioblastoma. Neurologic symptoms are often nonfocal such as headache, dizziness, paresthesias of extremities, and blurred vision. They are usually associated with elevated hematocrit and resolve following phlebotomy (Silverstein, Gilbert, & Wasserman, 1962). Rarely, persistent focal deficits will occur, likely due to increased viscosity and sludging in the cerebral microcirculation. In the presence of focal neurologic symptoms, evaluation for possible brain abscess or cardiogenic emboli is warranted in children with congenital heart disease or pulmonary AV fistulae.

Platelet Abnormalities

The most frequent causes of low platelets in children are idiopathic thrombocytopenic purpura (ITP), leukemia, and chemotherapy. In ITP, intracranial hemorrhage is the most frequent overall cause of morbidity and mortality. The risk of hemorrhage is directly proportional to the platelet count (Roach, 1989) and usually occurs with counts below 20,000. It is most likely to occur within days to weeks of diagnosis. When hemorrhage occurs later in the course of disease, systemic viral infection, with the production of antiplatelet antibodies, is often associated (Krivit, Tate, White, & Robinson, 1981; Roach, 1989). Bleeding may be intraparenchymal (affecting any portion of the cerebrum), subdural, or subarachnoid. Focal symptoms of intraparenchymal hemorrhage reflect the location of the bleeding and usually progress over hours, associated with a diminishing level of consciousness. Neck rigidity, headache, and altered mental status are the most common early findings in subarachnoid hemorrhage.

Children with ITP who develop any central nervous system findings should be emergently evaluated, both clinically and with a neuro-imaging study. The prophylactic avoidance of aspirin and antihistamines in these patients must be stressed. Initial treatment is with high-dose prednisone and platelet transfusions. If not successful in preventing progression of symptoms, splenectomy, followed by surgical evacuation of the hemorrhage, is frequently undertaken.

With aggressive management, a favorable outcome has been documented in a large number of cases (Woerner, Abildgaard, & French, 1981).

Increased numbers of circulating platelets in children are almost always secondary to an underlying systemic disorder. The many disorders associated with thrombocytosis include Kawasaki disease, infections, neoplasms, trauma, nutritional deficiency (especially iron deficiency), or drug effect due to steroids or chemotherapy (Addiego, Mentzer, & Dallman, 1974). Nonspecific neurologic symptoms—such as headache, dizziness, and altered mental status—occur most often, but seizures (focal or generalized), transient ischemic events, and stroke are also seen. Transient neurologic findings and associated headache can resemble a migraine attack. Symptoms may be secondary to the release of serotonin from breakdown of platelets or due to obstruction of cerebral microvasculature by platelets. Children appear to have less long-term neurologic morbidity from thrombocytosis than do adults. Symptoms often resolve with lowering of the platelet count. Therapy with aspirin or dypridamole is useful initially, followed by chemotherapy (i.e., hydroxyurea) for refractory thrombocytosis (Roach, 1989).

Leukemia, Cancers, and Chemotherapy

The leukemias are the most frequently encountered childhood malignancy. They are more often associated with cerebral infarction and intracranial hemorrhage than are solid tumors. Surprisingly, marked leukocytosis has not been associated with an increased incidence of cerebral infarction, despite elevated blood viscosity. Of 26 patients with white blood cell counts greater than level 100,000 in one study, none developed strokes (Packer, Rorke, Lange, Siegel, & Evans, 1985).

Several cerebrovascular syndromes have been identified in children with cancer: (1) vascular thromboses associated with disseminated intravascular coagulation (DIC); (2) a diffuse encephalopathy that is frequently mistaken to be of septic or metabolic etiology; and (3) focal or multifocal deficits due to infarction following venous or arterial thromboses.

Chemotherapy, particularly with L-Asparaginase, has been associated with both cerebral infarction and intracranial hemorrhage. Drug-induced suppression of clotting factor production by the liver is thought to be followed by a rebound doubled production of these factors, explaining the predisposition to both hemorrhage and intracerebral thrombosis. The many coagulation abnormalities encountered include low levels of fibrinogen, plasminogen, and antithrombin III, decreased factors IX and XI, increased factors V and VIII, and prolonged plasma clotting times (Packer et al., 1985; Priest, Ramsay, Latchaw, & Lockman, 1980; Priest, Ramsay, Steinherz, & Tubergan, 1982). The majority of cerebrovascular episodes occur in the third or fourth week of treatment, when hemostatic abnormalities are maximal. There is no method of anticipating which children will develop these potentially devastating complications.

Venous sinus thrombosis is one of the most common neurologic problems secondary to the chemotherapy-induced hypercoaguable state. Initial symptoms are nonspecific and include headache, fever, scalp vein prominence, and signs of increased intracranial pressure. With extension of the thrombus to cerebral cortical veins, progression to coma with generalized or focal seizures occurs (Lockman, Mastri, Priest, & Nesbit, 1980; Packer et al., 1985). Alternatively, arterial thrombosis with focal seizures and neurologic findings may occur. Diagnosis is confirmed by cerebral angiography, although evidence of abnormal cerebrospinal fluid on lumbar puncture, with elevated pressure, protein, and red blood cell count, is indicative. Therapy involves reducing intracranial pressure (Lockman et al., 1980), correcting coagulation abnormalities (with FFP, Vitamin K, and cryoprecipitate) (Priest et al., 1980), and preventing thrombus propagation (Lockman et al., 1980). The use of heparin for this purpose remains controversial, as intracerebral hemorrhage may further complicate the situation (Lockman et al., 1980).

High-dose methotrexate therapy has been associated with focal neurologic symptoms, thought to be due to embolic phenomena, in several children being treated for osteogenic sarcoma (Packer et al., 1985). Patients with neuroblastoma metastatic to the torcular region may develop focal neurologic deficits (seizures and obtundation) secondary to venous obstruction.

Intracranial hemorrhage may occur in association with hemorrhagic infarction or from intratumor bleed (in children with primary brain tumors or metastases), thrombocytopenia, or coagulation factor deficiencies.

Coagulation Disorders

Hemophilia is the most common and serious congenital disorder of coagulation, caused by deficiency of factor VIII (80%), IX (15%), or XI. Factor VIII deficiency (classic hemophilia) and factor IX deficiency are transmitted in an X-linked recessive manner (thus only affecting males) and are clinically more severe than factor XI deficiency, which is transmitted by autosomal dominant or recessive inheritance (Nelson et al., 1987). Patients present with excessive bruising and bleeding following minor injury. Hemorrhage into joint spaces (hemarthroses) and muscles is common. Prolonged clotting times are evident by laboratory testing. Intracranial hemorrhage is the most serious complication, occurring in 2 to 7.8% of hemophiliacs (Lutschg & Vassella, 1981), most often in those with severe factor deficiencies and in children less than 3 years of age. Fatal hemorrhage during infancy may occur without prior evidence of a bleeding disorder. A recent history of seemingly trivial closed-head injury is present in 50 to 75% of cases (Lutschg et al., 1981; Roach, 1989). Bleeding is more often intraparenchymal, subdural, or subarachnoid, with epidural and cerebellar hemorrhage less common.

Symptoms include headache, backache, stiff neck, vomiting, and seizures, which are often followed by focal neurologic signs. Emergent clinical evaluation is warranted, and factor replacement therapy should be administered immediately (and before further diagnostic evaluation) if intracranial hemorrhage is suspected. If hemorrhage is confirmed, a level of at least 30 to 50% of normal factor activity should be continued for 10 to 14 days (Roach, 1989).

Prophylactic factor replacement therapy for asymptomatic patients following minor closed-head injury has markedly reduced the incidence of intracranial hemorrhage. There is a mortality rate of 14 to 34% following intracranial hemorrhage, with neurologic sequelae in half of the survivors (Roach, 1989). Other, less common coagulation disorders that may cause intracranial hemorrhage include factor V deficiency, afibrinogenemia, and Von Willebrand's disease.

In contrast to the bleeding diathesis produced by deficiency of clotting factors, vascular thrombosis occurs when plasma proteins necessary to inhibit coagulation are deficient. Antithrombin III-heparin cofactor is a major inhibitor of activated coagulation factors. Deficiency is inherited in an autosomal dominant manner, and patients present with recurrent thromboembolic events most often beginning in young adulthood. Thrombosis may occur spontaneously, or following trauma, infections, burns, or childbirth (Ambruso, Jacobson, & Hatthaway, 1980). Lower extremity venous thrombosis is most common, but cerebral thromboses and pulmonary emboli also occur. Anticoagulation with heparin in the acute phase, followed by Coumadin, is often used.

Protein C and its cofactor protein S inhibit the clotting cascade by inactivating factors Va and VIIIa, as well as enhancing fibrinolysis. Deficiency of either is inherited autosomally and has been associated with venous and arterial thromboses in adults and children (Israels & Seshia, 1987).

Hemolytic Uremic Syndrome

Hemolytic uremic syndrome is defined by the triad of microangiopathic hemolytic anemia, thrombocytopenia, and uremia. Neurologic dysfunction occurs in approximately 35 to 50% of children (Sheth, Swick, & Haworth, 1986). Nonfocal neurologic symptoms—including an altered level of consciousness, behavioral changes, and generalized seizures—have been attributable to anoxia, hypertension, and metabolic abnormalities (including hyponatremia, acid-base changes, and hypocalcemia). Focal neurologic signs may be secondary to cerebral microvascular thrombi. The etiology of three cases of probable large-vessel strokes remains unclear (Trevathan & Dooling, 1987). As hemorrhagic infarction may occur, anticoagulation with heparin is discouraged (Roach, 1989).

NEUROPSYCHOLOGICAL FINDINGS

Cerebrovascular Disorders

Information regarding neuropsychological evaluation of adults following cerebrovascular occlusion and hemorrhage is available from many sources. In contrast, relatively little is published regarding neuropsychological assessment of children and adolescents with cerebrovascular disorders (CVD), and inferences must therefore be drawn from the adult literature as well as accessible studies of children. In general, the effects of cerebrovascular accidents in children tend to be better localized and circumscribed in comparison with the more widespread damage associated with trauma or infection. A summary of major neuropsychological findings in adults, adolescents, and children with vascular disorders involving major cerebral arteries is found in Table 8.1.

TABLE 8.1 Neuropsychological Findings in Vascular Disorders

Function	Anterior Cerebral	Middle Cerebral	Posterior Cerebral
Motor	Contralateral weakness or paralysis, typically most affecting the distal-lower extremity. Rapid alternating movements may be impaired or an inability to maintain them.	Contralateral paralysis with face and upper extremity more affected than lower.	Typically motor involvement not present except when proximal arteries are affected; then hemiballismus may result because of subthalamic nucleus lesion, cranial nerve palsy, or hemiparesis owing to involvement of the corticospinal tract as it passes down the brain stem.
Sensory	Absent or mild contralateral tactile loss.	Depending on extent of involvement, there may be contralateral auditory, visual, and tactile sensory disturbance.	If unilateral, then contralateral hemianopsia typically develops. Cortical blindness occurs if bilateral. Proximal occlusion may affect the thalamus, producing sensory disturbance, pain or both.
Language	Impaired articulation or disturbance in motor inertia may be present.	With left hemisphere involvement, may develop a Broca's, Wernicke's, global, or conduction aphasia depending on the site and extent of involvement.	If involves the left hemisphere, alexia without agraphia or other aphasic symptoms may occur.
Praxis	If anterior corpus callosum is affected, there may be left arm praxis.	Apraxia may occur with lesions in either hemisphere. Constructional apraxia (in the absence of aphasia) and dressing apraxia are common with right hemisphere involvement.	Constructional apraxia with right hemisphere involvement may occur.

Continued

TABLE 8.1 *Continued*

Function	Anterior Cerebral	Middle Cerebral	Posterior Cerebral
Spatial-Perceptual	Typically not affected.	If right hemisphere is affected, varying degrees of impairment may be present.	If right hemisphere is affected, primarily visuospatial functions will be impaired.
Memory	Some disturbance in new memory may be present.	With left hemisphere involvement greater tendency for disturbance in verbal memory; with right hemisphere greater tendency for visual memory disturbance.	Global amnesia may occur that is either transient or permanent. Permanent short-term memory deficits may also occur.
Gnosis	Infrequently may display features of anosognosia (failure to appreciate loss of function).	With right hemisphere involvement, may have greater tendency to develop topographagnosia (loss of direction) and anosognosia.	Typically not affected.
Behavior	Frontal lobe syndrome may develop with right hemisphere, prosody may be affected.	Impaired prosody if right hemisphere is involved.	No particular behavioral syndrome is characteristic.

Source: From *Diagnostic Clinical Neuropsychology* (pp. 107–127) by E. Bigler, 1984, Austin, TX: University of Texas Press. Reprinted by permission.

In Bornstein's (1986) review of the neuropsychological aspects of cerebrovascular disease, he concluded that there is not always a consistent relationship between the anatomic distribution of a vascular lesion and the degree and nature of neuropsychological impairment it may cause. This may be due, in part, to congenital anatomic variations in cerebral vasculature, rate of development of occlusive arterial disease, efficiency of collateral blood supply, and presence of additional medical risk factors that could compromise the cerebral vascular system.

Age at Onset

Of great importance is the effect of age at the time of injury on subsequent cognitive function. Hebb (1942) proposed that early brain insult disrupts intelligence more than later damage. His review of the literature led him to conclude that early injury may have a more generalized, rather than selective, effect on normal adult intelligence than late injury. However, Kennard (1942), based on her research with developing and mature monkeys, reported that better recovery or sparing of function is found if lesions in the motor areas occur early in development. The extent of sparing or loss of function varies not only with age of onset but also with age at testing and abilities measured by testing (Goldman, 1975; Nonneman & Isaacson, 1973).

Schneider (1979) concluded that children with early brain damage may lack the specific sensory and motor impairments observed in brain-injured adults but demonstrate persistent, subtle cognitive deficits not frequently found in later injury. Furthermore, anomalous sensory and motor functions—such as hyperasthesia, avoidance of diagonal pathwalking, and persistent mirror movements—are reported for children with lesions prior to one year of age (Rudel, Teuber, & Twitchell, 1966; Rudel & Teuber, 1971; Woods & Teuber, 1978). The anomalous motor function found by Woods and Teuber (1978) led Woods to state that the "earlier the lesion, the greater the reorganization of neural mechanisms underlying behavior" (personal communication, quoted in Schneider, 1979, p. 558).

Kennard (1942) suggested that sparing of function could be explained by alteration of neuronal connections. In support of Kennard's theory, Steward (1984) proposed that functionally significant rearrangements of neuronal connections may occur following brain injury, thus contributing to improved recovery. Variation in the extent or nature of this neuroplasticity might account for the differences in the functional consequences of injury in the young and old. Similarly, Schneider (1979) and colleagues found reorganization of brain connections by collateral sprouting of axons and redirected growth of axonal pathways in developing animals with lesions occurring soon after birth. Thus, he predicted that specific lesions in fetal and neonatal humans will result in behavioral anomalies of sensorimotor functions, cognitive functions, and emotional responses and expression.

One of the differential effects of pediatric versus adult brain injury is the possibility of delayed onset of deficits. Because early stroke impacts parts of the brain that may not be fully developed, the effects at times are not noticed until a later developmental stage. For example, if a toddler has an insult to the frontal lobe, it is not until the "executive control processes" (e.g., planning, directed attention) are expected to be functioning that such difficulties would become apparent. The child, who is continuing to develop, is faced with the challenge of recovery/improvement in the context of ongoing development. Thus, although results suggest that lesions occurring early in development may result in better recovery or general sparing of function, sensorimotor, intellectual, and behavioral deficits may be masked and become problematic as the child grows older. Such compromises are consistent with findings by Craft, Shaw, and Carlidge's report (1972) that even mildly injured infants, who demonstrated no difficulties at recovery, experienced intellectual, behavioral, and sensorimotor deficits at follow-up several years later.

Similarly, poorer recovery was found for children who were injured during the first year than during their second and third years of life (Raimondi & Hirschauer, 1984). Benton's (1962) review of the literature indicated that the greatest impairment for children with brain damage occurring early in life is in the areas of visual motor skills, perceptual motor speed, abstract reasoning, memory and learning of new information, and performance of complex, multi-element verbal and nonverbal tasks, which cannot be properly assessed until the child reaches school age.

Intellectual Functioning

Early studies of the general intellectual functioning of brain-injured children frequently attempted to diagnose brain damage using IQ (intelligence quotient) scores. A major difficulty with this approach is that IQ scores were created to provide a developmental evaluation and are not sensitive tests of brain damage (Dennis, 1985a). Dennis and colleagues have reported normal IQs in children and adolescents with infantile hemiplegia, hemidecortication, and congenitally absent corpus callosum (Dennis, 1980; Dennis, Lovett, & Wiegel-Crump, 1981; Dennis & Whitaker, 1976; Kohn & Dennis, 1974). However, despite normal IQ after brain damage early in life, anomalous patterns of cognitive functions are often found. For example, two studies report findings of children with early injury (including cerebrovascular disorders) who demonstrate normal verbal IQ but significant deficits in the understanding and use of both oral and written language (Dennis, Lovett, & Wiegel-Crump, 1981; Dennis & Whitaker, 1977). Thus, many important aspects of cognition, such as more complex linguistic skills, may not be predicted by IQ testing following brain injury that has occurred at an early age. Dennis's results (1985a, 1985b) suggest that IQ test scores are more sensitive to late-occurring brain damage than to disorders beginning early in life.

Several studies (Aram & Ekelman, 1986; Riva & Cazzaniga, 1986) have examined the relationship between age at onset of lesion and IQ by comparing children with unilateral lesions with onset prior to 1 year of age and those with lesion onset after 1 year of age. Results indicated that children with early left-hemisphere lesion onset had significantly lower verbal IQs (VIQs) and performance IQs (PIQs). Both early and late right-hemisphere lesions significantly lowered only PIQ, and the latter group showed increased distractibility. Similarly, Banich, Levin, Kim, and Huttenlocher (1990) evaluated 41 children, ranging in age from 6 to 18 years with congenital and acquired lesions. Results suggested that for congenitally hemiplegic children, IQ decreases, beginning at 6 to 8 years of age, which does not lend support to St. James-Roberts's (1981) hypothesis that higher intellectual functioning is associated with longer time period between onset and testing. Such findings may be partially explained by the requirement on intelligence measures for increased perceptual speed with age. Many children with early problems appear to "dement" at this age, as they never learn to master abstract concepts.

Language and Executive Control Processes
Acquired aphasia in childhood was long believed to be nonfluent, transient, and equally the result of left- and right-hemisphere damage (Woods & Teuber, 1978). Such assumptions evolved following Broca's (1861) original report of aphasia in an adult and were supported by Cotard (1868), Charcot's student, who noted language development in several patients with infantile hemiplegia and atrophy of the left cerebral hemisphere. Further support for this position was given with frequent reports of swift recovery from acquired aphasia in childhood (Clarus, 1874). Thus, the premise of equipotentiality for language function until approximately 9 to 11 years of age (Lenneberg, 1967) has continued until the last several years.

Research regarding the effets of age on language impairment has been inconclusive. Consistent with Kennard's findings, several authors report that language comprehension and production abilities are relatively spared by unilateral lesions occurring perinatally or in infancy (Annett, 1973; Vargha-Khadem, O'-Gorman, & Watters, 1985; Woods & Teuber, 1978). In Annett's study of 106 children, ages 5 to 18, with left- or right-sided hemiplegia, greater severity of speech deficits was found with increased age of onset. Similarly, Vargha-Khadem and colleagues reported poorer performance on tasks of auditory verbal comprehension and object naming with left hemisphere injuries acquired after 5 years of age.

Site of Lesion

The importance of localization of function has been long debated. Most recently, discussions have focused on whether changed behavior following a lesion is attributable to the loss of function of the damaged area or to the altered performance of remaining structures, which take over that function. Cognitive functions—such as language, visuospatial ability, and directed attention—are affected by lesions in numerous locations.

Intellectual Functioning
As with adults, the site of a lesion is the major factor influencing the outcome of cerebrovascular disorders in children. Previous attempts to relate lateralized brain damage to lowered verbal and nonverbal intelligence measures have usually produced inconsistent results. Dennis (1985b) proposed a number of factors that may partially explain such variability of findings. In her study of the relationship

between intellectual functioning and medical variables, laterality of the lesion predicted the relationship between VIQ and left-hemisphere injury but was not an adequate predictor of PIQ in the context of right-hemisphere damage. Dennis also
found that VIQ was most impacted by cortical damage, whereas subcortical injury
lowered PIQ.

The effects of site of lesion on intellectual functioning have been explored
by Aram and colleagues. Aram and Ekelman (1986) compared profiles for the
Wechsler Intelligence Scale for Children-Revised (WISC-R) for 18 left-lesioned
and 13 right-lesioned children, with clearly defined unilateral involvement
to normal matched controls. VIQ, PIQ, and FSIQ (full-scale IQ) were within
normal limits for all groups, and VIQ and PIQ discrepancy was not found to be
related to lesion laterality. However, right-lesioned children scored significantly
lower on all scales and were impaired on Kaufman's Perceptual Organization
factor. For both left- and right-lesioned subjects, the subtests that make up the
Freedom from Distractibility factor were significantly lower. Left-lesioned children showed a poorer performance on Digit Span and significantly higher performance on Picture Arrangement than on Information or Coding. In contrast,
right-lesioned children scored lower on all subtests, particularly Digit Span and
Picture Arrangement, but not on Comprehension.

Aram and Ekelman (1986) then compared groups with more specific lesion
localization (i.e., prerolandic vs. retrolandic, cortical vs. subcortical, left- vs.
right-sided lesions). They found that left subcortical impairment was associated
with significantly lower VIQ, compared to PIQ and FSIQ. In addition, children
with left subcortical injuries had lower Verbal Comprehension than Perceptual
Organization factors. All left-lesioned subjects, but particularly children with
retrolandic involvement, and all right-lesioned subjects had significantly lower
Freedom from Distractibility factors. Prerolandic involvement in three right-
lesioned children resulted in somewhat lower VIQ than PIQ, whereas subcortical involvement was associated with markedly lower PIQ than VIQ. Those children with only subcortical right-hemisphere lesions demonstrated particular
strength on the Verbal Comprehension factor.

Although rare, ischemic strokes have been reported not only in both hemispheres but also in vertebrobasilar areas and subcortical regions. In children,
large subcortical infarcts are more commonly described in the territory of the
basal ganglia and the internal capsule than the small lacunar infarcts, often seen
in this location in adults. A number of clinical features may be seen with these
larger subcortical infarcts, including unilateral motor and sensory deficits, unilateral visual and sensory neglect or inattention, athetosis, or dystonia. Additionally, confusion, dysphasia, dysarthria, seizures, constructional impairment,
and reading difficulties have been reported (Kappelle, Willemse, Ramos, & van
Gijn, 1989).

Language

The relationship between unilateral hemispheric lesions and language acquisition in children remains controversial. Hecaen (1983) reported that site of lesion
is a major factor in the development of language deficits. Anterior lesions (frontal

and/or rolandic) were associated with dysarthria and additional language deficits, including auditory and visual verbal comprehension, much more frequently than temporal lesions. Although numerous reports have emphasized the importance of the dominant hemisphere in language-related tasks, right hemisphere cerebrovascular accidents have been implicated, infrequently, in aphasic deficits.

The impact of right and left lateral ventricular dilatation following intraventricular hemorrhage was studied in 45 low birth weight (LBW) preterm infants (mean age = 16 months), 18 of whom suffered intraventricular hemorrhage (IVH) (Bendersky & Lewis, 1990). Analyses indicated that left, but not right, ventricular dilatation was inversely correlated with expressive, but not receptive language deficits. In general, more severe neonatal complications and lower socioeconomic status were associated with an increased likelihood of subsequent speech delay.

The effects of site of lesion on language was explored in eight left-lesioned and eight right-lesioned children (age range = 18 months to 8 years) (Aram, Ekelman, Rose, & Whitaker, 1985). Although both groups of lesioned subjects had depressed IQ score, most functioned within the normal range or above. Lexical comprehension and production were lowered in both groups but particularly in the right-lesioned subjects. In contrast, misarticulation and deficits in syntactic production were found in left-lesioned subjects in comparison with controls and with right-lesioned children. Fluency disorders were observed in both groups.

Visuospatial Skills

As with adults, visuospatial impairment has been found to be related to site of lesion in children. Impairment of spatial cognitive functioning, demonstrated by a restricted range of block play, was found in 18-to 42-month-old children with right-hemisphere injury by Stiles-Davis, Sugarman, and Nass (1985). Similarly, when 4 five-year-old children (2 with congenital left-hemisphere lesions and 2 with right-hemisphere lesions) were compared with 20 normal 3.5-to 5-year-olds in copying geometric forms and free drawings, the drawings of children with right-hemisphere injury were found to lack organization and configurational coherence, although no problems were found in the drawings of children with left-hemisphere damage (Stiles-Davis, Janowsky, Engel, & Nass, 1988). This is similar to the spatial dysfunction seen in adults with right parietal lesions. In the adult literature (Warrington, James, & Kinsbourne, 1966), subjects with left-hemisphere lesions were found to omit details in their drawing but this difficulty was not evident in the pediatric study.

Academic Skills

Although recovery of language and other cognitive abilities often occurs in children, difficulties in academic achievement following lateralized brain lesions may persist. In a study of 20 left-lesioned and 12 right-lesioned children, both groups showed decreased performance on the reasoning, perceptual speed, and memory clusters, and, for scholastic aptitude, were lower in all areas except that of general knowledge (Aram & Ekelman, 1988a). Left-lesioned subjects performed more poorly on written language tasks, in comparison to right-lesioned children's lower performances on reading, math, and written language.

The effects of lateralized lesions on reading and spelling were explored by Heaton, Schmitz, Avitable, and Lehrman (1987). They found that *Peabody Individual Achievement Test* (PIAT) performances were strongly related to the extent of brain damage within the left hemisphere, but not within the right. Both right- and left-hemisphere damaged groups were impaired on the Reading Comprehension and Spelling subtests relative to controls, whereas only the left-lesioned group was impaired on Reading Recognition. Reading and spelling deficits were associated with temporal-and occipital-lobe involvement in the left-lesion group, but specific lobe involvement was unrelated to PIAT performance in the right-lesioned group.

Developmental and acquired learning disabilities related to damage of the left hemisphere (e.g., alexia, agraphia, acalculia) have been well described in bcth children and adults (Albert, 1979; Kolb & Whishaw, 1990; Levin, 1979; Marcie & Hecaen, 1979). More recently, a learning disability of the right hemisphere has been described (Rourke, 1987; Tranel, Hall, Olson, & Tranel, 1987; Weintraub & Mesulam, 1983). The resulting pattern of dysfunction consists of deficits in non-verbal intellectual functioning, visuospatial skills, visual memory, and paralinguistic skills (e.g., inability to display affect). Additionally, individuals are noted to display shyness and chronic emotional and social difficulties. Consistent with this description, one case study of a 6½-year-old girl who was born prematurely and suffered a right-sided intraventricular hemorrhage found relatively stronger verbal than nonverbal abilities, with weaker numerical than linguistic skills and poor visual-motor integration (Sparrow, 1990).

Mood/Temperament

As with adults, relationships between affect and temperament and site of lesion have been found for children. Ten children with left-hemisphere damage (mean age = 21.9 months) and 9 children with right-hemisphere damage, whose lesions occurred prior to 12 months of age, were compared on the *Toddler Temperament Scale* (TTS) between the age of 1 to 3 years (Nass & Koch, 1987). Unilateral damage, confirmed on computerized tomography (CT), was found to be primarily related to prenatal infarctions of the middle cerebral artery. With the exception of the approach/withdrawal category (TTS), right-lesioned children showed more negative temperament, particularly in regard to rhythmicity (ability to keep to a schedule) and mood. Such findings are consistent with the adult literature (Ross & Rush, 1981) on the effects of right-hemisphere vascular lesions, indicating deficits in emotional output associated with dysphoric mood, flattened affect, aprosodic voice patterns, and dysfunctional gesturing.

Etiology

Little information is available regarding the comparative effects of etiology on neuropsychological outcome for children. In adults, differential impact of tumors and strokes was described in one study of 17 individually matched right-handed adult subjects on the basis of lesion location (Anderson, Damasio, & Tranel, 1990). They found that stroke victims had more severe language impairment and more frequent agraphia. Some tumor patients performed normally on neurpsychological tests, whereas stroke victims consistently demonstrated deficits relative to location. This is not unexpected concerning the mechanisms of each. Patients with infiltrating tumors often have preserved islands of unaffected brain close by, whereas strokes lead to complete cell death in the affected vascular territory.

A regression model utilizing multiple medical variables was used by Dennis (1985a, 1985b) to derive IQ estimates from Wechsler IQ scores of 407 subjects with brain damage early in life. Her data suggested that intermittent vascular ischemia (e.g., Moya-Moya syndrome), without other contributing factors, predicted an FSIQ and VIQ of approximately 84, with no significant effect on PIQ. In general, the more acute the lesion, the lower the VIQ. However, PIQ was most likely to be compromised by late onset (after 1 year of age), gradually occurring, midline subcortical tumors of brief duration.

Disorders Following Stroke

Aphasia

Speech disorders in children can be divided into developmental disorders (congenital) and acquired disorders (Ludlow, 1980). *Developmental disorders* of speech and language occur prior to the language acquisition (i.e., before 1 year of age), thus, children with developmental language disorders have never experienced normal language. *Acquired disorders* result from some form of cerebral insult after the emergence of language. Children with acquired aphasia disorders demonstrate normal language development prior to injury and, therefore, in this way, resemble adults.

Language is represented in the left hemisphere for approximately 98% of right-handed persons, and 68% of left-handed adults. The remaining individuals have language dominance in the right hemisphere, and a small minority have a shared dominance (between both hemispheres) (Pirozzolo, 1979). Similarly, aphasic disorders are found in comparable patterns for left-sided, right-sided, or bilateral lesions in right- and nonright-handed adults (Hicks & Kinsbourne, 1978; Satz, 1980). Children 5 years of age and older have been found to demonstrate patterns of aphasia for left- and right-sided lesions similar to adults (Krashen, 1973; Satz & Bullard-Bates, 1981).

The first published comparison of childhood and adult aphasias was made by Bernhardt (1897). "True aphasia is not rare in childhood: it is a frequent symptom of infantile cerebral hemiplegia, mostly transient, rarely permanent. It is mostly motor in type" (cited in Guttman, 1942, p. 205). In general, the incidence, type, and prognosis of aphasia in adults and children are significantly different.

Two major differences between children and adults with acquired aphasia should be emphasized. In children, (1) recovery is usually more rapid and extensive (Lennenberg, 1967) and (2) aphasia is usually of the nonfluent type, with primary features of mutism and lack of spontneity of speech (Fletcher & Taylor,

1984; Hecaen, 1976). It is also significant that acquired aphasia in children does not generally fit neatly into the well-established aphasia subtypes described in adults.

Aphasia in childhood was previously assumed to be invariably nonfluent and similar to Broca's aphasia (Broca, 1861; van Dongen & Visch-Brink, 1988). Although children most often present with nonfluent aphasia, cases of fluent aphasia are reported (Murdoch, 1990; Van Hout, Evrard, & Lyon, 1985; Woods & Teuber, 1978). Difficulties occur most commonly with expressive language, articulation, syntax, and the presence of a telegraphic style (Ludlow, 1980). Neologisms (which resolve rapidly) and paraphasias in both fluent and nonfluent aphasia occur with much less frequency than in adults (Hecaen, 1976, 1983; Murdoch, 1990; Visch-Brink & Van de Sandt-Koenderman, 1985). It remains unclear if such differences are attributable to age-related mechanisms or to age-independent factors, such as lesion site, type of lesion, or timing of assessment (Satz & Bullard-Bates, 1981). Recovery from acquired childhood aphasia most frequently occurs in the following sequence: mutism, decreased initiation of speech, nonfluent speech, telegraphic speech, impaired auditory comprehension, dysnomia, dysarthria, and reading and writing difficulties (Murdoch, 1990).

A review of the literature by Satz and Bullard-Bates (1981) led to the following conclusions regarding acquired childhood aphasia: (1) the risk of aphasia or language impairment is approximately the same in right-handed children and adults if the left hemisphere is damaged; (2) the risk of aphasia or language impairment is subtantially greater following left- versus right-sided brain injury regardless of age—at least after infancy; (3) the risk of aphasia after right hemisphere injury (crossed aphasia) is rare in both right-handed adults and children, particularly after ages 3 to 4 years and perhaps earlier; (4) the aphasia pattern, although predominantly nonfluent in a majority of children, is by no means constant and other aphasic patterns can coexist or appear independently, including disorders of auditory comprehension, writing, reading, and naming; (5) spontaneous recovery often occurs in children, but a majority of studies found unresolved aphasia (25 to 50%) one year after onset; and (6) even in cases of recovery from aphasia, serious cognitive and academic sequelae were found.

Studies of acquired aphasia secondary to vascular disorders in children suggest that the pattern of language symptoms is similar to those seen in aphasic adults (Aram, Rose, Rekate, & Whitaker, 1983; Dennis, 1980). Aram and colleagues (1983) described a left-hemisphere vascular lesion in the putamen, anterior limb of the internal capsule, and lateral portion of the head of the caudate nucleus in a right-handed 7-year-old girl. Symptoms, which were similar to adult aphasics with subcortical lesions, included right-sided hemiplegia, mutism, oral apraxia, and a comprehension deficit in the absence of dysarthria. Examination six months after onset revealed only mild hemiparesis and minor spelling problems.

Van Dongen and Visch-Brink (1988) reported the occurrence of neologisms and paraphasias during the first week of recovery for both children with traumatic brain injury and children with brain injury due to cerebrovascular accident, subdural empyema, or encephalitis resulting in acquired aphasia. However, a more severe aphasia was found in latter group, two of whom remained aphasic after one year, with decreased neologisms and paraphasias over time. Similarly, Guttman (1942) and Van Dongen and Loonen (1977) found that children with acquired aphasia due to vascular disorders recovered language less well than those with aphasia from traumatic head injuries.

In addition to the case studies described, Hecaen's (1983) sample of acquired childhood aphasia included four children with vascular etiology (hematoma due to ruptured angioma). All were aphasic with additional symptoms, including disorders of auditory comprehension, paraphasias, mutism, articulation, and naming. Reading and writing difficulties were also found. During periods of recovery ranging from one to eight years, the four children showed good improvement, with only naming and writing difficulties remaining. Similarly, Ludlow (1980) found that the effects of preschool language impairments are significant, resulting in placement of 60% of these children in special classes at 9 years of age.

Aphasia-Related Disorders

As described previously, aphasia is often associated with other disturbances of language and nonverbal function. The following aphasia-related disorders are found in children and should be considered in assessment of the child with aphasia: reading, writing (agraphia), acalculia, finger agnosia, right-left disorientation (Gerstmann syndrome), constructional disorders, and apraxia (Kaplan & Goodglass, 1981). In children, these difficulties are frequently identified as learning disabilities but they should also be considered in the broader framework of aphasia-related disorders.

Numerous reports have emphasized the importance of the occipital, parietal, and temporal lobes of the dominant hemisphere in such language-related tasks as reading, written language, and arithmetic. Other findings also suggest that frontal lobe damage can result in alexia that is not simply a reflection of motor speech impairment (Benson, 1977).

REHABILITATION

Cognitive rehabilitation is defined as a systematic effort to assist patients in overcoming intellectual deficits resulting from brain dysfunction. Such efforts consist of reinforcement and strengthening of previously learned patterns of cognitive behavior and the development and implementation of new cognitive patterns to compensate for neurological systems too impaired to function (Task Force on Head Injury, 1984).

A number of theoretical models of cognitive rehabilitation are available in the adult literature. These include such approaches as remedial strategies focused on improving test-specific deficits, groups or patterns of behavior, and behavioral engineering (Gray & Dean, 1989). These approaches will be discussed in greater detail later in the chapter. Pediatric cognitive rehabilitation is a relatively new field; thus, theories of cognitive rehabilitation specifically developed for children are quite limited. However, one approach supported by a number of authors is the use of remedial strategies that are designed to complement the child's current style of processing information (Hartlage & Reynolds, 1981; Hartlage & Telzrow, 1984).

The role of neuropsychologists in cognitive rehabilitation has previously been only in assessment and diagnosis of disorders related to cerebral dysfunction. More recently, the development of goals and treatment plans for cognitive, behavioral, and emotional sequelae have been added. A neuropsychologist's training in brain-behavior relationships places the clinician in a unique position to assist other members of the treatment team and the ongoing caregivers in understanding the child's strengths, limitations, and potential risks. Providing emotional support through therapy for pediatric patients and their families is also important in the adjustment process. The involvement of parents in the rehabilitation program is crucial in bridging the gap between professional and home care. Utilizing parents' knowledge of the child while training them in appropriate care and management of post injury is an important key to developing a consistent, workable treatment plan.

Child neuropsychology focuses on brain-behavior relationships in the developing brain, and, as such, is complicated by an ever-changing nervous system. Consideration of previously acquired skills is of interest for adults and older children but less so for younger children, who may not yet have acquired skills but may be impacted by delay in or inability to reach developmental milestones. Thus, *cognitive rehabilitation* and *cognitive retraining* are terms reserved for older children and adults with the goal of returning to an already acquired ability. With younger brain-impaired children, the focus may more aptly be described as *cognitive training*, in which skills are taught utilizing current abilities and without the assumption of prior competence (Brown & Morgan, 1987).

A developmental, idiographic approach to cognitive training based on the individual characteristics of each child is recommended by Brown and Morgan (1987). Variables for program development should include history, social environment, age and stage of cognitive development, level of preinjury functioning, present adaptive abilities, available family support, and motivational, behavioral, and personality factors.

School-age children with neurological impairment have the additional difficulty of returning to a learning environment, whereas adults often return to routinized work or home settings. The requirement for constantly learning new material is in the presence of an often reduced ability to learn and recall information. Additionally, the classroom setting is a distractible environment, and many of these children have an acquired attention deficit resulting from neurological impairment (as is the case in cerebrovascular disease). It is important for children in cognitive training programs to be evaluated in an educational setting prior to restarting school so that specific concerns can be addressed directly.

Familiarity with stages of cognitive development is essential, since some cognitive skills/systems do not develop prior to the age of injury and thus cannot adequately be assessed and addressed until after that time. For example, Golden

(1978) suggested that the tertiary sensory system (found in the parietal lobe and associated with integrating tactile and visual information used for coding the position of the body in extrapersonal space) is not developed until the child is 5 to 8 years of age (Kolb & Whishaw, 1990). Assessing such a deficit may not be feasible until several years following the neurological injury.

Deficit- versus Strength-Oriented Approaches

Consideration of deficit-oriented or strength-oriented training is one of the initial steps in developing any remedial program. Luria's theory (1973) was utilized in the development of four approaches to training a brain-impaired child (Golden & Anderson, 1979): (1) direct training of the deficit; (2) substitution of alternative skills (e.g., changing handedness); (3) substitution of more complex skills for the deficit, such as utilizing a computer to compensate for poor graphomotor skills; and (4) changing the environment. The first strategy is deficit oriented, whereas the second and third are strength oriented; the last is related to environmental engineering (i.e., changing the child's environment to accommodate the disabilities, rather than training the child). Most programs utilize both deficit- and strength-oriented approaches in cognitive training.

In deficit-oriented training (Golden & Anderson, 1979), direct training can consist of retraining the injured area or utilizing another part of the brain to acquire the skill. If damage allows partial use of the area, intensive and repeated practice may result in skill development. More extensive damage requires takeover by another part of the brain. The advantage is that deficits may ultimately be partially or completely resolved. The disadvantage of such an approach is the effort and time required. Rourke (1983) suggests that this approach is most appropriate with children (1) younger than 9 years old, due to the younger brain's putative capability for reorganization; (2) with mild adaptive weaknesses and psychological strengths, such as strong motivation; (3) whose deficits are likely to respond well to remediation (e.g., speech/language); and (4) whose strengths are too limited to utilize effectively, as in cases of global impairment.

A strength-oriented approach may be best utilized with children who (1) are older; (2) are younger but more uncooperative in treatment (because it requires less effort); (3) have marked deficits with an otherwise intact area of functioning; and (4) already have well-developed skills and require assistance in modifying circumscribed, specific weaknesses. Some strength-oriented approaches in the treatment of memory disturbances include the use of visual imagery (linking a word to a picture image evoked by a cue) and mnemonic elaborative training (which utilizes structured memory strategies and repeated presentations) (Leftoff, 1981).

Remediation of Academic Skills

The decision of which skills to remediate is best made in the context of relevance for the child. Since academic skills are necessary for the child's learning process, the educational skills of reading, writing, and arithmetic are priorities. Hartlage

(1981) proposed a neuropsychological model that utilizes a strength-oriented approach with learning-disabled children. Although not validated empirically, the commonalities between children with stroke and children with learning disabilities suggest that the model has relevance in this discussion. Hartlage's assumptions are as follows: (1) reading skills—particularly auditory sequencing, phonetic analysis, and comprehension—are primarily localized in the posterior regions of the dominant (usually left) hemisphere; (2) computation may be dependent on either hemisphere, depending on the complexity of skills involved; and (3) spelling is an aspect of language and depends heavily on the dominant hemisphere.

According to Hartlage's (1981) first assumption, if the right hemisphere is more efficient than the left, use of nonphonetic instruction based on visuospatial cues is likely to be more effective; and, if the left hemisphere is more intact, utilizing phonetic analysis and reading for comprehension are important. As the child becomes older, the focus on synthesis and comprehension increases. Aural comprehension approaches (e.g., use of tape-recorded material) may be used for young children with visuospatial difficulties. The second assumption suggests that the child with a strong left hemisphere would benefit from a focus on concepts, language formulation, and sequential logic; for the child with a capable right hemisphere, visually oriented models, such as flashcards and two-dimensional problems, are useful. The third assumption indicates that the child with a competent left hemisphere should be exposed to early linguistic aids; the child with a competent right hemisphere may profit from rote copying and use of a gestalt/whole-word approach.

Reading disability, or dyslexia, has been classified into three types: auditory-linguistic, visual-spatial, and mixed (Boder, 1973; Telzrow, 1985). The most common type is the auditory-linguistic, associated with left-hemisphere impairment; the visual-spatial, with the right hemisphere; and the mixed, with both left- and right-hemisphere involvement. Although not validated with children who are learning disabled or brain damaged, this approach suggests a strength-oriented approach utilizing the more intact skills, in a manner similar to Hartlage's (1981) model. Rourke and colleagues (Strang & Rourke, 1985; Sweeny & Rourke, 1985) have similarly applied this model to spelling and arithmetic and reported success in ameliorating difficulties by utilizing strengths of the child.

Behavioral and Cognitive Approaches

The skills of a neuropsychologist can also be applied in the development of cognitive and behavioral approaches for children to increase more adaptive skills and decrease difficult behaviors. Behavior therapy is considered to be the most effective treatment approach for a broad range of childhood disorders, including communication disorders (Mahoney & Carpenter, 1983), depression (Kaslow & Rehm, 1983), fears and phobias (Morris & Kratchowill, 1983), hyperactivity (Barkley, 1983), and academic problems (Hallahan, Lloyd, Kaufman, & Loper, (1983). Additional authors (Eames & Wood, 1985; Telzrow, 1985) have reported that behavioral treatment is the most useful approach for increasing prosocial behavior and enhancing long-term outcome with brain-injured children and adults. Integration of neuropsychological theory and behavioral principles can be utilized in addressing educational, behavioral, and adaptive concerns.

Behavior therapy covers a broad spectrum, from operant conditioning to the more recently developed cognitive behavioral techniques. Such principles as cuing, shaping, positive reinforcement, and generalization have been shown to be effective with brian-injured children and adults (Bolger, 1982). Parents of brain-damaged children have also been taught operant conditioning principles that they implement in behavior modification programs based on functional analysis of the behavior (Salzinger, Feldman, & Portnoy, 1970).

A more recent focus on cognitive psychology has resulted in attention to internal thought processes as mechanisms for change (Kendall & Braswell, 1985; Meichenbaum, 1977; Meyers & Craighead, 1984). This has evolved into the use of such strategies as modeling, problem-solving, self-control, and self-instruction training. *Modeling*, or observational learning, involves learning by watching another's behavior. *Problem solving* refers to leraning of certain "thinking" skills that increase the child's ability to deal overtly with challenging situations. With the *self-control* strategy, behavior is altered by changing and utilizing covert thought processes with such mechanisms as self-monitoring, self-evaluation, and self-reinforcement (refer to Meyers & Craighead for additional information). *Self-instruction training* (Meichenbaum & Goodman, 1971; Meichenbaum, 1977) involves teaching children to create statements that they repeat to themselves. It is based on the works of Luria (1961) and Vygotsky (1962), who proposed that the child's behavior is initially under the verbal control of adults but eventually comes under the child's control through overt, then covert, speech. Although initially designed for impulsive children, self-instruction training has been found to be effective in the treatment of attention, aggression, hyperactivity, fear, academic performance, and social competence in children (Kendall & Braswell, 1985; Meyers & Craighead, 1984; Webster & Scott, 1983).

Meichenbaum (1977) proposed a cognitive-functional approach in the treatment of learning-disabled children. This utilizes an analysis of cognitions (e.g., self-statements and images) subjects use to complete a task. He found that adequate performance by brain-damaged children was hindered by negative self-statements, task-irrelevant thoughts, and anxiety-engendering ideas. Poorer self-esteem was also more common in brain-injured children and manifested in the child's self-statements when approaching and performing a task, particularly with regard to frustration and failure. The process of change involves increasing the child's awareness of negative self-messages and the replacement of these with task-appropriate strategies, learned in therapy. Through the process of teaching the child to "talk positively" to himself or herself, thinking is changed in a positive direction, allowing better attention to tasks and mastery of skills.

Cognitive training using nonacademic tasks has been found to increase efficiency with both nonacademic and academic skills in children with and without learning difficulties (Kaufman & Kaufman, 1979). The authors give three suggestions for cognitive training: (1) in approaching the task, the child should be encouraged to verbalize the use of successive strategies, as learning the over-all strategies is more important than skill development in specific tasks; (2) tech-niques can be used with *all* children in a classroom; and (3) training should uti-lize material that is interesting and nonthreatening. For example, cognitive training, using verbalization and mental rehearsal of various sequences of a movement pattern, has resulted in improvement in motor skills, particularly on timed tasks in brain-injured children (Bawden, Knights, & Winogron, 1985; Haskell, Barrett, & Taylor, 1977). Cognitive strategies have also been found to be efficacious in generalizing verbal math problem solving and in self-monitor-ing of attention and accuracy, in learning-disabled adolescents (Montague & Bos, 1986; Rooney, Polloway, & Hallahan, 1985).

Although cognitive behavioral techniques have been shown to be effective with children who have learning and behavioral problems, significant brain im-pairment may be inconsistent with successful application of metacognitive skills necessary for such an approach. Thus, these approaches may not be useful for more seriously impaired children. A more traditional behavioral approach may be more effective in such cases.

Prognosis

It is generally believed that the consequences of cerebral lesions in childhood are less compromising than those occurring in adulthood (Teuber, 1975). In Satz and Bullard-Bates's (1981) review of the literature regarding prognosis of acquired childhood aphasia, they conclude that spontaneous recovery occurs in the ma-jority of children. More recently, however, authors have reported subtle but per-sistent deficits in general cognitive functioning, language, and academic skills in children, even when injury occurred early in life (i.e., intrauterine) (Aram & Ekel-man, 1988; Aram, Ekelman, Rose, & Whitaker, 1985; Rankin, Aram, & Horwitz, 1981; Vargha-Khadem, Gorman, & Watters, 1985).

Prognosis for recovery of cognitive function or reacquisition of lost functions depends primarily on the interactive effect of a number of variables, including the type, location, and extent of the damage (Rourke, Bakker, Fisk, & Strang, 1983). As previously discussed, younger age as a variable has been reported to predict more rapid improvement (Teuber, 1975). Individuals with relatively dis-crete lesions are more likely to have a good prognosis than those with bilateral or diffuse lesions (Golden, 1978). Miller and Miyamoto (1979) found that superficial or peripheral lesions result in a better prognosis than those in the deep or central areas. Additionally, brain stem involvement can result in persistent impairment of consciousness, alertness, and attention; language disorders can impair com-munication in the rehabilitation process. Individuals with mixed dominance have shown better adaptability to focal cerebral lesions due to increased decentraliza-tion of cortical functions.

Rehabilitation is generally assumed to be more effective with lesions of re-cent rather than remote onset (Jennett & Teasdale, 1981). Russell (1979) suggests that decisions regarding rehabilitation and prognosis should not be based on neuropsychological assessment immediately following a lesion, because of temporarily decreased function secondary to the lesion. Although most (adult) patients show the greatest recovery within the first six months, treatment long past this time often yields improvement (Lynch, 1984). It would be assumed that for many children ongoing assistance may be required for years, particularly regarding school transitions.

Limited information is available regarding recovery, developmental progress patterns, and effectiveness of early intervention in infants and preschoolers who experience acquired (vs. developmental or congenital) brain injuries (Raimondi & Hirschauer, 1984). One outcome study by Bagnato and Mayes (1986), which utilized interdisciplinary treatment, evaluated 7 multidisabled children with acquired brain injuries (e.g., traumatic brain injuries from automobile accidents) and 10 with congenital brain injuries (e.g., cerebral palsy, mental retardation) with a mean age of 33.8 months and range of 8 to 67 months. Assessments utilized the Bayley Scales of Infant Development (Bayley, 1969) and the Adaptive scale from the Gessell Developmental Schedules-Revised (GDS-R; Knobloch, Stevens, & Malone, 1980). Results indicated similar overall progress and recovery patterns for the two groups with significant overall changes in developmental rates, particularly in the cognitive area and least significant in gross motor skills. Significant global improvement in social responsiveness and social involvement was found, but heightened reactivity to stimuli, poor frustration tolerance, increased activity levels, low endurance for tasks, and deficits in goal-directed behavior and motivation persisted despite intervention.

While long-term sequelae follow some early lesions, Miller (1984) concluded that younger subjects tend to suffer less subsequent dysfunction. Severity of insult, while confounded by age and compensation, plays a critical role. In general, the more severe the insult, the more severe the dysfunction, although there was a trend toward positive results following earlier intervention. It may be concluded that no treatment seems to be universally efficacious, and it remains difficult to predict recovery with a large degree of accuracy.

In general, recovery appears to be more promising for children with cerebrovascular disorders than adults with comparable lesions. The efficacy of approaches for rehabilitation discussed in this chapter remains speculative, due to the limited research available with brain-damaged children, particularly due to cerebrovascular lesions. The value of any remedial strategy relies on the successful integration of a variety of techniques designed to foster development and reacquisition of skills in home and school settings.

REFERENCES

Adams, H. P., Subbiah, B., & Bosch, E. P. (1977). Neurologic aspects of hereditary hemorrhagic telangiectasia. *Archives of Neurology, 34*, 101–104.

Adams, R., & Victor, M. (1985). *Principles of neurology*, 3rd ed. New York: McGraw Hill.

Addiego, J. E., Mentzer, W. C., & Dallman, P. R. (1974). Thrombocytosis in infants and children. *The Journal of Pediatrics, 85*, 805–807.

Ahmann, P. A., Lazzara, H., Dykes, F. D., Brann, A. W., & Schwartz, J. F. (1980). Intraventricular hemorrhage in the high risk preterm infant: Incidence and outcome. *Annals of Neurology, 7,* 118–124.

Albert, M. L. (1979). Alexia. In K. M. Heilman & E. Valenstein (Eds.), *Clinical neuropsychology.* New York: Oxford University Press.

Ambruso, D. R., Jacobson, L. J., & Hathaway, W. E. (1980). Inherited antithrombin III deficiency and cerebral thrombosis in a child. *Pediatrics, 65,* 125–131.

Anderson, S. W., Damasio, H., & Tranel, D. (1990). Neuropsychological impairments associated with lesions caused by tumor or stroke. *Archives of Neurology, 47,* 397–405.

Annett, M. (1973). Laterality of childhood hemiplegia and the growth of speech and intelligence. *Cortex, 9,* 4–33.

Aram, D. M., & Ekelman, B. L. (1986). Cognitive profiles of children with early onset of unilateral lesions. *Developmental Neuropsychology, 2*(3), 155–172.

Aram, D. M., & Ekelman, B. L. (1988a). Scholastic aptitude and achievement among children with unilateral brain lesions. *Neuropsychologia 26*(6), 903–916.

Aram, D. M., & Ekelman, B. L. (1988b). Auditory temporal perception of children with left or right brain lesions. *Neuropsychologia, 26*(6), 931–935.

Aram, D. M., Ekelman, B. L., Rose, D. F., & Whitaker, H. A. (1985). Verbal and cognitive sequelae following unilateral lesions acquired in early childhood. *Clinical and Experimental Neuropsychology, 7*(1), 55–78.

Aram, D. M., Rose, D. F., Rekate, H. L., & Whitaker, H. A. (1983). Acquired capsular/striatal aphasia in childhood. *Archives of Neurology, 40,* 614–617.

Ariel, R., & Strider, M. A. (1983). Neuropsychological effects of general medical disorders. In C. J. Golden & P. J. Vicente (Eds.), *Foundations of clinical neuropsychology.* New York: Plenum Press (pp. 273–308).

Bagnato, S. J., & Mayes, S. D. (1986). Patterns of developmental and behavioral progress for young brain-injured children during interdisciplinary intervention. *Developmental Neuropsychology, 2*(3), 213–240.

Banich, M. T., Levin, S. C., Kim, H., & Huttenlocher, P. (1990). The effects of developmental factors on IQ in hemiplegic children. *Neuropsychologia, 28*(1), 35–47.

Barkley, R. A. (1983). Hyperactivity. In R. J. Morris & T. R. Kratchowill (Eds.), *The practice of child therapy.* New York: Pergamon Press.

Bawden, H. N., Knights, R. M., & Winogron, H. W. (1985). Speeded performance following head injury in children. *Journal of Clinical and Experimental Neuropsychology, 7,* 39–54.

Bayley, N. (1969). *Bayley Scales of Infant Development.* New York: Psychological Corporation.

Belman, A. L., Leicher, C. R., Moshe, S. L., & Mezey, A. P. (1985). Neurologic manifestations of Schoenlein-Henoch purpura: Report of three cases and review of the literature. *Pediatrics, 75,* 687–692.

Bendersky, M., & Lewis, M. (1990). Early language ability as a function of ventricular dilatation associated with intraventricular hemorrhage. *Developmental and Behavioral Pediatrics, 11*(1), 17–21.

Benson, D. F. (1977). The third alexia. *Archives of Neurology, 34,* 327–331.

Benton, A. L. (1962). Behavioral indices of brain injury in school children. *Child Development, 33,* 199–208.

Berg, R. A., & Linton, J. C. (1989). Neuropsychological sequelae of chronic medical disorders. In C. R. Reynolds & E. Fletcher-Janzen (Eds.), *Neuropsychological sequelae of chronic disorders.* New York: Plenum Press.

Bigler, E. (1984). *Diagnostic clinical neuropsychology.* Austin, TX: University of Texas Press (pp. 107–127).

Boder, E. (1973). Developmental dyslexia: A diagnostic approach based on three atypical reading-spelling patterns. *Developmental Medicine and Child Neurology, 15,* 630–687.

Bolger, J. P. (1982). Cognitive retraining: A developmental approach. *Clinical Neuropsychology, 4,* 66–70.

Bornstein, R. A. (1986). Neuropsychological aspects of cerebrovascular disease and its treatment. In G. Goldstein & R. E. Tartar (Eds.), *Advances in clinical neuropsychology* (Vol. 3). New York: Plenum Press.

Bousser, M. G., Chiras, J., Bories, J., & Gastaigne, P. (1985). Cerebral venous thrombosis—A review of 38 cases. *Stroke, 16,* 199–213.

Broca, P. (1861). Remarques sur le siege de la faculte' du language articule, suivies d'une observation d'aphemie (perte de parole). *Bulletin et memoires de la Societe Anatomique de Paris, 36*, 330–357.

Broderick, J. P., & Swanson, J. W. (1987). Migraine-related strokes. *Archives of Neurology, 44*, 868–871.

Brown, T. L., & Morgan, S. B. (1987). Cognitive training with brain-injured children: General issues and approaches. In J. M. Williams & C. J. Long (Eds.), *The rehabilitation of cognitive disabilities*. New York: Plenum Press.

Brust, J. C. M. (1981). Stroke: Diagnostic, anatomical and physiological considerations. In E. R. Kandel & J. H. Schwartz (Eds.), *The rehabilitation of cognitive disabilities*. New York: Plenum Press.

Clarus, A. (1874). Uber aphasie bei Kindern. *Jahresb Kinderheilkd, 7*, 369–400.

Cotard, J. (1868). Etude sur l'atrophie partielle du cerveau. these de Paris.

Craft, A., Shaw, D., & Carlidge, N. (1972). Head injuries in children. *British Medical Journal, 4*, 200–203.

Daniels, S. R., Bates, S., Luken, B. R., Benton, C., Third, Y., & Glueck, C. J. (1982). Cerebrovascular arteriopathy (arteriosclerosis) and ischemic childhood stroke. *Stroke, 13*, 360–364.

Dennis, M. (1980). Language acquisition in a single hemisphere: Semantic organization. In D. Caplan (Ed.), *Biological studies of mental processes*. Cambridge: MIT Press (pp. 159–185).

Dennis, M. (1985a). Intelligence after early brain injury I: Predicting IQ scores from medical variables. *Journal of Clinical and Experimental Neuropsychology, 7*(5), 526–554.

Dennis, M. (1985b). Intelligence after early brain injury II: IQ scores of subjects classified on the basis of medical history variables. *Journal of Clinical and Experimental Neuropsychology, 7*(5), 555–576.

Dennis, M., Lovett, M., & Wiegel-Crump, C. A. (1981). Written language acquisition after left or right hemidecortication in infancy. *Brain and Language, 12*, 54–91.

Dennis, M., & Whitaker, H. A. (1976). Language acquisition following hemidecortication: Linguistic superiority of the left over the right hemisphere. *Brain and Language, 3*, 404–433.

Eames, P., & Wood, R. (1985). Rehabilitation after severe brain injury: A follow-up study of a behavior modification approach. *Journal of Neurology, Neurosurgery, and Psychiatry, 48*, 613–619.

Eeg-Olofsson, O., & Ringheim, Y. (1983). Stroke in children. Clinical characteristics and prognosis. *Acta Pediatrica Scandinavia, 72*, 391–395.

Fletcher, J. M., & Taylor, H. (1984). Neuropsychological approaches to children: Towards a developmental neuropsychology. *Journal of Neuropsychology, 6*, 39–57.

Fults, D., & Kelly, D. (1984). Natural history of arteriovenous malformations of the brain: A clinical study. *Neurosurgery, 15*, 658–662.

Gold, A. M. (1984). Stroke in children. In L. P. Rowland (Ed.), *Merritt's textbook of neurology*, 7th ed. Philadelphia: Lea & Febiger.

Golden, C. J. (1978). *Diagnosis and rehabilitation in clinical neuropsychology*. Springfield, IL: C. C. Thomas.

Golden, C. J., & Anderson, S. (1979). *Learning disabilities and brain dysfunction: An introduction for educators and parents*. Springfield, IL: C. C. Thomas.

Goldman, P. S. (1975). Age, sex, and experience as related to the neural basis of cognitive development. In N. A. Buchwald & M. A. Brazier (Eds.), *Brain mechanisms in mental retardation*. New York: Academic Press (pp. 379–392).

Gorman, R. J., Saxon, S., & Snead, O. C. III. (1981). Neurologic sequelae of Rocky Mountain spotted fever. *Pediatrics, 67*, 354–356.

Gray, J. W., & Dean, R. S. (1989). Approaches to cognitive rehabilitation of children with neuropsychological impairment. In C. R. Reynolds & E. Fletcher-Janzen (Eds.), *Handbook of clinical child neuropsychology*. New York: Plenum Press.

Grotta, J. C., Manner, C., Pettigrew, L. C., & Yatsu, F. M. (1986). Red blood cell disorders and stroke. *Stroke, 17*, 811–817.

Guttman, E. (1942). Aphasia in children. *Brain, 65*, 205–219.

Haas, D. C., Pineda, G. S., & Lourie, H. (1975). Juvenile head trauma syndrome and their relationship to migraine. *Archives of Neurology, 32,* 727–730.

Hallahan, D. P., Lloyd, J. W., Kauffman, J. M., & Loper, A. B. (1983). Academic problems. In R. J. Morris & T. R. Kratchowill (Eds.), *The practice of child therapy.* New York: Pergamon Press.

Hartlage, L. C., & Reynolds, C. R. (1981). Neuropsychological assessment and the individuation of instruction. In G. W. Hynd & J. E. Obrzut (Eds.), *Neuropsychological assessment and the school-age child: Issues and procedures.* New York: Grune & Stratton (pp. 355–378).

Hartlage, L. C., & Telzrow, C. F. (1984). Rehabilitation of persons with learning disabilities. *Journal of Rehabilitation, 50,* 31–34.

Haskell, S. H., Barrett, E. K., & Taylor, H. (1977). *The education of motor and neurologically handicapped children.* New York: John Wiley & Sons.

Heaton, R. K., Schmitz, S. P., Avitable, N., & Lehrman, R. A. W. (1987). Effects of lateralized cerebral lesions on oral, reading comprehension, and spelling. *Journal of Clinical and Experimental Neuropsychology, 9*(6), 711–722.

Hebb, D. O. (1942). The effect of early and late brain injury upon test scores, and the nature of normal adult intelligence. *Proceedings of the American Philosophical Society, 85,* 275–292.

Hecaen, H. (1976). Acquired aphasias in children and the ontogenesis of hemispheric functional specialization. *Brain and Language, 3,* 114–134.

Hecaen, H. (1983). Acquired aphasia in children: Revisited. *Neuropsychologia, 21,* 581–587.

Hesselbrock, R., Sawaya, R., Tomsick, T., & Wadhwa, S. (1985). Superior sagittal sinus thrombosis after closed head injury. *Neurosurgery, 16,* 825–828.

Hicks, R. E., & Kinsbourne, M. (1978) Human handedness. In M. Kinsbourne (Ed.), *Asymmetrical function of the brain.* Cambridge: Cambridge University Press.

Huttenlocher, P. R., Moohr, J. W., Johns, L., & Brown, F. D. (1984). Cerebral blood flow in sickle cell cerebrovascular disease. *Pediatrics, 73,* 615–620.

Imai, W. K., Everhart, F. R., & Sanders, J. M. (1982). Cerebral venous sinus thrombosis: Report of a case and review of the literature. *Pediatrics, 70,* 965–970.

Israels, S. J., & Seshia, S. S. (1987). Childhood stroke associated with protein C or S deficiency. *The Journal of Pediatrics, 111*(4), 562–564.

Jennett, B., & Teasdale, G. (1981). *Management of severe head injuries.* Philadelphia: Davis.

Kaplan, E., & Goodglass, H. (1981). Aphasia-related disorders. *Acquired aphasia.* New York: Academic Press.

Kappelle, L. J., Willemse, J., Ramos, L. M. P., & van Gijn, J. (1969). Ischaemic stroke in the basal cell ganglia and internal capsule in childhood. *Brain Development, 11,* 283–292.

Kaslow, N. J., & Rehm, L. P. (1983). Childhood depression. In R. J. Morris & T. R. Kratchowill (Eds.), *The practice of child therapy.* New York: Pergamon Press.

Kaufman, D., & Kaufman, P. (1979). Strategy training and remedial techniques. *Journal of Learning Disabilities, 12,* 416–419.

Kelly, J., Mellinger, J., & Sundt, T. (1978). Intracranial arteriovenous malformations in childhood. *Annals of Neurology, 3,* 338–343.

Kendall, P. C., & Braswell, L. (1985). *Cognitive behavioral therapy for impulsive children.* New York: Guilford Press.

Kennard, M. (1942). Cortical reorganization of motor function. Archives of Neurology and Psychiatry, 48, 227–240.

Knobloch, H., Stevens, F., & Malone, A. F. (1980). *Manual of developmental diagnosis: The revised Gesell and Amatruda Developmental Neurologic Examination.* New York: Harper & Row.

Knudson, R., & Alden, E. (1979). Symptomatic arteriovenous malformation in infants less than 6 months of age. *Pediatrics, 64,* 238–241.

Kohn, B., & Dennis, M. (1974). Selective impairments of visuospatial abilities in infantile hemiplegics after right cerebral hemidecortication. *Neuropsychologia, 12,* 505–512.

Kolb, B., & Whishaw, I. Q. (1990). *Fundamentals of*

human neuropsychology. San Francisco: W. H. Freeman and Co.

Krashen, S. (1973). Lateralization of language learning and the critical period. Some new evidence. *Language Learning, 23*, 63–74.

Krivit, W., Tate, D., White, J. G., & Robinson, L. L. (1981). Idiopathic thrombocytopenic purpura and intracranial hemorrhage. *Pediatrics, 67*, 570–571.

Landry, S., & Fletcher, J. M. (1982). *Intraventricular hemorrhage in neonates: Developmental outcomes—second report.* Paper presented at the annual meeting of the International Neuropsychological Society, Pittsburgh, PA.

Leftoff, S. (1981). Learning functions for unilaterally brain damaged patients for serially and randomly ordered stimulus material: Analysis of retrieval strategies and their relationship to rehabilitation. *Journal of Clinical Neuropsychology, 3*(4), 301–313.

Lenneberg, E. H. (1967). *Biological foundations of language.* New York: John Wiley.

Lerer, R. J., & Kalavasky, S. M. (1973). Central nervous system disease associated with Mycoplasma pneumoniae infection. *Pediatrics, 52*, 658–668.

Levin, H. S. (1979). The acalculias. In K. M. Heilman & E. Valenstein (Eds.), *Clinical neuropsychology.* New York: Oxford University Press.

Lewis, D. W., & Tucker, S. H. (1986). Central nervous system involvement in cat scratch disease. *Pediatrics, 77*, 714–720.

Lockman, L. A., Mastri, A., Priest, J. R., & Nesbit, M. (1980). Dural venous sinus thrombosis in acute lymphoblastic leukemia. *Pediatrics, 66*, 943–947.

Ludlow, C. L. (1980). Children's language disorders. Recent research advances. *Annals of Neurology, 7*, 497–507.

Lupi-Herrera, E., Sanchez-Torres, G., Marcushamer, J., Mispireta, J. et al. (1977). Takayasu's arteritis. Clinical study of 107 cases. *American Heart Journal, 93*, 94–103.

Luria, A. R. (1961). The role of speech in the regulation of normal and abnormal behaviors. New York: Liveright.

Luria, A. R. (1973). *The working brain: An introduction to neuropsychology.* New York: Basic Books.

Lutschg, J., & Vassella, F. (1981). Neurological complications in hemophilia. *Acta Pediatrica Scandinavia, 70*, 235–240.

Lynch, W. J. (1984). A rehabilitation program for brain-injured adults. In B. A. Edelstein & E. T. Couture (Eds.), *Behavioral assessment and rehabilitation of the traumatically brain-damaged.* New York: Plenum Press.

Mahoney, G., & Carpenter, L. J. (1983). Communication disorders. In R. J. Morris & T. R. Kratchowill (Eds.), *The practice of child therapy.* New York: Pergamon Press.

Mannino, F. L., & Trauner, D. A. (1983). Stroke in neonates. *Journal of Pediatrics, 102*, 605–609.

Marcie, P., & Hecaen, H. (1979). Agraphia: Writing disorders associated with unilateral cortical lesions. In K. M. Heilman & E. Valenstein (Eds.), *Clinical neuropsychology.* New York: Oxford University Press.

Meichenbaum, D. (1977). *Cognitive-behavior modification: An integrative approach.* New York: Plenum Press.

Meichenbaum, D., & Goodman, J. (1971). Training impulsive children to talk to themselves: A means of developing self-control. *Journal of Abnormal Psychology, 77*(2), 115–126.

Menkin, M., & Schwartzman, J. R. (1977). Cerebral air embolism. *Archives of Neurology, 34*, 168–170.

Meyers, A. W., & Craighead, W. E. (1984). Cognitive behavior therapy with children: A historical, conceptual, and organizational overview. In A. W. Meyers & W. E. Craighead (Eds.), *Cognitive behavior therapy with children.* New York: Plenum Press.

Miller, E. (1984). *Recovery and management of neuropsychological impairments.* New York: John Wiley & Sons.

Miller, L. S., & Miyamoto, A. T. (1979). Computed tomography: Its potential as a predictor of functional recovery following stroke. *Archives of Physical Medicine and Rehabilitation, 60*, 108–109.

Montague, M., & Bos, C. S. (1986). The effect of cognitive strategy training on verbal math problem solving performance of learning disabled adolescents. *Journal of Learning Disabilities, 19*, 26–33.

Moore, P. A., & Cupps, T. R. (1983). Neurological

complications of vasculitis. *Annals of Neurology, 14,* 155–167.

Murdoch, B. E. (1990). *Acquired speech and language disorders.* New York: Chapman and Hall.

Nass, R., & Koch, D. (1987). Temperament differences in toddlers with early unilateral right- and left-brain damage. *Developmental Neuropsychology, 3*(2), 93–99.

Nelson, W., Behrman, R., & Vaughn, V. (Eds.) (1987). *Nelson textbook of pediatrics.* Philadelphia: W. B. Saunders.

Nonneman, A. J., & Isaacson, R. L. (1973). Task dependent recovery after early brain damage. *Behavioral Biology, 8,* 143–172.

Packer, R. J., Rorke, L. B., Lange, B. J., Siegel, K. R., & Evans, A. E. (1985). Cerebrovascular accidents in children with cancer. *Pediatrics, 76,* 194–201.

Pearl, P. (1987). Childhood stroke following intraoral trauma. *The Journal of Pediatrics, 110,* 574–575.

Pirozzolo, F. J. (1979). *The neuropsychology of developmental reading disorders.* New York: Praeger Publishers.

Portnoy, B., & Herion, J. (1972). Neurological manifestations in sickle-cell disease. *Annals of Internal Medicine, 76,* 643–652.

Prensky, A. L., & Sommer, D. (1979). Diagnosis and management of migraine in children. *Neurology, 29,* 506–510.

Priest, J., Ramsay, N., Latchaw, R., & Lockman, L. (1980). Thrombotic and hemorrhagic strokes complicating early therapy for childhood acute lymphoblastic leukemia. *Cancer, 46,* 1548–1554.

Priest, J., Ramsay, N., Steinherz, P., & Tubergen, D. (1982). A syndrome of thrombosis and hemorrhage complicating L-asparaginase therapy for childhood acute lymphoblastic leukemia. *The Journal of Pediatrics, 100,* 984–989.

Raimondi, A. J., & Hirschauer, J. (1984). Head injury in the infant and toddler: Coma scoring and outcome scale. *Child's Brain, 11,* 12–35.

Rankin, J. M., Aram, D. M., & Horwitz, S. J. (1981). Language ability in right and left hemiplegic children. *Brain and Language, 14,* 292–306.

Riva, D., & Cazzaniga, L. (1986). Late effects of unilateral brain lesions sustained before and after age one. *Neuropsychologia, 24,* 423–428.

Roach, E. (1989). Cerebrovascular disorders in children. *Current Opinion in Pediatrics, 1,* 278–283.

Roach, E. S., & Riela, A. R. (1988). *Pediatric cerebrovascular disorders.* New York: Futura Publishing.

Rooney, K., Polloway, E. A., & Hallahan, D. P. (1984). The use of self-monitoring procedures with low IQ learning disabled students. *Journal of Learning Disabilities, 18,* 384–389.

Ross, E. D., & Rush, A. J. (1981). Diagnosis and neuroanatomical correlates of depression in brain-damaged patients. *Archives of General Psychiatry, 38,* 1344–1354.

Rourke, B. P. (1983). Reading and spelling disabilities: A developmental neuropsychological perspective. In U. Kirk (Ed.), *Neuropsychology of language, reading, and spelling.* New York: Academic Press.

Rourke, B. P. (1987). The syndrome of nonverbal learning disabilities: The final common pathway of white matter disease/dysfunction? *The Clinical Neuropsychologist, 1*(3), 209–234.

Rourke, B. P., Bakker, D. J., Fisk, J. L., & Strang, J. D. (Eds.). (1983). *Child neuropsychology.* New York: Guilford Press.

Rudel, R. G., & Teuber, H. L. (1971). Spatial orientation in normal children and in children with early brain injury. *Neuropsychologia, 9,* 401–407.

Rudel, R. G., Teuber, H. L., & Twitchell, T. E. (1966). A note on hyperesthesia in children with early brain damage. *Neuropsychologia, 4,* 351–356.

Russell, E. (1979). *The chronicity effect.* Paper presented at the 7th annual meeting of the International Neuropsychological Society, New York.

Salzinger, K., Feldman, R. S., & Portnoy, S. T. (1970). Training parents of brain injured children in the use of operant conditioning procedures. *Behavior Therapy, 1,* 4–23.

St. James-Roberts, I. (1981). A reinterpretation of

hemispherectomy without functional plasticity of the brain. *Brain and Language, 14*, 292–306.

Sanchez-Torres, G., Marcushamer, J., Mispireta, J., Horwitz, S., & Vela, J. (1977). Takayasu's arteritis: A clinical study of 107 cases. *American Heart Journal, 93*, 94–103.

Sandok, B., Houser, O., Baker, H., & Holley, K. (1971). Fibromuscular dysplasia. *Archives of Neurology, 24*, 462–466.

Sarnaik, S., Soorya, D., Kim, J., Ravindranath, Y., & Lusher, J. (1979). Periodic transfusions for sickle cell anemia and CNS infarction. *American Journal of Disease in Childhood, 133*, 1254–1257.

Satz, P. (1980). Incidence of aphasia in left-handers: A test of some hypothetical models of speech organization. In J. Herron (Ed.), *Neuropsychology of left-handedness*. New York: Academic Press.

Satz, P., & Bullard-Bates, C. (1981). Acquired aphasia in children. In M. T. Sarno (Ed.), *Acquired aphasia*. New York: Academic Press.

Schneider, G. E. (1979). Is it really better to have your brain lesion early? A revision of the "Kennard Principle." *Neuropsychologia, 17*, 557–583.

Schoenberg, B. S. (1979). Risk factors for stroke in infants and children. In M. Goldstein et al. (Eds.), *Advances in neurology* (Vol. 25). New York: Raven Press.

Schoenberg, B. S., Mellinger, J. F., & Schoenberg, D. G. (1978). Cerebrovascular disease in infants and children: A study of incidence, clinical features, and survival. *Neurology, 28*, 763.

Sheth, K., Swick, H., & Haworth, N. (1986). Neurological involvement in hemolytic-uremic syndrome. *Annals of Neurology, 19*, 90–93.

Shucart, W., & Wolpert, S. (1974). Intracranial arterial aneurysms in childhood. *American Journal of Disease in Childhood, 127*, 288–293.

Silverstein, A., Gilbert, H., & Wasserman, L. (1962). Neurologic complications of polycythemia. *Annals of Internal Medicine, 57*, 909–914.

Sparrow, S. S. (1990). Nonverbal learning disability in children: Two case reports. *Journal of Clinical and Experimental Neuropsychology, 12*(1). (Abstract).

Steward, O. (1964). Lesion-induced neuroplasticity and the sparing or recovery of function following early brain damage. In C. R. Almli & S. Finger (Eds.), *Early brain damage* (Vol. 1). New York: Academic Press (pp. 59–77).

Stiles-Davis, J., Janowsky, J., Engel, M., & Nass, R. (1988). Drawing ability in four young children with congenital unilateral brain lesions. *Neuropsychologia, 26*(3), 359–371.

Stiles-Davis, J., Sugarman, S., & Nass, R. (1985). The development of spatial and class relations in four young children with early spatial constructive deficit. *Brain Cognition, 4*, 388–412.

Stockman, J., Nigro, M., Mishkin, M., & Oski, F. (1972). Occlusion of large cerebral vessels in sickle-cell anemia. *New England Journal of Medicine, 287*, 846–848.

Strang, J. E., & Rourke, B. P. (1985). Arithmetic disability subtypes: The neuropsychological significance of specific arithmetical impairment in childhood. In B. P. Rourke (Ed.), *Neuropsychology of learning disabilities: Essentials of subtype analysis*. New York: Guilford Press.

Swaiman, K. (1989). *Pediatric neurology: Principles and practice*. St. Louis: C. V. Mosby Co.

Sweeny, J. E., & Rourke, B. P. (1985). Spelling disability subtypes. In B. P. Rourke (Ed.), *Neuropsychology of learning disabilities: Essentials of subtype analysis*. New York: Guilford Press.

Task Force on Head Injury. (1984). *Standards for cognitive rehabilitation*. Erie, PA: American Congress of Rehabilitation Medicine.

Telzrow, C. F. (1985). The science and speculation of rehabilitation in developmental neuropsychological disorders. In L. D. Hartlage & C. F. Telzrow (Eds.), *The neuropsychology of individual differences: A developmental perspective*. New York: Plenum Press.

Teuber, H. L. (1975). Recovery of function after brain injury in man. In R. Porter & D. W. Fitzsimons (Eds.), *Outcome of severe damage of the central nervous system* (CIBA Foundation Symposium, No. 34). Amsterdam: Elsevier/Excerpta Medica.

Tranel, D., Hall, L. E., Olson, S., & Tranel, N. N. (1987). Evidence for a right-hemisphere developmental learning disability. *Developmental Neuropsychology, 3*(2), 113–127.

Trevathan, E., & Dooling, E. (1987). Large thrombotic strokes in hemolytic-uremic syndrome. *Journal of Pediatrics, 6*, 803–805.

van Dongen, H. R., & Loonen, M. C. B. (1977). Factors related to prognosis of acquired aphasia in children. *Cortex, 13*, 131–136.

van Dongen, H. R., & Visch-Brink, E. G. (1988). Naming in aphasic children: Analysis of paraphasic errors. *Neuropsychologia, 26*(4), 629–632.

Van Hoff, J., Ritchey, K., & Shaywitz, B. (1985). Intracranial hemorrhage in children with sickle cell disease. *American Journal of Disease in Children, 139*, 1120–1122.

van Hout, A., Evrard, P., & Lyon, G. (1985). On the positive semiology of acquired aphasia in children. *Developmental Medicine in Child Neurology, 27*, 231–241.

Vargha-Khadem, F., O'Gorman, A. M., & Watters, G. V. (1985). Aphasia and handedness in relation to hemispheric side, age and injury and severity of cerebral lesion during childhood. *Brain, 108*, 677–696.

Vasick, J., & Tew, J. (1982). Foreign body embolization of the middle cerebral artery: Review of the literature and guidelines for management. *Neurosurgery, 11*, 532–536.

Verret, S., & Steele, J. (1971). Alternating hemiplegia in childhood: A report of eight patients with complicated migraine beginning in infancy. *Pediatrics, 47*, 675–680.

Visch-Brink, E. G., & Van de Sandt-Koenderman, W. M. E. (1985). The occurrence of paraphasias in the spontaneous speech of children with an acquired aphasia. *Brain Language, 23*, 258–271.

Von Haam, E. (1934). Pathology of intracranial hemorrhage in the newborn child. *American Journal of Obstretric Gynecology, 27*, 184–201.

Vygotsky, L. S. (1962). *Thought and language.* New York: Wiley.

Walton, J. N. (1977). *Brain's diseases of the nervous system,* 8th ed. New York: Oxford University Press.

Warrington, E. S., James, M., & Kinsbourne, M. (1966). Drawing disability in relation to laterality of cerebral lesion. *Brain, 89*, 53–82.

Webster, J. S., & Scott, R. R. (1983). The effects of self-instructional training on attentional deficits following head injury. *Clinical Neuropsychology, 5*(2), 69–74.

Weintraub, S., & Mesulam, M.-M. (1983). Developmental learning disabilities of the right hemisphere: Emotional, interpersonal, and cognitive components. *Archives of Neurology, 40*, 463–468.

Woerner, S., Abildgaard, C., & French, B. (1981). Intracranial hemorrhage in children with idiopathic thrombocytopenic purpura. *Pediatrics, 67*, 453–459.

Wood, D. (1978). Cerebrovascular complications of sickle cell anemia. *Stroke, 9*, 73–75.

Woodhurst, W., Robertson, W., & Thompson, G. (1980). Carotid injury due to intraoral trauma: Case report and review of the literature. *Neurosurgery, 6*, 559–563.

Woods, B. T., & Teuber, H. L. (1978). Changing patterns of childhood aphasia. *Annals of Neurology, 3*, 273–280.

9

ISSUES AND APPROACHES IN THE NEUROPSYCHOLOGICAL TREATMENT OF CHILDREN WITH LEARNING DISABILITIES

STEPHEN R. HOOPER   W. GRANT WILLIS

BRENDA H. STONE

INTRODUCTION

The field of child neuropsychology has made considerable progress over the past 20 years with respect to theoretical conjectures, neurodevelopmental issues, assessment methods, and gaining an increased understanding of a variety of brain-based disorders. The contribution of neuropsychological models and principles to the treatment planning of children and adolescents also has been impressive, particularly within the educational arena. In fact, treatment planning may represent the one area in which child neuropsychology actually surpasses its adult counterpart. Although Rourke, Bakker, Fisk, and Strang (1983, p. 153) noted about 10 years ago that there seemed to be "more questions than answers with respect to the remediation of brain-related deficiencies," the field of child neuropsychology has continued to progress in its attempts to address many of these questions. Further, the field has grown significantly with respect to what is known about how brain damage or dysfunction hinders classroom performance, educational progress, and psychological development, and, conversely, what should be asserted with respect to implementing specific intervention techniques.

Historically, neuropsychological assessment has been used to identify the presence, pattern, nature, and possible site(s) of brain damage or dysfunction (Beaumont, 1983). More recent efforts, however, have begun to focus on the functional capacities of the child in order to plan and implement intervention programs (Lyon, Moats, & Flynn, 1988). Indeed, Tramontana and Hooper (1988) noted that the field of child neuropsychology currently appears to be stressing "ecological validity" or, more generally, the application of neuropsychological assessment findings to an individual's everyday functioning (e.g., school performance, social functioning). In this regard, the primary purpose of a neuropsychological assessment should be not only on generating accurate and detailed descriptions of a child's functioning but also on making prescriptive statements regarding the types of interventions and/or environments that will facilitate maximal adaptive functioning. Consequently, child neuropsychologists increasingly are finding themselves in the position of having to make pertinent recommendations for interventions for children diagnosed with neurologically based learning problems.

This chapter addresses many of the issues pertaining to neuropsychologically based treatment approaches for children with learning disorders, with a particular focus on specific learning disabilities. Definitional issues are discussed with respect to learning disabilities along with related epidemiological findings. The neurological basis of learning disabilities is presented, with a particular emphasis being placed on recent findings from postmortem and neuroimaging studies. Given the importance of neuropsychological assessment to the development of treatment programs, this chapter also highlights several of the major approaches to neuropsychological assessment and related assessment-treatment issues and concerns for this population. Finally, a major portion of this chapter is devoted to selected neuropsychologically based treatment approaches, with a particular emphasis being placed on research findings pertinent to children with learning disabilities.

DEFINITIONAL ISSUES

Definitions of *learning disabilities* have been controversial since Kirk (1963) first introduced the term approximately 30 years ago. For example, about 10 years later Cruickshank (1972) published a list of 40 different terms used to describe these disorders, and Vaughan and Hodges (1973) complied a list of approximately 38 definitions. More recently, Epps, Ysseldyke, and Algozzine (1983) described 14 different ways to define learning disabilities in an operation manner and examined the differential impact of each of these definitions on the number of students identified for special educational services. Given these definitional concerns, Benton (1974) has concluded that the study of learning disabilities "is truly a mare's nest," and Hooper and Willis (1989) have referred to it as a "confusing quagmire."

Although the definition of learning disabilities that is recognized by most state departments of education continues to be the one asserted by the Education for All Handicapped Children Act of 1975 (i.e., PL 94-142, U.S. Office of Education, 1977), there are numerous problems associated with this "official" definition. For example, this definition is too general, clearly lacks operation criteria, and conceptualizes learning disabilities as a unitary phenomenon. Further, given these concerns, it contributes little in the way of addressing issues relevant to etiology, prognosis, or treatment. More recent definitions have attempted to address these concerns (Hammill, Leigh, McNutt, & Larsen, 1981), but they, too, remain vague with respect to operational criteria.

The most recent definition of learning disabilities has been proposed by the Interagency Committee on Learning Disabilities (ICLD), a multidisciplinary group mandated by the Health Research Extension Act of 1985 (PL 99-158). This definition states the following:

> *Learning disabilities is a generic term that refers to a heterogeneous group of disorders manifested by significant difficulties in the acquisition and use of listening, speaking, reading, writing, reasoning, or mathematical abilities, or of social skills. These disorders are intrinsic to the individual and presumed to be due to central nervous system dysfunction. Even though a learning disability may occur concomitantly with other handicapping conditions (e.g., sensory impairment, mental retardation, social and emotional disturbance), with socioenvironmental influences (e.g., cultural differences, insufficient or inappropriate instruction, psychogenic factors), and especially with attention deficit disorder, all of which may cause learning problems, a learning disability is not the direct result of those conditions or influences. (Wyngaarden, 1987, p. 222)*

The ICLD definition is important because of its inclusion of several key points. First, the proposed definition directly recognizes the heterogeneous nature of learning problems, and indirectly encourages clinicians and researchers to examine the multidimensional aspects of learning. This is consistent with emergent work addressing learning disability subtypes (e.g., Feagans, Short, & Meltzer, 1991; Hooper & Willis, 1989; Rourke, 1985) and research denoting the dissociable nature of many academic skills (Leong, 1989). Second, the definition acknowledges the neurobiological basis hypothesized to be related to these disorders of learning and, thus, at least begins to address current research findings in this regard. Third, the definition allows for a specific learning disability to exist concurrently with other disabling conditions, with a particular emphasis on attention-deficit hyperactivity disorder (ADHD). Finally, this definition includes deficiencies in social skills within the parameters of learning disabilities that undoubtedly will create additional diagnostic dilemmas for those working with children and adolescents referred for learning problems. Despite these noteworthy points, the ICLD definition lacks specific operational criteria and, consequently, will offer little in the way of guidance to the clinician and researcher.

Attempts have been made to address this lack of operational criteria in diagnosing learning disabilities but, generally, they have not met with much success. For example, inherent in nearly all definitions of learning disabilities is the concept of an intraindividual difference, or discrepancy, between academic achievement and academic aptitude, in favor of the latter. The concept of discrepancy was proposed in an effort to operationalize the diagnosis of learning disabilities (Bateman, 1966; McCarthy, 1975) and, consequently, a plethora of discrepancy formulas subsequently were generated. With all of these proposed formulas, however, there is no consensus of protocol, no accounting for the significant variability that can be demonstrated by children with learning disabilities, and the exact parameters of quantification are less than clear.

Shepard (1983) argued that the various formulas developed to date are seriously flawed, both logistically and methodologically, in that they typically assume that all children should be functioning at or above grade/age-level expectancies. Various factors—such as high correlations between the ability and achievement tests selected, statistical regression, test reliability, and developmental variables—also can exert a significant effect on the discrepancy formulas and influence diagnostic accuracy (Epps et al., 1985). In fact, Epps and colleagues (1983) reported that 85% of the school-age population could be classified as learning disabled using one or more of the current discrepancy formulas. Even the regression method of discrepancy determination, which has been cited as perhaps least subject to error and misinterpretation among the various approaches, has been noted to have serious methodological, statistical, and psychometric deficiencies when used as the sole criterion for learning disability identification (Shepard, 1980).

Given the preceding concerns, the Board of Trustees of the Council for Learning Disabilities (1987) voiced strong opposition to the use of discrepancy formulas in the identification of learning disabilities, and further suggested that these formulas should be phased out. Alternatively, when mandated by state of local agencies, it was warned that these formulas should be used only with extreme caution and should be viewed as only one source of information. Thus, the lack of a standard, operational, and methodologically adequate definition of learning disabilities remains elusive, with current efforts providing continued obstruction to the clinical and theoretical progress in understanding this heterogeneous group of disorders. Efforts to improve this situation, however, continue to be explored (Boyan, 1985; Stanovich, 1991; Tittemore, Lawson, & Inglis, 1985).

EPIDEMIOLOGY

Although definitional difficulties will continue to be debated, it is clear that children and adolescents manifesting learning disabilities represent an increasing number, with many having significant education, social, and perhaps psychiatric needs. With the increased survival rate of many high-risk infants, estimates have been projected to increase exponentially. Figures from the U.S. Department of Education (1984) revealed that children with learning disabilities account for 38% of all special education recipients, with males outnumbering females by a ratio of about 3 or 4 to 1 (however, see Shaywitz, Shaywitz, Fletcher, & Escobar, 1990), making this the number-one disability in terms of categorical funding (Doris, 1986).

The difficulties presented by the lack of an accepted operational definition of learning disabilities, however, will affect any attempts to determine prevalence rates. In this regard, Cruickshank (1983) stated that there does not exist "a single adequate epidemiological study of learning disabilities in the world literature." Nonetheless, some efforts have been asserted, particularly with respect to the concepts of underachievement and severe learning impairment. For example, over 25 years ago, Myklebust and Boshes (1969) found approximately a 7 to 8% rate of underachievement in a sample of 2,700 third- and fourth-grade students with average general intellectual abilities. More recently, Kaufman and Kaufman (1983) noted approximately a 2 to 3% rate of severe learning impairment in a test standardization sample of 2,000 children ages 6 through 16. Generally, prevalence estimates of learning disabilities vary considerably, but most researchers would agree that some 3 to 6% of school-age children most likely suffer some form of a learning disability (e.g., Keogh, 1986). While it is recognized that a number of factors can affect estimates of prevalence—such as geographic location (Keogh, 1986), language characteristics (Hynd & Cohen, 1983), and inheritance (Smith, Pennington, Kimberling, & Ing, 1990)—the number of children with learning disabilities probably exceeds the combined total of children who have cerebral palsy, epilepsy, and severe mental retardation (Duane, 1979).

NEUROLOGICAL BASIS OF LEARNING DISABILITIES: RECENT FINDINGS

A number of physiological, psychological, and sociological factors have been implicated in the etiology of learning disabilities (Gaddes, 1985); however, from an historical perspective, most learning disabilities have been presumed to be due to central nervous system deficit or dysfunction. For example, it has been 100 years since Hinshelwood (1895), Morgan (1896), and Bastian (1898) described learning problems in children that resembled deficits typically found in adults with known brain damage.

Based on these observations, it was postulated that some developmental anomaly existed in the brains of these children in the region of the left parietal-occipital cortex. This postulated deficit was believed to disrupt the functioning of the cortical pathways important in learning, particularly in learning to read fluently. In addition, Hinshelwood (1909) reported a series of cases that implicated genetic linkages in learning disorders. Many of the single-factor theories of learning disabilities (e.g., Orton, 1928) also contributed to the presumptive role of neurological factors directly and indirectly influencing learning and generated an impressive amount of research (see Hooper & Willis, 1989).

Currently, empirical support for the neurological basis of learning disabilities is accumulating across multiple levels of analysis. While a significant amount of this literature has been conducted at the neuropsychological (e.g., Gaddes, 1985; Hooper & Willis, 1989; Obrzut & Hynd, 1991; Rourke, 1985) and neurophysiological levels (e.g., Duffy, Denckla, Bartels, Sandini, & Keissling, 1980; Galin, Herron, Johnstone, Fein, & Yingling, 1988) in support of a neurological basis for learning disorders, a considerable literature also has evolved at the neuroanatomical level. Findings at the neuroanatomical level of analysis provide the strongest support for the neurological basis of learning disorders. Although an exhaustive review is beyond the scope of this chapter, several highlights of the postmortem and neuro-imaging literature require mentioning.

Postmortem Findings

It has long been accepted that disturbances in the overall growth of the brain (e.g., microcephaly, megalencephaly), various dysplasias of the cerebral cortex (e.g., agyria, pachygyria, polymicrogyria), and dysplasias of the cerebral hemispheres (e.g., holoprosencephaly, agenesis) may be associated with mental retardation (Crome, 1960; Freytag & Lindenberg, 1967; Jellinger, 1972; Malamud, 1964). It has been only in the last two decades, however, that significant advances in neuropathology have allowed for an articulation of what kind of anomalous development might be associated with learning disabilities. Further, based on a theory advanced by Geschwind (1984) and Geschwind and Galaburda (1985a, 1985b, 1985c) that suggested that alterations in fetal development could result in aberrations in neurological development, postmortem studies of individuals with learning disabilities were deemed important to uncovering direct linkages between neurostructural phenomenon and functional learning problems.

Drake (1968) provided the first postmortem report on a child with severe learning and behavioral problems. Despite the fact that Drake's autopsy report was based primarily on gross unaided inspection, he found an abnormal convolutional pattern in the left parietal lobe—a finding consistent with earlier notions. He also reported that the corpus callosum was thinned and stretched. While these findings were consistent with existing theory and represented important initial findings, they were largely ignored until some 11 years later.

In a landmark investigation, Galaburda and Kemper (1979) reported on a case of a developmental dyslexic who had a long history of academic failure. He died as a young adult and the comprehensive autopsy revealed results that complemented those reported by Drake (1968). Pathological findings from serial brain sections revealed areas of disordered cortical layering, a large area of polymicrogyria (i.e., clustering of many small convolutions) in the region of the left planum temporale and other focal cellular abnormalities. Most importantly, all of the cortical regions known to be involved in the functional system of reading (Hynd & Hynd, 1984) were affected to some degree by these neurodevelopmental anomalies. Further investigation of this case by Galaburda and Eidelberg (1982) provided evidence that the neurodevelopmental anomalies also may have occurred subcortically, with particular disruption of the cytoarchitecture noted bilaterally in the regions of the medial geniculate nucleus and lateral posterior nucleus of the thalamus.

Since these early reports, additional postmortem cases of individuals with learning disabilities have been reported, each with a unique distribution of cortical and subcortical anomalies (Galaburda, Sherman, Rosen, Aboitiz, & Geschwind, 1985). As Galaburda and colleagues (1985) reported, however, there are a number of striking similarities among these cases. One of the most significant findings in the postmortem studies was the presence of symmetry in the region of the planum temporale and parieto-occipital cortex. In fact, all seven of the brains studied by Galaburda and his colleagues had symmetrical plana. In addition, neuronal ectopias (i.e., brain warts), polymicrogyria, and other dysplasias consistently were noted. Normative evidence suggests that these developmental anomalies are rarely found in normal brains (Kaufman & Galaburda, 1989) and, developmentally, these cellular abnormalities most likely occur between the fifth to the seventh month of fetal gestation (Galaburda et al., 1985). Both experimental (Dvorak, Feit, & Jurankova, 1978) and clinical reports (Caviness, Evrard, & Lyon, 1978) suggest that this is an important period for the development of these anomalies.

Another significant finding was the bilateral disruption in the medial-geniculate and posterior nuclei of the thalamus (Galaburda & Eidelberg, 1982; Galaburda et al., 1985). Because these nuclei may be related to language functions, Hynd and Semrud-Clikeman (1989) hypothesized that these nuclei might be involved in allocating and focusing attentional resources on linguistic tasks. Significant involvement of frontal regions bilaterally also was found, and this would be consistent with emergent data implicating the frontal cortex in the functioning of the linguistic system (Kelly, Best, & Kirk, 1989), and perhaps other learning functions as well (Semrud-Clikeman & Hynd, 1990).

Although the postmortem studies are few in number, these data are vitally important in providing direct evidence as to the neurological factors that may be associated with learning disabilities. The significance of these studies cannot be understated with respect to their ability to address the presumptive role of neurological factors in learning disabilities; however, the exact relationship of these findings to specific functions (e.g., language, reading, etc.) remain largely speculative at this time.

Neuro-Imaging Findings

The neuro-imaging studies do not have the capability to reveal cellular anomalies, but they do allow for a noninvasive way to examine brain morphology. With regard to learning disabilities, however, it has never been suggested that the brains of these individuals would show obvious signs of brain damage or large lesions of developmental origin. What has been suggested is that the brains of these individuals would show deviations in normal patterns of asymmetry in those brain regions known to be important in language and language-dependent functions, such as selected components of reading and arithmetic (Geschwind, 1984).

For the majority of individuals, the brain is characterized by normal patterns of asymmetry. Evidence indicates that approximately 75% of normal brains have right frontal regions that are larger in volume than the left frontal region (Weinberger, Luchins, Morihisa, & Wyatt, 1982). The region of the left planum temporale is larger than the right in about 66% of normal brains (Geschwind & Levitsky, 1968). Further, the majority of normal brains also evidence a larger posterior region on the left side (LeMay, 1981). Neurobiological theory would predict that children and adolescents with language deficits would show less asymmetry or even reversed asymmetry in those regions known to be important to language (e.g., planum temporale, posterior cortex). The notion is that at a structural level there is a less developed neurological system to support the complex language processes and associated functions.

A number of studies using either computerized tomography (CT) or magnetic resonance imaging (MRI) of the brain have been conducted to examine this hypothesis. Hier, LeMay, Rosenberger, and Perlo (1978) were perhaps the first investigators to report CT results with 24 dyslexics. They found that only 33% of the dyslexics had a wider left posterior region, whereas 67% had either symmetrical or reversed asymmetry of the posterior region. Similarly, Leisman and Ashkenazi (1980) reported that all of their dyslexics ($n = 10$) had either symmetry or reversed asymmetry of the posterior region. In a follow-up study, Rosenberger and Hier (1980) found that a brain asymmetry index correlated with verbal-performance IQ discrepancies such that lower verbal IQ was associated with symmetry or reversed asymmetry of the posterior region in the dyslexics. Haslam, Dalby, Johns, and Rademaker (1981) found 54% of their dyslexic sample to have symmetry or reversed asymmetry of the left posterior region; however, they did not find a relationship with verbal abilities.

More recently, two studies have reported on patterns of asymmetry in the region of the plana and possible relationships to neurolinguistic performance in children with dyslexia. Larsen, Hoien, Lundberg, and Odegaard (1990) used MRI to examine the size and patterns of plana asymmetry in their sample. They found that 70% of their dyslexic sample had symmetry in the region of the plana, whereas only 30% of the normals exhibited this pattern. They also found that when symmetry or reversed asymmetry in the region of the plana was evident, there was associated deficits in phonological processing.

Hynd, Semrud-Clikeman, Lorys, Novey, and Eliopulos (1990) also employed MRI techniques to investigate the relative specificity of patterns of plana morphology in dyslexics, a normal control group, and a clinic control group of children diagnosed as having attention-deficit disorder with hyperactivity (ADD/H) but who did not have reading problems. Similar to Larsen and associates (1990), Hynd and colleagues found 90% of the dyslexics to have either symmetry or reversed asymmetry of the plana. Underscoring the notion that this pattern of plana morphology may be unique to dyslexics, they found 70% of both the normals and ADD/H children had a left plana larger than the right, while only 10% of the dyslexics did. In a follow-up examination, Semrud-Clikeman, Hynd, Novey, and Eliopulos (1991) found this pattern to be associated with significant deficits in confrontational naming, rapid naming, and neurolinguistic processes in general.

Despite the great clinical and methodological heterogeneity of these studies, several tentative conclusions have been proffered. First, neuro-imaging techniques revealed very few abnormalities in the gross brain morphology of children with learning disabilities. The brains of children with learning disabilities, especially dyslexia, do not seem to have any obvious structural defect or lesion that would provide a definitive marker for learning problems. Second, these neuro-imaging techniques did reveal a robust finding of significant deviations in normal patterns of brain asymmetry for children with learning problems. The specific findings implicating symmetry or reversed asymmetry of the plana appear consistent with the results from autopsy studies. Finally, several studies suggested important relationships between these patterns of brain symmetry or reversed asymmetry and neurolinguistic functions, although this latter brain-behavior trend requires further substantiation.

Summary of Recent Findings

To date, postmortem and neuro-imaging studies provide support for the historical conceptualization that learning disabilities are due to neurological factors. They also support the presumptive role of neurological factors in this group of disorders espoused by the most recent definition of learning disabilities (Wyngaarden, 1987). Although these studies are not without methodological problems (Hynd & Semrud-Clikeman, 1989), the accumulating evidence remains provocative, yet productive, with respect to understanding the neurological basis of learning problems.

NEUROPSYCHOLOGICAL ASSESSMENT-TREATMENT ISSUES

The neuropsychological assessment of learning disabilities presents an assessment challenge because these disorders typically involve presumed rather than documented brain dysfunction. Consequently, children and adolescents with learning disabilities should be expected to show less overall impairment than individuals with known brain damage. Consideration of the multifaceted nature of learning disorders requires a comprehensive approach to assessment.

For example, Hynd, Connor, and Nieves (1988) advocated that a neuropsychological assessment battery should reflect tasks constructed around a wide array of functions, particularly with respect to identifying specific strengths and weaknesses. These investigators also suggested that a battery should be flexible in order to address referral questions efficiently, especially for children referred for specific learning problems. More generally, Taylor (1988) noted that it is important to recognize the strengths and weaknesses of a particular set of neuropsychological procedures so as to maximize potential treatment recommendations. In this regard, neuropsychological assessment strategies for the learning disabled can be divided into several different approaches: fixed batteries, eclectic batteries, and special purpose measures (Tramontana & Hooper, 1988).

Neuropsychological Assessment Approaches

Fixed Battery Approach

This approach attempts to provide a comprehensive assessment of brain function using an invariant set of validated test procedures. The composition of the battery is neither tailored to the presenting characteristics of an individual patient nor to specific clinical hypotheses. Rather, the emphasis is on administering as many of the designated procedures as the individual's condition will permit. Individual variability is assumed to be measured reasonably well when the battery is designated to assess a broad array of human capabilities. Moreover, the use of a fixed battery across individuals provides a standard data base on which different clinical groups can be compared. Fixed batteries, such as the Halstead-Reitan Neuropsychological Battery (HRNB) and the Luria-Nebraska Neuropsychology Battery (LNNB), currently represent some of the most commonly used approaches in neuropsychological assessment.

Although there have been a number of criticisms levied against the current fixed battery approaches (Tramontana & Hooper, 1988) (see Chapter 2), the application of fixed batteries to learning disabled population has proven fruitful. In particular, they have been useful in discriminating between heterogeneous groups of learning disabled children and normals (Batchelor & Dean, 1992; Geary & Gilger, 1984, 1985; Geary, Jennings, Schultz, & Alper, 1984; Hyman, 1983; Lewis, Garland, & Hutchens, 1991; Lewis & Lorion, 1988; Selz & Reitan, 1979; Strom, Gray, Dean, & Fischer, 1987; Teeter, Boliek, Obrzut, & Malsch, 1986). They also have been used successfully in the derivation of learning disability subtypes (Batchelor & Dean, 1992; Nolan, Hammeke, & Barkley, 1983; Snow & Hynd, 1985), although not consistently (Morgan & Brown, 1988). With respect to learning disability subtyping, the work of Rourke and colleagues has been particularly noteworthy (e.g., Rourke, 1985).

Eclectic Battery Approach

This approach attempts to preserve the quantitative nature of neuropsychological assessment by selecting standardized tests that, when considered collectively, measure a broad range of neuropsychological functions. There generally is at least an implicit outline of the relevant functions and abilities that should be assessed routinely (e.g., Lezak, 1995; Spreen & Strauss, 1991; Taylor, 1988). Any of a variety of available test, however, may be selected to quantify the extent of deficit in each of the functional areas of interest. The psychometric properties of individual tests (e.g., reliability, validity, normative standards), as well as their abilities to complement the overall battery are factors that guide test selection. Professionals constructing eclectic batteries, however, should be aware that these collections of instruments, although designed around broad-band neuropsychological constructs, may not accurately reflect true profile differences. This is because data are compared across different normative samples, and the empirical relationships among measures only can be estimated.

Despite these concerns, eclectic batteries probably have been used most frequently in the study of learning disabilities. One of the main reasons for their popularity is that they allow for flexibility in test selection, thus minimizing the time required to conduct assessments. Another reason is that these batteries generally have shown remarkable similarity to the factor structure of the fixed neuropsychological test batteries (Sutter & Battin, 1983; Sutter, Bishop, & Battin, 1986). Although several eclectic batteries have been proposed for the study of learning disabilities (Aaron, 1981; Mattis, French, & Rapin, 1975; Obrzut, 1981; Wilson & Risucci, 1986), this kind of battery can assume any form as long as key neuropsychological constructs are covered with respect to breadth and depth of assessment. These batteries have been particularly useful in the construction of subtype treatment paradigms in the learning disability literature (Bakker, Bouma, & Gardien, 1990; Lyon, 1983, 1985).

Special Purpose Measures

In addition to fixed and eclectic battery approaches to neuropsychological assessment of children with learning disabilities, there are many individual measures and specialized test batteries available to assess more specific aspects of functioning. Examples include Benton's Motor Impersistence Battery and the Judgment of Line Orientation Test (Benton, Hamsher, Varney, & Spreen, 1983), the Goldman-Fristoe-Woodcock Auditory Skills Battery (Goldman, Fristoe, Woodcock, 1974), the Wide Range Assessment of Memory and Learning Test (Adams & Sheslow, 1990), the Gordon Diagnostic System (Gordon, McClure, & Post, 1983), and the Wisconsin Card Sorting Test (Heaton, 1981), to name only a few. There also are procedures for assessing specific aspects of learning disabilities, such as dichotic listening paradigms (Hugdahl, in press), metacognitive techniques (Wiener, 1986), and the Boder Test of Reading-Spelling Patterns (Boder & Jarrico, 1982).

Special purpose neuropsychological measures typically are designed to assess selected aspects of an individual's functioning (e.g., visual-spatial functions, visual vigilance, etc.). As such, they should be used as only part of a more comprehensive neuropsychological battery or as screening devices to determine the likelihood of the presence of impairment in a selected domains. However, their potential contribution to effective treatment planning for children and adolescents with learning disabilities appears fruitful.

Assessment-Treatment Issues and Concerns

Regardless of the approach selected, the primary goals of most neuropsychological assessments are (1) to determine the impact of brain damage/dysfunction on cognitive functioning, (2) to diagnose those with brain damage/dysfunction and those without, and (3) to understand how various kinds of neuropathology affect behavior. More generally, Boll (1981) noted that the primary goal of neuropsychology is to describe brain-behavior relationships in a reliable and valid manner. In addition, Boll asserted that the development of empirically valid remediation and rehabilitation procedures should be another primary goal of neuropsychological assessment.

The shift in focus of neuropsychological assessment as a diagnostic or classification enterprise to a process designed to gain specific treatment strategies truly embodies an effort to increase the clinical relevance of neuropsychology, particularly in an educational setting. It is clear, however, that the majority of the assessment batteries, procedures, and general approaches to assessment were designed to obtain detailed descriptive information, and not necessarily prescriptive information (Lyon & Moats, 1988; Lyon et al., 1988). Given this relatively recent shift in the field from gaining detailed diagnostic descriptions from a neuropsychological assessment to detailed prescriptions, there has been concomitant scrutiny of the instruments and approaches to assessment that are available to clinicians and researchers. Lyon and associates (1988) point out several major issues in this regard.

First, Lyon and colleagues note that most of the standardized batteries used for assessment (e.g., HRNB, LNNB) are typically downward extensions of batteries initially developed on adult populations. Although this is a standard criticism levied against many child neuropsychological assessment tools, its relevance for treatment planning is particularly important. Indeed, if tasks and items are based on adult models of brain functioning, then their predictive power for children and adolescents may be compromised because of their potential lack of sensitivity to neurodevelopmental processes. Further, many of the tasks may be useful for the focal effects that can be seen in many types of adult neuropathology; however, their utility for identifying the more generalized effects of pediatric neurological disorders may be significantly lessened. This is particularly important for the subtle neurodevelopmental anomalies that have been associated with children and adolescents with learning disabilities. Finally, many of the adult-based tasks may have little relevance (i.e., ecological validity) to the daily tasks encountered by children and adolescents.

Second, although the fixed and eclectic neuropsychological assessment approaches are designed to be comprehensive, most of the these approaches utilize static measures of functioning. Although a considerable amount of detailed, descriptive information can be across a wide array of neuropsychological functions (e.g., attention, language, memory), it is rare that the qualitative aspects of a child's functioning are addressed. This concern is echoed in many of the traditional psychoeducational assessment practices that occur in schools and pediatric clinics. The quality of *how* a child passes or fails an item or task, the strategies that are employed for retrieving old information or learning new information, the child's level of awareness of these strategies, and the generalization of these strategies to school-related or social activities are rarely incorporated into traditional psychoeducational or neuropsychological assessment practices. This kind of information nicely complements the descriptive diagnostic profile of strengths and weaknesses, although more frequent assessment probes may be required, and seems vital for treatment planning. Relatedly, Lyon and Toomey (1985) suggested that the accurate description of child and adolescent brain-behavior relationships does not by itself guarantee linkage to successful treatment strategies.

The third concern raised by Lyon and colleagues (1988) reflects another age-old criticism against neuropsychological assessment; that is, tasks comprising a neuropsychological battery primarily assess general cognitive abilities and not unique or specific functions (e.g., Hynd, Snow, & Becker, 1986). Given this concern, the utility of using information generated from current neuropsychological batteries remains suspect, particularly given the lack of treatment efficacy for specific intellectual measures and the concept of IQ in general (Ysseldyke &

Mirkin, 1981). This concern also has been reiterated by Lezak (1988). Relatedly, the poor normative data available for many of the neuropsychological batteries also raises many questions with respect to their reliability and validity, not to mention their application to treatment planning.

Fourth, with respect to children and adolescents with learning problems, most of the neuropsychological assessment techniques were not designed specifically for this heterogeneous group of disorders. In addition to not directly addressing the neurodevelopmental nature of most of these learning problems, few of the approaches are hypothesis driven with respect to this population nor do they include procedures that thoroughly evaluate selected areas of dysfunction (e.g., language-based deficiencies). Although other neuropsychological assessment approaches have potential for application to learning disabilities, such as the qualitative- (Luria, 1973) and process-oriented (Milberg, Hebben, & Kaplan, 1986) approaches, they have not been thoroughly examined with respect to their merit with this population.

Finally, there are a variety of additional assessment-treatment issues that should be addressed for this population. For example, there are a number of social-environmental concerns, such as socioeconomic status and family factors, that can make neuropsychological assessment results less clear and, ultimately, interfere with the development and/or implementation of a treatment program. Social-emotional functioning also should be included in a thorough neuropsychological assessment and, subsequently, incorporated into any treatment planning. This is particularly important, given the debilitating or habilitating effects that emotional factors can have on neurocognitive functions. Most importantly, however, in order to relate assessment findings directly to treatment planning and outcome variables, the phenotypic (i.e., behavioral) expression of the different kinds of learning problems must be clearly defined, characterized, and classified (Lyon et al., 1988). Lastly, neuropsychological assessment of children with learning disabilities should not stand alone but, rather, should be complemented by other kinds of assessment. These assessment-treatment issues are important with respect to planning and modifying specific neuropsychological interventions for a child with a learning disability.

SPECIFIC NEUROPSYCHOLOGICAL TREATMENT APPROACHES

Although a large number of approaches to the treatment of learning disorders have been advanced over the years (e.g., Ylvisaker, Szekeres, & Hartwick, in press; Alley & Deshler, 1979), this section will review only neuropsychologically based treatment approaches. These neuropsychologically based approaches have received various levels of research support; some are well-grounded empirically, others are primarily clinical or, at best, speculative. Four kinds of examples are discussed here: developmental, behavioral, strength, and deficit approaches to treatment. Finally, some associated treatment approaches and issues are noted as they relate to children with learning disorders.

Developmental Neuropsychological Approach

Rourke, Fisk, and Strang (1986) proposed a developmental neuropsychological remediation/habilitation approach that comprises seven stages. This approach, shown in Figure 9.1, is useful for conceptualizing the treatment and management of individuals with learning disorders because it provides a strong link with the neuropsychological assessment of these disorders. In this sense, it also provides a foundation for conceptualizing treatment strategies for particular kinds of learning disorders (i.e., subtypes), especially when those disorders are identified using neuropsychological methods.

The stages of this approach successively lead from specifying the nature of the relationship between the child's neuropsychological functioning and neurological deficits to evaluating a realistic treatment intervention. Evaluating the intervention is related closely to the initial stage of this approach. This provides a particularly strong assessment-treatment linkage, and emphasizes that it is the recursive relationship between stages that characterizes effective therapeutic programs. The stages are outlined here with specific reference to learning disorders.

Brain-Behavior Relationships

Given the marked discontinuities in human development, understanding brain-behavior relationships, particularly in children, is truly a complex matter. It is clear that there is no direct relationship between extent of brain impairment and behavioral deficit. Instead, this relationship is moderated by a variety of factors, some of which are known or suspected, such as the age of the individual and the site of the lesion, and others of which currently are unknown. The first stage of this approach involves specifying this relationship. Although research evidence is useful toward this endeavor, individual differences obfuscate broad generalizations. Each case must be investigated individually and thoroughly. Both the details of the brain impairment (i.e., history) and a comprehensive neuropsychological profile must be considered.

In the case of most developmental learning disorders, of course, there usually are no definitive or classical hard signs of brain impairment. Other cases of acquired learning disorders, however, may be associated with these signs as documented by various neuro-imaging procedures. Regardless of the assumed or documented nature of the lesion, it is useful to consider the consequences of its etiology in terms of prognosis, because prognosis inextricably is connected with treatment. Here, important issues include those associated with anticipated deterioration versus improvement of function; the level, extent, and chronicity of the brain lesion; and any potential secondary effects or sequelae. Particularly important for learning disorders is the age at which the brain impairment was sustained. In the case of developmental learning disorders, for example, the lesion often is assumed to be present at least from birth, perhaps resulting from neurodevelopmental errors (Galaburda et al., 1985). Again, although the precise effects of the age of impairment on the interaction of brain-behavior relationships is unknown, it is reasonable to expect differential effects of earlier versus later lesions. For example, individuals with developmental learning disorders

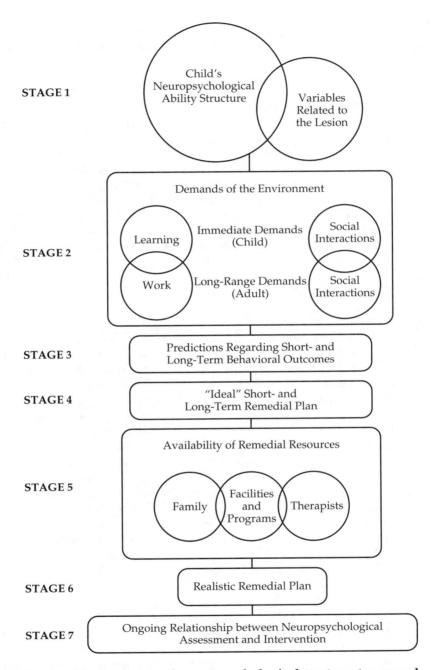

FIGURE 9.1   A developmental neuropsychological treatment approach.

Source: From *The Neuropsychological Assessment of Children: A Treatment-Oriented Approach* by B. P. Rourke, J. L. Fisk, and J. D. Strang, 1986, New York: Guilford Press. Copyright © 1986 Guilford Press. Reprinted by permission.

(i.e., presumably present from birth) probably have experienced very different learning histories than individuals who have acquired learning problems due to craniocerebral traumata subsequent to the school-age years.

The consideration of a comprehensive neuropsychological function profile involves a thorough evaluation. Here, it is important to consider not only academic skills but also neurocognitive, linguistic, and social-emotional factors in these evaluations. Additionally, Rourke and associates (1983) particularly emphasized the assessment of sensory-perceptual and motor functions for childhood evaluations. This is because serious developmental consequences may accrue in the presence of fundamental sensory-perceptual or sensorimotor impairments. Similar to any evaluation, when selecting measures of these functions, clinicians need to be concerned with psychometric issues. Of particular relevance to treatment are criterion-related validities that address the developmental demands with which the child is and will be confronted. Given the ultimate treatment goal, it is important to elicit the best possible level of performance (i.e., as opposed to a typical level). This facilitates an understanding of the conditions that influence the presentation, persistence, and remission of academic as well as other (e.g., psychosocial, metacognitive, adaptive) problems.

Environmental Demands
In the second stage of the approach, formal and informal environmental demands are considered. For children, of course, a major formal environment is the school. The school presents both general (e.g., conduct, social-interactive) and specific (e.g., academic skills) demands, many of which are particularly challenging for children with learning disorders. Competence in these general and specific school-related demands substantially contributes to self-esteem and the potential for postschool success. It is important, therefore, for interventions to address these demands. Treatment plans, however, should not focus exclusively on the school environment. Instead, clinicians also must recognize the importance of informal environmental demands (both general and specific) and the contribution of nonschool-related environments toward the development of prosocial and adaptive behaviors. These other environments should neither be excluded from nor transgressed by interventions for learning disorders. Understanding the beneficial roles of informal as well as formal environments helps the clinician to maintain a balanced perspective between the long-term and short-term demands confronted by the individual with a learning disorder.

Prognosis
The third stage of the approach involves predictions about long-term and short-term behavioral outcomes. These kinds of predictions, or prognoses, are essential to well-informed treatment planning. In fact, Rourke and colleagues (1986) asserted that if clinicians are unable to proffer educated predictions about probable outcomes, then they should refrain from developing treatment interventions. Of course, this does not mean that accurate predictions are easily conceived. For example, preliminary evidence (Spreen & Haaf, 1986) suggests that particular kinds of learning disorders identified during childhood (i.e, a linguistic-deficit subtype

of a learning disability) may develop more global impairments in adulthood. In contrast, other kinds of learning problems identified during childhood (e.g., a visual-perceptual deficit subtype of a learning disability) may continue to show similar profiles of impairment into adulthood.

Other research suggests that particular kinds of learning disorders can be predicted from variables during the preschool years (Tramontana, Hooper, & Selzer, 1988). Still other research (see Hooper & Willis, 1989, for a review) indicates that particular kinds of learning disorders may predispose individuals toward distinctive kinds of social-emotional problems (or perhaps vice-versa). This kind of research should be considered concomitantly with variables that are unique to individual cases when predicting long-term and short-term behavioral outcomes for these individuals, particularly given the poor (Schonhaut & Satz, 1983) or, at best, equivocal (Spreen, 1988) outcomes for this group of learning disorders.

Treatment Intervention Plan

The fourth through sixth stages of the approach involve developing the intervention plan. Here, ideal plans are mitigated by available resources to derive a realistic treatment intervention. In formulating ideal plans, Rourke and associates (1986) emphasized that both long-term and short-term treatment requirements should be considered. Particularly when considered from a developmental perspective, these requirements may be at variance with one another. Thus, the overall plan should address issues such as foci changes in intervention as well as times when particular strategies should be terminated and others initiated.

Once developed, the ideal intervention plan must be considered in terms of the resources required versus the resources available for effective implementation. The family may be among the most influential resources available, although this very powerful system unfortunately frequently is omitted from consideration in favor of professional efforts. Other resources, of course, include teachers, specialists/therapists, support services (i.e., "related services" as defined by the rules and regulations for Public Law 94-142), various school and community programs, and specialized facilities and equipment, among others. Sometimes these resources are less than ideal but can be adapted to the existing circumstances. With some exceptions, public school districts can be remarkably creative and responsive to the unique needs of children with learning disorders. This creativity and responsiveness can be mobilized for the mutual benefit of both the school district and the child through skilled consultation efforts that show sensitivity to systemic and individualized issues of importance in the school milieu (Idol & West, 1987; West & Idol, 1987).

Evaluation of Effectiveness

The final stage in this approach emphasizes the ongoing, or recursive, relationship between neuropsychological assessment and treatment. Established interventions are evaluated in terms of effectiveness by neuropsychological performance changes. Such evaluations, for example, may signal that minor adjustments or major changes are required in the intervention plan. This kind of follow-up is especially important when considered from a developmental perspective and our currently limited understanding of the ontogeny of brain-behavior relationships in children with and without learning disorders.

Behavioral-Neuropsychological Approach

Another neuropsychologically based treatment approach that has been proposed involves the integration of two major disciplines. At one time, scientific progress required that the disciplines of behavior and neurology be studied separately. For example, in 1938, Skinner emphasized the distinct nature of these two disciplines, asserted that the science of behavior was independent of neurology, and urged that behavioral science be established as a separate field of study. Currently, however, many have come to believe that the time has come for a rapprochement of these two disciplines. Indeed, as our knowledge base has expanded, the artificial boundaries once established between neurology and psychology have become increasingly less tenable. The treatment of children with learning disorders perhaps provides one of the most cogent examples of the importance of such a rapprochement.

Behavioral neuropsychology is a specialty that integrates principles of behavior therapy with neuropsychology (Horton, 1989; Horton & Puente, 1986). It is based on the ideas that a neuropsychological perspective can (1) contribute to the understanding of the etiology of behavior and (2) facilitate functional analyses of particular behavioral deficits (Horton, 1979). Both of these ideas are useful in formulating treatment interventions for children with learning disorders. Toward this goal, it is helpful to conceptualize behavioral-neuropsychological approaches to treatment within the framework of the "S-O-R-K-C" heuristic originally presented by Lindsley (1964) and discussed by others (Goldfried & Sprafkin, 1976; Kanfer & Phillips, 1970; Mash & Terdal, 1988).

S-O-R-K-C Framework

This framework provides a convenient classification of the variables of interest in a functional (i.e., behavioral) analysis of a problem (e.g., a particular kind of learning disorder). Within this framework, S designates the antecedent stimuli that signal the occurrence of the behavior or provide the opportunity for its occurrence. Discriminative stimuli, for example, are considered in terms of this designation.

The O designates organismic variables that influence behavior. These include neuropsychological, genetic, personality, medical, and other variables considered to be intrinsic to the individual. It is through these organismic variables that neuropsychological information is integrated effectively within a more general behavioral treatment paradigm.

The third component of the heuristic, R, designates the response class—that is, those behaviors targeted in the treatment intervention plan. Covert as well as overt behaviors are appropriate targets for these plans and, in the case of learning disorders, can include a variety of metacognitive, academic, motoric, linguistic, and social-adaptive responses. Response classes typically are defined clearly, often in an operational manner, for behaviorally oriented treatments. Here, aspects to consider include the rates, durations, topographies, and magnitudes of behaviors, as well as the common properties that interrelate behaviors within a response class.

Finally, K designates the contingencies by which the response class is linked to C, the response-controlling consequences. Specification of contingencies involves clarifying the schedule of reinforcement that maintains the response class. Consequences may include positive and negative reinforcement as well as punishment and response-cost stimuli.

Treatment Implications

When treatment is considered from the perspective of the S-O-R-K-C heuristic, neuropsychological and behavioral approaches appear quite compatible. As Barkley (1984) identified, behaviorism emphasizes environmental antecedents and consequences in the functional analysis of behavior, whereas neuropsychology emphasizes the role of the central nervous system. Treatment goals of both disciplines, however, are similar, whereas differences primarily are related to variables selected for manipulation. For example, behavioral (R) change can result from either central nervous system (O) or environmental (S, K, C) change. Theoretically, all aspects are important for the thorough understanding and effective management of behavior, but continued empirical efforts are needed to evaluate the effectiveness of behavioral neuropsychology approaches for the treatment of childhood learning disorders.

Neuropsychological Strength Approach

The neuropsychological strength approach (e.g., Hartlage & Reynolds, 1981; Hartlage & Telzrow, 1983; Kamphaus & Reynolds, 1987; Reynolds, 1981, 1986) also has been advocated for the treatment of children with learning disorders. This approach is essentially an individualized aptitude-by-treatment paradigm, where teaching is directed toward specific problem areas (e.g., reading, social skills). Instructional methods that are congruent with the child's neuropsychological processing strengths (e.g., simultaneous cognitive processing) are used, whereas those that are more congruent with weaknesses (e.g., successive cognitive processing) generally are avoided or bypassed. Rationale for this approach include its intuitive appeal, tenuous neurodevelopmental empirical support, and the circumvention of stress and anxiety that often are associated with approaches that focus on areas of weakness.

Aptitude-by-Treatment Interaction (ATI)

ATI approaches have been prevalent in the field of special education for many years. For these approaches, particular instructional methods are matched with particular learning styles or profiles. For example, a different teaching method would be used for a child with auditory learning problems than for a child with visual learning problems. Unfortunately, research clearly indicates that treatment approaches based on these kinds of ATI paradigms are ineffective (Arter

& Jenkins, 1979; Forness & Kavale, 1983; Glass, 1983; Kampwirth, 1979; Larivee, 1981; Lewis, 1983; Ysseldyke & Mirkin, 1982). Howell (1986, p. 326) even called ATI approaches "a pervasive . . . affliction in special education," and Lakin (1983, p. 236) identified the continued use of these approaches as, "a professional disgrace, given the wealth of [refuting] evidence. . . . "

In contrast, others (e.g., Hartlage & Reynolds, 1981; Kamphaus & Reynolds, 1987; Reynolds, 1986) have argued that the neuropsychological strength approach differs from these more traditional ATI approaches in at least two important ways. First, many traditional ATI approaches have identified perceptual or cognitive-processing deficits and focused instructional efforts on circumventing those deficits. Second, in focusing on perceptual/cognitive deficits, these approaches have neglected direct instruction of content skills. For the neuropsychological strength approach, however, identified strengths are used solely to determine how specific subject matter should be taught. Consequently, perceptual and cognitive processing do not become foci of treatment. Instead, behavioral and psychoeducational analyses of academic tasks are used to determine exactly what should be taught. Thus, in contrast to traditional ATI approaches, the neuropsychological strength approach uses identified learner aptitudes to determine how to teach, rather than what to teach.

There is an additional difference between traditional ATI approaches and the neuropsychological strength approach. When a neurocognitive function is considered in terms of Guilford's (1985) structure-of-intellect model, three facets are conceptualized. These are (1) content, or characteristics of the input stimulus; (2) operation, or characteristics of the neurocognitive process; and (3) product, or characteristics of the output response. In terms of the aptitude variable in ATI paradigms, the traditional focus has been on contents and products (e.g., auditory-oral, visual-motor). In contrast, the neuropsychological strength approach tends to focus on operations (e.g., successive, simultaneous).

Specific ATI approaches to reading instruction have been proposed for children with developmental dyslexia (e.g., Boder, 1971, 1973; Mattis, 1981; Mattis, French, & Rapin, 1975; Hynd, 1986; Hynd & Cohen, 1983). These approaches are based on research showing different patterns of psychometric performance for particular subtypes of dyslexia (see Hooper & Willis, 1989). For example, Boder suggested that a particular subtype of dyslexia, characterized by weaknesses in auditory processing, would respond better to whole-word approaches to reading instruction than to more phonics-based teaching strategies. Interventions capitalizing on the tactile-perceptual aspects of learning also were suggested for this subtype of dyslexia. Here, Boder believed that a phonics approach to reading instruction was contraindicated and should not be attempted until an adequate sight-word foundation had been developed. In contrast, Boder suggested that a different subtype of dyslexia, characterized by visual-processing deficiencies, would respond best to a phonics-based approach to reading instruction. Tactile-kinesthetic strategies also were suggested as possible avenues for initiating the reading process for young children with these kinds of learning problems. Similarly, Mattis and associates also provided differential treatment suggestions for each of the specific dyslexic subtypes identified in their model, and Hynd proposed subtype-to-treatment matches based on a neurolinguistic subtyping model developed by Marshall (1984).

Research Evidence

Of course, the ultimate value of the neuropsychological strength approach will be supported or refuted empirically. Unfortunately, there are very few studies that address this issue at the present time, and results of the available preliminary investigations are equivocal (cf., Ayres, Cooley, & Severson, 1988; Cohen, Krawiecki, & DuRant, 1987; Flynn, 1987; Kaufman & Kaufman, 1983; Lyon, 1983, 1985). All of these studies carry certain methodological limitations such as small sample sizes, inability to control for teacher characteristics and previous educational experiences, and incompletely crossed experimental designs. As Teeter (1989) noted, however, these kinds of methodological problems are not unique to the neuropsychological strength approach. Instead, they more generally influence nearly all research efforts to evaluate the effectiveness of treatments that are based on cognitive-neuropsychological theories. Even so, despite current market demands for remedial programs based on the neuropsychological strength approach (e.g., Kaufman sequential or simultaneous [K-SOS]; Kaufman, Kaufman, & Goldsmith, 1984), the clinical application of this approach to treating children with learning disorders should be practiced cautiously.

Continued research efforts clearly are required. In addition to the methodological issues identified, another consideration for future research in this area concerns the clear separation of facets of the aptitude variable selected for study within the ATI paradigm. Here, cognitive operations assessed by tasks in many commonly administered assessment instruments (e.g., K-ABC, WISC-R) often are confounded by modality-specific contents and operations (Willis, 1985). For example, most standardized tasks of simultaneous cognitive processing involve a visual content and a motor product, whereas most standardized tasks of successive cognitive processing involve an auditory content and an oral product. Partitioning effects to distinct aptitude variables may be particularly important given the possibility that interactions among facets (e.g., cognitive processing strategies by stimulus-response modalities) may contribute to differential functional cerebral organization (Willis & Hynd, 1987).

Neuropsychological Deficit Approach

In contrast to neuropsychological strength approaches to the treatment of learning disorders, deficit approaches attempt to ameliorate relatively weak perceptual and cognitive processes. Thus, whereas the strength approach broadly can be characterized as circumventive, the deficit approach primarily is remedial.

Early Approaches

Most of the early deficit approaches to the treatment of learning disorders have fallen into disfavor. This is because a wide variety of studies now clearly has demonstrated that these kinds of approaches are ineffective (Cook & Welch, 1980; Hallahan & Cruickshank, 1973; Hammill & Larsen, 1974; Hicks, 1980; Liberman

& Shankweiler, 1979; Sowell, Parker, Poplin, & Larsen, 1979; Vellutino, 1979). Most of these early interventions, frequently referred to as process-training approaches, were based on the premise that learning disorders were due to fundamental perceptual-motor (e.g., Kephart, 1971), visual-perceptual (e.g., Frostig & Horne, 1964), or psycholinguistic (e.g., Kirk & Kirk, 1971) processing deficiencies. Remediation was focused on ameliorating these fundamental perceptual/cognitive deficits. Currently, of course, these interventions are notorious for their overwhelming lack of empirical support.

Contemporary Approaches
Several more recent neuropsychological deficit approaches to treating learning disorders, however, have been advanced (Affolter & Stricker, 1980; Ayres, 1972; Bakker, 1979; Reitan, 1980; Tomatis, 1978). Bakker (1979), for example, proposed a developmental "balance model" that describes two subtypes of reading disorders. He reviewed evidence that he interpreted to suggest that the right cerebral hemisphere is a primary mediator in the beginning stages of learning to read. This was based largely on the perhaps dubious assumption that reading appears to be more visual-perceptual and less linguistic during these early stages of the reading process. As the demands of learning to read become more linguistically complex, however, he believed that the reading process begins to be mediated more by left cerebral hemisphere strategies. Some children, however, may show an overuse of visual-perceptual (putatively right hemisphere) strategies and poor emergence of linguistic-semantic (putatively left hemisphere) strategies. In contrast, other children may be relatively insensitive to the visual-perceptual features of text, even when first learning to read. Bakker labeled these children "P-dyslexics" (perceptual dependence) and "L-dyslexics" (linguistic dependence), respectively. Thomlinson-Keasey and Kelly (1979a, 1979b) advanced this kind of classification in spelling and arithmetic domains as well.

Bakker, Moerland, and Goekoop-Hoefkens (1981) and Bakker (1984) provided some preliminary support for a neuropsychological deficit (i.e., remedial) approach using cerebral hemispheric stimulation to alter event-related potentials to improve reading scores in P-dyslexics and L-dyslexics. Subsequently, Bakker and Vinke (1985) found significant differences between the two dyslexic subtypes on event-related potentials and reading tasks following direct and indirect stimulation of the cerebral hemispheres.

In a later field experiment, Bakker and associates (1990) found that for P-dyslexics, a putative left hemisphere-specific stimulation improved reading fluency relative to a control treatment, whereas for L-dyslexics, a putative right hemisphere-specific stimulation improved reading accuracy relative to an undefined control treatment. The potential importance of these findings, however, is difficult to estimate given the significant methodological problems inherent in this study. For example, among other problems, the treatment of control P-dyslexics and L-dyslexics was "left to the discretion" (p. 436) of the 56 different remedial teachers involved in the study, the hemispheric specificity of the experimental treatments was questionable at best, and different dependent measures were evaluated for the two experimental treatments. It is unclear why a two-by-two crossed design (i.e., subtype by treatment design) was not used for this experiment.

As another example, Reitan (1980) also proposed a neuropsychologically based remedial program, which he called Reitan Evaluation of Hemispheric Abilities and Brain Improvement Training (REHABIT). There are three phases of this program, the last of which involves deficit-area training for language and verbal abilities; abstract thinking, reasoning, and problem-solving skills; and visual-spatial, motor, and sequential abilities. Remedial materials are selected from a variety of tracts for training general abstraction abilities based on the results of neuropsychological evaluation. There are no published studies currently available that have evaluated this program empirically (Teeter, 1989), however; thus, its clinical application cannot be recommended.

Primary Prevention

As illustrated by all of the approaches discussed so far, most treatments for children with learning disorders involve secondary or tertiary interventions. A major goal of these kinds of interventions is to reduce the number of currently existing cases of particular learning disorders (Zins, Conyne, & Ponti, 1988). Secondary interventions involve the identification and treatment of problems before they have serious consequences (Brown, Pryzwansky, & Schulte, 1987), whereas tertiary interventions are initiated once a disorder is established and its symptoms are differentially diagnosable (Lorion, 1983). The intent of a tertiary intervention is to treat the identified disorder, minimize its duration, and decrease its impact (Lorion, 1983). Unfortunately, as Shapiro (1988) noted, many of these kinds of interventions may be "too little too late" (p. 601). In addition, many methods currently used to identify and to classify learning disorders have been criticized as ineffective and inefficient (Maher & Illback, 1983). Increases in the number of children being placed in special education, reductions in resources for public educational programs, and demands for accountability all have focused attention on the need for alternative intervention approaches (Algozzine, Christenson, & Ysseldyke, 1982; Haynes & Jenkins, 1986; Maher & Illback, 1983).

Primary prevention is an alternative intervention approach that has the potential to alleviate many of the problems inherent in current service-delivery methods. The goal of primary prevention is to reduce the number of new cases of a disorder in a given population (Caplan, 1964). As Brown and colleagues (1987) asserted, criteria for selecting an intervention should include maximizing the chance of achieving the intended goal and minimizing its cost. Primary prevention interventions may help to address concerns (such as those about effectiveness and cost) directed at many current approaches (Curtis, Zins, & Graden, 1987; Zins et al., 1988). Progressing from interventions that focus on treating existing learning disorders to those that have potential to prevent them may prove to be both more effective and more efficient. In order to maximize the effectiveness of primary prevention interventions, however, programs should have sound theoretical and empirical bases. Additionally, these interventions should include opportunities for a student to make frequent, correct responses to materials at that student's instructional level (Shapiro, 1988).

An example of primary prevention techniques can be seen in work implicating the importance of phonological processing in the reading process. Perhaps the highest incidence of childhood learning disorders involves the area of reading, and the importance of language-based skills in reading has been well documented (Brady, 1986; Liberman & Shankweiler, 1985; Perfetti, 1985; Stanovich, 1985; Wagner & Torgesen, 1987). Numerous studies indicate that children who are poor readers perform significantly below good readers on a variety of language tasks, but they perform comparably to good readers on non-language tasks (Brady, 1986). One aspect of language that seems to be especially significant is phonological processing. Poor readers and children classified as reading disabled often experience problems in this area (Stanovich, 1988). Several phonological processing abilities have been identified as being associated with success at learning to read, one of which is a metaphonological ability called *phonological awareness.* This refers to an explicit recognition of the sound structure of one's language (Mattingly, 1972).

Phonological awareness may be particularly important because selected aspects of reading require explicit recognition of phonological segments. The fact that those segments are embedded in syllables and, for many phonemes, cannot be readily isolated makes this recognition difficult to achieve (Brady, in press; Liberman & Shankweiler, 1985). According to Crowder (1982), a basic task of the beginning reader is to learn that graphemes (i.e., symbols) represent phonemes (i.e., sounds). In order to grasp this connection, a child must recognize that spoken words are composed of sequences of individual sounds (Lewkowicz, 1980).

As might be expected, phonological awareness appears to be a developmental phenomenon. Although children capably use language to communicate before they begin school, their awareness of language structure is implicit. They can produce and understand language without having an explicit awareness of its phonological structure (Perfetti, 1985). The ability to segment both syllables and phonemes increases gradually; however, phoneme analysis is significantly more difficult than syllable analysis and therefore typically is mastered at a later age (Liberman, Shankweiler, Fischer, & Carter, 1974).

There is an emerging body of research demonstrating a relationship between phonological awareness and reading success (e.g., Fox & Routh, 1980; Liberman et al., 1974; Stanovich, Cunningham, & Cramer, 1984). Stanovich (1986) speculated that early problems with phonological awareness may have cumulative adverse effects and hypothesized that "if there is a specific cause of reading disability at all, it resides in the area of phonological awareness" (p. 393). Given the putative importance of phonological awareness to reading acquisition, several investigators have studied whether phonological awareness can be taught to prereaders. Results of these training studies suggest that phonological awareness can be taught and can facilitate later reading and spelling acquisition (Ball & Blachman, 1988; Bradley & Bryant, 1983, 1985; Lundberg, Frost, & Petersen, 1988; Treiman & Baron, 1983).

Although a causal link between phonological awareness and reading success has not yet been firmly established, it is reasonable to speculate that activities designed to teach phonological awareness might provide useful interventions aimed at preventing reading problems. These kinds of intervention not only might benefit children who, without phonological awareness training, may become reading disabled but also potentially could improve the reading skill of those children who may have more global deficits. Past research has suggested that, with appropriate strategies, even very young children can begin to understand that language comprises individual sounds (Ball & Blachman, 1988; Bradley & Bryant, 1983, 1985; Lundberg, Frost, & Petersen, 1988). Thus, in order to reduce the risk of children experiencing reading failure, phonological awareness interventions could be introduced before formal reading instruction is begun (i.e., at the preschool or kindergarten level).

Data about the difficulty level of the wide variety of tasks that have been used to assess phonological awareness ability provide information germane to potential intervention programs. Examples of such tasks include (1) recognition or production of rhyme, (2) phoneme segmentation, (3) phoneme deletion, and (4) discrimination and matching of sounds (Lewkowicz, 1980; Yopp, 1988). These data suggest that, at least for kindergartners, rhyming tasks are easiest, and tasks requiring discrimination and matching of sounds and symbols are more difficult. Tasks requiring phoneme segmentation are slightly more difficult than discrimination/matching tasks, and tasks requiring the deletion of phonemes are the most difficult (Stanovich et al., 1984; Yopp, 1988).

Thus, for example, an intervention designed to train phonological awareness might begin with easier tasks (e.g., rhyme). Once these tasks are mastered, more difficult tasks could be introduced (e.g., discrimination/matching, segmentation, deletion). Individual phonological awareness tasks also could be arranged hierarchically and introduced in a systematic way. Here, segmentation tasks could be introduced at the compound-word or syllable level before progressing to segmentation at the phoneme level. Associating plastic letters with letter sounds could be used to create a link between sounds and symbols in an effort to enhance phonological awareness (Bradley & Bryant, 1983, 1985). Another aspect of such a primary prevention intervention also might include articulation awareness training (Lindamood & Lindamood, 1975). This kind of training focuses on how sounds are produced by helping children to attend explicitly to speech sounds and to identify the motor characteristics inherent in the production of those speech sounds. Thus, articulation training may facilitate the acquisition of phonological awareness (Lindamood & Lindamood, 1975; Stone, 1990).

Related Treatment Approaches and Issues

A variety of other neuropsychologically based approaches has been advanced for the treatment of learning disorders. One area that has received relatively recent attention concerns particular subtypes of learning disorders and, in particular, subtypes of learning disabilities (Hooper & Willis, 1989). Although this literature currently is sparse, it is clear that direct and accurate matching of subtypes to specific treatment regimens shows good instructional potential for the treatment of individuals with learning disorders. Of course, the few studies that have been conducted (e.g., Cohen, Krawiecki, & DuRant, 1987; Flynn, 1987; Lyon, 1983, 1985; Simeon et al., 1980; Spijer, DeJong, & Bakker, 1987), however, also suggest that simple matching of subtypes to treatments will not account for all of the variability in treatment response. Rather, other variables also play important roles. If childhood learning disorders are conceptualized multidimensionally, then it also is reasonable to conceptualize their treatment multidimensionally. Thus, subtype to treatment matching actually may represent only one of the many components of a comprehensive treatment intervention approach.

Other components may include particular pharmacologic strategies such as the use of analeptics (e.g., methylphenidate or Ritalin; DuPaul, Barkley, & McMurray, 1991), nootropics (e.g., Piracetam; Wilsher, Atkins, & Manfield, 1985), or even tricyclic antidepressants (e.g., imipramine or Tofranil; Forness & Kavale, 1988); various cognitive-behavioral interventions (e.g., Harter, 1982; Meichenbaum, 1976; Ryan, Weed, & Short, 1986); and EMG (Carter & Russell, 1985) and EEG (Lubar et al., 1985) biofeedback techniques. Still other components may include the important social-emotional, school, and family factors that influence the interactive teaching-learning process.

For example, the behavior of children with learning disorders frequently is characterized by particular patterns of social-emotional maladjustment (Hooper & Willis, 1989). Moreover, the influence of these features may be potentiated by increasing age (Kistner & Osborne, 1987; Tramontana, Hooper, & Nardolillo, 1988). Thus, by adolescence or even earlier (e.g., during the latency period of development), the child's response to treatment may be adversely influenced by factors such as poor motivation, apathy, and behavioral difficulties. School-related factors, of course, also are likely to influence treatment response, independent of the particular intervention approach selected. Here, the way in which the child interacts with the teacher, the teacher's instructional style (e.g., directive, nondirective), particular curricula and materials, prior learning history, and the context in which treatment is delivered all may influence treatment response. Finally, it also is important to consider family-related factors. Clearly, the functioning of the child's family system, as well as the placement of education in the family's hierarchy of needs are likely to influence how that child approaches the learning task. Other family issues center around homework and the use of leisure time. This latter issue may be especially significant for some children who experience learning problems because particular associated behaviors (e.g., low self-esteem, poor interpersonal skills) may hinder cooperative participation in structured social activities (e.g., Pearl, 1987).

SUMMARY AND CONCLUSIONS

This chapter has attempted to outline the multitude of issues that confront researchers and clinicians with respect to the neuropsychological treatment of children and adolescents with learning disabilities. As such, definitional issues were addressed with respect to this heterogeneous group of disorders, and recent findings supporting the neurological basis of these problems were discussed, with a particular emphasis being placed on harder neurological findings. Major neuropsychological assessment approaches were mentioned, particularly with respect to their relevance for the assessment of learning problems, and a variety of assessment-specific treatment issues were enumerated. A major portion of this chapter was devoted to the specific neuropsychologically based treatment approaches that currently appear applicable for children with learning problems.

From this discussion, it is clear that the definitional issues confronting the field of learning disabilities pose significant challenges for professionals interested in the interaction between assessment and treatment, particularly with an increased emphasis being placed on the ecological validity of assessment strategies. At present, many of the current assessment approaches remain grounded in description, and only recently have been advanced with respect to their utility for prescription. Although the comprehensive nature of many of the current approaches to neuropsychological assessment lends itself to the development of more refined, homogeneous subtypes of learning disabilities, and ultimately to detailed descriptions of a child's strengths and weaknesses, the application of this information to specific treatment strategies remains largely a clinical endeavor with little in the way of significant research findings.

Despite these concern, several research efforts have been initiated with respect to the neuropsychological treatment of learning disabilities, with efforts addressing hemispheric stimulation (Bakker et al., 1990) and phonological processing (Lundberg et al., 1988) representing "cutting-edge" attempts in this regard. Although somewhat provocative, these efforts clearly suggest that there is merit to treatment efforts based on neurological and neuropsychological functioning. However, it is equally clear that using solely a neuropsychological treatment approach may not take into account other treatment concerns that might be relevant for a particular individual (e.g., social-emotional factors, familial issues, pharmacological needs). Consequently, a multidimensional treatment approach, such as the one suggested by Rourke and associates (1986), may be most beneficial at this time. In the future, however, it will be essential that the field move towards developing neuropsychologically based treatment programs that are guided by scientific findings and theory. This will not only address the cognitive, educational, social, affective, and perhaps familial dimensions in a systematic fashion for an individual child but it also will contribute to advancing the field with respect to the sophistication of assessment-treatment linkages.

REFERENCES

Aaron, P. G. (1981). Diagnosis and remediation of learning disabilities in children: A neuropsychological key approach. In G. W. Hynd & J. E. Obrzut (Eds.), *Neuropsychological assessment and the school-age child: Issues and procedures* (pp. 303–334). New York: Grune & Stratton.

Adams, W., & Sheslow, D. (1990). *WRAML: The Wide Range Assessment of Memory and Learning*. Wilmington, DE: Jastak Associates, Inc.

Affolter, F., & Stricker, E. (Eds.). (1980). *Perceptual processes as prerequisites for complex human behaviour: A theoretical model and its application to therapy*. Bern: Huber.

Algozzine, B., Christenson, S., & Ysseldyke, J. E. (1982). Probabilities associated with the referral to placement process. *Teacher Education and Special Education, 5,* 19–23.

Alley, G. R., & Deshler, D. D. (1979). *Teaching the learning disabled adolescent: Strategies and methods.* Denver: Love Publishing.

Arter, J. A., & Jenkins, J. R. (1979). Differential diagnostic-prescriptive teaching: A critical appraisal. *Review of Educational Research, 49,* 517–555.

Ayres, A. A., Cooley, E. J., & Severson, H. H. (1988). Educational translation of the Kaufman Assessment Battery for Children: A construct validity study. *School Psychology Review, 17,* 113–124.

Ayres, A. J. (1972). *Sensory integration and learning disorders.* Los Angeles, CA: Western Psychological Services.

Bakker, D. J. (1979). Hemispheric differences and reading strategies: Two dyslexias? *Bulletin of the Orton Society, 29,* 84–100.

Bakker, D. J. (1984). The brain as an independent variable. *Journal of Clinical and Experimental Neuropsychology, 6,* 1–16.

Bakker, D. J., Bouma, A., & Gardien. C. J. (1990). Hemisphere-specific treatment of dyslexia subtypes: A field experiment. *Journal of Learning Disabilities, 23,* 433–438.

Bakker, D. J., Moerland, R., & Goekoop-Hoefkens, M. (1981). Effects of hemisphere-specific stimulation on the reading performance of dyslexic boys: A pilot study. *Journal of Clinical and Experimental Neuropsychology, 3,* 155–159.

Bakker, D. J., & Vinke, J. (1985). Effects of hemispheric-specific stimulation on brain activity and reading in dyslexics. *Journal of Clinical and Experimental Neuropsychology, 7,* 505–525.

Ball, E., & Blachman, B. (1988). Phoneme segmentation training: Effect on reading readiness. *Annals of Dyslexia, 38,* 208–225.

Barkley, R. A. (1984). Learning disabilities. In E. J. Mash & L. G. Terdal (Eds.), *Behavioral assessment of childhood disorders* (pp. 441–482). New York: Guilford Press.

Bastian, H. C. (1898). *A treatise on aphasia and other speech defects.* London: H. K. Lewis.

Batchelor, E. S., & Dean, R. S. (1992). Empirical derivation and classification of children with learning disorders. *Archives of Clinical Neuropsychology.*

Bateman, B. D. (1966). Learning disorders. *Journal of Educational Research, 5,* 36.

Beaumont, J. G. (1983). *Introduction to neuropsychology.* New York: Guilford Press.

Benton, A. L. (1974). Clinical neuropsychology of childhood: An overview. In R. M. Reitan & L. A. Davison (Eds.), *Clinical neuropsychology: Current status and applications* (pp. 47–52). New York: John Wiley & Sons.

Benton, A. L., Hamsher, K., Varney, N. R., & Spreen, O. (1983). *Contributions to neuropsychological assessment: A clinical manual.* New York: Oxford University Press.

Board of Trustees of the Council for Learning Disabilities. (1987). The CLD position statements. *Journal of Learning Disabilities, 20,* 349–350.

Boder, E. (1971). Developmental dyslexia: A diagnostic screening procedure based on three characteristic patterns of reading and spelling. In B. Bateman (Ed.), *Learning disorders* (Vol. 4). Washington, DC: Special Child Publications.

Boder, E. (1973). Developmental dyslexia: A diagnostic approach based on three atypical reading-spelling patterns. *Developmental Medicine and Child Neurology, 15,* 663–687.

Boder, E., & Jarrico, S. (1982). *The Boder Test of Reading-Spelling Patterns.* New York: Grune & Stratton.

Boll, T. J. (1981). The Halstead-Reitan Neuropsychological Test Battery. In S. B. Filskov & T. J. Boll (Eds.), *Handbook of clinical neuropsychology* (pp. 577–607). New York: Wiley.

Boyan, C. (1985). California's new eligibility criteria: Legal and program implications. *Exceptional Children, 52,* 131–141.

Bradley, L., & Bryant, P. (1983). Categorizing sounds and learning to read a causal connection. *Nature, 301,* 419–421.

Bradley, L., & Bryant, P. (1985). *International Academy for Research in Learning Disabilities Monograph Series (No. 1). Rhyme and reason in reading and spelling.* Ann Arbor: The University of Michigan Press.

Brady, S. (1986). Short-term memory, phonological processing and reading ability. *Annals of Dyslexia, 36,* 138–153.

Brady, S. (in press). The role of working memory in reading disability. In S. Brady & D. Shankweiler (Eds.), *Phonological processes in literacy: A tribute to Isabelle Y. Liberman.* Hillsdale, NJ: Lawrence Erlbaum Associates.

Brown, D., Pryzwansky, W. B., & Schulte, A. C. (1987). *Psychological consultation: Introduction to theory and practice.* Boston: Allyn and Bacon.

Caplan, G. (1964). *Principles of preventive psychiatry.* New York: Basic Books.

Carter, J. L., & Russell, H. L. (1985). Use of EMG biofeedback procedures with learning disabled children in a clinical and an educational setting. *Journal of Learning Disabilities, 18,* 214–216.

Caviness, V. S., Evrard, P., & Lyon, G. (1978). Radial neuronal assemblies, ectopia and necrosis of developing cortex: A case analysis. *Acta Neuropathologia, 41,* 67–72.

Cohen, M. , Krawiecki, N., & DuRant, R. H. (1987). The neuropsychological approach to the remediation of dyslexia. *Archives of Clinical Neuropsychology, 2,* 163–173.

Cook, J. M., & Welch, M. W. (1980). Reading as a function of visual and auditory process training. *Learning Disabilities Quarterly, 3,* 76–87.

Crome, L. (1960). The brain in mental retardation. *British Medical Journal, 1,* 897–904.

Crowder, R. G. (1982). *The psychology of reading.* New York: Cambridge University Press.

Cruickshank, W. M. (1972). Some issues facing the field of learning disability. *Journal of Learning Disabilities, 5,* 380–388.

Cruickshank, W. M. (1983). Straight is the bamboo tree. *Journal of Learning Disabilities, 16,* 191–197.

Curtis, M. J., Zins, J. E., & Graden, J. L. (1987). Prereferral intervention programs: Enhancing student performance in regular education settings. In C. A. Maher & J. E. Zins (Eds.), *Psychoeducational interventions in the schools.* New York: Pergamon Press.

Doris, J. (1986). Learning disabilities. In S. J. Ceci (Ed.), *Handbook of cognitive, social, and neuropsychological aspects of learning disabilities* (pp. 3–54). Hillsdale, NJ: Lawrence Erlbaum Associates.

Drake, W. (1968). Clinical and pathological findings in a child with a developmental learning disability. *Journal of Learning Disabilities, 1,* 468–475.

Duane, D. D. (1979). Toward a definition of dyslexia: A summary of views. *Bulletin of the Orton Society, 29,* 56–64.

Duffy, F. H., Denckla, M. B., Bartels, P. H., Sandini, G., & Kiessling, L. S. (1980). Dyslexia: Automated diagnosis by computerized classification of brain electrical activity. *Annals of Neurology, 7,* 421–428.

DuPaul, G. J., Barkley, R. A., & McMurray, M. B. (1991). Therapeutic effects of medication on ADHD: Implications for school psychologists. *School Psychology Review, 20,* 203–219.

Dvorak, K., Feit, J., & Jurankova, Z. (1978). Experimentally induced microgyria and status verrucosus deformis in rats: Pathogenesis and interrelation histological and autoradiographical study. *Acta Neuropathologia, 44,* 1211–1229.

Epps, S., Ysseldyke, J. E., & Algozzine, B. (1983). Impact of different definitions of learning disabilities on the number of students identified. *Journal of Psychoeducational Assessment, 1,* 341–352.

Epps, S., Ysseldyke, J. E., & Algozzine, B. (1985). An analysis of the conceptual framework underlying definitions of learning disabilities. *Journal of School Psychology, 23,* 133–144.

Feagans, L. V., Short, E. J., & Meltzer, L. J. (Eds.). (1991). *Subtypes of learning disabilities.* Hillsdale, NJ: Lawrence Erlbaum Associates.

Flynn, J. (1987). *Neurophysiologic characteristics of dyslexic subtypes and response to remediation.* Grant awarded by the Initial Teaching Alphabet Foundation. Roslyn, NY.

Forness, S. R., & Kavale, K. A. (1983). Remediation of learning disabilities: Part one. Issues and concepts. *Learning Disabilities, 11,* 141–152.

Forness, S. R., & Kavale, K. A. (1988). Psychopharmacologic treatment: A note on classroom effects. *Journal of Learning Disabilities, 21,* 144–147.

Fox, B., & Routh, D. (1980). Phonemic analysis and severe reading disability in children. *Journal of Psycholinguistic Research, 9,* 115–119.

Freytag, E., & Lindenberg, R. (1967). Neuropathologic findings in patients of a hospital for the mentally retarded. A study of 359 cases. *Johns Hopkins Medical Journal, 121,* 379–392.

Frostig, M., & Horne, D. (1964). *The Frostig Program for the Development of Visual Perception. Teacher's guide.* Chicago: Follett.

Gaddes, W. H. (1985). *Learning disabilities and brain function: A neuropsychological approach* (2nd ed.). New York: Springer-Verlag.

Galaburda, A. M., & Eidelberg, D. (1982). Symmetry and asymmetry in the human posterior thalamus: II. Thalamic lesions in a case of developmental dyslexia. *Archives of Neurology, 39,* 333–336.

Galaburda, A. M., & Kemper, T. L. (1979). Cytoarchitectonic abnormalities in developmental dyslexia: A case study. *Annals of Neurology, 6,* 94–100.

Galaburda, A. M., Sherman, G. F., Rosen, G. D., Aboitiz, F., & Geschwind, N. (1985). Developmental dyslexia: Four consecutive cases with cortical anomalies. *Annals of Neurology, 18,* 222–233.

Galin, D., Herron, J., Johnstone, J., Fein, G., & Yingling, C. (1988). EEG alpha asymmetry in dyslexics during speaking and block design tasks. *Brain and Language, 35,* 241–253.

Geary, D. C., & Gilger, J. W. (1984). The Luria-Nebraska Neuropsychological Battery–Children's Revision: Comparison of learning disabled and normal children matched on Full Scale IQ. *Perceptual and Motor Skills, 58,* 115–118.

Geary, D. C., & Gilger, J. W. (1985). The Luria-Nebraska Neuropsychological Battery–Children's Revision: An instrument for school psychologists? *School Psychology Review, 14,* 383–384.

Geary, D. C., Jennings, S. M., Schultz, D. D., & Alper, T. G. (1984). The diagnostic accuracy of the Luria-Nebraska Neuropsychological Battery-Children's Revision for 9 to 12 year old learning disabled children. *School Psychology Review, 13,* 375–380.

Geschwind, N. (1984). Cerebral dominance in biological perspective. *Neuropsychologia, 22,* 675–683.

Geschwind, B., & Galaburda, A. M. (1985a). Cerebral lateralization: Biological mechanisms, associations, and pathology, I. A hypothesis and a program for research. *Archives of Neurology, 42,* 428–459.

Geschwind, B., & Galaburda, A. M. (1985b). Cerebral lateralization: Biological mechanisms, associations, and pathology, II. A hypothesis and a program for research. *Archives of Neurology, 42,* 521–552.

Geschwind, B., & Galaburda, A. M. (1985c). Cerebral lateralization: Biological mechanisms, associations, and pathology, III. A hypothesis and a program for research. *Archives of Neurology, 42,* 634–654.

Geschwind, N., & Levitsky, W. (1968). Human brain: Left-right asymmetries in temporal speech region. *Science, 161,* 186–187.

Glass, G. V. (1983). Effectiveness of special education. *Policy Studies Review, 2,* 65–78.

Goldfried, M. R., & Sprafkin, J. N. (1976). Behavioral personality assessment. In J. T. Spence, R. C. Carson, & J. W. Thiabaut (Eds.), *Behavioral approaches to therapy* (pp. 295–321). Morristown, NJ: General Learning Press.

Goldman, R., Fristoe, M., & Woodcock, R. W. (1974). *Manual for the Goldman-Fristoe-Woodcock Auditory Skills Test Battery.* Circle Pines, MN: American Guidance Service.

Gordon, M., McClure, F. D., & Post, E. M. (1983). *Interpretive guide to the Gordon Diagnostic System.* DeWitt, NY: Gordon Systems.

Guilford, J. P. (1985). The structure-of-intellect model. In B. B. Wolman (Ed.), *Handbook of intelligence: Theories, measurements and applications* (pp. 225–266). New York: John Wiley.

Hallahan, D. P., & Cruickshank, W. M. (1973). *Psychoeducational foundations of learning disabilities.* Englewood Cliffs, NJ: Prentice-Hall.

Hammill, D. D., & Larsen, S. C. (1974). The effectiveness of psycholinguistic training. *Exceptional Children, 41,* 5–15.

Hammill, D. D., Leigh, J. E., McNutt, G., & Larsen, S. C. (1981). A new definition of learning disabilities. *Learning Disability Quarterly, 4,* 336–342.

Harter, S. (1982). A developmental perspective on some parameters of self-regulation in children. In P. Karoly & F. H. Kanfer (Eds.), *Self-

management and behavior change: From theory to practice. New York: Pergamon Press.

Hartlage, L. C., & Reynolds, C. R. (1981). Neuropsychological assessment and the individualization of instruction. In G. W. Hynd & J. E. Obrzut (Eds.), *Neuropsychological assessment and the school-aged child: Issues and procedures* (pp. 355–378). New York: Grune & Stratton.

Hartlage, L. C., & Telzrow, C. F. (1983). The neuropsychological basis of educational intervention. *Journal of Learning Disabilities, 16,* 521–528.

Haslam, R. H., Dalby, J. T., Johns, R. D., & Rademaker, A. W. (1981). Cerebral asymmetry in developmental dyslexia. *Archives of Neurology, 38,* 679–682.

Haynes, M. C. & Jenkins, J. R. (1986). Reading instruction in special education resource rooms. *American Educational Research Journal, 23,* 161–190.

Heaton, R. K. (1981). *Manual for the Wisconsin Card Sorting Test.* Odessa, FL: Psychological Assessment Resources.

Hicks, C. (1980). The ITPA Visual Sequential Memory Task: An alternative interpretation and the implications for good and poor readers. *British Journal of Educational Psychology, 50,* 16–25.

Hier, D. B., LeMay, N., Rosenberger, P. B., & Perlo, V. P. (1978). Developmental dyslexia: Evidence for a subgroup with a reversal of cerebral asymmetry. *Archives of Neurology, 35,* 90–92.

Hinshelwood, J. (1895). Word-blindness and visual memory. *Lancet, 1,* 1506–1508.

Hinshelwood, J. (1909). Four cases of congenital word-blindness occurring in the same family. *British Medical Journal, 22,* 1229–1232.

Hooper, S. R., & Willis, W. G. (1989). *Learning disability subtyping. Neuropsychological foundations, conceptual models, and issues in clinical differentiation.* New York: Springer-Verlag.

Horton, A. M. (1979). Behavioral neuropsychology: Rationale and research. *Clinical Neuropsychology, 1,* 20–23.

Horton, A. M. (1989). Child behavioral neuropsychology. In C. R. Reynolds & E. Fletcher-Janzen (Eds.), *Handbook of clinical child neuropsychology* (pp. 521–533). New York: Plenum Press.

Horton, A. M., & Puente, A. E. (1986). Behavioral neuropsychology with children. In J. E. Obrzut & G. W. Hynd (Eds.), *Child neuropsychology: Clinical practice* (Vol. 2; pp. 299–316). Orlando, FL: Academic Press.

Howell, K. W. (1986). Direct assessment of academic performance. *School Psychology Review, 15,* 324–335.

Hugdahl, K. (in press). Considerations in the use of dichotic listening with children. In M. G. Tramontana & S. R. Hooper (Eds.), *Advances in child neuropsychology* (Vol. I). New York: Springer-Verlag.

Hyman, L. M. (1983). *An investigation of the neuropsychological characteristics of learning disabled children as measured by the Luria-Nebraska (Children).* Doctoral dissertation, University of Southern California, Los Angeles.

Hynd, C. R. (1986). Educational intervention in children with developmental learning disorders. In J. E. Obrzut & G. W. Hynd (Eds.), *Child neuropsychology: Clinical practice* (Vol 2; pp. 265–297). Orlando, FL: Academic Press.

Hynd, G. W., & Cohen, M. (1983). *Dyslexia: Neuropsychological theory, research, and clinical differentiation.* New York: Grune & Stratton.

Hynd, G. W., Connor, R. T., & Nieves, N. (1988). Learning disability subtypes: Perspectives and methodological issues in clinical assessment. In M. G. Tramontana & S. R. Hooper (Eds.), *Assessment issues in child neuropsychology* (pp. 281–312). New York: Plenum Press.

Hynd, G. W., & Hynd, C. R. (1984). Dyslexia: Neuroanatomical/neurolinguistic perspectives. *Reading Research Quarterly, 19,* 482–498.

Hynd, G. W., & Semrud-Clikeman, M. (1989). Dyslexia and brain morphology. *Psychological Bulletin, 106,* 447–482.

Hynd, G. W., Semrud-Clikeman, M., Lorys, A., Novey, E. S., & Eliopulos, D. (1990). Brain morphology in developmental dyslexia and attention deficit disorder/hyperactivity. *Archives of Neurology, 47,* 919–926.

Hynd, G. E., Snow, J., & Becker, M. G. (1986). Neuropsychological assessment in clinical child psychology. In B. Lahey & A. Kazdin

(Eds.), *Advances in clinical child psychology* (Vol. 9). New York: Plenum Press.

Idol, L., & West, J. F. (1987). Consultation in special education: Part II. Training and practice. *Journal of Learning Disabilities, 20,* 474–494.

Jellinger, J. (1972). Neuropathological features of unclassified mental retardation. In J. B. Cavanaugh (Ed.), *The brain in unclassified mental retardation* (pp. 283–321). Baltimore: Williams & Wilkins.

Kamphaus, R. W., & Reynolds, C. R. (1987). *Clinical and research applications of the K-ABC.* Circle Pines, MN: American Guidance Service.

Kampwirth, T. J. (1979). Teaching to preferred modalities: Is it worth it? *Claremont Reading Conference,* 163–176.

Kanfer, F. H., & Phillips, J. S. (1970). *Learning foundations of behavior therapy.* New York: John Wiley.

Kaufman, W. E., & Galaburda, A. M. (1989). Cerebrocortical microdysgenesis in neurologically normal subjects: A histopathologic study. *Neurology, 39,* 238–244.

Kaufman, A. S., & Kaufman, N. L. (1983). *K-ABC interpretive manual.* Circle Pines, MN: American Guidance Service.

Kaufman, A. S., Kaufman, N. S., & Goldsmith, B. Z. (1984). *K-SOS: Kaufman sequential or simultaneous.* Circle Pines, MN: American Guidance Service.

Kelly, M. S., Best, C. T., & Kirk, N. (1989). Cognitive processing deficits in reading disabilities: A prefrontal cortical hypothesis. *Brain and Language, 11,* 275–293.

Keogh, B. K. (1986). A marker system for describing learning disability samples. In S. J. Ceci (Ed.), *Handbook of cognitive, social, and neuropsychological aspects of learning disabilities* (Vol. 1, pp. 81–94). Hillsdale, NJ: Lawrence Erlbaum Associates.

Kephart, N. C. (1971). *The slow learner in the classroom* (2nd ed.). Columbus, OH: Charles E. Merrill.

Kirk, S. A. (1963). Behavioral diagnosis and remediation of learning disabilities. *Proceedings of the Conference on Exploration into the Problems of the Perceptually Handicapped Child.* Chicago: Perceptually Handicapped Children.

Kirk, S. A., & Kirk, W. D. (1971). *Psycholinguistic learning disabilities: Diagnosis and remediation.* Urbana: University of Illinois Press.

Kistner, J., & Osborne, M. (1987). A longitudinal study of LD children's self-evaluations. *Learning Disability Quarterly, 10,* 258–266.

Lakin, K. C. (1983). A response to Gene V. Glass. *Policy Studies Review, 2,* 233–239.

Larivee, B. (1981). Modality preference as a model for differentiating beginning reading instruction: A review of the issues. *Learning Disability Quarterly, 4,* 180–188.

Larsen, J. P., Hoien, T., Lundberg, I., & Odegaard, H. (1990). MRI evaluation of the size and symmetry of the planum temporale in adolescents with developmental dyslexia. *Brain and Language.*

Leisman, G., & Ashkenazi, M. (1980). Aetiological factors in dyslexia: IV. Cerebral hemispheres are functionally equivalent. *International Journal of Neuroscience, 11,* 157–164.

LeMay, M. (1981). Are there radiological changes in the brains of individuals with dyslexia? *Bulletin of the Orton Society, 31,* 135–141.

Leong, C. K. (1989). Neuropsychological models of learning disabilities. Contributions to remediation. In C. R. Reynolds & E. Fletcher-Janzen (Eds.), *Handbook of clinical child neuropsychology* (pp. 335–355). New York: Plenum Press.

Lewis, R. B. (1983). Learning disabilities and reading: Instructional recommendations from current research. *Exceptional Children, 50,* 230–241.

Lewis, R. D., Garland, B., & Hutchens, T. A. (1991). Identification of learning disabilities: Accuracy of aptitude/achievement discrepancy criteria vs. the Luria-Nebraska Neuropsychological Battery. *Journal of Psychoeducational Assessment, 9,* 130–139.

Lewis, R. D., & Lorion, R. P. (1988). Discriminative effectiveness of the Luria-Nebraska Neuropsychological Battery for LD adolescents. *Learning Disability Quarterly, 11,* 62–70.

Lewkowicz, N. K. (1980). Phonemic awareness training: What to teach and how to teach and how to teach it. *Journal of Educational Psychology, 72,* 686–700.

Lezak, M. D. (1983). *Neuropsychological assessment*

(2nd ed.). New York: Oxford University Press.

Lezak, M. D. (1988). IQ: RIP. *Journal of Clinical and Experimental Neuropsychology, 10*, 351–361.

Liberman, I. Y., & Shankweiler, D. (1979). Speech, the alphabet, and teaching to read. In L. Resnick & P. Weaver (Eds.), *Theory and practice of early reading* (Vol. 1, pp. 109–132). Hillsdale, NJ: Lawrence Erlbaum Associates.

Liberman, I. Y., & Shankweiler, D. (1985). Phonology and the problems of learning to read and write. *Remedial and Special Education, 6*, 8–17.

Liberman, I. Y., & Shankweiler, D., Fischer, F. W., & Carter, B. (1974). Explicit syllable and phoneme segmentation in the young child. *Journal of Experimental Child Psychology, 18*, 201–212.

Lindamood, C. H., & Lindamood, P. C. (1975). *The A.D.D. Program: Auditory Discrimination in Depth.* Boston: Teaching Resources Corporation.

Lindsley, O. R. (1964). Direct measurement and prosthesis of retarded behavior. *Journal of Education, 147*, 62–81.

Lorion, R. P. (1983). Evaluating preventive interventions: Guidelines for the serious social change agent. In R. D. Felner, L. A. Jason, J. N. Moritsugu, & S. S. Farber (Eds.), *Preventive psychology: Theory, research, and practice* (pp. 251–272). New York: Pergamon Press.

Lubar, J. F., Bianchini, K. J., Calhoun, W. H., Lambert, E. W., Brody, Z. H., & Shabsin, H. S. (1985). Spectral analysis of EEG differences between children with and without learning disabilities. *Journal of Learning Disabilities, 18*, 403–408.

Lundberg, I., Frost, J., & Petersen, O. (1988). Effects of an extensive program for stimulating phonological awareness in preschool children. *Reading Research Quarterly, 23*, 263–284

Luria, A. R. (1973). *The working brain: An introduction to neuropsychology.* New York: Basic Books.

Lyon, G. R. (1983). Learning disabled readers: Identification of subgroups. In H. R. Myklebust (Ed.), *Progress in learning disabilities* (Vol. 5, pp. 103–133). New York: Grune & Stratton.

Lyon, G. R. (1985). Identification and remediation of learning disability subtypes: Preliminary findings. *Learning Disabilities Focus, 1*, 21–35.

Lyon, G. R., & Moats, L. C. (1988). Critical issues in the instruction of the learning disabled. *Journal of Consulting and Clinical Psychology, 56*, 830–835.

Lyon, G. R., Moats, L., & Flynn, J. M. (1988). From assessment to treatment. Linkage to interventions with children. In M. G. Tramontana & S. R. Hooper (Eds.), *Assessment issues in child neuropsychology* (pp. 113–142). New York: Plenum Press.

Lyon, G. R., & Toomey, L. C. (1985). Neurological, neuropsychological, and cognitive-developmental approaches to learning disabilities. *Topics in Learning Disabilities, 2*, 1–15.

Maher, C. A., & Illback, R. J. (1983). Planning for organizational change in schools. Alternative approaches and procedures. *School Psychology Review, 12*, 460–466.

Malamud, N. (1964). Neuropathology. In H. A. Stevens & R. Heber (Eds.), *Mental retardation* (pp. 429–452). Chicago: University of Chicago Press.

Marshall, J. C. (1984). Toward a rational taxonomy of the developmental dyslexias. In R. N. Malatesha & H. A. Whitaker (Eds.), *Dyslexia: A global issue* (pp. 45–58). The Hague: Nijhoff.

Mash, E. J., & Terdal, L. G. (1984). Behavioral assessment of childhood disturbance. In E. J. Mash & L. G. Terdal (Eds.), *Behavioral assessment of childhood disorders* (pp. 3–76). New York: Guilford Press.

Mattingly, I. G. (1972). Reading, the linguistic process, and linguistic awareness. In J. Kavanagh & I. Mattingly (Eds.), *Language by ear and by eye* (pp. 133–147). Cambridge, MA: MIT Press.

Mattis, S. (1981). Dyslexia syndromes in children: Toward the development of syndrome-specific treatment programs. In F. J. Pirozzolo & M. C. Wittrock (Eds.), *Neuropsychological and cognitive processes in reading* (pp. 93–107). New York: Academic Press.

Mattis, S., French, J. H., & Rapin, I. (1975). Dyslexia in children and young adults: Three independent neuropsychological syndromes. *Developmental Medicine and Child Neurology, 17*, 150–163.

McCarthy, J. M. (1975). Children with learning disabilities. In J. J. Gallagher (Ed.), *The application of child development research to exceptional children* (pp. 299–317). Reston, VA: The Council for Exceptional Children.

Meichenbaum, D. (1976). Cognitive factors as determinants of learning disabilities: A cognitive functional approach. In R. Knights & D. Bakker (Eds.), *The neuropsychology of learning disorders: Theoretical approaches*. Baltimore, MD: University Park Press.

Milberg, W. P., Hebben, N., & Kaplan, E. (1986). The Boston process approach to neuropsychological assessment of neuropsychiatric disorders. In I. Grant & K. M. Adams (Eds.), *Neuropsychological assessment of neuropsychiatric disorders* (pp. 65–86). New York: Oxford University Press.

Morgan, S. B., & Brown, T. L. (1988). Luria-Nebraska Neuropsychological Battery–Children's Revision: Concurrent validity with three learning disability subtypes. *Journal of Consulting and Clinical Psychology, 56,* 463–466.

Morgan, W. P. (1896). A case of congenital word-blindness. *British Medical Journal, 2,* 1978.

Myklebust, H. R., & Boshes, B. (1969). *Final report, minimal brain damage in children.* Washington, DC: U.S. Department of Health, Education, and Welfare.

Nolan, D. R., Hammeke, T. A., & Barkley, R. A. (1983). A comparison of the patterns of the neuropsychological performance in two groups of learning disabled children. *Journal of clinical Child Psychology, 12,* 13–21.

Obrzut, J. E. (1981). Neuropsychological assessment in the schools. *School Psychology Review, 10,* 331–342.

Obrzut, J. E., & Hynd, G. W. (Eds.). (1991). *Neuropsychological foundations of learning disabilities. A handbook of issues, methods, and practice.* San Diego, CA: Academic Press.

Orton, S. T. (1928). Specific reading disability—Strephosymbolia. *Journal of the American Medical Association, 90,* 1095–1099.

Pearl, R. (1987). Social cognitive factors in learning-disabled children's social problems. In S. J. Ceci (Ed.), *Handbook of cognitive, social, and neuropsychological aspects of learning disabilities* (Vol. 2, pp. 273–294). Hillsdale, NJ: Lawrence Erlbaum.

Perfetti, C.A. (1985). *Reading ability.* New York: Oxford University Press.

Reitan, R. M. (1980). *REHABIT—Reitan evaluation of hemispheric abilities and brain improvement training.* Tucson: Reitan Neuropsychological Laboratory and University of Arizona.

Reynolds, C. R. (1981). Neuropsychological assessment and the habilitation of learning: Consideration in the search for aptitude X treatment interactions. *School Psychology Review, 10,* 343–349.

Reynolds, C. R. (1986). Transaction models of intellectual development, yes. Deficit models of remediation, no. *School Psychology Review, 15,* 256–260.

Rosenberger, P. B., & Hier, D. B. (1980). Cerebral asymmetry and verbal intellectual deficits. *Annals of Neurology, 8,* 300–304.

Rourke, B. P. (Ed.). (1985). *Neuropsychology of learning disabilities: Essentials of subtype analysis.* New York: Guilford Press.

Rourke, B. P., Bakker, D. J., Fisk, J. L., & Strang, J. D. (1983). *Child neuropsychology: An introduction to theory, research, and clinical practice.* New York: Guilford Press.

Rourke, B. P., Fisk, T. L., & Strang, J. D. (1986). *The neuropsychological assessment of children: A treatment-oriented approach.* New York: Guilford Press.

Ryan, E. B., Weed, K. A., & Short, E. J. (1986). Cognitive behavior modification: Promoting active, self-regulatory learning styles. In J. K. Torgeson & B. Y. L. Wong (Eds.), *Psychological and educational perspectives on learning disabilities* (pp. 367–397). Orlando, FL: Academic Press.

Schonhaut, S., & Satz, P. (1983). Prognosis of children with learning disabilities: A review of follow-up studies. In M. Rutter (Ed.), *Developmental neuropsychiatry* (pp. 542–563). New York: Guilford Press.

Selz, M., & Reitan, R. M. (1979). Rules for neuropsychological diagnosis: Classification of brain function in older children. *Journal of Consulting and Clinical Psychology, 47,* 258–264.

Semrud-Clikeman, M., & Hynd, G. W. (1990).

Right hemispheric dysfunction in nonverbal learning disabilities: Social, academic, and adaptive functioning in adults and children. *Psychological Bulletin, 107,* 196–209.

Semrud-Clikeman, M., Hynd, G. W., Novey, E. S., & Eliopulos, D. (1991). Dyslexia and brain morphology: Relationships between neuroanatomical variation and neurolinguistic performance. *Learning and Individual Differences.*

Shapiro, E. S. (1988). Preventing academic failure. *School Psychology Review, 17,* 671–613.

Shaywitz, S. E., Shaywitz, B. H., Fletcher, J. M., & Escobar, M. D. (1990). Prevalence of reading disability in boys and girls: Results of the Connecticut longitudinal study. *Journal of the American Medical Association, 264,* 998–1002.

Shepard, L. (1980). An evaluation of the regression discrepancy method for identifying children with learning disabilities. *Journal of Special Education, 14,* 79–91.

Shepard, L. (1983). The role of measurement in educational policy: Lessons from the identification of learning disabilities. *Educational measurement: Issues and practice, 2,* 4–8.

Simeon, J., Waters, B., & Resnick, M., et al. (1980). Effects of Piracetam in children with learning disorders. *Psychopharmacology Bulletin, 16,* 65–66.

Skinner, B. F. (1938). *The behavior of organisms.* New York: Appleton-Century.

Smith, S., Pennington, B., Kimberling, W. J., & Ing, P. S. (1990). Familial dyslexia: Use of genetic linkage data to define subtypes. *Journal of the American Academy of Child and Adolescent Psychiatry, 29,* 204–213.

Snow, J. H., & Hynd, G. W. (1985). A multivariate investigation of the Luria-Nebraska Neuropsychological Battery–Children's Revision with learning disabled children. *Journal of Psychoeducational Assessment, 3,* 101–109.

Sowell, V., Parker, R., Poplin, M., & Larsen, S. (1979). The effects of psycholinguistic training on improving psycholinguistic skills. *Learning Disability Quarterly, 2,* 69–77.

Spijer, G., DeJong, A., & Bakker, D. J. (1987). Piracetam and Piracetam plus hemisphere-specific stimulation: Effects on the reading performance of two subtyped dyslexic boys

[Abstract]. *Journal of Clinical and Experimental Neuropsychology, 9,* 275–276.

Spreen, O. (1988). Prognosis of learning disability. *Journal of Consulting and Clinical Psychology, 56,* 836–842.

Spreen, O., & Haaf, R. G. (1986). Empirically derived learning disability subtypes: A replication attempt and longitudinal patterns over 15 years. *Journal of Learning Disabilities, 19,* 170–180.

Spreen, O., & Strauss, E. (1991). *A compendium of neuropsychological tests. Administration, norms, and commentary.* New York: Oxford University Press.

Stanovich, K. E. (1985). Explaining the variance in reading ability in terms psychological processes: What have we learned? *Annals of Dyslexia, 35,* 67–96.

Stanovich, K. E. (1986). Matthew effects in reading: Some consequences of individual differences in the acquisition of literacy. *Reading Research Quarterly, 21,* 360–407.

Stanovich, K. E. (1988). Explaining the differences between the dyslexic and the garden-variety poor reader: The phonological-core variable-difference model. *Journal of Learning Disabilities, 21,* 590–604.

Stanovich, K. E. (1991). Developmental reading disorder. In S. R. Hooper, G. W. Hynd, & R. E. Mattison (Eds.), *Developmental disorders: Diagnostic criteria and clinical assessment* (pp. 173–208). Hillsdale, NJ: Lawrence Erlbaum Associates.

Stanovich, K. E., Cunningham, A. E., & Cramer, B. B. (1984). Assessing phonological awareness in kindergarten children: Issues of task comparability. *Journal of Experimental Child Psychology, 38,* 175–190.

Stone, B. H. (1990). *Phonological processing abilities: Their interrelations in the presence and absence of phonological awareness training.* Unpublished manuscript, University of Rhode Island, Kingston.

Strom, D. A., Gray, J. W., Dean, R. S., & Fischer, W. E. (1987). The incremental validity of the Halstead-Reitan Neuropsychological Battery in predicting achievement for learning-disabled children. *Journal of Psychoeducational Assessment, 2,* 157–165.

Sutter, E. G., & Battin, R. (1983). Using traditional psychological tests to obtain neuropsychological information on children. *International Journal of Clinical Neuropsychology, 6,* 115–119.

Sutter, E. G., Bishop, P. C., & Battin, R. R. (1986). Factor similarities between traditional psychoeducational and neuropsychological test batteries. *Journal of Psychoeducational Assessment, 4,* 73–82.

Taylor, H. G. (1988). Neuropsychological testing: Relevance for assessing children's learning disabilities. *Journal of Consulting and Clinical Psychology, 56,* 795–800.

Teeter, P. A. (1989). Neuropsychological approaches to the remediation of educational deficits. In C. R. Reynolds & E. Fletcher-Janzen (Eds.), *Handbook of clinical child neuropsychology* (pp. 357–376). New York: Plenum Press.

Teeter, P. A., Boliek, C. A., Obrzut, J. E., & Malsch, K. (1986). Diagnostic utility of the critical level formula and clinical scales of the Luria-Nebraska Neuropsychological Battery–Children's Revision with learning disabled children. *Developmental Neuropsychology, 2,* 125–135.

Tittemore, J. A., Lawson, J. S., & Inglis, J. (1985). Validation of a learning disability index (LDI) derived from a principal components analysis of the WISC-R. *Journal of Learning Disabilities, 18,* 449–454.

Tomatis, A. (1978). *Education and dyslexia.* France-Quebec: Les Editions.

Tomlinson-Keasey, C., & Kelly, R. R. (1979a). Is hemispheric specialization important to scholastic achievement? *Cortex, 15,* 97–107.

Tomlinson-Keasey, C., & Kelly, R. R. (1979b). A task analysis of hemispheric functioning. *Neuropsychologia, 17,* 345–351.

Tramontana, M. G., & Hooper, S. R. (1988). Child neuropsychological assessment. Overview of current status. In M. G. Tramontana & S. R. Hooper (Eds.), *Assessment issues in child neuropsychology* (pp. 3–38). New York: Plenum Press.

Tramontana, M. G., Hooper, S. R., & Nardolillo, E. (1988). Behavioral manifestations of neuropsychological impairment in children with psychiatric disorders. *Archives of Clinical Neuropsychology.*

Tramontana, M. G., Hooper, S. R., & Selzer, C. S. (1988). Research on the preschool prediction of later academic achievement. *Developmental Review, 8,* 89–146.

U.S. Department of Education, Division of Educational Services. (1984). *Sixth annual report to Congress on the implementation of Public Law 94–142: The Education for All Handicapped Children Act.* Washington, DC: Author.

U.S. Office of Education. (1977). Assistance to states for education of handicapped children: Procedures for evaluating specific learning disabilities. *Federal Register, 42,* 65082–65085.

Vaughan, R. W., & Hodges, L. A. (1973). A statistical survey into a definition of learning disabilities. *Journal of Learning Disabilities, 6,* 658–664.

Vellutino, F. R. (1979). *Dyslexia: Theory and research.* Cambridge, MA: MIT Press.

Wagner, R., & Torgesen, J. (1987). The nature of phonological processing and its causal role in the acquisition of reading skills. *Psychological Bulletin, 101,* 192–212.

Weinberger, D. R., Luchins, D. J., Morihisa, J., & Wyatt, R. J. (1982). Asymmetrical volumes of the right and left frontal and occipital regions of the human brain. *Neurology, 11,* 97–100.

West, J. F., & Idol, L. (1987). School consultation: Part I. An interdisciplinary perspective on theory, models, and research. *Journal of Learning Disabilities, 20,* 388–408.

Wiener, J. (1986). Alternatives in the assessment of the learning disabled adolescent: A learning strategies approach. *Learning Disabilities Focus, 1,* 97–107.

Willis, W. G. (1985). Successive and simultaneous processing: A note on interpretation. *Journal of Psychoeducational Assessment, 4,* 343–346.

Willis, W. G., & Hynd, G. W. (1987). Lateralized interference effects: Evidence for a processing style by modality interaction. *Brain and Cognition, 6,* 112–126.

Wilsher, C., Atkins, G., & Manfield, P. (1985). Effect of Piracetam on dyslexic's reading ability. *Journal of Learning Disabilities, 18,* 19–25.

Wilson, B. C., & Risucci, D. A. (1986). A model for clinical-quantitative classification. Generation I: Application to language-disordered preschool children. *Brain and Language, 27,* 281–309.

Wyngaarden, J. E. (1987). *Learning disabilities: A report to the Congress.* Washington, DC: National Institute of Health, Interagency Committee on Learning Disabilities.

Ylvisaker, M., Szekeres, S. F., & Hartwick, P. (in press). Cognitive rehabilitation following traumatic brain injury in children. In M. G. Tramontana & S. R. Hooper (Eds.), *Advances in child neuropsychology.* New York: Springer-Verlag.

Yopp, H. (1988). The validity and reliability of phonemic awareness tests. *Reading Research Quarterly, 23,* 159–177.

Ysseldyke, J. E., & Mirkin, P. K. (1981). The use of assessment information to plan instructional interventions: A review of the research. In C. R. Reynolds & T. B. Gutkin (Eds.), *Handbook of school psychology* (pp. 395–409). New York: Wiley.

Zins, J. E., Conyne, R. K., & Ponti, C. R. (1988). Primary prevention: Expanding the impact of psychological services in schools. *School Psychology Review, 17,* 542–549.

10

CHILDHOOD MEDICAL CONDITIONS IMPACTING ON CENTRAL NERVOUS SYSTEM FUNCTION

KELLI S. WILLIAMS   J. MICHAEL WILLIAMS

A variety of medical disorders will cause brain injury as part of the general effects of the illness. Also, numerous treatments of these illnesses can have complimentary or independent deleterious effects on brain functions. These effects can range from transient ischemia and mild neurological manifestations to severe, permanent brain lesions with consequent neurological impairment. For example, cardiac illnesses may be associated with transient ischemic attacks that produce mild hemiparesis that recovers quickly. This illness may be treated with medications that mildly impair cognition, or the patient may sustain a cerebral vascular accident following a surgical intervention. Many other illnesses are associated with a mix of transient and permanent cerebral impairment that may be the direct result of the illness or a side effect of treatments.

This area is associated with great controversy. This is due to the uncertainties of the relationship between the illnesses and the impairment of brain function, the great variability in the manifestations of the illnesses, the generalized effects of the illness on cognitive test performance (e.g., fatigue), the low base rate of cognitive impairment, and the great range of impairment that is possible with each illness. It is difficult to generalize for an individual illness because of these factors. For example, occlusive cardiac illness is very common among adults, and coronary bypass surgery is often used as a treatment. However, probably less than 5% of cardiac patients who receive bypass surgery have any transient or permanent brain impairment. This base rate results in measurement difficulties, and generalizations are difficult from studies using the typical pre-post outcome method because so few patients with the general disorder have measurable differences on the dependent measures (Kimball, 1972; Savageau, Stanton, Jenkins, & Klein, 1982).

Regardless of these factors, a large number of medical disorders may directly involve the central nervous system at some level of illness severity or at some point in the progress of the illness. Also, many illnesses are associated with complications that result in injury to the nervous system. Finally, virtually all medications and a number of other treatment methods may result in damage to the central nervous system if some unforeseen treatment-related event occurs. If the medications are prescribed at very high levels, if some accident occurs in the use of medication, or if a surgery intervention is complicated by sepsis or other events, then the brain may be injured and neuropsychological impairment will result.

This chapter will cover five major illnesses that result in direct injury of the central nervous system or treatments for these illnesses that are associated with possible neurological complications. Other chapters of this volume will cover other illnesses that have direct consequences for brain function (e.g., brain tumor) and many of the points covered here will also appear on the other chapters. Our selection of illnesses was based on the notion that the illnesses are not commonly associated with brain injury but may result in enough cases that they warrant separate consideration. Certainly, many other illnesses could be presented, but either they are discussed in other chapters, there are too few cases with neuropsychological impairment, or there are yet essentially no neuropsychological studies of the illness, especially among children. The illnesses included were asthma, acquired immune deficiency syndrome (AIDS), diabetes, childhood leukemia, and chronic renal disease.

ASTHMA

Asthma is the most common chronic disease among children. Onset typically occurs before age 5, although it can occur at any time throughout life. The disease is characterized by a hypersensitivity of the lungs that results in constriction or obstruction that is typically intermittent, variable, and reversible. This obstruction can be due to swelling of small or large airways, smooth muscle constriction, swelling of mucosa or tissue, and dried mucus plugs (Chai, 1975; King, 1980).

Symptoms of asthma include labored breathing, wheezing, and coughing. Attacks can last as little as several minutes to as long as days or weeks and can be mild to severe. Severe asthmatic attacks can lead to increased risk of brain damage through hypoxia (Berman, Pierson, Shapiro, & Simons, 1975). It is possible that loss of consciousness and cyanosis that can occur during severe asthmatic attacks causes subsequent seizures and abnormal EEGs (Nellhaus, Neuman, Ellis, & Pernat, 1975). The basal ganglia are especially vulnerable to anoxia, and children with asthma may show some psychomotor disturbance (Prigatano & Levin, 1988).

There are few neuropsychological studies of the cognitive effects of asthma in children. A number of studies have reported maladaptive behavior in asthmatic children, which may have been the cause of hypoxia-related brain damage (Isbister & Mayer, 1970; Nellhaus et al., 1975). However, none of these studies used neuropsychological assessment instruments. Dunleavy and Baade (1980) examined a sample of severely asthmatic children in an attempt to elucidate patterns of neuropsychological deficits. They used the Halstead Neuropsychological Test Battery for Children (Reitan, 1964, 1966) as their assessment instrument, and compared 19 severely asthmatic children to 19 matched controls, aged 9 to 14 years. Results showed a significant difference between the two groups, which the authors attributed to possible brain damage asthmatics suffer during severe attacks. They did not find a relationship between anti-asthmatic medication and neuropsychological test performance (Dunleavy, 1981). The asthmatic children were significantly more impaired on tasks of visualizing and remembering spatial configurations, incidental memory, and planning and executing visual and tactile motor tasks. Seven of the asthmatic children were found to be mildly impaired on the battery of tests.

Although Dunleavy and Baade (1980) did not find a significant effect for medication usage in their sample of asthmatic children, other authors have argued that this is an important influence on performance (Suess & Chai, 1981). Corticosteroids and theophylline are often used as a treatment for severe asthma, and have been shown to have central nervous system (CNS) effects (Bacal, Linegar, Denton, Gourdeau, 1959; Gillin, Jacobs, Fram, & Snyder, 1972; Glaser, 1953; Glaser, Kornfeld, & Knight, 1955; Henkin, 1970; Hoefer & Glaser, 1950; Kopell, Willner, Landi, Warrick, & Edwards, 1970; Nolke, 1956; Soifer, 1957). A number of studies have addressed this issue, but results are inconclusive due to flaws in experimental design such as poor selection and diagnostic criteria, failure to control confounding variables, and inadequate selection of assessment tools (Creer & Gustafson, 1989; Furukawa, DuHamel, & Weiner, 1988; Kasenberg & Bloom 1987; McLoughlin, Nall, Isaacs, Petrosko, Karibo, & Lidney, 1983; Rachelefsky, Wo, & Adelson, 1986; Rappaport, Coffman, Guare, Fenton, Degraw & Twarog, 1989; Seuss, Stump, Chai, & Kalisker, 1986; Springer, Goldenberg, Dov, & Godfrey, 1985). A recently well-designed double-blind study of theophylline effects indicated no significant findings on parent's teachers' or children's ratings of behavior or mood, or on tests of cognitive processing (Schlieper, Alcock, Beaudry, Feldmanm, & Leikin, 1991). However, there were more negative additional comments made by parents and teachers during the theophylline phase of the study suggesting that the measures used were not sensitive to the specific types of behaviors asthmatic children experience. Also, there appeared to be a pattern of individual differences among the asthmatic children and this suggested that children who already had attentional or achievement problems were more vulnerable to adverse effects of theophylline treatment.

AIDS

Acquired immune deficiency syndrome (AIDS) is caused by retroviruses identified as human immunodeficiency virus (HIV). Pediatric AIDS occurs when children are born to women infected with the AIDS virus or when children receive infected blood transfusions, which are frequently used as treatment for the complications of prematurity and hemophilia. AIDS may also be contracted through breast milk, through sexual abuse by an infected person, or by playing with infected needles. The pattern of AIDS that occurs in children is similar to that in adults. Children with the AIDS virus can either manifest the full-blown disease, which is characterized by the presence of opportunistic infections and/or Kaposi's sarcoma, or they may have the AIDS-related complex (ARC) which lacks the opportunistic infections (Epstein et al., 1985; Klug, 1986; Seligman, 1986).

Accurate diagnosis of HIV infection in infants is difficult. Children younger than 6 months of age have immature B-cells that cannot mount an antibody response (Klug, 1986). Antibodies from the mother remain in the infant's blood, which further complicates the diagnosis. Infants also have a different pattern of infections than adults with the AIDS virus, making the disease appear different (Byers, 1989). Initial symptoms of both AIDS and ARC include microcephaly, neurological abnormalities, interstitial pneumonitis, hepatosplenomegaly, lymphadenopathy, recurrent diarrhea, parotitis, rashes, fever, and fungal and bacterial infections such as meningitis, strep, staph, salmonella, urinary and ear infections, and oralpharyngeal thrush (Klug, 1986; Seligman, 1986; Ultmann et al., 1985).

Complications of HIV infection include failure to thrive, opportunistic infections such as cytomegalic virus (CMV), subacute encephalitis, and progressive calcification of the basal ganglia evident on computerized tomography (CT) scan (Epstein et al., 1985). Such complications can result in a loss of or failure to attain developmental milestones and neurological impairment, including dementia, weakness, spasticity, and seizures (Ammann et al., 1983; Belman et al., 1984; 1986; Epstein et al., 1985; Rubinstein et al., 1983). Children born infected with AIDS are often small for gestational age and have medical complications. If they were infected early in their prenatal development, they often have dysmorphic features (Klug, 1986).

The prevalence of central nervous system involvement in children infected with HIV has been estimated to range from 50 to 93% (Belman et al., 1986; Epstein et al., 1986). It appears that HIV infection in children has a more profound effect on brain function than is true in adults with the virus. It has been hypothesized that the brain is the primary site of HIV infection in children (Epstein, Sharer, & Goudsmit, 1988). Neurologic complications include encephalopathy, microcephaly, bilateral pyramidal tract signs, and occasionally extrapyramidal and cerebellar signs (Belman et al., 1985, 1986; Epstein et al., 1985, 1986; Ultmann et al., 1985, 1987). Diamond and colleagues (1987) summarized four characteristic courses of encephalopathy in children with AIDS or ARC: (1) full-blown encephalopathy, (2) subacute progressive course, (3) subacute stepwise course, and (4) static course. Courses 1 and 2 were more typical of children with AIDS, whereas courses 3 and 4 were typically found in children with ARC. However, cases to the exception of these were noted in both AIDS and ARC (Epstein et al., 1986; Ultmann et al., 1987).

The etiology of neurological complications from HIV infection can be related to the HIV virus itself (Ho et al., 1985; Koenig et al., 1986; Resnick et al., 1985;

Shaw et al., 1985) or to secondary complications stemming from immunosuppression. Cytomegalic virus (CMV has been a common secondary infectious source in both children and adults, and it is known that CMV can produce a profound encephalopathy, although the mechanisms of this are not well understood. There are also several other factors that may contribute to the cognitive sequelae of AIDS and ARC. These include prenatal factors such as drug abuse in the mother and poor prenatal care, which have been shown to have deleterious effects on the cognitive development of children (Clarren & Smith, 1978; Jones et al., 1973; Lifschitz et al., 1985; Rosen & Johnson, 1982); medical factors such as nutritional and metabolic deficiencies, which can result from the chronic diarrhea often associated with AIDS (Ultmann et al., 1985); chronic use of multiple medications that may cause cognitive sequelae; recurrent otitis media, which can result in hearing impairments and can lead to language delays; hypoxia as a result of the interstitial lung disease, which is common among AIDS suffers (Ultmann et al., 1985); and deprivation from formal learning and socialization experiences due to chronic hospitalizations (Diamond et al., 1987).

Although the neurological complications of HIV infection have been fairly well characterized in several studies (Belman et al., 1985, 1986; Epstein et al., 1985, 1986; Ultmann et al., 1985, 1987), the neuropsychological sequelae in pediatric cases have not been as well examined. In adults, AIDS dementia is characterized by impaired concentration and memory, psychomotor retardation, and flat affect followed by global cognitive impairment (Faulstich, 1986; Navia, Jordan, & Price, 1986). Neuropsychological studies of children with HIV have used a variety of assessment batteries making comparison between and even within studies difficult. However, results generally indicate motor, perceptual motor functions, and expressive speech to be more affected than other cognitive areas. Abstract reasoning and verbally mediated skills are relatively spared (Belman et al., 1985; Diamond et al., 1987; Epstein et al., 1986; Ultmann et al., 1985, 1987).

Epstein and associates (1985) reported on a series of four children with AIDS who developed a progressive encephalopathy and associated neurological disorder. The clinical features were similar to those seen in adults with AIDS. All of the children had a loss of milestones as well as bilateral weakness with pyramidal tract signs and impaired brain growth. Other symptoms were ataxia, cortical blindness, seizures, and myoclonis.

Ultmann and colleagues (1985) reported on the developmental abnormalities of 16 infants and children with AIDS and ARC. Both groups were consistently delayed in motor development and most of the children showed delayed acquisition of milestones. Several of the AIDS children actually lost developmental milestones, which did not occur in the ARC group. Psychometric testing indicated the AIDS group had more severe cognitive dysfunction as compared to the ARC group, and CNS involvement was documented in all patients with AIDS. The ARC group showed more variability in their course of illness.

Belman and colleagues (1988) reported on the neurologic syndromes found in 61 of 68 children with AIDS and ARC. The most common symptoms were microencephaly, cognitive deficits, and bilateral pyramidal tract signs. Cognitive assessment included the Bayley Scales of Infant Development, the Stanford-Binet

Intelligence Test, or the Kaufman Assessment Battery for Children, depending on the age of the child. Of the group, 11 patients developed an encephalopathy that began insidiously. Disease course was manifested by loss of interest in play, loss of previously acquired developmental milestones, apathy, and progressive bilateral pyramidal tract signs. Also, 31 children had a neurological course that was characterized by a slowing down of cognitive maturation. Of these children, 13 then developed further neurologic deterioration; 4 children had a slowing down of cognitive development, which then improved, although they still remained impaired on measures of IQ. Neuroradiologic findings in the children who had progressive neurological declines indicated atrophy and white matter attenuation in all cases. In addition, 10 of the patients had bilateral symmetric calcification of the basal ganglia, and 2 also had calcifications in the frontal lobes.

INSULIN DEPENDENT DIABETES MELLITUS (IDDM)

This chronic disease is the second most prevalent in childhood, after asthma (Ryan, 1988). It is estimated that there are 435,000 individuals with IDDM, with 19,000 new cases diagnosed each year (Carter Center, 1985). The primary age range of diagnosis is 10 to 14 years of age (LaPorte et al., 1981). Insulin dependent diabetes mellitus, or Type I diabetes, is also known as "juvenile-onset" diabetes and is characterized by the inability of the pancreas to produce insulin. Without insulin, the body is incapable of metabolizing carbohydrates, which leads to dangerously high levels of blood glucose.

The initial symptoms of Type I diabetes are excessive urination and water and food intake in conjunction with rapid weight loss. If the person is not treated, acute complications ensue, which may include severe dehydration, ketoacidosis, diabetic coma, and death (Drash & Becker, 1978). Chronic high levels of blood glucose can result in damage to large and small blood vessels. Treatment involves administration of insulin along with diet regulation and exercise. However, incorrect administration and regulation of insulin treatment can lead to hypoglycemia or very low blood sugar levels. Hypoglycemia can result in fine motor tremor, confusion, weakness, and loss of consciousness ("insulin coma") (Miller & Sperling, 1986).

There have been several neuropsychological studies of children with IDDM, but the results are mixed and inconclusive. Proposed risk factors for neuropsychological sequelae include early age at onset of disease, poor metabolic control, extended duration of the illness, number of hypoglycemic seizures, school deprivation, and personality factors.

The research on age of onset suggests that the developing nervous system may be more sensitive to metabolic fluctuations, and therefore IDDM may produce cognitive deficits among very young children (Ryan & Morrow, 1987). Ack, Miller, and Weil (1961) found that children diagnosed with IDDM before the age of 5 showed an average 10-point difference in IQ scores than healthy siblings. Children older when diagnosed showed no measurable difference with siblings.

These differences were not related to the length of time the child had had the disease. Ryan and Morrow (1987) also found age at onset to be an important variable, with deficits across a wide range of cognitive areas including attention, memory, problem solving, visuospatial and visuomotor abilities.

Metabolic control is crucial because the brain relies on an available source of serum glucose from the blood that is not stored in large quantities in the brain. Among diabetic children, the amount of glucose circulating in the blood stream can fluctuate based on diet, insulin dose, and exercise (Miller & Sperling, 1986). This fluctuating level of glucose availability could have immediate effects on psychomotor performance, reaction time, and concentration (Holmes, Hayford, Gonzalez, & Weydert, 1983; Homes et al., 1984; Ryan & Morrow, 1987). Diabetic children can experience dramatic fluctuations in attentional abilities throughout the day. Poor metabolic control may also result in hypoglycemia and chronic disorders of the vasculature.

Another risk factor is the number of episodes of hypoglycemia that a child may suffer early in life. EEG studies have also indicated a significantly higher number of abnormal EEGs among diabetic children who have had a history of severe hypoglycemic or hyperglycemic episodes (Eeg-Olofsson & Peterson, 1966; Haumont, Dorchy, & Pelc, 1979). Neuropsychological studies have yet to specifically examine this factor.

LEUKEMIA

Leukemia is a form of cancer in which abnormal white blood cells develop in bone marrow and proliferate, preventing the production of normal blood cells. This leads to the early symptoms of the disease, which include anemia, bone pain, lethargy, and easy bruising. The cause of leukemia is not currently known, although viruses, carcinogens, and heredity factors have been implicated. Incidence in children peaks at age 4 years, and the diagnosis is more prevalent among boys than girls. There are two major types of leukemia in children: acute lymphoblastic leukemia (ALL) and acute myelocytic leukemia (AML). ALL is the prevalent type, occurring in approximately 95% of cases and being the less severe of the two.

The average life expectancy for children with leukemia improved significantly with the introduction of prophylactic treatments of the central nervous system (CNS). Systemic chemotherapy apparently did not penetrate the blood-brain barrier and eradicate leukemic foci. The leukemia would then become active following systemic therapy and the child would have a CNS relapse (Simone, 1972). CNS prophylactic treatments were developed to address this problem. They most often consist of cranial irradiation or intrathecal methotrexate, singly, or in some combination (Allen, 1978). The most common radiation doses are 1,800 or 2,400 rads spread over a 10- to 14-day period, and intrathecal methotrexate is usually administered over a 1- to 2-month period. The use of such prophylactic treatment helped to increase the 5-year survival rate from essentially 0% to approximately 50%, and the risk of relapse is significantly diminished (Simone, Aur, Hustu, Verzosa, & Pinkel, 1978).

Although prophylactic treatments represented a major breakthrough, concerns over the possible neurotoxic effects of these treatments emerged. Cranial irradiation and intrathecal methotrexate are both known to cause significant microangiopathy, demyelination, and cerebral necrosis (Bleyer, 1981; Crosley, Rorke, Evans, & Nigro, 1978). The treatments are presently given amid concern that therapeutic dosage levels might result in CNS injury and neurological impairment.

Approximately 40 studies have examined the neuropsychological outcome of CNS prophylactic treatment. They vary considerably in methodological factors such as sample size, age at testing, selection of control groups, choice of intellectual tests, and selection of subjects. Due to common clinical constraints associated with this chronic, severe illness, these methodological problems are often unavoidable. However, they have been a source of considerable confusion and strongly influence the conclusions that can be drawn from the studies.

In terms of overall level of performance, most studies found that leukemic children performed at least in the average range. Studies that found intellectual impairment defined it simply as the significant difference between leukemic and control or comparison subjects. Typically, the leukemic sample performed in the average range and the comparison subjects performed in the bright normal range. Williams and Davis (1986) discovered a compelling selection bias among these studies. Virtually none of the studies using random selection found impairment. Some 85% of studies using nonrandom selection found positive results. This suggests that leukemic patients with intellectual problems were selectively referred to study groups using nonrandom selection and/or assignment. Analyses of these subjects only fostered the generalization that all leukemic children have deficits.

Comparison of type of CNS prophylaxis have largely found negative results (e.g., Williams et al., 1986). Many studies are consistent in finding that leukemic children who acquire leukemia at an earlier age have a different history of illness. In particular, the school history of younger children is greatly disrupted and factors such as this may account for differences.

Only one study examined the specific effects of CNS relapse on neuropsychological function. As previously described, some children may sustain a leukemic relapse following initially successful systemic and CNS prophylactic treatment. These children receive extremely intensive treatment subsequent to the relapse. They may also relapse repeatedly and then receive further systemic and CNS treatment. Mulhern and colleagues (1987) discovered that these children sustain unequivocal intellectual impairment. The mean full-scale IQ for the 40 children in the sample was 88. Some 20% of the sample was mentally retarded and required special education intervention. The best predictors of IQ following treatment were the number of radiation therapy courses, age, and the presence of cerebral pathology measured by computed tomography (CT).

In summary, it is clear that extremely high dosage levels of irradiation and intrathecal methotrexate injure the CNS and cause intellectual impairment. However, conventional dosage levels for CNS prophylaxis given in a single course probably does not result in permanent brain injury or intellectual deficits.

END-STAGE RENAL DISEASE

A number of illnesses will result in severe renal insufficiency or failure. Among these are bilateral Wilm's tumor and congenital renal hypoplasia. The "end-stage" care for these illnesses includes chronic dialysis or transplantation. End-stage renal disease and its treatment is associated with a few clinical syndromes that probably have a CNS component and neuropsychological impairment. Prominent among these are uremia, dialysis disequilibrium, and dialysis dementia.

Uremia refers to the increase in metabolic waste products in the blood associated with acute or chronic renal failure. This may result in a general encephalopathy, the severity of which varies with the degree of renal failure. Acute renal failure produces alteration of brain electrolyte concentrations, decreased oxygen consumption, disruption of transport mechanisms, and an increase in brain urea concentrations (Arieff, 1981). Acute renal encephalopathy is associated with acute confusion, fatigue, memory deficits, and decreased motor coordination. If untreated, the renal failure will result in delirium, coma, and death (Marshall, 1979).

The metabolic changes associated with chronic uremia are less severe. A number of related illnesses often accompany chronic uremia (e.g., hypertension and diabetes) and these may independently produce cerebral impairment.

Dialysis disequilibrium refers to the unique cerebral metabolic dysfunction that often accompanies hemodialysis. Electrolytic imbalance, tissue swelling, and increased cerebral spinal fluid pressure produce neurological symptoms, including headache, nausea, restlessness, tremors, seizures, and disorientation. These symptoms usually occur toward the end of dialysis or up to 24 hours later. Manifestations of dialysis disequilibrium are strongly influenced by manipulation of the dialysis technique. The syndrome can be prevented and/or treated by careful attention to blood flow rates and duration of dialysis.

A small number of chronically dialysized patients develop severe progressive *dialysis dementia* that is characterized by dysarthria, myoclonus, apraxia, seizures, disorientation, memory disorder, and delirium (Alfrey et al., 1972). This disorder occurs following at least two years of dialysis treatment and the condition is associated with mortality within one to two years of further treatment. The onset of symptoms can occur from one to seven years after dialysis is begun, with a mean of four years. Speech disturbance may be the initial feature, or occur later. This begins as an intermittent hesitancy of speech (stuttering and slurring) and may progress to aphasia. Agraphia and apraxia may also be present. Subtle changes in personality occur early in the course and give the appearance of depression. The syndrome may progress to include agitation, disorientation, hallucinations, flat affect, confusion, and decreased interest in surroundings (Scheiber & Ziesat, 1976). Progressive dementia follows.

The study of etiological factors has focused on the accumulation of toxic metabolites, including trace aluminum and medication-related metabolites, normal pressure hydrocephalus, neurotransmitter deficiencies, and other electrolytic imbalance (Arieff, 1981).

Neuropsychological studies have revealed a pattern of generalized cognitive impairments for renal patients. These deficits are reflected in lower general intelligence, memory ability, attention, and psychomotor speed (Hart, Pederson, Czerwinski, & Adams, 1983; Ryan, Souheaver, & DeWolfe, 1980: Souheaver, Ryan, & DeWolfe, 1982). The deficits are nonspecific and may be partially attributable to the generalized effects of chronic illness. There is also a suggestion that attention deficits and psychomotor speed are correlated with the severity of renal illness (Teschan, Ginn, Bourne, & Ward, 1976; Treischmann & Sand, 1971). Illness severity was assessed by serum creatinine and BUN levels. Some improvement of cognitive function has also been associated with the onset of dialysis treatment and kidney transplant (Teschan et al., 1974).

Studies of adults undergoing chronic hemodialysis have not shown consistent findings of impairment. For example, English and associates (1978) found evidence of mild cognitive impairment on the WAIS but a number of other studies found essentially no impairment (e.g., Winokur, Czaczkes, & Kaplan De-Nour, 1973). These studies differed widely in methodology and it is difficult to draw summary conclusions regarding their findings difficult.

Very few studies have specifically examined the neuropsychological effects of renal disease among children. Presumably many of the etiological factors and cerebral impairment associated with renal failure in adults applies to children. For example, Foley, Polinski, Gruskin, Baluarte, and Grover (1981) documented progressive cerebral encephalopathy in their clinic where infants and children with chronic renal disease are treated. From a sample of 72 patients, they discovered encephalopathy in 5 patients. These patients demonstrated a stereotyped pattern of symptoms. Initial findings consisted of a delay in motor development, dysmetria and tremor in infants, and ataxia in ambulatory children. Over a period ranging from 6 to 12 months, all patients manifested extremity and facial myoclonus and motor seizures followed by generalized convulsions. A decrease in memory, language, and other cognitive function preceded the seizures, and cognitive impairment persisted during the interictal period. Over approximately 9 months, 3 patients progressed to an end-stage that included progressive bulbar failure with loss of swallow function and chronic vegetative state with lack of response to visual and auditory stimuli. Death occurred in 2 of these patients. The remaining patient who attained the latter stage remained in a vegetative state for two years. One patient received intelligence tests and IQ scores dropped from 90 to 45. Neurological symptoms and cognitive decline persisted even after successful dialysis treatment or renal transplant had reduced uremia.

Serial EEG studies revealed progressive slowing with superimposed sharp waves and atypical spike-wave discharges. These signs were correlated with attenuation in motor function, cognitive ability, and seizure disorder. Computed tomography scans of patients in the later stages revealed ventricular dilatation and cortical atrophy.

Another study (Rasburg, Fennell, Eastman, Garin, & Richards, 1979) examined the pre-to-post effects of hemodialysis in cognitive function among 14 children with end-stage renal disease but no overt dementia. This study used a continuous performance attention task, a problem-solving task, and a paired associates memory test. The renal patients were compared to normal volunteers from a local school and matched the renal patients on age, gender, and IQ. The study found no differences pre- and postdialysis, or in comparison to control subjects.

The findings from these studies suggest that both children and adults who experience renal disease probably do not sustain significant brain injury unless they experience severe, acute renal complications, or such chronic disease and treatment that they sustain encephalopathy or progressive dementia. This occurs for approximately 3% of patients in end-stage disease who have experienced renal failure and dialysis treatment for at least two years. Of course, there are probably levels of cognitive impairment short of frank dementia that are experienced by some renal patients. Such impairment may be associated with acute renal insufficiency or illness, and the generalized effects of severe chronic illness on cognitive function. However, these studies suggest that the encephalopathy and progressive dementia is a profoundly different manifestation of renal disease than such mild or transient cognitive impairment. Dialysis dementia is poorly understood at this point. It probably represents the end point of a neurodegenerative process that precipitates small neuronal and other tissue loss that accumulates over the continued course of renal disease and treatment. The final result is cerebral atrophy and profound neurological compromise similar to the course of other neurodegenerative dementia-related illnesses.

EMOTIONAL CONSEQUENCES OF MEDICAL DISORDERS IN CHILDREN

Children can have a wide range of emotional reactions to chronic illness. Some children cope very well, while others show severe emotional consequences. Most of the current literature suggests that adjustment depends on a variety of intrapersonal (age, personality, intelligence), disease-related (severity, chronicity), and environmental factors (family support, financial) (Eiser, 1985). Also, the manner in which the child is educated about the disease can have implications for adjustment.

In terms of intrapersonal factors, a child's cognitive developmental level has been posited as an important predictor of coping with disease. Bibace and Walsh (1980, 1981) interviewed children ranging in age from 4 to 11 years, and found different explanations of disease consistent with Piaget's stages of cognitive development—prelogical, concrete logical, and formal logical. As children advance through these stages, they become increasingly more aware of the differentiation between self and other. Children in the prelogical stage tend to believe illness is due to external concrete phenomena such as contagion. The concrete logical child begins to observe some relationship between the cause of illness and its effects. However, reasons for illness are still seen as something outside the body with very little understanding of how the body actually functions. Finally, the formal logical child is characterized by a clear differentiation between self and other, and disease can be understood in terms of physiological aspects. Bibace and Walsh (1981) suggest that explanations of disease should be kept very concrete and focused on the visible aspects of disease management until a child has reached the stage of formal operations (approximately age 11). At that point, children can comprehend more physiologically based explanations of their illness.

Kellerman, Zeltzer, Ellenberg, Dash, and Rigler (1980) reported that locus of control in children with a variety of chronic illnesses was an important variable to consider. Results of their work indicated that those illness groups who do not have any control over their medical procedures but rather are the recipients of treatment have perceptions of greater externality of control. For example, leukemic children have very little control over their illness and tend to feel helpless and dependent. In contrast, diabetic children can exert some control over their disease through diet and self-administration of medicine. Their perceptions of control are more internalized.

There are also disease-related variables that may be important when considering the emotional consequences of each illness. For example, the social attitudes about cancer set this disease apart from other chronic illnesses in terms of the degree of pessimism associated with it (Mitchielutte & Diseker, 1982). The diagnosis of leukemia may be so emotion-laden as to have a very traumatic effect on the patient and family, and it has been reported that leukemic children never believe that they are completely cured, so they never feel completely normal (Peck, 1979; Zeltzer, Kellerman, Ellenberg, Dash & Rigler, 1980).

AIDS is similar to cancer in terms of the social connotations of the illness. AIDS is associated with great fear among the general population and patients with a diagnosis of AIDS are ostracized. AIDS also has some unique psychosocial complications. Parents of AIDS children are often infected with the disease themselves and may die or be too ill to care for their children. Infectious disease precautions also result in increased isolation for the AIDS child. All these may have serious implications for adjustment.

Diabetic children are constantly reminded that they have a chronic illness by their need to continually monitor food intake, exercise, and take insulin treatments. In addition, they must live with the fact that even with good dietetic control, the nature of their disease predisposes them to a variety of life-threatening and disabling complications.

Several studies have concluded that the less severely ill children have higher degrees of maladjustment than do severely ill children (Eiser, 1985). The reasons for this may be that children who are severely ill do not have high expectations placed on them, either by themselves or by others. Children who are less severely afflicted continue to compete with normal peers and may experience stress related to feeling less adequate. This constant failure often results in low self-esteem and subsequent inadequate adjustment. Indeed, parents of less severely ill children may be perceived as not needing as much support as those with severely ill children, when this may not be the case. This state of affairs leads to poorer adjustment among family members, including the chronically ill child.

In terms of educating the child about their disease, it is important to take into account the cognitive developmental level, as discussed earlier. Also, it must be realized that children experience anxiety related to their diagnosis and prognosis. Before 1970, it was widely thought that fatally ill children under the age of 10 did not experience or express death- or illness-related anxiety (Richmond & Waisman, 1955). At that time, the practice among health-care professionals was to keep the children unaware of their diagnosis. Waechter's (1971) work was a major break from this viewpoint, and her findings influenced much of the later research. Her hypothesis was that children who are not told their diagnosis are still aware of its seriousness, though unable to overtly express their fears. It is now generally believed that children should be kept informed about their illness and prognosis in order to avoid the development of erroneous beliefs.

A GENERAL MODEL FOR NEUROPSYCHOLOGICAL ASSESSMENT OF MEDICAL DISORDERS

The disorders presented in this chapter are characterized by great diversity in type and level of cognitive impairment and the degree to which extraneous factors, such as psychological distress, influence test performance. Patients with these disorders will manifest the extreme ranges of cognitive performance, from superior levels of ability among completely intact patients, to extremely low levels of ability, which is characteristic of many of these disorders at their end-stage, or otherwise associated with severe illness and neurological complications.

The assessment of cognitive function must span the broad range of ability present among children with these disorders. Some children will have mild, subtle deficits, while others will manifest severe impairment, equivalent to mental retardation. Children with the illnesses described here are also often followed over time and many children will start with subtle deficits and then decline to lower levels of ability as the illness worsens. Finally, since these illnesses may affect any part of the brain, the assessment must be comprehensive and must be designed to assess virtually all cognitive constructs. A battery that meets these design specifications should be organized according to major cognitive constructs and appropriate levels of ability (see Table 10.1).

The assessment of subtle impairment is usually accomplished by full assessment of neuropsychological function, cognitive/academic abilities, and emotional/behavior problems (see Chapter 2).

As the illness worsens, the assessment is abbreviated and will usually be conducted only for descriptive purposes. This abbreviation of the assessment usually results from the decreased need for elaborate information and to the lower ability level and cooperation of the child. Many formal intellectual and neuropsychological tests were not designed for low-ability levels and many patients

TABLE 10.1 General Features and Assessment of Progressive Cognitive Decline

General Severity Level	Living Situation	Typical Everyday Behavior	Example of Assessment Strategy	Purpose of Evaluation	General Benchmark Events
Mild, reflecting subtle cognitive impairment	Independent at home	Forgets novel material	IQ testing, parent rating scales, tests of academic skills, & neuropsychological tests	Diagnostic (e.g., psychological) distress vs. neurological impairment	Parents & teachers first note problems in memory or academic skills
Moderate, reflecting clear neurological impairment	Supervised at home	Forgets material that is repeated	Parent rating scales, IQ, and academic testing only	Description of functional levels	Child severely lags behind age peers and is placed in some special classes
Severe, reflecting dementia and/or localized neurological impairment	Constant dependent care at home	Forgets all new information	Parent rating scales and mental status examination	Description of functional levels	Child is placed in only special education classes or home-bound programs
Very severe, usually reflecting dementia	Constant dependent care at home or in an institutional setting	Cannot recall remote and well-learned information and the child may have focal neurological deficits	Parent rating sclaes and mental status examination	Description of functional levels	Child receives special education classes in an institutional setting or as part of a home-bound program

cannot take them at a certain point in the progression of their illness. When this occurs, the examiner must rely on mental status testing, neurologic screening, and the parent rating scales to describe the patient's abilities.

As part of the general examination, it is imperative to assess psychological distress and behavior problems among children with medical disorders. These factors are important in their own right but may also influence cognitive test performance to the point when the results are invalid. These constructs are usually assessed among children using behavior rating scales. Occasionally, older children are administered self-reports. The most commonly used behavior rating scale is the Achenbach Child Behavior Checklist (Achenbach, McConaughy, & Howell, 1987). This checklist is in widespread clinical use and includes a large number of descriptions of psychological distress and behavior problems among children. It also consists of self-report, parent rating, and teacher rating forms. Another popular self-report instrument is the Personality Inventory for Children (Wirt, Lachar, Klinedinst, & Seat, 1977). Although psychological distress is common among children with chronic illness, usually they do not manifest distress or psychopathology at the levels of most children referred for psychological evaluation or treatment in the general population. Consequently, it is difficult to characterize their problems using assessment tools designed for more extreme disorders or the typology of childhood disorders described in the *Diagnostic and Statistical Manual of Mental Disorders (DSM-IV)* by the American Psychiatric Association (1995).

Strategies for treating CNS dysfunction associated with systemic or remote organ disease begin with proper diagnoses of primary and secondary medical conditions. Appropriate medical treatment should follow. For children with asthma, bronchodilators are used as needed. In cases of AIDS, AZT is often indicated. Diabetes is managed with insulin or insulin substitutes. Severe renal disease typically requires dialysis. Leukemia is treated with radiation and/or chemotherapy. The philosophy herein being that if the primary medical condition is well managed, secondary effects on the CNS will be minimized.

It may be hypothesized that the severity and chronicity of the remote system or organ illness is likely linked to the degree of neuropsychological deficits identified. However, because of frequent changes in metabolic conditions, neuropsychological functions may vary. Rehabilitation efforts may well require psychopharmacologic agents, cognitive rehabilitation, psychotherapy, and family therapy. From this view, treatment is designed to address symptoms and deficits evidenced from neuropsychological testing. Medications in concert with family therapy, psychotherapy, and behavioral interventions are usually required to treat adjustment and neurobehavioral problems. Cognitive rehabilitation efforts and special education are typically designed on a case-by-case basis to help remediate and/or compensate for the information processing deficits demonstrated. The decision to implement remedial or compensatory strategies depends on several factors, including age of the child, severity of CNS dysfunction, stage of recovery, prognosis for recovery and survival, and nature of presenting symptoms and deficits. Little data exist, linking neuropsychological test data to treatment outcomes, for the medical disorders discussed in this chapter. Clearly, this is fertile ground for future research.

REFERENCES

Achenbach, T.M., McConaughy, S.H., & Howell, C.T. (1987). Child/adolescent behavioral and emotional problems: Implications of cross-informant correlations for situational specificity. *Psychological Bulletin, 213–232.*

Ack, M., Miller, I., & Weil, W.B. (1961). Intelligence of children with diabetes mellitus. *Pediatrics, 28,* 764–770.

Alfrey, A.C., Mishell, J.M., Burks, J., Contiguglia, S.R., Rudolph, H., Lewin, E., & Holmes, J.H. (1972). Syndrome of dyspraxia and multifocal seizures associated with chronic hemodialysis. *Transactions, American Society for Artificial Internal Organs, 18,* 257–261.

Allen, J.C. (1978). The effects of cancer therapy on the nervous system. *Journal of Pediatrics, 93,* 903–909.

American Psychiatric Association. (1995). *Diagnostic and statistical manual of mental disorders (4th ed., Revised).* Washington, DC: Author.

Ammann, A.J., Cowan, M.J., Wara, O.W., Weintrub, P., Dritz, S., Goldman, H., Perkins, H.A. (1983). Acquired immunodeficiency in an infant: Possible transmission by means of blood products. *Lancet, 1,* 956–958.

Arieff, A.I. 9181). Neurological complications of uremia. In B. Brennan & F. Rector (Eds.), *The kidney* (pp. 2307–2343). Philadelphia W.B. Saunders.

Bacal, H., Linegar, K., Denton, R., & Gourdeau, R. (1959). Aminophylline poisoning in children. *Canadian Medical Association Journal, 80,* 6.

Belman, A.L., Diamond, G., Dickson, D., Horoupian, D., Llena, H., Langos, G., & Rubinstein, A. (1988). Pediatric acquired immunodeficiency syndrome: Neurologic syndromes. *American Journal of Diseases in Children, 142,* 29–35.

Belman, A.L., Lantos, G., Horoupian, D., et al. (1986). Calcification of the basal ganglia in infants and children. *Neurology, 36,* 1192–1199.

Belman A.L., Novick, B., Ultmann, M.H., Spiro, A., Rubinstein, A., Horoupian, D.S., & Cohen, H. (1984). Neurological complications in children with acquired immune deficiency syndrome. *Annals of Neurology, 16,* 414.

Belman, A.L., Ultmann, N.H., Horoupian, D.S., Novick, B., Spiro, A., Rubinstein, A., Kurtzberg, D., & Cone-Wesson, B. (1985). Neurologic complications in infants and children with AIDS. *Annals of Neurology, 18,* 560-566.

Bibace, R., & Walsh, M.E. (1980). Development of children's concepts of illness. *Pediatrics, 66,* 913–917.

Bibace, R., & Walsh, M.E. 1981). Children's conceptions of illness. In R. Bibace & M.E. Walsh (Eds.), *New directions for child development* (pp. 31–48). San Francisco: Jossey-Bass.

Bierman, C., Pierson, W., Shapiro, G., & Simons, E. (1975). Brain damage from asthma in children. *Journal of Allergy and Clinical Immunology, 55,* 126.

Bleyer, W.A. (1981). Neurologic sequelae of methotrexate and ionizing radiation: A new classification. *Cancer Treatment Reports, 65,* 89–98.

Byers, J. (1989). AIDS in children: Effects on neurological development and implications for the future. *The Journal of Special Education, 23,* 5–16.

Carter Center. (1985). Closing the gap: The problem of diabetes mellitus in the United States. *Diabetes Care, 8,* 391–406.

Chai, H. (1975). Management of severe chronic perennial asthma in children. *Advances in Asthma and Allergy, 2,* 1–12.

Clarren, S.K., & Smith, D.W. (1978). The fetal alcohol syndrome. *New England Journal of Medicine, 298,* 1063–1067.

Creer, T., & Gustafson, K. (1989). Psychological problems associated with drug therapy in childhood asthma. *Journal of Pediatrics, 115,* 850–855.

Crosley, C.J., Rorke, L.D., Evans, A., & Nigro, M.

(1978). Central nervous system lesions in childhood leukemia. *Neurology, 28,* 678–685.

Diamond, G.W., Kaufman, J., Belman, A.L., Cohen, L., Cohen, H. J., & Rubinstein, A. (1987). Characterization of cognitive functioning in a subgroup of children with congenital HIV infection. *Archives of Clinical Neuropsychology, 2,* 245–256.

Drash, A.L., & Becker, D. (1978). Diabetes mellitus in the child: Course, special problems, and related disorders. In H.M. Katzen & R.J. Mahler (Eds.), *Diabetes, obesity, and vascular disease: Metabolic and molecular interrelationships* (pp. 615–643). New York: Wiley.

Dunleavy, R.A. (1981). Neuropsychological correlates of asthma: Effect of hypoxia or drugs? *Journal of Consulting and Clinical Psychology, 49,* 137.

Dunleavy, R.A., & Baade, L.E. (1980). Neuropsychological correlates of severe asthma in children 9–14 years old. *Journal of Consulting and Clinical Psychology, 48,* 214–219.

Eeg-Olofsson, O., & Peterson, I. (1966). Childhood diabetic neuropathy: A clinical and neuropsychological study. *Acta Paediatrica Scandinavia, 55,* 163–176.

Eiser, C. 9185). *The psychology of childhood illness.* New York: Springer-Verlag.

English, A., Savage, R.D., Britton, P.G., Ward, M. K., & Kerr, D.N.S. (1978). Intellectual impairment in chronic renal failure. *British Medical Journal, 1,* 888–890.

Epstein, L.G., Sharer, L.R., & Goudsmit, J. (1988). Neurological and neuropathological features of human immunodeficiency virus infection in children. *Annals of Neurology, 23,* 19–23.

Epstein, L.G., Sharer, L.R., Joshi, V.V., Fojas, M.M., Koenigsberger, M.R., & Oleske, J.M. (1985). Progressive encephalopathy in children with acquired immune deficiency syndrome. *Annals of Neurology, 17,* 488–496.

Epstein, L.G., Sharer, L.R., Oleske, J.M., Connor, E.M., Goudsmit, J., Bagdon, L., Robert-Guroff, M., & Koenigsberger, M.R. (1986). Neurologic manifestations of human immunodeficiency virus infection in children. *Pediatrics, 78,* 678–687.

Faulstich, M.E. (1986). Acquired immune deficiency syndrome: An overview of central nervous system complications and neuropsychological sequelae. *International Journal of Neuroscience, 30,* 249–254.

Foley, C.M., Polinsky, M.S., Gruskin, A.B., Baluarte, H.J., & Grover, W.D. (1981). Encephalopathy in infants and children with chronic renal disease. *Archives of Neurology, 38,* 656–658.

Furukawa, C., DuHamel, T., & Weiner, L. (1988). Cognitive and behavioral findings in children taking theophylline. *Journal of Allergy and Clinical Immunology, 81,* 83–88.

Gillin, J.C., Jacobs, L.S., Fram, D.H., & Snyder, F. (1972). Acute effect of a glucocorticoid on normal human sleep. *Nature, 237,* 398–399.

Glaser, G.H. (1953). Psychotic reactions induced by corticotropin (ACTH) and cortisone. *Psychosomatic Medicine, 15,* 280–291.

Glaser, G.H., Kornfeld, D.S., & Knight, R.P. (1955). Intravenous hydrocortisone, corticotropin and the electroencephalogram. *Archives of Neurology and Psychiatry, 73,* 338–344.

Hart, R.P., Pederson, J.A., Czerwinski, A.W., & Adams, R.L. (1983). Chronic renal failure, dialysis and neuropsychological function. *Journal of Neuropsychology, 4,* 301–312.

Haumont, D., Dorchy, H., & Pelc, S. (1979). EEG abnormalities in diabetic children: Influence of hypoglycemia and vascular complications. *Clinical Pediatrics, 18,* 750–753.

Henkin, R.I. (1970). The effects of corticosteroid and ACTH on sensory systems. *Progress in Brain Research, 32,* 270–294.

Ho, D.D., Rota, T.R., Schooley, R.T., Kaplan, H.C., Allan, J.D., Groopman, J.E., Resnick, L., Felsenstein, D., Andrews, C.A., & Hirsch, M.S. (1985). Isolation of HTLV-III from cerebrospinal fluid and neural tissues of patients with neurologic syndromes related to the acquired immunodeficiency syndrome. *New England Journal of Medicine, 313,* 1493–1497.

Hoefer, P.F., & Glaser, G.H. (1950). Effects of pituitary adrenocorticotropic hormone (ACTH) therapy. Electroencephalographic and neuropsychiatric changes in fifteen patients. *Journal of the American Medical Association, 14,* 620–624.

Holmes, C.S., Hayford, J.T., Gonzalez, J.L., &

Weydert, J.A. (1983). A survey of cognitive functioning at different glucose levels in diabetic persons. *Diabetes Cares, 6,* 180–185.

Holmes, C.S., Koepke, K.M., Thompson, R.G., Gyves, P.W., & Weydert, J.A. (1984). Verbal fluency and naming performance in type I diabetics at different blood glucose concentrations. *Diabetes Care, 7,* 454–459.

Isbister, C., & Mayer, L. (1970). Asthma and special learning difficulty. *Medical Journal of Australia, 2,* 917–918.

Jones, R.L., Smith, D.W., Ulleland, C.W., Streissguth, A.P. (1973). Patterns of malformations in offspring of chronic alcoholic mothers. *Lancet, 1,* 1267–1271.

Kasenberg, D., & Bloom, L. (1987). Potential neuropsychological side effects of theophylline in asthmatic children. *Pediatric Asthma and Allergy Immunology, 1,* 165–173.

Kellerman, J., Zeltzer, L., Ellenberg, L., Dash, J., & Rigler, D. (1980). Psychological effects of illness in adolescence. I. Anxiety, self-esteem and perception of control. *Journal of Pediatrics, 97,* 126–131.

Kimball, C. P. (1972). The experience of open-heart surgery. *Archives of General Psychiatry, 27,* 57–63.

King, N.J. (1980). The behavioral management of asthma and asthma-related problems of children: A critical review of the literature. *Journal of Behavioral Medicine, 3,* 169–189.

Klug, R.M. (1986). AIDS beyond the hospital Part 2: Children with AIDS. *American Journal of Nursing, 86,* 1126–1132.

Koenig, S., Gendelman, H.E., Orenstein, J.M., Dal Canto, M.C., Pezeshkpour, G.H., Yungbluth, M., Janotta, F., Aksamit, A., Martin, M.A., & Fauci, A.S. (1986). Detection of AIDS virus in macrophages in brain tissue from AIDS patients with encephalopathy. *Science, 233,* 1089–1093.

Kopell, B.S., Willner, W.K., Landi, D., Warrick, G., & Edwards, D. (1970). Cortisol effect on average evoked potential, alpha rhythm, time estimation, and two-flash fusion threshold. *Psychosomatic Medicine, 32,* 39.

LaPorte, R.E., Fishbein, H.A., Drash, A.L., Kuller, L.H., Schneider, B.B., Orchard, T.J., & Wagener, D.K. (1981). The Pittsburgh insulin-dependent diabetes mellitus registry: The incidence of insulin-dependent diabetes mellitus in Allegheny county, Pennsylvania (1965–1976). *Diabetes, 30,* 279–284.

Lifschitz, M.H., Wilson, G.W., Smith, E.O., Desmond, M.M. (1985). Factors affecting head growth and intellectual function in children of drug addicts. *Pediatrics, 75,* 269–274.

Marshall, J.R. (1979). Neuropsychiatric aspects of renal failure. *Journal of Clinical Psychiatry, 40,* 81–85.

McLoughlin, J., Nall, M., Isaacs, B., Petrosko, J., Karibo, J., & Lidney, G. (1983). The relationship of allergies and allergy treatment to school performance and student behavior. *Annals of Allergy, 51,* 506–510.

Miller, J.D., & Sperling, M.A. (1986). Diabetes mellitus in children. In V.C. Kelley (Ed.), *Practice of Pediatrics, 6,* 1–19. New York: Harper and Row.

Michielutte, R., & Diseker, R.A. (1982). Children's perceptions of cancer in comparison to other chronic illness. *Journal of Chronic Diseases, 35,* 843–852.

Mulhern, R. K., Ochs, J., Fairclough, D., Wasserman, A. L., Davis, K. S., & Williams, J. M. (1987). Intellectual and academic achievement status after CNS relapse: A retrospective analysis of 40 children treated for acute lymphoblastic leukemia. *Journal of Clinical Oncology, 5,* 933–940.

Navia, G.A., Jordan, B.D., & Price, R.W. (1986). The AIDS dementia complex: I. Clinical features. *Annals of Neurology, 19,* 517–524.

Nellhaus, G., Neuman, I., Ellis, E., & Pirnat, G. (1975). Asthma and seizures in children. *Pediatric Clinics of North America, 22,* 89–100.

Nolke, A. (1956). Severe toxic effects from aminophylline and theophylline suppositories in children. *Journal of the American Medical Association, 616,* 693–697.

Peck, B. (1979). Effects of childhood cancer on long term survivors and their families. *British Medical Journal, 1,* 1327–1329.

Prigatano, G.P., & Levin, D.C. (1988). Pulmonary System. In R.E. Tarter, D.H. Van Thiel, & K.L. Edwards (Eds.), *Medical neuropsychology: The impact of disease on behavior.* New York: Plenum Press.

Rachelefsky, G., Wo, J., & Adelson, J. (1986). Behavior abnormalities and poor school performance due to oral theophylline use. *Pediatrics, 78,* 1133–1138.

Rappaport, L., Coffman, H., Guare, R., Fenton, T., Degraw, C., & Twarog, F. (1989). Effects of theophylline on behavior and learning in children with asthma. *American Journal of Diseases in Children, 143,* 368–372.

Rasbury, W.C., Fennell, R.S., Eastman, B.G., Garin, E.H., & Richards, G. (1979). Cognitive performance of children with renal disease. *Psychological Reports, 45,* 231–239.

Reitan, R.M. (1964). Relationships between neurological and psychological variables and their implications for reading instructions. In H.A. Robinson (Ed.), *Meeting individual differences in reading.* Chicago: University of Chicago Press.

Reitan, R.M. (1966). Problems and prospects in studying the psychological correlates of brain lesions. *Cortex, 2,* 127–154.

Reitan, R.M. (1971). Trail making test results for normal and brain-damaged children. *Perceptual and Motor Skills, 33,* 575–581.

Resnick, L., di Margo-Veronese, F., Schupbach, J., Tourtellotte, W.W., Ho, D.D., Muller, F., Shapshak, P., Vogt, M., Groopman, J.E., Markham, P.D., & Gallo, R.C. (1985). Intra-blood-brain barrier synthesis of HTLV-III infection in brains of children and adults with AIDS encephalopathy. *Science, 227,* 177–182.

Richmond, J.B., & Waisman, H.A. (1955). Psychologic aspects of management of children with malignant diseases. *American Journal of Disease in Children, 89,* 42–47.

Rosen, T.S., & Johnson, H.L. (1982). Children of methadone-maintained mothers: Follow-up to 18 months of age. *Journal of Pediatrics, 101,* 192–196.

Rubinstein, A., Sicklick, M., Gupta, A., Bernstein, L., Klein, N., Rubinstein, E., Spigland, I., Fruchter, L., Litman, N., Lee, H., & Hollander, M. (1983). Acquired immunodeficiency with reversed T4/T8 ratios in infants born to promiscuous and drug-addicted mothers. *Journal of the American Medical Association, 249,* 2350–2356.

Ryan, C.M. (1988). Neurobehavioral disturbances associated with disorders of the pancreas. In R.E. Tarter, D.H. Van Thiel, & K.L. Edwards (Eds.), *Medical neuropsychology: The impact of disease on behavior* (pp. 121–158). New York: Plenum.

Ryan, C., & Morrow, L. (1987). Neuropsychological characteristics of children with diabetes. In M.L. Wolraich & D.K. Routh (Eds.), *Advances in developmental and behavioral pediatrics* (Vol. VIII). Greenwich, CT: JAI Press.

Ryan, C., & Morrow, L. (1987). Self-esteem in diabetic adolescents: Relationship between age at onset and gender. *Journal of Consulting and Clinical Psychology, 54,* 730–731.

Ryan, J.J., Souheaver, G.T., & DeWolfe, A.S. (1980). Intellectual deficit in chronic renal failure. A comparison with neurological and medical psychiatric patients. *The Journal of Nervous and Mental Disease, 168:12.* 763–767.

Savageau, J. A., Stanton, B., Jenkins, C. D., & Klein, M. D. (1982). Neuropsychological dysfunction following elective cardiac operation. *Journal of Thoracic and Cardiovascular Surgery, 84,* 585–594.

Scheiber, S.C., & Ziesat, H. (1976). Brief communication: Clinical and psychological test findings in cerebral dyspraxia associated with hemodialysis. *The Journal of Nervous and Mental Disease, 162,* 212–214.

Schlieper, A., Alcock, D., Beaudry, P., Feldman, W., & Leikin, L., (1991). Effect of therapeutic plasma concentrations of theophylline on behavior, cognitive processing, and affect in children with asthma. *The Journal of Pediatrics, 118,* 449–455.

Seligman, J. (1986). Babies born with AIDS. *Newsweek, 22,* 70–71.

Seuss, W.M., & Chai, H. (1981). Neuropsychological correlates of asthma: Brain damage or drug effects? *Journal of Consulting and Clinical Psychology, 49,* 135–136.

Seuss, W., Stump, N., Chai, H., & Kalisker, A. (1986). Mnemonic effects of asthma medication in children. *Journal of Asthma, 23,* 291–296.

Shaw, G.M., Harper, M.E., Hahn, B.H., Epstein, L.G., Gajdusek, D.C., Price, R.W., Navia, B.A., Petito, C.K., O'Hara, C.J., Groopman, J.E., Cho, E.S., Oleske, J.M., Wong-Staal, F., &

Gallo, R.C. (1985). HTLV-III infection in brains of children and adults with AIDS encephalopathy. *Science, 227,* 177–182.

Simone, J.V. (1972). Treatment of children with acute lymphocytic leukemia. *Advances in Pediatrics, 19,* 13–28.

Simone, J.V., Aur, R.J.A., Hustu, H.O., Verzosa, M.S., & Pinkel, D. (1978). Three to ten years after cessation of therapy in children with leukemia. *Cancer, 42,* 839–844.

Soifer, H. (1957). Aminophylline toxicity. *Journal of Pediatrics, 50,* 657.

Souheaver, G.T., Ryan, J.J., & DeWolfe, A.S. (1982). Neuropsychological pattern in uremia. *Journal of Clinical Psychology, 38,* 490–496.

Sparrow, S.S., Balla, D.A., & Cicchetti, D.V. (1984). *Vineland adaptive behavior scales.* Circle Pines, MN: American Guidance Service.

Springer, C., Goldenberg, B., Dov, I., & Godfrey, S. (1985). Clinical physiologic and psychologic comparison of treatment by cromolyn or theophylline in childhood asthma. *Journal of Allergy and Clinical Immunology, 76,* 64–69.

Teschan, P.E., Ginn, H.E., Bourne, J.R., & Ward, J.W. (1976). Neurobehavioral responses to "middle molecule" dialysis and transplantation. *Transactions, American Society for Artificial International Organs, 22,* 190–194.

Teschan, P.E., Ginn, H.E., Walker, P.J., Fristoe, M., & Ward, J.W. (1974). Quantified functions of the nervous system in uremic patients on maintenance dialysis. *Transactions, American Society for Artificial International Organs, 20,* 388–389.

Trieschmann, R.B., & Sand, P.L. (1971). WAIS and MMPI correlates of increasing renal failure in adult medical patients. *Psychological Reports,* 29, 1251–1262.

Ultmann, M.H., Belman, A.L., Ruff, H.A., Novick, B.E., Cone-Wesson, B., Cohen, H.J., & Rubinstein, A. (1985). Developmental abnormalities in infants and children with acquired immune deficiency syndrome (AIDS) and AIDS-related complex. *Developmental Medicine and Child Neurology, 27,* 563–571.

Ultmann, M.H., Diamond, G.W., Ruff, H.A., Belman, A.L., Novick, B.E., Rubinstein, A., & Cohen, H.J. (1987). Developmental abnormalities in children with acquired immunodeficiency syndrome (AIDS): A follow-up study. *International Journal of Neuroscience, 32,* 661–667.

Waechter, E. (1971). Children's awareness of a fatal illness. *American Journal of Nursing, 75,* 86–87.

Williams, J.M., & Davis, K.S. (1986). Central nervous system prophylactic treatment for childhood leukemia: Neuropsychological outcome studies. *Cancer Treatment Reviews, 13,* 113–127.

Winokur, M.Z., Czaczkes, J.W., & Kaplan De-Nour, A. (1973). Intelligence and adjustment to chronic hemodialysis. *Journal of Psychosomatic Research, 17,* 29–34.

Wirt, R.D., Lachar, D., Klinedinst, J.K., & Seat, P.D., (1984). *Multidimensional description of child personality: A manual for the Personality Inventory for Children* (rev. ed.). Los Angeles: Western Psychological Services.

Zeltzer, L., Kellerman, J., Ellenberg, L., Dash, J., & Rigler, D. (1980). Psychological effects of illness in adolescence. II. Impact of illness in adolescents: Crucial issues and coping styles. *Journal of Pediatrics, 97,* 132–138.

11

DISORDERS OF ATTENTION

ROGER LIGHT

ROBERT F. ASARNOW

ALLAN RIBBLER

PAUL SATZ

RICHARD LEWIS

ELIZABETH NEUMANN

The format of this chapter is unique in this book. Rather than focusing on a particular disease process that may cause a multitude of neuropsychological symptoms, this chapter concentrates on disorders of attention. Including a chapter focusing exclusively on attentional problems, regardless of etiology, is warranted due to the ubiquitous nature of these disorders after acquired brain injury (ABI). In the context of this chapter, ABI refers to central nervous system (CNS) dysfunction from known neurological substrates (e.g., head injury, brain tumors, stroke, etc.), as opposed to congenital disabilities or developmental disorders of unknown etiology (e.g., attention-deficit hyperactive disorder [ADHD], developmental disability, or learning disability). Many disorders seen by pediatric neuropsychologists have as a cardinal or secondary symptom, problems in some aspects of attentional functioning. Disorders of controversial etiology—such as schizophrenia, pervasive developmental disorder, conduct disorder, depression, ADHD, and learning disabilities—are reported to have attentional deficits as prominent symptoms (Asarnow & Sherman, 1984; Barkely, 1988a; Mash & Terdal, 1987). Attentional deficits have also been reported in children after most, if not all, disorders associated with identifiable CNS dysfunction. Specifically, attentional deficits have been reported after head injury (Levin, 1987; Ryan et al., 1995), treated leukemia (Brouwers et al., 1984), seizure disorders (Holdsworth & Whitmore, 1974), hypoxia/anoxia (O'-Dougherty et al., 1984), encephalitis (Koskiniemi et al., 1983), toxic/lead poisoning (Needleman et al., 1979, Hartman, 1988), tumors (Mulhern, Crisco, & Kun, 1983; Silverman & Patrick, 1990), Tourettes/tic disorders (Barkley, 1988b), and stroke (Aram, 1986).

An important, but under investigated, question is the extent to which there are qualitatively different disorders of attention associated with different types of acquired CNS insults or developmental problems. There exists considerable question about the core problem in children with attention-deficit hyperactive disorder (Douglas, 1983). The relationship between this controversial developmental disorder and acquired attentional deficits has been largely ignored. Although the study of ADHD may be the most investigated of all childhood disorders, this chapter will not review this extensive literature. The ADHD literature has been thoroughly reviewed elsewhere (see Barkley, 1988; Douglas, 1983). Rather, the goal of this chapter is to elucidate the characteristics of attentional deficits found after acquired brain injury, using at times the information gathered from investigations of ADHD, together with the types of interventions that have been attempted to circumvent disorders of attention. In addition, an outline of what remains to be done in the assessment and treatment of attentional disorders in brain-injured children is presented.

Despite the apparent ubiquity of attentional deficits in children after CNS disruption, there exists no accepted definition of what is meant by *attentional functioning* or *attentional deficits*. This confusion appears to arise from several sources. Part of the problem is inherent in the construct of attention itself. Numerous attempts have been offered to define *attention* but they typically are vague and of limited practical utility (see Barkley, 1988; Gronwall, 1987). A universally accepted definition has not yet emerged that could lead to successful quantification, assessment, and interventions for attentional deficits. A major source of these definitional problems emanates from the fact that attention is not a unitary entity (Posner & Petersen, 1990; Davies, Jones, & Taylor, 1984; Zubin, 1975; Piontrowski & Calfee, 1979; Barkley, 1988; Douglas, 1983). For successful measurement and intervention, attentional functioning must be considered from a multifactorial approach.

Traditionally, clinicians and researchers have poorly defined the construct of attention. With rare exception (see Mirsky, 1989, 1991; Posner, 1987; Barkley, 1988a), most pediatric psychologists are similarly vague in their treatment of this construct. The problem is exacerbated by the fact that attention is not a "pure" or basic function but rather a group of processes dependent on many other components. It is difficult to evaluate attention independent of other cognitive functions such as sensory/perceptual functioning, psychomotor speed, executive skills, and motivational factors. For example, performance on most timed response tasks that are purported to assess attentional functioning (e.g., choice reaction time, continuous performance, or Stoop Tests) is directly related to a child's motor and psychomotor speed (Gronwall, 1987). Therefore, if a brain injury affects either psychomotor speed (often a sign of brain dysfunction), motor functioning, or attentional processes, time-dependent performance will suffer.

The assessment of which skills (or subskills) are impaired is limited by available tests and research into what they actually measure. Assessment limitations hamper speculation about potential interventions, due to the confounding interrelationship of these vague constructs. These confounding influences can be partially adjusted for with the hierarchical assessment approach. For example, if the most basic measure available is used for the evaluation of individual skills (e.g., the finger-tapping test for motor speed), the confounding role of potential mediating factors can be evaluated.

Given these definitional ambiguities, the problems one confronts in the measurement of attentional processes is significant. Since the measurement of attentional processes is so problematic, the phase of formulation of diagnostic labels and attentional remediation techniques becomes extremely difficult. Evaluating the efficacy of these attentional interventions becomes nearly impossible. Because of the difficulties encountered at each level of this hierarchy, it is easy to understand why so few studies are reported that investigate attentional functioning. In particular, there exists a conspicuous lack of studies examining the efficacy of attentional interventions with the ABI child.

Another serious problem in the study of attentional functioning in children (including both assessment and intervention) is the assumption (often implicit) that these processes are independent of developmental stages. Undoubtedly, this is not the case. Children learn to sustain attention for longer periods as perceptual and cognitive abilities develop (Gibson & Rader, 1979). Simultaneously, children become better at dividing and focusing their attention as they mature. The qualitative and quantitative developmental changes in all aspects of attention functioning must be considered in any assessment or intervention into attentional deficits. For an excellent review of these issues, refer to Barkley (1988a).

This chapter will proceed as follows. First, a multifactorial model of attentional processes will be presented. This section will include brief discussions of the measures used to evaluate the various facets of attention as well as current issues and problems in its evaluation. The second section of the chapter will review issues in treatment of attentional problems in the ABI child. This section will include general methods of remediation of attentional deficits currently available, as well as a brief review of outcome studies. The final section will present the results of a project conducted by the authors. The Neuro-Cognitive Re-education Project (NCRP) is presented as an illustration of assessment and intervention with the attention deficits found in mild and severe head-injured children. This section illustrates the multifactorial approach to studying attention, as well as the problems encountered in attempting to remediate the attentional deficits found in children who have suffered a brain injury. This project is not presented as a model study in this field; rather, it is included to illustrate the issues one encounters in this type of research.

COMPONENTS OF ATTENTION

Traditional divisions of attention could lead to a comprehensive definition of *attention* as a flexible state of cognitive alertness directed toward stimuli over time and in the face of competing stimuli associated with a task-appropriate response. Such a definition considers the most popular subdivisions of attention (i.e., arousal/alertness, sustained attention, selective attention, shifting attention, and impulsivity or inhibition of responses). Unfortunately, such an ungainly definition attempts to make a unitary construct out of a process that is divisible, although the feasibility of assessment of these components separately via different tests or measures has yet to be firmly established. Some unique variance is found in different tests that purport to measure the same underlying subdivision of attention, indicating that many tests of attention do not measure exactly the same construct (Shum et al., 1990). This unique variance is also reportedly separate from that found in a standard neuropsychological battery (Grant et al., 1990; Mirsky et al., 1991). Nevertheless, the various components of attention as measured by currently available tests are not independent (Klee & Garfinkel, 1983; Bremer & Stern, 1976; Barkley, 1988a).

The correlations between some measures of the subcomponents of attention appear low such as between sustained and selective attention (Morey, 1969). In addition, differentiating different components of attention does allow one to begin to operationally define this elusive construct. Such definitions allow for the development of intervention methods that can be theoretically generated and that have the potential to be experimentally validated. In the sections that follow, we will briefly describe some of the more important components of attention.

Arousal/Alertness

The most basic attentional process is arousal level (Gronwall, 1987) and the related concept of alertness (Piontkowski & Calfee, 1979). Typically, arousal is clinically evaluated by observational measures (e.g., Pediatric Glasgow Coma Scale, Simpson & Reilly, 1982) or parent/teacher interviews or questionnaires (e.g., Achenbach & Edelbrock, 1983). Levels of alertness interpretation are typically made via judgments based on a clinician's perception of the child's involvement with an intervention or assessment. Many neuropsychological tests have behavioral observation sections that have an ordinal listing of arousal and alertness categories (e.g., alert, lethargic, obtunded, comatose) but the criteria are often poorly outlined and highly subjective.

The dramatic shift in arousal from sleep to conscious states are moderated by more subtle shifts in attention (Posner, 1986). Alertness level has been extensively studied in laboratory settings using EEG and a variety of reaction time tasks (see Posner, 1986). A distinction has made between phasic and tonic alertness (Posner, 1975). *Phasic alertness* refers to the rapid variations in attention, often under volitional control, after an abrupt warning signal. *Tonic alertness* refers to the slower changes in vigilance that occurs throughout the day or over an individuals developmental lifetime. Diurnal rhythms vary during the day with many autonomic changes. For example, body temperature (which varies systematically according to time of day) and performance on many tasks are inversely correlated (Posner, 1986). Clinical experience discourages many pediatric neuropsychologists from testing children in the early morning or late afternoon and evenings, to optimize their performance. It is likely that the poorer performance often observed at these times relates, at least in part, to tonic alertness factors. The time of day that a child is tested is rarely quantified as a relevant factor in clinical evaluations, although diurnal factors have a significant influence on attentional performance.

A consensus exists that most attentional measures in use in child neuropsychology today are flawed, of limited selectivity and sensitivity, and nonsystematic. This is clearly the case in the evaluation of alertness and arousal. Behavior rating scales and behavior checklists have been used clinically to evaluate many aspects of attentional functioning. The most commonly used of these are the Conners Rating Scales (Goyette, Conners, & Ulrich, 1978) and the Child Behavior Checklists (Achenbach & Edelbrock, 1983). Both of these measures include numerous questions about general level of arousal and alertness. A major weakness of these questionnaires, as they are currently used, is their reliance on global measures of attention. Although multiple aspects of attention are often evaluated, only a single summary score is derived.

Although more validation studies are clearly warranted, the use of such measures in neuropsychological assessment and interventions offers promise. One brief and easily completed checklist of attentional functioning (including alertness) that could be easily integrated into clinical and research neuropsychological evaluations is Edelbrock's Child Assessment Profile (see Barkley, 1988a).

Psychophysiological measurement of arousal and alertness has been traditionally ignored by neuropsychologists. The level of sensitivity to stimulation, as measured by physiologic indicators (e.g., electrodermal response, muscle tone, body temperature), is related to performance (Piontkowski & Calfee, 1979; Posner, 1986). The use of sophisticated measures of alertness and the precursors of cognition via auditory or visual event related potentials (e.g., contingent negative variation [CNV] or processing negativity) could offer much to a traditional neuropsychological assessment and intervention as a covariate or dependant measure of attentional functioning (Papanicolaou, 1987). Sophisticated methods of EEG brain mapping and use of autonomic measure to determine level of tonic and phasic alertness while performing cognitive tasks also may have potential applications, although many questions remain in this area.

Sustained Attention/Vigilance

Though often used interchangeably in the literature, the terms *sustained attention*, *concentration*, and *vigilance* have been used to describe a wide range of only partially overlapping aspects of attentional functioning. These concepts are generally used to describe the maintenance of cognitive performance over time. The formal definition of *sustained attention* is the ability to distinguish target stimuli from background noise when they are presented successively over time (Parasuraman & Davies, 1984). One everyday example of this task is the air traffic controller responding to airplanes on the screen and ignoring other signals (noise) for long periods (Green, Nuechterlein, & Gaier, 1992; Davies, Jones, & Taylor, 1984).

The classic measure of vigilance is the Continuous Performance Test (CPT) (Rosvold et al., 1956). This test has been used extensively with children, although primarily in the areas of ADHD and childhood overt schizophrenia (Grant et al., 1990; Asarnow & Sherman, 1984). Although evidence exists that the CPT measures unique variance not assessed by traditional neuropsychological tests in children (Grant et al., 1990), some investigators have suggested that the test may be less specific than previously thought (Trommer et al., 1988; Wolf et al., 1987, 1989). Nevertheless, the CPT is commonly used in research studies, and numerous computerized versions are now available for research and clinical purposes (Gordon, 1983; Klee & Garfinkel, 1983; Lindgren & Lyons, 1984; Asarnow & Betts, 1984; Cegalis & Bowlin [VIGIL], 1993; Greenberg & Crosby (TOVA), 1992; Sanford & Turner [IVA], 1993). Despite the increasing interest in the CPT, widespread use in clinical interventions and outcome studies has not occurred, although the test itself demonstrates some promise with brain-injured children (see Light et al., 1987). Problems with the various forms of the CPT include hardware incompatibility, monitor difference, and overall comparability of normative data.

Another computerized test that has been reported to measure a child's ability to sustain attention is described by Schiff and Knopf (1985). Simple and choice reaction time tasks have been mechanically and computer administered to children, and are believed by some to assess sustained attention (Van Zomeren, 1981; Gronwall & Wrightson, 1974). However, this test requires initiation, activation, and persistence, all components of attention. The self-paced Serial Reaction Test has also been used to assess these attentional functions (Sykes, Douglas, & Morgenstern, 1973). The Paced Auditory Serial Addition Test (PASAT) (Gronwall, 1977) has been modified for use with children (Children's Paced Auditory Serial Addition Test; CHIPASAT) (Johnson, Johnston, & Middleton, 1988). In adults, this test has been found to be a sensitive measure of sustained attention disrupted by even mild head injury, although replication in children has not, as of yet, been attempted. A computerized version of the PASAT, including modifications for use with children, has also recently become available (Paced Auditory Serial Attention Test (PASAT); Cegalis & Birdsall, 1993).

Common problems with the tests include the need for additional equipment that is typically not available in neuropsychological assessments (due to the expense and inconvenience). In addition, most of these tests have limited normative data available for most age groups and populations and some of the tests (such as the PASAT) are too complex for most children. These problems have contributed to their limited use in clinical interventions, with most of these potentially useful tests relegated to the laboratory.

In part, due to these problems, the typical pediatric neuropsychologist has assessed the attentional functions of sustained attention/vigilance using behavioral observation, rating scales, checklists (described previously), paper-and-pencil tests, or cognitive tasks that may require many skills other than attentional functioning. Among the most commonly used of these types of tests are cancellation or underlining tasks (Keough & Margolis, 1976; Rourke & Orr, 1977; Mesulam, 1985) and serial arithmetic tasks (Talland, 1965; Lezak, 1983). Sequential processing tasks (e.g., Trail Making Test A; Lezak, 1983), auditory perception/discrimination tests (e.g., Seashore Rhythm Test; Reitan & Wolfson, 1985), and some memory tests (e.g., Visual Continuous Recognition Memory Test [Hannay & Levin, 1988]; and Letter Span [Ruff, 1985]) have also been used clinically to assess aspects of sustained attention. Whether these measures primarily evaluate sustained attention is still to be determined (see Shum, McFarland, & Bain, 1990).

Direct observation of behavior for evaluating attentional decrements over time (sustained attention) typically has not been utilized in neuropsychological evaluation. Systematic behavioral observation of ADHD children has been reported, typically in school setting (Ross & Ross, 1982; Barkley et al., 1988). The use of behavioral assessment of attentional functioning of ABI children in naturalistic settings may be a beneficial addition to both assessment and intervention.

Given the current state of research in these areas, it would seem prudent to utilize a multivariate and hierarchical approach toward evaluating sustained attention for both clinical and intervention purposes. Such evaluations could include computer and traditional neuropsychological tests, direct observation, the use of behavioral rating scales or checklists, and a clear understanding of specific cognitive functions underlying each task presented so that cognitive deficits can be clearly dissociated.

Selective/Focused/Divided Attention

Selective attention is considered a critical factor in the functioning of children and adults, although the assessment of these attentional components are not as developed as those for sustained attention (Barkley, 1988a). The formal definition of *selective attention* is the distinguishing of target stimuli from noise when they are presented concurrently (Parasuraman & Davies, 1984). The everyday situation of attending to a single conversation at a cocktail party when internal and external distractions are always present illustrates selective attention and the related concept of freedom from distractibility (Green et al., 1990).

Divided attention is typically thought of as reflecting an active focusing on multiple tasks or task demands with simultaneous responses required (Sohlberg & Mateer, 1989), although multiple target stimuli can also be selectively attended to. Divided attention has been assessed in several dual task methodologies (see Kinsbourne & Hiscock, 1977; van Strien & Bouma, 1988). Although these techniques are not popular among pediatric neuropsychologists, a considerable amount of research has been performed on adults. Some investigators report that certain dual task measurements serve as an indicator of cerebral dominance, although other interpretations have been advanced (Simon & Sussman, 1987).

A test that measures a concept closely related to selective attention is the Span of Apprehension Test (SAT; Estes & Taylor, 1966). A child's span of apprehension refers to the amount of information a child can process from briefly presented visual stimuli (usually letters). The SAT can be administered with either a tachistoscope or a computer. Again, this test has been successfully used in the evaluation of ADHD (Denton & McIntyre, 1978) and in child psychopathology (Asarnow & Sherman, 1984), but only rarely in children with ABI (Light et al., 1987).

Other experimental and research measures of selective and focused attention that have yet to find their way into general clinical practice include dichotic listening (Loiselle et al., 1980; Hugdahl et al., 1990), digit-span distractibility (Oltmanns & Neale, 1975), Ruff 2 and 7 Selective Attention (Ruff, 1985), and the computer-administered Visual Selective Attention Tests (Miller, Satz et al., 1990). These tests were developed on adult population and their generalizability to children has yet to be established. Although some computerized measures of selective attention are commercially available (Gordon, 1983), their use in standard neuropsychological assessment and intervention is currently limited.

In clinical practice, selective/focused attention and freedom from distractibility are typically assessed using measures developed for other purposes, and only indirectly assess these factors. Behavioral observation during testing sessions is a popular technique for selective attention assessment, and in vivo observation, usually in school settings, is also occasionally performed (Barkley, 1988a). As with sustained attention assessment, behavioral rating scales and checklists include items related to selective attention. Several versions of the Stroop test (Stroop, 1935; MacLeod, 1991) have been described as assessing aspects of selective attention (Mclean et al., 1983). Another visual measure reported to assess aspects of selective attention is the Children's Embedded Figures Test (Witkin et al., 1971; Douglas & Peters, 1979). One of the few auditory selective attention tests used clinically is the Goldman-Fristoe-Woodcock Test of Auditory Discrimination (Woodcock, 1976). The Cognitive Assessment System (Das & Naglieri, 1987) includes subtests that are reported to assess both visual and auditory selective attention (Snyder, Das et al., 1990).

Other tests that are commonly included in a pediatric neuropsychological evaluation and have been suggested as tapping aspects of selective attention include the coding subtest of the WISC-R (Wechsler, 1974), the Symbol Digit Modalities test (Smith, 1973), the Knox Cubes (Bornstein, 1983), and the Trail Making Test (Reitan & Wolfson, 1985). It is important to recognize that what these measures actually assess is open to debate (see Shum et al., 1990). Clearly, these tasks are not pure measures of selective and focused attention. The "attentional triad" from the WISC-R is often referred to as a measure of freedom from distractibility. How well these measures assess freedom from distractibility, though, has been under some scrutiny (Kaufman, 1975; Steward & Moely, 1983; Ownby & Matthews, 1985; Schwartz et al., 1990) but the general consensus is that many factors other than attention are involved with performance on the "attentional triad."

In a departure from most attention theorists, Mirsky (1989), on the basis of factor analytic studies, suggested the area typically called selective/focused attention actually consists of focusing, executing, and perceptual motor speed. He found that the tests that load on this factor include letter cancellation, trail making, Stroop, and coding/symbol digit tests.

In general, the evaluation of selective, focused, and divided attention has consisted of indirect and poorly validated measurement in clinical practice. The practical utility of experimental computer-administered tests has yet to be established. Given our current knowledge, the most prudent course is to base evaluation strategies on multiple measures and to generate interventions based on developmental and hierarchical strategies.

Shifting or Alternating Attention

The ability to change the focus of attention from one stimulus or set of task demands to another is typically called *shifting attention*. This concept is related to the notions of alternating attention, cognitive flexibility, and resistance to perseveration. An everyday example of shifting attention is the secretary in a busy office who must type letters, answer phones, and respond to requests from others.

The assessment of the ability to shift attention has received limited attention in the experimental literature dealing with the evaluation of children. It is an area neglected in the assessment of ADHD children, and consequently very little research has been reported. This is particularly unfortunate in the assessment and treatment of the ABI child, since the tendency toward perseveration is one of the cardinal symptoms of organic dysfunction at least in adults (Levin & Eisenberg, 1987).

The assessment of the ability to shift attention in experimental research has typically focused on the "overlearned reversal" technique. In this paradigm many trials of a task are offered after which the contingencies are suddenly changed and the demands of the task are reversed or altered. Such procedures have been used with the CPT (Light et al., 1987; Schwartz et al., 1990), choice reaction time tasks (Gronwall, 1987), and the Selective Attention Test (Miller, Satz et al., 1990).

In clinical settings, evaluation of shifting/alternating attention typically consists of observation during testing of a child's performance when tasks are changed. Some standard adult neuropsychological tests are reported to measure aspects of shifting attention and have been used with at least older children. Such tests include the Trail Making Test B (Reitan & Wolfson, 1985) or the various versions of the Wisconsin Card Sorting Test (Grant & Berg, 1981; Heaton, 1981). Apparently, many factors besides the ability to shift attention are present in measures purported to evaluate this skill. Additional research on finding valid assessment measures of shifting attention is warranted. In addition, the need for further development of intervention strategies aimed at remediating problems in the ABI child with shifting or alternating of attention is essential.

Cognitive Style/Response Inhibition/Impulsivity

The ability to inhibit responding, although not always considered a subtype of attention, has been found to be particularly disrupted in ADHD children (Douglas,

1983) and can be regarded as a factor in the manner in that a child attends to his or her environment. The tendency to respond quickly or impulsively has also been called impulsive cognitive style (in contrast to a reflective style) (Kagan, 1966). Impulsivity is a frequently reported sequelae of brain injury in children (e.g., Lehr & Lantz, 1990), which underscores the importance of its evaluation and treatment in the ABI child.

Experimental research in impulsivity typically utilizes delayed response tasks (DRT) (Douglas, 1983) or direct reinforcement of latency (DRL) tasks (Barkley, 1988a). While some of these computer-administered delayed reaction time tests are available for clinical use with children (Gordon et al., 1983; Lindgren & Lyons, 1984) they have rarely been applied to the ABI child.

Again, in clinical practice, impulsivity is often assessed only via direct observation by the examiner or the rehabilitation specialist during sessions. The ability to delay responding and impulsivity are heavily weighted in behavior rating scales and checklist (e.g., Conner's Rating Scales; Achenback's Checklists) and their use in the assessment and intervention of ABI children with impulse control problems is appropriate. As noted earlier, only global measures of attention are available from these questionnaires and direct measures of impulsivity are not available with standard administration.

The most widely used measure of impulsivity is the Matching Familiar Figures Test (MFF; Kagan et al., 1964). While many studies have been published reporting deficits in the ADHD child and the sensitivity of the MFF in assessing medication effects in ADHD children (e.g., Quay & Brown, 1980), this test has not found its way into standard clinical practice with the ABI child.

Closely related to the construct of impulsivity is the notion of inhibiting responses. Although few researchers have addressed this issue, Mesulam (1985) discussed this notion within the paradigm introduced by Luria. Inability to select the appropriate response may result in an impulsive erroneous response. Inhibition of inaccurate responses can be assessed using Luria's Go-NoGo task in the motor modality, Stroop interference condition ofr modalities. The validation of measures of impulsivity and inhibition of inappropriate responses in intervention and outcome studies to remediate the negative adaptive effects in the ABI child is likely to be a useful direction to proceed. Previous suggestions of utilization of multiple validated measures are once again appropriate in the area of impulsivity.

TREATMENT STRATEGIES FOR THE REMEDIATION OF DEFICITS OF ATTENTION

As noted earlier, the majority of intervention studies in the treatment of disorder of attention emerges from the field of ADHD research. Many of the techniques used in the treatment of attentional deficits in ADHD children hold promise in the remediation of attentional deficits in the ABI child, but validation studies on their efficacy are limited. Very few outcome studies have been performed that have sought to investigate the potential remediation strategies that are available in attacking the attention-deficits observed in the ABI child. Many general strategies and some specific programs exist that hold promise in the treatment of attentional disorders in the ABI child. Some are in use in clinical and educational settings, but studies of their efficacy are rare.

The treatments currently available for ADHD children use one of three basic approaches: (1) medical interventions (e.g., Wender, 1987), (2) behavioral modification (e.g., Becker, 1972), and (3) cognitive behavioral (e.g., Douglas, Parry et al., 1976; Cameron & Robinson, 1980). Examples of each of these interventions will be described separately here. In addition, a set of interventions that include the previously mentioned techniques have emerged from rehabilitation settings and will also be discussed.

These interventions often include training directed not only toward the child but also teachers (Piontkowski & Calfee, 1979; Cobb & Hops, 1973) and parents (Lavin, 1989). Many of these interventions developed for the ADHD child have been attempted clinically with the ABI child, although not systematically. In addition, outcome studies of the efficacy of these interventions with the ABI child are rare.

Current interventions in use with the ABI survivor for remediation of attentional deficits are based on medical interventions, behavioral treatments, cognitive behavioral interventions, or brain-injury rehabilitation principles. Each of these intervention approaches will be discussed separately, although in clinical practice more than one type of interventions may be used simultaneously.

Medical Interventions

The efficacy of medical interventions in the treatment of attentional deficits in the ABI child has been relatively unresearched. Although the treatment of the ADHD child with stimulant medication has widespread support (Wender, 1987; Weingartner, Langer et al., 1980), such treatment, even in that population, is not without its problems and detractors (e.g., Lavin, 1989; Sprague & Sleator, 1977). Improvement on certain attentional measure and in selected academic tasks is observed (Douglas, 1983), but investigation of the long-term outcomes reveal few differences between those on medications and those receiving no treatment (Weiss & Hechtman, 1993). In addition, the generalizability of treatment has been questioned (Rumain, 1988) and the potential side effects are significant (*Physicians' Desk Reference*, 1995; Lavin, 1989).

Given the potential problems with stimulant treatment in the ADHD child, their use in the ABI (acquired brain injury) patient should be approached with caution. Although limited trials have been reported on the use of stimulants in brain-injured adults (e.g., Lipper & Tuchman, 1976), the use of stimulants with the ABI child has not been well researched. Their use in both child and adult brain-injured patients is currently based only on clinical judgment (Glenn, 1986; Gualtieri & Evans, 1988). Although stimulants such as Amantadine may have direct effects on increasing or improving modulation of arousal and may have application in emergence from coma, without controlled stimulant drug trials on brain-injured children the use of stimulant medications should be approached judiciously. Because of the increased risk of seizures in an individual with brain injury, the administration of medication that can induce or exacerbate a seizure disorder, such as stimulants (*Physicians' Desk Reference*, 1995), should be handled carefully. The effects of many medications currently used with ABI patients (such as barbiturates, benzodiazepines, antihistamines, neuroleptics, anticonvulsant, and antidepressants) can have adverse effects on cognition and learning as well as on attentional functioning (Cope, 1986; Ludwig, 1989). Therefore, the use of any medication with a survivor of brain injury can further interfere with their functioning and should be used with caution.

In the child with an acquired brain injury, regardless of etiology or treatment, the likelihood of seizure activity increases with severity of injury (Feeney & Walker, 1979). Many types of seizures (e.g., petit mal, partial complex) or other abnormal brain wave patterns can interfere with a child's attentional functioning. Aarts, Binnie, and colleagues (1984) reported cases in which generalized epileptiform EEG discharges, that had no overt clinical symptoms, were found to lead to transitory cognitive impairment with particular disruption during encoding of information. The blank stare associated with petit mal seizures not only appears to others as inattentiveness but will also limit the amount of information processed and properly encoded. Therefore, the treatment of these abnormal brain wave patterns and the clinical manifestation of seizure and subthreshold seizure patterns with anticonvulsant medication can result in improvement in attentional functioning in those with epileptiform activity. The use of carbamazepine is becoming increasingly preferred as an anticonvulsant because of its perceived minimal effect on cognition (Cope, 1986). Some evidence exists that it may even improve arousal and alertness in some cases (Evans & Gualtieri, 1985). The use of anticonvulsants when abnormal electrical activity is not present, though, is debatable.

Behavioral Modification

Behavioral interventions for problems in attention have been utilized extensively in both children (e.g., Becker, 1972) and adults (e.g., Wood, 1987). Behavioral interventions include operant conditioning, contingency management, and environmental manipulations. Basic operant approaches for improving attention have been used frequently in classroom settings for many types of children. One of the first documented operant interventions to improve attending time in distractible children was reported by Patterson (1965). In this study, Patterson used visual cues and candy as reinforcers in increasing the attending time of a distractible child. The use of visual, verbal, or physical cues and reinforcement to increase attentional behaviors has been reported by many educational researchers with many types of children. One of the common targets of these interventions is the learning disabled (LD) child (Quay et al., 1967; Walker & Buckley, 1968; Coleman, 1970; Willis & Crowder, 1972; Glynn, Thomas, & Shee, 1973; Argulewicz,

1982). Due to many factors, including limited educational placement options and incomplete school screening of medical history, a significant proportion of those labeled as LD may have, in fact, acquired a brain injury that contributed to their disability. (See Chapter 3 for more details on educational placement option for the ABI child.)

The use of token economies and operant shaping has also been reported as effective in increasing attentional behaviors in distractible children (Bushell et al., 1968; McKenzie et al., 1968; Packard, 1970; Wagner & Guyer, 1971; Novy et al., 1973). Modeling appropriate attending behaviors and training attentional skills has also been reported in LD children in the classroom setting (Argulewicz, 1982; McCarney, 1989). For further information on behavioral interventions in the classroom, the reader may refer to the many instructional manuals that are available (e.g., McCarney, 1989; Piontkowski & Calfee, 1979).

hemi-inattention Although hemi-inattention or neglect is rare in children and often rapidly resolved (Barkley, 1988a), the persistence of such deficits in a child would severely limit their educational and functional performance. Behavioral methods have been successful in improving visual field scanning in adults (Diller & Weinberg, 1977); however, there is a lack of data reported for the treatment of hemi-inattention in children.

Another type of behavioral intervention includes manipulating the child's environment to make it more conducive to attending behavior. Modification of the learning environment that have been reported include a more structured school program. Other interventions include reduced environmental stimuli, reduced space, and the use of novel teaching materials that were considered motivating and interesting (Cruickshank et al., 1961; Berlyne, 1960). Introduction of a variety of tasks and the providing of feedback has also been attempted to improve classroom alertness (Keele, 1973). The manipulation of seating assignments has been reported to improve attentional behaviors (Schwebel & Cherlin, 1972).

In general, behavioral interventions have been shown to improve attending behavior in classroom settings (i.e., in the settings of training or intervention), although generalization of these improvements to academic performance has not been established (Argulewicz, 1982). In addition, the efficacy of behavioral intervention on improving attentional functioning with ABI children has not been confirmed. Research into the use of these techniques in the ABI survivor certainly warrants further study, although the results from their use in other populations (e.g., ADHD and LD children) do not suggest that these approaches alone will eliminate the attentional deficits observed.

Cognitive-Behavioral Interventions

The majority of interventions that have been attempted to improve attentional functioning can be labeled as *cognitive-behavioral modification (CBM)*. The developmental notions of verbal control of motor behavior were outlined by Vygostsky (1962) and Luria (1961, 1982). The methods of Luria have been frequently utilized and extended in the remediation of attentional problems (e.g., Palkes,

Stewart, & Kahana, 1968; Bender, 1976) (see Pressley et al., 1983, for a review). The original self-instructional techniques, using self-talk and self-monitoring strategies, were developed to train impulsive children to better control themselves (Meichenbaum & Goodman, 1971). CBM interventions differ from operant approaches in that they utilize internal processes of cognition and language to alter behavior and function.

The techniques of self-instruction for improving attentional functioning have been attempted with many types of preschool and school children with attention and impulse control problems (e.g., Meichenbaum, 1974; Genshaft & Hirt, 1979; Finch et al., 1975; Douglas et al., 1976; Arnold & Forehand, 1978; Bornstein & Quevillon, 1976; Parrish & Erickson, 1981). These techniques have also been reported successful in reducing impulsive behavior in older children (Snyder & White, 1979). Kendall and associates have investigated cognitive-behavioral interventions intensively with children with impulsivity and attentional deficits (Kendall & Braswell, 1985; Kendall, 1982; Kendall & Finch, 1979; Kendall & Zupan, 1981). In particular, these researchers have investigated the pertinent components and necessary elements of successful CBM interventions with impulsive children. While positive outcome results are reported by many of these researchers, the dependent measures have typically included standardized tests (e.g., MFF), rather than functional outcome measures. Criticisms of self-instructional interventions for improving attentional performance include questions about the generalization of improvements to academic performance (e.g., Albert, 1970). Few systematic outcome studies have been performed utilizing self-instructional interventions exclusively with ABI children.

An intervention that may be considered either medical or cognitive behavioral is biofeedback or relaxation training. A study by Omizo and Michael (1982) investigated the effects of biofeedback-induced relaxation training on ADHD children. Increased attention to task and reduced impulsivity in the experimental group was reported. The use of relaxation procedures to improve attentional functioning in ABI children, particularly in those displaying signs of anxiety, is an innovative concept that merits investigation.

Although the interventions of Feuerstein (1980) were not developed to address attentional functioning directly, they include teaching the individual to remain on task and monitor attentional processes. The notion of a "mediated learning experience," the basis of Feuerstein's Instrumental Enrichment (IE) cognitive intervention, is based on using a trainer to act as the subject's attentional mechanism. The mediator is an experienced person who interposes himself or herself between the child and the external stimuli and interprets appropriately and selectively by consciously framing, selecting, focusing, and sequencing objects or events (Feuerstein et al., 1981). Systematic implementation of the instrumental enrichment procedures with the ABI child may advance our understanding of the factors that result in improved attentional functioning, although IE is very labor intensive and requires individual or small-group sessions.

Given the results from ADHD outcome studies, many of these CBM approaches to intervention may be successful methods of improving attentional functioning in the ABI child within a multimodal framework. Nevertheless, considerable work remains to be done. Efficacy studies are necessary to determine whether the interventions are helpful. Comparisons between the various cognitive-behavioral interventions are also essential to determine which approaches to intervention work with each type of deficit in the different subtypes of brain-injured children.

Brain Injury Rehabilitation Intervention

The majority of rehabilitation centers currently utilize some combination of the interventions previously discussed. Interventions specifically developed for use with brain-injury survivors with attentional deficits are described here. These interventions are addressed separately to emphasize that they have been specifically, if not systematically, employed with brain-injury survivors. Rehabilitation of the adult brain-injury survivor has expanded tremendously in the past 10 years. According to the National Head Injured Foundation (NHIF), there are more than 600 brain-injury rehabilitation facilities in the United States. Few of these programs address systematically the remediation of attentional problems directly in ABI children. Those that do typically base their interventions on the principles of overlearning or overpractice using tasks that have attentional demands. The use of overlearning with the brain-injured has several drawbacks, including failing to capitalize on the development of compensation strategies (see discussion section of this chapter).

In the adult literature, there has been, in recent years, some investigation into the efficacy of attentional interventions with brain-injury survivors (Ponsford & Kinsella, 1988; Ben-Yishay, Diller, & Rattok, 1978; Malec et al., 1984; Sohlberg & Mateer, 1987; Wood, 1986, 1987). However, there have been no such systematic investigations on the efficacy of attentional interventions with ABI children.

One approach used in some rehabilitation setting is Attention Process Training (APT) developed by Sohlberg and Mateer (1987, 1989). Although this program was developed for adult brain injury survivors, APT has been used clinically with children in a few settings. One particular advantage of APT is the theoretical basis on which it was developed. APT considers the subcategories of attention arranged in a hierarchical fashion. At the most basic level of this hierarchy is focused attention, followed by sustained, selective, alternating, and divided attention. Programs are available for improving skills in each of these areas.

While APT has not been formally validated for use with children (Mateer, personal communication), it is now being used on a trial basis in certain school districts. It is Mateer's impression that the procedure can be used with children as young as age 7. Williams (1989) used APT with a group of six children (aged 8 to 11) having attentional and learning deficits. Results of this study showed improvement in attentional processes, although the degree of generalization to academic improvement was less clear. The results also showed that age related to treatment efficacy. Campbell (1990) reported success using the APT program with a 15-year-old adolescent.

A major drawback of the APT program for children is the reliance on formulations derived from treating adults. Several of the APT modules assume skills are present that would have evolved in the adult survivor but would be in various stages of development in children. Children may not have the educational and cognitive prerequisites necessary for benefiting fully from all APT modules. For example, several of the modules assume a working knowledge of arithmetic functions, while others require a knowledge of the months in the year, which may not be found in the ABI child. Further validation studies are necessary regarding the use of APT in the ABI child. It may have limited use with younger children, but the program may be beneficial with older children and adolescents. An approach using the hierarchical formulation of APT combined with a developmental perspective, would be a major contribution to the remediation of pediatric attentional deficits.

A general cognitive rehabilitation program outlined in Haarbauer-Krupa and asociates (1985) includes a section for improving selective attention and comprehension. Although limited in scope, the interventions presented represent those currently performed in many rehabilitation facilities. This work is presented as a chapter in a book edited by Ylvisaker (1985) and remains one of the few available concerning rehabilitation issues for the brain-injured child.

Many rehabilitation settings utilize computer programs for improving attention, often to the exclusion of other types of interventions. Many types of programs are available in both the public domain and from proprietary sources. The programs of Gianutsos and Klitzner (1981) have found considerable use in rehabilitation settings for attentional remediation with children and adults (e.g., REACT). Other sources of computer-based software concerned with attentional remediation are available from Soft Tools (Bracy, 1983–93), BrainTrain (Sanford et al., 1985–93) and CoolSpring Software (Williams, 1992). IBM has also developed cognitive rehabilitation software (THINKable/2, 1993; THINKable/DOS 1994). THINKable is a combination of hardware and software focusing on cognitive remediation with an emphasis on attention and memory skills. For a review of the use of microcomputers in cognitive retraining, refer to Bradley and associates (1993).

As with most interventions in rehabilitation settings, these computer programs rely on massed and spaced practice and overlearning as the primary mechanism of improving attentional performance. The advent of computer programs that encourages a child to use individual cognitive strength areas and suggests compensation methods for improving attentional functioning would reflect significant progress.

THE NEURO-COGNITIVE RE-EDUCATION PROJECT (NCRP)

The NCRP was supported by the Handicapped Children Early Education Program (HCEEP) through the National Institute on Disability and Rehabilitation Research (NIDRR) (formally the National Institute of Handicapped Research). The project sought to investigate, in mildly and severely head-injured children (ages 4 to 10), the efficacy of a neuropsychologically and educationally based intervention program. Interventions were developed in four categories (problem solving/executive, memory, behavioral, and attentional functioning). This individualized home and school tutoring program was developed with the goal of improving the cognitive prerequisites for learning, as opposed to providing domain- and subject-specific education. Instructional approaches were interactive and modeled after the style used by Wilson and colleagues (1982). Examples of the type of attentional interventions included in the training program are included in the Appendix at the end of this chapter. For more details on the general evaluation and intervention program, refer to Light and associates (1987); Asarnow and associates (1991); and Lewis and associates (submitted for publication).

The NCRP attentional components are presented to illustrate the issues involved in a multifactorial approach to the assessment and remediation of attentional deficits in the ABI child. Brevity and economy necessitated including only a subset of the attentional measures described previously. The NCRP attentional measures consisted of the Child Behavior Checklist (CBCL; Achenbach & Edelbrock, 1983) and computerized versions of the Continuous Performance Test (CPT; Asarnow & Betts, 1984) and the Span of Apprehension Test (SAT; Asarnow & Betts, 1984). The attentional factor from the CBCL samples a child's caregiver's perception of the child's arousal, sustained, and selective attention processes and derives a single summary score for attentional functioning. The CPT was designed to assess sustained attentional abilities using a signal detection model. The CPT allows for the evaluation of a sensitivity measure (d'5), sensitivity changes over time, and response criterion (Beta). This CPT version also included an over-learned reversal condition that allowed the assessment of the child's ability to shift attention. The SAT measures the span of perception, a concept similar to but not identical to selective attention (see Selective Attention section of this chapter).

There were 22 children included in the attentional evaluation portion of the NCRP. Of these, 10 were classified as mild to moderately head-injured (post-traumatic amnesia (PTA) of less than 5 hours) and 12 were classified as severely head injured (PTA greater than 7 days). The children in the attentional assessment group included most but not all of the same patients entered into the intervention study. Not all children received the computerized neuropsychological tests and not all those assessed were included in the tutoring project. The intervention group included 15 head-injured children and the nonintervention control group included 6 head-injured children.

Patients were entered into the project if they met the following inclusionary criteria: (1) they were between 4 years and 10 years 11 months at the time of initial testing; (2) they had experienced a medically documented closed-head injury; (3) PTA had abated at least one year before testing (to minimize the effects of spontaneous recovery); (4) at the time of testing, the child's general level of cognitive functioning was at least 30 months (as measured by the Kaufman Assessment Battery for Children, Kaufman & Kaufman, 1983); (5) adequate use of at least one hand; and (6) no gross defects in vision or hearing. Children with any history of CNS insult or disease, developmental delay, or behavior problems prior to the head injury were excluded from the study.

The results from the initial attentional testing section of the NCRP indicated that severely head-injured children had deficits in both sustained and selective attention. Their deficits were not confined to attentional functioning, since deficits were also seen in memory (Lewis et al., submitted for publication) and in adaptive functioning (Asarnow et al., 1991). The severely head-injured children performed significantly worse than the mild head-injured children and the control group in CPT sensitivity and in SAT accuracy. However, in some target locations of the SAT (in the area of the fixation point), the severe patients performed within normal limits. It is tempting to hypothesize that the severely head-injured children in this study had retained the ability to focus visually and execute this task but were impaired in their ability to disengage and move their visual attention. Alternatively, their speed of disengaging and shifting attention may have been impaired by the severity of their injuries.

The mild head-injured patients were not significantly different from the control group in response sensitivity (d'5) on the CPT or in accuracy on the SAT. A tendency for a reduced response criteria was found, with a decreased beta (B) relative to the control and severely head-injured groups, but this trend did not reach statistical significance. Interestingly, those mild head-injured children who had the lowest beta scores were also the children who had excess rates of behavioral problems (Asarnow et al., 1991). Replication of this study with a larger longitudinal cohort sample has recently been completed, with results forthcoming. Very preliminary results are available in Zaucha and associates (1993) and Light and associates (1993). The tendency for a decreased response threshold in some mildly head-injured children, if confirmed, could offer a potential explanation for the subjective complaints (e.g., increased behavioral problems and academic difficulties) reported by some researchers and clinicians after even relatively mild head trauma (Asarnow et al., 1991; Lundvar & Nestvold, 1985; Klonnof et al., 1977; Horowitz et al., 1983).

The results of the CBCL data revealed that both the mild and severely head-injured groups had similarly excessive rates of behavioral problems, although these problems were not confined to the attentional domain.

The effects of the intervention project on attentional functioning, as measured by the neuropsychological tests were limited (see Light et al., 1987). Significant differences between pre- and posttesting were not found on any of the neuropsychological measures of attention in the intervention group in comparison to the control group. However, significant improvements were noted in adaptive functioning, as measured by the Vineland Adaptive Behavior Scale (Sparrow, Bolla, & Cicchetti, 1984). In particular, significant improvements in the adaptive behavior composite score and the communication domain were found. One explanation for the observed results is that while functional improvement after cognitive remediation may be present, neuropsychological tests may not be the best measures of outcome. Such instruments are typically developed to remain stable over time (i.e., have high test-retest reliability) and are developed to assess underlying CNS functioning that may not be expected to change from such cognitive interventions. Consequently, such tests may be resistant to state-related changes and to new learning. Therefore, the exclusive use of such tests in outcome research should be discouraged. The need for multiple outcome measures, with a particular emphasis on using functionally based measures and observations, is illustrated by this study.

It is important to note that the intervention method used in the NCRP included more than just attentional interventions. Individualized components were also included that addressed executive functioning, memory skills, and behavioral functioning. Therefore, it cannot be concluded that the attentional component was, in itself, associated with the observed improvement in adaptive functioning. In addition, the sample size of the groups was extremely small and the results require replication. The assessment of differing subcomponents of cognitive interventions, as well as the comparison of the efficacy of different attentional interventions on the ABI child, would be a logical direction for further research. Such controlled outcome studies would be a major contribution to our knowledge about remediation of attentional deficits found in the brain-injured child. As noted by Ryan and colleagues (Chapter 6 of this book), the focus of evaluation and intervention on functional performance, considering education and home needs, of the head-injured child is critical.

DISCUSSION

Much clinical and basic research is needed in the area of evaluation and remediation of attentional deficits after acquired brain-injury in children. A review of the assessment literature supports the need to treat attentional functioning as a multifactorial process. The need for clear, objective, and standardized definitions of what is meant by the various divisions of attention is evident. Available literature indicates that, although attention is a difficult construct to define, a general consensus has emerged that attentional processes can be disrupted by many different types of acquired brain injury. Furthermore, the potential benefits from thorough and competent evaluation of attentional processes in these populations is obvious.

The subjective and poorly validated measures in current use should be replaced by more completely investigated assessment procedures. Standard clinical and research neuropsychological protocols should include multiple objective and subjective measures that differentially assess the various factors of attention. These measures should include computer-administered tests, as well as tasks that more closely parallel functional performance (e.g., tasks that approximate a school classroom setting). In addition, the use of parent- or teacher-completed questionnaires could be expanded and their concurrent and predictive validity should be investigated. One of the major drawbacks of available questionnaires and behavioral checklists for the evaluation of attentional functioning is their reliance on a single summary score of attention. As noted previously, treating attention as a unitary process has severe limitations. The derivation of subscales assessing the various components of attention could lead to major progress. Including direct in vivo behavioral observation in both research and clinical assessment could also yield significant and clinically relevant information.

Standard neuropsychological tests of attention can be improved considerably. How well the currently available tests assess the various attentional factors is, at present, poorly understood. Further validation of existing tests, with an emphasis on the development of reliable normative data in children, is also necessary. A critical need exists for new instruments that measure more directly the subtypes of attention, such as sustained and selective attention. The use of a hierarchical approach to neuropsychological evaluation could also help unconfound the complex interacting factors in attentional processes. Considerable potential also exists in the concurrent assessment of psychophysiological (e.g., electrodermal responsivity) and neurodiagnositic processes (e.g., brain mapping) in the evaluation of attentional functioning.

Because of the many needs in the assessment of attentional functioning, it is not surprising that current intervention procedures are similarly limited. Intervention methods are not well validated on either children or adults. Many of those in use with ABI children have been developed for the adult brain-injury survivor. The failure to consider the developmental differences between attentional processes in children and adults severely limits the utility of such procedures. Many interventions described in this chapter hold promise for significantly improving the functioning in many ABI children; however systematic treatment outcome studies are still unavailable. This is true not only in the area of attentional functioning but also in pediatric cognitive rehabilitation in general (Lehr et al., 1990; Light et al., 1987). Some of the procedures holding promise with ABI children are Attention Process Training, cognitive behavioral interventions, and mediated learning interventions. None of these interventions, however, has been systematically validated with this population. Without such data, the prudent course for the clinician is to provide multiple types of intervention. The use of medical, behavioral, cognitive-behavioral, and rehabilitation techniques may all be warranted until the successful components of these interventions are established. The introduction of different types of interventions sequentially, using single subject design and multiple baseline methods, is appropriate both practically and from a research design standpoint.

The linking of the results of a neuropsychological evaluation to the specific interventions is of critical importance. Such linkage could circumvent the tendency, so prevalent currently in rehabilitation, to use only overlearning for the amelioration of attentional problems. The typical intervention now in use requires the child to practice a task involving some attentional skill repeatedly. The use of such overlearning techniques assumes that the brain is like a "muscle" and will get "stronger" from practice. This is the basis of most educational approaches and may work well with the cognitively intact child but may be less efficient with the brain-injured child. When an area of the brain that subserves a particular function is damaged, teaching to that area repeatedly makes less sense than utilizing compensation strategies that capitalize on the intact portions of the brain. The use of neuropsychological data to determine the relative strength areas in a child could lead to interventions that may be more successful for that individual. For example, if a child has strengths in verbal mediation and language-based skills and deficits in visuo-spatial functioning, the use of language based interventions, such as the self-instructional techniques, are more logical than the visuo-spatial techniques involved with many computer-based interventions.

In addition, the use of family, educational, and more functional-based interventions must be incorporated into the recovery of the ABI child. As discussed in Chapter 6, the critical learning environment for a child is in the home and in school. The involvement of parents and teachers in the implementation of interventions for improving attentional functioning can only help increase the probability of generalized progress.

The critical step for advancing our understanding of attentional deficit remediation will be the investigation of which intervention approaches are best with what type of attentional problems in different groups of brain-injured children. In addition, further investigation of subtypes of attentional problems in ABI children is also necessary. The determination of whether CNS injuries from different etiologies have different symptom manifestations and respond differentially to interventions is still unknown. The assessment of whether different types of intervention are differentially effective at different ages also remains to be performed.

As with most of the disorders discussed in this book, many questions remain to be answered. There are factors that make the disorders of attention somewhat more difficult to investigate. Not the least of these are conceptual and definitional problems. A concerted effort will be required by clinicians, educators, and researchers to standardize the concepts of attentional functioning. Only then will significant advancement be possible toward the development of procedures for the amelioration of the attentional deficits that are found after brain-injury in children.

APPENDIX: SAMPLE ATTENTIONAL TASKS
NEURO-COGNITIVE RE-EDUCATION PROJECT

Task 1: Clapping

Focus on: Sustained and Shifting Auditory Attention
For problems remaining on task, shifting tasks when asked, and following verbal directions.
Skills needed: Child can hear and understand words.
                Child can repeat words when asked.
Objective: Child will learn to attend to auditory stimuli by counting or tapping to keep on task. In addition, child will learn to change tasks as required. Child will learn to generalize using these skills into the classroom.
Materials: Auditory Association Sheets (such as that on page 37 of Wilson and colleagues, 1983) consisting of words from the vocabulary of the child with randomly interspersed target words (i.e., *spoon*), as well as other words to do with the category from which the target word belongs (e.g., *eating [plate, fork, spoon, etc.]*). These

words should be arranged in four columns of 15 to 20 words each. If utilizing a modification of the following lesson (as described under Modifications), additional items may be needed (e.g., plastic spoons, doll coat, and other toys).

Instructional Plan

TEACHER: "I'd like us to play a new game today. This is a very special listening game. I will say some words and I want you to listen to them. When I say a special word, I would like you to clap your hands. For example, if our special word was (say the child's name), then every time I say your name, you clap your hands. Let's try it."

Teacher (T) and child (C) have a practice session. T says a number of names interspersing C's name and waits for C to clap on name. Once C understands the task, then T can continue with the Auditory Association Sheets. If C is having a difficult time understanding the directions, see Modifications.

T: "Great. Now let's try this game with some other words. And remember, you need to listen really well to make sure to clap on our very special word."

T begins with the Auditory Association Sheet (Target word is *spoon*).

T: "Our special word that I want you to listen for and clap on is *spoon*. Can you repeat that for me?"

C: "Spoon."

T: "Good. Now let me say that word and you clap on it right after I say it."

T says word spoon. C claps on word.

T: "Excellent. Now if I said the words *night, hello, chair,* and *sandwich,* would you clap?"

C: "No."

T: "That's right. Now tell me, which word will you clap on?"

C: "Spoon."

T: "Great. Let's get started. Every time you clap, I will make a mark on my paper so that I know when you clapped."

T reads words off the first column on the Auditory Association Sheet. Pace is around one word every 3 to 5 seconds to begin with (unless this seems very slow to C). T records each time C claps. If C is performing well and understanding the instructions, then T continues with the second list, again recording each time C claps. After this, T indicates to C when C clapped and if it was only on the word spoon, if there were errors.

A reasonable criteria may be 80% correct. Therefore, if C clapped 80% correctly, then T and C may continue on to the last two columns on the sheet. (T may want to set up different criteria according to C's abilities, strengths, weaknesses, and motivations.) If C had more than 20% errors, then the first two columns may need to be repeated either with additional cues from T to C or just to reinforce this task and listening skill.

If/when continuing onto the last two columns on the sheet, T says:

T: "Now that you have listened to my words so well, and clapped on the word *spoon*, I think it's time for us to do another listening game. This time, I will say another group of words, but I don't, *do not*, want you to clap on the word *spoon*, even if I say it. I want you to clap on every word that has something to do with eating, except for the word *spoon*. Let's think of some words that have to do with eating. How about *knife*? "

T and C together discuss the different words that have to do with eating.

T: "Okay, now remember, I've changed the rules of the game on you. Instead of clapping on *spoon*, like you did before, this time you will clap on all the words I say that have something to do with eating—except for which word?"

C: "Spoon."

T: "Great. Here we go."

T begins reading the list of words in column 3, and records C's claps. If C is meeting criteria (80% correct or whatever T has determined is appropriate for C), then T continues onto column 4. If C is not meeting criteria then perhaps the rules need to be explained again, C needs more cues, or more repetition of the exercise.

At the conclusion of the task, T and C summarize what was done regarding listening, clapping, etc. and how to generalize this listening behavior to classroom (see Generalizations).

Modifications

1. If C is having a difficult time understanding the rules of the game, then T can modify the words and use lists of names interspersing C's name into the list. C's task is to clap each time her or his own name is mentioned. For some children, this modification is much simpler and successful. After T and C have done the task several times with names (having C clap on his or her own name), then the second component can be introduced, where C claps on all the other names, not on her or his own name. When C is comfortable and confident with this part of the task, then T can introduce the Spoon worksheet.

2. T can introduce variations to clapping, depending on C's ability level. If C needs concrete objects to hold, then T may bring plastic spoons for the Spoon sheet and have C drop a spoon each time C hears the word *spoon*. Then, C could drop a plastic utensil, except for spoon, on the third- and fourth-column word lists (the shifting attention section). For other Association Sheets, T and C could decide what C will use to drop, or hide, or collect, etc. After C is competent with this task using manipulatives, then T could introduce this task with clapping.

3. Another variation of this task is to have C count the number of times a word is said. This is dependent, of course, on C's ability to count. C could tap with fingers every time a word was said and then total the amount. Feedback on accuracy could be shared with C.

4. If C is having difficulty shifting attention on the last two columns, a variation can be introduced to assist this shift. T could ask C to clap on all the words that are not *spoon*, regardless if they have anything to do with eating. In this way, C begins to learn to listen and react to words that are different than the initial "special word." After C is competent at clapping at all but the *spoon* word, then T could introduce the change of clapping at only the words related to eating.

5. Another variation on this task is related to pacing of the spoken word. As C becomes competent at the initial pace of T reciting the words and responding correctly, then T could pace the words at a faster speed, thereby introducing another dimension to this attention task.

6. For some learners, in particular those learners with some auditory difficulties, it is helpful to have them repeat each word after T has stated it. This is a good way for T to monitor if C has heard the words correctly. In addition, it is another attention maintaining device for C.

Generalizations

1. T and C should discuss when it is necessary to listen carefully to what the teacher is saying in class. Also, after reading some of the words on the Association List, T and C can discuss how some words, instructions, etc. sound similar but are really very different. For example, *spoon* and *moon* sound very similar; however, they have different meanings and are used at different times. In addition, one cannot be substituted for the other because if just wouldn't make sense to "eat with a moon" or "see a beautiful spoon in the sky at night." T and C could make up some classroom directions that sound similar but still very different. The importance of good listening can be emphasized.

2. A variation of this discussion would be for T and C to think of similar yet different directions in real-life situations such as walking across the street. If someone didn't listen and thought that he or she could walk when the red light was red instead of green, he or she could get hurt very badly. If a doctor didn't listen to what a patient was saying and checked his or her ear instead of eye, the person might get the wrong medication. T and C could think of many examples, even far-fetched ones, to make the point that listening is important.

3. To help generalize, T could introduce stories that are of a similar theme and discuss what happens to characters that aren't paying attention. For example, Richard Scarry's story of *The Absent Minded Rabbit* is an excellent example of what can happen to a rabbit who isn't watching where he is walking. The generalization can be made that it is important to be attentive in all areas and senses, such as with one's eyes and ears, and even with one's nose to detect certain smells.

4. T should help C generalize the "Thinking Trick" of clapping or tapping, a hand movement, that helps keep C attentive to the task at hand. T and C could discuss when during the day could C use this technique. If this technique is too loud and may disturb people around them, then discuss what else C could do to help stay on task.

5. The concept of shifting attention can be generalized to many situations in a school or home. The idea of changing tasks, going from math to reading to music, etc. should be discussed. Also, the difficulty in stopping what one is doing when perhaps one wants to continue should also be discussed. The idea that C could continue the activity at another time perhaps or that maybe next time C needs to work faster to finish a task or begin on time, etc. could be discussed. T and C could simulate different times of the day when C has to shift attention to different tasks, and now C could do that smoothly. C may discover that certain cues are helpful, such as: "In a couple of minutes we will be doing something else. Let's clean this up." If C has some difficulty in shifting attention during a school day, T may remind C that it is not very different from the game of listening to words that C did so well on.

6. If C has been repeating each word after T, then this type of "Thinking Trick" should also be generalized to other situations. For example, after the teacher has given some instructions in class, C should repeat them to himself or herself or perhaps an aide, etc. to make sure that C heard them correctly and knows what to do. This can be generalized to written instructions as well. C can repeat an instruction that was read and continue to repeat it as often as necessary throughout the written exercise (such as a math or spelling page). This could be practiced with T and C simulating classroom situations.

Measuring Success

T could use the Success Chart to measure how many times C was successful in clapping at the correct times, and the changes in this over time. In addition, T could use the Strategy Chart to note if C is clapping, tapping, or using his or her hands in another fashion to stay on task.

Home Program

I CAN (task related) clap on the word *spoon* whenever I hear it.

I LEARNED (Thinking Trick) to use my hands to help me listen.

I AM LEARNING (generalization) to listen very carefully when my teacher (or mom or dad) is talking to me.

REFERENCES

Aarts, J.H.P., Binnie, C.D., Smit, A.M., & Kins, J.W. (1984). Selective cognitive impairment during focal and generalized epileptiform EEG activity. *Brain, 107*, 293–308.

Achenbach, T.M., & Edelbrock, C. (1983). *Manual for the Child Behavior Checklist and Revised Child Behavior Profile*. Burlington, VT: Thomas Achenbach.

Albert, J.A. (1970). Modification of the impulsive conceptual style (Doctoral dissertation. University of Illinois, 1969). *Dissertation Abstracts International, 30*, 3377B. (University Microfilms No. 70–778).

Aram, D.M. (1986). Cognitive profiles of children with early onset of unilateral lesions. *Developmental Neuropsychology, 2*, 155–172.

Argulewicz, E.N. (1982). Effects of an instructional program designed to improve attending behaviors of learning disabled students. *Journal of Learning Disabilities, 15*, 23–27.

Arnold, S., & Forehand, R. (1978). A comparison of cognitive training and response cost procedures in modifying cognitive styles of impulsive children. *Cognitive Therapy and Research, 2*, 183–187.

Asarnow, R.F., & Betts, B. (1984). *Span of Apprehension and Continuous Performance Test: User's Manual*. Los Angeles: Medcomp.

Asarnow, R.F., Satz, P., Light, R., Lewis, R., & Neumann, E. (1991). Behavior problems and adaptive functioning in children with mild and severe closed-head injury. *Pediatric Psychology, 16*, 543–555.

Asarnow, R.F., & Sherman, T. (1984). Studies of visual information processing in schizophrenic children. *Child Development, 55*, 249–261.

Barkley, R.A. (1988a). Attention, In M.G. Tramontana & S.R. Hooper (Eds.), *Assessment Issues in Child Neuropsychology*. New York: Plenum Press.

Barkley, R.A. (1988b). Tic disorders and Tourettes syndrome. In E. Mash & L. Terdal (Eds.), *Behavioral Assessment of Childhood Disorders* (2nd ed.). New York: Guilford Press.

Barkley, R.A., Fischer, M., Newby, R.F., & Breen, M.J. (1988). Development of a multi-method clinical protocol for assessing stimulant drug responding in ADD children. *Journal of Clinical Child Psychology, 17*, 14–24.

Becker, W.C. (1972). Applications of behavioral principles in typical classrooms, In C.E. Thoresen (Ed.), *Behavior Modification in Education*. The 71st Yearbook of the National Society for the Study of Education. Chicago: University of Chicago Press.

Bender, N. (1976). Self-verbalization versus tutor verbalization in modifying impulsivity. *Journal of Educational Psychology, 68*, 347–354.

Ben-Yishay, Y., Diller, L., & Rattok, J. (1978). A modular approach to optimizing orientation, psychomotor alertness and purposive behaviour in severe head trauma patients. In *Working Approaches to Remediation of Cognitive Deficits in Brain Damaged Persons. Rehabilitation Monograph No. 59* (pp. 63–67). Institute of Rehabilitation Medicine, New York University Medical Center.

Berlyne, D.E. (1960). *Conflict, Arousal, and Curiosity*. New York: McGraw-Hill.

Boll, T.J. (1983). Minor head injury in children: Out of sight but not out of mind. *Journal of Clinical Child Psychology, 12*, 74–80.

Bornstein, P., & Quevillon, R. (1976). The effects of a self-instructional package on overactive preschool boys. *Journal of Applied Behavior Analysis, 9*, 179–188.

Bornstein, R.A. (1983). Construct validity of the Knox Cube Test as a neuropsychological measure. *Journal of Clinical Neuropsychology, 5*, 105–114.

Bracy, O.L. (1983–93). *Soft Tools*. Indianapolis: NeuroScience Publishers.

Bradley, V.A., Welch, J.L., & Skilbeck, C.E. (1993). *Cognitive Retraining Using Microcomputers*. Hillsdale, NJ: Lawrence Erlbaum.

Bremer, D.A., & Stern, J.A. (1976). Attention and distractibility during reading in hyperactive boys. *Journal of Abnormal Child Psychology, 4*, 381–387.

Brouwers, P., Riccardi, R., Poplack, D., & Fedio, P. (1984). Attentional deficits in long term survivors of childhood acute lymphoblastic leukemia (ALL). *Journal of CLinical Neuropsychology, 6*, 325–336.

Bushell, D., Wrobel, P.A., & Michaelis, M.L. (1968). Applying group contingencies to the classroom study behavior of preschool children. *Journal of Applied Behavior Analysis, 1*, 55–61.

Cameron, M.I., & Robinson, M.J. (1980). Effects of cognitive training on academic and on-task behavior in hyperactive children. *Journal of Abnormal Child Psychology, 8*, 405–419.

Campbell, T (1990). *Cognitive remediation with the brain-injured adolescent*. Paper presented at the annual conference of the National Head Injury Foundation, New Orleans, LA.

Cegalis, J.A., & Birdsall, W. (1993). *Paced Auditory Serial Attention Test (PASAT): Multimedia Software.* Nashua, NH: For Thought, Ltd.

Cegalis, J.A., & Bowlin, J. (1993). *Vigil: Continuous Performance Test (CPT).* Nashua, NH: For Thought, Ltd.

Cobb, J.A., & Hops, H. (1973). Effects of academic survival skills training on low achieving first graders. *Journal of Educational Research, 67,* 108–113.

Cognitive Rehabilitation. (Various Dates). (Computer Programs). Indianapolis, IN: Neuro-Science Publishers.

Coleman, R. (1970). A conditioning technique applicable to elementary school classrooms. *Journal of Applied Behavior Analysis, 3,* 293–297.

Cope, D.N. (1986). The pharmacology of attention and memory. *Journal of Head Trauma Rehabilitation, 1,* 34–42.

Cruickshank, W.M., Bentzen, F.A., Ratzburg, F.H., & Tannhauser, M.T. (1961). *A Teaching Method for Brain Injured and Hyperactive Children.* Syracuse: Syracuse University Press.

Das, J.P., & Naglieri, J. (1987). *Cognitive Assessment System.* New York: Psychological Corporation.

Davies, D.R., Jones, D.M., & Taylor, A. (1984). Selective-and sustained-attention tasks: Individual and group differences. In R. Parasuraman & D.R. Davies (Eds.), *Varieties of Attention.* Orlando, FL: Academic Press.

Denton, C.L., & McIntyre, C.W. (1978). Span of apprehension in hyperactive boys. *Journal of Abnormal Child Psychology, 6,* 19–24.

Diller, L., & Weinberg, J. (1977). Hemi-attention in rehabilitation: The evaluation of a rationale remediation program. In R. Friedland (Ed.), *Advances in Neurology.* New York: Raven Press.

Douglas, V.I. (1983). Attentional and cognitive problems. In M. Rutter (Ed.), *Developmental Neuropsychiatry.* New York: Guilford.

Douglas, V.I., Parry, P., Marton, P., & Garson, C. (1976). Assessment of a cognitive training program for hyperactive children. *Journal of Abnormal Child Psychology, 4,* 389–410.

Douglas, V.I., & Peters, K.G. (1979). Toward a clearer definition of the attentional deficit of hyperactive children. In G.A. Hale & M. Lewis (Eds.), *Attention and the Development of Cognitive Skills.* New York: Plenum Press.

Estes, W.K., & Taylor, H.A. (1966). Visual detection in relation to display size and redundancy of critical elements. *Perception and Psychophysics, 1.*

Evans, R.W., & Gualtieri, C.T. (1985). Carbamazepine: A neuropsychological and psychiatric profile. *Clinical Neuropharmacology, 8,* 221–241.

Feeney, D.M., & Walker, A.E. (1979). The prediction of post-traumatic epilepsy. *Archives of Neurology, 36,* 8–12.

Feuerstein, R. (1980). *Instrumental Enrichment: An Intervention Program for Cognitive Modifiability,* Baltimore: University Park Press.

Feuerstein, R., Miller, R., Hoffman, M.B., Rand, Y., Mintzker, Y., & Jensen, M.R. (1981). Cognitive modifiability in adolescence: Cognitive structure and the effects of intervention, *The Journal of Special Education, 15,* 269–287.

Finch, A., Wilkinson, M., Nelson, W., & Montgomery, L. (1975). Modification of an impulsive cognitive tempo in emotionally disturbed boys. *Journal of Abnormal Child Psychology, 3,* 49- 52.

Genshaft, J., & Hirt, M. (1979). Race effects in modifying cognitive impulsivity through self-instruction and modeling. *Journal of Experimental Child Psychology, 27,* 185–194.

Gianutsos, R., & Klitzner, C. (1981). *Computer Programs for Cognitive Rehabilitation.* Bayport, NY: Life Science Associates.

Gibson, E., & Rader, N. (1979). Attention: Perceiver as performer. In G. Hale & M. Lewis (Eds.), *Attention and Cognitive Development.* New York: Plenum Press.

Glynn, E.L., Thomas, J.D., & Slee, S.M. (1973). Behavioral self-control of on-task behavior in an elementary classroom. *Journal of Applied Behavior Analysis, 6,* 105–113.

Gordon, M. (1983). *The Gordon Diagnostic System.* DeWitt, NY: Gordon Systems.

Goyette, C.H., Conners, C.K., & Ulrich, R.F. (1978). Normative data for Revised Conners

Parent and Teacher Rating Scales. *Journal of Abnormal Child Psychology, 6*, 221–236.

Glenn, M.B. (1986). Update on pharmacology: CNS stimulants: Applications for traumatic brain-injury. *Journal of Head Trauma Rehabilitation. 4*, 74–76.

Grant, D.A. & Berg, E.A. (1981). *The Wisconsin Card Sort Test*. Odessa, FL: Psychological Assessment Resources.

Grant, M.L., Ilai, D., Nussbaum, N.L., & Bigler, E.D. (1990). The relationship between continuous performance tasks and neuropsychological test in children with attention-deficit and hyperactive disorder. *Perceptual and Motor Skills, 70*, 435–445.

Green, M.F., Nuechterlein, K.H., & Gaier, D.J. (1992). Sustained and selective attention in schizophrenia. *Progress in Experimental Personality and Psychopathology Research, 15*, 290–313.

Greenberg, L.M. & Crosby, R.D. (1992). *A summary of developmental normative data on the Test of Variables of Attention (TOVA)*. Minnesota: University of Minnesota.

Gronwall, D. (1977). Paced Auditory Serial Addition Task: A measure of recovery from concussion. *Perceptual and Motor Skills, 44*, 367–373.

Gronwall, D. (1987). Advances in the assessment of attention and information processing after head injury. In H. S. Levin, J. Grafman, & H. M. Eisenberg (Eds.), *Neurobehavioral Recovery From Head Injury*. New York: Oxford University Press.

Gronwall, D., & Wrightson, P. (1974). Delayed recovery of intellectual functioning after minor head injury. *Lancet, 2*, 995–997.

Gualtieri, C.T., & Evans, R.W. (1988). Stimulant treatment for the neurobehavioural sequelae of traumatic brain-injury. *Brain Injury, 2*, 273–290.

Haarbauer-Krupa, J., Moser, L., Smith, G.J., Sullivan, D.M., & Szekeres, S.F. (1985). Cognitive rehabilitation therapy: Middle stages of recovery. In M. Ylvisaker (Ed.), *Head Injury Rehabilitation: Children and Adolescents*. San Diego: College Hill Press.

Hannay, H.J., & Levin, H.S. (1988). Visual continuous recognition memory in normal and closed-head-injured adolescents. *Journal of Clinical and Experimental Neuropsychology, 11*, 444–460.

Hartman, D.E. (1988). *Neuropsychological Toxicology*. New York: Pergamon Press.

Heaton, R.K. (1981). *A Manual for the Wisconsin Card Sort Test*. Odessa, FL: Psychological Assessment Resources.

Holdsworth, L., & Whitmore, K. (1974). A study of children with epilepsy attending ordinary schools: I. Their seizure patterns, progress, and behavior in school. *Developmental and Child Neuropsychology, 16*, 746–758.

Horowitz, I., Costeff, H., Sadan, N., Abraham, E., Geyer, S., & Najenson, T. (1983). Childhood head injuries in Israel: Epidemiology and outcome. *International Rehabilitation Medicine, 5*, 32–36.

Hugdahl, K., Andersson, L., Asbjornsen, A., & Dalen, K. (1990). Dichotic listening, forced attention, and brain asymmetry in righthanded and lefthanded children. *Journal of Clinical and Experimental Neuropsychology, 12*, 539–548.

Johnson, D.A., Roethig-Johnston, K., & Middleton, J. (1988). Development and evaluation of an attentional test for head-injured children–1. Information processing capacity in a normal sample. *Journal of Child Psychology and Psychiatry, 29*, 199–208.

Kagan, J. (1966). Reflection-impulsivity: The generality of dynamics of conceptual tempo. *Journal of Abnormal Psychology, 7*, 17–24.

Kagan, J., Rosman, B., Day, D., Albert, J., & Phillips, W. (1964). Information processing in the child: Significance of analytic and reflective attitudes. *Psychological Monographs, 78* (1, Whole No. 578).

Kaufman, A.S. (1975). Factor analysis of the WISC-R at eleven age levels between 6½ and 16½ years. *Journal of Consulting and Clinical Psychology, 43*, 135–147.

Kaufman, A. & Kaufman, N. (1983). *Kaufman Assessment Battery for Children*. Circle Pines, MN: American Guidance Service.

Keele, S.W. (1973). *Attention and Human Performance*. Pacific Palisades, CA: Goodyear.

Kendall, P.C. (1982). Individual versus group cognitive-behavioral self-control training: 1-year follow-up. *Behavior Therapy, 13*, 241– 247.

Kendall, P.C., & Braswell, L. (1985). *Cognitive Behavioral Therapy for Impulsive Children*. New York: Guilford Press.

Kendall, P.C., & Finch, A.J. (1979). Analyses of changes in verbal behavior following a cognitive-behavioral treatment for impulsivity. *Journal of Abnormal Child Psychology, 7*, 455-463.

Kendall, P.C., & Zupan, B.A. (1981). Individual versus group application of cognitive-behavioral self-control procedures with children. *Behavior Therapy, 12*, 344–359.

Keough, B.K., & Margolis, J.S. (1976). A component analysis of attentional problems of educationally handicapped boys. *Journal of Abnormal Child Psychology, 4*, 349–359.

Kinsbourne, M., & Hiscock, M. (1977). Does cerebral dominance develop? In S. Segalowitz & F. Gruber (Eds.), *Language Development and Neurological Theory*. New York: Academic Press.

Klee, S.H., & Garfinkel, B.D. (1983). The computerized continuous performance task: a new measure of inattention. *Journal of Abnormal Child Psychology, 11*, 487–496.

Klonoff, H., Low, M.D., & Clark, C. (1977). Head injuries in children: A prospective five year follow-up. *Journal of Neurology, Neurosurgery and Psychiatry, 40*, 1211–1219.

Koskiniemi, M., Donner, M., & Pettay, O. (1983). Clinical appearance and outcome in mumps encephalitis in children. *Acta Paediatr Scand, 72*, 603–609.

Lavin, P. (1989). *Parenting the Overactive Child: Alternatives to Drug Therapy*. New York: Madison Books.

Lehr, E. & Lantz, J.A. (1990). Behavioral Components. In E. Lehr (Ed.), *Psychological Management of Traumatic Brain Injury in Children and Adolescents*. Rockville, MD: Aspen.

Lewis, R.S., Satz, P., Asarnow, R.F., Light, R. & Haist, F. (1994) Verbal memory impairment in children with mild and severe closed-head injury. Submitted for publication.

Levin, H. S., & Eisenberg, H. M. (1987). *Neurobehavioral Recovery from Head Injury*. New York: Oxford University Press.

Lezak, M. (1983). *Neuropsychological Assessment*. New York: Oxford University Press.

Light, R., Asarnow, R.F., Satz, P., Zaucha, K., & Lewis, R. (1993). UCLA studies of mild closed-head injury in children and adolescents: III—Behavioral and academic outcomes. *Journal of Clinical and Experimental Neuropsychology, 15(1)*, 20–21.

Light, R., Neumann, E., Lewis, R., Morecki-Oberg, C., Asarnow, R., & Satz, P. (1987). An evaluation of a neuropsychologically based re-education project for the head-injured child. *Journal of Head Trauma Rehabilitation, 2*, 11–25.

Lindgren, S.D., & Lyons, D.A. (1984). *Pediatric Assessment of Cognitive Efficiency (PACE)*. Iowa City: University of Iowa, Department of Pediatrics.

Lipper, S., & Tuchman, M.M. (1976). Treatment of chronic post-traumatic organic brain syndrome with dextroamphetamine: First reported case. *Journal of Nervous and Mental Disorders, 162*, 366–371.

Loiselle, D.L., Stamm, J.S., Maitinsky, S., & Whipple, S.C. (1980). Evoked potentiation and behavioral signs of attentive dysfunctions in hyperactive boys. *Psychophysiology, 17*, 193–201.

Ludwig, B. (1989). Psychopharmacologic management of the difficult patient. *Journal of Neurologic Rehabilitation, 3*, 147–149.

Lundar, T., & Nestvold, K. (1985). Pediatric head injuries caused by traffic accidents: A prospective study with 5-year follow-up. *Child's Nervous System, 1*, 24–28.

Luria, A.R. (1961). *The Role of Speech in the Regulation of Normal and Abnormal Behavior*. New York: Pergamon.

Luria, A.R. (1982). *Language and Cognition*. New York: Wiley.

MacLeod, C.M. (1991). Half a century of research on the Stroop: An integrated review. *Psychology Bulletin, 109*, 163–203.

Malec, J., Jones, R., Rao, N., & Stubbs, K. (1984). Video-game practice effects on sustained attention in patients with craniocerebral trauma, *Cognitive Rehabilitation, 2*, 18–23.

Mash, E., & Terdal, L. (1987). *Behavioral Assessment of Childhood Disorders* (2nd ed.). New York: Guilford Press.

McCarney, S.B. (1989). *The Learning Disability*

Intervention Manual. Columbia, MO: Hawthorne Educational Services.

McKenzie, H.S., Clarke, M., Wolfe, M.M., Kothera, R., & Benson, C. (1968). Behavior modification of children with learning disabilities using grades as tokens and allowances as back up reinforcers. *Exceptional Children, 34,* 745–752.

Mclean, A., Temkin, A.R., Dikmen, S., & Wyler (1983). The behavioral sequelae of head injury. *Journal of Clinical Neuropsychology, 5,* 361–376.

Meichenbaum, D.H. (1974). *Cognitive-Behavior Modification.* New York: Plenum Press.

Meichenbaum, D.H., & Goodman, J. (1971). Training impulsive children to talk to themselves. *Journal of Abnormal Psychology, 77,* 115–126.

Mesulam, M. (1985). *Principles of Behavioral Neurology.* Philadelphia: F.A. Davis.

Miller, E.N., Satz, P., Van Gorp, W., Visscher, B., & Dudley, J. (1990). Computerized screening for HIV-related cognitive decline in gay men: Cross-sectional analyses and one-year follow-up. *Journal of Clinical and Experimental Neuropsychology, 12,* 48 Abstract.

Mirsky, A.F. (1989). The neuropsychology of attention: Elements of a complex behavior. In E. Perecmen (Ed.), *Integrating Theory and Practice in Clinical Neuropsychology.* Hillsdale, NJ: Erlbaum.

Mirsky, A.F., Anthony, B.J., Duncan, C.C., Ahearn, M.B., & Kellam, S.G. (1991). Analysis of the elements of attention: A neuropsychological approach. *Neuropsychology Review, 2,* 109–145.

Morey, N. (1969). *Attention: Selective Process in Vision and Hearing.* London: Hutchinson.

Mulhern, R.K., Crisco, J.J., & Kun, L.E. (1983). Neuropsychological sequelae of childhood brain tumors: A Review. *Journal of Clinical Child Psychology, 12,* 66–73.

Needleman, H.L., Gunnoe, C., Leviton, A., Reed, R., Peresie, H., Maher, C., & Barrett, P. (1979). Deficits in psychologic and classroom performance of children with elevated dentine lead levels. *New England Journal of Medicine, 300,* 689–695.

Novy, P., Burnett, J., Powers, M., & Sulzer-Azaroff, B. (1973). Modifying attending-to-work behavior of a learning disabled child. *Journal of Learning Disabilities, 6,* 20–24.

O'Dougherty, M., Nuechterlein, K.H., & Drew, B. (1984). Hyperactivity and hypoxic children: Signal detection, sustained attention, and behavior. *Journal of Abnormal Psychology, 93,* 178–191.

Oltmanns, T.F., & Neale, J.M. (1975). Schizophrenic performance when distractors are present: Attentional deficits or differential task difficulty? *Journal of Abnormal Psychology, 84,* 205–209.

Omizo, M.M., & Michael, W.B. (1982). Biofeedback-induced relaxation training and impulsivity, attention to task, and locus of control among hyper active boys. *Journal of Learning Disabilities, 15,* 414–416.

Ownby, R.L., & Matthews, C.G. (1985). On the meaning of the WISC-R third factor: Relations to selected neuropsychological measures. *Journal of Consulting and Clinical Psychology, 53,* 531–534.

Packard, R.G. (1970). The control of "classroom attention": A group contingency for complex behavior. *Journal of Applied Behavior Analysis, 3,* 13–28.

Palkes, H., Stewart, M., & Kahana, B. (1968). Porteus maze performance after training in self-directed verbal commands. *Child Development, 39,* 817–826.

Papanicolaou, A.C. (1987). Electrophysiological methods for the study of attentional deficits in head injury. In H.S. Levin, J. Grafman & H.M. Eisenberg (Eds.), *Neurobehavioral Recovery from Head Injury.* New York: Oxford University Press.

Parasuraman, R., & Davies, D.R. (1984). *Varieties of Attention.* Orlando: Academic Press.

Parrish, J.M, & Erickson, M.T. (1981). A comparison of cognitive strategies in modifying the cognitive style of impulsive third-grade children. *Cognitive Therapy and Research, 5,* 71-84.

Patterson, G.R. (1965). An application of conditioning techniques to the control of a hyperactive child. In L.P. Ullman & L. Krasner (Eds.), *Case Studies in Behavior Modification.* New York: Holt, Rinehart, & Winston.

Physicians' Desk Reference (49th ed.). (1995). E. R. Barnhart (Publisher). Oradell, N.J.: Medical Economics Company.

Piontkowski, D., & Calfee, R. (1979). Attention in the classroom. In G. Hale & M. Lewis (Eds.), *Attention and Cognitive Development.* New York: Plenum Press.

Ponsford, J.L., & Kinsella, G. (1988). Evaluation of a remedial programme for attentional deficits following closed-head injury. *Journal of Clinical and Experimental Neuropsychology, 10,* 693–708.

Posner, M.I. (1975). Psychobiology of attention. In M.S. Gazzaniga & C. Blakemore (Eds.), *Handbook of Psychobiology.* New York: Academic Press.

Posner, M.I. (1986). *Chronometric Explorations of Mind.* New York: Oxford University Press.

Posner, M.I. (1987). Hierarchical distributed networks in the neuropsychology of selective attention. In A. Carumazza (Ed.), *Advances in Cognitive Neuropsychology* (Vol. I). Hillsdale, NJ: Erlbaum.

Posner, M.I. & Petersen, S.E. (1990). The attention system of the human brain. *Annual Review of Neuroscience, 13,* 25–42.

Pressley, M., Reynolds, W.M., Stark, K.D., & Gettinger, M. (1983). Cognitive strategy training and children's self-control. In M. Pressley & J.R. Levin (Eds.), *Cognitive Strategy Research: Psychological Foundations.* New York: Springer-Verlag.

Quay, L.C., Sprague, R.L., Werry, J.S., & McQueen, M.M. (1967). Conditioning visual orientation of conduct problem children in the classroom. *Journal of Experimental Child Psychology, 5,* 512–517.

Quay, L.C., & Brown, R.T. (1980). Hyperactive and normal children and the error, latency, and double median split scoring procedure of the Matching Familiar Figures Test. *Journal of School Psychology, 18,* 12–16.

Reitan, R.M., & Wolfson, D. (1985). *The Halstead Reitan Neuropsychological Test Battery: Theory and Clinical Interpretation.* Tucson: Neuropsychology Press.

Ross, D.M., & Ross, S.A. (1982). *Hyperactivity: Current Issues, Research, and Theory.* (2nd ed.). New York: Wiley.

Rosvold, H.E., Mirsky, A., Sarason, I., Brausome, E.D., & Beck, L.H. (1956). A continuous performance test of brain damage. *Journal of Consulting Psychology, 20,* 343–350.

Rourke, B.P., & Orr, R.R. (1977). Prediction of the reading and spelling performance of normal and retarded readers: Four-year follow-up. *Journal of Abnormal Child Psychology, 5,* 9–20.

Ruff, R.M. (1985). *San Diego Neuropsychological Test Battery* (Manual). San Diego: University of California, San Diego.

Rumain, B. (1988). Efficacy of behavior management versus methylphenidate in a hyperactive child: The role of dynamics. *American Journal of Orthopsychiatry, 58,* 466–469.

Ryan, T.V., LaMarche, J.A., Barth, J.T., & Boll, T.J. (1995). Neuropsychological consequences of pediatric head trauma. In R.S. Dean & E.S. Batchelor (Eds.), *Pediatric Neuropsychology: Interfacing Assessment and Treatment for Rehabilitation.* Boston: Allyn and Bacon.

Sanford, J.A., Browne, R.J., & Turner, A. (1985–93). *Captain's Log: Cognitive Training System (Version 2.5).* Richmond, VA: BrainTrain.

Sanford, J.A., Browne, R.J., & Turner, A. (1993). *Attention Skills: Next Generation.* Richmond, VA: BrainTrain.

Sanford, J.A., & Turner, A. (1993). *Intermediate Visual and Auditory Attention Test (IVA).* Richmond, VA: BrainTrain.

Schiff, A.R., & Knopf, I.J. (1985). The effect of task demands on attention allocation in children of different ages. *Child Development, 56,* 621–630.

Schwartz, S.T., Healey, J.M., Wolf, L.E., Pascualvaca, D.M., Newcorn, J.H., Sharma, V., & Halperin, J.M. (1990). Inattention and cognitive flexibility: Implications for understanding the processing deficits of ADHD children. *Journal of Clinical and Experimental Neuropsychology, 11(1),* 102.

Schwartz, S.T., Healey, J.M., Halperin, J.M., Wolf, L.E., Pascualvaca, D.M., Newcorn, J., & Sharma, V. (1990). Is the "attentional triad" of the WISC-R related to attention? *Journal of Clinical and Experimental Neuropsychology, 12(1),* 27.

Schwebel, A.I., & Cherlin, D.L. (1972). Physical and social distancing in teacher-pupil relationships. *Journal of Educational Psychology, 63,* 543–550.

Shum, D.H.K., McFarland, K.A., & Bain, J.D. (1990). Construct validity of eight tests of attention: Comparison of normal and closed head-injured samples. *The Clinical Neuropsychologist, 4*, 151–162.

Silverman, C.L., & Thomas, P.R.M. (1990). Long-term neuropsychologic and intellectual sequelae in brain tumor patients, In M. Deutsch (Ed.), *Management of Childhood Brain Tumors*. Hingham, MA: Kluwer Academic Publishers.

Simon, T.J., & Sussman, H.M. (1987). The dual task paradigm: Speech dominance or manual dominance? *Neuropsychologia, 25*, 559–569.

Simpson, D., & Reilly, P. (1982). Pediatric coma scale. *Lancet, 2*, 450.

Smith, A. (1973). *Symbol Digit Modalities Test*. Los Angeles: Western Psychological Services.

Snyder, J., & White, M. (1979). The use of cognitive self-instruction in the treatment of behaviorally disturbed adolescents. *Behavior Therapy, 10*, 227–235.

Snyder, T.J., Das, J.P., Mishra, R.K., & Lowrengel, M. (1990). Attentional measures in relation to Conners Teacher Rating. *Journal of Clinical and Experimental Neuropsychology, 11(1),* 70 Abstract.

Sohlberg, M.M., & Mateer, C.A. (1987). Effectiveness of an attention-training program. *Journal of Clinical and Experimental Neuropsychology, 9*, 117–130.

Sohlberg, M.M., & Mateer, C.A. (1989). *Introduction to Cognitive Rehabilitation*. New York: Guilford Press.

Sparrow, S., Bolla, D., & Cicchetti, D. (1984). *Vineland Adaptive Behavior Scales*. Circle Pines, MN: American Guidance Service.

Sprague, R.L., & Sleator, E.K. (1977). Methylphenidate in hyperkinetic children: Differences in dose effects on learning and social behavior. *Science, 198*, 1274–1276.

Stewart, K.J., & Moely, B.E. (1983). The WISC-R third factor: What does it mean? *Journal of Consulting and Clinical Psychology, 51*, 940–941.

Stroop, J.R. (1935). Studies of interference in serial verbal reactions. *Journal of Experimental Psychology, 18*, 643–662.

Sykes, D.H., Douglas, V.I., & Morgenstern, G. (1973). Sustained attention in hyperactive children. *Journal of Child Psychology and Psychiatry, 14*, 213–220.

Talland, G.A. (1965). *Deranged Memory*. New York: Academic Press.

THINKable/2 & THINKable/DOS. (1993–94). *Software Package (Computer Programs)*. San Antonio: Psychological Corporation.

Trommer, B.L., Hoeppner, T.B., Lorber, R., & Armstrong, K. (1988). Pitfalls in the use of a continuous performance test as a diagnostic tool in attentional deficit disorder. *Journal of Developmental and Behavioral Pediatrics, 9*, 339–346.

Van Strien, J.W., & Bouma, A. (1988). Cerebral organization of verbal and motor functions in left-handed and right-handed adults: Effects of concurrent verbal tasks on unimaual tapping performance. *Journal of Clinical and Experimental Neuropsychology, 10*, 139–156.

Van Zomeren, A.H. (1981). *Reaction time and attention after closed head injury*. Lisse: Swets & Zeitlinger.

Van Zomeren, A.H., & Deelman, B.G. (1978). Long-term recovery of visual reaction time after closed head injury. *Journal of Neurology, Neurosurgery, and Psychiatry, 41*, 452–457.

Vygotsky, L.S. (1962). *Thought and Language*. New York: Wiley.

Wagner, R.R., & Guyer, B.P. (1971). Maintenance of discipline through increasing children's span of attending by means of a token economy. *Psychology in the Schools, 8*, 285–289.

Walker, H.M. & Buckley, N.K. (1968). The use of positive reinforcement in conditioning attending behavior. *Journal of Applied Behavior Analysis, 1*, 245–250.

Wechsler, D. (1974). *Manual: Wechsler Intelligence Scale for Children-Revised*. San Antonio: Harcourt Brace Jovanovich.

Weingartner, H., Langer, D., Grice, J., & Rapoport, J.L. (1982). Acquisition and retrieval of information in amphetamine treated hyperactive children. *Psychiatry Research, 6*, 21–29.

Weiss, G., & Hechtman, L.T. (1993). *Hyperactive Children Grown Up: ADHD in Children, Adolescents, and Adults*. New York: Gilford Press.

Wender, P.H. (1987). *The Hyperactive Child, Adolescent, and Adult: Attention Deficit Disorder Through the Life Span*. New York: Oxford University Press.

Williams, D.J. (1989). *A Process-Specific Training Program in the Treatment of Attention Deficits in Children.* Unpublished doctoral dissertation, University of Washington.

Williams, J.M. (1992). *Software for Psychological Testing & Education.* Walkersville, MD: Cool-Spring Software.

Willis, J., & Crowder, J. (1972). A portable device for group modification of classroom attending behavior. *Journal of Applied Behavior Analysis, 5*, 499–504.

Wilson, C., Hall, D., & Watson, D.L. (1982). *Teaching Children Self-Control: A Teachers Manual for Grades 1,2,3 Using Cognitive Behavior Modification and Relaxation Techniques.* San Diego, CA: San Diego County Superintendent of Schools.

Witkin, H.A. Oltman, P., Raskin, E., & Karp, S. (1971). *Manual for the Children's Embedded Figure Test.* Palo Alto: Consulting Psychologists Press.

Wolf, L.E., & Halperin, J.M. (1987). Assessment of attention in psychiatrically disturbed children: What are we really measuring? *Journal of Clinical and Experimental Neuropsychology, 9(1).*

Wolf, L.E., Pascualvaca, D.M., Schwartz, S.T., Healey, J.M., Newcorn, J., Sharma, V., &

Halperin, J.M. (1989). Continuous performance test measures of sustained attention. *Journal of Clinical and Experimental Neuropsychology, 11(1)*, 30.

Wood, R.L. (1986). Rehabilitation of patients with disorders of attention. *Journal of Head Trauma Rehabilitation, 1*, 43–54.

Wood, R.L. (1987). *Brain Injury Rehabilitation: A Neurobehavioral Approach.* London: Croom Helm.

Woodcock, R.W. (1976). *Goldman-Fristoe-Woodcock Auditory Skills Test Battery Technical Manual.* Circle Pines, MN: American Guidance Service.

Ylvisaker, M. (Ed.)(1985). *Head Injury Rehabilitation: Children and adolescents.* San Diego: College-Hill Press.

Zaucha, K., Asarnow, R.F., Satz, P., Light, R., & Lewis, R. (1993). UCLA studies of mild closed-head injury in children and adolescents: II—Neuropsychological Outcome. *Journal of Clinical and Experimental Neuropsychology, 15(1)*, 20.

Zubin, J. (1975). The problem of attention in schizophrenia. In M. Kietzman, S. Sutton, & J. Zubin (Eds.), *Experimental Approaches to Psychopathology.* New York: Academic Press.

12

SEIZURE DISORDERS

CARL B. DODRILL **MOLLY H. WARNER**

INTRODUCTION

A chapter on the neuropsychological aspects of epilepsy is most appropriate for this volume since not only is epilepsy one of the most common neurological disorders but 75% of all epileptic seizures begin in people prior to their eighteenth birthday (Dreifuss, 1989). Furthermore, this medical problem can have a major adverse impact on both patient and family.

In this chapter, we will initially cover the International Classification of Epileptic Seizures, the natural history and prognosis of seizures from childhood to adulthood, the cognitive and behavioral impacts of medication given to stop seizures, surgery for epilepsy, and alternate methods of seizure control beyond medication and surgery. Finally, neuropsychological testing in children will be covered with an emphasis on intervention, particularly within the school setting.

TYPES OF EPILEPTIC SEIZURES IN CHILDHOOD

Epilepsy can be defined as repeated spontaneous seizures. Seizures are the observed phenomena of epilepsy, and the International Classification System is the best recognized way of classifying these attacks (Commission on Classification

A portion of the research reported in this chapter was supported by NIH grants NS 17111 and NS 24823 awarded by the National Institute of Neurological Disorders and Stroke, PHS/DHHS. Address reprint requests to Carl B. Dodrill, Ph.D., Regional Epilepsy Center (ZA–50), Harborview Medical Center, 325 Ninth Avenue, Seattle WA 98104.

and Terminology, 1985). This system recognizes three basic domains of seizures: partial, generalized, and unclassified.

Partial (Local, Focal) Seizures

Partial seizures are attacks in which the spell begins in a circumscribed portion of one cerebral hemisphere (a "part" of the brain). The area that is involved will determine how the seizure is manifested. As long as the seizure remains in a limited area, it does not result in the complete dysfunction of the person. Partial seizures are subclassified into three groups, primarily according to whether or not consciousness is impaired.

Simple partial seizures do not involve the impairing of consciousness. According to the International Classification System, they can be manifest primarily with motor, somatosensory, autonomic, or psychic symptoms. Such attacks frequently involve the involuntary movement of an extremity, unusual sensations in one part of the body, the subjective perception of an *aura* (a warning that a seizure is about to occur), or some combination of the three. In children, such warnings may result in a fear response and sudden unusual emotional changes. This is true whether or not the attack introduces a larger and more evident seizure. As long as the attack remains simple partial, the child is typically able to maintain some ability to respond and to communicate.

Complex partial seizures vary remarkably in their manifestations, but they routinely involve some type of impairment of consciousness. They may begin as simple partial seizures that progress to clouding of consciousness, or they may begin on their own without a preceding simple partial seizure. They may have all the features of simple partial seizures including motor, somatosensory, autonomic, and psychic changes, and they can also involve automatisms (repetitive but essentially purposeless movements such as fumbling with items on a desk, picking at one's clothing, etc.). This may be a continuation of an activity that was ongoing when the seizure started, or it may be a new repetitive activity. The child often has impairment of the ability to talk and/or understand, routinely cannot carry out planned or organized activities, and later may or may not be aware that the seizure has occurred. These attacks can often be distinguished from absence seizures since they are usually much longer and routinely last from 10 seconds to several minutes.

Partial seizures secondarily generalized occur when the electrical disturbance associated with either a simple partial or a complex partial seizure generalizes to the cerebral hemispheres as a whole. Often, this results in a convulsion with tonic extension of the extremities followed by clonic movements that are essentially bilateral and symmetric (tonic-clonic seizures).

Overall, partial seizures are an important part of the childhood epilepsies, and the reader should not conclude that they are any less significant because they are not always as dramatic in their outward manifestation as some of the generalized seizures. On the contrary, they frequently do lead to generalized attacks, they can be very disabling, and they can also be most difficult to control.

Generalized Seizures

Generalized seizures are those in which both cerebral hemispheres are involved approximately equally. If such involvement is from the very start of the attack, the seizure is said to be *primarily* generalized, whereas if the generalization occurs after a partial seizure, the attack is *secondarily* generalized.

Generalized seizures may be divided according to those that are *convulsive* and those that are *nonconvulsive*. Convulsive seizures include tonic-clonic seizures (previously called *grand mal*), which often start with sudden marked increased muscle tone resulting in a sudden bilateral extension of the extremities, sometimes with a cry if the muscles around the rib cage contract. This is usually followed by a clonic phase in which there are repetitive jerks of the extremities, which gradually slow until they stop altogether as the seizure subsides. Tonic seizures may occur alone, as may clonic, but all are considered convulsive. In this same group are myoclonic seizures, which are single or multiple, involuntary, sudden, and brief bilateral and symmetrical contractions of the extremities. They often occur at the time of going to sleep or awakening from sleep.

Nonconvulsive seizures often take the form of absence (previously called *petit mal*) or atypical absence attacks. The hallmark of the absence attack is a sudden onset, essentially complete interruption of ongoing activities, and often with a stare. The attack typically lasts only a very few seconds, and it comes to a sudden end rather than a gradual conclusion, as is often seen in partial seizures. The child may or may not be able to resume activities at the place left off just prior to the spell. Atypical absence seizures may include some automatisms, psychic changes, and motor components, and they can be difficult to distinguish from complex partial seizures. Atypical seizures constitute a significantly different disorder than simple absence, and they require significantly different drug regimens.

The final type of nonconvulsive seizure is the atonic attack during which there is a sudden loss of muscle tone. The child may suddenly and without warning drop to the floor if walking, or the loss in muscle tone may be fragmentary such as that which leads to a head drop.

Unclassified Epileptic Seizures

This category includes all spells that cannot be classified into the two basic categories due either to incomplete data or to the inability to classify seizures because of their unusual nature. Some types of neonatal seizures are included here.

This synopsis of the classification system is brief and is primarily intended to give an overview of epileptic seizures. The reader should be aware, however, that there are also a number of epileptic syndromes of childhood which, in addition to the usual type(s) of seizure, often also have a typical response to antiepileptic drugs, a natural history, a family history, and a prognosis. The most common of these will be referred to in the next section. More detailed discussions are found elsewhere (Dreifuss, 1989; Roger, Dravet, Bureau, Dreifuss, & Wolf, 1985).

NATURAL HISTORY AND PROGNOSIS OF EPILEPTIC SEIZURES IN CHILDHOOD

The natural history and prognosis of epileptic seizures is an interesting but complex topic. Following a child for even a few years is fraught with difficulties, not the least of which that the child may have passed into adulthood. At the minimum, the child has likely moved across developmental stages and this factor alone may significantly affect the type of attack experienced or even if one is experienced (Dreifuss, 1989). Furthermore, the drug treatment routinely given is deliberately designed to alter the natural course of the disorder. While it is therefore frequently not possible to make a precise prognostic statement for any particular child with epilepsy, one can identify various prognostic indicators that are of some value.

Epilepsy Syndromes

There are several syndromes of seizures in childhood that have excellent prognoses. Routinely, these types are of unknown etiology and often they are generalized by nature. Included here are benign neonatal convulsions with or without a familial basis, benign myoclonic epilepsy in infancy, and childhood absence epilepsy. One common focal type of seizure that falls within this group is that of benign epilepsy with centrotemporal spikes, which clinically consists of brief, simple, partial hemifacial motor seizures. Only rarely do any of these types constitute a persisting problem, and the child usually spontaneously remits, frequently after reaching a certain age.

Epilepsy syndromes other than those mentioned tend to have a prognosis that is variable or unknown. These syndromes include childhood epilepsy with occipital paroxysms, childhood absence epilepsy, and juvenile myoclonic epilepsy. Among the groups with the least optimistic outlooks are West syndrome (infantile spasms, arrest of psychomotor development, and hypsarrhythmia), Lennox-Gastaut syndrome (multiple types of frequent generalized seizures poorly controlled and mental retardation), progressive myoclonic epilepsy (severe bilateral clonic jerks with or without other seizure types), and epilepsy with continuous spike-waves during slow-wave sleep (Commission on Classification and Terminology, 1989). In these epilepsy syndromes, mental deterioration in at least a portion of the cases has been reported (Bourgeois et al., 1983; Rodin, Schmaltz, & Twitty, 1986). Also, there is a greater tendency for partial seizures to recur than generalized attacks (Hauser & Hesdorffer, 1990), and the prognosis is less optimistic when more than one type of seizure has been experienced, at least in adults (Okuma & Kumashiro, 1980). It is clear that epilepsy syndromes are complexly related to natural history and prognosis.

Etiology

Seizures are more likely to recur if they are symptomatic (a cause for them has been identified) than if they are idiopathic (no cause has been identified). In one study of children with epilepsy divided into these two groups (Shinnar et al., 1990), the cumulative risk of recurrence 36 months after an initial attack was 60% for symptomatic epilepsies but only 36% for idiopathic conditions. Similar findings have been reported in other populations (Annegers et al., 1986; Hauser et al., 1990).

Other Factors

Electroencephalograms (EEGs) that are abnormal and epileptiform are associated with an increased likelihood of recurrent seizures as opposed to normal EEGs. Although the relationship between family history of epilepsy and probability of recurrent attacks is complex, an especially potent predictor of increased probability of recurrent spells is the combination of an epileptiform EEG and a positive family history (Hauser & Hesdorffer, 1990). These investigators report that no relationship between age at onset of the first attack and likelihood of repeated attacks has been established. Likewise, duration of the first attack, prescription of medication after the first attack, and sex of patient do not predict recurrence.

Overall, prognosis in epilepsy is multifactorial. Since Gowers's influential writings of the mid-nineteenth century, professionals have tended to conclude that the prognosis for epilepsy generally is grim in part because of the tendency to study patients associated with hospitals and institutions (Shorvon, 1984). Community-based samples result in decidedly more positive deductions, and it appears that as many as 60% of patients with epilepsy ultimately achieve remission of seizures lasting at least several years (Hauser & Hesdorffer, 1990; Okuma & Kumashiro, 1980). Thus, one should not be unduly pessimistic about this disorder generally.

EFFECTS OF ANTIEPILEPTIC DRUGS ON ABILITIES AND BEHAVIOR

This is an important area if for no other reason than parents commonly blame antiepileptic medications for many of their children's cognitive and behavioral difficulties. Whereas this cannot be justified in most cases, the area is complex and one in which a great deal more needs to be known. Since in our society there is more reluctance to subject children to experimental treatment protocols than adults, less than one-third of all studies in this area deal with children or adolescents (Dodrill, 1991). The result is that most available information was obtained with adults, and even though it may not be strictly applicable to children, it is difficult to cover the topic without at least some reference to such data.

The two areas in which study of drug effects has been undertaken pertains to impacts on abilities of various types and on behavior, including various aspects of adjustment. In order to prepare a summary of the literature, it was reviewed and all studies of the effects of antiepileptic drugs on abilities and behavior in children were included where there were formal measures of abilities and/or behavior such as tests or behavioral rating scales. Papers offering informal and unsystematic observations about perceived changes in these areas were *not* included. Studies in languages other than English or papers presented at professional meetings were included if an abstract in English was available that gave the information essential for this review. Such information had to include an indication that children or adolescents were used, a listing of which tests or rating procedures were applied, and fundamental conclusions in terms of the effects of the drug(s) in question on abilities and/or adjustment.

Using the criteria for study selection just stated, a total of 37 investigations were found: 9 reported on the effects of the drugs on abilities alone, 10 presented results on the effects on behavior alone, and 18 presented findings dealing with both realms. A summary of all of these studies is given in Table 12.1. It will be noted that the studies are listed according to whether their results provided positive (+), neutral (0), or negative (-) effects with respect to a certain drug or group of drugs. The barbiturates include phenobarbital (Luminol, Mebaral) and primidone (Mysoline). Carbamazepine (Tegretol), phenytoin (Dilantin), and valproic acid (Depakene, Depakote) were considered individually, and all other medications (ethosuximide—Zarontin; sulthiame—Conadil, Ospolot; Benzedrine) were considered as a group.

While recognizing that not all studies are of equal value and should not be given equal weight, several conclusions are evident from Table 12.1. Perhaps the most obvious of these is that the barbiturates are by far associated with the most negative findings, and this is true for both abilities and behavior. Of 16 negative conclusions reached concerning the effects of all drugs on mental abilities, 12 related to the barbiturates. Decreases in alertness, psychomotor skills, motor speed, memory, and general mental abilities were most frequently reported. With respect to behavior, negative conclusions were reached in 10 studies concerning all drugs, *every one of which* pertained to barbiturates. This is truly impressive. The conclusions from these behavioral studies were that phenobarbital resulted in an increase in oppositional and antagonistic behaviors, temper tantrums, anger, irritability, dependency, unhappiness, and an inability to be pleased. The conclusion concerning the barbiturates is very clear: Their use should be avoided whenever possible.

The most favorable drug studied was carbamazepine. Favorable conclusions offered by the investigators often resulted from a comparison of this agent with another drug such as the barbiturates. Thus, the conclusions reached are often relative and they should *not* necessarily be interpreted to mean that this drug actually improves functioning in an absolute sense. Such a contention, previously

TABLE 12.1 Summary of Studies of Cognitive and Behavioral Effects of Antiepileptic Drugs

		Area of Impact	
Drug/Drug Group	**Drug Effect**	*Cognitive / ability*	*Behavioral / adjustmental*
Barbiturates	+		
	0	Mitchell & Chavez (1986)	Mitchell & Chavez (1986); Pellock et al. (1987); Schain et al. (1981)
	-	Byrne et al. (1987); Camfield et al. (1979); Corbett et al. (1985); Farwell et al. (1990); Hellström & Barlach-Christoffersen (1980); Nolte et al. (1980); Özdirim et al. (1978); Pellock et al. (1987); Rodin et al. (1986); Schain et al. (1977); Schain et al. (1981); Vining et al. (1987)	Brent et al. (1987); Camfield et al. (1979); Corbett et al. (1985); Hellström& Barlach-Christoffersen (1980); Lindsley & Henry (1942); Miles et al. (1988); Özdirim et al. (1978); Schain et al. (1977); Vining et al. (1987)
Carbamazepine	+	Corbett et al. (1985); Holcombe et al. (1987); Jacobides (1978); O'Dougherty et al. (1987); Pellock et al. (1987); Schain et al. (1977); Schain et al. (1981)	Brent et al. (1987); Corbett et al. (1985); Cull & Trimble (1989); Groh (1976); Jacobides (1978); Miles et al. (1988); Schain et al. (1977)
	0	Mitchell & Chavez (1986); Rett (1976); Stores & Williams (1987); Aman et al. (1990)	Aman et al. (1990); Holcombe et al. (1987); Mitchell & Chavez (1978); Pellock et al. (1987); Rett (1976); Schain et al. (1981); Stores & Williams (1987)
	-		

Continued

TABLE 12.1 *Continued*

		Area of Impact	
Drug/Drug Group	Drug Effect	Cognitive / ability	Behavioral / adjustmental
Phenytoin	+	Goldberg & Kurland (1970)	Goldberg & Kurland (1970); Lindsley & Henry (1942)
	0	Holcombe et al. (1987); Rodin et al. (1986); Looker & Conners (1970)	Holcombe et al. (1987); Klein & Greenberg (1967); Lefkowitz (1969); Looker & Conners (1970); Miles et al. (1988); Özdirim et al. (1978); Pellock et al. (1987)
	-	Corbett et al. (1985); Nolte et al. (1980); Pellock et al. (1987); Stores & Hart (1976)	
Valproic acid	+	Vining et al. (1987)	Jeavons & Clark (1974); Vining et al. (1987)
	0	Aman et al. (1987); Stores & Williams (1987)	Herranz et al. (1982); Stores & Williams
	-		
All other drugs	+	Smith et al. (1968)—ethosuximide	Al-Kaisi & McGuire (1974)—sulthiame; Corbett et al. (1985)—sulthiame; Lindsley & Henry (1942)—benzedrine; Moffat et al. (1970)—sulthiame
	0		Smith et al. (1968)—ethosuximide; Stores & Hart (1976)
	-		

held with respect to cognitive skills (e.g., Dalby, 1975), is no longer generally accepted. With respect to behavior and adjustment, note should be made that it is now commonly accepted that with adults, this drug *is* of significant assistance in affective disorders, including manic-depressive and depressive problems (Ballenger, 1988), whereas the other medications (with the possible exception of valproic acid) are not. The value of carbamazepine in childhood psychiatric disorders is presumed although it has not been well studied (Evans, Clay & Gualtieri, 1987; Evans & Gualtieri, 1985). In fact, there has been a tendency to prescribe carbamazepine for children with almost any kind of behavioral or brain-related problem in the hope that somehow the need will be met (Evans et al., 1987). As might be suspected, the results have varied substantially, but since negative behavioral effects are not commonly reported, the practice continues.

Phenytoin does not appear to be associated with significant behavioral changes, either positive or negative (it has not been possible to replicate the positive findings of the early studies reported in Table 12.1). The results in the cognitive area are much more controversial, however. The reader's attention is drawn to two points. First, even for adults where much more work has been done, there is considerable dispute as to the cognitive effects of this agent. For example, the conclusions reached by Dodrill and Troupin (1991), Meador and associates (1990), and Yusko and Verma (1991) contrast sharply with those of Duncan and colleagues (1990) and Trimble (1987). Second, those studies arriving at negative conclusions concerning the cognitive effects of phenytoin in children often demonstrate significant design limitations such as contaminating factors and small numbers of subjects. Final conclusions concerning the cognitive effects of phenytoin have not yet been reached. In the opinion of these writers, however, there are few significant adverse effects of this drug on mental abilities beyond that which can be related to speed of response when serum levels are no higher than the therapeutic range (Dodrill & Temkin, 1989).

The one other medication deserving special comment is sodium valproate. Although few studies have been done with this relatively recent drug, the results of some of these have been quite encouraging (Vining et al., 1987). Ultimately, it may be shown that this agent is not only effective in controlling especially generalized seizures but that it also has very few adverse cognitive and behavioral side effects.

NEUROLOGICAL SURGERY FOR EPILEPSY IN CHILDREN

In certain cases where seizures have proven intractable to drug therapy and are not a manifestation of a condition that is likely to remit spontaneously, neurosurgery may be an appropriate intervention. The most common surgical procedure is that of cortical resection surgery, the object of which is to remove a discrete epileptic focus in an expendable brain area. When this extends to most or all of a hemisphere, it is called *hemispherectomy*. In special applications, *corpus callosotomy* may be performed by which the corpus callosum is cut to control spread of seizures from one cerebral hemisphere to the other (see review by Green, Adler, & Erba 1988). Although relief from seizures is frequently reported from these procedures, and although it stands to reason that stopping seizures should improve quality of life for both patient and family, as yet only anectotal information is available on the psychosocial impact of successful pediatric epilepsy surgery. This is an area that deserves much more attention in the future.

ALTERNATIVE TREATMENT STRATEGIES FOR MANAGING SEIZURES

Seizures may be viewed as merely one form of behavior of the organism, and since psychologists often set about to modify behavior, it might be reasonable to assume that, by using behavioral strategies, they could also modify seizure frequency. An operant conditioning paradigm might be especially appropriate here, especially if conditions or behaviors that routinely appear prior to a seizure can be identified. Building on such a rationale, efforts dating back as far as 30 years have been made to reduce seizure frequency by psychological rather than by medical or surgical techniques. As early as 1977, at least 12 different procedures in this area had been used with varying degrees of success (Mostofsky & Balaschak, 1977). Most of these techniques can be reduced to two general approaches, each of which will be summarized here.

Alteration of Brain Waves through Conditioning

Epilepsy is obviously an electrical problem related to the brain, and in many cases there are characteristic wave forms that appear just prior to the beginning of a seizure. It is possible to reinforce the occurrence of alternative wave forms that are incompatible with the patterns characteristic of epilepsy. A number of investigators have attempted to do this, most of whom published only a single paper. One clear exception to this is that of Sterman and colleagues, who published several investigations from 1970 (Sterman et al., 1970) through 1988 (Lantz & Sterman, 1988). These investigators began with the observation that cats could be trained to produce SMR (sensorimotor rhythm, μ, a 12- to 14-Hz rhythm appearing over the sensorimotor cortex). SMR is of significance because it is believed to activate thalamic and cortical inhibition, which in turn inhibits seizures. Furthermore, these investigators observed that SMR appears during the voluntary suppression of movement. Seeking a human analogue, Sterman and colleagues established that in humans, a rhythm resembling the SMR can be recorded over the sensorimotor cortex, which can be brought under operant control through biofeedback techniques.

Over the years, a series of individual patients have been trained by Sterman and colleagues to reduce their seizure frequencies using these techniques (Sterman et al., 1972, 1974; Lanz & Sterman, 1988). Others have attempted to pick up the general technique at least in somewhat modified form. An example is that of

Wyler and associates (1979), who attempted to reduce seizure frequency by a somewhat similar technique in a series of 23 patients. This series is perhaps the largest that has ever been reported, and it contrasts with most papers that report on 1 to 4 patients. The benefit was limited, however, and these investigators abandoned the procedure.

Reduction of Seizure Frequency through Other Procedures

A number of investigators have attempted to bring seizures under behavioral control through procedures not dependent on the monitoring of brain waves. Several of these have observed that various events or conditions have tended to precipitate seizures in given persons. For example, events perceived as stressful by the person with epilepsy and major life changes are common precipitants of seizures, and this has been documented prospectively (Temkin & Davis, 1984) and retrospectively (Webster & Mawer, 1989). An obvious approach is to assist the patient with stress-management techniques, which, although probably quite effective with some patients, does not necessarily stand up to rigorous evaluation and follow-up (Tan & Bruni, 1986).

Moving from more general to more specific interventive methods, it is noted that fairly sophisticated behavioral techniques have been developed to reduce seizures in specific cases. With children, for example, symptom discrimination, countermeasures, contingent relaxation, and positive reinforcement were used with three children with a consequent reduction of both seizures and EEG paroxysmal activity (Dahl et al., 1988). This occurred following the use of customized countermeasure techniques that emphasized performing behaviors antagonistic to the development of an attack. Although this procedure had to be customized for each child, it provided seizure control in each case.

Evaluation of Alternative Methods of Seizure Control

It is interesting to note that every one of the techniques described has been met by success in certain cases but that, as far as is known to these authors, nowhere is any one of these techniques routinely in use. The reasons for this disparity are not hard to find: (1) most procedures are adapted only to selected cases, such as where specific warnings or precipitating factors can be identified; (2) the amount of professional time required to set up and execute a treatment program for even one patient is extremely high; and (3) in many cases, such as those involved with EEG biofeedback, although the patient may learn the rudiments about how to control brain waves, the training sessions are very short relative to 24 hour days, and the rest of the time the person may in fact be on an extinction schedule without the continued reinforcement of appropriate brain wave patterns. The result is that although in selected cases these and other techniques have promise, it is unlikely that they will be used on large numbers of cases in the foreseeable future. In the typical case, it is much more economical for both patient and physician to use appropriate medication if reasonable control can be achieved by so doing. Where it cannot, in selected cases these procedures might be chosen as alternatives.

USES OF NEUROPSYCHOLOGICAL TESTS IN CHILDREN WITH EPILEPSY

Probably the most frequently asked questions of a neuropsychologist who is treating a young person with epilepsy are: Why isn't this child doing better in school? and How can we help? Although the range of abilities of children with seizure disorders is considerable, the ones whom the neuropsychologist sees are generally those who are having difficulty in one or more areas. Integrated neuropsychological and psychosocial evaluation can provide the basis for sound, coordinated intervention in school (Strang, 1990) and at home.

Cognitive and Academic Assessment

Although intellectual functioning of children with seizures has been of interest for many years, research on neuropsychological functioning of children with epilepsy has been a focus for a considerably shorter time. In the United States, most reports have included tests from the Halstead Neuropsychological Test Battery for Children (9–14) or the Reitan-Indiana Neuropsychological Test Battery for Children (5–8) (Reitan & Davison, 1974), downward extensions of the Halstead-Reitan Neuropsychological Battery for Adults. The Luria-Nebraska Neuropsychological Battery-Children (LNNB-C; Golden, 1981) has been reported in one study (Hermann et al., 1988).

Compared to normal children, those with epilepsy are more likely to test poorly on intellectual and neuropsychological measures, and to require academic remediation (Farwell et al., 1985). Earlier age at seizure onset, longer duration of seizures and the presence of more than one seizure type have been associated with greater intellectual, neuropsychological and academic impairment (Farwell et al., 1985; Hermann et al., 1988; O'Leary et al., 1981; Rodin, 1989; Seidenberg et al., 1986, 1988). Individuals whose seizures remain refractory are more likely to experience difficulties throughout their life spans, with education limited and vocational choices restricted.

With regard to localization of seizure focus in temporal lobe epilepsy, Camfield and colleagues (1984) could find no differences on intellectual, neuropsychological, academic, or personality measures between children with pure left versus right foci, although memory measures sensitive to verbal versus visual-spatial modalities were not administered. It should be noted here that measurement of memory, an important construct in neuropsychological evaluation of adults with epilepsy, has been difficult to measure across a wide age spread in children due to the paucity of well-normed, multimodal memory tests. It is hoped that studies on memory in children with epilepsy will be forthcoming using newly developed tests (Delis et al., 1989; Sheslow & Adams, 1990).

Seidenberg and associates (1986) reported that 10 to 33% of a sample of 122 children with epilepsy were making less academic progress than expected for age and intellectual level in word recognition, reading, comprehension, and especially mathematics and spelling. Age of the child, age of seizure onset, the presence of generalized seizures, and lifetime total seizure frequency emerged as the strongest predictive correlates for these academic areas. In another paper, the same group of investigators found that duration of seizure disorder was inversely related to academic success (Seidenberg et al., 1988). Unsuccessful children showed specific impairments in verbal and language abilities and attention/concentration, compared to the successful group. Girls appear to be better readers than boys (Stores & Hart, 1976; Holdsworth & Whitmore, 1974), but this does not appear to hold true across all subjects (Seidenberg et al., 1986). Problems with attention and concentration are frequent complaints (Stores, 1977).

Objective Assessment of Behavior and Psychosocial Functioning

A number of assessment instruments have been used to characterize emotional and psychosocial aspects of epilepsy. The most frequently reported is the Child Behavior Checklist (CBCL; Achenbach & Edelbrock, 1983), designed to record parental observations of the behavioral problems and social competencies of children ages 4 through 16. Summary T-scores of Social Competence, overall Behavior Problems, and Internalizing versus Externalizing behavioral difficulties can be compared across sex and age, and have been particularly useful in research settings. Other forms of this checklist are the Teacher's Report Form for children ages 6 through 16 (Achenbach & Edelbrock, 1986) and the Youth Self Report for children ages 11 through 18 (Achenbach & Edelbroch, 1987).

Relationships between behaviors and other biological, psychosocial, medical, and demographic factors are complex. Hermann and colleagues (1988, 1989), using the CBCL with a large sample, found that the most powerful independent factor correlating with Behavior Problems was degree of seizure control, followed by parents' marital state and male sex (associated with more behavioral difficulties). Social Competence was related to the duration of seizures and median family income, while earlier age at onset was related to increased Total Externalizing Behavior Problem scores. In a prospective study, Mitchell and associates (1990) found that poor Social Competence scores were associated with high seizure frequency, a history of partial seizures, and poor seizure control, although scores on Behavior Problem scales were not related to seizure variables. Austin (1989) reported that poorly adapted children (as identified by scores on the CBCL) experienced more seizures and were more likely to come from single-parent homes than better adapted children with epilepsy. Family stress levels, resources, attitudes, and adaptation were all associated with behavioral adaptation.

Other objective emotional and behavioral measures that have been used in studies of children with epilepsy include the Personality Inventory for Children (PIC; Wirt et al., 1977; Camfield et al., 1984) and the Vineland Adaptive Behavior Scales (VABS; Sparrow et al., 1984, 1985), which is a developmental schedule concerned with an individual's ability to look after his or her practical needs and to take responsibility. It is particularly useful with younger or cognitively impaired children (Strang, 1990).

As opposed to instruments designed to assess general behavioral or psychiatric problems, the Adolescent Psychosocial Seizure Inventory (APSI; Batzel et al., 1991) was developed to address the particular needs and difficulties experienced by adolescents with seizure disorders. This is an empirically developed self-report inventory patterned after the adult version, the Washington Psychosocial Seizure Inventory (WPSI; Dodrill et al., 1980). Scales measuring family support, emotional and interpersonal adjustment, school adjustment, vocational outlook, adjustment to seizures, medical management of seizures, antisocial activity, and overall psychosocial functioning are provided, while three validity indices aid in interpretation of the profile. Scores on the APSI have been associated with biographical and seizure history variables (Batzel et al., 1989).

Intervention

Although children with epilepsy as a group may have more academic and psychosocial difficulties than children without seizures, each child is different, and intervention must be based on assessment of the individual situation.

Following a neuropsychological evaluation, the first feedback session is often best with the parents. An adolescent with epilepsy may join the session as is deemed appropriate, or may be seen separately. Review of test scores and implications for everyday functioning should be checked against parental observations of the child's behavior and abilities in a variety of contexts. Referral questions should be addressed here: To what extent may behavioral problems be influenced by the child's cognitive make-up? Can deficiencies in school work be explained by the child's neuropsychological profile? Do concentration, sustained attention, and ability to recall material represent problem areas? To what extent do seizures themselves, as opposed to the child's interictal interactional style, contribute to social and emotional problems? Do medication levels contribute to a child's difficulties (this factor is frequently the target of parental blame)?

With school-related problems, the most effective interventions are the product of coordination between parents and all concerned professionals. The ideal form of communication is a face-to-face meeting with all adults involved. This will include the parent(s), the neuropsychologist (equipped with appropriate medical information), the school psychologist, the special education teacher (if appropriate), the regular room teacher(s), and the school nurse. The purposes of such a team meeting are (1) to share observations and concerns about the child's performance and abilities, through test results, schoolwork, and behaviors; (2) to share information about the child's seizure disorder, medical treatment, and possible effects on functioning; and (3) to generate an intervention scheme. A written neuropsychological report is useful, but knowledge of the school setting is necessary for effective implementation of recommendations.

The building of team effort for the benefit of the child with seizures is of considerable importance. It is imperative that the neuropsychologist be knowledgeable about the roles played by each professional within the educational organization and the processes by which children are qualified to receive special help. Many parents are confused by the system and experience frustration when they attempt to get help for their child through inappropriate channels. The neuropsychologist can facilitate smooth relations between parents and school staff in helping to open lines of communication and clarifying for parents the roles played by various school staff.

Typically, school personnel have not been provided with sufficient information about epilepsy and how to deal with its manifestations (Gadow, 1982). Seizures at school may be disruptive to the classroom setting, thus a coordinated plan for how to deal with them must be developed. Issues of responsibility for the child's safety must be addressed. School staff must know when it is appropriate to send for the parent or medics, and how soon the postictal child will typically be able to attend to schoolwork. Some teachers, particularly those in regular classrooms, may be uncomfortable dealing with seizures and intolerant of the disruption to their schedules and to the rest of the class; information and familiarity may help here.

The administration of medications at school also requires coordination between adults. With regard to fine-tuning of medical treatment, teachers are in a position to observe for drowsiness on the part of the child, a sign that medication dosages may be high; this should be communicated to the physician via the parent. A record of seizure frequency and type may be useful to the physician if medications require adjusting, although the keeping of extra records must not become burdensome to the teacher who has a multitude of other responsibilities.

Three interrelated aspects of the child's interictal functioning at school should be addressed in any intervention scheme: cognitive abilities, behavior, and self-esteem. The educational program should reflect the needs of the child as determined by testing by the school psychologist, the neuropsychologist, and other allied services (speech therapy, occupational therapy etc.), as needed. Cognitive issues that the neuropsychologist may be able to elucidate include attention span under ideal testing conditions, memory abilities, the quantity and complexity of material that a child may be able to process at a sitting, the child's strengths and weaknesses in different modes of learning, organizational skills, and abilities in expression in different modes (verbal vs. written). Observations by school staff include most of preceding as well as the child's abilities to concentrate and acquire information in classroom settings, and performance in classroom, test, and homework situations. Parental input should include the child's ability to carry out school assignments at home, including the time and effort required, organizational skills, and reactions both to the assignments and to parental input and help.

The overall goal of an educational plan should be to maximize the child's successes in learning and to minimize the failures. The design of the plan should integrate the child's needs with the resources available to the school district, with the pragmatic recognition that resources vary from area to area. Creativity is a particularly important ingredient to successful plans, especially in resource-poor districts. In a regular classroom, quantity of work expected of the child or a supervised, structured study time at school may be the only adjustment needed. Among the most commonly found models for an individual education plan (IEP) may include a pull-out program where the child meets with a resource room teacher for work on certain topics each day, an aide in the regular classroom, or placement in a self-contained special education classroom. School districts vary in how they integrate instruction for their students with milder learning problems with those without learning difficulties; it is with these particular children with seizures that the most creative educational solutions are usually needed. The best educational options for the bright or retarded children are usually easier to determine.

For older adolescents, the relevance of the educational plan to future vocational options is an important consideration. For those individuals whose cognitive limitations clearly rule out a future competitive work situation, emphasis in school on acquisition of everyday living skills is of prime importance. The long-term educational goal for all children with epilepsy is maximal independence and productivity as adults. However, safety remains a primary issue when considerations are given to driving privileges and vocational situations where use of power tools, climbing, operating heavy or mobile mechinery, and electricity are involved.

Problems of social behavior and self-esteem of the schoolchild with epilepsy need to be addressed in a coordinated plan. Successes in the academic setting help boost self-esteem; the importance of structuring the educational plan so that the child can achieve short-term goals cannot be overemphasized. Interpersonal relations may be problematic if the child has deficits in reading subtle social cues, particularly if he or she reacts with behaviors inappropriate to the occasion. Direct teaching in how to handle social situations may be useful. Some school districts offer social skills programs; the topic may also be addressed in special education settings. The team should address how best to inform the child's classmates about seizures in school; ostracism stemming from such episodes increases during adolescence, worsened by ignorance and fear on the part of peers.

Other Sources of Support

In some metropolitan areas, social support for families and adolescents is available through an epilepsy society; the Epilepsy Foundation of America (4351 Garden City Drive, Landover, MD 20785, 1–800–EFA–1000) can provide contacts for specific geographical areas as well as a wealth of useful information. Some school districts have parent organizations for families of special needs children, which may serve to connect families with children with epilepsy. Self-help books that deserve frequent recommendation to families are those by Buchanan

(1987), Freeman, Vining, and Pillas (1990), Gumnit (1990), and Jan, Zeigler, and Erba (1983). Professionals working with such families are urged to have one or more of these books readily available.

CONCLUSIONS

This chapter has shown that neuropsychological factors are very important in working with children with epilepsy. The seizures themselves, the medications taken, and the underlying brain dysfunction can contribute to a myriad of neuropsychological, emotional, and psychosocial problems that require a coordinated effort of parents and professionals alike. The neuropsychologist, armed with information about areas of strengths and weaknesses in brain-related abilities as well as a basic knowledge of epilepsy, has a most important role in seeing that the best is done for these children and their families. The involvement of an neuropsychologist on a routine basis is urged before significant behavioral, psychiatric, and academic problems develop.

REFERENCES

Achenbach, T. M., & Edelbrock, C. (1983). *Manual for the Child Behavior Checklist and Revised Child Behavior Profile*. Burlington, VT: University of Vermont.

Achenbach, T. M., & Edelbrock, C. (1986). *Manual for the Teacher's Report Form and Teacher Version of the Child Behavior Profile*. Burlington VT: University of Vermont.

Achenbach, T. M., & Edelbrock, C. (1987). *Manual for the Youth Self Report and Profile*. Burlington, VT: University of Vermont.

Al-Kaisi, A. H., & McGuire, R. J. (1974). The effect of sulthiame on disturbed behaviour in mentally subnormal patients. *British Journal of Psychiatry, 124,* 45–49.

Aman, M. G., Werry, J. S., Paxton, J. W., & Turbott, S. H. (1987). Effect of sodium valproate on psychomotor performance in children as a function of dose, fluctuations in concentration, and diagnosis. *Epilepsia, 28,* 115–124.

Aman, M. G., Werry, J. S., Paxton, J. W., Turbott, S. H., & Steward, A. W. (1990). Effects of carbamazepine on psychomotor performance in children as a function of drug concentration, seizure type, and time of medication. *Epilepsia, 31,* 51–60.

Annegers, J. F., Shirts, S. B., Hauser, W. A., & Kurland, L. T. (1986). Risk of recurrence after an initial unprovoked seizure. *Epilepsia, 27,* 43–50.

Austin, J. K. (1989) . Factors associated with poor psychosocial adaptation to childhood epilepsy. *Epilepsia, 30,* 731.

Ballenger, J. C. (1988). The clinical use of carbamazepine in affective disorders. *Journal of Clincal Psychiatry, 49* (Suppl.), 13–19.

Batzel, L. W., Dodrill, C. B., Dubinsky, B. L., Zeigler, R. G., Connolly, J. E., Freeman, R. D., Farwell, J. R., & Vining, E. P. G. (1991). An objective method for the assessment of psychosocial problems in adolescents with epilepsy. *Epilepsia, 32,* 202–211.

Batzel, L. W., Dodrill, C. B., & Farwell, J. R. (1989). Relation of biographical and seizure history variables to adolescent psychosocial adjustment in epilepsy. *Epilepsia, 30,* 731.

Bourgeois, B. F. D., Prensky, A. L., Palkes, H. S., Talent, B. K., & Busch, S. G. (1983). Intelligence in epilepsy: A prospective study in children. *Annals of Neurology, 14,* 438–444.

Brent, D. A., Crumrine, P. K., Varma, R. R., Allan, M., & Allman, C. (1987). Phenobarbital treatment with major depressive disorder in children with epilepsy. *Pediatrics, 80,* 909–917.

Buchanan, N. (1987). *Epilepsy and You: Information for People with Epilepsy, Parents, Teachers and Other Interested Persons.* Sydney, Australia: Williams & Wilkins.

Byrne, J. M., Camfield, P. R., Clark-Touesnard, M. C., & Hondas, B. J. (1987). Effects of phenobarbital on early intellectual and behavioral development: A concordant twin case study. *Journal of Clinical and Experimental Neuropsychology, 9,* 393–398.

Camfield, C. S., Chaplin, S., Doyle, A-B, Shapir, S. H., Cummings, C., & Camfield, P. R. (1979). Side effects of phenobarbital in toddlers: Behavioral and cognitive aspects. *Journal of Pediatrics, 95,* 361–365.

Camfield, P. R., Gates, R., Ronen, G., Camfield, C., Ferguson, A., & MacDonald, G. W. (1984). Comparison of cognitive ability, personality profile, and school success in epileptic children with pure right versus left temporal lobe EEG foci. *Annals of Neurology, 15,* 122–126.

Commission on Classification and Terminology, International League Against Epilepsy. (1985). Proposal for classification of epilepsies and epileptic syndromes. *Epilepsia, 26,* 268–278.

Commission on Classification and Terminology of the International League Against Epilepsy. (1989). Proposal for revised classification of epilepsies and epileptic syndromes. *Epilepsia, 30,* 389–399.

Corbett, J. A., Trimble, M. R., & Nichol, T. C. (1985). Behavioral and cognitive impairments in children with epilepsy: The long-term effects of anticonvulsant therapy. *Journal of the American Academy of Child Psychiatry, 24,* 17–23.

Cull, C. A., & Trimble, M. R. (1989). Effects of anticonvulsant medications on cognitive functioning in children with epilepsy. In B. Hermann & M. Seidenberg (Eds.), *Childhood Epilepsies: Neuropsychological, Psychosocial and Intervention Aspects.* (pp. 83–103). Chichester: John Wiley.

Dahl, J., Melin, L., & Leissner, P. (1988). Effects of a behavioral intervention on epileptic seizure

behavior and paroxysmal activity: A systematic replication of three cases of children with intractable epilepsy. *Epilepsia, 29,* 172–183.

Dalby, M. A. (1975). Behavioral effects of carbamazepine. In J. K. Penry & D. D. Daly (Eds.), *Advances in Neurology: Complex Partial Seizures and Their Treatment* (Vol. 11, pp. 331–344). New York: Raven Press.

Delis, D. C., Kramer, J. H., Kaplan, E., & Ober, B. A. (1989). *California Verbal Learning Test: Children's Version, Research Addition.* San Antonio: The Psychological Corporation.

Dodrill, C. B. (1991). Behavioral effects of antiepileptic drugs. In D. Smith, D. Treiman, & M. R. Trimble (Eds.), *Advances in Neurology: Neurobehavioral Problems in Epilepsy* (Vol. 55, pp. 213–224). New York: Raven Press.

Dodrill, C. B., Batzel, L. W., Queisser, H. R., & Temkin, N. (1980). An objective method for the assessment of psychological and social problems among epileptics. *Epilepsia, 21,* 123–135.

Dodrill, C. B., & Temkin, N. (1989). Motor speed is a contamin- ating variable in evaluating the "cognitive" effects of phenytoin. *Epilepsia, 30,* 453–457.

Dodrill, C. B., & Troupin, A. S. (1991). Neuropsychological effects of carbamazepine and phenytoin: A reanalysis. *Neurology, 41,* 141–143.

Dreifuss, F. E. (1989). Childhood epilepsies. In B. P. Hermann & M. Seidenberg (Eds.), *Childhood Epilepsies: Neuropsychological, Psychosocial and Intervention Aspects* (pp. 1–13). Chichester: John Wiley.

Duncan, J. S., Shorvon, S. D., & Trimble, M. R. (1990). Effects of removal of phenytoin, carbamazepine, and valproate on cognitive function. *Epilepsia, 31,* 584–591.

Evans, R. W., Clay, T. H., & Gualtieri, C. T. (1987). *Journal of the American Academy of Child and Adolescent Psychiatry, 26,* 2–8.

Evans, R. W., & Gualtieri, C. T. (1985). Carbamazepine: A neuropsychological and psychiatric profile. *Clinical Neuropharmacology, 8,* 221–241.

Farwell, J. R., Dodrill, C. B., & Batzel, L. W. (1985). Neuropsychological abilities of children with epilepsy. *Epilepsia, 26,* 395–400.

ref.

Farwell, J. R., Lee, Y. J., Hirtz, D. G., Sulzbacher, S. I., Ellenberg, J. H., & Nelson, K. B. (1990). Phenobarbital for febrile seizures—effects on intelligence and on seizure recurrence. *New England Journal of Medicine, 322,* 364–369.

Freeman, J. M., Vining, E. P. G., & Pillas, D. J. (1990). *Seizures and Epilepsy in Childhood: A Guide for Parents.* Baltimore, MD: Johns Hopkins University Press.

Gadow, K. D. (1982). School involvement in the treatment of seizure disorders. *Epilepsia, 23,* 215–224.

Goldberg, J. B., & Kurland, A. A. (1970). Dilantin treatment of hospitalized cultural-familial retardates. *Journal of Nervous and Mental Disease, 150,* 133–137.

Golden, C. J. (1981). The Luria-Nebraska children's battery: Theory and initial formulation. In G. Hynd & J. Obrzut (Eds.), *Neuropsychological Assessment and the School-Age Child: Issues and Procedures* (pp. 277–302). New York: Grune & Stratton.

Green, R. C., Adler, J. R., & Erba, G. (1988). Epilepsy surgery in children. *Journal of Child Neurology, 3,* 155–166.

Groh, C. (1976). The psychotropic effect of Tegretol in non- epileptic children, with particular reference to the drug's indications. In W. Birkmayer (Ed.), *Epileptic Seizures-Behavior-Pain* (pp. 259–263). Bern: Hans Huber.

Gumnit, R. J. (1990). *Living Well with Epilepsy.* New York: Demos Publications.

Hauser, W. A., & Hesdorffer, D. C. (1990). *Epilepsy: Frequency, Causes, and Consequences.* New York: Demos Publications.

Hauser, W. A., Rich, S. S., Annegers, J. F., & Anderson, V. E. (1990). Seizure recurrence after a first unprovoked seizure: An extended followup. *Neurology, 40,* 1163–1170.

Hellström, B., & Barlach-Christoffersen, M. (1980). Influence of phenobarbital on the psychomotor development and behaviour in preschool children with convulsions. *Neuropädiatrie, 11,* 151–160.

Hermann, B. P., Desai, B., & Whitman, S. (1988). Epilepsy. In V. Van Hasselt, P. Strain, M. Hersen (Eds.), *Handbook of Developmental and Physical Disabilities* (pp. 247–270). New York: Pergamon Press.

Hermann, B. P., Whitman, S., Hughes, J. R., Melyn, M. M., & Dell, J. (1988). Multietiological determinants of psychopathology and social competence in children with epilepsy. *Epilepsy Research, 2,* 51–60.

Hermann, B. P., Whitman, S., & Dell, J. (1989). Correlates of behavior problems and social competence in children with epilepsy, aged 6–11. In B. Hermann & M. Seidenberg (Eds.), *Childhood Epilepsies: Neuropsychological, Psychosocial and Intervention Aspects* (pp. 143–157). Chichester: John Wiley.

Herranz, J. L., Arteaga, R., & Armijo, J. A. (1982). Side effects of sodium valproate in monotherapy controlled by plasma levels: A study of 88 pediatric patients. *Epilepsia, 23,* 203–314.

Holcombe, V., Summit, N. J., Brandt, J., Carden, F., Johnson, K., Ris, D., Vail, R., & Strollo, A. (1987). Effects of Tegretol or phenytoin on cognitive function and behavior in epileptic children younger than six years. *Neurology, 37* (Supp. 1), 92.

Holdsworth, L., & Whitmore, K. (1974). A study of children with epilepsy attending ordinary schools. I. Their seizure patterns, progress and behaviour in school. *Developmental Medicine and Child Neurology, 16,* 746–758.

Jacobides, G. M. (1978). Alertness and scholastic achievement in young epileptics treated with carbamazepine (Tegretol). In H. Meinardi & A. J. Rowan (Eds.), *Advances in Epileptology: 1977* (pp. 114–119). Amsterdam: Swets & Zeitlinger B.V.

Jan, J. E., Zeigler, R. G., & Erba, G. (1983). *Does Your Child Have Epilepsy?* Baltimore, MD: University Park Press.

Jeavons, P. M., & Clark, J. E. (1974). Sodium valproate in treatment of epilepsy. *British Medical Journal, 2,* 584–586.

Klein, D. F., & Greenberg, I. M. (1967). Behavioral effects of diphenylhydantoin in severe psychiatric disorders. *American Journal of Psychiatry, 124,* 847–848.

Lantz, D., & Sterman, M. B. (1988). Neuropsychological assessment of subjects with uncontrolled epilepsy: Effects of EEG feedback training. *Epilepsia, 29,* 163–171.

Lefkowitz, M. M. (1969). Effects of diphenylhydantoin on disruptive behavior: Study of male delinquents. *Archives of General Psychiatry, 20,* 643–651.

Lindsley, D. B., & Henry, C. E. (1942). The effect of drugs on behavior and the electroencephalograms of children with behavior disorders. *Psychosomatic Medicine, 4,* 140–149.

Looker, A., & Conners, C. K. (1970). Diphenylhydantoin in children with severe temper tantrums. *Archives of General Psychiatry, 23,* 80–89.

Meador, K. J., Loring, D. W., Huh, K., Gallagher, B. B., & King, D. W. (1990). Comparative cognitive effects of anticonvulsants. *Neurology, 40,* 391–394.

Miles, M. V., Tennison, M. B., & Greenwood, R. S. (1988). Assessment of antiepileptic drug effects on child behavior using the Child Behavior Checklist. *Journal of Epilepsy, 1,* 209–213.

Mitchell, W. G., Baker S. A., & Guzman, B. L. (1990). Social competence in children with epilepsy. *Epilepsia, 31,* 664.

Mitchell, W. G., & Chavez, J. M. (1986). Phenobarbital versus carbamazepine for partial seizures in children. *Epilepsia, 27,* 639–640.

Moffatt, W. R., Siddiqui, A. R., & MacKay, D. N. (1970). The use of sulthiame with disturbed mentally subnormal patients. *British Journal of Psychiatry, 117,* 673–678.

Mostofsky, D. I., & Balaschak, B. A. (1977). Psychobiological control of seizures. *Psychological Bulletin, 84,* 723–750.

Nolte, R., Wetzel, B., Br gmann, G., & Brintzinger, I. (1980). Effects of phenytoin and primidone monotherapy on mental performance in children. In S. I. Johannessen, P. L. Morselli, C. E. Pippenger, A. Richens, D. Schmidt, & H. Meinardi (Eds.), *Antiepileptic Therapy: Advances in Drug Monitoring* (pp. 81–88). New York: Raven Press.

O'Dougherty, M., Wright, F. S., Cox, S., & Walson, P. (1987). Carbamazepine plasma concentration relationship to cognitive impairment. *Archives of Neurology, 44,* 863–867.

Okuma, T., & Kumashiro, H. (1980). Natural history and prognosis of epilepsy. In J. A. Wada & J. K. Penry (Eds.), *Advances in Epileptology: The Xth Epilepsy International Symposium* (pp. 135–141). New York: Raven Press.

O'Leary, D. S., Lovell, M. R., Sackellares, J. C., Berent, S., Giordani, B., Seidenberg, M., & Boll, T. J. (1981). Effects of age of onset of partial and generalized seizures on neuropsychological performance in children. *Journal of Nervous and Mental Disease, 171,* 624–629.

O'Leary, D. S., Seidenberg, M., Berent, S., & Boll, T. J. (1981). Effects of age at onset of tonic-clonic seizures on neuropsychological performance in children. *Epilepsia, 22,* 197–204.

Özdirim, E., Renda, Y., & Epir, S. (1978). Effects of phenobarbital and phenytoin on the behaviour of epileptic children. In H. Meinardi, & A. J. Rowan (Eds.), *Advances in Epileptology: 1977* (pp. 120–123). Amsterdam: Swets & Zeitlinger B.V.

Pellock, J. M., Culbert, J. P., Garnett, W. R., Crumrine, P. K. Kaplan, A. M., Frost, M. M., O'Hara, K. A., Driscoll, S. M., Alvin, R., Handen, B., Horowitz, I. W., & Hamer, R. M. (1987). Assessment of cognitive and behavioral effects of carbamazepine, phenytoin, and phenobarbital in school-aged children. *Epilepsia, 28,* 597.

Reitan, R. M., & Davison, L. A. (1974). *Clinical Neuropsychology: Current Status and Applications.* Washington, DC: V. H. Winston & Sons.

Rett, A. (1976). The so-called psychotropic effect of Tegretol in the treatment of convulsions of cerebral origin in children. In W. Birkmayer (Ed.), *Epileptic Seizures-Behavior-Pain* (pp. 194–204). Bern: Hans Huber.

Rodin, E. (1989). Prognosis of cognitive functions in children with epilepsy. In B. Hermann & M. Seidenberg (Eds.), *Childhood Epilepsies: Neuropsychological, Psychosocial and Intervention Aspects.* Chichester: John Wiley.

Rodin, E. A., Schmaltz, S., & Twitty, G. (1986). Intellectual functions of patients with childhood-onset epilepsy. *Developmental Medicine and Childhood Neurology, 28,* 25–33.

Roger, J., Dravet, C., Bureau, M., Dreifuss, F. E., & Wolf, P. (1985). *Epileptic Syndromes in Infancy, Childhood and Adolescence.* Paris: John Libbey Eurotext.

Schain, R. J., Shields, W. D., & Dreisbach, M. (1981). Carbamazepine and cognitive functioning. *Book of Abstracts: Thirteenth Epilepsy International Congress* (p. 250). Kotyo, Japan.

Schain, R. J., Ward, J. W., & Guthrie, D. (1977). Carbamazepine as an anticonvulsant in children. *Neurology, 27,* 476–480.

Seidenberg, M. (1989). Academic achievement and school performance of children with epilepsy. In B. Hermann & M. Seidenberg (Eds.), *Childhood Epilepsies: Neuropsychological, Psychosocial and Intervention Aspects.* Chichester: John Wiley.

Seidenberg, M., Beck, N., Geisser, M., Giordani, B., Sackellares, J. C., Berent, S., Dreifuss, F. E., & Boll, T. J. (1986). Academic achievement of children with epilepsy. *Epilepsia, 27,* 753–759.

Seidenberg, M., Beck, N., Geisser, M., O'Leary, D. S., Giordani, B., Berent, S., Sackellares, J. C., Dreifuss, F. E., & Boll, T. J. (1988). Neuropsychological correlates of academic achievement of children with epilepsy. *Journal of Epilepsy, 1,* 23–29.

Sheslow, D., & Adams, W. (1990). *Wide Range Assessment of Memory and Learning: Administration manual.* Wilmington, DE: Jastak Associates, Inc.

Shinnar, S., Berg, A. T., Mosh,, S. L., Petix, M., Maytal, J., Kang, H., Goldensohn, E. S., & Hauser, W. A. (1990) Risk of seizure recurrence following a first unprovoked seizure in childhood: A prospective study. *Pediatrics, 85,* 1076–1085.

Shorvon, S. D. (1984). The temporal aspects of prognosis in epilepsy. *Journal of Neurology, Neurosurgery, and Psychiatry, 47,* 1157–1165.

Smith, W. L., Philippus, M. J., & Guard, H. L. (1968). Psychometric study of children with learning problems and 14–6 positive spike EEG patterns, treated with ethosuximide (Zarontin) and placebo. *Archives of Diseases of Childhood, 43,* 616–619.

Sparrow, S., Balla, D. A., & Cichetti, D. V. (1984). *Vineland Adaptive Behavior Scales—Interview Edition, Expanded Form Manual.* Circle Pines, MN: American Guidance Service.

Sparrow, S., Balla, D. A., & Cichetti, D. V. (1985). *Vineland Adaptive Behavior Scales—Classroom Edition manual.* Circle Pines, MN: American Guidance Service.

Sterman, M. B., & Friar, L. (1972). Suppression of seizures in an epileptic following sensorimotor EEG feedback training. *Electroencephalography and Clinical Neurophysiology, 33,* 89–95.

Sterman, M. B., Macdonald, L. R., & Stone, R. K. (1974). Biofeedback training of the sensorimotor electroencephalogram rhythm in man: Effects on epilepsy. *Epilepsia, 15,* 395–416.

Stores, G. (1977). Behaviour disturbance and type of epilepsy in children attending ordinary school. In J. K. Penry (Ed.), *Epilepsy: Proceedings of the Eighth International Symposium* (pp. 245–249). New York: Raven Press.

Stores, G., & Hart, J. (1976). Reading skills of children with generalized or focal epilepsy attending ordinary school. *Developmental Medicine and Child Neurology, 18,* 705–716.

Stores, G., & Williams, P. (1987). A controlled study of the behavioural effects of carbamazepine and valproate used as single treatment in children with epilepsy. *Book of abstracts: Seventeenth Epilepsy International Congress* (p. 116). Jerusalem.

Strang, J. D. (1990). Cognitive deficits in children: Adaptive behavior and treatment techniques. *Epilepsia, 31* (Suppl. 4), S54-S58.

Tan, S-Y, & Bruni, J. (1986). Cognitive behavioral therapy with adult patients with epilepsy: A controlled outcome study. *Epilepsia, 27,* 225–233.

Temkin, N. R., & Davis, G. R. (1984). Stress as a risk factor for seizures among adults with epilepsy. *Epilepsia, 25,* 450–456.

Trimble, M. R. (1987). Anticonvulsant drugs and cognitive function: A review of the literature. *Epilepsia, 28* (Suppl. 3), S37-S45.

Vining, E. P. G., Mellits, E. D., Dorsen, M. M., Cataldo, M. F., Quaskey, S. A., Spielberg, S. P., & Freeman, J. M. (1987). Psychologic and behavioral effects of antiepileptic drugs in children: A double-blind comparison between phenobarbital and valproic acid. *Pediatrics, 80,* 165–174.

Webster, A., & Mawer, G. E. (1989). Seizure frequency and major life events in epilepsy. *Epilepsia, 30,* 162–167.

Wirt, R. D., Lachar, D., Klinedinst, J. K., & Seat, P. D. (1977). *Multidimensional Description of*

Child Personality. Los Angeles: Western Psychological Services.

Wyler, A. R., Robbins, C. A., & Dodrill, C. B. (1979). EEG operant conditioning for control of epilepsy. *Epilepsia, 20,* 279–286.

Yusko, M. J., & Verma, N. P. (1991). Carbamazepine offers no psychotropic advantage over phenytoin in adult epileptic subjects. *Neurology, 41* (Suppl. 1), 216.

13

CONGENITAL MENTAL RETARDATION

KENNETH D. MCCOY   **JANET M. ARCENEAUX**

RAYMOND S. DEAN

DEFINITION ISSUES

Mental retardation is most commonly defined as a general subaverage intellectual functioning, accompanied by deficits or impairments in adaptive behavior with an onset before age 18 (American Psychiatric Association, 1987; Grossman, 1983). Assessment of general intellectual functioning most often relies on a standardized intelligence battery. To meet the criteria set by the *Diagnostic and Statistical Manual of Mental Disorders, Third Edition, Revised* (DSM-III-R; American Psychiatric Association, 1987), the patient must obtain an intelligence quotient (IQ) of 70 or below, which is an arbitrary score, merely reflecting two standard deviations below the population mean. However, various measures of IQ have different psychometric features and can produce different IQ scores for the same patient. This fact emphasizes the rather arbitrary diagnostic criteria for the diagnosis of mental retardation.

The American Association of Mental Deficiency (AAMD) (Grossman & Tarjan, 1987) definition of *mental retardation* requires that both the level of intelligence and level of adaptive behavior be considered concurrently in diagnoses. Adaptive behavior is defined by the AAMD as the degree of effectiveness of behavior in confronting the requirements of the social and natural environment. In contrast with standardized intellectual tests that offer a precise score, there are very few adaptive behavior measures that satisfy accepted psychometric standards (Sattler, 1990).

The definition and diagnosis of mental retardation is complicated because it is test bound. For example, in public schools, even if a child has an IQ of 70 (a score that is not within the range for mental retardation criteria) and an adaptive behavior score of 65, the child may still meet criteria for mental retardation.

CLASSIFICATION

Mental retardation is classified into subcategories, depending on the degree of impairment, as measured by an IQ test. It must be noted that there exists ambiguity pertaining to the cut-off scores of these subcategories. This can produce confusion in communication and research (e.g., prevalence rates). For example, some researchers consider IQ scores of less than 50 as severe. McLaren and Bryson (1987) overview research on epidemiology and conclude that the prevalence rate for severe mental retardation, IQ less than 50, is consistent with prior research (e.g., Abramowicz & Richardson, 1975; d'Anthenaise & Salbreux, 1979; Bernsen, 1976; Darragh, 1982). The prevalence rate for severe mental retardation is 3 to 4 individuals per 1,000 (McLaren & Bryson, 1987). However, when using the AAMD or the *DSM-III-R* classification system, "severe" is an obtained IQ score of 20 to 35 to 40, which would result in a different prevalence rate than that based on an IQ score of 50.

When discussing mental retardation, the classification proposed by Grossman (1983) defines the classification used by the American Psychiatric Association, where mental retardation is divided into subcategories that consider the severity of the disorder. These classifications are borderline, mild, moderate, severe, and profound.

Borderline mental retardation, sometimes referred to as the slow learner (Sinclair & Forness, 1983), is seen to exist when a patient's IQ score is between 84 and 71. The prevalence rate is approximately 6 to 7% of the general population (Kaplan & Sadock, 1988). This category is thought to be related more to environmental factors, such as "cultural deprivation," rather than to any specific neurological dysfunction. The classification of borderline is no longer considered a valid subcategory (Sinclair & Forness, 1983). However, it is still often used because individuals in the category may experience various types of adaptive difficulties (Kaplan & Sadock, 1988).

A subject is considered *mildly mentally retarded* when the obtained IQ score falls between 70 and 50–55. Mild mentally retarded is equivalent to the previously referred educational term, *educable mentally retarded* (Sinclair & Forness, 1983). This is the largest subgroup and it encompasses about 85% of all mentally retarded patients (Heber, 1970). The prevalence rate for mild mental retardation, as overviewed by McLaren and Bryson (1987), is approximately 3.7 to 5.9 per 1,000. However, this estimate for mild retardation is much less than the 2 to 3% that would be predicted by a normal distribution of IQ scores (Dingman & Tarjan, 1960). Although the etiology is not entirely understood, some believe that it is due to genetic factors, others to environmental factors, and still others believe that it is an interaction of the two (Zigler & Hodapp, 1986). Mildly retarded children can be difficult to distinguish from normal functioning children until the schoolyears, when they fail to achieve the academic level of their peers. The expectation for these patients is an academic achievement of about sixth-grade level. They can live fairly independent lives in their adult years.

According to this system, the diagnosis of *moderately mentally retarded* is made when the patient's IQ score falls between 50–55 and 35–40. Moderate mental retardation is equivalent to the previously referred educational classification, *trainable mentally retarded* (Sinclair & Forness, 1983). Trainable is not a popular label as a classification because it implies that these patients are unable to learn or benefit from formal classroom educational efforts. According to McLaren and Bryson's (1987) overview of epidemiology, the prevalence rate is approximately 2 per 1,000. Individuals within this category have not only impaired intelligence but often also have physical and neurological impairments (Brantley, 1988). In fact, many of these cases of mental retardation are caused by biological abnormalities (Kaplan & Sadock, 1988). Generally, the moderately retarded can be expected to function at the second-grade academic level, and as adolescents and adults, can be expected to live independently in a supervised group home. With intervention, these patients often learn to perform some type of skilled or semi-skilled work.

Patients with IQ scores that range from 35–40 to 20–25 are considered to be *severely mentally retarded.* Severe mental retardation encompasses about 3 to 4% of the total population of mentally retarded (Heber, 1970). The prevalence rate is considered to be about 1.3 per 1,000 (McLaren & Bryson, 1987). These patients usually develop only minimal oral communication and generally show poor motor development. Most often, these patients do not gain much beyond readiness skills for the academic subjects. They usually adapt well to their community and homes but require close supervision. Mental retardation in this category is most often related to biological abnormalities (Kaplan & Sadock, 1988).

Profound mental retardation is diagnosed with an IQ score below 20–25 (American Psychiatric Association, 1987; Grossman, 1983). Profound levels of mental retardation are found in 1 to 2% of the patients with mental retardation (Heber, 1970). Based on the prediction from a normal distribution of IQ scores, the prevalence rate should be about 0.4 per 1,000 (McLaren & Bryson, 1987). Profoundly retarded individuals generally display minimal capacity for sensorimotor functioning, and will require nursing care and supervision. Extensive repetition and training is required for these patients to acquire basic communication skills, motor development, and minimal self-care. Individuals within this category usually show clear organic cerebral abnormalities (Hicks & Berg, 1988).

Public schools are affected by the arbitrary definitions in that the definitions are based on ranges and not a definite score. Thus, difficulties ensue in applying diagnostic criteria. In addition, public schools must also consider other factors such as adaptive behavior. Although each state has individual guidelines for the placement of children into exceptional children's programs, most schools adhere to this rule of thumb: If a child is two standard deviations below the mean on a standardized intelligence test and is deficient in adaptive behavior, he or she qualifies for special education. These individuals may require a full-time placement or may only require a part-time resource room. In addition, the schools are mandated to appropriately serve each child's educational needs in the least restrictive environment (PL 94-142, 1975). Therefore, according to the law, not only must the educational needs of the child be satisfied but also these needs be satisfied in the least restrictive environment.

ETIOLOGY

Since mental retardation is diagnosed on the bases of IQ scores, it does not represent a single disorder. Clearly, mental retardation may be either a primary diagnosis or secondary to a number of other disorders. Indeed, mental retardation may be the result of multifaceted etiologies. How mental retardation is etiologically categorized is frequently idiosyncratic and subjective. This review of the etiology of retardation will utilize three categories, which are often not mutually exclusive. These three categories are cultural-familial issues, genetic factors, and pre-, peri-, and postnatal insults.

Cultural-Familial Issues

The patients within this group have IQs that fall within the range of 50 to 70 (i.e., mildly mentally retarded) and make up about 75% of the mentally retarded population (Kaplan & Sadock, 1988). It is believed that the etiology of this group of mentally deficient individuals is primarily one of cultural and/or psychosocial deprivation. Mild retardation is significantly higher in the low socioeconomic class, sometimes with family members displaying similar symptoms. The existence of adverse conditions is not uncommon within the low socioeconomic class, creating an environment ripe for negative developmental and pathogenic effects (Kaplan & Sadock, 1988).

Genetic Causes of Mental Retardation

Some cases of mental retardation can be traced to some type of genetic abnormality (Warkany, Lemire, & Cohen, 1981; Zigler & Hodapp, 1986; Hicks & Berg, 1988). Genetic aberrations may result in chromosomal and metabolic defects. Often, fetuses with gross genetic abnormalities are spontaneously aborted. However, those that survive may have biochemical and/or structural brain abnormalities (Baumeister & MacLean, 1979).

Chromosomal abnormalities comprise the largest number of known genetic causes of mental retardation (Heber, 1970; Hicks & Berg, 1988; Zigler & Hodapp, 1986; Warkany et al., 1981). Each human cell contains 46 chromosomes, which are comprised of 23 matched pairs. Half of the 46 chromosomes are received from the mother, and half are received from the father. The 23 matched pairs of chromosomes consist of 22 pairs of autosome and 1 pair of sex chromosome (either X or

Y), which determine the sex of the child. Following conception, during the process of cell division, chromosomal defects can occur (Berg, 1988).

Trisomies are one of the most common etiologies of the chromosomal disorders. Trisomy disorders are characterized by an extra chromosome (47 rather than 46). Trisomy 18 (Edward's syndrome), Trisomy 13 (Patau's syndrome) and Trisomy 21 (Down syndrome) are all examples of this type of chromosomal disorder (Mikkelsen, 1988).

The most common type of chromosomal disorder resulting in mental retardation is *Trisomy 21*. Three primary chromosome abnormalities have been identified in patients with Down syndrome. The first abnormality is a supernumerary 21 chromosome, and occurs in approximately 90 to 95% of Down syndrome cases (Pueschel & Thuline, 1983). This abnormality occurs when either the egg or the sperm contributes one too many chromosomes. As a result, the extra chromosome attaches to the 21st pair and fails to separate, producing a pattern of mental and physical abnormalities (Zellweger & Patil, 1987; Swaiman & Jacobson, 1984). The second abnormality involves translocation, in which the long extensions of chromosome 21 attach in place of the short extensions on chromosomes 14 or 21, and occasionally 13, 15, or 22. Translocation occurs in approximately 4 to 6% of Down syndrome patients (Pueschel & Thuline, 1983). The third abnormality is mosaicism. This is the result of both normal and trisomic cells in the blood and other tissue. This abnormality occurs in approximately 1 to 2% of the cases of Down syndrome (Pueschel & Thuline, 1983).

The occurrence of Down syndrome in the United States is approximately 1 per 1,000 births (Gray & Dean, 1991) and is rarely found within the African-American population (Santrock & Yussen, 1992). It has been widely recognized that the increased aging of the mother significantly increases the risk of Down syndrome (Pueschel & Thuline, 1983). However, using staining methods, Thuline and Pueschel (1982) were able to trace 75% of the trisomy 21 cases they examined, and found both maternal and paternal origin.

Using amniocenteses, Down syndrome can be diagnosed in utero. However, diagnosis is most often made on the bases of physical characteristics soon after birth. These physical characteristics include short stature, upward eye slant with epicanthal folds, white spots around the iris of the eye, flatness of the back of the head, flat nose, protruding deeply fissured tongue, small low-set ears, short broad fingers, and a simian crease in the palm of the hands (Swaiman & Jacobson, 1984; Zellweger & Patil, 1987). Down syndrome patients also suffer from muscular hypotonia (muscle tone weakness), joint hyperlaxity, and nystagmus. The gait of Down syndrome patients is usually clumsy and slightly dysmetric (Zellweger & Patil, 1987).

The neurological features of individuals with Down syndrome consist of small brain, abnormal neuronal growth and migration, inadequate synaptogenesis, and reduced myelination. Approximately 10% of the patients with Down syndrome suffer a seizure disorder. As the individual matures and enters the second and third decades of life, a loss in intellectual and social functioning is experienced. This change in cognitive functioning is very similar to presenile dementia and resembles the symptoms of Alzheimer's disease (Swaiman & Jacobson, 1984).

EEG abnormalities include slow background activity, spikes and waves, polyspikes, and focal paroxysmal discharges. Somatosensory, auditory, and visual evoked potentials in individuals with Down syndrome are different from normal individuals, suggesting diffuse brain dysfunction.

Patients with Down syndrome exhibit mild to severe mental retardation (Brantley, 1988). However, the majority of these patients fall within the moderate to severe range (Kaplan & Sadock, 1988).

Trisomy 18 (Edwards syndrome) is the second most common autosomal disorder and occurs in approximately 1 in 3,000 to 1 in 5,000, with a female to male ratio of 3:1 (Pueschel & Thuline, 1983). Mortality rate is high for these individuals, and death occurs in 90% of these patients within the first year, with males surviving an average of 2 to 3 months, and females 10 months. Death usually occurs due to congenital heart disease (Pueschel & Thuline, 1983). In addition to mental retardation, other clinical signs are low birth weight, hypertonicity, microcephaly, harelip and/or cleft palate, ear defects, and congenital heart defects (Krompotic, 1978).

Trisomy 13 (Pautau syndrome) occurs in approximately 1 in 8,000 to 1 in 5,000 live births (Pueschel & Thuline, 1983). These individuals exhibit severe mental retardation. Neonates with this disorder most often demonstrate excessive tics and episodes of apnea. Other physical complications can include seizures, microcephaly, scalp defects, abnormal ears, deafness, microphthalmia, and coloboma. Life expectancy is approximately 130 days, with a 92% mortality rate within the first year (Abuelo, 1983). Death usually occurs due to cardiac complications.

Patients with *trisomy 8* exhibit mild to severe mental retardation with a female to male ratio of 1:3 (Pueschel & Thuline, 1983). Physical complications and/or abnormalities include seizures, plagiocephaly, agenesis of the corpus callosum, low-set abnormal ears, micrognathia, long slender trunk, narrow pelvis, skeletal anomalies, deep skin furrows over palms and soles, and joint contractures. Individuals with trisomy 8 appear to have a normal life expectancy.

Individuals with chromosome 5 disorders, or "cri du chat" (cat cry), exhibit a remarkable feature in which the infant has a high-pitched cat-like cry (Pueschel & Thuline, 1983). Symptoms of this disorder include severe developmental retardation, failure to thrive, seizures, and hypotonia. Patients may also exhibit microcephaly, ocular hypertelorism, and epicanthal folds. The development of congenital heart disease occurs in approximately 20% of this population (Swaiman & Jacobson, 1984). Life expectancy is into adulthood (Pueschel & Thuline, 1983).

Another principal area of chromosomal abnormalities relates to the sex chromosomes. As stated previously, one pair of the 23 pairs of chromosomes determines the sex of the child. The chromosome from the mother will always be an X chromosome, whereas the chromosome from the father can be either, an X or a Y chromosome. If the embryo has received two X chromosomes, a female will develop; however, if the combination received is one X and one Y, then the result will be a male.

Fragile X syndrome is the second most common chromosomal disorder that causes mental retardation (Fryns, 1988). It occurs in approximately 1 per 5,500 live births (Webb, Crawley & Bundey, 1990). This disorder is a result of a defect in the X chromosome. The defected portion is located at the distal end of the X chromosome, and appears to remain attached to the body of the chromosome by only a thin mangled membrane.

Fragile X syndrome primarily affects males, and is characterized by such physical characteristics as small stature, large head, a long narrow face, ear anomalies, and large testicles. These patients also evidence mental retardation, ranging from mild to moderate. Speech and language difficulties are common, and include articulation deficits, echolalia, and perseveration. Often, behavioral problems are also present, such as self-abusive behavior, hyperactivity, self-isolation, and bizarre behaviors (Swaiman & Jacobson, 1984; Zellweger & Patil, 1987).

Klinefelter syndrome is the second most common sex-linked genetic disorder. It affects males exclusively (Brantley, 1988), and occurs in approximately 1 per 1,000 live births (Apgar & Beck, 1974). Patients affected by this disorder have either 47 or 48 chromosomes (Grossman & Tarjan, 1987), involving two possible combinations. The combinations consist of either XXY or XXXY. Individuals with the XXXY combination generally display more severe signs of mental retardation than individuals with the XXY combination.

Symptoms of Kleinfelter syndrome may include mild to moderate mental retardation, essential tremor, choreiform dyskinesis, microcephaly, and learning and speech problems (Zellweger & Patil, 1987). Volavka, Mednick, Rasmussen, and Sergeant (1977) also found abnormalities of visual, auditory, and somatosensory evoked responses. In addition, these individuals have small testes, small slender stature or obesity, female-like breasts, and behavioral problems that resemble antisocial behavior that ranges from mild to severe (Swaiman & Jacobson, 1984). This disorder may not be readily apparent until the male reaches adolescence and displays a delay in secondary sexual development (Swaiman & Jacobson, 1984; Zellweger & Patil, 1987).

Turner syndrome occurs almost exclusively in females (Brantley, 1988) at a rate of approximately 1 per 3,000 live births (Menkes, 1985). Approximately 18% of these patients exhibit mental retardation in the mild range. In many cases, the verbal score is actually higher than the performance score due to a spatial perception difficulty (Brantley, 1988), a pattern not often seen in the general mentally retarded population.

Phenylketonuria (PKU) is a genetically based, metabolic disorder in which the patient is unable to metabolize phenylalanine (Swaiman & Jacobson, 1984). Phenylalanine is an amino acid that is essential for development and growth. This disorder occurs in approximately 1 per 14,000 live births (Abuelo, 1983; Brantley, 1988).

Children with untreated PKU usually have blue eyes, blonde hair, and severe mental retardation (Baumeister, 1967). Other complications consist of behavioral and neurological problems (Abuelo, 1983). Treatment consists of a life-long, strict diet of phenylalanine free foods. Early detection (i.e., at infancy) is imperative because it can prevent deficiency or significantly improve it (Baumeister, 1967). Damage by PKU toxicity seems to be complete by the age of 3; in fact, the IQ of patients who began treatment subsequent to 160 weeks of age were the same as those untreated (Baumeister, 1967).

Natal Causes of Mental Retardation

Previously discussed endogenous etiologies have focused on genetic factors. However, there are many etiologies of mental retardation that, although not genetic, can occur during pregnancy or delivery.

There are a number of risk factors prior to pregnancy, but age of the mother at time of conception is one of the most salient factors (Gray & Dean, 1991). Conception after the age of 35 increases the risk of perinatal complications (Naeye, 1983). A study by Kajanoja and Widholm (1978) compared 558 women over 40 years of age to a group of younger mothers. They found that the older mothers had significantly higher incidence of premature births, breech births, and infants with congenital abnormalities. In fact, Cohen, Newman, and Friedman (1980) showed that mothers over the age of 35 years had twice as many labor abnormalities than mothers 20 years old or less.

Adolescent mothers are another group who are at high risk of premature births, stillbirths, and infant mortality (Dwyer, 1974). In addition, children born of adolescent mothers have a higher risk of motor and cognitive delays (Broman, 1978).

During pregnancy, risk factors that can affect growth and development and result in mental retardation include maternal drug use, infections, and traumas. Primary prenatal factors that affect the unborn fetus and may cause mental retardation are drug use, infection, and malnutrition. Although these factors can occur at any time during pregnancy, occurrence during the first trimester is more likely to produce more gross abnormalities. Indeed, the first trimester is the time of fastest growth of the central nervous system, and by the third month, mature glia cells are present (Gray & Dean, 1991). Drugs and toxic substances can result in complications during pregnancies, including bleeding, stillbirths, and premature delivery (Brantley, 1988).

A growing concern has been the mother's use of drugs and toxic substances, such as alcohol. Fetal alcohol syndrome (FAS), a collection of abnormalities, is the result of ethanol use during the gestation period. It is estimated, for an alcoholic mother, the risk of producing an infant with some type of defect is as high as 35% (Kaplan & Sadock, 1988). Even moderate use can increase the occurrence of growth abnormalities and microcephaly by as much as five times the normal rate (Hanson, 1977).

There are three primary characteristics of FAS (Grossman & Tarjan, 1987). The first characteristic is central nervous dysfunction. This results in mental retardation, developmental delays, microcephaly, impaired coordination, hypotonia, irritability in infants, and attention-deficit disorders. The second characteristic is growth deficiency. Both zinc and magnesium are vital nutrients in growth process, and alcohol can deprive the body of these nutrients. The third characteristic is dysmorphic features. Some FAS children are born with genital abnormalities, joint anomalies, drooping eyelids, crossed eyes, flat midface, low nasal bridge, and epicanthic folds. Prognosis is poor for children with severe mental retardation due to FAS. However, most children with mental retardation due to FAS fall within the borderline to moderate range (Grossman & Tarjan, 1987).

Although the full effects of this syndrome are not yet fully understood, the occurrence of this disorder does appear to be rapidly growing. Whether this growth is due to an actual increase of the event, improved ability to recognize the disorder, or both is not yet clear.

Viral infections are another factor that may affect the developing fetus and result in major birth defects. Not all infections are transferred from the mother to the fetus; however, there is a 50% greater chance of fetal infection if contracted in the first trimester (Naeye & Tafari, 1983). Infections contracted in the first trimester pose a greater risk to the fetus than infections contracted in the latter trimesters (Monif, Egan, & Held, 1972). Three such viruses that have been shown to be connected with fetal complications are CMV (cytomegalovirus), herpes simplex, and rubella (Gray & Dean, 1991).

CMV has been shown to produce adverse effects such as developmental disorders and mental retardation (Naeye & Tafari, 1983). Herpes simplex, which is in the same family of viruses as CMV, can result in death. The consequence for those infants who survive this infection can be seizures, microcephaly, and psychomotor disorders (Torphy, Ray, & McAlister, 1970). The rubella virus can have devastating effects, such as deafness, CNS dysfunction, behavioral disorders, or death (Gumpel, 1972; Miller, Cradock-Watson, & Pollock, 1982).

Trauma is another cause of mental retardation. One such trauma is irradiation. Exposure can occur when pregnant women receive x-rays or treatment for tumors. Irradiation exposure has long been known to cause congenital brain defects, abnormalities of the central nervous system (Goldstein & Murphy, 1929), and microcephaly (Warkany et al., 1981). Irradiation to the central nervous system of a neonate may result in microencephaly, malformations of the eyes, mental retardation and/or behavior deficits.

Maternal trauma, such as physical injury, suffocation, or carbon monoxide poisoning can adversely affect the fetus. Although the specific cause of damage is not always clear, it is a reasonable to assume that any physical trauma to the mother could produce a premature detachment of the placenta and result in secondary anoxia and premature delivery (Koch, 1967).

The perinatal period (e.g., the interval of time beginning after the 28th week of pregnancy through 28 days following birth) is also a very crucial period in the neonate's development. During this period, the neonate can be subjected to various hazardous influences that could result in long-term consequences.

Complications that can occur during the birth process is of continuing concern for the neonate. Birth is a traumatic process, and numerous possibilities for injury—resulting in cognitive and behavioral disorders—exist (McCurry, Silverton,

& Mednick, 1991). For example, premature separation from the placenta, placental previa producing massive bleeding, or placental compression or prolapse can result in anoxia. Anoxia can produce long-term physical and/or neuropsychological consequences (McCurry, Silverton, & Sarnoff, 1991). The passage through the narrow birth canal itself, as well as the use of forceps during delivery, can result in cerebral damage and neurobehavioral defects. Although the advancements of medical technology have significantly reduced the number of cases, medical technology has not completely eliminated them.

Another perinatal risk factor is the weight of the fetus at birth (Drillien, 1971; Commey & Fitzhardinge, 1979). Studies indicate that premature/low birth weight infants, when compared to control groups, have a higher rate of various types of disabilities (Telzrow, 1991). These include blindness, deafness, cerebral palsy, and mental retardation in the moderate, severe, and profound ranges (Telzrow, 1991). In addition, data indicate that the lower the birth weight, the greater the chance of severe disabilities (Robinson & Robinson, 1965; Wiener, Rider, Oppel, Fischer, & Harper, 1965). Elements that can adversely affect birth weight are mother's age at time of conception, poor health, genetic predisposition, low socioeconomic background, obesity, and poor nourishment.

The postnatal period is a crucial time for the development of the brain. Postnatal factors that can result in mental retardation include such things as closed-head injuries, tumors, malnutrition, toxic substances, asphyxia, and environmental and social problems. Boldt (1948) found that within an institutionalized population of mentally retarded, 1.5% had a history of some postnatal trauma.

Many postnatal factors that can produce mental retardation can be prevented. The use of child restraints in automobiles can reduce the risk of mental retardation through closed-head injury (Grossman & Tarjan, 1987). Education and screening has reduced the cases of mental retardation due to lead poisoning resulting from ingestion of paint flakes. However, auto emissions and the production of lead-based products is a major source of lead poisoning (Grossman & Tarjan, 1987).

NEUROPSYCHOLOGY OF MENTAL RETARDATION

Although the study of the neuropsychological functioning of the mentally retarded population has much to offer toward increasing the knowledge and understanding of this population, this area has been slow in developing. Benton (1970) and Tramontana (1983) offer several possible reasons for this slow development. First, administering neuropsychological batteries, such as the Halstead-Reitan Neuropsychological Battery (HRNB), to this population is cumbersome. The battery can take quite some time, which is stressful and tedious for the mentally retarded patient, who already has a low tolerance for frustration. Second, there is very little information concerning the neuroanatomical and neurophysiological correlates of behavior in this population. Third, there is a lack of good neuropsychological normative data for this population.

Many have argued that mental retardation is virtually always related to some type of brain dysfunction, even with mild severity (Masland, 1958; Tredgold & Soddy, 1963; Baumeister & MacLean, 1979). Luria (1963) contended that organicity should not be inferred exclusively by either symptomology or risk factors. This appears to be concurrent with contemporary views of mental retardation, which holds that there is some degree of brain pathology and central nervous system dysfunction in most cases (Hynd & Obrzut, 1986). Indeed, in a postmortem analysis of institutionalized mentally retarded patients, Crome (1960) showed some type of structural brain abnormality was found in virtually all cases. Other postmortem studies have supported this conclusion, showing some type of brain anomaly or neurostructural damage (Malamud, 1964; Freytag & Lindenberg, 1967; Jellinger, 1972). These studies have substantiated dysfunction in the axonal, dendritic, synaptic processes, pyramidal motor neurons, and hippocampal region. Damage in any one of these areas may manifest itself as dysfunction in processing information, attributed to the misfiring within the connections in the brain. Problems in motor functions and memory would also exist, resulting in impairment in the learning process. These data support the current persuasion of brain dysfunction throughout all ranges of mental retardation (Hynd & Obrzut, 1986). However, it is imperative to recognize the existence of cultural-familial retardation as the result of adverse environmental influences (Grossman, 1983).

Snart, O'Grady, and Das (1982) studied a group of moderately mentally retarded subjects comprising three categories based on etiology. The first category was patients with medically diagnosed brain damage. The diagnoses included hydrocephalus, cerebral agenesis, cerebral atrophy, meningitis, anoxia, PKU, and cerebral palsy. The second category was patients diagnosed with Down syndrome. The third category was patients who had no specific organic etiology of mental retardation but who were classified as culturally and environmentally deprived. They found that both the medically diagnosed brain-damaged group and the culturally and environmentally deprived group performed better in areas of successive processing than did the Down syndrome group. This supported Bilowsky and Share's (1965) results showing greater deficit for individuals with Down syndrome is in the area of auditory sequential memory. These authors further speculated that this deficit could be a possible explanation for the difficulty with language development for Down syndrome individuals. Snart and associates (1982) argued that language development depends on successive coding with simultaneous coding and planning, which contributes to higher-level thought processes and organization.

Down syndrome patients would be expected to show impairment on such a battery as the HRNB, depending on the severity and/or the effected cerebral area. Indeed, because performance of the mentally retarded is consistently lower than the general population, neither meaningful patterns nor relationships are easily obtained (Reitan & Wolfson, 1992). Therefore, it would be expected that individuals who are diagnosed with moderate to profound mental retardation would show overall gross impairment; that is, the impairment index would most likely be greater than 0.5. However, a proclivity toward specific difficulties—such as concept formation, concept alternations, tactile retention and memory, and auditory discrimination for verbal stimuli—does exist.

Many patients with Turner's syndrome demonstrate a parietal lobe dysfunction. Specifically, Reske-Nielsen, Christensen, and Nielsen (1982) reported microgyria in the posterior-inferior parts of the right parietal lobe and adjacent areas of the occipital and temporal lobes. Using electroencephalographic studies, Tsuboi and Nielsen (1985), showed dysrhythmia compatible with immaturity of the cerebral cortex. Other neurological factors include ptosis and neurosensory hearing loss, which is usually caused by chronic ear infections.

Money (1973) found that Turner's syndrome patients had difficulty with visuo-constructive tasks such as with the Bender-Gestalt, Benton Visual Retention Test, and the Block Design and Object Assembly subtests of the Wechsler Intelligence Scale for Children-Revised (WISC-R). He concluded that these patients were susceptible to right parietal lobe dysfunction. This could result in deficits exhibited by personality changes, perceptual impairments, and constructional difficulties (Kolb & Whishaw, 1990). Pennington, Heaton, Karzmarck, Pendleton, Lehman, and Shucard (1985) demonstrated that patients with Turner's syndrome display learning difficulties in mathematics, geometry, and abstract subject matter. Other neuropsychological deficits include visual dysgnosia, visual-spatial disability, right-left disorientation, defective figure recognition, and defective word fluency (Money, 1973; Kolb & Heaton, 1975; Silbert, Wolff, & Lilientahal, 1977; Waber, 1979; Reske-Nielsen et al., 1982; Netley & Rovet, 1982; Pennington et al., 1985).

Considering the available instruments, a "good" instrument for assessing IQ in the severe and profound population does not exist. Sattler (1990) notes that the Stanford Binet: Fourth Edition has a lower floor than the Wechsler scales; however, this is not true for all age levels. Neither of the instruments was designed for use with the severe and profound populations. Therefore, assessment must depend on adapting IQ tests outside the age range of the mentally retarded patient.

Other factors that make the use of the present IQ batteries difficult in the assessment of mental retardation are cultural influence and lack of educational opportunities. Either of these factors can influence an IQ score and prevent a valid assessment of cerebral damage.

Reitan and Wolfson (1992) argued that use of the standardized IQ test alone is not enough to classify patients as mentally retarded. They proposed the use of a comprehensive neuropsychological evaluation to assess the full range of cognitive and intellectual abilities. Using the HRNB, Reitan and Wolfson (1992) argued against a unidimensional approach to the diagnosis of mental retardation (e.g., the use of an IQ test). The data suggested that to make inferences about brain dysfunction, a wide band approach is necessary. Moreover, the neuropsychological battery allows one to account for both interindividual differences and intraindividual differences (Reitan & Wolfson, 1992). Unlike the simple IQ assessment, a full neuropsychological examination allows differential diagnosis of etiologies and differences in the severity of particular impairments. There has been evidence for some time that neuropsychological differences exist between mentally retarded individuals at the same IQ levels (Matthews & Reitan, 1961; Matthews & Reitan, 1962; Trites, 1986). Such data strengthens the argument against a unidimensional approach.

Understanding neuropsychological functioning of mentally retarded patients offers valuable information for understanding motoric, perceptual, mnestic, and cognitive functioning (Hooper & Boyd, 1986). Benton (1970) has argued for the utility of neuropsychological data in researching mental retardation subtypes useful in understanding the etiology and ability deficits. Results of the neuropsychological examination can assist in bridging the gap between the neuroanatomy and functioning of the mentally retarded. Presently, it is being used with some success in educational/vocational treatment planning (Reed, 1979).

Unfortunately, there is very little information on the neuropsychological functioning of the mentally retarded population. However, data that do exist suggest specific types of impairments unique to mental retardation. In one early study, Matthews (1974) assessed a large sample of mentally retarded patients using the HNRB. The results indicated that many of the tests in the battery correlated highly with the patient's full-scale IQ score. In this study, impairment was seen to extend beyond intelligence test to most cognitive and sensory areas. Matthews (1974) demonstrated that the mental retarded subjects had a significantly higher performance IQs than verbal IQs. This is to be expected, as verbal IQ depends more on crystallized intelligence. So, too, the results of the HRNB suggested that for both the adult and child, mental retarded patients are impaired on mental flexibility, concept formation, verbal auditory discrimination, and undirected motor speed.

More recently, McCaffrey and Issac (1985) administered the Luria-Nebraska neuropsychological battery to a sample of mentally retarded patients and found that mentally retarded subjects had signs of either unilateral or bilateral frontal lobe dysfunction. These deficits were in the specific areas of planning and regulation of simple behavioral tasks. The subjects also demonstrated difficulties with programming and execution of a task. In general, the subjects had additional cortical dysfunction involving the remaining areas of the brain with specific impairments in mental flexibility.

Matthews and Reitan (1961) examined two groups of adult mental retarded patients. The first group consisted of mentally retarded individuals with a history of deficits before the age of 3. The second group had recently sustained brain damage. The results showed that the Category Test was more impaired for the mentally retarded sample than for the brain-damaged sample. The researchers concluded that mentally retarded patients were more impaired in general abstraction ability, although they could perform well in more concrete tasks, than were the brain-damaged patients. This finding is consistent with those subtests analyses of intelligence measures (Sattler, 1990). Indeed, individuals with mental retardation do perform better on more concrete tasks than abstract tasks. Considering subtests five and six of the Category Test, mentally retarded patients seemed to learn more with repeated exposure than did the brain-damaged sample. Matthews and Reitan (1961) concluded that mentally retarded subjects tend to profit more from their experiences if there is repeated exposure to the stimuli than do the brain-damaged patients.

In another study using the same design, Matthews and Reitan (1962) compared the performance of two groups of mentally retarded patients using the Tactile Performance Test (TPT). As in the previous study (Matthews & Reitan, 1961), the first group consisted of mentally retarded subjects with a history of deficits before the age of 3. The second group of subjects had recently sustained brain damage. The mentally retarded subjects in this study tended to have better performance on the TPT than on the Category Test. Considering that the mentally retarded usually have more highly developed psychomotor skills than abstract abilities, this may help to explain the reason the mentally retarded patients demonstrated a tendency to improve on the TPT with the successive trials.

Sattler (1990) argued that the goal of a psychological evaluation for a mentally retarded patient differs little from other groups. The need is to consider and understand the reasons for the deficit in functioning both cognitively and socially. In addition, evaluations are also conducted to identify and describe strengths and weaknesses. Reitan and Wolfson (1992) stress that the use of the neuropsychological battery is important, even with individuals who are mildly mentally retarded, because many impairments are neurologically based. Indeed, when only an individual intelligence test is given for diagnosis, such as the WISC-R, it does not provide adequate breadth.

A comprehensive neuropsychological examination assesses a wide range of brain-behavior functions (Reitan & Wolfson, 1992). As such, a comprehensive examination should consist of a compilation of cognitive, social, emotional, and neurological measures. Consistent with these goals, it is important to utilize the best of what is presently available. It is for this reason that wide-band neuropsychological battery offers all the vital information necessary in an evaluation.

Further research of neuropsychological functioning of the mentally retarded is essential. Consideration of these functions would result in high-utility information useful in identifying patterns for various mental retardation subtypes. Indeed, Matthews (1962) found differences in groups of mentally retarded patients with varying etiologies. Knowledge of these functions can assist in identifying and understanding various disorders and their etiologies. In addition, understanding of the brain-behavior relationship offers potential for compensatory and rehabilitation planning for the mentally retarded patients.

SCHOOL RESPONSIBILITIES

Education for children with handicapping or disabling conditions continues to evolve since the passage of the Education for All Handicapped Children Act (PL 94-142, 1975), now referred to as Individuals with Disabilities Education Act (IDEA). The intent of this law is to ensure that all children, regardless of any disabling condition, should receive appropriate education. Public Law 99-457 is an amendment to PL 94-142, which mandates that services be provided to help young children at risk of developmental delays.

Pearman, Huang, Barnhart, and Melblom (1992) pointed out that the intent of this law was not to create separate programs for various disabling conditions but to ensure quality education. However, individual diagnostic classifications have evolved in an attempt to identify disabling conditions that separate these children from "nondisabled" students. Will (1986) argued that separate programs have not been successful because they are based on the assumption that children with disabilities cannot benefit from regular classroom instruction. The "education reform movement" is an effort to integrate all students into the same curriculum through the concept of inclusion. Hilton and Liberty (1992) argue that inclusion is more than just locating students with disasbilities in the same building with nondisabled students.

Currently, school placements and educational programming are governed by the individual state and vary throughout the United States. Actual placement depends on the decisions made by a case conference committee. For the most part, the norm is to break placement for the mentally retarded into three classifications. First, there is a placement for the mildly mentally handicapped (often referred to as MIMH), which is for children who exhibit scores that are at least two standard deviations below the mean on an IQ test and have mild impairment on an adaptive behavior measure. A second placement is for the moderately mentally handicapped (MOMH), which requires that a student score at least three standard deviations below the mean on a standardized IQ test and a measure of adaptive behavior. A final placement is for the severe and profound mentally handicapped (often referred to as S & P). Placement in S & P requires that the individual score below four standard deviations below the mean on a standardized IQ and adaptive behavior measures.

Assessment and placement is paramount in building appropriate educational programs and interventions for the mentally retarded (Smith & Dowdy, 1992). Assessment and intervention must be concurrently considered to develop meaningful programs (Polloway & Smith, 1992; Smith, Price, & Marsh, 1986; Luftig, 1989). If weaknesses and strengths are identified but not considered in the intervention, then the assessment has little value other than diagnosis. Awareness of this necessary link, between assessment and treatment, has recently increased (Smith & Dowdy, 1992; Reitan & Wolfson, 1988). In fact, the development of curriculum-based assessment (CBA) is a good example of this movement. CBA provides a means of relating intervention directly to school-related instruction, and is developed through an analysis of what is taught in the classroom (Bigge, 1988). Thus, the content of the individualized educational program (IEP) for mentally retarded students should reflect the strengths and weaknesses identified through assessment.

Proponents of CBA claim that there are several advantages in using this approach. The advantages include an assessment that is specific, is based on the student's curriculum, directly results in instructional programs, can be developed easily and economically, is used frequently to monitor progress, and will assist in revising the IEP (Smith & Dowdy, 1992). However, Patton, Payne, and Beirne-Smith (1986) have argued that CBA lacks relevance for secondary school programming and transition into postsecondary settings.

Considering intervention from a neuropsychological point of view, Reitan and Wolfson (1988) are also proponents of linking assessment and intervention. They have developed a structured program for retraining neuropsychological abilities using the Reitan Evaluation of Hemispheric Abilities and Brain Improvement Training (REHABIT) (Reitan & Wolfson, 1988). Reitan and Wolfson's REHABIT approach uses the Halstead Reitan Neuropsychology Battery, which allows for identification of the patients neuropsychological impairments and assists in a remediation plan that is tailored to the individual (Reitan & Wolfson, 1992).

Although, Reitan and Wolfson view both children and adults from the same theoretical framework, they do recognize that the evaluation of children is more complex. However, involving rehabilitation, the materials for REHABIT are essentially the same for children and adults. The theory that guides REHABIT holds that the highest level of neuropsychological functioning is represented by the general cerebral cortical area (Reitan & Wolfson, 1988). The authors argue that REHABIT goes beyond traditional rehabilitation systems that emphasize the left cortical hemisphere functions, and fails to focus on many of the neuropsychological deficits found in the evaluation (Reitan & Wolfson, 1992).

REHABIT has five tracks of remediation. However, the pattern of deficits identified through the evaluation with the HRNB may require that one track be emphasized over another. This type of remediation plan would require that each individual undergo a complete neuropsychological evaluation to gather information about both strengths and weaknesses. They stress the importance of the neuropsychological evaluation as the first step in rehabilitation, because this allows the characterization of the strengths and weaknesses as a basis for designing a program for cognitive retraining (Reitan & Wolfson, 1988). In contrast to the previously discussed program of CBA, REHABIT uses existing procedures that engage in a routine implementation of a standard set of techniques designed to address an array of cognitive deficits presumed to be characteristic of all cases of brain damage. Indeed, mentally retarded children do not constitute a homogeneous group. Instead, each may present with different levels of impairment and have a diverse array of strengths and weaknesses. We cannot assume that the children are all alike and have the same needs.

REHABIT is appropriate for serving individuals with mental retardation because it approaches each individual as a unique case to find specific cognitive strengths and weaknesses. Moreover, REHABIT could easily be adapted in the school system where teachers are already trained to offer educational programming to the mentally retarded. Since REHABIT is based on data from the HRNB, it requires school personnel to receive training in administration and interpretation of the HRNB. Furthermore, it requires that school psychologists have an understanding of brain-behavior relationships.

Preliminary research looking at the effectiveness of REHABIT has shown that individuals have gained in neuropsychological functioning after completing REHABIT (Reitan & Wolfson, 1988). It is apparent that this approach is fairly new and more research is needed to validate its utility. We do know that mentally retarded patients differ in abilities and processing skills. Rather than general basic skills programming, this approach recognizes individual differences. This value of an individualized approach to habilitation of mentally retarded children will probably be most effectively utilized in clinical populations presenting with mild retardation. Patients at this level of functioning are more likely to have more variations in performance on neuropsychological testing, resulting in relative strengths and weaknesses. Wherein strengths can be identified, compensatory strategies may be developed for older children.

Task analysis, in tandem with behavioral rehearsal and reinforcement techniques, have also been demonstrated as effective habilitation techniques for the retarded population's learning activities of daily living. Other associative learning strategies—combining behavioral reinforcement with visual, auditory, and/or tactual cues—may facilitate development of more complex communications skills such as interfacing with computers or other technology that could be designed as supportive orthotics. Clearly, creative research efforts will be required to investigate novel approaches to using neuropsychological test results to develop treatment plans for mentally retarded children.

REFERENCES

Abramowicz, H. K., & Richardson, S. A. (1975). Epidemiology of severe mental retardation in children: Community studies. *American Journal of Mental Deficiency, 80,* 18–39.

Abuelo, D. N. (1983). Genetic disorders. In J. L Matson & J. A. Mulick (Eds.), *Handbook of mental retardation* (pp. 105–120). New York: Pergamon Press.

American Psychiatric Association. (1987). *Diagnostic and statistical manual of mental disorders* (3rd ed.-Revised). Washington, DC: Author.

d'Anthenaise, M., & Salbreux, R. (1979). Prevalence de la deficience mentale profonde chez l'enfant. *Neuropsychiatrie de l'Enfance, 27,* 45–58.

Apgar, V. & Beck, J. (1974). *Is my baby all right?* New York: Trident Press.

Baumeister, A. (1967). Problems in comparative studies of mental retardates and normals. *American Journal of Mental Deficiency, 71,* 869–875.

Baumeister, A. A., & MacLean, W. E. (1979). Brain damage and mental retardation. In N. R. Ellis (Ed.), *Handbook of mental deficiency, psychological theory and research.* Hillsdale, NJ: Lawrence Erlbaum Associates.

Benton, A. L., (1970). Neuropsychological aspects of mental retardation. *Journal of Special Education, 4,* 3–11.

Berg, J. M. (1988). Genetic counseling in mental retardation: Realities and implications. In E. K. Hicks and J. M. Berg (Eds.), *The Genetics of Mental Retardation* (pp. 139–148). The Netherlands: Kluwer Academic Publishers.

Bernsen, A. H. (1976). Severe mental retardation in the county of Arhus, Denmark. A community study on prevalence and provision of service. *Acta Psychiatrica Scandinavica, 54,* 43–66.

Bigge, J. (1988). *Curriculum based instruction for special education students.* Mountain View, CA: Mayfield.

Bilowsky, D., & Share, J. (1965). The ITPA and Down syndrome: An exploratory study. *American Journal of Mental Deficiency, 70,* 78–82.

Boldt, W. H. (1948). Postnatal cerebral trauma as an etiological factor. *American Journal of Mental Deficiency, 53,* 247–267.

Brantley, D. (1988). *Understanding mental retardation.* Springfield, IL: Charles C. Thomas.

Broman, S. H. (June, 1978). *Outcome of adolescent*

pregnancy: A report from the collaborative peri-natal project. Paper presented at the Workshop on Developmental Followup on Infants Born at Risk, 13th Annual Conference of the Association for the Care of Children in Hospitals, Washington, DC.

Cohen, W. R., Newman, L., & Friedman, E. A. (1980). Risk of labor abnormalities with advancing maternal age. *Obstetrics and Gynecology, 55,* 414- 416.

Commey, J. O. O., & Fitzhardinge, P. M. (1979). Handicap in the preterm small-for-gestational-age infant. *The Journal of Pediatrics, 94,* 779–786.

Crome, L. (1960). The brain and mental retardation. *British Medical Journal, 1,* 897–904.

Darragh, P. M. (1982). The prevalence and prevention of severe mental handicap in Northern Ireland. *Irish Medical Journal, 75,* 16–19.

Dingman, H. F., & Tarjan, G. (1960). Mental retardation and the normal distribution curve. *American Journal of Mental Deficiency, 64,* 991–994.

Drillien, C. M. (1971). Prognosis of infants of very low birth weight. *Lancet, 10,* 697–703.

Dwyer, J. F. (1974). Teenage pregnancy. *American Journal of Obstetrics and Gynecology, 118,* 373–378.

Education for All Handicapped Children Act of 1975 (Public Law 94-142), 20 U.S.C. 1401 et seq.

Freytag, E., & Lindenberg, R. (1967). Neuropathologic findings in patients of a hospital for the mentally deficient. A study of 359 cases. *John Hopkins Medical Journal, 121,* 379–392.

Fryns, J. P. (1988). X-linked mental retardation and fragile X (q27): Pitfalls and difficulties in diagnosis and genetic counseling. In E. K. Hicks & J. M. Berg (Eds.), *The genetics of mental retardation* (pp. 149–156). The Netherlands: Kluwer Academic Publishers.

Goldstein, L. & Murphy, D. P. (1929). Etiology of the ill health in children born after maternal pelvic irradiation. Part II. Defective children born after postconception pelvic irradiation. *American Journal Roentgenol, 22.*

Gumpel, S. (1972). Clinical and social status of patients with congenital rubella. *Archives of Disabled Children, 47,* 330–334.

Gray, J., & Dean, R. S. (1991). Behavioral implications of perinatal communications: An Overview. In J. W. Gray & R. S. Dean (Eds.), *Neuropsychology of perinatal complications* (pp. 1–22). New York: Springer.

Grossman, H. J. (Ed.). (1983). *Classification in mental retardation.* Washington, DC: American Association on Mental Deficiency.

Grossman, H. J., & Tarjan, G. (Eds.). (1987). *AMA handbook on mental retardation.* Chicago, IL: American Medical Association.

Hanson, J. W. (1977). Unpublished manuscript.

Heber, R. (1970). *Epidemiology of mental retardation.* Springfield, IL: Charles C. Thomas.

Hicks, E. K., & Berg, J. M. (1988). *The genetics of mental retardation.* The Netherlands: Kluwer Academic Publishers.

Hilton, A., & Liberty, K. (1992). The challenge of ensuring educational gains for students with severe disabilities who are placed in more integrated settings. *Education and Training in Mental Retardation, 27*(2), 167–175.

Hooper, S. R., & Boyd, T. A., (1986) Neurodevelopmental learning disabilities. In J. E. Obrzut & G. W.

Hynd (Eds.), *Child neuropsychology: Vol. 2. Clinical practice.* Orlando, FL: Harcourt Brace Jovanovich.

Hynd, G. W., & Obrzut, J. E. (1986). Clinical child neuropsychology: Issues and perspectives. In J. E. Obrzut & G. W. Hynd (Eds.), *Child neuropsychology: Vol. 2. Clinical practice.* Orlando, FL: Harcourt Brace Jovanovich.

Jellinger, J. (1972). Neuropathological features of unclassified mental retardation. In J. B. Cavanaugh (Ed.), *The brain in unclassified mental retardation.* Baltimore: Williams & Wilkins.

Kajanoja, P., & Widholm, O. (1978). Pregnancy and delivery in women aged 40 and over. *Obstetrics and Gynecology, 51,* 47–51.

Kaplan H. I., & Sadock, B. J. (1988). *Synopsis of psychiatry.* Baltimore, MD: Williams & Wilkins.

Koch, R. (1967). The multidisciplinary approach to mental retardation. In A. A. Baumeister (Ed.), *Mental retardation* (pp. 20–38). Chicago: Aldine.

Kolb, B., & Whishaw, I. Q. (1990). *Fundamentals of human neuropsychology* (3rd ed.). New York: W. H. Freeman.

Kolb, J. E., & Heaton, R. K. (1975). Lateralized neurologic deficits and psychopathology in a Turner syndrome patient. *Archives of General Psychiatry, 32*(9), 1198–1200.

Krompotic, E. (1978). Cytogenetic counseling in mental retardation. In C. H. Carter (Ed.), *Medical aspects of mental retardation* (pp. 476–495). Springfield, IL: Charles C. Thomas.

Luftig, R. L. (1989). *Assessment of learners with special needs.* Boston: Allyn and Bacon.

Luria A. R. (1963). *The mentally retarded child.* New York: Pergamon Press.

Luria A. R. (1973). *The working brain.* New York: Basic Books.

Malamud, N. (1964). Neuropathology. In H. A. Stevens & R. Heber (Eds.), *Mental retardation: A review of research.* Chicago: University of Chicago Press.

Masland, R. L. (1958). The prevention of mental subnormality. In R. L. Masland, S. B. Sarason, & T. Gladwin (Eds.), *Mental subnormality.* New York: Basic Books.

Matthews, C. G. (1974). Applications of neuropsychological test methods in mentally retarded subjects. In R. M. Reitan & L. A. Davison (Eds.), *Clinical neuropsychology: Current status and applications.* Washington, DC: Hemisphere Publishing.

Matthews, C. G., & Reitan, R. M. (1961). Comparisons of abstraction ability in retardates and in patients with cerebral lesions. *Perceptual and Motor Skills, 13,* 327–333.

Matthews, C. G., & Reitan, R. M. (1962). Psychomotor abilities of retardates and patients with cerebral lesions. *American Journal of Mental Deficiency, 66,* 607–612.

McCaffrey, R. J., & Isaac, W. (1985). Preliminary data on the presence of neuropsychological deficits in adults who are mentally retarded. *Mental Retardation, 23*(2), 63–66.

McCurry, C., Silverton, L., & Sarnoff, A. M. (1991). Psychiatric consequences of pregnancy and birth complications. In J. W. Gray & R. S. Dean (Eds.), *Neuropsychology of perinatal complications* (pp. 186–203). New York: Springer.

McLaren, J., & Bryson, S. E. (1987). Review of recent epidemiological studies of mental retardation: Prevalence, associated disorders, and etiology. *American Journal of Mental Retardation, 92*(3), 243–254.

Menkes, J. H. (1985). *Textbook of child neurology* (3rd ed.). Philadelphia: Lea & Febiger.

Mikkelsen, M. (1988). Chromosomal findings in first trimester chorionic villi biopsy. In E. K. Hicks & J. M. Berg (Eds.), *The genetics of mental retardation* (pp. 23–32). The Netherlands: Kluwer Academic Publishers.

Miller, E., Cradock-Watson, J. E., & Pollock, T. M. (1982). Consequences of confirmed maternal rubella at successive stages of pregnancy. *Lancet, 2,* 781–785.

Money, J. (1973). Turners syndrome and parietal lobe functions. *Cortex, 9,* 387–393.

Monif, G. R., Egan, E. A., & Held, B. (1972). The correlation of maternal cytomegalovirus infection during varying stages in gestation with neonatal development. *Journal of Pediatrics, 80,* 17–24.

Naeye, R. L. (1983). Maternal age, obstetric complications, and the outcome of pregnancy. *Obstetrics and Gynecology, 61,* 210–216.

Naeye, R. L., & Tafari, N. (1983). *Risk factors in pregnancy and diseases of the fetus and newborn.* Baltimore: Williams & Wilkins.

Netley, C., & Rovet, J. (1982). Atypical hemispheric lateralization in Turner syndrome subjects. *Cortex, 18*(3), 377–384.

Patton, J. R., Payne, J. S., & Beirne-Smith, M. (1986). *Mental retardation* (2nd ed.). Columbus, OH: Merrill.

Pearman, E. L., Huang, A. M., Barnhart, M. W., & Melblom, C. (1992). Educating all students in school: Attitudes and beliefs about inclusion. *Education and Training in Mental Retardation, 27*(2), 176–182.

Pennington, B. F., Heaton, R. K., Karzmarck, P., Pendleton, M. G., Lehman, R., & Shucard, D. W. (1985). The neuropsychological phenotype in Turner syndrome. *Cortex, 21*(3), 391–404.

Polloway, E. A., & Smith, T. E. C. (1992). *Teaching language skills to students with mild disabilities.* Denver: Love Publishing.

Pueschel, S. M., & Thuline, H. C. (1983). Chromosome disorders. In J. L. Matson & J. A. Mulick

(Eds.), *Handbook of mental retardation* (pp. 121–141). New York: Pergamon Press.

Reed, H. B. C. (1979). Biological defects and special education: An issue in personnel preparation. *Journal of Special Education, 13*(1), 9–33.

Reitan, R. M., & Wolfson, D. (1988). The Halstead-Reitan Neuropsychological Test Battery and REHABIT: A model for integrating evaluation and remediation of cognitive impairment. *Cognitive Rehabilitation, 6*, 10–17.

Reitan, R. M., & Wolfson, D. (1992). *Neuropsychological evaluation of older children.* Tucson, AR: Neuropsychology Press.

Reske-Nielsen, E., Christensen, A. L., & Nielsen, J. (1982). A neuropathological and neuropsychological study of Turner's syndrome. *Cortex, 18*(2), 181- 190.

Robinson, N. M., & Robinson, N. B. (1965). A follow-up study of ex-premature and control children at school age. *Pediatrics, 35*, 425–433.

Santrock, J. W., & Yussen, S. R. (1992). *Child development* (5th ed.). Dubuque, IA: William C. Brown.

Sattler, J. M. (1990). *Assessment of children* (4th ed.). San Diego, CA: Author.

Silbert, A., Wolff, P. H. & Lilientahal, J. (1977). Spatial and temporal processing in patients with Turner's syndrome. *Behavior Genetics, 7*(1), 11- 21.

Sinclair, E., & Forness, S. (1983). Classifications: Educational issues. In J. L. Matson & J. A. Mulick (Eds.), *Handbook of mental retardation* (pp. 171- 184). New York: Pergamon Press.

Smith, T. E., & Dowdy, C. (1992). Future based assessment and intervention for students with mental retardation. *Education and Training in Mental Retardation, 27*(3), 255–260.

Smith, T. E. C., Price, B. J., & Marsh, G. E. (1986). *Mildly handicapped children and adults.* St. Paul: West.

Snart, F., O'Grady, M., & Das, J. P. (1982). Cognitive processing by subgroups of moderately mentally retarded children. *American Journal of Mental Deficiency, 86*(5), 465–472.

Swaiman, K. F., & Jacobson, R. I. (1984). Developmental abnormalities of the central nervous system. In A. B. Baker & R. J. Joynt (Eds.), *Clinical neurology: Vol. 4.* Philadelphia: Lippincott.

Telzrow, C. F. (1991). Impact of perinatal complications on education. In J. W. Gray & R. S. Dean (Eds.). *Neuropsychology of perinatal complications* (pp. 161–185). New York: Springer.

Thuline, H. C., & Pueschel, S. M. (1982). Cytogenetics in Down's syndrome: In S. M. Pueschel & J. E. Rynders (Eds.), *Down syndrome: Advances in biomedicine and the behavioral sciences.* Cambridge: The Ware Press.

Torphy, D. E., Ray, C. G., & McAlister, R. (1970). Herpes simplex virus infection in infants: A spectrum of disease. *Journal of Pediatrics, 76*, 405–409.

Tramontana, M. G. (1983). Application of neuropsychological methods in the evaluation of coexisting mental retardation and mental illness. In F. J. Menolascino & B. M. McCann (Eds.), *Mental health and mental retardation: Bridging the gap.* Baltimore: University Park Press.

Trites, R. L. (1986). Neuropsychological variables and mental retardation. *Psychiatric Clinics of North America, 9*, 723–731.

Tredgold, R. F., & Soddy, K. (1963). *Textbook of mental deficiency.* Baltimore: Williams & Wilkens.

Tsuboi, T., & Nielsen, J. (1985). Electroencephalographic examination of 64 Danish Turner girls. *Acta-Neurologica-Scandinavica, 72*(6), 590–601.

Volavka, J., Mednick-S. A., Rasmussen, L., & Sergeant, J. (1977). *Electroencephalography and Clinical Neurophysiology, 43*(6), 798–801.

Waber, D. P. (1979). Neuropsychological aspects of Turner's syndrome. *Developmental Medicine and Child Neurology, 21*(1), 58–70.

Warkany, J., Lemire, R. J., & Cohen, M. M., Jr. (1981). *Mental retardation and congenital malformations of the central nervous system.* Chicago: Year Book Medical Publishers.

Webb, T., Crawley, P., & Bundey, S. (1990). Folate treatment of a boy with fragile-X syndrome. *Journal of Mental Deficiency Research, 34*(1), 67-73.

Wehman, P. (1992). Transition of young people with disabilities: Challenges of the 1990's.

Education and Training in Mental Retardation, 27(2), 112–118.

Wiener, G., Rider, R. V., Oppel, W. C., Fischer, L. K., & Harper, P. A. (1965). Correlates of low birth weight: Psychological status at six to seven years of age. *Pediatrics, 35*, 434–444.

Will, M. C. (1986). Educating children with learning problems: A shared responsibility. *Exceptional Children, 52*, 411–415.

Zellweger, H., & Patil, S. R. (1987). Chromosomal anomalies excluding Down syndrome. In P.

J. Vinken, G. W. Bruyn, & H. L. Klawans (Eds.), *Handbook of clinical neurology: Revised series 6.* New York: Elsevier Science.

Zellweger, H., & Patil, S. R. (1987). Down syndrome. In P. J. Vinken, G. W. Bruyn, & H. L. Klawans(Eds.), *Handbook of clinical neurology: Revised series 6.* New York: Elsevier Science.

Zigler, E., & Hodapp, R. M. (1986). *Understanding mental retardation.* New York: Cambridge University Press.

14

FUTURE CONSIDERATIONS FOR REHABILITATION RESEARCH AND OUTCOME STUDIES

ERVIN S. BATCHELOR, JR.

This brief essay addresses current issues influencing research and outcome studies in rehabilitation settings, and some of the concurrent complications. An argument is made for comprehensive longitudinal data collection to be instituted for specific diagnostic categories of pediatric neurologic disorders and later to be used in a multivariate format to predict outcome variables important to all interested parties.

Behavioral scientists have long struggled with paradigms for outcome studies, given the rigors of the scientific method of research. The relatively recent application of multivariate statistics in neurobehavioral science reflects researchers' attempts to develop and evaluate models proposed to account for multifactorial relationships between intrapersonal and extrapersonal variables. Indeed, outcome in the rehabilitation setting is uniformly a multivariate issue.

In a recent review of outcome studies conducted for brain-injured adults, Evans and Ruff (1992) described a number of outcome variables ranging from pre- and postneuropsychological test scores to subjective patient report of abilities, independent living status, and employability obtained via questionnaires. Based on my and others' (e.g., Ris & Noll, 1994) literature search, there have been precious few outcome studies that have applied analysis of covariance models in determining the effects of treatment on success in clinical pediatric neurologic populations (e.g., Adunsky, Hershkowitz, Rabbi, Asher-Sivron & Ohry, 1992). To my knowledge there are few, if any, researchers that have utilized neurobiological, neuropsychological, and neurodevelopmental test data together, to develop and evaluate treatment plans. In a laboratory environment, such an approach would be ideal because it would allow scientists to more carefully consider the effects of illness and treatment on neurobiological and neuropsychological development. From this view, researchers would also be assisted in formulating models of aberrant neurological development for specific clinical pediatric populations, which may eventually lead us to more exacting models of treatment for rehabilitation. Many researchers have argued for a similar approach (e.g., Dennis, 1987; Ris & Noll, 1994; Tupper & Rosenblood, 1984). Unfortunately, there are a cadre of other variables that impact the nature and form of outcome-based studies in the rehabilitation setting that may limit future researchers' attempts to pursue such a strategy.

The most commonly disputed issue in researchers' collaboration is definition of subject matter. This notion has been widely argued in the learning disability and attention-deficit disorder literature. Outcome in rehabilitation research clearly has different meanings depending on the authors' and audience's orientations. For pediatric clinical populations that permit, researchers have published some studies of pre- and postperformance on measures of cognitive, motivational/emotional, and behavioral function (Ris & Noll, 1994). However, service providers have tended to focus on outcome constructs such as employment and independent management of activities of daily living as criteria for discharge, all of which are mitigated by funding (Adunsky et al., 1992; Frattali, 1993). Naturally, third-party payers have been persistently concerned about length of stay, costs, and effectiveness in allocation of resources (Frattali, 1993, Leiter, 1994). Families and consumers have struggled with the quality of programs and treating professionals' potential for helping the patient maximize functional capacity for independence in managing various aspects of their environment; long- and short-term potential for independent living; and public school placement and work, while trying to balance financial demands associated with treatment and long-term care (Frattali, 1993; Leonard, Johnson, & Brust, 1993). Because the overwhelming majority of research with children conducted thus far has addressed more scientifically oriented short-term goals, rather than applied long-term outcome issues, many of the fundamental questions germane to the definition of outcome considered by service providers, consumers, and third-party payers have been overlooked.

This state of affairs presents future researchers with an extremely difficult set of circumstances to evaluate. From this view, the notion of outcome must incorporate neurobiological, neurodevelopmental, neuropsychological adaptive/ functional issues and cost over the period of time the patient requires treatment for a given diagnostic category. Long-term prospective outcome studies would be required for each diagnostic category. While short-term outcome variables could be considered in concert to address the concerns of each interested party (i.e., researchers, service providers, families, patients, and third-party payers), the challenge of evaluating these concerns over the course of development becomes horrendous.

Most of the functionally based assessment tools used as dependent variables to measure rehabilitation outcome produce ordinal data (see Frattali, 1993, for a review). Clearly, ordinal data do not qualify for further application using multivariate procedures. However, if these short-term outcome variables are later used as independent variables, the design must change to accommodate the quality of data as ordinal. This being the case, it becomes much more difficult to establish causal or correlative links between early interventions and long-term outcomes to follow. Hence, the results become less powerful.

In fact, erroneous conclusions regarding cost effectiveness may be easily drawn from short-term outcome variables rated on an ordinal scale (Merbitz, Morris, & Grip, 1989). Merbitz and colleagues insightfully point out that as patients move along an ordinal scale of measurement, it is impossible to delineate the meaningfulness of the differences between scores. Further, they argue that variations in hours of treatment a patient may take to reach different scores on the same measure via different treatment strategies may significantly vary, and may not take into account any host of other intervening or interacting variables. Thus, to infer that cut-off scores derived from indices based on ordinal rated functional scales should be used as criteria for admission or discharge may well be fraudulent (Frattali, 1993). The issue gets increasingly cumbersome when one attempts to evaluate short-term and long-term outcomes in light of costs for services. Once diagnosed and initially treated, the family will incur additional ongoing expenses over the course of development, and perhaps into adulthood unless there is a cure without residuals. Few studies have considered the evaluation of maintenance care for patients with chronic disabilities and the associated costs.

The pre- and postmorbid independent intervening and interacting variables occurring over the course of development present an equally complicated aspect of the problem. They may be divided into two groups: extrinsic and intrinsic factors. The most salient extrinsic factors include socioeconomic status (SES) (e.g., Batchelor, Gray, Dean, & Lowery, 1988; Brown, Chadwick, Shaffer, Rutter, & Traub, 1981), time lapse between accurate diagnosis and treatment, quality and appropriateness of comprehensive service delivery and follow-up services, iatrogenic effects of treatment, case management, parents' and families' ability to accept the patients' conditions and properly move into the role of caregiver, community-based attitudes and expectations for development and recovery, public and private insurance policies determining funding for treatment. The important premorbid intrinsic factors are discussed in Chapter 2 of this book. The postmorbid intrinsic variables may include course of illness, morbidity and mortality, increased risk in some populations (e.g., tumors, cerebrovasular disorders, and brain injury) to experience recurrence of the condition, and potential for secondary medical complications, which may also affect central nervous system functioning.

As one can surmise based on this discussion, models for future research of outcome should be all inclusive of the extrinsic factors just identified. However, differences in intrinsic factors specific to each diagnostic category, and the quality of short-term outcome data will require special consideration prior to establishing long-term research paradigms.

First, functional assessment tools would have to be designed to accommodate dependent variables such as living status, educational/program placement, and independence in activities of daily living on interval scales of measurement. In this way, functional assessment could be integrated into a multivariate design to answer short-term and long-term outcome questions.

Second, standardized pre-, post-, and serial neuropsychological test batteries could be developed for each diagnostic category to determine cognitive, motivational/emotional, and behavioral changes associated with onset of illness, acute, post acute, community reintegration treatment interventions, and ongoing follow-up care. Serial neuropsychological testing would also contribute to more sophisticated models of neurobiological and neurodevelopmental aberrations for different clinical populations. In tandem, serial neuropsychological test scores and interval-based functional outcome measures could be considered across time to parse out the effects of different stages of treatment in the developmental/recovery process, while simultaneously controlling for other extrinsic and intrinsic variables (e.g., SES, insurance funding, community attitudes, quality of community-based resources, age of onset, extent of lesion, etc.).

Prospective longitudinal data should therefore be collected and logically regressed against final outcome measures based on path analysis models to determine effectiveness of a given treatment strategy. Depending on variables specific to a give diagnostic condition, different treatment strategies could be compared in multivariate analysis of covariance to evaluate cost effectiveness. Granted, this postulation is a rough sketch of how longitudinal outcome research could be conducted to satisfy the needs of different groups who might be interested in outcome research. The preceding discussion offers one researcher's perspective of the bare minimum requirements for longitudinal outcome studies conducted in the pediatric population with neurologic disorders. Easier said than done, and others see it quite differently.

Some have argued that it is unwise to wait for more sophisticated research instruments and paradigms, given a political climate where legislators and policy-makers are strongly advocating national health-care reform (Kane, 1991). In 1990, the United States Congress mandated changes in Medicare reimbursement rates for rehabilitation services to reflect cost containment. This policy has led to a number of other mandates that make reimbursement conditional on outcomes derived from functional assessment. In times past, the private insurance industry has followed the trends set by Congress in reforming Medicare policy. Consequently, this issue is foreboding for many providers and consumers of rehabilitation. In response, there have been a flurry of publications that attempted to frame functional assessment within the definitions of impairment, disability, and handicap provided by the World Health Organization (WHO) (e.g., Ashley, Persel, & Krych 1993; Wilkerson, Bativia, & DeJong, 1992).

Other researchers opposing this trend have emphasized the difference between assessment of impairment versus the assessment of disability (Frattali,

1993). These researchers have used more traditional measures with strong psychometric properties to assess impairment (abnormality of psychological, physiological, or anatomical structure or function at the organ level). Functional measures have been applied in cases of disability (restriction in or lack of ability to perform a daily task; a functional consequence of impairment), whereas the measurement of handicap (a social, economic, or environmental disadvantage resulting from impairment or disability) has been less well established.

Indeed, policy-makers, payers, and even providers have not heeded clarification of these distinctions and have been relatively disinterested in this line of research (Badley, 1993; Frattali, 1993). The currently accepted rating systems for impairments, disabilities, and handicaps can be found in the International Classification of Impairments, Disabilities and Handicaps (ICIDH) (WHO, 1980). Impairment ratings are first considered as dichotomous, but further attention may be given in describing the degree of impairment. Disability ratings are provided on a 0 to 9 ordinal-based scale: not disabled, difficulty in performance, aided performance, and so on. The equivalent of a prognostic scale rating expected course of recovery is also ordinal based. The handicap scale is again dichotomous with availability for further description of limitations. From a brief overview of this system, it is relatively easy to recognize that these rating procedures offer little to researchers in the way of meaningful data for application in a multivariate design. Although the ICIDH is currently under revision, policy-makers and payers will probably be slow and resistant to fund or accept any future research projects targeted at changing rating systems that require complicated and expensive longitudinal data collection.

Instead, policy-makers and payers are moving to place the burden of research necessary to demonstrate efficacy of treatment onto providers in the private sector, which may well lead to publication of inaccurate data. Furthermore, this approach encourages production of fraudulent results, given the extent of competitiveness in today's private health-care industry. Finally, this strategy results in an increase in cost to the consumer and payers to cover the expense of research in the local market, which is exactly what health-care reform advocates seek to avoid. From this view, haste makes more expense, innocent children and families may suffer, and science may be detoured and compromised due to political forces that establish policy of funding based on ignorance of short-sighted forethought.

Should policy-makers and providers continue with this line of thinking, there will be more expensive problems to manage in the long run. As technology advances, more and more children will survive trauma and illnesses with neurological sequelae. If proper funding for maximizing potential for development is not available, some of these children will eventually end up costing the government more money through other social programs, after parents have exhausted their resources. Scientist practitioners and service providers must expedite a united effort in order to educate the public about the potential complications for drastic changes in funding policies for health-care delivery in the pediatric rehabilitation environment.

REFERENCES

Adunsky, A., Hershkowitz, M., Rabbi, R., Asher-Sivron, L., & Ohry, A., (1992). Functional recovery in young stroke patients. *Archives of Physical Medicine and Rehabilitation, 73,* 859–862.

Ashley, M. J., Persel, C. S., & Krych, D. K. (1993). Changes in reimbursement climate: Relationship among outcome, cost and payor type in the post acute rehabilitation environment. *Journal of Head Trauma Rehabilitation, 8*(4), 30–47.

Baley, E. M. (1993). An introduction to the concepts and classifications of the international classification of impairments, disabilities, and handicaps. *Disability and Rehabilitation, 15*(4), 161–178.

Batchelor, E. S., Gray, J., Dean, R. S., & Lowery, R. (1988). Interactive effects of socioeconomic factors and perinatal complications. *NASP Program Abstracts, F-169,* 115–116.

Brown, G., Chadwick, O., Shaffer, D., Rutter, M., & Traub, M., (1981). A prospective study of children with head injuries: III Psychiatric sequelae. *Psychiatric Medicine, 11,* 63–78.

Dennis, M., (1987). Using language to parse the young damaged brain. *Journal of Clinical and Experimental Neuropsychology, 9,* 723–753.

Evans, R. W., & Ruff, R. M. (1992). Outcome and value: A perspective on rehabilitation outcomes achieved in acquired brain injury. *Journal of Head Trauma Rehabilitation, 7*(4), 24–36.

Frattali, C. M. (1993). Perspectives on functional assessment. *Disability and Rehabilitation, 15*(1), 1–9.

Kane, R. L. (1991). Update on assessment: Perspectives from consumers, practitioners, policy makers and payers. Presentation at National Health Policy Forum Session, Washington, DC.

Leiter, P. (1994). Rehabilitation outcome strategy in 1994 and beyond. *Physical Rehab Update, 3*(1), 1–6.

Leonard, B. J., Johnson, A. L., & Brust, J. D. (1993). Caregivers of children with disabilities: A comparison of those managing "OK" and those needing more help. *Children's Health Care, 22*(2), 93–105.

Merbitz, C., Morris, T., & Grip, J. C. (1989). Ordinal scales and foundations of misinference. *Archives of Physical Medicine & Rehabilitation, 70,* 308–312.

Ris, D., & Noll, R. B., (1994). Long-term neurobehavioral outcome in pediatric brain tumor patients: Review and methodological critique. *Journal of Clinical and Experimental Neuropsychology, 16*(4), 21–42.

Tupper, D. E., & Rosenblood, L. K (1984). Methodological considerations in the use of attribute variables in neuropsychological research. *Journal of Clinical Neuropsychology, 6,* 441–453.

Wilkerson, D. L., Bativia, A. I., & DeJong, G., (1992). The use of functional status measure for payment of rehabilitation services. *Archives of Physical Medicine and Rehabilitation, 73,* 11–120.

World Health Organization (WHO). (1980). *The international classification of impairments, disabilities and handicaps—A manual relating to the consequences of disease.* Geneva, Switzerland: Author.

INDEX